Praise for

# The Wealth and Poverty of Nations

"Truly wonderful. No question that this will establish David Landes as preeminent in his field and in his time."  —John Kenneth Galbraith

"David Landes's new historical study of the emergence of the current distribution of wealth and poverty among the nations of the world is a picture of enormous sweep and brilliant insight. The sense of historical contingency does not detract from the emergence of repeated themes in the encounters which led to European economic leadership. The incredible wealth of learning is embodied in a light and vigorous prose which carries the reader along irresistibly."
—Kenneth Arrow

"David Landes has written a masterly survey of the great successes and failures among the world's historic economies. He does it with verve, broad vision, and a whole series of sharp opinions that he is not shy about stating plainly. Anyone who thinks that a society's economic success is independent of its moral and cultural imperatives obviously has another think coming."  —Robert Solow

"Mr. Landes writes with verve and gusto. . . . This is indeed good history."  —Douglass C. North, *Wall Street Journal*

"You cannot even begin to think about problems of economic development and convergence without knowing the story that Landes tells. . . . I know of no better place to start thinking about the wealth and poverty of nations."  —J. Bradford DeLong, *Washington Post*

"Enormously erudite and provocative. . . . Never less than scintillating, witty, and brilliant."  —*Kirkus Reviews*

*Also by* DAVID S. LANDES

BANKERS AND PASHAS
THE UNBOUND PROMETHEUS
REVOLUTION IN TIME

#  The
# Wealth and Poverty
# of Nations

*Why Some Are So Rich
and Some So Poor*

**DAVID S. LANDES**

**W·W·NORTON & COMPANY**

*New York   London*

For information about permission to reproduce selections from this book, write to
Permissions, W. W. Norton & Company, Inc.,
500 Fifth Avenue, New York, NY 10110.

The text of this book is composed in Galliard
with the display set in Modern MT Extended
Composition and manufacturing by the Haddon Craftsmen, Inc.
Book design by Jacques Chazaud
Cartography by Jacques Chazaud

Library of Congress Cataloging-in-Publication Data

Landes, David S.
The wealth and poverty of nations : why some are so rich and some
so poor / by David S. Landes.
p. cm.
Includes bibliographical references and index.
ISBN 0-393-04017-8
1. Wealth—Europe—History. 2. Wealth—History. 3. Poverty—
Europe—History. 4. Poverty—History. 5. Regional economic
disparities—History. 6. Economic history. 7. Economic
development—Social aspects. I. Title.
HC240.Z9W45 1998
330.1'6—dc21 97-27508
CIP
ISBN 0-393-31888-5 (pbk.)

W. W. Norton & Company, Inc., 500 Fifth Avenue, New York, N.Y. 10110
www.wwnorton.com

W. W. Norton & Company Ltd., 10 Coptic Street, London WC1A 1PU

2 3 4 5 6 7 8 9 0

*For my children and grandchildren,
with love.*

. . . the causes of the wealth and poverty of nations—the grand object of all enquiries in Political Economy.

—Malthus to Ricardo, letter of 26 January 1817*

* J. M. Keynes, *Collected Works*, X, 97–98, quoted in Skidelsky, *John Maynard Keynes: The Economist as Saviour 1920–1937*, p. 419. My thanks for this quotation to Morton Keller.

# Contents

# Preface and Acknowledgments

My aim in writing this book is to do world history. Not, however, in the multicultural, anthropological sense of intrinsic parity: all peoples are equal and the historian tries to attend to them all. Rather, I thought to trace and understand the main stream of economic advance and modernization: how have we come to where and what we are, in the sense of making, getting, and spending. That goal allows for more focus and less coverage. Even so, this is a very big task, long in the preparing, and at best represents a first approximation. Such a task would be impossible without the input and advice of others—colleagues, friends, students, journalists, witnesses to history, dead and alive.

My first debt is to students and colleagues in courses at Columbia University, the University of California at Berkeley, Harvard University, and other places of shorter stays. In particular, I have learned from working and teaching in Harvard's undergraduate programs in Social Studies and the Core Curriculum. In both of these, teachers come into contact with students and assistants from the full range of concentrations and other faculties and have to field challenges from bright, contentious, independent people, unintimidated by differences in age, rank, and experience.

Second, thanks largely to the sympathetic understanding of Dr. Alberta Arthurs, this work received early support from the Rockefeller Foundation, which funded research and writing and brought a number of scholars together for inspiration and intellectual exchange in its beautiful Villa Serbelloni in Bellagio, Italy—there where the younger Pliny once reconciled beauty, work, and leisure on the shores of Lake Como. Easy to succumb. The meeting led to publication of *Favorites of Fortune* (eds. Patrice Higonnet, Henry Rosovsky, and myself) and gave me the opportunity to write a first essay on the recent econometric historiography of European growth. Among the people who helped me then and on other occasions, my two co-editors, Higonnet and Roskovsky; also Robert Fogel, Paul David, Rudolf Braun, Wolfram Fischer, Paul Bairoch, Joel Mokyr, Robert Allen, François Crouzet, William Lazonick, Jonathan Hughes, François Jequier, Peter Temin, Jeff Williamson, Walt Rostow, Al Chandler, Anne Krueger, Irma Adelman, and Claudia Goldin.

The Rockefeller Foundation also supported two thematic conferences—one on Latin America in 1988 and another on the role of gender in economic activity and development the following year. Among those who contributed to these stimulating dialogues, exercises in rapid-fire instruction, I want to cite David Rock, Jack Womack, John Coatsworth, David Felix, Steve Haber, Wilson Suzigan, Juan Dominguez, Werner Baer, Claudia Goldin, Alberta Arthurs, and Judith Vichniac.

I also owe a debt of gratitude to Armand Clesse and the Luxembourg Institute for European and International Studies. Mr. Clesse has become one of the key figures in the mobilization of scholars and intellectuals for the discussion and analysis of contemporary political, social, and economic problems. His main theme is the "vitality of nations," which has been interpreted broadly to mean just about anything relevant to national performance. The product has been a series of conferences, which have not only yielded associated volumes but promoted a growing and invaluable network of personal contacts among scholars and specialists. A Clesse conference is a wonderful mixture of debate and sociability—a usually friendly exercise in agreement and disagreement. In 1996, Mr. Clesse organized just such a meeting to deal with the unfinished manuscript of this book. Among those present: William McNeill, global historian and successor in omniscience to that earlier historian of Greece, Arnold Toynbee; Stanley Engerman, America's economic history reader and critic extraordinary; Walt Rostow, perhaps the only scholar to return to original scholarship after government service; Rondo Cameron, lone crusader against the concept and term of Industrial Revolution; Paul Bairoch and Angus Maddison, collectors and calculators of the numbers of growth and productivity.

A similar meeting, on "The Singularity of European Civilization," was held in June 1996 in Israel, under the sponsorship of the Yad Ha-Nadiv Rothschild Foundation (Guy Stroumsa, coordinator), bringing some of the same people plus another team, medieval and other: Patricia Crone, Ron Bartlett, Emanuel Sivan, Esther Cohen, Yaacov Metzer, Miriam Eliav-Feldon, Richard Landes, Gadi Algazi, et al.

Other venues where I was able to try out some of this material were meetings in Ferrara and Milan (Bocconi University) in 1991; the III Curso de Historia de la Técnica in the Universidad de Salamanca in 1992 (organizers Julio Sánchez Gómez and Guillermo Mira); a Convegno in 1993 of the Società Italiana degli Storici dell'Economia (Vera Zamagni, secretary) on the theme of "Innovazione e Sviluppo"; several sessions of the Economic History Workshop at Harvard; the "Jornadas Bancarias" of the Asociación de Bancos de la República Argentina in Buenos Aires in 1993 on "Las Estrategias del Desarrollo"; a congress in Hull, England, in 1993 (Economic History Society, Tawney Lecture); a conference in Cambridge University on "Technological Change and Economic Growth" (Emma Rothschild, organizer) in 1993; Jacques Marseille and Maurice Lévy-Leboyer's colloquium (Institut d'Histoire économique, Paris, 1993) on "Les performances des entreprises françaises au XX$^e$ siècle"; a conference on "Convergence or Decline in British and American Economic History" at Notre Dame University in 1994 (Edward Lorenz and Philip Mirowski organizers, Donald McCloskey promoter); a session on the Industrial Revolution (John Komlos organizer) at the Eleventh International Economic History Congress in Milan in 1994; and a session at the Social Science History Association in Atlanta in 1994.

Also lectures in the universities of Oslo and Bergen in 1995 (Kristine Bruland and Fritz Hodne, organizers); a symposium in Paris in 1995 on the work of Alain Peyrefitte (*"Valeurs, Comportements, Développement, Modernité,"* Raymond Boudon organizer) dealing *inter alia* with regional differences in European economic development; further symposia in 1995 on "The Wealth and Poverty of Nations" in Reggio Emilia and the Bocconi University in Milan (Franco Amatori, organizer).

Also a conference in the University of Oslo in 1996 on "Technological Revolutions in Europe, 1760–1860" under the direction of

Kristine Bruland and Maxine Berg; in 1996, too, at the Fondazione Eni Enrico Mattei in Milan on "Technology, Environment, Economy and Society" (Michele Salvati and Domenico Siniscalco, organizers). And in 1997, a planning meeting in Madrid for the forthcoming Twelfth International Economic History Congress on the theme "Economic Consequences of Empire 1492–1989" (Leandro Prados de la Escosura and Patrick K. O'Brien, organizers).

Each of these encounters, needless to say, focused on those points of particular interest to the participants, with gains to my understanding of both the larger theme and its special aspects.

Given the multiplicity of these meetings plus a large number of personal conversations and consultations, it is not easy to pull together a comprehensive list of those who have helped me on these and other occasions. My teachers first, whose lessons and example have stayed with me: A. P. Usher, M. M. Postan, Donald C. McKay, Arthur H. Cole. Also my colleagues in departments of economics and history in Columbia University (Carter Goodrich, Fritz Stern, Albert Hart, and George Stigler especially); in the University of California at Berkeley (Kenneth Stampp, Hans Rosenberg, Richard Herr, Carlo Cipolla, Henry Rosovsky, and Albert Fishlow especially); and at Harvard (Simon Kuznets, C. Crane Brinton, Alexander Gerschenkron, Richard Pipes, David and Aida Donald, Benjamin Schwartz, Harvey Leibenstein, Robert Fogel, Zvi Griliches, Dale Jorgensen, Amartya Sen, Ray Vernon, Robert Barro, Jeff Sachs, Jess Williamson, Claudia Goldin, Daniel Bell, Nathan Glazer, Talcott Parsons, Brad DeLong, Patrice Higonnet, Martin Peretz, Judith Vichniac, Stephen Marglin, Winnie Rothenberg).

Nor should I forget the extraordinary stimulation I received from a year at the Center for Advanced Study in the Behavioral Sciences in Palo Alto. This was in 1957–58, and I was the beneficiary of a banner crop of economists: Kenneth Arrow, Milton Friedman, George Stigler, Robert Solow (four future winners of the Nobel Prize!). Get a paper past them, and one was ready for any audience.

And then, in addition to those colleagues mentioned above, others at home and abroad. In the United States: William Parker, Roberto Lopez, Charles Kindleberger, Liah Greenfield, Bernard Lewis, Leila Fawaz, Alfred Chandler, Peter Temin, Mancur Olson, William Lazonick, Richard Sylla, Ivan Berend, D. N. McCloskey, Robert Brenner, Patricia Seed, Margaret Jacob, William H. McNeill, Andrew Kamarck, Tibor Scitovsky, Bob Summers, Morton and Phyllis Keller, John Kautsky, Richard Landes, Tosun Arıcanlı. In Britain: M. M. Postan, Lance

Beales, Hrothgar John Habakkuk, Peter Mathias, Barry Supple, Berrick Saul, Charles Feinstein, Maxine Berg, Patrick K. O'Brien, P. C. Barker, Partha Dasguppa, Emma Rothschild, Andrew Shonfield. In France: François Crouzet, Maurice Lévy-Leboyer, Claude Fohlen, Bertrand Gille, Emmanuel Leroy-Ladurie, François Furet, Jacques LeGoff, Joseph Goy, Rémy Leveau, François Caron, Albert Broder, Pierre Nora, Pierre Chaunu, Rémy Prudhomme, Riva Kastoryano, Jean-Pierre Dormois. In Germany: Wolfram Fischer, Hans Ulrich Wehler, Jürgen Kocka, John Komlos. In Switzerland: Paul Bairoch, Rudolf Braun, J.-F. Bergier, Jean Batou, François Jequier. In Italy: Franco Amatori, Aldo de Madalena, Ester Fano, Roby Davico, Vera Zamagni, Stefano Fenoaltea, Carlo Poni, Gianni Toniolo, Peter Hertner. In Japan: Akira Hayami, Akio Ishizaka, Heita Kawakatsu, Isao Sutō, Eisuke Daitō. In Israel: Shmuel Eisenstadt, Don Patinkin, Yehoshua Arieli, Eytan Shishinsky, Jacob Metzer, Nahum Gross, Elise Brezis. And elsewhere: Herman van der Wee, Francis Sejersted, Erik Reinert, H. Floris Cohen, Dharma Kumar, Gabriel Tortella, Leandro Prados de la Escosura, Kristof Glamann. To all these and others I owe suggestions, criticisms, data, insights. We have not always agreed, but so much the better.

I want to give special thanks to my extraordinary editor, Edwin Barber, who not only challenged and improved the text but taught me a few things about writing. It's never too late to learn.

Finally, I want to thank my wife, Sonia, who has sweetly put up with years of heaping books, offprints, papers, letters, and other debris. Even multiple work studies have not been big enough, and only the computer has saved the day. Now for the cleanup.

# Introduction

> No new light has been thrown on the reason why poor countries are poor and rich countries are rich.
> —Paul Samuelson, in 1976[1]

In June of 1836, Nathan Rothschild left London for Frankfurt to attend the wedding of his son Lionel to his niece (Lionel's cousin Charlotte), and to discuss with his brothers the entry of Nathan's children into the family business. Nathan was probably the richest man in the world, at least in liquid assets. He could, needless to say, afford whatever he pleased.

Then fifty-nine years old, Nathan was in good health if somewhat portly, a bundle of energy, untiring in his devotion to work and indomitable of temperament. When he left London, however, he was suffering from an inflammation on his lower back, toward the base of his spine. (A German physician diagnosed it as a boil, but it may have been an abscess.)[2] In spite of medical treatment, this festered and grew painful. No matter: Nathan got up from his sickbed and attended the wedding. Had he been bedridden, the wedding would have been celebrated in the hotel. For all his suffering, Nathan continued to deal with business matters, with his wife taking dictation. Meanwhile the great Dr. Travers was summoned from London, and when he could not cure the problem, a leading German surgeon was called in, presumably to open and clean the wound. Nothing availed; the poison spread; and on 28 July 1836, Nathan died. We are told that the Roth-schild pigeon post took the message back to London: *Il est mort.*

Nathan Rothschild died probably of staphylococcus or streptococ-cus septicemia—what used to be called blood poisoning. In the ab-sence of more detailed information, it is hard to say whether the boil (abscess) killed him or secondary contamination from the surgeons' knives. This was before the germ theory existed, hence before any no-tion of the importance of cleanliness. No bactericides then, much less antibiotics. And so the man who could buy anything died, of a routine infection easily cured today for anyone who could find his way to a doc-tor or a hospital, even a pharmacy.

Medicine has made enormous strides since Nathan Rothschild's time. But better, more efficacious medicine—the treatment of illness and repair of injury—is only part of the story. Much of the increased life expectancy of these years has come from gains in prevention, cleaner living rather than better medicine. Clean water and expedi-tious waste removal, plus improvements in personal cleanliness, have made all the difference. For a long time the great killer was gastroin-testinal infection, transmitted from waste to hands to food to digestive tract; and this unseen but deadly enemy, ever present, was reinforced from time to time by epidemic microbes such as the *vibrio* of cholera. The best avenue of transmission was the common privy, where contact with wastes was fostered by want of paper for cleaning and lack of washable underclothing. Who lives in unwashed woolens—and woolens do not wash well—will itch and scratch. So hands were dirty, and the great mistake was failure to wash before eating. This was why those religious groups that prescribed washing—the Jews, the Mus-lims—had lower disease and death rates; which did not always count to their advantage. People were easily persuaded that if fewer Jews died, it was because they had poisoned Christian wells.

The answer was found, not in changed religious belief or doctrine, but in industrial innovation. The principal product of the new tech-nology that we know as the Industrial Revolution was cheap, washable cotton; and along with it mass-produced soap made of vegetable oils. For the first time, the common man could afford underwear, once known as body linen because that was the washable fabric that the well-to-do wore next to their skin. He (or she) could wash with soap and even bathe, although too much bathing was seen as a sign of dirt-iness. Why would clean people have to wash so often? No matter. Per-sonal hygiene changed drastically, so that commoners of the late nineteenth and early twentieth century often lived cleaner than the kings and queens of a century earlier.

The third element in the decline of disease and death was better nutrition. This owed much to increases in food supply, even more to better, faster transport. Famines, often the product of local shortages, became rarer; diet grew more varied and richer in animal protein. These changes translated among other things into taller, stronger physiques. This was a much slower process than those medical and hygienic gains that could be instituted from above, in large part because it depended on habit and taste as well as income. As late as World War I, the Turks who fought the British expeditionary force at Gallipoli were struck by the difference in height between the steak- and mutton-fed troops from Australia and New Zealand and the stunted youth of British mill towns. And anyone who follows immigrant populations from poor countries into rich will note that the children are taller and better knit than their parents.

From these improvements, life expectancy has shot up, while the differences between rich and poor have narrowed. The major causes of adult death are no longer infection, especially gastrointestinal infection, but rather the wasting ailments of old age. These gains have been greatest in rich industrial nations with medical care for all, but even some poorer countries have achieved impressive results.

Advances in medicine and hygiene exemplify a much larger phenomenon: the gains from the application of knowledge and science to technology. These give us reason to be hopeful about the problems that cloud present and future. They even encourage us toward fantasies of eternal life or, better yet, eternal youth.

Yet these fantasies, when science-based, that is, based on reality, are the dreams of the rich and fortunate. Gains to knowledge have not been evenly distributed, even within rich nations. We live in a world of inequality and diversity. This world is divided roughly into three kinds of nations: those that spend lots of money to keep their weight down; those whose people eat to live; and those whose people don't know where the next meal is coming from. Along with these differences go sharp contrasts in disease rates and life expectancy. The people of the rich nations worry about their old age, which gets ever longer. They exercise to stay fit, measure and fight cholesterol, while away the time with television, telephone, and games, console themselves with such euphemisms as "the golden years" and the *troisième âge*. "Young" is good; "old," disparaging and problematic. Meanwhile the people of poor countries try to stay alive. They do not have to worry about cholesterol and fatty arteries, partly because of lean diet, partly because they die early. They try to ensure a secure old age, if old age there be, by having lots of children who will grow up with a proper sense of filial obligation.

The old division of the world into two power blocs, East and West, has subsided. Now the big challenge and threat is the gap in wealth and health that separates rich and poor. These are often styled North and South, because the division is geographic; but a more accurate signifier would be the West and the Rest, because the division is also historic. Here is the greatest single problem and danger facing the world of the Third Millennium. The only other worry that comes close is environmental deterioration, and the two are intimately connected, indeed are one. They are one because wealth entails not only consumption but also waste, not only production but also destruction. It is this waste and destruction, which has increased enormously with output and income, that threatens the space we live and move in.

How big is the gap between rich and poor and what is happening to it? Very roughly and briefly: the difference in income per head between the richest industrial nation, say Switzerland, and the poorest nonindustrial country, Mozambique, is about 400 to 1. Two hundred and fifty years ago, this gap between richest and poorest was perhaps 5 to 1, and the difference between Europe and, say, East or South Asia (China or India) was around 1.5 or 2 to 1.[3]

Is the gap still growing today? At the extremes, clearly yes. Some countries are not only *not* gaining; they are growing poorer, relatively and sometimes absolutely. Others are barely holding their own. Others are catching up. Our task (the rich countries), in our own interest as well as theirs, is to help the poor become healthier and wealthier. If we do not, they will seek to take what they cannot make; and if they cannot earn by exporting commodities, they will export people. In short, wealth is an irresistible magnet; and poverty is a potentially raging contaminant: it cannot be segregated, and our peace and prosperity depend in the long run on the well-being of others.

How shall the others do this? How do we help? This book will try to *contribute to* an answer. I emphasize the word "contribute." No one has a simple answer, and all proposals of panaceas are in a class with millenarian dreams.

I propose to approach these problems historically. I do so because I am a historian by training and temperament, and in difficult matters of this kind, it is best to do what one knows and does best. But I do so also because the best way to understand a problem is to ask: How and why did we get where we are? How did the rich countries get so rich? Why are the poor countries so poor? Why did Europe ("the West") take the lead in changing the world?

A historical approach does not ensure an answer. Others have thought about these matters and come up with diverse explanations. Most of these fall into one of two schools. Some see Western wealth and dominion as the triumph of good over bad. The Europeans, they say, were smarter, better organized, harder working; the others were ignorant, arrogant, lazy, backward, superstitious. Others invert the categories: The Europeans, they say, were aggressive, ruthless, greedy, unscrupulous, hypocritical; their victims were happy, innocent, weak—waiting victims and hence thoroughly victimized. We shall see that both of these manichean visions have elements of truth, as well as of ideological fantasy. Things are always more complicated than we would have them.

A third school would argue that the West-Rest dichotomy is simply false. In the large stream of world history, Europe is a latecomer and free rider on the earlier achievements of others. That is patently incorrect. As the historical record shows, for the last thousand years, Europe (the West) has been the prime mover of development and modernity.

That still leaves the moral issue. Some would say that Eurocentrism is bad for us, indeed bad for the world, hence to be avoided. Those people should avoid it. As for me, I prefer truth to goodthink. I feel surer of my ground.

# THE WEALTH AND POVERTY
# OF NATIONS

# ~ 1 ~

# Nature's Inequalities

Geography has fallen on hard times. As a student in elementary school, I had to read and trace maps, even draw them from memory. We learned about strange places, peoples, and customs, and this long before anyone had invented the word "multiculturalism." At the same time, at higher levels far removed, schools of economic and cultural geography flourished. In France, no one would think of doing a study of regional history without first laying out the material conditions of life and social activity.[1] And in the United States, Ellsworth Huntington and his disciples were studying the ways that geography, especially climate, influenced human development.

Yet in spite of much useful and revealing research, Huntington gave geography a bad name.[2] He went too far. He was so impressed by the connections between physical environment and human activity that he attributed more and more to geography, starting with physical influences and moving on to cultural. In the end, he was classifying civilizations hierarchically and assigning the best—what he defined as best—to the favors of climate. Huntington taught at Yale University and not coincidentally thought New Haven, Connecticut, had the world's most invigorating climate. Lucky man. The rest of the world went down from there, with the lands of the peoples of color toward or at the bottom of the heap.

Yet in saying these things, Huntington was simply echoing the tradition of moral geography. Philosophers easily linked environment with temperament (hence the long-standing contrast between cold and hot, between sober thoughtfulness on the one hand, ebullient pleasure seeking on the other); while the infant discipline of anthropology in the nineteenth century presumed to demonstrate the effects of geography on the distribution of merit and wisdom, invariably most abundant in the writer's own group.[3] In our own day, the tables are sometimes reversed, and Afro-American mythmakers contrast happy, creative "sun people" with cold, inhuman "ice people."

That kind of self-congratulatory analysis may have been acceptable in an intellectual world that liked to define performance and character in racial terms, but it lost credibility and acceptability as people became sensitized and hostile to invidious group comparisons. And geography lost with it. When Harvard simply abolished its geography department after World War II, hardly a voice protested—outside the small group of those dismissed.[4] Subsequently a string of leading universities—Michigan, Northwestern, Chicago, Columbia—followed suit, again without serious objection.

These repudiations have no parallel in the history of American higher education and undoubtedly reflect the intellectual weaknesses of the field: the lack of a theoretical basis, the all-embracing opportunism (more euphemistically, the catholic openness), the special "easiness" of human geography. But behind those criticisms lay a dissatisfaction with some of the results. Geography had been tarred with a racist brush, and no one wanted to be contaminated.

And yet, if by "racism" we mean the linking, whether for better or worse, of individual performance and behavior to membership in a group, especially a group defined by biology, no subject or discipline can be less racist than geography. Here we have a discipline that, confining itself to the influence of environment, talks about anything but group-generated characteristics. No one can be praised or blamed for the temperature of the air, or the volume and timing of rainfall, or the lay of the land.

Even so, geography emits a sulfurous odor of heresy. Why? Other intellectual disciplines have also propagated nonsense or excess, yet no other has been so depreciated and disparaged, if only by neglect. My own sense is that geography is discredited, if not discreditable, by its nature. It tells an unpleasant truth, namely, that nature like life is unfair, unequal in its favors; further, that nature's unfairness is not easily remedied. A civilization like ours, with its drive to mastery, does not like to be thwarted. It disapproves of discouraging words, which geographic comparisons abound in.[5]

Geography, in short, brings bad tidings, and everyone knows what you do to that kind of messenger. As one practitioner puts it: "Unlike other history . . . the researcher may be held responsible for the results, much as the weather forecaster is held responsible for the failure of the sun to appear when one wishes to go to the beach."[6]

Yet we are not the wiser for denial. On a map of the world in terms of product or income per head, the rich countries lie in the temperate zones, particularly in the northern hemisphere; the poor countries, in the tropics and semitropics. As John Kenneth Galbraith put it when he was an agricultural economist: "[If] one marks off a belt a couple of thousand miles in width encircling the earth at the equator one finds within it *no* developed countries. . . . Everywhere the standard of living is low and the span of human life is short."[7] And Paul Streeten, who notes in passing the instinctive resistance to bad news:

> Perhaps the most striking fact is that most underdeveloped countries lie in the tropical and semi-tropical zones, between the Tropic of Cancer and Tropic of Capricorn. Recent writers have too easily glossed over this fact and considered it largely fortuitous. This reveals the deepseated optimistic bias with which we approach problems of development and the reluctance to admit the vast differences in initial conditions with which today's poor countries are faced compared with the pre-industrial phase of more advanced countries.[8]

To be sure, geography is only one factor in play here. Some scholars blame technology and the rich countries that have developed it: they are charged with inventing methods suited to temperate climates, so that potentially fertile tropical soil remains fallow. Others accuse the colonial powers of disrupting the equatorial societies, so that they have lost control of their environment. Thus the slave trade, by depopulating large areas and allowing them to revert to bush, is said to have encouraged the tsetse fly and the spread of trypanosomiasis (sleeping sickness). Most writers prefer to say nothing on the subject.

One must not take that easy way out. The historian may not erase or rewrite the past to make it more pleasing; and the economist, whose easy assumption that every country is destined to develop sooner or later, must be ready to look hard at failure.[9] Whatever one may say about the weakening of geographical constraints today in an age of tropical medicine and high technology, they have not vanished and were clearly more powerful earlier. The world has never been a level playing field, and everything costs.

We begin with the simple, direct effects of environment and go on to the more complex, more mediated links.

Climate first. The world shows a wide range of temperatures and temperature patterns, reflecting location, altitude, and the declination of the sun. These differences directly affect the rhythm of activity of all species: in cold, northern winters, some animals simply curl up and hibernate; in hot, shadeless deserts, lizards and serpents seek the cool under rocks or under the earth itself. (That is why so many desert fauna are reptiles: reptiles are crawlers.) Mankind generally avoids the extremes. People pass, but do not stay; hence such names as the "Empty Quarter" in the Arabian desert. Only greed—the discovery of gold or petroleum—or the duties of scientific inquiry can overcome a rational repugnance for such hardship and justify the cost.

In general the discomfort of heat exceeds that of cold.* We all know the fable of the sun and wind. One deals with cold by putting on clothing, by building or finding shelter, by making fire. These techniques go back tens of thousands of years and account for the early dispersion of humanity from an African origin to colder climes. Heat is another story. Three quarters of the energy released by working muscle takes the form of heat, which the body, like any machine or engine, must release or eliminate to maintain a proper temperature. Unfortunately, the human animal has few biological devices to this purpose. The most important is perspiration, especially when reinforced by rapid evaporation. Damp, "sweaty" climes reduce the cooling effect of perspiration—unless, that is, one has a servant or slave to work a fan and speed up evaporation. Fanning oneself may help psychologically, but the real cooling effect will be canceled by the heat produced by the motor activity. That is a law of nature: nothing for nothing; or in technical terminology, the law of conservation of energy and mass.

The easiest way to reduce this waste problem is not to generate heat; in other words, keep still and don't work. Hence such social adaptations as the siesta, which is designed to keep people inactive in the

---

* In general. It is easier to stay warm if one has the means—the appropriate clothing and housing. Faujas de Saint Fond, a French traveler of the late eighteenth century, remarks that whereas English cultivators lived snug and warm thanks to coal fuel, French peasants often kept to bed in winter, thereby aggravating their poverty by forced idleness.

heat of midday. In British India, the saying had it, only mad dogs and Englishmen went out in the noonday sun. The natives knew better.

Slavery makes other people do the hard work. It is no accident that slave labor has historically been associated with tropical and semitropical climes.* The same holds for division of labor by gender: in warm lands particularly, the women toil in the fields and tend to housework, while the men specialize in warfare and hunting; or in modern society, in coffee, cards, and motor vehicles. The aim is to shift the work and pain to those not able to say no.

The ultimate answer to heat has been air conditioning. But that came in very late—really after World War II, although in the United States it was known before in cinemas, doctors' and dentists' offices, and the workplaces of important people such as the denizens of the Pentagon. In America, air conditioning made possible the economic prosperity of the New South. Without it, cities like Atlanta, Houston, and New Orleans would still be sleepy-time towns.

But air cooling is a costly technology, not affordable by most of the world's poor. Moreover, it simply redistributes the heat from the fortunate to the unfortunate. It needs and consumes energy, which generates heat in both the making and using (nothing for nothing), thereby raising the temperature and humidity of uncooled surroundings—as anyone knows who has walked near the exhaust vent of an air conditioner. And of course, for most of history it was not available. The productivity of labor in tropical countries was reduced accordingly.†

So much for direct effects. Heat, especially year-round heat, has an even more deleterious consequence: it encourages the proliferation of life forms hostile to man. Insects swarm as the temperature rises, and parasites within them mature and breed more rapidly. The result is faster transmission of disease and development of immunities to countermeasures. This rate of reproduction is the critical measure of the danger of epidemic: a rate of 1 means that the disease is stable—one

---

* Cf. Adam Smith, *Wealth of Nations,* Book IV, ch. 7, Part 2: "In all European colonies the culture of the sugar-cane is carried on by negro slaves. The constitution of those who have been born in the temperate climate of Europe could not, it is supposed, support the labour of digging the ground under the burning sun. . . . "
† Not everyone would agree. Cf. Blaut, *The Colonizer's Model,* p. 70, who says that it has become clear, "from many sources of evidence including physiological studies, that human bodies of all sorts can labor as effectively in the tropics as elsewhere if the bodies in question have had time to adjust to tropical conditions." Blaut is ideologically opposed to the notion that the favors of nature may be unequally distributed.

new case for one old. For infectious diseases like mumps or diphtheria, the maximum rate is about 8. For malaria it is 90. Insect-borne diseases in warm climes can be rampageous.[10] Winter, then, in spite of what poets may say about it, is the great friend of humanity: the silent white killer, slayer of insects and parasites, cleanser of pests.

Tropical countries, except at higher altitudes, do not know frost; average temperature in the coldest month runs above 18°C. As a result they are a hive of biological activity, much of it destructive to human beings. Sub-Saharan Africa threatens all who live or go there. We are only beginning to know the extent of the problem because of the appearance of new nations with armies and medical examinations for recruits. We now know for example that many people harbor not one parasite but several; hence are too sick to work and are steadily deteriorating.

One or two examples will convey the gruesome picture.

Warm African and Asian waters, whether canals or ponds or streams, harbor a snail that is home to a worm (schistosome) that reproduces by releasing thousands of minute tailed larvae *(cercariae)* into the water to seek and enter a mammal host body through bites or scratches or other breaks in the skin. Once comfortably lodged in a vein, the larvae grow into small worms and mate. The females lay thousands of thorned eggs—thorned to prevent the host from dislodging them. These make their way to liver or intestines, tearing tissues as they go. The effect on organs may be imagined: they waste the liver, cause intestinal bleeding, produce carcinogenic lesions, interfere with digestion and elimination. The victim comes down with chills and fever, suffers all manner of aches, is unable to work, and is so vulnerable to other illnesses and parasites that it is often hard to say what is killing him.

We know this scourge as snail fever, liver fluke, or, in more scientific jargon, as *schistosomiasis* or *bilharzia,* after the physician who first linked the worm to the disease in 1852. It is particularly widespread in tropical Africa, but afflicts the whole of that continent, plus semitropical areas in Asia and, in a related form, South America. It poses a particular problem wherever people work in water—in wet rice cultivation, for example.[11]

In recent decades, medical science has come up with a number of partial remedies, although the destructive power of these vermicides makes the cure almost as bad as the disease. The same for chemical attacks on the snail host: the molluscicides kill the fish as well as the snails. The gains of one year are canceled by the losses of the next: schistosomiasis is still with us. It was even deadlier in the past.

Better known is *trypanosomiasis*—a family of illnesses that includes nagana (an animal disease), sleeping sickness, and in South America Chagas' disease. The source of these maladies is trypanosomes, parasitic protozoans so named because of their augur-shaped bodies; they are borers. The *Trypanosoma brucei* is also "a wily beast, with a unique ability to alter its antigens."[12] We now know a hundred of these; there may be thousands. Now you see it, now you don't. The body's immune system cannot fight it, because it cannot find it. The only hope for resistance, then, is drugs—still in the experimental stage—and attacks on the vector.

In the case of African trypanosomiasis, the vector is the tsetse fly, a nasty little insect that would dry up and die without frequent sucks of mammal blood. Even today, with powerful drugs available, the density of these insects makes large areas of tropical Africa uninhabitable by cattle and hostile to humans. In the past, before the advent of scientific tropical medicine and pharmacology, the entire economy was distorted by this scourge: animal husbandry and transport were impossible; only goods of high value and low volume could be moved, and then only by human porters. Needless to say, volunteers for this work were not forthcoming. The solution was found in slavery, its own kind of habit-forming plague, exposing much of the continent to unending raids and insecurity. All of these factors discouraged intertribal commerce and communication and made urban life, with its dependence on food from outside, just about unviable. The effect was to slow the exchanges that drive cultural and technological development.* (Table 1.1 shows data on tropical and semitropical diseases.)

---

* Some scholars would not agree with this historical sequence. They see the slave trade as not indigenous but rather imported by the European demand for labor. This trade "changed trypanosomiasis from an endemic disease to which both humans and cattle had some immunity and exposure, which was kept in check by the relatively full occupation of lands into a devastating disease that, since the end of the last century, has indeed prevented the development of animal husbandry in some areas of Africa." Blaut, *The Colonizer's Model*, pp. 79–80, who miscites Giblin, "Trypanosomiasis Control." (Giblin is concerned, not with the effects of Atlantic slaving beginning in the sixteenth century, but rather those of colonial administration from the 1890s [pp. 73–74], a very different story.) Even on this later period, scholars disagree. Cf. Waller, "Tsetse Fly," p. 100.

Note, moreover, that there is abundant testimony to the existence of slavery in Africa long before the coming of the Europeans, as well as of an active slave trade by Arabs seeking captives for Muslim lands. Gordon, *Slavery*, pp. 105–27. On the other hand, whatever the origins and effects of these earlier manifestations, the Atlantic trade certainly aggravated them. Cf. Law, "Dahomey and the Slave Trade"; and Lovejoy, "Impact." Even here, however, Eltis, *Economic Growth*, p. 77, disagrees.

TABLE 1.1. Scope and Incidence of Tropical Diseases, 1990

| Disease | Countries Affected | Number Infected ('000) | Number at risk ('000,000) |
|---|---|---|---|
| Malaria | 103 | 270,000 | 2,100 |
| Schistosomiasis | 76 | 200,000 | 600 |
| Lymphatic filariasis | 76 | 90,000 | 900 |
| River blindness | 34 | 17,000 | 90 |
| Chagas' disease | 21 | 16–18,000 | 90 |
| Leishmaniasis | 80 | 12,000 | 350 |
| Leprosy | 121 | 10–12,000 | 1,600 |
| African sleeping sickness | 36 | 25 | 50 |

SOURCE: World Health Organization (WHO), Special Program for Research and Training in Tropical Diseases, 1990, cited in Omar Sattaur, "WHO to Speed Up Work on Drugs for Tropical Diseases," p. 17.

To be sure, medicine has made great strides in combatting these maladies. Its role goes back almost to the beginning of the European presence: Europeans, physically unprepared for the special rigors and dangers of warm climes, brought doctors with them. In those early days, of course, ignorant if well-intentioned physicians did more harm than good; but they did put people out of their misery. Not until the second half of the nineteenth century did the germ theory of disease lay the basis for directed research and effective prevention and treatment. Before that, one relied on guesswork empiricism and imagination. These techniques, fortunately, were not haphazard. The stress on observation and the reality principle—you can believe what you see, so long as you see what I see—paid off beyond understanding.

Take the biggest killer worldwide: malaria. Before the discovery of microbic pathogens, physicians attributed "fevers" to marshy miasmas—wrong cause, but not an unreasonable inference from proximity. So the French in Algeria, appalled by losses to illness, undertook systematic drainage of swamps to get rid of bad air *(malaria)*. These projects may or may not have cleared the air, but they certainly banished mosquitoes. Military deaths from malaria fell by 61 percent in the period 1846–48 to 1862–66, while morbidity fell even more sharply from the 1830s to the 1860s.[13] Such measures, moreover, yielded beneficial side effects. We do not have figures for civilians, but their health must also have improved, natives as well as French colonists. Say what you will about French policies and actions in Algeria, they enabled millions of Algerians to live longer and healthier. (To which an Algerian Muslim might reply, drainage also increased the land available for European colonists.)

The Algerian experience illustrates the gain to environmental improvement: better to keep people from getting sick than to cure them once ill. Over the past century, medicine and public hygiene in alliance have made an enormous difference to life expectancy—the figure for tropical and poor populations have been converging with those of kinder, richer climes. Thus in 1992 a baby born in a low-income economy (population over 1 billion people if one excludes China and India) could expect to live to fifty-six, whereas one born in a rich country (population 828 million) could look forward to seventy-seven years. This difference (37.5 percent longer), not small but smaller than before, will get smaller yet as poor countries grow richer and gains in longevity in rich societies bump up against a biological ceiling and the environmental diseases of affluence.[14] The most decisive improvements have occurred in the care of infants (under one year): a fall in mortality from 146 per thousand live births in 1965 in the poorest countries (114 in China and India) in 1965 to 91 in 1992 (79 in India, 31 in China). Still, the contrast with rich countries remains: their low infant death rates fell even faster, 25 to 7, over the same period.[15] They can't go much lower.

All of this does not justify complacency. Modern medicine can save babies and keep people alive longer, but that does not necessarily mean they are healthy. Indeed, mortality and morbidity are statistically contradictory. Dead people do not count as ill, as the researcher for the American tobacco industry implied when he argued straightfacedly that estimates of the high health costs of smoking should be reduced by smokers' shorter life expectancy. So, conversely, for the tropics: antibiotics, inoculations, and vaccinations save people, but often to live sickly lives. The very existence of a specialty known as tropical medicine tells the character of the problem. As much as this field has accomplished, the bill, among scientific researchers as well as among indigenous victims and sundry imperialists, has been high.[16]

Meanwhile prevention is costly and treatment often entails a protracted regimen of medication that local facilities cannot supply and that patients find hard to use. As of 1990, most people with tropical illnesses lived in countries with average annual incomes of less than $400. Their governments were spending less than $4 per person on health care. No surprise, then, that pharmaceutical companies, which say it costs about $100 million to develop a drug or vaccine and bring it to market, are reluctant to cater for that kind of customer.[17] Even in rich countries, the cost of medication can exceed patients' resources and the tolerance of medical insurance. The latest therapies for AIDS, for example, cost $10,000 to $15,000 a year for a lifetime—an unthinkable fortune for Third World victims.[18]

Finally, habits and institutions can favor disease and thwart medical solutions. Diseases are almost invariably shaped by patterns of human behavior, and remedies entail not only medication but changes in comportment. There's the rub: it is easier to take an injection than to change one's way of living. Look at AIDS in Africa. In contrast to other places, the disease afflicts women and men equally, originating overwhelmingly in heterosexual contacts. Epidemiologists are still seeking answers, but among the suggested factors are: widespread and expected male promiscuity; recourse to anal sex as a technique of birth control; and the persistent wound of female circumcision (clitorectomy), intended as a deterrent to sexual pleasure and appetite. None of these vectors is properly medical, so that all the doctors can do is alleviate the suffering of victims and delay the onset of the full-blown disease. Given the poverty of these societies, this is not much.

Aside from material constraints, modern medicine must also reckon with ideological and religious obstacles—everywhere, but more so in poorer, technically backward societies. Traditional nostrums and magical invocations may be preferred to foreign, godless remedies. A science-oriented Westerner will dismiss such practices as superstition and ignorance. Yet they may offer psychosomatic relief, and native potions, even if not chemically pure and concentrated, do sometimes work. That is why modern scientists and drug companies spend money exploring the virtues of exotic *materia medica.*

The pattern of occasional empiricist success, in combination with anticolonist resentment and a sentimental attachment to indigenous culture (to say nothing of the vested interest of old-style practitioners), has given rise to political and anthropological criticisms of tropical (modern) medicine and a defense, however guarded, of "alternative" practice.[19] For Africa, this literature argues that tropical medicine, in its overweening pride and its contempt for indigenous therapies, has done less than it might have; further, that Europe-drawn frontiers and European-style commercial agriculture have wiped out traditional barriers to disease vectors (bugs, parasites, etc.). Even "perfectly sensible" measures of public health may offend indigenous susceptibilities, while medical tests and precautions may be seen as condescending and exploitative.[20]

Water is another problem. Tropical areas generally average enough rainfall, but the timing is often irregular and unpredictable, the downpours anything but gentle. The drops are large; the rate of fall torrential. The averages mean nothing when one goes from one extreme to the other, from one year or season or one day to the next.[21] In northern Nigeria, 90 percent of all rain falls in storms of over 25 mm. per hour; that makes half the average monthly rainfall at Kew Gardens, outside London. Java has heavier pours: a quarter of the annual rainfall comes down at 60 mm. per hour.

In such climes, cultivation does not compete easily with jungle and rain forest: these treasure houses of biodiversity favor every species but man and his limited array of crops. The result is a kind of war that leaves both nature and man losers. Attempts to cut down valuable plants and timber take the form of wasteful, slashing hunts. Nor does the exuberance of the jungle offer a good clue to what is possible under cultivation. Clear and plant, and the unshaded sun beats down; heavy rains pelt the ground—their fall unbroken by leaves and branches—leach out soil nutrients, create a new kind of waste. If the soil is clayey, composed in large part of iron and aluminum oxides, sun plus rain bakes the ground into a hard coat of armor. Two or three years of crops are followed by an indefinite forced fallow. Newly cleared ground is rapidly abandoned, and soon the vines and tendrils choke the presumptuous dwellings and temples. Again towns cannot thrive, for they need to draw on food surpluses from surrounding areas. Urbanization in Africa today, often chaotic, rests heavily on food imports from abroad.

At the other extreme, dry areas turn to desert, and the sands of the desert become an implacable invader, smothering once fertile lands on the periphery. Around 1970, the Sahara was advancing into the Sahel at the rate of 18 feet an hour—in geological terms, a gallop.[22] Such expansions of wasteland are a problem in all semi-arid climes: on the Great Plains of the United States (remember the Okies of Steinbeck's *Grapes of Wrath*), in the Israeli Negev and the lands just east of the Jordan, in western Siberia. Less rainfall, and the crops die of thirst and the topsoil blows away. In temperate latitudes, however, the crops come back when rainfall picks up; tropical and semitropical deserts are less forgiving.

One answer to irregular moisture is storage and irrigation; but this is countered in these regions by incredibly high rates of evaporation. In the Agra region of India, for example, rainfall exceeds the current needs of agriculture for only two months in the year, and the excess held in the soil in those wet months dries up in only three weeks.

It is no accident, then, that settlement and civilization followed the rivers, which bring down water from catchment areas and with it an annual deposit of fertile soil: thus the Nile, the Indus, the Tigris and Euphrates. These centers of ancient civilization were first and foremost centers of nourishment—though the Bible reminds us that even the Egyptians had to worry about famine. Not all streams are so generous. The Volta drains over 100,000 square kilometers in West Africa—half the area of Great Britain—but when low, averages at its mouth a meager flow of only 28 cubic meters per second, as against 3,500–9,800 at the peak. Drought in the Volta basin comes at the hottest and windiest time of year, and loss of water to evaporation is discouragingly high.[23]

Then we have the catastrophes—the so-called once-in-a-hundred-year floods and storms and droughts that happen once or twice every decade. In 1961–70, some twenty-two countries in "climatically hostile areas" (flood-prone, drought-prone, deserts) suffered almost $10 billion in damages from cyclones, typhoons, droughts, and similar disasters—almost as much as they got in loans from the World Bank, leaving just about nothing for development. The cyclone of 1970 in Bangladesh, which is a sea-level plain and easily awash, killed about half a million and drove twice that number from their homes. In India, which has been striving to achieve 2–3 percent annual growth in food crops, one bad growing season can lower output by over 15 percent.[24] The impact of such unexceptional exceptions can be extremely costly even to rich societies, witness the losses due to Hurricane Andrew in 1992 and the great midwestern floods of 1993 and 1997 in the United States. For marginally poor populations living on the edge of subsistence, the effects are murderous. We know something about these if there are television cameras present; if not, who hears or sees the millions who drown and starve? And if they are unheard and unseen, who cares?

Life in poor climes, then, is precarious, depressed, brutish. The mistakes of man, however well intentioned, aggravate the cruelties of nature. Even the good ideas do not go unpunished. No wonder that these zones remain poor; that many of them have been growing poorer; that numerous widely heralded projects for development have failed abysmally (one hears more of these before than after); that gains in health peter out in new maladies and give way to counterattacks by old.

Africa especially has had a hard struggle against these handicaps, and although much progress has been made, as mortality rates and life expectancy data show, morbidity remains high, nourishment is inadequate, famine follows famine, and productivity stays low. Once able to feed its population, it can do so no longer. Foreign aid is primarily food aid. People there operate at a fraction of their potential. Government cannot cope. In view of these stubborn natural burdens, the amazing thing is that Africans have done so well as they have.

Yet it would be a mistake to see geography as destiny. Its significance can be reduced or evaded, though invariably at a price. Science and technology are the key: the more we know, the more can be done to prevent disease and provide better living and working conditions. We can clearly do more today than yesterday, and the prognosis for tropical areas is better than it used to be. Meanwhile improvement in this area requires awareness and attention. We must take off the rose-colored glasses. Defining away or ignoring the problem will not make it go away or help us solve it.

## "I Have Always Felt Reinforced and Stimulated by the Temperate Climate"

Personal experiences can be misleading, if only because of the variance among individuals. One person's discomfort is another's pleasure. Still, the law of heat exhaustion applies to all, and few manage to work at full capacity when hot and wet. Here is a Bangladeshi diplomat recalling his own experience and that of compatriots when visiting temperate climes:

"In countries like India, Pakistan, Indonesia, Nigeria and Ghana I have always felt enervated by the slightest physical or mental exertion, whereas in the UK, France, Germany or the US I have always felt reinforced and stimulated by the temperate climate, not only during long stays, but even during brief travels. And I know that all tropical peoples visiting temperate countries have had a similar experience. I have also seen hundreds of people from the temperate zone in the tropics feeling enervated and exhausted whenever they were not inside an air-conditioned room.

"In India and other tropical countries I have noticed farmers, industrial labourers, and in fact all kinds of manual and office workers working in slow rhythm with long and frequent rest pauses. But in the temperate zone I have noticed the same classes of people working in quick rhythm with great vigour and energy, and with very few rest pauses. I have known from personal experience and the experience of other tropical peoples in the temperate zone that this spectacular difference in working energy and efficiency could not be due entirely or even mainly to different levels of nutrition."[25]

# 2

# Answers to Geography: Europe and China

The unevenness of nature shows in the contrast between this un-happy picture and the far more favorable conditions in temperate zones; and within these, in Europe above all; and within Europe, in western Europe first and foremost.

Take climate. Europe does have winters, cold enough to keep down pathogens and pests. Winter's severity increases as one moves east into continental climes, but even the milder versions fend off festering morbidity. Endemic disease is present, but nothing like the disablers and killers found in hot lands. Parasitism is the exception. Some have argued that this exemption accounts for the vulnerability of Europeans to epidemic plagues: they were not sufficiently exposed to pathogens to build up resistance.

Even in winter, West European temperatures are kind. If one traces lines of equal temperature around the globe (isotherms), nowhere do they bend so far north as along Europe's Atlantic coast. The mean winter temperature in coastal Norway, north latitude 58 to 71 degrees, exceeds that in Vermont or Ohio, some 20 degrees closer to the equator. As a result, Europeans were able to grow crops year round.

They were assisted here by a relatively even rainfall pattern, distributed around the year and rarely torrential: "it droppeth as the gentle rain from heaven." This is a pattern found only exceptionally around the globe. Summer rain falls abundantly right across the Eurasian landmass; winter rain, no. Precipitation coming off the Atlantic in the winter fails by the time it gets to the plains of Central and Eastern Europe. The landlocked steppes of Asia starve for water; hence such places as the Gobi Desert. Southern and eastern China are saved by rains coming up from the seas off Indochina; the same for the southeastern United States, heir to moisture from the Gulf of Mexico.

This dependable and equable supply of water made for a different pattern of social and political organization from that prevailing in riverine civilizations. Along rivers, control of food fell inevitably to those who held the stream and the canals it fed. Centralized government appeared early, because the master of food was master of people. (The biblical account of Joseph and Pharaoh tells this process in allegory. In order to get food, the starving Egyptians gave up to Pharaoh first their money, then their livestock, then their land, then their persons [Genesis 47:13–22].) Nothing like this was possible in Europe.

This privileged European climate was the gift of the large warm current that we know as the Gulf Stream, rising in tropical waters off Africa, working its way westward across the Atlantic and through the Caribbean, then recrossing the Atlantic in a generally northeast direction. The clockwise rotation is produced by the spin of the earth in combination with water rising as it warms; in the southern hemisphere, equatorial currents go counterclockwise (see Map 1). In both hemispheres, equatorial currents proceed from east to west, bearing heat and rich marine life with them.

Normally north and south equatorial currents should be roughly equal in volume, but in the Atlantic, an accident of geology turns the north equatorial into the largest such oceanic flow in the world. This accident: the shape taken by South America as tectonic continental plates parted and the Americas broke off from the African landmass, specifically, the great eastward bulge of Brazil (roughly corresponding to the eastward bend in the Atlantic coast of Africa). Brazil's salient splits the south equatorial current and sends roughly half of it northward to join its northern counterpart, producing a huge warm-water mass that washes finally against the coasts of Ireland and Norway (see Map 1). This geological good fortune gives western Europe warm winds and gentle rain, water in all seasons, and low rates of evaporation—the makings of good crops, big livestock, and dense hardwood forests.

To be sure, Europe knows more than one climate. Rainfall is heaviest and most equable along the Atlantic, there where the moisture-laden west winds leave the water for land. As one moves east toward the Polish and Russian steppe, climate becomes more "continental," with wider extremes of both moisture and temperature. The same for the Mediterranean lands: the temperatures are kind, but rain is sparser, more uneven. In Spain, Portugal, southern Italy, and Greece, the soil yields less, olive trees and grapes do better than cereals, pasture pays more than agriculture. Some would argue that these geographical handicaps led to poverty, even to industrial retardation, in southern as against northern Europe.[1] (We shall see later that other, cultural reasons may have been at least as important.)

If so, why was Europe so slow to develop, thousands of years after Egypt and Sumer? The answer, again, is geography: those hardwood forests. Edmund Burke spoke well when he contrasted the Indians and the English: "a people for ages civilized and cultivated . . . while we were yet in the woods."[2] Not until people had iron cutting tools, in the first millennium before our era (B.C.E.), could they clear those otherwise fertile plains north of the Alps. No accident, then, that settlement of what was to become Europe took place first along lakeshores (what we know as lacustrine settlements, often on stilts) and on grasslands—not necessarily the most fertile lands, but the ones accessible to primitive, nonferrous technology. Only later could Europe grow enough food to sustain denser populations and the surpluses that support urban centers of cultural exchange and development. Even so, most of the forest remained, even gaining when population shrank in the centuries following the fall of Rome. The folk memory comes down to us in legend and tale, in *Little Red Riding Hood, Hansel and Gretel, Tom Thumb,* and other stories of woods and wolves and witches and danger close by.

As these tales make clear, it would be a mistake to present the European geographic environment as idyllic. Europe knew famine and disease, long waves of cooling and warming, epidemics and pandemics. Peasants knew they could survive one and perhaps two bad crops, but after that came starvation. Here again the forest played a crucial role—source of berries, nuts, even acorns and chestnuts. And here too the steady water meant that farming was not marginal, that a dry spell would soon be followed by a return of rain and crops. One has to look at the dry places, there where cultivation is a gamble and the land risks turning into desert—not only the areas south of the invasive Sahara, or the lands east of the Jordan River on the northern margin of the Arabian desert, but the American plains west of the 100th meridian, or the

Siberian steppe where Khrushchev tried to grow wheat, or the cotton lands around Lake Baikal—to get a sense of how narrow the edge where rains are fickle and rare.

This favorable environment enabled Europeans to leave more of the land for forest and fallow and so raise livestock without seeking far for pasture. Their animals were bigger and stronger than those of other lands. The Mongolian pony, scourge of the steppe, stood tiny next to a European battle steed; the same for Arab mounts. Much of India could not breed horses at all because of the climate. Yet both small and large animals offered advantages. The Mongol and Tartar could move easily across their empty inland sea, striking fast and hard against the sedentary populations round. The European horse, carrying an armored warrior, amounted to a living tank, irresistible in charges, unbeatable in set combat.

The conflict between these two tactics gave rise to some of the greatest battles in history. In 732, Charles Martel, grandfather of Charlemagne and Frankish Mayor of the Palace, led an army of mounted knights against the Arab invaders near Tours and set a westward limit to what had seemed irresistible Muslim expansion.* Some four hundred fifty years later, in 1187, the Saracen troops of Saladin let the European knights charge down at them at the Horns of Hattin, stepping aside at the last moment to let them through. By then the crusader mounts, which had been carrying their riders all day in the blazing sun, were exhausted. The Saracens had only to close and cut down the Europeans from the rear. So ended the crusading kingdom of Jerusalem and Christian feudal power in the Holy Land.

In the long run, however, the Europeans won. Larger animals meant an advantage in heavy work and transport. Dray horses could plow the clayey soils of the great northern plain (the horse is more powerful than the ox, that is, it moves faster and does more work in less time), while moving fresh crops to urban markets. Later on they would haul field guns to war and into combat. European herds were typically larger and yielded lots of animal fertilizer (as against the human night soil employed in East Asia). This enabled more intensive cultivation and larger crops, which gave more feed, and so on in an upward spiral. As a result, Europeans kept a diet rich in dairy products, meat, and animal proteins. They grew taller and stronger while staying relatively free of

---

* Gibbon, the great historian of the *Decline and Fall of the Roman Empire,* by way of emphasizing the momentousness of this victory, remarked that had the Arabs won, all of Europe would now be reading the Koran and all the males circumcised.

the worm infestations that plagued China and India.* (Only a few years ago, one fifth of all Chinese who received blood transfusions came down with hepatitis, because donors' livers had been ravaged by parasites and blood screening was incompetent.)³ Healthier Europeans lived longer and worked closer to their potential.†⁴

This is not to say that European crop yields *per area* or population *densities* were higher than those in warm irrigation societies. The gains from animal fertilizer, plowing (which brings nutrients up from below), and fallow could not match the fertile silt of the Nile, the Euphrates, or the Indus; even less, the alluvial deposits of the Yellow and Yangtze rivers, and the multiple cropping made possible by year-round warmth.** On the other hand, irregular interruptions in riverine cultivation, whether by want or excess of water or by enemy action against irrigation systems, could hurt far more than dry or wet spells in a rainy climate.‡ Averages are deceiving. Monsoon rains, generous over time, vary a lot from season to season and year to year. Floods and droughts are the norm. In China and India, repair and replenishment were that much more urgent. Even without catastrophe, the demand for labor in the rainy season and the big yields of wet cultivation promoted high densities of population—30 times that of Africa per unit of arable, 40

---

* Eric Jones, *The European Miracle*, pp. 6–7: "Faeces discharged into water made China the world reservoir of lung, liver and intestinal flukes and the Oriental schistosome, all serious causes of chronic illness. Human excreta were used as a fertiliser, and soil-transmitted helminth infestation was an occupational hazard for the farmer. According to Han Suyin there was ninety per cent worm infestation among children in Peking in the early twentieth century and worms were visible everywhere on paths and alongside buildings. . . . Anti-social customs apart, this was the penalty for a dense population operating irrigation agriculture in a warm climate, with inadequate sources of fertiliser." India, with the unhygienic habit of defecating in public space, often in streams and rivers that also served for washing and drinking, may have been in even worse shape.

† Jones, *European Miracle*, who cites Narain, *Indian Economic Life*, pp. 332–33. But Narain's data come from the late nineteenth and early twentieth centuries, when Europe had made substantial progress over earlier mortality levels. The differences between Europe and Asia had presumably been smaller five hundred or a thousand years earlier.

** The Yangtze alone deposits more silt than the Nile, Amazon, and Mississippi combined; and the Yellow River deposits three times that of the Yangtze—Link, "A Harvest," p. 6.

‡ Because of dependence on artifice, such societies were highly vulnerable. It has been argued, for example, that the destruction (fourteenth century) by Timur and his Tartar hordes of the cisterns and water delivery systems of Persia was never repaired and turned a once populous, fertile land into a waste. The kingdoms and peoples of that area never recovered.

times that of Europe, 100 times that of America.[5] Hence early and al-most universal marriage, without regard to material resources.*

In contrast, Christian and especially western Europe accepted celibacy, late marriage (not until one could afford it), and more widely spaced births. Medieval Europeans saw children as a potential burden in time of need. Recall the stories of Hansel and Gretel and Tom Thumb—the children left in the forest to die far from the eyes of their parents. The riverine civilizations maximized population; the Euro-peans focused on small households and strategies of undivided inher-itance and interfamilial alliance.

So, numbers alone do not tell the story, and some would say that when health and animal support are factored in, Europe may have brought more energy to agriculture (per area of cultivation) than the much more numerous populations of Asia. Such peasant throngs, moreover, tempted Asian rulers to undertake ostentatious projects based on forced labor. These would one day be the wonder and scan-dal of European visitors—great tourist attractions—astonishing by the contrast between overweening wealth and grinding poverty. "The splendours of Asian courts, the religious and funerary monuments and hydraulic engineering works, the luxury goods and skilled craftsman-ship seemed merely to testify that political organisation could squeeze blood out of stones if the stones were numerous enough."[†]

The Europeans did not have to build pyramids.** Europe, particu-larly western Europe, was very lucky.

---

*  In effect, this pattern of maximum reproduction enhanced political power, in terms both of combat fodder and of material for territorial expansion. In the last analysis, this was the story of Chinese aggrandizement over less prolific societies.

†  Jones, *The European Miracle*, p. 5. Jones cites one apologist as arguing that many of these projects may not have involved that many workers after all, that they may have been spread out over time and taken generations to complete, and that the laborers may have been volunteers motivated by religious fervor (p. 10). Anyone who can be-lieve that will believe anything: these projects typically used armed overseers and en-tailed spectacularly high death rates. On the losses that went with construction of the Grand Canal and the Great Wall of China—we are talking of millions of dead—see *ibid.*, p. 9.

** That's not quite true: the Europeans also had their despotisms. Visitors today to the great basilica at Vézelay may be interested to learn that the serfs who were conscripted to build it rose three times in revolt against the church authorities. Animals also paid; cf. the cathedral at Laon, which stands atop a hill and has in its tower the statues of four oxen, facing north, south, east, and west, commemorating the beasts that died haul-ing up stone from the plain below. But better oxen than people. And that was a kind of apology.

For a more recent example, cf. the railway line (1840s) from St. Petersburg to Moscow—a corpse for every tie.

Now look at China, where "agriculture teems . . . and mankind swarms."[6]

Anyone who wants to understand world economic history must study China, the most precocious and long the most successful developer of all. Here is a country with some 7 percent of the earth's land area that supports some 21 percent of the world's population. The old Chinese slogan puts it succinctly: "The land is scarce and the people are many."[7]

Some two thousand years ago, perhaps 60 million people crowded what was to become the northern edge of China—a huge number for a small territory. This number more or less held over the next millennium, but then, from about the tenth to the beginning of the thirteenth century, almost doubled, to around 120 million. At that point came a setback, due largely to the pandemics also scourging Europe and the Middle East; and then, from a trough of 65–80 million around 1400, the number of Chinese rose to 100–150 million in 1650, 200–250 million in 1750, over 300 million by the end of the eighteenth century, around 400 million in 1850, 650 million in 1950, and today 1.2 billion, or more than one fifth of the world total. This extraordinary increase is the result of a long-standing (up to now) reproductive strategy: early, universal marriage and lots of children. That takes food, and the food in turn takes people. Treadmill.

This strategy went back thousands of years, to when some peoples at the eastern end of the Asian steppe exchanged nomadic pastoralism for the higher yields of sedentary agriculture. From the beginning, their chiefs saw the link between numbers, food, and power. Their political wisdom may be inferred from (1) their mobilization of potential cultivators, assigned to (planted in) potentially arable soil; (2) their storage of grain to feed future armies; (3) their focus on food supply to fixed administrative centers (as against camps). On these points, we have "The Record of the Three Kingdoms," which tells of state warfare around the year 200 of our era:

> Ts'ao Ts'ao said: "It is by strong soldiers and a sufficiency of food that a state is established. The men of Ch'in took possession of the empire by giving urgent attention to farming. Hsiao-wu made use of military colonies to bring order to the western regions. This is a good method used by former generations." In this year he recruited commoners to farm state colonies around Hsu [in central Honan] and obtained a million measures of grain. Then he . . . marched out on campaign in every direction. There was no

need to expend effort on the transport of grain. In consequence he destroyed the swarms of bandits [the forces of rival political chiefs] and brought peace to the empire.

A half century later, according to the same source, "it was desired to extend the area under cultivation and to amass a supply of grain that would make it possible to destroy the 'bandits.' " To do this, "it would also be necessary to excavate canals to provide water for irrigation, to make possible the accumulation of large supplies of grain for the troops, and to serve as routes for the transport of the government grain. . . . " Some calculations follow: "Within six or seven years thirty million measures of grain would be stockpiled on the Huai. This would be enough to feed 100,000 men for five years. Wu would thus be conquered and [Wei] arms prevail everywhere."[8] And so it was.

This erratic seesaw of labor-hungry soil and food-hungry labor inevitably brought times and places of want, even famine. No room for animals. Around 300 C.E. a memorialist named Shu Hsi complained:

> The situation is especially bad in the San-Wei, and yet grazing lands for pigs, sheep, and horses are spread throughout this region. All of these should be done away with, so that provision may be made for those with no or little land. . . . All the pasturages should be removed, so that horses, cattle, pigs, and sheep feed on the grass of the empty plains, while the men who roam about in search of a living may receive land from the bounty of the state.[9]

Clearly, Chinese agriculture could not run fast enough. State and the society were always striving for new land and higher yields, making and using people in order to feed people. Under the emperor T'ai-wu (reigned 424–52, so, over a century later), the government was not going to leave anything to chance. Peasants without oxen were forced to sell their labor for the loan of oxen. Families were listed, numbers were counted, labor duties and performance clearly recorded. "Their names were written up at the place where they worked, so that it was possible to distinguish between their varying degrees of success. They were also forbidden to drink wine, to attend theatrical entertainments, or to abandon agriculture for wine-making or trade."[10]

No time, then, for fun or money. Only for growing food and making children.

Viewed over time, the treadmill process shows a number of stages:

1. The Chinese, or Han people, as they came to call themselves, started in the north, in the forests edging the barren inner Asian steppe. They cleared the land (by fire?) and worked it as hard as they could; but what with irregular rainfall and no trees to hold the soil, severe erosion soon killed the yield. They then moved, not into the open dry lands to the west, which could not support an already dense population, but south, on to the loess soils along the upper Yellow River.*

2. Loess agriculture was a school for water control and irrigation technology. It prepared the way for the next move, into the wetter, more fertile, but also more precarious river basin environment of the lower Yellow River and its branches.† There the Han came to know rice, a crop that yielded many more calories per area, although the traditional cereals—millet, sorghum, barley—remained important. Wheat came later.

By about 500 B.C.E. the Chinese had learned to improve the supply and use of water by means of artificial devices and arrangements; were making use of draft animals (above all, the water buffalo) for plowing; were weeding intensively; and were putting down animal waste, including night soil, as fertilizer. All of this required prodigious labor, but the work paid off. Yields shot to a high of 1,100 liters of grain per hectare, which would have left a substantial surplus for the maintenance of nonfood producers. The Chinese energy system was in place.

3. Between the eighth and thirteenth centuries of our era came a second agricultural revolution. The Han people kept moving south, into

---

* Loess is a loose loam, ranging from clayey soil to sand, fertile if well watered, well suited to cereal crops. It was not the richest land within reach, but rich enough, and it possessed the virtue of being easy to work because it did not carry heavy timber and could be cleared and cultivated with nonmetal instruments.

In the western parts of North China, the primary loess deposits run as much as 250 meters deep. The soil is fine and friable, hence easily plowed—see Bray, "Swords into Plowshares," p. 23. On the critical importance of ease of cultivation as against potential fertility in the early stages of agriculture, see above on the European experience. On China, see Lattimore, *Inner Asian Frontiers*, pp. 29–30. In his n.8 he cites Wittfogel to the effect that Egyptian agriculture began, not in the Nile delta, but upstream around what was to become the site of Memphis. Also the agricultural anthropologist-archeologist Carl Sauer, who stressed the importance of a soil "amenable to few and weak tools," and noted that the American Indians first cultivated poorer but more workable soils.

† Irregular precipitation upstream led to large variations in the volume of water, and the build-up of alluvial deposits at the great eastward bend had the Yellow River changing course all over the place as it splashed and poured into the Great Plain. Hence the nickname: China's Sorrow.

the Yangtze basin and beyond, pushing slash-and-burn, itinerant aboriginals aside or before. Most of these eventually found shelter in the mountains and other areas unsuited to intensive cultivation. They still live there—China's largest minority.

In this wetter, warmer clime, mild winters and long summers permitted full double cropping: winter wheat, for example, harvested in May, and summer rice planted in June and harvested in October or November. Where conditions permitted, the Chinese went beyond this, over to rice gardening in submerged paddies. Taking quicker-growing varieties, they got three or more crops per year. To do this, they saved and applied every drop of dung and feces; weeded incessantly; and maximized land use by raising seedlings in nurseries (high density) and then transplanting the mature shoots (needing more space) to the rice fields. In economic terms, they substituted labor for land, using sixty and eighty persons per hectare where an American wheat farmer would use one, and obtaining yields double and triple the already good results achieved in dry farming—as much as 2,700 liters per hectare. At the maximum, a thousand people could live on the food produced by a square kilometer. "By the thirteenth century China thus had what was probably the most sophisticated agriculture in the world, India being the only conceivable rival."[11]

All of this left little room for animals, except those needed for plowing and hauling and as mounts for the army. The pig was another exception—China's great scavenger and primary source of meat for the rich man's table. But few cattle or sheep: the Chinese diet knew little of dairy products or animal protein, and wool clothing was largely unknown. When the British tried to sell their woolens to the Chinese, they were told their cloths were too scratchy for people used to cotton and silk. They surely were.

4. Later innovations added marginally to the Chinese granary. In the seventeenth and eighteenth centuries, new plants were taken from distant lands—peanuts, potatoes, sweet potatoes, yams. These grew well in dryer uplands, but in the last analysis, they were only a supplement to a rice complex that could no longer keep up with demand.*

5. The overwhelming concentration on rice yielded a mix of good and bad. The appetite of rice for nutrients (particularly phosphate and

---

* Ingenuity and labor can still increase farm output, if not of rice and cereals, then of accessory crops. See Emily M. Berstein, "Ecologists Improve Production in Chinese Farming Village," *N.Y. Times,* 10 August 1993, p. C4, *re* increase in fish crop and savings in fertilizer.

potash) is lower than that of other food staples; its labor requirements greater. Its caloric yield per acre exceeds that of temperate zone grains such as wheat, rye, and oats; its protein content, however, is only about half as high.[12] Rice is a tough grain: it grows in diverse habitats and is the only cereal that will give good yields on poor soil year after year so long as it gets enough water. On the other hand, the wading in water paddies and the use of human feces as fertilizer has meant high exposure to schistosomes and other nasty parasites, with loss to productivity and hence higher labor requirements.

This labor-intensive, water-intensive energy model had important consequences for Chinese history. For one thing, reliance on the indigenous population meant that the Chinese never sought to incorporate foreign slaves into their workforce. (To be sure, many of their own population lived in bondage, though they were not chattel slaves.) For another, they did expand by sheer force of numbers. It was very hard for sparsely distributed, less organized, and technically less advanced groups to keep the Chinese out.

At the same time, the management of water called for supralocal power and promoted imperial authority. This link between water and power was early noted by European observers, going back to Montesquieu and reappearing in Hegel, later copied by Marx. The most detailed analysis, though, is the more recent one of Karl Wittfogel, who gave to water-based rule the name of Oriental despotism, with all the dominance and servitude that that implies.[13] (Others have offered analogous arguments, prudently shorn of portentous social and cultural implications.)[14]

The hydraulic thesis has been roundly criticized by a generation of Western sinologists zealous in their political correctness (Maoism and its later avatars are good) and quick to defend China's commitment to democracy. Wittfogel is the preferred target. One scholar sees in his thesis a lightly disguised program for neo-imperialism: "Clearly the action message of this theory is to recommend and justify intervention."[15] Presumably these protestations of loyalty aim to convince Chinese, if not Western, readers, for almost all these critics of the water connection are courting the favor of an umbrageous regime, dispenser of invitations and access.

The facts gainsay them. The anti-hydraulics point to evidence that the early centers of Chinese population did not rely much on irrigation; that then and later, much water was drawn from wells rather than brought in; and that some aspects of water management were always locally conceived and financed—as though such activity somehow contradicted the ultimate responsibility of the higher authorities in this domain, especially in conscripting and assigning labor for the larger tasks: the big dikes, dams, and canals, flood control, repair and relief. Such interventions went far beyond local possibilities. The stakes were huge. For one thing, the more daring the alteration of nature, the greater the scope and cost of failure or catastrophe.[16] For another, it was food surpluses that sustained the machinery of government.

This was the reality. As one team of scholars put it, repudiating Wittfogel the while, "There must be irrigable land available, adequate social hegemony and state control, and so on."[17] Yes indeed.

# 3

# European Exceptionalism:
# A Different Path

Europe was lucky, but luck is only a beginning. Anyone who looked at the world, say a thousand years ago, would never have predicted great things for this protrusion at the western end of the Eurasian landmass that we call the continent of Europe. In terms popular among today's new economic historians, the probability at that point of European global dominance was somewhere around zero. Five hundred years later, it was getting close to one.

In the tenth century, Europe was just coming out of a long torment of invasion, plunder, and rapine, by enemies from all sides. From what we now know as Scandinavia, the Norsemen or Vikings, marine bandits whose light boats could handle the roughest seas and yet sail up shallow rivers to raid and pillage far inland, struck along the Atlantic coasts and into the Mediterranean as far as Italy and Sicily. Others went east into Slavic lands, establishing themselves as a new ruling class (the Rus, who gave their name to Russia and ruled that somber land for some seven hundred years), and eventually penetrating almost to the walls of Constantinople.

So terrifying were these marauders, so ruthless their tactics (taking pleasure in tossing babes in the air and catching them on their lances, or smashing their heads against the wall), that the very rumor of their arrival loosened the limbs and loins of the population and sent their leaders, including their spiritual guides, in headlong flight, carrying their movable wealth with them. The clerics did leave their parishioners some newly composed prayers for protection by the Almighty, but the altar was not a good refuge, for the Vikings knew where the plunder lay and headed straight for churches and castles.

Also coming from the sea, across the Mediterranean, were Saracens (Moors), who set up mountain bases in the Alps and on the Côte d'Azur, and went out from these to raid the trade routes between northern and southern Europe. These fastnesses, hard of access and yet linked to Muslim lands by the sea, were inexpugnable, and folk legend has it that to this day some villagers in the high Alps carry the color and appearance of their Maghrebin origins.

Finally, from the east overland, but highly mobile for all that, rode the Magyars or Hungarians, one more wave of invaders from Asia, pagans speaking a Ural-Altaic language (a distant cousin of Turkish), sweeping in year after year, choosing their targets by news of European dissensions and dynastic troubles, swift enough to move in a single campaign from their Danubian bases into eastern France or the foot of Italy. Unlike the Norsemen, who were ready to settle into base camps for a period of years, the better to hunt and find, or who even established themselves quasi-permanently as rulers in part of England, in Normandy (which took their name), and in Sicily, the Hungarians went out and back, hauling their booty and slaves along with them in wagons or on pack animals.

No one will submit to that kind of abuse indefinitely. The Europeans learned to counter these thrusts, with or without the help of their leaders, who were only too quick to make their own deals with the invaders on the backs of their peasants. Instead of trying to keep the Norsemen out, the villagers let them in, trapped them, fell on them from all sides.* The Hungarians, too swift to deal with when they came in, were slow going out; a few ambushes of the overproud, overloaded trains convinced them that there must be better ways to make a living. As for the Saracens, the solution lay, as in Muslim lands, in military escorts for mule and wagon trains (caravans). In short, the Europeans raised the price of aggression. In all these instances, ironically, the Europeans were assisted by enemy headquarters. Over the years, the northern tribes and the Hungarian invaders settled down and became

---

* This is the theme of, though not the inspiration for, the film *The Magnificent Seven*. Comparable situations lead to comparable tactics.

domesticated. Kingdoms replaced nomadic war camps, and their rulers looked with disfavor on these swaggering "captains," with their private armies and tales of derring-do, returning from their raids with booty and brags, and threatening the peace. Kings do not need career troublemakers. A mix of threat and reward succeeded in persuading rogues and pirates that more was to be gained by being landlords and shearing sheep at home than by being warlords and killing sheep abroad.

It has been suggested that this end to danger from without launched Europe on the path of growth and development. This is the classical economists' view: increase is natural and will occur wherever opportunity and security exist. Remove the obstacles, and growth will take care of itself. Others would argue that freedom from aggression is a necessary but not sufficient condition. Growth and development call for enterprise, and enterprise is not to be taken for granted. Besides, medieval Europe did not lack for impediments to such initiatives.

To get an idea of the larger character of this process, one has to see the Middle Ages as the bridge between an ancient world set in the Mediterranean—Greece and then Rome—and a modern Europe north of the Alps and Pyrenees. In those middle years a new society was born, very different from what had gone before, and took a path that set it decisively apart from other civilizations.

To be sure, Europe had always thought of itself as different from the societies to the east. The great battles between Greeks and Persians—Salamis, Thermopylae—have come down in folk memory and in the classes of yesteryear as symbolic of the combat between West and East, between the free city (the *polis*, which gives us our word "politics") and aristocratic empires,[1] between popular sovereignty (at least for free men) and oriental despotism (servitude for all). In those days one was taught that the Greeks invented democracy, the word and the idea. This is still the conventional wisdom, though substantially modified by an awareness of Greek slavery and of their exclusion of women from the political process (though not from public space).

Linked to the opposition between Greek democracy and oriental despotism was that between private property and ruler-owns-all. Indeed, that was the salient characteristic of despotism, that the ruler, who was viewed as a god or as partaking of the divine, thus different from and far above his subjects, could do as he pleased with their lives and things, which they held at his pleasure. And what was true for the ruler was true for his henchmen. The martial aristocracy typically had a monopoly of weapons, and ordinary folk were careful not to offend them, arouse their cupidity, or even attract their attention; to look them in the eye was an act of impudence that invited severest punishment.

Today, of course, we recognize that such contingency of ownership stifles enterprise and stunts development; for why should anyone invest capital or labor in the creation or acquisition of wealth that he may not be allowed to keep? In the words of Edmund Burke, "a law against property is a law against industry."[2] In Asian despotisms, however, such arrangements were seen as the very raison d'être of human society: what did ordinary people exist for, except to enhance the pleasure of their rulers?

Certainly not to indulge a will of their own. The experience of the people of Balkh (central Asia) is emblematic. It so happened their ruler was away making war on the Indians, and a nomadic people nearby took advantage of his absence to seize the city. The inhabitants put up a good fight, defending not only their own houses and families but those of the absent ruler; but they lost. When the ruler returned, he retook the city; and when he learned of his subjects' valor, he scolded them. War, he lectured, was not their affair; their duty was to pay and obey whoever ruled them. The leaders of the common folk duly apologized and promised not to repeat their *lèse-majesté*.[3]

In these circumstances, the very notion of economic development was a Western invention. Aristocratic (despotic) empires were characteristically squeeze operations: when the elites wanted more, they did not think in terms of gains in productivity. Where would these have come from? They simply pressed (and oppressed) harder, and usually found some hidden juice. Sometimes they miscalculated and squeezed too hard, and that could mean flight, riot, and opportunities for rebellion. These autocracies, though defined as divine, were not immortal. Meanwhile only societies with room for multiple initiatives, from below more than from above, could think in terms of a growing pie.

The ancient Greeks distinguished between free and unfree, not so much in terms of material benefits (they were not particularly keen on economic enterprise, which they associated with metics and other crass people), or even in terms of the advantages of their own system, as of the wrongness of the other, which they saw as tyranny. And yet the Greeks succumbed to despotism, most spectacularly in the empire created by Alexander and ruled by his Asian and Egyptian successors; and later the Romans went the same way, sliding all too easily into tyrannical autocracy. In final form, the classical Mediterranean world came to resemble politically the civilizations to the east—a powerful and small elite surrounded by clients, servants, and slaves, and headed by an autocrat. But only resembled. Dissenters knew this was wrong, spoke up and wrote, and suffered for their presumption. The republican ideal died hard.

Meanwhile property rights had to be rediscovered and reasserted after the fall of Rome. This world, which we know as medieval—the time between—was a transitional society, an amalgam of classical legacy, Germanic tribal laws and customs, and what we now call the Judaic-Christian tradition. All of these provided support for institutions of private property. The Germanic custom was that of a nomadic community, with each warrior master of his modest possessions—kept modest by constant movement. Nothing was so special and valuable as to give rise to issues of ownership or to the ambitions of power.*

Which is not to say that there were not other incentives to power; or that the condition of these nomadic peoples was immutable. In the course of their wanderings and conquests, such issues did arise. Every French grammar school student used to learn the story of the vase of Soissons, a beautiful object robbed from a church by the Franks in war against the Gauls. The chief Clovis wanted to return it, by way of giving pleasure to a Christian woman who had won his fancy, but the soldier who had taken it (or had been awarded it in the division of the booty) refused. It was his by right, and he broke it in front of Clovis to make his point. In effect, he told his chief, what's yours is yours and what's mine is mine. The next time the troops were drawn up in array, Clovis stopped before the vase-breaker and asked him what was wrong with his sandal; and when the man bent down to look, Clovis shattered his skull with a battle-ax. In effect, what's yours is yours, but you are mine.†

Tensions and ambiguities, then. But what mattered in the long run were the constraints imposed by political fragmentation and general insecurity. In the centuries that followed the end of empire, the arm of authority was short. Power derived in principle from the freely con-

---

* "The acquisition of valuable and extensive property, therefore, necessarily requires the establishment of civil government. Where there is no property, or at least none that exceeds the value of two or three days labour, civil government is not so necessary."— Adam Smith, *Wealth of Nations,* Book 5, ch. 1, Part 2. Smith was thinking here of the protection of private property; but these considerations also apply to the uses of power.

† After years of telling of this apocryphal exchange (versions vary, but that's folklore), French teachers were afraid to ask their students who broke the vase of Soissons, because there would always be one wiseacre in the class to deny it. Cf. Bonheur, *Qui a cassé,* p. 77.

sented allegiance of the group or an elite within it and was correspondingly limited. To be sure, the tradition of election gave way to hereditary rule (the Germans were much influenced by Roman example, or rather principle). But old customs and appearances died hard: the ruler, even when designated by birth, was nominally elected. So he was earthly, human rather than divine, and his power the same.

Some did seek to restore the empire that had been. The dream of Rome reborn never died.[4] Had they succeeded, one might have expected a revival of arbitrary despotism. But such efforts broke down in the face of poor communication, inadequate transport, challenges to legitimacy, the contrary power of local rulers, the triumph of reality over fantasy. In this context, private property was what could be held and defended. Sometimes it was seized by force, just as today someone might be mugged and robbed. But the principle never died: property was a right, and confiscation, no more than plunder, could not change that.

The concept of property rights went back to biblical times and was transmitted and transformed by Christian teaching. The Hebrew hostility to autocracy, even their own, was formed in Egypt and the desert: was there ever a more stiff-necked people? Let me cite two examples, where the response to popular initiative is directly linked to the sanctity of possessions. When the priest Korach leads a revolt against Moses in the desert, Moses defends himself against charges of usurpation by saying, "I have not taken one ass from them, nor have I wronged any one of them" (Numbers 16:15). Similarly, when the Israelites, now established in the Land, call for a king, the prophet Samuel grants their wish but warns them of the consequences: a king, he tells them, will not be like him. "Whose ox have I taken, or whose ass have I taken?" (I Samuel 12:3).

This tradition, which set the Israelites apart from any of the kingdoms around and surely did much to earn them the hostility of nearby rulers—who needs such troublemakers?—tended to get lost in Christianity when that community of faith became a church, especially once that Church became the official, privileged religion of an autocratic empire. One cannot well bite the hand that funds. Besides, the word was not getting out, for the Church early decided that only qualified people, certain clerics for example, should know the Bible. The Good Book, with its egalitarian laws and morals, its prophetic rebukes of power and exaltation of the humble, invited indiscipline among the faithful and misunderstanding with the secular authorities. Only after censorship and edulcoration could it be communicated to the laity. So that it was not until the appearance of such heretical sects as the Waldensians (Waldo, c. 1175), the Lollards (Wiclif, c. 1376), Lutherans (1519 on), and Calvinists (mid-sixteenth), with their emphasis on personal religion and the translation of the Bible into the vernacular, that this Judaic-Christian tradition entered explicitly into the European political consciousness, by way of reminding rulers that they held their wealth and power of God, and then on condition of good behavior. An inconvenient doctrine.

Yet Western medieval Christianity did come to condemn the pretensions of earthly rulers—lesser monarchs, to be sure, than the emperors of Rome. (The Eastern Church never talked back to the Caesars of Byzantium.)* It thereby implicitly gave protection to private property. As the Church's own claims to power increased, it could not but emphasize the older Judaic principle that the real owner of everything was the Lord above, and the newer Christian principle that the pope was his vicar here below. Earthly rulers were not free to do as they pleased, and even the Church, God's surrogate on earth, could not flout rights and take at will. The elaborate paperwork that accompanied the transfer of gifts of the faithful bore witness to this duty of good practice and proper procedure.

All of this made Europe very different from civilizations around.

In China, even when the state did not take, it oversaw, regulated, and repressed. Authority should not have to depend on goodwill, the right attitude, personal virtue. Three hundred years before the Common Era, a Chinese moralist was telling a prince how to rule, not by winning the affection of his subjects but by ensuring their obedience. A prince cannot see and hear everything, so he must turn the entire empire into his eyes and ears. "Though he may live in the deepest retreat of his palace, at the end of tortuous corridors, nothing escapes him, nothing is hidden from him, nothing can escape his vigilant watch."[5] Such a system depends on the honesty and capacity of the living eyes and ears. The ruler is at the mercy of ambitious subordinates, whose capacity for deception and hypocrisy is unbounded. The weakness of autocracy is in the human raw material. Fortunately.

One scholar, impervious to euphemisms, terms the system "totalitarian":

---

* This split between western and eastern Europe is only one aspect of a profound chasm that still exists. And most people in eastern Europe know which side of the line they want to be on. Hence the expansion of "central" Europe to include everyone outside Russia. Also the inclusionary plans of the European Union and NATO.

No private undertaking nor any aspect of public life could escape official regulation. In the first place there was a whole series of state monopolies. . . . But the tentacles of the Moloch state, the omnipotence of the bureaucracy, extended far beyond that. . . . This welfare state superintended, to the minutest detail, every step its subjects took from the cradle to the grave.[6]

Despotisms abounded in Europe, too, but they were mitigated by law, by territorial partition, and within states, by the division of power between the center (the crown) and local seigneurial authority.[7] Fragmentation gave rise to competition, and competition favored good care of good subjects. Treat them badly, and they might go elsewhere.

Ecumenical empires did not fear flight, especially when, like China, they defined themselves as the center of the universe, the hearth and home of civilization, and everything outside as barbarian darkness. There was no other place to go, so that symbolic boundaries were enough, like the "willow palisade," a low wall that ran from the Great Wall to the sea and separated China from the Mongol-Tartar lands to the north. In a poem on the subject, the Qian Long emperor makes this point: "In our erection of boundaries and regulation of people, ancient ways are preserved, / As it is enough simply to tie a rope to indicate prohibition. . . . Building it is the same as not having built it: / Insofar as the idea exists and the framework is there, there is no need to elaborate."[8]

The contest for power in European societies (note the plural) also gave rise to the specifically European phenomenon of the semi-autonomous city, organized and known as commune. Cities of course were to be found around the world—wherever agriculture produced sufficient surplus to sustain a population of rulers, soldiers, craftsmen, and other nonfood producers. Many of these urban nodes came to acquire great importance as markets, to say nothing of their role as administrative centers. But nothing like the commune appeared outside western Europe.[9]

The essence of the commune lay, first, in its economic function: these units were "governments of the merchants, by the merchants, and for the merchants";[10] and second, in its exceptional civil power: its ability to confer social status and political rights on its residents—rights crucial to the conduct of business and to freedom from outside interference. This meant everything in a hierarchical, agrarian society that held most of the population in thrall, either by personal dependence on local lords or ties to place. It made the cities gateways to freedom, holes in the tissue of bondage that covered the countryside. *Stadtluft macht frei* ran the medieval dictum—city air makes one free. Literally: when the count of Flanders tried to reclaim a runaway serf whom he ran across in the market of Bruges, the bourgeois simply drove him and his bully boys out of the city.

The consequences were felt throughout the society. Under this special dispensation, cities became poles of attraction, places of refuge, nodes of exchange with the countryside. Migration to cities improved the income and status not only of the migrants but of those left behind. (But not their health. The cities were dirty, crowded, and lent themselves to easy contagion, so that it was only in-migration that sustained their numbers and enabled them to grow.) Serf emancipation in western Europe was directly linked to the rash of franchised villages and urban communes, and to the density and proximity of these gateways. Where cities and towns were few and unfree, as in eastern Europe, serfdom persisted and worsened.

Why did rulers grant such rights to rustics and townsmen, in effect abandoning (transferring) some of their own powers? Two reasons above all. First, new land, new crops, trade, and markets brought revenue, and revenue brought power.[11] (Also pleasure.) Second, paradoxically, rulers wanted to enhance their power within their own kingdom: free farmers (note that I do not say "peasants") and townsmen *(bourgeois)* were the natural enemies of the landed aristocracy and would support the crown and other great lords in their struggles with local seigneurs.

Note further that European rulers and enterprising lords who sought to grow revenues in this manner had to *attract* participants by the grant of franchises, freedoms, and privileges—in short, by making deals. They had to *persuade* them to come.[12] (That was not the way in China, where rulers moved thousands and tens of thousands of human cattle and planted them on the soil, the better to grow things.) These exemptions from material burdens and grants of economic privilege, moreover, often led to political concessions and self-government. Here the initiative came from below, and this too was an essentially European pattern. Implicit in it was a sense of rights and contract—the right to *negotiate* as well as *petition*—with gains to the freedom and security of economic activity.

Ironically, then, Europe's great good fortune lay in the fall of Rome and the weakness and division that ensued. (So much for the lamentations of generations of classicists and Latin teachers.) The Roman dream of unity, authority, and order (the *pax Romana*) remained, in-

deed has persisted to the present. After all, one has usually seen fragmentation as a great misfortune, as a recipe for conflict; it is no accident that European union is seen today as the cure for the wars of
yesterday. And yet, in those middle years between ancient and modern,
fragmentation was the strongest brake on wilful, oppressive behavior.
Political rivalry and the right of exit made all the difference.[13]

One other fissure helped: the split between secular and religious. Unlike Islamic societies, where religion was in principle supreme and the
ideal government that of the holy men, Christianity, craving imperial
tolerance, early made the distinction between God and Caesar. To each
his own. This did not preclude misunderstandings and conflicts: nothing is so unstable as a dual supremacy; something's got to give. In the
end, it was the Church, and this meant yielding to Caesar what was
Caesar's and then a good part of what was God's. Among the things
that gave, homogeneous orthodoxy: where authority is divided, dissent
flourishes. This may be bad for certainty and conformity, but it is surely
good for the spirit and popular initiatives.

Here, too, fragmentation made all the difference. The Church succeeded in asserting itself politically in some countries, notably those of
southern Europe, not in others; so that there developed within Europe
areas of potentially free thought. This freedom found expression later
on in the Protestant Reformation, but even before, Europe was spared
the thought control that proved a curse in Islam.

As for China, which had no established faith and where indeed an extraordinary religious tolerance prevailed, the mandarinate and imperial court served as custodians of a higher, perfected lay morality and in
that capacity defined doctrine, judged thought and behavior, and stifled dissent and innovation, even technological innovation. This was a
culturally and intellectually homeostatic society: that is, it could live
with a little change (indeed, could not possibly stifle all change); but
as soon as this change threatened the status quo, the state would step
in and restore order. It was precisely the wholeness and maturity of this
inherited canon and ethic, the sense of completeness and superiority,
that made China so hostile to outside knowledge and ways, even where
useful.

One final advantage of fragmentation: by decentralizing authority, it
made Europe safe from single-stroke conquest. The history of empire
is dotted with such coups—one or two defeats and the whole ecumenical autocracy comes tumbling down. Thus Persia after Issus (333
B.C.E.) and Gaugamela (331 B.C.E.); Rome after the sack by Alaric

(410); and the Sassanian empire after Qadisiya (637) and Nehawand (642). Also Aztec Mexico and Inca Peru.

Europe, in contrast, did not have all its eggs in one basket.* In the thirteenth century the Mongol invaders from the Asian steppe made short work of the Slavic and Khazar kingdoms of what is now Russia and Ukraine, but they still had to cut their way through an array of central European states, including the new kingdoms of their predecessors in invasion—the Poles, Lithuanians, Germans, Hungarians, and Bulgars—before they could even begin to confront the successor states of the Roman empire. This they might well have done had they not been distracted by troubles back home; but they would have paid dearly for further gains, especially in forested areas. Shortly thereafter the Turks, who had established themselves in Anatolia, began to expand into Europe, conquering the Balkans, then the lower Danube Valley, and getting twice to the walls of Vienna, capital of Germany's eastern march. In the course of these advances, they subdued the Serbs. the Bulgars, the Croats, the Slovenes, the Albanians, the Hungarians, and sundry other peoples of that confused and quarrelsome palimpsest. But that was it; by the time they got to Vienna, they had reached the limit of their resources.[†]

Part of the brittleness of these empires, of course, derived from their exploitative, surplus-sucking character and the indifference of subjects to the identity of their rulers: one despot was the same as the next; one foreign clan as arrogant and predatory as another. Why should the inhabitants of Persia care what happened to Darius at the hands of Alexander? Or what happened nine hundred years later to the Sassanian monarchy at the hands of the Arabs? Why should the tired, oppressed Roman "citizens" of the last days of empire care whether Rome fell? Or the subject tribes of Mexico, for that matter, care what happened to Moctezuma? The classical Greeks (−5th century), who saw

* Already in late Roman times, Germanic tribes fought as allies alongside imperial forces to repel later invaders: thus Salian Franks, Visigoths, and others, with the Roman general Aetius against Attila's Huns at the so-called Battle of Chalons (somewhere near Troyes) in 451. Attila and his Huns have come down in European tradition as quintessential symbols of barbarism and savagery. But today's Turks do not feel that way: Attila is one of their favorite names.

† When they got to Vienna the second time, in 1683, the Turks found themselves facing not only Germans but the Poles of Sobieski. Europeans could work together when they thought they faced a common enemy. That this was a last gasp is shown by the rapid Ottoman retreat thereafter. In a short sixteen years, they left Hungary and pulled back to Bosnia and Serbia, thus giving up the middle Danube Valley to Christian settlement (Treaty of Karlowitz).

themselves as the defenders of freedom against Asian tyranny, perceived this indifference as their secret weapon:

> Where there are kings, there must be the greatest cowards. For men's souls are enslaved and refuse to run risks readily and recklessly to increase the power of somebody else. But independent people, taking risks on their own behalf and not on behalf of others, are willing and eager to go into danger, for they themselves enjoy the prize of victory.[14]

Once the Europeans found themselves reasonably secure from outside aggression (eleventh century on), they were able, as never before and as nowhere else, to pursue their own advantage. Not that internal violence ceased from the land. The tenth and eleventh centuries were filled with baronial brigandage, eventually mitigated by popular, Church-supported revulsion and outrage that found expression in mass "peace" assemblies; and, from the top down, subdued by stronger central government allied with urban interests.[15] Time and money were on the side of order. So was the diversion of brawlers to external frontiers (cf. the Crusades). The economist would say that once the exogenous shocks ended, the system could take care of its endogenous troublemakers.

There ensued a long period of population increase and economic growth, up to the middle of the fourteenth century, when Europeans were smitten by the plague (the "Black Death") in its bubonic and pneumonic forms and a third or more of the people died; a half when you count the losses inflicted by sequellae. That was a jolt, but not a full stop. The one hundred fifty years that followed were a period of rebuilding, further technological advance, and continued development. In particular, these centuries saw the further expansion of a civilization that now found itself stronger than its neighbors, and the beginnings of exploration and conquest overseas.

This long multicentennial maturation (1000–1500) rested on an economic revolution, a transformation of the entire process of making, getting, and spending such as the world had not seen since the so-called Neolithic revolution. That one (c. −8000 to −3000) had taken thousands of years to work itself out. Its focus had been the invention of agriculture and the domestication of livestock, both of which had enormously augmented the energy available for work. (All economic [industrial] revolutions have at their core an enhancement of the supply of energy, because this feeds and changes all aspects of human activity.) This shift away from hunting and gathering, bringing a leap in the supply of nourishment, permitted a substantial growth of population and a new pattern of concentrated settlement. It was the Neolithic revolution that made possible towns and cities, with all that they yielded in cultural and technical exchange and enrichmentment.

The medieval economic revolution also built on gains in the production and application of energy and concomitant increases in work. First, food supply: this was a period of innovation in the techniques of cultivation. I say innovation rather than invention because these new techniques went back earlier. Thus the wheeled plow, with deep-cutting iron share, had come in with the German invaders; but it had seen limited use in a world of limited animal power and low population density. Now it spread across Europe north of the Loire, opened up the rich river valleys, turned land reclaimed from forest and sea into fertile fields, in short did wonders wherever the heavy, clayey soil resisted the older Roman wooden scratch plow, which had worked well enough on the gravelly soils of the Mediterranean basin.

The wheeled plow turning heavy soil called for animals to match. We have already had occasion to speak of these big, stall-fed oxen such as were found nowhere else, and these large dray horses, more powerful if not stronger than the ox. These living, mobile engines offered a great advantage in a land-rich, labor-scarce economy. For time too was scarce: agricultural work has peaks of activity at sowing and harvest when one must seize good weather and get the seed in or crops out. Especially was this true of European communal agriculture, where scattered and intermingled holdings and open fields made for much to-and-fro and one peasant's haste was the haste of all his neighbors. Strong, quick animals could make all the difference, and cultivators pooled resources to get the right livestock.

Along with these superior techniques went, as both cause and effect, a more intensive cultivation, in particular, a shift from a two-field (one half left fallow every year) to a three-field system of crop rotation (winter grain, spring grain, and one third fallow). This yielded a gain of one third in land productivity (one sixth of total cultivable land, but one third of the half previously under cultivation), which further contributed to the ability to support livestock, which increased the supply of fertilizer, which nourished yields, and so on in ascending cycle. Given the character of land distribution and the collective use of draft animals, this critical change called for strong communal leadership and cooperation, made easier by example and results.

How much of this was response to population pressure and how much a stimulus to increase is hard to say. No doubt both. But it would seem that over time, population began to outstrip the means of sustenance, because these centuries also saw a great effort to increase arable, whether by forest clearing (assarts) or reclamation of land from water, by diking, drainage, and pumping. All these call for enormous energy and capital, and their success testifies not only to private and collective initiative but to the ingenuity of a society that was learning to substitute machines for animal and human power. In particular, the windmill, tireless and faithful, was the key to the successful pumping of fens and polders. It was the windmill that made Holland.

Historians rightly emphasize gains in land productivity and output in a society overwhelmingly rural because compelled to devote most of its resources to feeding itself. Yet these advances were essentially permissive. It was the urban minority that held most of the seeds and secrets of transformation—technical, intellectual, political. To be sure, the towns and cities were themselves shaped by the countryside: immigrants from the fields brought with them values, habits, and attitudes that made more sense on the land and then set them as a straitjacket on urban activity. Thus the organization of tradesmen and craftsmen in corporate guilds assumed a zero-sum game—one man's increase was another's diminution—like pieces in a bounded field. Besides, the urban setting itself made it necessary to ration space and time, again with an eye to discouraging self-aggrandizement. So, no stealing a march and selling before a certain hour or after another; no price competition; no trade-off of quality and solidity for cheapness; no buying low ("jewing down," in popular parlance—bad habits always belong to someone else) to sell high; in short, no market competition. Everyone who did his job was entitled to a living. Laudable but static. The aim was an egalitarian social justice, but it entailed serious constraint on enterprise and growth—a safety net at the expense of income.

That was the principle. One should always assume that rules, then as now, were made to be broken. Business, like love, laughs at locksmiths. So in medieval Europe, where the move toward guild controls was as much a response to free dealing as the expression of an older morality. Cities and towns sprang up thick and ambitious; in France, the Low Countries, the Rhineland, rulers encouraged them by generous grants of privilege. But attempts to sustain local monopoly were thwarted by the growth of suburbs (*faubourgs*), where urban rules did not apply. There outsiders and Jews settled in, and journeymen worked for masters who had outgrown their shop. There market restrictions did not hold. Hence pairings like Hamburg-Altona and Nürnberg-Fürth: old wealth, new wealth; decorum, disorder; tight access, free entry.

One inevitable consequence of active trade was selection by merit. This ran against the parity principle (equality of results), but it was not possible to impose uniformity of performance. Some craftsmen simply did better work and attracted buyers beyond their capacity. At the same time, the very effort to restrain competition by limiting access to mastership meant talent unemployed. It did not take much to bring together such masters and journeymen. Since the journeymen were often not permitted to work in the master's city shop (limits on size), they worked *en chambre* or in the suburbs. Here was the beginning of putting-out and division of labor, with substantial gains in productivity.

Urban closure was also thwarted by the spread of industrial production to the countryside. Agriculture, with its seasonal and irregular pattern of activity, offered a pool of untapped labor, the greater because outside the cities constraints on the use of female and child workers no longer applied. Women and children, grossly underpaid, gave more product for the penny. Early on (thirteenth century), then, merchants began to hire cottage workers to perform some of the more tedious, less skilled tasks. In the most important branch, the textile manufacture, peasant women did the spinning on a putting-out basis: merchants gave out (put out) the raw material—the raw wool and flax, and, later, cotton—and collected the finished yarn.

This shift to outsourcing initially encountered little resistance from urban workers; but when merchants started putting-out yarn to cottage weavers, they were attacking one of the most powerful vested interests of the day, the guild weavers of the towns. Then the fat was in the fire. In Italy, the autonomous cities, which held political control over the surrounding countryside, managed to destroy much of this "unfair" competition. In the Low Countries, the other great medieval center of cloth manufacture, urban weavers marched into the villages to break cottage looms; and although the country weavers fought back, the putting-out system was held in check for centuries. The one country where putting-out had a free field was England, where local political autonomies made it hard for the monarchy to sustain corporate (guild) claims to monopoly and where guilds were quickly reduced to ceremonial fraternities. By the fifteenth century, more than half the nation's woolen cloth was being made in rural cottages. This recourse to cheap labor lowered costs over competitors abroad, so that by the sixteenth century a country that had once been largely an exporter of primary products, including raw wool, was well on its way to becoming the premier manufacturing nation of Europe.

The economic expansion of medieval Europe was thus promoted by a succession of organizational innovations and adaptations, most of them initiated from below and diffused by example. The rulers, even local seigneurs, scrambled to keep pace, to show themselves hospitable, to make labor available, to attract enterprise and the revenues it generated. At the same time, the business community invented new forms of association, contract, and exchange designed to secure investment and facilitate payment. In these centuries a whole new array of commercial instruments came into use; commercial codes were elaborated and enforced; and partnership arrangements were devised to encourage alliances between lenders and doers, between the men who supplied the funds and merchandise and those who went to distant lands to sell and to buy. Almost all of this "commercial revolution" came from the mercantile community, bypassing where necessary the rules of this or that city or state, inventing and improvising new venues for encounter and exchange (ports and outports, *faubourgs,* local markets, international fairs), creating in short a world of its own like an overlay on the convoluted, inconvenient mosaic of political units.

They got thereby substantially enhanced security, a sharp reduction in the cost of doing business (what the economist calls "transaction costs"), a widening of the market that promoted specialization and division of labor. It was the world of Adam Smith, already taking shape five hundred years before his time.

# 4

# The Invention of
# Invention

When Adam Smith came to write about these things in the eighteenth century, he pointed out that division of labor and widening of the market encourage technological innovation. This in fact is exactly what happened in the Europe of the Middle Ages—one of the most inventive societies that history had known. Some may be surprised: for a long time one saw these centuries as a dark interlude between the grandeur of Rome and the brilliance of the Renaissance. That cliché no longer holds in matters technological.[1]

A few examples:

1. *The water wheel*. It had been known to the Romans, who began to do interesting things with it during the last century of the empire, when the conquests were over and the supply of slaves had shrunk almost to nothing. By then it was too late; order and trade were breaking down. The device may well have survived on Church estates, where it freed clerics for prayer. In any event, it was revived in the tenth and eleventh centuries, multiplying easily in a region of wide rainfall and ubiquitous watercourses. In England, that peripheral, backward island, the Domesday census of 1086 showed some 5,600 of these mills; the Continent had many more.

Even more impressive is the way waterpower technique advanced.

Millwrights increased pressure and efficiency by building dams and ponds and by lining the wheels up to utilize the diminishing energy for a variety of tasks, beginning with those that needed the most power, and descending. At the same time, the invention or improvement of accessory devices—cranks, toothed gears—made it possible to use the power at a distance, change its direction, convert it from rotary to reciprocating motion, and apply it to an increasing variety of tasks: hence not only grinding grain, but fulling (pounding) cloth, thereby transforming the woolen manufacture; hammering metal; rolling and drawing sheet metal and wire; mashing hops for beer; pulping rags for paper. "Paper, which was manufactured by hand and foot for a thousand years or so following its invention by the Chinese and adoption by the Arabs, was manufactured mechanically as soon as it reached medieval Europe in the thirteenth century. . . . Paper had traveled nearly halfway around the world, but no culture or civilization on its route had tried to mechanize its manufacture."[2] Europe, as nowhere else, was a power-based civilization.

2. *Eyeglasses.* A seemingly banal affair, the kind of thing that appears so commonplace as to be trivial. And yet the invention of spectacles more than doubled the working life of skilled craftsmen, especially those who did fine jobs: scribes (crucial before the invention of printing) and readers, instrument and toolmakers, close weavers, metal-workers.

The problem is biological: because the crystalline lens of the human eye hardens around the age of forty, it produces a condition similar to farsightedness (actually presbyopia). The eye can no longer focus on close objects. But around the age of forty, a medieval craftsman could reasonably expect to live and work another twenty years, the best years of his working life . . . if he could see well enough. Eyeglasses solved the problem.

We think we know where and when the first spectacles appeared. Crude magnifying glasses and crystals *(lapides ad legendum)* had been found earlier and used for reading.[3] The trick was to improve them so as to reduce distortion and connect a pair into a wearable device, thus leaving the hands free. This apparently first happened in Pisa toward the end of the thirteenth century. We have a contemporary witness (1306) who says he knew the inventor:

> Not all the arts [in the sense of arts and crafts] have been found; we shall never see an end of finding them. Every day one could discover a new art. . . . It is not twenty years since there was discovered the art of making

spectacles that help one to see well, an art that is one of the best and most
necessary in the world. And that is such a short time ago that a new art that
never before existed was invented. . . . I myself saw the man who discovered and practiced it and I talked with him.[4]

These convex lenses were obviously not uniform or of what we would
call prescription quality. But here medieval optical technology, however
primitive, was saved by the nature of the difficulty: the lenses to correct presbyopia do not have to be extremely accurate. Their function
is primarily to magnify, and although some magnify more than others,
just about any and all will help the user. This is why people will occasionally borrow glasses in a restaurant to read the menu, and why five-
and-dime stores can put out boxes of such spectacles for sale. The
buyer simply tries a few and picks the most suitable. Myopes (short-
sighted people) cannot do that.

That was the beginning. By the middle of the fifteenth century, Italy,
particularly Florence and Venice, was making thousands of spectacles,
fitted with concave as well as convex lenses, for myopes as well as pres-
byopes. Also, the Florentines at least (and presumably others) understood that visual acuity declines with age and so made the convex
lenses in five-year strengths and the concave in two, enabling users to
buy in batches and change with time.

Eyeglasses made it possible to do fine work and use fine instruments.
But also the converse: eyeglasses encouraged the invention of fine instruments, indeed pushed Europe in a direction found nowhere else.
The Muslims knew the astrolabe, but that was it. The Europeans went
on to invent gauges, micrometers, fine wheel cutters—a battery of
tools linked to precision measurement and control. They thereby laid
the basis for articulated machines with fitted parts.

Close work: when other civilizations did it, they did it by long ha-
bituation. The skill was in the hand, not the eye-and-tool. They
achieved remarkable results, but no piece was like any other; whereas
Europe was already moving toward replication—batch and then mass
production. This knowledge of lenses, moreover, was a school for further optical advances, and not only in Italy. Both telescope and microscope were invented in the Low Countries around 1600 and spread
quickly from there.

Europe enjoyed a monopoly of corrective lenses for three to four
hundred years. In effect they doubled the skilled craft workforce, and
more than doubled it if one takes into account the value of experience.[5]

3. *The mechanical clock.* Another banality, so commonplace that we

take it for granted. Yet Lewis Mumford quite correctly called it "the key-machine."[6]

Before the invention of this machine, people told time by sun (shadow sticks or dials) and water clocks. Sun clocks worked of course only on clear days; water clocks misbehaved when the temperature fell toward freezing, to say nothing of long-run drift as a result of sedimentation and clogging. Both of these devices served reasonably well in sunny climes; but north of the Alps one can go weeks without seeing the sun, while temperatures vary not only seasonally but from day to night.

Medieval Europe gave new importance to reliable time. The Church first, with its seven daily prayer offices, one of which, matins, was in spite of its name a nocturnal rite and required an alarm arrangement to wake clerics before dawn. (Hence our children's round, *Frère Jacques:* Brother Jacques has overslept and failed to sound the bells for matins.)* And then the new cities and towns had their temporal servitudes. Squeezed by their walls, they had to know and order time in order to organize collective activity and ration space. They set a time to wake, to go to work, to open the market, close the market, leave work, and finally a time to put out fires (*couvre-feu* gives us our word "curfew") and go to sleep.

All of this was compatible with the older devices so long as there was only one authoritative timekeeper; but with urban growth and the multiplication of time signals, discrepancy brought discord and strife. Society needed a more dependable instrument of time measurement and found it in the mechanical clock.

We do not know who invented this machine or where. It seems to have appeared in Italy and England (perhaps simultaneous invention) in the last quarter of the thirteenth century. Once known, it spread rapidly, driving out the water clocks; but not solar dials, which were needed to check the new machines against the timekeeper of last resort. These early versions were rudimentary, inaccurate, and prone to breakdown—so much so that it paid to buy a clockmaker along with the clock.

Ironically, the new machine tended to undermine ecclesiastical authority. Although Church ritual had sustained an interest in timekeep-

---

* The English and German versions of the verse (and maybe others) traduce the meaning by saying that "morning bells are ringing." The point is, they are not ringing.

ing throughout the centuries of urban collapse that followed the fall of
Rome, Church time was nature's time. Day and night were divided
into the same number of parts, so that except at the equinoxes, day and
night hours were unequal; and then of course the length of these hours
varied with the seasons. But the mechanical clock kept equal hours, and
this implied a new time reckoning. The Church resisted, not coming
over to the new hours for about a century. From the start, however, the
towns and cities took equal hours as their standard, and the public
clocks installed in the towers and belfries of town halls and market
squares became the very symbol of a new, secular municipal authority.
Every town wanted one; conquerors seized them as specially precious
spoils of war; tourists came to see and hear these machines the way they
made pilgrimages to sacred relics. New times, new customs.

The clock was the greatest achievement of medieval mechanical ingenuity. Revolutionary in conception, it was more radically new than
its makers knew. This was the first example of a digital as opposed to
an analog device: it counted a regular, repeating sequence of discrete
actions (the swings of an oscillating controller) rather than tracked
continuous, regular motion such as the moving shadow of a sundial or
the flow of water. Today we know that such a repeating frequency can
be more regular than any continuous phenomenon, and just about all
high-precision devices are now based on the digital principle. But no
one could have known that in the thirteenth century, which thought
that because time was continuous, it ought to be tracked and measured
by some other continuity.

The mechanical clock had to meet the unsparing standards of earth
and sun; no blinking or hiding its failures. The result was relentless
pressure to improve technique and design. At every stage, clockmakers led the way to accuracy and precision: masters of miniaturization,
detectors and correctors of error, searchers for new and better. They remain the pioneers of mechanical engineering—examples and teachers
to other branches.

Finally, the clock brought order and control, both collective and
personal. Its public display and private possession laid the basis for
temporal autonomy: people could now coordinate comings and goings
without dictation from above. (Contrast the military, where only officers need know the time.) The clock provided the punctuation marks
for group activity, while enabling individuals to order their own work
(and that of others) so as to enhance productivity. Indeed, the very notion of productivity is a by-product of the clock: once one can relate

performance to uniform time units, work is never the same. One moves from the task-oriented time consciousness of the peasant (one job after another, as time and light permit) and the time-filling busyness of the domestic servant (always something to do) to an effort to maximize product per unit of time (time is money). The invention of the mechanical clock anticipates in its effects the economic analysis of Adam Smith: increase in the wealth of nations derives directly from improvement of the productive powers of labor.

The mechanical clock remained a European (Western) monopoly for some three hundred years; in its higher forms, right into the twentieth century. Other civilizations admired and coveted clocks, or more accurately, their rulers and elites did; but none could make them to European standard.

The Chinese built a few astronomical water clocks in the Tang and Sung eras—complicated and artful pieces that may have kept excellent time in the short run, before they started clogging. (Owing to sediment, water clocks keep a poor rate over time.) These monumental machines were imperial projects, done and reserved for the emperor and his astrologers. The Chinese treated time and knowledge of time as a confidential aspect of sovereignty, not to be shared with the people. This monopoly touched both daily and year-round time. In the cities, drums and other noisemakers signaled the hours (equal to two of our hours), and everywhere the imperial calendar defined the seasons and their activities. Nor was this calendar a uniform, objectively determinable datum. Each emperor in turn had his own calendar, placed his own seal on the passage of time. Private calendrical calculation would have been pointless.

These interval hour signals in large cities were no substitute for continuing knowledge and awareness. In particular, the noises were not numerical signifiers. The hours had names rather than numbers, and that in itself testifies to the absence of a temporal calculus. Without a basis in popular consumption, without a clock trade, Chinese horology regressed and stagnated. It never got beyond water clocks, and by the time China came to know the Western mechanical clock, it was badly placed to understand and copy it. Not for want of interest: the Chinese imperial court and wealthy elites were wild about these machines; but because they were reluctant to acknowledge European technological superiority, they sought to trivialize them as toys. Big mistake.

Islam might also have sought to possess and copy the clock, if only to fix prayers. And as in China, Muslim horologers made water clocks well in advance of anything known in Europe. Such was the legendary clock that Haroun-al-Raschid sent as a gift to Charlemagne around the year 800: no one at the Frankish court could do much with it, and it disappeared to ignorance and neglect. Like the Chinese, the Muslims were much taken with Western clocks and watches, doing their best to acquire them by purchase or tribute. But they never used them to create a public sense of time other than as a call to prayer. We have the testimony here of Ghiselin de Busbecq, ambassador from the Holy Roman Empire to the Sublime Porte in Constantinople, in a letter of 1560: " . . . if they established public clocks, they think that the authority of their muezzins and their ancient rites would suffer diminution."[7] Sacrilege.

4. *Printing*. Printing was invented in China (which also invented paper) in the ninth century and found general use by the tenth. This achievement is the more impressive in that the Chinese language, which is written in ideographs (no alphabet), does not lend itself easily to movable type. That explains why Chinese printing consisted primarily of full-page block impressions; also why so much of the old Chinese texts consists of drawings. If one is going to cut a block, it is easier to draw than to carve a multitude of characters. Also, ideographic writing works against literacy: one may learn the characters as a child, but if one does not keep using them, one forgets how to read. Pictures helped.

Block printing limits the range and diffusion of publication. It is well suited to the spread of classic and sacred texts, Buddhist mantras, and the like, but it increases the cost and risk of publishing newer work and tends to small printings. Some Chinese printers did use movable type, but given the character of the written language and the investment required, the technique never caught on as in the West. Indeed, like other Chinese inventions, it may well have been abandoned for a time, to be reintroduced later.[8]

In general, for all that printing did for the preservation and diffusion of knowledge in China, it never "exploded" as in Europe. Much publication depended on government initiative, and the Confucian mandarinate discouraged dissent and new ideas. Even evidence of the falsity of conventional knowledge could be dismissed as appearance.[9] As a result, intellectual activity segmented along personal and regional lines, and scientific achievement shows surprising discontinuities. "The great mathematician Chu Shih-chieh, trained in the northern school, migrated south to Yang-chou, where his books were printed but he could find no disciples. In consequence, the more sophisticated of his achievements became incomprehensible to following generations. But the basic scientific texts were common property everywhere."[10] Basic texts, a kind of canonical writ, are not enough; worse, they may even chill thought.

Europe came to printing centuries after China. It should not be thought, however, that printing made the book and invented reading. On the contrary, the interest in the written word grew rapidly in the Middle Ages, especially after bureaucracy and the rise of towns increased demand for records and documents. Government rests on paper. Much of this verbiage, moreover, was written in the vernacular, shattering the hieratic monopoly of a dead but sacred tongue (Latin) and opening the way to wider readership and a literature of dissent.

As a result, scribes could not keep up with demand. All manner of arrangements were conceived to increase reading material. Manuscripts were prepared and bound in separable fascicles; that divided the labor of writing while enabling several people to read the book at the same time. And as in China, block printing came in before movable type, yielding flysheets more than books and once again copiously illustrated. So when Gutenberg published his Bible in 1452–55, the first Western book printed by movable type (and arguably the most beautiful book ever printed), he brought the new technique to a society that had already vastly increased its output of writing and was fairly panting after it. Within the next half century, printing spread from the Rhineland throughout western Europe. The estimated output of incunabula (books published before 1501) came to millions—2 million in Italy alone.

In spite of printing's manifest advantages, it was not accepted everywhere. The Muslim countries long remained opposed, largely on religious grounds: the idea of a printed Koran was unacceptable. Jews and Christians had presses in Istanbul but not Muslims. The same in India: not until the early nineteenth century was the first press installed. In Europe, on the other hand, no one could put a lid on the new technology. Political authority was too fragmented. The Church had tried to curb vernacular translations of sacred writ and to forbid dissemination of both canonical and noncanonical texts. Now it was overwhelmed. The demons of heresy were out long before Luther, and printing made it impossible to get them back in the box.

5. *Gunpowder.* Europeans probably got this from the Chinese in the early fourteenth, possibly the late thirteenth century. The Chinese

knew gunpowder by the eleventh century and used it at first as an in-
cendiary device, both in fireworks and in war, often in the form of
tubed flame lances. Its use as a propellant came later, starting with inefficient bombards and arrow launchers and moving on to cannon
(late thirteenth century). The efficiency and rationality of some of
these devices may be inferred from their names: "the eight-sided magical awe-inspiring wind-and-fire cannon" or the "nine-arrows, heart-
penetrating, magically-poisonous fire-thunderer."[11] They were
apparently valued as much for their noise as for their killing power. The
pragmatic mind finds this metaphorical, rhetorical vision of technology
disconcerting.

The Chinese continued to rely on incendiaries rather than explosives,
perhaps because of their superior numbers, perhaps because fighting
against nomadic adversaries did not call for siege warfare.* Military
treatises of the sixteenth century describe hundreds of variations: "sky-
flying tubes," apparently descended from the fire lances of five hundred
years earlier, used to spray gunpowder and flaming bits of paper on the
enemy's sails; "gunpowder buckets" and "fire bricks"—grenades of
powder and paper soaked in poison; other devices packed with chemicals and human excrement, intended to frighten, blind, and presumably disgust the enemy; finally, more lethal grenades filled with metal
pellets and explosives.[12] Some of these were thrown; others shot from
bows. One wonders at this delight in variety, as though war were a display of recipes.

The Chinese used gunpowder in powder form, as the name indicates, and got a weak reaction precisely because the fine-grain mass
slowed ignition. The Europeans, on the other hand, learned in the
sixteenth century to "corn" their powder, making it in the form of
small kernels or pebbles. They got more rapid ignition, and by mixing
the ingredients more thoroughly, a more complete and powerful explosion. With that, one could concentrate on range and weight of pro-
jectile; no messing around with noise and smell and visual effects.

This focus on delivery, when combined with experience in bell
founding (bell metal was convertible into gun metal, and the techniques of casting were interchangeable), gave Europe the world's best
cannon and military supremacy.[13]

---

* The Chinese would seem to have been more afraid of rebellion from within than
invasion from without. More modern armaments might fall into the wrong hands, and
these included those of the generals. Cf. Hall, *Powers and Liberties,* pp. 46–47.

As these cases make clear, other societies were falling behind Europe even before the opening of the world (fifteenth century on) and the great confrontation.* Why this should have been so is an important historical question—one learns as much from failure as from success. One cannot look here at every non-European society or civilization, but two deserve a moment's scrutiny.

The first, Islam, initially absorbed and developed the knowledge and ways of conquered peoples. By our period (roughly 1000 to 1500), Muslim rule went from the western end of the Mediterranean to the Indies. Before this, from about 750 to 1100, Islamic science and technology far surpassed those of Europe, which needed to recover its heritage and did so to some extent through contacts with Muslims in such frontier areas as Spain. Islam was Europe's teacher.

Then something went wrong. Islamic science, denounced as heresy by religious zealots, bent under theological pressures for spiritual conformity. (For thinkers and searchers, this could be a matter of life and death.) For militant Islam, the truth had already been revealed. What led *back* to the truth was useful and permissible; all the rest was error and deceit.[14] The historian Ibn Khaldūn, conservative in religious matters, was nonetheless dismayed by Muslim hostility to learning:

> When the Muslims conquered Persia (637–642) and came upon an indescribably large number of books and scientific papers, Sa'd bin Abi Waqqas wrote to Umar bin al-Khattab asking him for permission to take them and distribute them as booty among the Muslims. On that occasion, Umar wrote him: "Throw them in the water. If what they contain is right guidance, God has given us better guidance. If it is error, God has protected us against it."[15]

Remember here that Islam does not, as Christianity does, separate the religious from the secular. The two constitute an integrated whole. The ideal state would be a theocracy; and in the absence of such fulfillment, a good ruler leaves matters of the spirit and mind (in the widest sense) to the doctors of the faith. This can be hard on scientists.

As for technology, Islam knew areas of change and advance: one

* For reasons well worth exploring in the context of the history of ideas and the invention of folklore, a number of scholars have recently tried to propagate the notion that European technology did not catch up to that of Asia until the late eighteenth century. The most active source at the moment is the H-World site on the Internet—a magnet for fallacies and fantasies.

thinks of the adoption of paper; or the introduction and diffusion of new crops such as coffee and sugar; or the Ottoman Turkish readiness to learn the use (but not the making) of cannon and clocks. But most of this came from outside and continued to depend on outside support. Native springs of invention seem to have dried up. Even in the golden age (750–1100), speculation disconnected from practice: "For nearly five hundred years the world's greatest scientists wrote in Arabic, yet a flourishing science contributed nothing to the slow advance of technology in Islam."[16]

The one civilization that might have surpassed the European achievement was China. At least that is what the record seems to show. Witness the long list of Chinese inventions: the wheelbarrow, the stirrup, the rigid horse collar (to prevent choking), the compass, paper, printing, gunpowder, porcelain. And yet in matters of science and technology, China remains a mystery—and this in spite of a monumental effort by the late Joseph Needham and others to collect the facts and clarify the issues. The specialists tell us, for example, that Chinese industry long anticipated European: in textiles, where the Chinese had a water-driven machine for spinning hemp in the twelfth century, some five hundred years before the England of the Industrial Revolution knew water frames and mules;[17] or in iron manufacture, where the Chinese early learned to use coal and coke in blast furnaces for smelting iron (or so we are told) and were turning out as many as 125,000 tons of pig iron by the later eleventh century—a figure reached by Britain seven hundred years later.[18]

The mystery lies in China's failure to realize its potential. One generally assumes that knowledge and know-how are cumulative; surely a superior technique, once known, will replace older methods. But Chinese industrial history offers examples of technological oblivion and regression. We saw that horology went backward. Similarly, the machine to spin hemp was never adapted to the manufacture of cotton, and cotton spinning was never mechanized. And coal/coke smelting was allowed to fall into disuse, along with the iron industry as a whole. Why?

It would seem that none of the conventional explanations tells us in convincing fashion why technical progress was absent in the Chinese economy during a period that was, on the whole, one of prosperity and expansion. Almost every element usually regarded by historians as a major contributory cause to the industrial revolution in north-western Europe was also present in China. There had even been a revolution in the relations between social classes, at least in the countryside; but this had had no important effect on the techniques of production. Only Galilean-Newtonian science was missing; but in the short run this was not important. Had the Chinese possessed, or developed, the seventeenth-century European mania for tinkering and improving, they could easily have made an efficient spinning machine out of the primitive model described by Wang Chen. . . . A steam engine would have been more difficult; but it should not have posed insuperable difficulties to a people who had been building double-acting piston flame-throwers in the Sung dynasty. The crucial point is that nobody tried. In most fields, agriculture being the chief exception, Chinese technology stopped progressing well before the point at which a lack of scientific knowledge had become a serious obstacle.[19]

Why indeed? Sinologists have put forward several partial explanations. The most persuasive are of a piece:

• The absence of a free market and institutionalized property rights. The Chinese state was always interfering with private enterprise—taking over lucrative activities, prohibiting others, manipulating prices, exacting bribes, curtailing private enrichment. A favorite target was maritime trade, which the Heavenly Kingdom saw as a diversion from imperial concerns, as a divisive force and source of income inequality, worse yet, as an invitation to exit. Matters reached a climax under the Ming dynasty (1368–1644), when the state attempted to prohibit all trade overseas. Such interdictions led to evasion and smuggling, and smuggling brought corruption (protection money), confiscations, violence, and punishment. Bad government strangled initiative, increased the cost of transactions, diverted talent from commerce and industry.

• The larger values of the society. A leading sociological historian (historical sociologist) sees gender relations as a major obstacle: the quasi-confinement of women to the home made it impossible, for example, to exploit textile machinery profitably in a factory setting. Here China differed sharply from Europe or Japan, where women had free access to public space and were often expected to work outside the home to accumulate a dowry or contribute resources to the family.[20]

• The great Hungarian-German-French sinologist, Etienne Balazs, would stress the larger context. He sees China's abortive technology as part of a larger pattern of totalitarian control. He does not explain this by hydraulic centralism, but he does recognize the absence of freedom, the weight of custom, consensus, what passed for higher wisdom. His analysis is worth repeating:

. . . if one understands by totalitarianism the complete hold of the State and its executive organs and functionaries over all the activities of social life, without exception, Chinese society was highly totalitarian. . . . No private initiative, no expression of public life that can escape official control. There is to begin with a whole array of state monopolies, which comprise the great consumption staples: salt, iron, tea, alcohol, foreign trade. There is a monopoly of education, jealously guarded. There is practically a monopoly of letters (I was about to say, of the press): anything written unofficially, that escapes the censorship, has little hope of reaching the public. But the reach of the Moloch-State, the omnipotence of the bureaucracy, goes much farther. There are clothing regulations, a regulation of public and private construction (dimensions of houses); the colors one wears, the music one hears, the festivals—all are regulated. There are rules for birth and rules for death; the providential State watches minutely over every step of its subjects, from cradle to grave. It is a regime of paper work and harassment [*paperasseries et tracasseries*], endless paper work and endless harassment.

The ingenuity and inventiveness of the Chinese, which have given so much to mankind—silk, tea, porcelain, paper, printing, and more—would no doubt have enriched China further and probably brought it to the threshold of modern industry, had it not been for this stifling state control. It is the State that kills technological progress in China. Not only in the sense that it nips in the bud anything that goes against or seems to go against its interests, but also by the customs implanted inexorably by the *raison d'Etat*. The atmosphere of routine, of traditionalism, and of immobility, which makes any innovation suspect, any initiative that is not commanded and sanctioned in advance, is unfavorable to the spirit of free inquiry.[21]

In short, no one was trying. Why try?

Whatever the mix of factors, the result was a weird pattern of isolated initiatives and sisyphean discontinuities—up, up, up, and then down again—almost as though the society were held down by a silk ceiling. The result, if not the aim, was change-in-immobility; or maybe immobility-in-change. Innovation was allowed to go (was able to go) so far and no farther.

The Europeans knew much less of these interferences. Instead, they entered during these centuries into an exciting world of innovation and emulation that challenged vested interests and rattled the forces of conservatism. Changes were cumulative; novelty spread fast. A new sense of progress replaced an older, effete reverence for authority. This intoxicating sense of freedom touched (infected) all domains. These were years of heresies in the Church, of popular initiatives that, we can see now, anticipated the rupture of the Reformation; of new forms of expression and collective action that challenged the older art forms, questioned social structures, and posed a threat to other polities; of new ways of doing and making things that made newness a virtue and a source of delight; of utopias that fantasized better futures rather than recalled paradises lost.

Important in all this was the Church as custodian of knowledge and school for technicians. One might have expected otherwise: that organized spirituality, with its emphasis on prayer and contemplation, would have had little interest in technology. Surely the Church, with its view of labor as penalty for original sin, would not seek to ease the judgment. And yet everything worked in the opposite direction: the desire to free clerics from time-consuming earthly tasks led to the introduction and diffusion of power machinery and, beginning with the Cistercians, to the hiring of lay brothers *(conversi)* to do the dirty work. Employment fostered in turn attention to time and productivity. All of this gave rise on monastic estates to remarkable assemblages of powered machinery—complex sequences designed to make the most of the waterpower available and distribute it through a series of industrial operations. A description of work in the abbey of Clairvaux in the mid-twelfth century exults in this versatility: "cooking, straining, mixing, rubbing [polishing], transmitting [the energy], washing, milling, bending." The author, clearly proud of these achievements, further tells his readers that he will take the liberty of joking: the fulling hammers, he says, seem to have dispensed the fullers of the penalty for their sins; and he thanks God that such devices can mitigate the oppressive labor of men and spare the backs of their horses.[22]

Why this peculiarly European *joie de trouver*? This pleasure in new and better? This cultivation of invention—or what some have called "the invention of invention"? Different scholars have suggested a variety of reasons, typically related to religious values:

1. The Judeo-Christian respect for manual labor, summed up in a number of biblical injunctions. One example: When God warns Noah of the coming flood and tells him he will be saved, it is not God who saves him. "Build thee an ark of gopher wood," he says, and Noah builds an ark to divine specifications.

2. The Judeo-Christian subordination of nature to man. This is a sharp departure from widespread animistic beliefs and practices that saw something of the divine in every tree and stream (hence naiads and dryads). Ecologists today might think these animistic beliefs preferable

to what replaced them, but no one was listening to pagan nature worshippers in Christian Europe.

3. The Judeo-Christian sense of linear time. Other societies thought
of time as cyclical, returning to earlier stages and starting over again.
Linear time is progressive or regressive, moving on to better things or
declining from some earlier, happier state. For Europeans in our period, the progressive view prevailed.

4. In the last analysis, however, I would stress the market. Enterprise
was free in Europe. Innovation worked and paid, and rulers and vested
interests were limited in their ability to prevent or discourage innovation. Success bred imitation and emulation; also a sense of power that
would in the long run raise men almost to the level of gods. The old
legends remained—the expulsion from the Garden, Icarus who flew
too high, Prometheus in chains—to warn against hubris. (The very notion of *hubris*—cosmic insolence—is testimony to some men's pretensions and the efforts of others to curb them.)

But the doers were not paying attention.

# 5

# The Great Opening

The greatest thing since the creation of the world, except for the incarnation
and death of Him who created it, is the discovery of the Indies.
—FRANCISCO LOPEZ DE GOMARA, *History of the Indies*

There is one historical event which everybody knows. Even those whose
predilections do not turn toward history know that Christopher Columbus
discovered America. This general knowledge of one fact indicates how that
singular achievement, the discovery of a New World, has captivated the sentiment of all Europe and all America as the most notable event in secular history.
—F. A. KIRKPATRICK, *The Spanish Conquistadores*

"You're a lost civilization!" crowed the anthropologist to the Indian chief.
"We don't mind being lost," answered the chief. "It's being found that scares
us."

Not long ago the world was getting ready to celebrate the five
hundredth anniversary of Columbus's discovery of America. One
group after another competed to honor the man and the achievement.
In the United States, which some would have named Columbia, where
some seventy cities and towns and a large number of fair and fraternal
institutions bear the discoverer's name, where people of Italian descent have vied with Hispanics to draw merit and honor from their
countryman (whether by descent or adoption), one could reasonably
expect a repetition *en grand* of the quadricentennial of 1892: a world's
fair (the Columbian Exposition); mementos galore; and the following
year, richly colored issues of commemorative stamps.

People felt good about Columbus in those days, and the expectation
was that 1992 would be bigger and better (500 beats 400); but then
something, everything, went wrong. Columbus, symbol of historical
achievement, midwife of a new world, turned out to be a political embarrassment. It emerged—but there had been rumblings of dissent for
years—that many people did not see the Admiral of the Ocean Sea as
a hero, the European arrival in the New World as a discovery, the anniversary of this event as occasion for celebration.[1]

On the contrary. Columbus was now portrayed as a villain; the Europeans as invaders; the native inhabitants as innocent, happy people reduced to bondage and eventually wiped out by the rapacious, disease-carrying white man.[2] In Berkeley, California, long a secessionist, irreverent (or rather, differently reverent) municipal enclave with its own foreign policy, the City Council renamed Columbus Day Indigenous Peoples' Day and offered two performances of an opera entitled *Get Lost (Again), Columbus,* the work of a Native American composer named White Cloud Wolfhawk.[3] Two years later, by way of affirming a choice, Mexico decided to issue commemorative coins in honor of the Aztecs and "a civilization of incredible sophistication in the arts, science and culture."[4] No praise for conquistadors.

Now, it was obviously not possible to erase or reverse history. No one was planning to evacuate and return to Europe; it was too late for Columbus to find his way. But there was enough anti-Columbus sentiment, especially in politically correct circles, to make rejoicing as out of place as a jig at a wake. So, no pageants; no souvenirs; no T-shirts and logos; no product endorsements; no reenactments (who could agree on the terms?); no oratory; no stamps; no coins; no prizes. And when the National Gallery of Art in Washington, D.C., decided to do a quincentenary exhibit with thick glossy-paper catalogue, it did an ABC—Anything But Columbus.[5] The exhibit covered the rest of the world, the other events of 1492 and years around. The most important event of all was deliberately omitted. History eviscerated.

As in most iconoclastic subversions of tradition, the attack on Columbus—or more accurately, on what followed his arrival—contains much truth, much nonsense, and some irrelevancy.

The *truth* lies in the unhappy fate of the indigenous peoples the Europeans found in the New World. With rare, trivial, and ineffectual exceptions, they were treated with contempt, violence, and sadistic brutality. They were almost wiped out by the microbes and viruses the Europeans unknowingly brought with them. Their land and culture and dignity were taken from them. They have nothing to celebrate.

The *nonsense* lies in quibbles about discovery: How could Columbus have discovered the New World? It was always there. The natives knew their land. It was they who had discovered it long before.* (We may

---

* Jean Ziegler, *La victoire des vaincus,* p. 101, cites a Russian novel of the 1960s, *Ajvanhu,* by Juryi Rychten (the Polish translation is dated 1966) that has its Siberian hero complain: "I have never been able to understand how anyone can discover land that

not have a new Columbus stamp, but the U.S. Post Office, swift-to-stroke and politically irreproachable, issued a commemorative in 1992 recalling the Asians who crossed over to North America some tens of thousands of years ago, the ancestors of the American Indians.) Besides, Columbus clearly did not know where he was going. In 1492, the indigenous peoples discovered Columbus.

But of course they did, just as he discovered them. Encounter goes two ways. To note the reciprocity, however, does not justify throwing out one side of the pair.[6]

This kind of cavil, interestingly enough, is a major issue in mathematics. The research mathematician finds and reveals new theorems and proofs. He calls them "truths." Has he discovered them? Or created them? Were they always there to be found—inscribed from eternity in the great "Book," as Paul Erdös called it? Or do they exist only by virtue of being invented? No matter. The mathematician has found/created them, and mathematical thought and imagination are thereby altered.[7] So with Columbus's discovery: once the news got back, thinking about the world and its peoples—the human imagination—was changed forever.

The *irrelevancy* lies in the argument that emphasis on the Columbian discovery Europeanizes a world process of encounter and exchange; that this Eurocentrism induces an easy triumphalism, leading historians to accentuate the false positive (the great age of exploration) and ignore the true negative (the catastrophic consequences of invasion).

Some of this complaint is true, but a good historian tries to keep his balance. The opening of the New World (for Europe it was new) *was* an exchange, but asymmetric. The European epiphany was the one that mattered. Europe it was that initiated the process, responded to the discovery, and set the agenda for further developments. On the operative level—*who did to whom*—this was a one-way business.

As for the self-congratulatory grandeur of these events, people, big and small, snatch at prestige where they may; and once invented, myths die hard. Yet the heroic discovery myths have not commanded the assent of scholars for many years—certainly not in the professional literature. Ever since Carl Sauer and Woodrow Borah and the California school of economic geography announced, on the basis of archeolog-

---

is already inhabited by people. . . . It's as though I went to Yakutsk and announced that I had discovered that city. Tht would hardly please the Yakuts." (NB: This is translation at three removes—Russian to Polish to French to English. But I don't think it traduces the original.)

ical remains, that the coming of the white man and his fellow-traveling pathogens (smallpox, influenza, etc.) had brought death to nine tenths of a Mexican Indian population of perhaps 25 million, no one has been able to look at the story in the same complacent way.*

These nomenclatorial dissents are a form of expiation and political mobilization. They aim to delegitimate rather than illuminate. The target is European (Western) dominion and the gains therefrom. The purpose: to impute guilt, provoke consciences, justify reparations. We can do better by asking what happened and why.

The discovery of the New World by Europeans was not an accident. Europe now held a decisive advantage in the power to kill. It could deliver its weapons wherever ships could take them; and thanks to new navigational techniques, European ships could now go anywhere.

Here let us pause a moment to consider the larger implications of this inequality. I would put forward a law of social and political relationships, namely, that three factors cannot coexist: (1) a marked disparity of power; (2) private access to the instruments of power; and (3) equality of groups or nations. Where one group is strong enough to push another around and stands to gain by it, it will do so. Even if the state would abstain from aggression, companies and individuals will not wait for permission. Rather, they will act in their own interest, dragging others along, including the state.

That is why imperialism (the domination by one group of another) has always been with us.† It is the expression of a deep human drive.

---

* The one exception to this disenchantment has been a persistent gratification in the spread of Christianity to a world of pagan religion, human sacrifice, and cannibalism. Far be it from me to defend these older practices. Still, the historian must note that those proffered "salvation" paid a high price and might put a different value on the exchange.

† Some would argue that all of this is patently untrue. The world is composed of a diversity of nations of unequal size and strength, and one does not see the strong always dominating or exploiting the weak. That is correct; but such forbearance is in large part conditioned by the balance of power. Nations will join forces if necessary to prevent hegemony; hence a rational calculus of forbearance. But it is a fragile calculus, liable to errors of appreciation. Thus it took many centuries to arrive at such an equilibrium in Europe, but twice in this century the balance has been challenged, with tragic results. The recent Gulf War was also the result of such a miscalculation (based on misinformation); and the reasons for the huge response were, first, the nature of the stakes (oil), and second, the conviction that it was important to affirm the principle of what used to be called collective security.

On this equilibrium power model of imperialism, see Landes, "Some Thoughts on the Nature of Economic Imperialism" and "An Equilibrium Model of Imperialism."

There are other, finer sentiments: the altruistic impulse, ideals of solidarity, the golden rule. But such noble ideals, even when sanctioned and propagated by organized religion, have been honored as much in the breach as in the observance. Indeed, the loftiest principles, including religion, have all too often been invoked in the cause of aggression. Only a deliberate decision by political authority, not merely to abstain from such behavior but to prevent members of the group from engaging in it, can thwart this impulse.

No central authority existed in medieval Europe to take such a decision. On the contrary, competing sovereignties gave ample opportunity for private initiatives in war, and personal ties—feudal obligations and loyalties—helped warriors mobilize for depredation. And so it was that Europe, after centuries of compression and victimization at the hands of invaders, passed to the attack from the eleventh century on. The Crusades (First Crusade, 1096) were a manifestation of this outward push. They were promoted in part as a way of sublimating internecine violence and turning it abroad. This was a bellicose society.

And what well-chosen adversaries! The Crusades renewed the centuries-old war of Christendom against Islam, of faith against faith, carried into the heart of the enemy camp. In theory, no cause was more holy; but in the event and as always, the idealistic goal was cover for arrant thuggery and cupidity. Three good days of rapine and murder in Greek Constantinople, with assorted massacres of Jews and Christians along the way (but were Eastern Christians really Christian?), were worth all the loot of Jerusalem and the precarious comforts of petty kingdoms in Anatolia and Muslim Palestine.*

The crusader invasion did not take. The Muslims expelled the intruders and have cherished that success ever since as a sign of divine judgment. But the war against the Muslim was going on in other places too, most notably in Spain, where over the course of the following centuries (final victory, Granada 1492) Christian kingdoms had increasing success against a multitude of jealous successor sheikhdoms. These were the debris of el-Andalus: "every qa'id and man of influence who could command a score of followers or possessed a castle to retire to in case of need, styled himself sultan and assumed the insignia of royalty."[8]

In this intermittent combat, the Muslims were handicapped by their dependence on Berber soldiers brought over from North Africa—mer-

---

* When the crusaders took Jerusalem in 1099, they sacked, raped, and massacred; whereas when Saladin recaptured the city for the Muslims in 1187, he spared it.

cenaries short on loyalty to the rulers who engaged them. Against these stood Christian barons and bullies, given to victimizing peasants and clerics, whom the Castilian monarch, on the understandable advice of the Church, sent to war against the infidel. It was a repeat of the motivation of the First Crusade to the Holy Land: better them than us. Bumblers on both sides, which is why the struggle took so long. But logistics and demography favored the Christians. "Christendom was spreading slowly south, as if by a process of titration rather than flood."⁹

In the end, civilization succumbed and ferocity triumphed. Cordoba, once the greatest center of learning in Europe, fell in 1236; Seville, the great economic metropolis of el-Andalus, in 1248. Both were taken almost in a fit of absent-mindedness: Ferdinand III of Castile did not really think he was ready to roll up the Moors in the valley of the Guadalquivir. The emir made a deal to withdraw as Ferdinand's vassal to the tiny mountain stronghold of Granada, which hung on by pursuing a strategy of timorous collaboration and systematic indifference to the fate of fellow Muslims in other parts. As ye sow . . . when it was Granada's turn to go (1490–92), its appeals for help went unanswered. So the last Moorish ruler of Granada negotiated a well-paid exit and left Spain scorned by his own mother: she knew a coward when she saw one.

The victors in this *reconquista* were Portugal, which liberated its territory from the Muslims by the mid-fourteenth century, and Castile, an expansionist frontier state of *caballero* pastoralists (what we would call cowboys) and roughnecks and soldiers of fortune for whom the great Moorish cities of the south, with their marble palaces and cool fountains, green gardens and centers of learning, were an irresistible target.¹⁰

And after *reconquista*, then what? Well, the land had to be grabbed up and resettled, estates bounded and exploited, peasants (especially Muslim cultivators) set to work for their new lords. And the kingdom had to be Christianized, for Queen Isabella was a passionate believer. Whatever concessions to Islam had been made by way of negotiating the surrender of Grenada, no such commitment could long hold against the claims of true faith. The Church, through the Holy Office of the Inquisition, to say nothing of lay spies and snitches, kept very busy. Converts from Judaism, most of them involuntary, hence untrustworthy, had to be kept under close surveillance; the same for ex-Muslims. Castilian society was afflicted with a pious prurigo, a scabies of the spirit.

Yet all of that left energy for further campaigning and adventure. Demobilization does not come easy for men who know little but the sword and the horse, the camaraderie of combat, the thrill of killing and the joys of rapine. Even before the final expulsion of the Moor from the Iberian peninsula, Portugal and Spain were moving on to probe and attack beyond the water. The first targets were islands in the Mediterranean and the shores of North Africa. King Jaime I of Aragon took the Balearics in 1229–35 and boasted of it later as "the best thing man has done in the last hundred years." The Portuguese in turn took Ceuta in 1415; Casablanca in 1463; Tangiers in 1471.

War has a way of legitimating its cause and celebrating its conquests. So with these new crusaders: poets sang their praises and they sublimated their violence in chivalric codes and posturing. Maritime expeditions took on special virtue and merit: "There was more honor," said Jaime I, in conquering a single kingdom "in the midst of the sea, where God has been pleased to put it," than three on dry land. By the end of the century, his chronicler was bragging that no fish could go swimming without the king's permission.[11]

It takes money to fight. The pattern of these "noble" quests was that of the traditional, feudal "business" enterprise. Some baron—what one historian calls an "aristocratic hooligan"—set off at the head of a war band with the ruler's blessing and sometimes his money, often in ships furnished by merchants near and far, to grab what he could grab. What he could take and hold was his, subject to distribution of spoil and rewards to his men, dividends to his backers, and a commitment of support and loyalty to his overlord.

The choice of targets was not random. These brigands began with the closest places, the most accessible. An economist would say: low cost of entry. These targets, moreover, were held by infidels, and this alone sanctified the venture. The Muslims call the non-Muslim world the *Dar el-Harb,* the House of the Sword, thereby designating it as fair game for conquest. The Christians had no such term, but acted as though they had.

Beyond these nearby victims lay an alluring array of distant temptations: gold that came by camel from no one knew where across the African desert; spices imported from the Indian Ocean through the Red Sea and the Persian Gulf, then overland to ports in the Levant, passing through numerous hands along the way and rising in price with every transaction; fabulous silks come by caravan all the way from China. All of these precious things were held ransom by Muslim traders. Could a way be found to bypass these infidel middlemen, one might grow rich in the service of God.

Those were only the known treasures of the East, things people could hold in their hands. Rumor and legend told of greater wonders, the stuff of dreams: on the other side of Africa, the kingdom of Prester John, a Christian enclave in the world of Islam; somewhere nearby, the lost paradise of Eden; farther east, the land of Xanadu; and going west, well, that was the unknown. Most people understood the world was round and that one could in theory go east by sailing west. But the Atlantic was a terrifying ocean for those used to the waters of the inland sea. Even the seaboard populations saw only the awful emptiness. Names like Land's End and Finisterre were more than mere statements of topographical fact.

Where there is ignorance, fantasy reigns. The west was the place of the Blessed Isles, of the mysterious Atlantis now sunk beneath the waves—of magical realms guarded by monsters and whirlpools and sea spouts—all the hazards that realism and imagination could put together. It took tremendous courage to venture into the ocean sea, well beyond any of the landmarks that dotted the portolan maps and gave reassurance from point to coastal point. The Viking voyages, west and north and west again, testify to their seamanship and courage; also to an intimate knowledge of the water (its color, moods, and depths, even its bottom) and the fauna (the fish and birds) that enabled them to know the presence of land long before they saw it and thus to island-hop around the top of the Atlantic. The Genoese and other Italians came later, learning first to round Iberia and sail to England. By the fourteenth century, in the company of Portuguese and Basques, they found the near Atlantic isles: the Azores, Madeiras,[12] Canaries—all but the last, which lie close to the African mainland, uninhabited.* (The Cape Verde Islands, which lie south of Bojador at north latitude 15°, were not found by Europeans until the mid-fifteenth century; São

---

* In the Canaries, the Spanish found natives still living in the stone age. These Guanches, as they were called, after some early, unhappy experiments in coexistence, made ferocious resistance and in spite of drastic inferiority in weapons (clubs vs. steel and guns), held the invaders off for more than a century. The Canaries were not fully subdued until after Columbus.
   The Guanches posed a theological and spiritual problem. Were they human? Did they have a soul? Did they live according to law? Could they be Christian? The major reason for these moralistic excursions was the justification of conquest and enslavement. The Spanish had a need for legitimation; they wanted a blessing on their enterprises and always got it.

Tome, in the Gulf of Guinea, was not opened to settlement until the 1490s.)

These tiny islands do not seem much today. They have been reduced to outposts, visited only by tourists or by residents returning from studies or jobs on the mainland. In the decades following their discovery, however, they represented a major addition to European space. Note that the Canaries were known to the ancient Romans, who learned of them from the king of Mauretania. They did not add to Roman space. It takes a mix of knowledge, means, and need to turn discovery into opportunity.

All were there in the fifteenth century. In particular, the southern islands (Madeiras and Canaries) proved superbly suited to the cultivation of sugar cane, destined to become Europe's greatest money crop. Europeans first encountered this plant in the Middle East, where the Arabs had brought it from India and thence into the Mediterranean, to Cyprus, Crete, and the Maghreb. Returning crusaders in turn introduced it into Europe—into Greece, Sicily, the Portuguese Algarve.

Sugar is powerfully addictive, naturally pleasing to the palate (not a learned taste) and comforting to the human psyche. It cost a great deal at first and was limited to pharmaceutical uses; one bought it at the apothecary's, and most Europeans got their sweetness from fruit and honey. But this was not the first time that a medicinal substance came to appeal to the healthy as well as the sick. Thanks to spreading cultivation, price fell to the point where sugar could be found at the grocer's. Now it began to be used as a condiment with all manner of fare; as the German saying had it, there's no food can be spoiled by sugar. (Germans still cook that way.) It also proved useful as a preservative or flavor camouflage in a world of easy spoilage. In the fifteenth and sixteenth centuries, sugar was a luxury: mistresses locked the loaves up to keep them from the servants; but it was becoming a necessity, spreading from the top of the social hierarchy on down.

As successful as the Mediterranean centers of cultivation were, they could not compare with the Atlantic islands, for reasons both climatic and social. Sugar cane grows best in tropical or subtropical climes. It needs a lot of regular water, and it likes steady heat—both found in these near-equatorial lands set down in the path of rain-heavy trade winds. It also takes a lot of hard gang labor, the sort of thing shunned by free men, so that cultivators preferred slaves where available. This is what the crusaders found when they captured such Mediterranean islands as Cyprus: the Arab sugar industry ran on slave labor, most of it brought in from East Africa.

But this regime could not easily be installed in Christian Europe, where it would have entailed a reversion to earlier, now unacceptable institutions. Slavery had long since given way to serfdom, in part because Christians were not supposed to be held as slaves (among other things because chattel status was incompatible with the sacrament of marriage), in part because the supply of pagan or infidel slaves was small and unreliable—also self-liquidating by conversion. Blacks, to be sure, might be seen as an exception. One might question whether they had a soul, whether they could become Christian. We know the Portuguese had no qualms importing black slaves for domestic service or for labor in the cane fields of the coastal plain; some 10 percent of the population of Lisbon in the mid-sixteenth century was apparently black.[13] Yet many (how many?) of these were eventually manumitted, and they merged into the population at large. The institution of black slavery, in spite of occasional "blackamoor" servants come down to us in oil paintings of elegant interiors, never took hold in Europe. If Europeans were going to use black slaves for field work, they wanted it done far away.

The Atlantic islands were far away. Here was a *tabula rasa,* a laboratory for new social arrangements. One can follow the progression. The Azores and Madeiras were initially peopled by European settlers or by unfree persons who had no choice in the matter—convicts, prostitutes, victims and orphans of religious persecution.* The Cape Verde Islands, on the other hand, off the coast of Gambia, were ideally placed to tap the slave trade that flourished a short reach away, and were soon shipping blacks to Lisbon and to some of the other islands.

When African slavers found that the white man, come for gold and pepper, was also interested in this human commodity, they were ready. In the quarter century before Columbus, the Cape Verde Islands and to a lesser extent the Madeiras became a testing ground for slave sugar plantations, to be followed by São Tome in the sixteenth century. Those planters tough enough to drill and squeeze labor while standing up to hardship and climate made fortunes; so did the Italian mer-

---

* The recent Argentine practice of taking the children of "disappeared" (note the transitive verb) political adversaries, including babies born in prison, and then giving them to their jailers or even the policemen who murdered the parents, to rear as their own, has long antecedents. Cf. this shipload of the "converted" children of Jews banished from Portugal in the expulsion of 1497, wrenched from their parents and saved for the next world, sent to the Cape Verde Islands because volunteer settlers were not available—Fernandez-Armesto, *Before Columbus,* p. 201. White men went in to these tropical lands, but few came out.

chant shippers. Meanwhile the Portuguese crown took a third or more of the gross in the form of license fees, sugar contracts, and taxes. These plantations then served as models for later, even more profitable developments in the New World.

The Atlantic islands enormously extended Europe's reach. In a few bold leaps, seamen found sailing platforms hundreds of miles westward and southward, launching pads into the unknown, harbors home. Here were oases in the ocean desert: they eased the pain and made the impossible possible. Was it luck or forethought that led Columbus to the farthest Canary isle, right in the path of the great easterlies, before setting out? Whatever; he found himself on the boulevard of the equatorial trades, and those warm, steady winds drove him across the Atlantic in a month.

Crazy. But in 1492 the Spanish thought they could do anything. Columbus was a maverick. He wanted to go to Asia by going west, which held no interest for Portugal. But the plan made sense to Spain, which had agreed to divide the world with Portugal and had conceded the eastern (African) route to its rival—another testimony to the hubris of these kingdoms. For Spain, it was westward ho! or nothing. Columbus happened to underestimate his task: he thought the world much smaller than it was. But that was not a bad way to begin; the ocean was in fact narrower than he thought.

What Columbus found was a new world. Even on his deathbed he did not believe that, thinking he had come on an archipelago off the coast of China and Cipangu (Japan). Nor did he know that beyond the islands lay two large landmasses, the continents that came to be known as North and South America. He found naked or near-naked people still living in the Stone Age, who cut their hands at first grasping the Spaniards' swords by the blade.[14] He brought some of them back to Spain as specimens—like animals for a zoo.

What Columbus did not find was great treasure of gold or silk or spices or any of the other valuables associated with the Orient. Gold above all he wanted, not so much for himself (he wanted rank and fame more) as for his monarchs, for he understood that nothing was so likely to keep the crown interested and supportive.

The scarcity of gold was a disappointment, but he made the best of things and assured that these islands could be an abundant source of slaves; that they were moreover eminently suitable for sugar cultivation, which he knew from the Canaries and Madeiras. They would also support livestock; and so it went. Caribbean history after the coming of the

white man was in large part the replacement of people by cattle, followed by a repeopling with black slaves to work the sugar plantations.

The process of depopulation was hastened by massacre, barbarous
cruelty, deep despair. The natives committed suicide, abstained from
sex, aborted their fetuses, killed their babies. They also fell by the tens
and hundreds of thousands to Old World pathogens (smallpox, influenza). The Spanish debated whether the savages they encountered
had a soul and were human; but the record makes clear where the savagery lay. When Columbus met his first Indians, he could not get over
their trust and friendliness; to this the Spaniards, frustrated for gold, returned bestialities unworthy of beasts:

> They came with their Horsemen well armed with Sword and Launce,
> making most cruel havocks and slaughters. . . . Overrunning Cities and Vil-
> lages, where they spared no sex nor age; neither would their cruelty pity
> Women with childe, whose bellies they would rip up, taking out the Infant
> to hew it in pieces. They would often lay wagers who should with most dex-
> terity either cleave or cut a man in the middle. . . . The children they would
> take by the feet and dash their innocent heads against the rocks, and when
> they were fallen into the water, with a strange and cruel derision they would
> call on them to swim. . . . They erected certains Gallowses . . . upon every
> one of which they would hang thirteen persons, blasphemously affirming
> that they did it in honour of our Redeemer and his Apostles, and then
> putting fire under them, they burnt the poor wretches alive. Those whom
> their pity did think to spare, they would send away with their hands half cut
> off, and so hanging by the skin.[15]

No need to multiply these testimonies. The reader would only recoil
from so much blood and evil. They were all there: the spontaneous expressions of wanton brutality; the random, carefree, thoughtless murders; the good-natured competition in imagining torments; the
refinements of pain; the unprovoked explosions of collective killer
frenzy; the hatred for life.

One surprise here: rationality was absent, even in the treatment of
valuable labor. Very early on, a group of Dominican friars wrote the
king of Spain complaining that so many miners died of hunger on
forced marches from one site to another that later groups needed no
guide to follow. (Tom Thumb dropped pebbles to mark the way; the
Spaniards left corpses.) The same letter spoke of a shipload of over
eight hundred Indians brought to a place called Puerto de Plata (Silver Harbor) and held on board for two days before being disembarked.
Under what conditions? No details, but six hundred of them are said

to have died and been thrown overboard, to float like planks on the waves. African slaves would have a higher survival rate.[16]

Nothing like this would be seen again until the Nazi Jew hunts and killer drives of World War II. Within decades, the native Arawaks (Tainos) and Caribs were largely wiped out.*

The Caribbean conquest, of course, only began the story. The Spanish thirst for gold and treasure was unassuaged; the enterprise of factious malcontents irrepressible. Mission leaders, agents of the Spanish crown, found that one of the best ways to deal with disobedience and rebellion was to ship the troublemakers off to unknown shores. Let them hunt the Fountain of Youth; with luck they might die in the search. The desperate readiness and hardiness of these adventurers surpass belief. The history of Spanish conquest, then, is in part a story of ill-starred voyages and futile marches into legend and oblivion. But also of lucky strikes like Mexico and Peru. One find, even one report, could provoke and justify a dozen expeditions. Such were the ingredients of empire: power, greed, and mission, seasoned with credulity, wrath, and madness.

⤙ ⤚

# Black Gold[17]

The gold that found its way from somewhere in Africa to the Mediterranean coast held European merchants in thrall. They went to places like Tunis to trade silver and arms, textiles and leather, rice and figs, nuts and wine (presumably for re-export) for grain and fodder, oils, fats, semolina, and honey; and then—to balance payments—for gold. Gold dust, gold ingots, gold coins (Moorish ducats). Not only did the yellow metal cast an almost hypnotic lure, the rate of exchange made these transactions extremely lucrative.

---

* The extent of this holocaust is a subject of disagreement. High estimates of the population of the Caribbean islands at the time of Columbus' arrival run into the millions, over a million for Hispaniola (Haiti) alone. These are based on a count supposedly done by Bartholomew Columbus (the admiral's brother) in 1496 and repeated as authority in subsequent reports—Sauer, *The Early Spanish Main,* pp. 65–67. What kind of count this was is impossible to say. On the other hand, Sauer, p. 204, states that plague and disease were not reported in the islands until 1518, at which time the native population of Hispaniola was down to some eleven thousand. How, then, had the missing persons been extinguished? By brutality, murder, forced labor in placer gold mines, a precipitous fall in births. Still, it is hard to understand how even a busy colony of sadists, butchers, and taskmasters could kill so many (that is, over a million) so fast.

Silver traded for gold at 10 to 1 in Tunis in the first half of the fourteenth century, but that same gold would buy 13 units of silver in the markets of Valencia. Such a disparity could not last; active trade makes a working market, and a market makes for homogeneous prices. By the middle of the fourteenth century, the ratio was 10.5:1 in Naples, 11:1 in Florence. The influx from Africa was such that much of the western Mediterranean went over to a gold standard, as reflected in new coinages: the *pierrale d'oro* in Sicily, the *reial d'oro* in Majorca, the *alfonsino* in Sardinia (1339), the gold florin in Aragon (1346).

Literary and cartographic sources dating back to the mid-thirteenth century attest to the Latin fascination with this gold and its unknown mother lode. The suppliers, however, took pains to keep the source secret—no doubt wisely, for they correctly surmised that the Christian infidels would kill and die for gold. We know now that the gold came from deep in the interior of West Africa, somewhere along the upper reaches of the Niger and near the headwaters of the Gambia and Senegal rivers. The story has it that the blacks who mined the gold exchanged it by "dumb" barter: the buyers left trade goods at an appointed place and then withdrew, and the miners then took the goods and left what they felt was an appropriate amount of gold in payment. The mystery, needless to say, was an invitation to fantasy. Some said the gold grew there like carrots; others affirmed that it was brought up from under the ground by diligent and serviable ants; others that it was mined by naked men who lived in holes.

In any event, the precious metal had to pass from its source through the legendary African kingdom of Mali, which controlled access to Timbuktu and the cross-Sahara camel routes and was the farthest "upstream" source known to the Mediterranean merchants. There the bullion traders paid a heavy tribute to the local middlemen and the ruler, known as the Mansa; as the story has it, Mali took the nuggets and left the dust to the traders. (A mill to grind and flake the nuggets might have proved handy.) From time to time, the Mansa and his agents tried to increase revenue by forcing the diggers to produce more. Such efforts foundered on the passive resistance of the miners, who just stopped delivering.

In the meantime, the Mansa was getting more than enough for his *laisser-passer*. One Mansa, by name Musa (Arabic for Moses), went on pilgrimage to Mecca in 1324. Such a trip took more than a year, and the Mansa was determined to do it in style. He stayed three months in Egypt, and the visit was remembered for centuries thereafter. He gave 50,000 dinars to the Sultan, who was not above taking so princely a gift, and thousands of ingots to the shrines he visited and the officials who entertained and ministered to him. By the end of his stay, we are told, the value of gold in Egypt had fallen by 10 to 25 percent.

Though the Mansa had come with a fortune in expense money—eighty to one hundred camels bearing 300 pounds of gold each (equals from 110 to 135 million of our dollars!)—he was penniless by the end of his pilgrimage and had to borrow for his return. His creditors were well reimbursed for their confidence, at 700 dinars for every 300 he had borrowed.

The opulence impressed. Arab authors such as Ibn-amir Hajib and Ibn Battuta have left us detailed accounts of the Mali king and kingdom. The Mansa, they tell us, commanded more devotion from his people than any ruler anywhere. He was the living embodiment of majesty—from the way he held himself and walked to the way his subjects showed their abject humiliation in his presence, prostrating themselves, touching their heads to the ground, greeting his every word with murmurs of wonder and approval. Let no man enter his presence informally dressed; let no one even sneeze. Such signs of impertinence brought death.

The legend of the Mansa's greatness reached Europe at second hand. Maps, particularly the *Catalan Atlas* of 1375, showed the ruler enthroned like a European monarch, crown on head, orb and scepter in hand. "So abundant is the gold that is found in his country," the *Catalan Atlas* noted, "that this lord is the richest and noblest king in all the land." This admiration and esteem were not to last. The gold trade diminished; Mali declined. In the later fourteenth century, when the Portuguese got down to the African "gold coast" and were able to penetrate Gambia, the successors of Mansa Musa came to be seen as crude, pretentious stereotypes. *Sic transit.*

## The Importance of Being Covered

Nakedness was not a trivial consideration: it was construed in the beginning as a sign of edenic innocence. Columbus, for example, was initially enraptured.[18] "They go naked as the day they were born," he wrote, "the women as well as the men." And: "We Christians said they were remarkably beautiful, the men as well as the women." And: "This beauty was moral as well as physical. . . . They are the most pleasant and peaceful people in the world."

Along with beauty went innocence. "The Admiral said he could not believe that a man could have ever beheld people so good of heart, so generous and timid, because they all gave away everything they had to us Christians and ran to give us whatever they had as soon as they saw us." And: "In exchange for anything you give them, no matter how trifling, they immediately give you all their possessions." And: "They do not covet other people's property. . . . Whatever you ask for that belongs to them, they never refuse. On the contrary, they ask you to help yourself, and show so much love that you give them your heart." And: "They are very gentle and know nothing of evil. They know nothing of killing one another."[19]

But such an idyllic image could not long survive the test of experience. In particular, one thing these generous people were not ready to give away, and that was their women. And that was the one thing that, after months at sea, these horny Spaniards wanted above all, more even than gold. Also, the same innocents who were ready to give freely of their possessions assumed the Spanish would do the same. So they took, which the Spanish defined as theft. The very Columbus who had waxed rhapsodic on arrival soon repented himself of his credulity and offered some practical advice to his men: "During your voyage to Cibao, if an Indian steals anything at all, you must punish him by cutting off his nose and his hands, because these are the parts of the body that they cannot hide."

So now the noble savage had become the savage, pure and simple. What else could he be? No one could live up to scriptural myths in the presence of some of the most ruthless rogues ever let loose on unsuspecting victims. Pascal Bruckner argues persuasively that the Indian was "condemned from the very beginning because he had been declared perfect." This new, and for the white man far more congenial, image was reinforced, moreover, by other aspects of Indian culture—in particular their alleged recourse to cannibalism. Some scholars would deny the existence of such practice, at least for the Indians of the Caribbean. (There would seem to be no doubt of it in Mexico or Central America.) How credible such denials are is hard to say; it is, after all, very hard to prove a negative, but it is clear that anthropologists are sometimes motivated here by a need to see the European-Amerindian encounter in black and white, with all the wickedness on one side and only virtue on the other.[20]

Sometimes the defense is indirect. The social anthropologist David Maybury-Lewis cites as representative and influential in this regard a work by Hans Staden, *True History and Description of the Land of the Savage, Naked and Ugly Maneating Peoples of the New World of America* (1557), and goes on to say that the Tupinamba Indians, who had held Staden captive, "regularly and ritually ate their prisoners." "It was considered," he goes on, "a heroic death. A captive warrior, who in some cases might have been living with his captors for years and might have even raised a family there, was led out and clubbed to death in a ceremonial duel, after which the entire community ate him to partake of his heroic essence."[21]

Maybury-Lewis further notes that the same Tupinamba were horrified by the cruelty of Europeans, as evinced by the routine use of torture in trial and punishment and the practice of slavery; and then goes on to deplore the one-sidedness of European judgments and policy. But of course it is very hard for any of us "to see ourselves as others see us." Relativism—the power of sympathy— becomes us and is a particular virtue of ethnological scholarship. But one must not expect to find it generally. In sixteenth-century Europe, it was confined to a few clerics, whose arguments were best appreciated when recollected in tranquility.

⁓ ⁓

# History and Legend

The tale of Spanish misdeeds and crimes in the conquest of the Americas is so appalling that it has been a source of retrospective embarrassment and mortification. What kind of people were these, who could perpetrate so much cruelty and treachery? The answer, as outlined above, lay in social selection and history. On the one hand, the kind of adventures that lay ahead in the New World attracted the most daring, hungry, knavish members of Spanish society, many of them blackguards who thought little of their own lives and even less of those of others. On the other, the Spanish historical experience, the protracted war against enemies without (the *reconquista*) and within (the persecution of religious difference), could not but promote ends over means and extinguish sentiments of decency and humanity. To which Tzvetan Todorov would add the factor of distance: the Spanish were operating far from home and exercising their power and wrath on strangers, on an Other defined as subhuman and hence outside or beneath the rules that governed comportment even against an enemy. In such circumstances, anything goes; nothing is forbidden. So they competed in imagining and doing evil, which thus fairly exploded in collective frenzies. Todorov adds: "The 'barbarity' of the Spanish has nothing atavistic or animal about it; it is perfectly human and announces the arrival of modern times."[22]

Unhappy the day that brought together this monumental amorality and the opportunity of conquest, that placed much weaker peoples in the merciless hands of greedy, angry, unpredictably cruel men.

In the effort to mitigate, if not excuse, this record of evil, apologists, many of them descendants of these conquistadors, have followed two lines of argument. One is to discredit the charges by labeling them as myth or exaggeration. Hence recourse to the term *leyenda negra* (black legend): black, thus by implication excessive (is anything ever completely black?); and legend rather than history. The aim is to dismiss rather than disprove, because disproof is impossible. (The same tactic and the same terminology have been employed to discredit the argument that Spanish intolerance and religious fanaticism at home, culminating in the obsession with racial purity [*limpieza de sangre*], and the pursuit of heresy even into the solitude of dreams, crippled the nation's capacity for inquiry and learning. Here, too, it is easier to dismiss bad news than to rebut.)

The second approach is to point out the misdeeds of other colonizers, in particular the Anglo-Saxon, Protestant Nordamericanos, whose strategy of conquest was different and whose victims were fewer, but whose capacity for cruelty and hypocrisy was supposedly similar.* As though the misdeeds of others excused one's own crimes. This line of argument is not unrelated to

* Is that really so? The British colonists in North America were capable of cold murder; but hot torment and torture? And if one asks who can measure these things, there does seem to me a significant operational difference here, namely, that if I were an Indian, I would rather have died at British than at Spanish hands. Dead is dead, but that way I might go to my death swiftly and reasonably whole.

subsequent issues of power and the politics of imperialism. For many Latin American historians and ideologues, it has been vital to emphasize the wickedness of the *gringos* who came to dominate the Americas. Better, then, to lay the misfortunes of the Amerindian populations at their door, if only by implication.[23]

# — 6 —

# Eastward Ho!

Of all the great Events that have happened in the World of late Ages, those which concern the Voyages and Discoveries, made by the *Europeans* in the fifteenth and sixteenth Centuries, do justly challenge the Preference. . . . In the Merit and Glory of these Achievements, the *Portugueze,* without all Controversy are intitled to the first and principal Share . . . it must be confessed, that they first set on Foot the Navigation of the Ocean, and put it into the Heads of other Nations, to go on the Discovery of distant Regions.

Other Nations were so far from being as early as the *Portugueze* in Attempts of this Kind, that these latter had been carrying on their Enterprizes, near fourscore Years, before any of their Neighbours seem to have thought of foreign Discoveries . . . the several Events showed, that the Designs were the Results of solid Reasoning, and formed on the most rational Grounds.
—THOMAS ASTLEY, *Voyages and Travels*

Like the Spanish, the Portuguese began by island-hopping. Down the western coast of Africa, aiming at an end run around the Muslims into the Indian Ocean. The first reaches were easy. Southing, their sails swelled with the trade winds. But that meant trouble getting back to Lisbon. It was a stroke of genius not to beat their way upwind but rather to swing out west and north and return via the Azores.

The same but different beyond the Canaries. Now southing proved difficult, as winds and currents turned contrary. The trouble began around Cape Bojador (27° N.), symbolic boundary between creation and chaos, where struggling waters made the sea seem to boil. A decade of probes (1424–34) turned back at this invisible barrier.[1]

But still the Portuguese pressed on, voyage after voyage, league after league. At first they thought that no one lived along that arid coast; but then they encountered a few natives, took some prisoners, learned of slavery, saw new opportunities for profit. For profit was the heart of the matter: as Prince Henry's biographer-hagiographer Zurara put it, " . . . it is evident that [no sailor or merchant] would want to go to a place where he did not stand to make money."[2]

The South Atlantic is like no other ocean. On the African side it is not bordered by a convenient continental shelf; currents and winds run

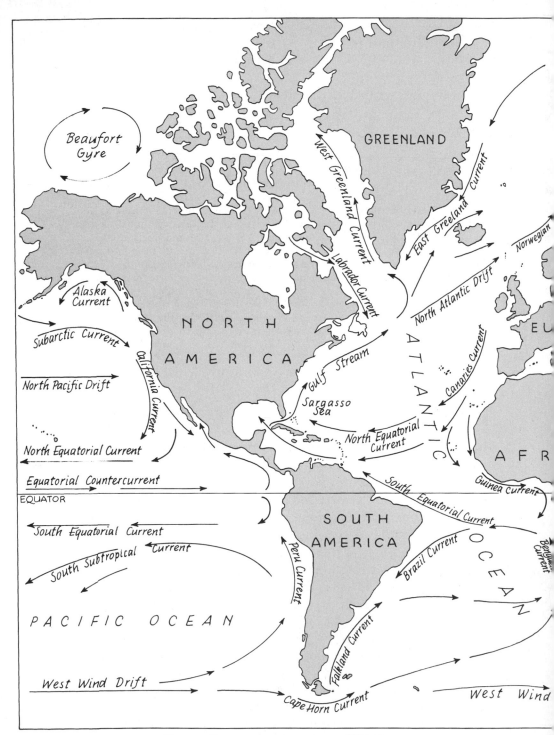

OCEAN CURRENTS AROUND THE WORLD
These currents, along with prevailing winds, dictated shipping routes
in the Age of Sail.

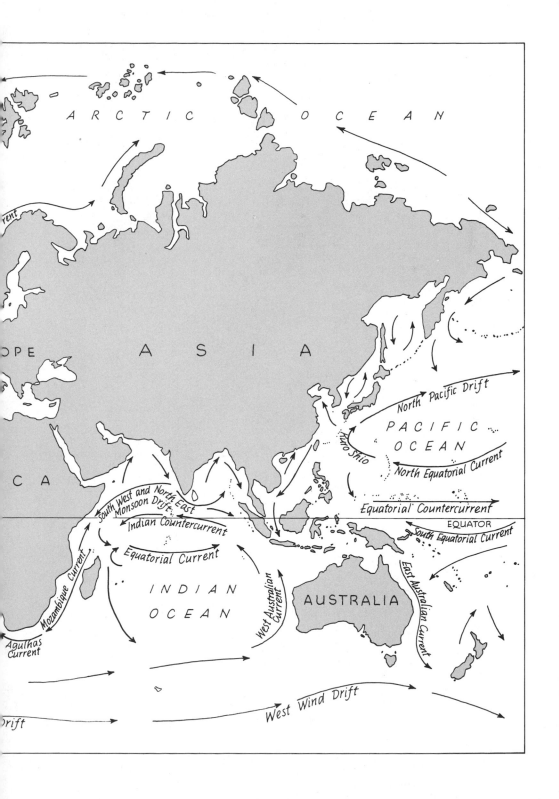

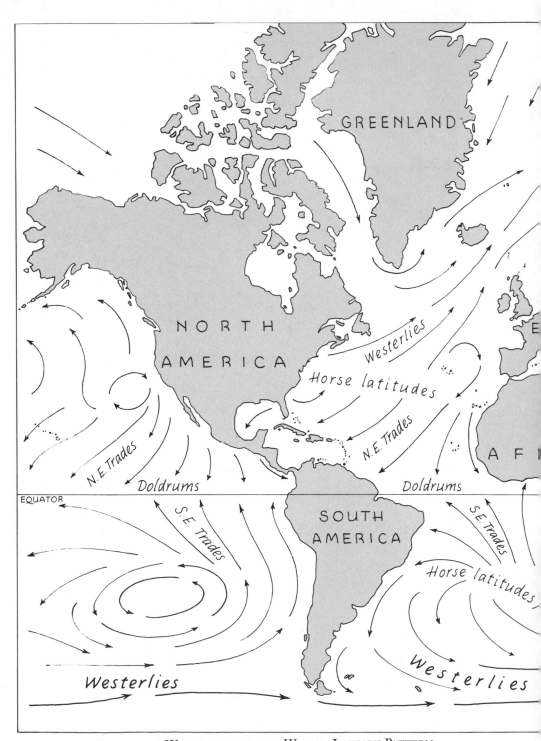

PREVAILING WINDS AROUND THE WORLD, JANUARY PATTERN
Calms and doldrums are found where countervailing winds meet.
To be avoided.

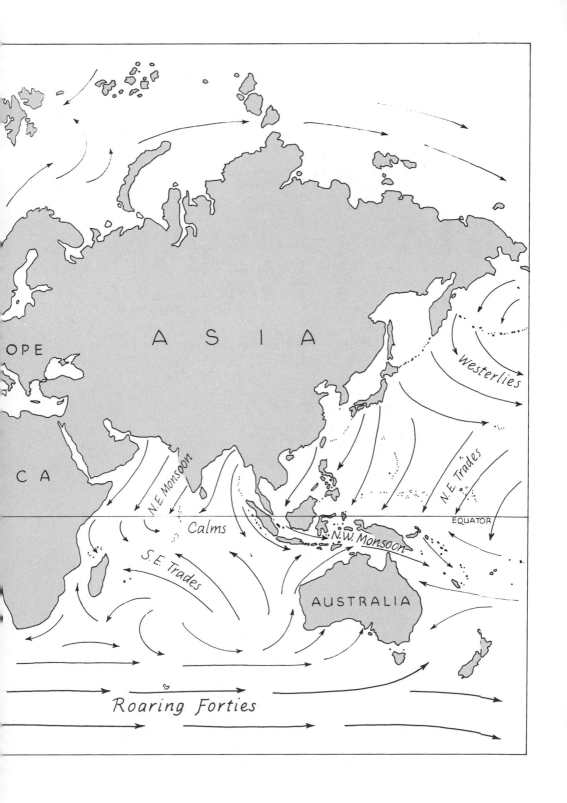

ASIA

OPE

CA

Westerlies

N.E. Monsoon

N.E. Trades

Calms

EQUATOR

S.E. Trades

N.W. Monsoon

AUSTRALIA

Roaring Forties

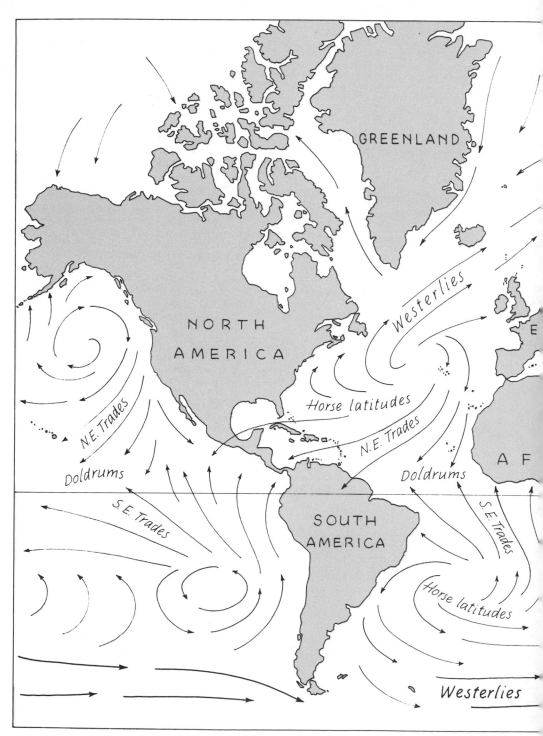

PREVAILING WINDS, JUNE PATTERN

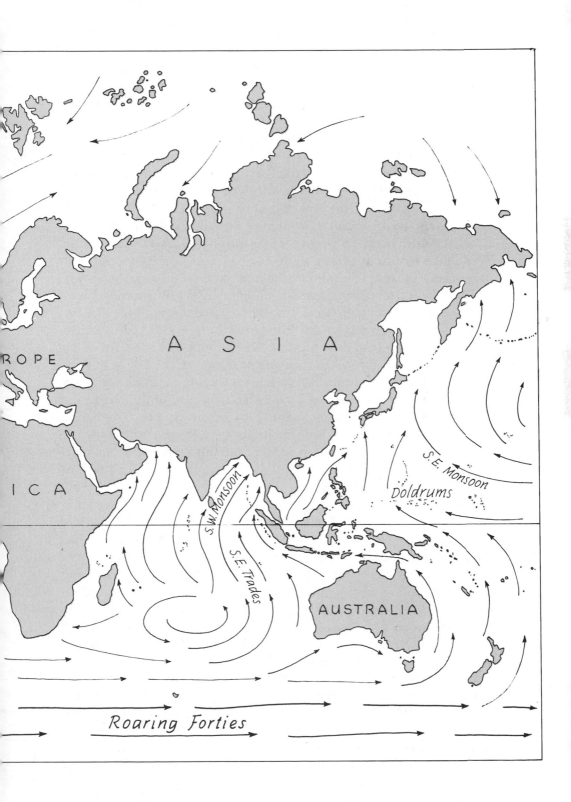

against southing ships, and the coastline is dreary-arid. Once one gets past the Cape Verdes, moreover, one finds little in the way of harbor and refreshment between Guinea and the Cape. Time-honored techniques of coasting, then, highly effective in the North Atlantic, Mediterranean, Indian Ocean, and China seas, do not work here. This is high-seas navigation.[3] (See Maps 1, 2, and 3.)

Here the earlier experience of the Portuguese in using the trade winds to ease their return home from the islands paid off, but in a different direction. After decades of beating and tacking their way south, they filled their sails and took the audacious step of swinging well out to the west, clear across the ocean to Brazil, before turning back to the southeast. This added hundreds of leagues to the route and meant weeks, even months out of sight of land; but the effect was to shorten the voyage and give them clear sailing around the point of Africa into friendlier seas.

One must not think of this as luck. The Portuguese could do this because they had learned to find the latitude. In the North Atlantic, sailors had always read their location north-south by the height of the Pole star. As they approached the equator, however, the Pole star stood too low in the sky, and they had to rely on the sun for guidance. Here the problem was complicated by the changing position of the sun in the sky: in European summer, it stood farther north, hence higher; in winter, farther south. This variance in position, known as declination, had to be taken into account in reading the sun's altitude as the measure of latitude. Here Iberia's position as frontier and bridge between civilizations paid off. In the fourteenth and fifteenth centuries, Arab and Jewish astronomers there (the key figure was Abraham Zacut) prepared convenient tables of solar declination for the use of navigators.[4]

Once one could find the latitude, both at sea and on land, one had the key to the oceans; for now one could know position north-south; and if one also knew the latitude of the destination, one could get there by sailing to and then following the parallel. (Occasional problem: should one turn east or west?) The most important information that Bartolomeu Dias brought back from his voyage (1488) was the coordinate of the southern tip of Africa. Knowing that, the Portuguese could find their way there from any part of the South Atlantic.

These explorations had taken the Portuguese the better part of a century. Some of this was the work of the Portuguese crown and its devout, single-minded prince (we are told that he died a virgin) come down to us as Henry the Navigator, who built a marine research station at Sagres on a promontory overlooking the ocean and directed decades of inquiry into the science and technique of steering and sailing on the high seas. Some of it was the work of private shippers and seamen, who saw riches at the end of their bowsprit. All of it depended on improvements in the art of shipbuilding: caravels, longer and sleeker, rather than broad, cargo-bearing cogs; stern rudders; a mix of square and lateen sails; a marriage of Atlantic and Mediterranean techniques. When Dias returned from the southern tip of Africa, he also brought with him ideas that went into the ships (no longer called caravels) used by Vasco da Gama a decade later. Ten years more saw further modifications. Every trip was an experience, an incentive to emendation.

Ocean sailing further depended on instrumentation: the compass for direction; the astrolabe and cross-staff for measuring altitudes of celestial bodies; devices for sighting with back turned to the sun; sandglasses for timing and estimating speed. And, lest we forget, all sailing depended on the tenacity of hard-bitten sailors. These fellows, a strange crowd, had plenty of opportunity to regret signing on. They sickened and often died of scurvy on these endless voyages, nagged Virgin and saints with numberless Hail Mary's and repetitious litanies, sought to appease the sea with superstitious gestures; and then, feet once more on dry land, wages spent on booze and sex, pockets empty, allowed themselves to be tempted again. That was the way of a seafaring man. (Besides, the crimps were always waiting to pounce.)

The Portuguese strategy, doing by knowing, made good sense. Each trip built on the ones before; each time, they went a little farther; each time they noted their latitude, changed their maps, and left a marker of presence. Psychological barriers made some steps more difficult: thus Cape Bojador; also the Cape of Storms, later renamed of Good Hope (symbolism was important). Gradually, fear yielded to reason and method. The decision to sail west, almost to the coast of South America, before going east was the most inventive and audacious of all, showing tremendous confidence in their ability to find their way. (By comparison, Columbus had a cakewalk.) Better to keep moving than to tack and stand. No wind like a following wind; no sail like a full sail.

The Portuguese push to the Indies is not understandable without taking account of men such as Vasco de Gama, sailor and seaman from childhood, man of hard head and hard measures. We do not know as much about Gama as we should like, but one story of his pre-Indies career tells much about his character. The year was 1492, and Gama was about thirty. A Portuguese caravel carrying gold from El Mina (on the west coast of Africa) had been seized by a French privateer, even though the two countries were at peace. What to do? The Portuguese king's counselors advised diplomacy: send an emissary to plead for the

ship and its gold. King John was not pleased: "I have no desire to see
a messenger of mine ill received or made to kick his heels in ante-
rooms. That would be more grievous to me than the loss of the gold."

So King John sent for Gama, "a man in whom he had confidence,
who had seen service in the fleets and in the affairs of the sea." The sea
was Portugal's great school, and not only in matters of navigation.
The next morning Gama and a hastily assembled posse were on the
quay at Setubal, where ten French ships were berthed, loading rich
merchandise. All of them were seized; their cargoes taken and placed
under seal; their men brought ashore. Nothing more was needed. The
French shipowners made petition to the king of France. The king of
France sent the caravel back and the gold, to the last ounce. And the
king of Portugal released the French ships and their cargoes, to the last
ell and cask.[5]

Columbus's discovery of a new world shocked the Portuguese. Like
Sputnik to the Americans. After all, they could have had him and had
turned him down. Decades of painful, costly exploration reaching
around Africa, and here the Spanish found a new world (or maybe
Asia) on the first try. No justice. Time to get going: in July of 1497 a
small flotilla of four ships under the command of Vasco da Gama set
forth from Lisbon to follow on the aborted initiative of Bartolomeu
Dias and, rounding Africa, to find India. The voyage would take them
over 27,000 miles and over two years; and only fifty-four of the original crew of one hundred seventy returned alive.

This costly probe did not prove a commercial success. To da Gama's
astonishment, the merchants he encountered in India were Muslims and
had no intention of trading with Christian infidels; what's more, the
glass beads, trinkets, and shirts he had brought with him for barter or
sale, though eminently attractive to natives of the Caribbean, were near
to worthless in India, which knew the difference between trash and
precious things and made far better fabrics than Europe. So da Gama returned more or less empty-handed. The little he did bring back was a
prize of war; in his eagerness and desperation, he attacked and captured
a small Muslim vessel with a cargo of spices. Not a good precedent: from
that point on, the Portuguese would rely on force to establish themselves in the Indian Ocean rather than on market competition.

Much more important, da Gama brought back news—two kinds of
news. The first: that Europeans were stronger than the natives; they
had better ships and better guns. The second: that although he had not
been able to trade, spices aplenty were to be had for prices that

promised huge profits. A hundredweight of pepper could be had in Calicut for three ducats. After passing through the hands of a half-dozen intermediaries and paying substantial fees and bribes to kings, sheikhs, and officials along the way, it sold in Venice for 80. Against that kind of gain, what was the cost of outfitting a fleet? And what the value of seamen's lives?

This was Portugal's revenge. King Manuel wrote his fellow monarchs, Ferdinand and Isabella ("Most high and excellent Prince and Princess, most potent Lord and Lady!"), to tell them about "large cities, large buildings and rivers, and great populations"—no naked savages here—and to brag of spices, precious stones, and "mines of gold." Nothing of scurvy and death, nothing of Muslim merchants and commercial disappointment. Here was the kind of place that Columbus had been looking for and did not find. Stick that in your craw.

In early 1500, less than six months after da Gama's triumphal return, the Portuguese sent out a second fleet to the Indies—thirteen ships this time and one thousand two hundred men, including soldiers—under the command of Pedro Alvares Cabral. They sent him to make money and told him not to look for trouble; but if a hostile vessel should try to do him harm, he was not to let it come near, but rather to stand off and blow it out of the water.

Nothing better illustrates awareness of superiority. For it is well known that those who possess stronger arms can kill from a distance at no risk to themselves; whereas those in a position of weakness must close and rely on personal valor and strength to gain a victory. Cabral's instructions signaled a new balance of world power. The Asians, so much more numerous than the Portuguese, also richer and in many ways more civilized, would not have understood this, could not have imagined it. Yet there it was: *Europe could now plant itself anywhere on the surface of the globe within reach of naval cannon.**

The Portuguese went at their task with method that would have warmed the heart of Prince Henry. Here were curiosity and appetite ra-

---

* This decisive superiority of European armament in 1500, along with other technological advantages already discussed, sticks in the craw of scholars who want to believe that European global hegemony was a lucky accident. As one iconoclast has proclaimed: "My 1400–1800 book 'shows' that Asia was way ahead of Europe till 1800 and that Europe joined/climbed up on Asia using American money. The 'expansion' of Europe and its progress/advantage over Asia from 1500 is a Eurocentric myth." Andre Gunder Frank, University of Toronto, on the Internet, H-World @msu.edu, 7 June 1996.

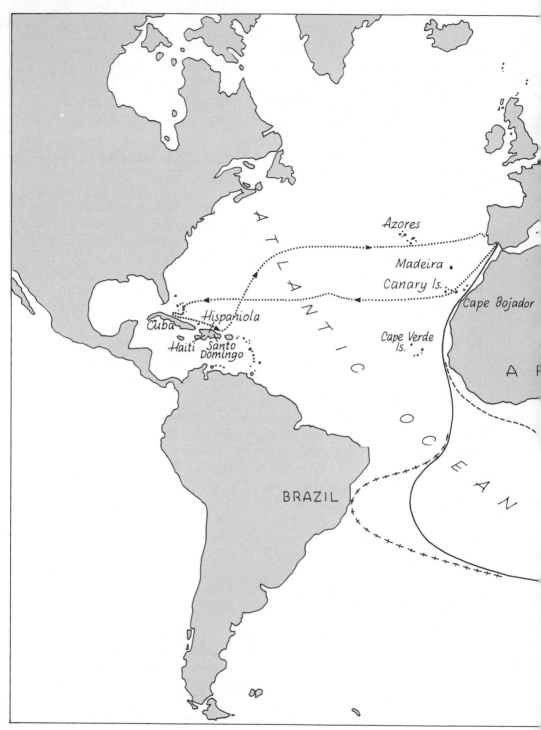

THE AGE OF DISCOVERY: ROUTES OF MAJOR VOYAGES
Note the way wind and current dictated the choice of route. Better to sail
long and fast than tack and fight a shorter distance.

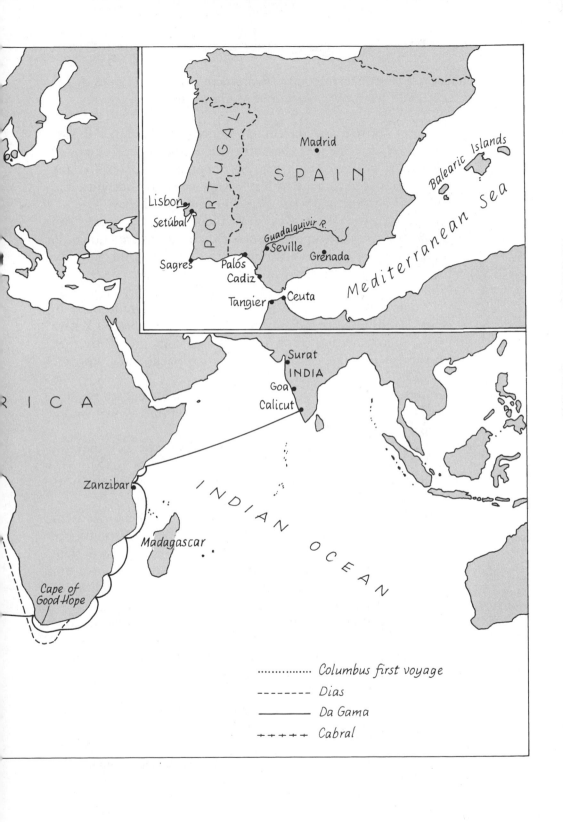

PORTUGAL

SPAIN

Madrid

Lisbon
Setúbal

Guadalquivir R.
Seville
Sagres
Palos
Cadiz
Grenada

Tangier
Ceuta

Balearic Islands

Mediterranean Sea

Surat
INDIA
Goa
Calicut

AFRICA

Zanzibar

INDIAN OCEAN

Madagascar

Cape of
Good Hope

............ Columbus first voyage

-------- Dias

————— Da Gama

+ + + + + Cabral

tionalized, as in the instructions *(Regimento)* to Diogo Lopes de Se-
queira in 1508 for the exploration of Madagascar:

1. The fleet was to follow the circumference of the island, with special attention to the west coast (the side facing Africa); enter and
   study every port, reconnoiter means of entry and exit, explore the
   possibilities of anchorage with reference to winds, currents, and
   nature of bottom; and *write all of this down* [my italics].
2. First contact with the natives: show them a range of articles and
   metals (spices, wax, copper) to see if these things are known on
   the island; and if there, ask how to get to them and trade for
   them. Find out what they would want in exchange.
3. Find out what if any other ships come in to these ports. Where do
   they come from? What do they carry? Do they trade these in
   other islands or carry different things to different places? Where
   do the merchants and crews of these ships come from? Are they
   Muslim or pagan *("gentiles")*? White or black? How are they
   dressed? Do they come armed?
4. Are these other ships big or small? What kind? What are the seasons of their coming and going? The rhythm (annual, more
   often)? Their way of navigating?
5. Does the island have its own vessels, and if so, where do they go,
   what do they carry, what do they seek?
6. What does the island produce, what will the natives take for it?
   Are these things dear or cheap?
7. Political structure: what kinds of kings or lords, whether Muslim
   or pagan? How do they live? How do they administer justice?
   What do they possess? Do they hold treasure? What kind of state
   and dignity, and how do they maintain it? What military force and
   arms: elephants or horses, weapons, firearms, artillery of any kind?
   Are the soldiers timid or warlike?
8. Are there Muslim rulers apart, independent; and do they recognize the pagan rulers?
9. Is the population Muslim or pagan? If the latter, how do the Muslims live with them? Are there Christians as in India?* Do they
   know St. Thomas?
10. What are the customs? Are they, in part at least, like those of the
    Malabars?

---

* The first Portuguese to arrive in India were misled by native idolatry into thinking
that Hinduism was an exotic form of Christianity.

11. Are there cities, towns, or villages of special importance? Are they fortified? How is the land inhabited?
12. Money? Is there some standard tender, or are there simply "moneys," like those of Manicongo [Africa?]? In this regard do they trade copper as a commodity, and in that case, what things are made of it? In particular, is it used for casting guns and if so, what kind? Also in that case, how do they make gunpowder?

A similar questionnaire for Malacca (Malay peninsula) adds a detailed question about the Chinese who traded in those parts: vessels and techniques of navigation? arms and style of war? trade, merchants, trading posts, merchandise, prices? political power? clothing and manners? size and shape of China?[6]

These systematic inquiries went back in Portugal at least to 1425, beginning with the exploration of the Canaries. In 1537, Pedro Nuñes, cosmographer to King João III, boasted in recollection: "It is evident that the discoveries of coasts, islands, continents has not occurred by chance, but to the contrary, our sailors have departed very well informed, provided with instruments and rules of astronomy and geometry."[7] The contrast with Spain is marked. The Spanish did not adopt this methodical approach until the last quarter of the sixteenth century. Either they did not need it (no competition; simpler navigation), or it did not accord with their tradition and style. Whereas the Portuguese sealed claims of possession by asserting discovery, that is, by entering latitudes on maps, the Spanish asserted material facts. They planted crosses, "converted" natives, built Christian edifices, installed tribunals and jails. As for objectives, the Spanish aimed at treasure; the Portuguese, at profits from trade. Two views of empire.

The history of European commercial and political expansion into the Indian Ocean and East Asia is dominated by the question of a might-have-been. What if the sixteenth century were not a period of Asian political disarray, of war in India between native states and Turcoman invaders, of Chinese isolationism, a low as it were, exposing Asia to the ruthless thrusts of these invaders? The Chinese "absence" hurt especially.

From 1405 to 1431, the Chinese undertook at least seven major naval expeditions to explore the waters of Indonesia and the Indian Ocean. These voyages aimed to show the Chinese flag, bestow awareness and knowledge of the Celestial Kingdom on the barbarians, receive homage and tribute, and collect for the emperor those few rarities not available within his borders. In particular, the ships brought back exotic zoological specimens—giraffes, zebras, ostriches; also jewels and potent animal, vegetable, and mineral substances to enrich the Chinese pharmacopeia.

The relationship of these voyages to trade is not entirely clear. The ships carried valuable commodities (silks, porcelain) that were intended for exchange, but apparently not in the open market; rather, in the context of gift giving: tribute from the barbarians, benevolence from the Chinese. On the other hand, the sorties were apparently intended to open the way to normal trade, and merchants did come along to make their own deals. Independent trading voyages followed, presumably profiting from enhanced Chinese prestige. But if trade was one of the objectives, this was a very costly way to go about it. In effect the Chinese people were paying for the profits of the officials who organized the treasure fleets and promoted private trade, so much indeed that the burden of these voyages came to exceed the empire's means.[8]

These flotillas far surpassed in grandeur the small Portuguese fleets that came later. The ships were probably the largest vessels the world had seen: high multideck junks (but that is a misleading term) acted as floating camps, each carrying hundreds of sailors and soldiers, testimony to the advanced techniques of Chinese shipbuilding, navigation, and naval organization.[9] The biggest were about 400 feet long, 160 wide (compare the 85 feet of Columbus's *Santa Maria*), had nine staggered masts and twelve square sails of red silk. These were the so-called treasure ships, built for luxury, fitted with grand cabins and windowed halls—accommodations fit for the representatives of the Son of Heaven and the foreign dignitaries who would accompany them back to China. Other ships met other needs: eight-masted "horse ships" carrying mounts to South Asia, which for climatic reasons could not easily raise these animals, along with building and repair materials; seven-masted supply ships, carrying principally food; six-masted troop transports; five-masted warships for naval combat; and smaller fast boats to deal with pirates. The fleet even included water tankers, to ensure a fresh supply for a month or more.

The first of these fleets, that of the eunuch admiral Zheng He (Cheng-ho) in 1405, consisted of 317 vessels and carried 28,000 men.[10] From 1404 to 1407, China undertook an orgy of shipbuilding and refitting. Whole seaboard provinces were drawn into the effort, while inland forests were stripped for timber. Hundreds of households of carpenters, smiths, sailmakers, ropemakers, caulkers, carters and haulers, even timekeepers, were moved by fiat, grouped into teams, domiciled in yards next to their work. Since the shipwrights and their apprentices were generally illiterate, learning proceeded by example, using handcrafted models whose parts fitted perfectly without nails. No detail was too small to escape the planning of the shipwrights: overlapping planks, multiple layers, joints between planks caulked with jute and covered with sifted lime and tung oil, iron nails sealed against rust, special woods for every purpose, even large "dragon eyes" painted on the prow so that the ship could "see" where it was going. These eyes, plus a good, balanced stern rudder and heavy ballast, the whole guided by navigational experience and folkloric wisdom, would take the ship from port to port. The work itself was done in huge drydocks (China here anticipated European technology by hundreds of years) opening onto the Yangtze (Yangzi). In this way, over a period of three years, the Chinese built or refitted some 1,681 ships. Medieval Europe could not have conceived of such an armada.[11]

Yet this Chinese opening to the sea and the larger world came to naught, indeed was deliberately reduced to naught.* In the 1430s a new emperor reigned in Peking, one who "knew not Joseph." A new, Confucian crowd competed for influence, mandarins who scorned and distrusted commerce (for them, the only true source of wealth was agriculture) and detested the eunuchs who had planned and carried out the great voyages. For some decades, the two groups vied for influence, the balance shifting now one way, now the other. But fiscality and the higher Chinese morality were on the Confucian side. The maritime campaign had strained the empire's finances and weakened its authority over a population bled white by taxes and corvée levies.

The decision (early fifteenth century) to move the capital to Peking made things worse: new city walls, a palace compound of over nine thousand rooms, peasants liable in principle for thirty days service but kept at work for years running. The transportation bill alone—moving the court from Nanking, some eight hundred miles—drove tax surcharges upward.[12] A few conscientious officials spoke up, but the imperial courtiers stifled them by severe and humiliating penalties. A prefect who protested the extra requisitions was put in a cage and wheeled in disgrace to the capital to be interrogated by the emperor. So much for duty. Meanwhile, on the northwest frontier, a changing but unchanging cast of nomadic raiders gave the empire no peace, draining resources and demanding undivided attention.

* They also explored the east coast of Asia as far north as Kamchatka, but there too decided to abstain. (Once you've seen an ice floe, you've seen 'em all.)

So, after some decades of tugging and hauling, of alternating celebration and commemoration on the one hand, of contumely and repudiation on the other, the decision was taken not only to cease from
maritime exploration but to erase the very memory of what had gone
before lest later generations be tempted to renew the folly. From 1436,
requests for the assignment of new craftsmen to the shipyards were refused, while conversely, foreigners asking for the renewal of customary
gifts were turned down, presumably for reasons of economy. For want
of construction and repair, public and private fleets shrank. Pirates
flourished in unguarded waters (the Japanese were particularly active),
and China placed ever more reliance on inland canal transport. By
1500, anyone who built a ship of more than two masts was liable to the
death penalty, and in 1525 coastal authorities were enjoined to destroy all oceangoing ships and to arrest their owners. Finally in 1551,
it became a crime to go to sea on a multimasted ship, even for trade.[13]

The abandonment of the program of great voyages was part of a
larger policy of closure, of retreat from the hazards and temptations of
the sea. This deliberate introversion, a major turning point in Chinese
history, could not have come at a worse time, for it not only disarmed
them in the face of rising European power but set them, complacent
and stubborn, against the lessons and novelties that European travelers would soon be bringing.

Why? Why did China not make that little extra effort that would
have taken it around the southern end of Africa and up into the Atlantic? Why, decades and even centuries after the arrival of European
visitors in Chinese waters, were there no Chinese vessels in the harbors
of Europe? (The first such vessel, a vehicle for diplomacy, visited London for the Great Exhibition of 1851.)

As always, there are several reasons. The result, in sociological jargon, is overdetermined.

To begin with, the Chinese lacked range, focus, and above all, curiosity. They went to show themselves, not to see and learn; to bestow
their presence, not to stay; to receive obeisance and tribute, not to
buy. They were what they were and did not have to change. They had
what they had and did not have to take or make. Unlike the Europeans,
they were not motivated by greed and passion. The Europeans had a
specific target: the wealth of the Indies. They had to get around Africa;
that was the point of the exercise. The Chinese did not have to. They
could find what they wanted in the Indian Ocean, and what they
wanted was so trivial that it was not an appetizer but a dessert.[14]

At the same time, this desire to overawe meant that costs far exceeded returns. These voyages reeked of extravagance. Whereas the first profits (the first whiff of pepper) and the promise of even greater ones to come were a powerful incentive to Western venturers, in China the pecuniary calculus said no. This reconsideration, in its way, was very much like that currently faced in the United States by such projects as the supercollider and the space station.

The vulnerability of the program—here today, gone tomorrow—was reinforced by its official character. In Europe, the opportunity of private initiative that characterized even such royal projects as the search for a sea route to the Indies was a source of participatory funding and an assurance of rationality. Nothing like this in China, where the Confucian state abhorred mercantile success. The opening to the sea, moreover, entailed huge outlays for defense against piracy: the more active the ships, the greater the temptation to corsairs.* For the Chinese government, then, the traders were free riders, getting rich at imperial expense.

Hence the decision to turn from the sea. In 1477, a powerful eunuch named Wang Zhi, head of the secret police, asked for the logs of the great voyages by way of renewing interest in naval expeditions. In response, the vice-president of the Ministry of War confiscated the documents and either hid or burned them. Challenged on this mysterious disappearance, he denounced the records as "deceitful exaggerations of bizarre things far removed from the testimony of people's eyes and ears"—so, unbelievable. As for the things the treasure ships brought home, "betel, bamboo staves, grape-wine, pomegranates and ostrich eggs and suchlike odd things," they obviously did nothing for China. These voyages to the West Ocean had wasted "myriads of money and grain," to say nothing of "myriads" of lives. And that was that.

The question remains: Suppose the Chinese had not given up on trade and exploration, suppose the Portuguese had arrived in the Indian Ocean to find these huge Chinese ships ruling the seas? Or even more, suppose the Chinese had not stopped somewhere around the Mozambique channel but had gone around the Cape into the Atlantic, thereby opening maritime links to West Africa and Europe? Those are the kinds of counterfactual that have come to fascinate historians and econo-

---

* The Yellow and South China seas have always been a notorious nursery of pirates. Witness the terrible fate of many of the so-called boat people fleeing Vietnam in recent years.

mists, not so much because one can ever know the answers but for their heuristic value. Looking backward, we think we know what happened. Looking forward, we have to contemplate diverse outcomes. Such questions focus attention on cause and effect, help us distinguish between major and minor, direct and indirect influences, suggest possibilities otherwise overlooked.

On the possibility of continued Chinese maritime expansion, for example, one has to consider the possibility of violence, of competition decided by force. On the surface, the Chinese were immeasurably stronger and richer. Who could stand up to them? Yet reality ran the other way. The Chinese had learned the secret of gunpowder before the Europeans, but the Europeans had better guns and greater firepower, especially at a distance. The Chinese had bigger ships, but the Europeans were better navigators. If we compare the two sides around 1400, the Chinese might have come out on top, at least in the Indian Ocean or South China Sea. (Even a strong animal has trouble defeating his weaker prey close to home.) But fifty years later, even in Asian waters, the Europeans would have run circles around the Chinese vessels. Of course, the Chinese might have learned by experience and eventually met the Europeans with comparable weapons and ships. That is one of the problems with hypotheticals: they are open-ended, and confidence levels diminish with speculation.

Isolationism became China. Round, complete, apparently serene, ineffably harmonious, the Celestial Empire purred along for hundreds of years more, impervious and imperturbable. But the world was passing it by.

# ～ 7 ～

# From Discoveries to Empire

The news of Columbus's find spread fast thanks to the power of the printing press.* Nothing speaks so eloquently to the reality of this discovery than the excitement and wonder it aroused. The world had opened up, transforming European self-awareness. Who are we? Who are they? Theologians and moralists posed questions about the nature of the "savages" found in these distant lands and the appropriate way to deal with them. For artists, the New World provided a plethora of images and themes, not only in itself but also as part of the new oecumene. For cartographers, maps became ephemera, repeatedly redrawn to new information. The sea monsters and ornamental flourishes disappeared to make way for new landmasses of increasingly accurate shape.

New land invites action. The rulers of Spain saw and held the prospect of a great empire. This had no obvious connection with the holy war of Christendom against Islam, but was nevertheless seen as an extension of divinely blessed and papally sanctioned crusade. Even dis-

---

* Columbus himself made a point of spreading the news. After his return to Spain in March 1493, his letter of discovery was printed thirteen times—once in Spanish, nine times in Latin, three times in Italian. Gomez, *L'invention*, p. 95.

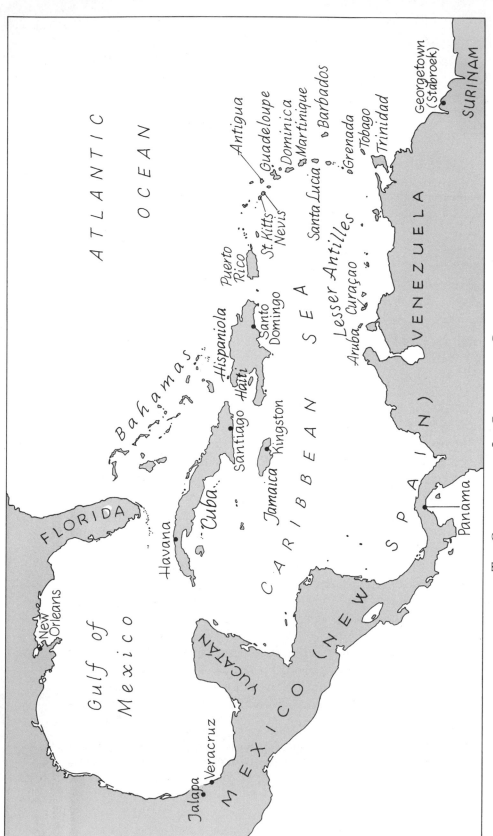

THE CARIBBEAN AND ITS CONTINENTAL BORDERS

Note the difference between the larger islands (the Great Antilles) and the chain of
smaller places to the east (the Lesser Antilles).

appointment turned into attraction, for it meant that the treasure was still to be found. Columbus, the bumbler, just didn't know where to look. This was just the beginning, and the rewards would go to the quickest. Merchant venturers bought and fitted old ships, built new ones, hired crews from a hundred leagues around. In trouble? Start over across the water. Men-at-arms and freelance *caballeros,* roughnecks, rogues, and ruffians, came forward to seek or remake their fortune. These people cherished the legends and fables of "chivalric romance"—the comic books of that age—tales of Amazons, headless and cynocephalous monsters, or better yet, of El Dorado (the Man of Gold). The Amazon legend was a particular favorite, combining as it did the themes of female and male prowess. These woman warriors were reported everywhere, always beyond the next cordillera or on an island some days journey away. In one instance, they were said to be coming to Spain, ten thousand of them, to get themselves pregnant "by the men of our nation, whose reputation for gallantry is well established."* The very extravagance of these tales and promises made for credence. Anything and everything was possible in those distant lands.

For a quarter of a century, the Spanish sailed about the Caribbean, touching the continents to south and north, always disappointed not to find the treasures that presumably lay just beyond the next landfall. They comforted themselves for the nonce with slaves, botanical novelties, exotic fauna, pieces of gold that hinted at mother lodes. Messengers went back to Spain with jewels and nuggets, by way of inducing the crown to send back reinforcements, animals, weapons. Meanwhile parties of conquistadors planted themselves, their flag, their cross; established "cities" in the legalistic tradition of the European commune and named them after divinities, saints, and sundry sacred objects; traded colored beads for gold pebbles; took part in native rivalries and played one tribe against another. They fought, terrorized, tortured, and killed the natives; bedded their wives, daughters, and Spanish-made relicts; and brought many a pagan soul to salvation, often at the same time as they extinguished the body. And always they asked after gold. Their persistence says much for their appetite . . . and

---

* This may have been intended as a consolation for those who could not get to the New World and meet the Amazons on their home turf. From a letter of 1533 from Martin de Salinas, official in Valladolid, to the secretary of Charles V—Gomez, *L'invention,* pp. 120–21. Legend had it that Amazons coupled two or three times a year in order to have children, then gave the male babies away.

their folly: Adam Smith describes this "sacred thirst" as "perhaps the most disadvantageous lottery in the world."[1]

Seek, and ye shall find. Sailing along the coast of Yucatán in the second decade of the sixteenth century, the Spanish encountered Indians like none seen before. These were dressed in cotton garments and lived in towns built of stone. They did not know hard metal, neither bronze nor iron, but they had weapons—slings, poison darts, clubs set with razor-sharp pieces of obsidian—and they were not so easy to kill and intimidate as the islanders. So the Spanish spoke softer, traded and cajoled, and they learned of a land somewhere to the west, over the mountains, where ruled a great king, rich in ornament and glittering treasure. Each contact confirmed the promise, partly because the ruler of this land, unbeknownst to the strangers, had given orders to appease them with gifts in the hope of inducing them to go away. This, needless to say, was a big mistake.

Now party followed party northward and westward along the Mexican coast. It was a matter of chance that the leader of the decisive exploratory flotilla was a man named Hernando Cortés—sometime rapscallion student in Salamanca, precocious and prodigious wencher with a weakness for the most dangerous kind of woman—another man's wife. Cortés had good reason to get out of Spain. He was handsome and virile, a charmer, intriguer, and diplomat, the kind of natural leader who would give his life for his men and whose men would follow him to hell. It took such a man to bring and hold together a band of a few hundred and with them (plus later reinforcements) conquer the mightiest power in North America.

Even so, Cortés only begins the story. History is not a simple epic of derring-do. People matter, but the Aztec empire collapsed for deeper reasons. The most important lay in the very nature of tributary empires, which differ from kingdoms and nations by their ethnic diversity and want of sympathetic cohesion. The we/they division separates rulers from ruled and one member group from another; not members from outsiders. Such units are necessarily an expression of naked power. They rest on no deep loyalty; enjoy no real legitimacy; extort wealth by threat of pain. So, although they have the appearance of might, it is only appearance, and the replacement of one gang of tyrants by another is often welcomed by common folk who hope against hope that a change will relieve their oppression. In reality, the brilliance of these constructs is but glitter; their apparent hardness a brittle shell.

So with the Aztecs, alias the Mexica. They were a small group, a rough nomadic people come into the sedentary areas of the south from primitive desert lands to the north (what is now the southwestern United States). They found no welcome and even served a time as slaves to a more civilized people on the shores of the great lake of the valley of Mexico (a lake long since dried up and today the precarious, subsiding seat of the world's most populous city). Slavery was a school for war and power. When the Aztecs broke free, they fled into reed-choked fastnesses and sheltered there until they grew in numbers and strength. When they came out, originally because they needed drink-able water, they conquered one people after another, using a combination of art, prowess, and above all a terror that unstrung their adversaries and brought them to surrender before they were defeated.[2]

Aztec terror took the form of the industrialization of blood sacrifice. This is a touchy subject, which anthropologists and ideologues of *indigenista* have preferred to avoid or ignore, if not to excuse. Yet one cannot understand the strengths and weaknesses of the Aztec empire, its rise and fall, without dealing with this hate-provoking practice. Human sacrifice for religious purposes was general to the area (including Mayan lands to the south) and reflected a belief that the sun god in particular needed human blood for nourishment. Unfed, he might not rise again. Other gods also needed offerings: of babies and children, for example, to ensure the fertility of crops or an abundance of rain; the tears of the victims were a promise of water.[3]

Such symbolic gestures (perceived as acts of consubstantial nourishment) needed few victims. Adult flesh came primarily from capture in battle, and the victim was presented and told to think of himself as a hero in a noble cause: this is what we were born to. Some scholars have pretended that these heart and blood donors did think of themselves that way, but it should be noted that they needed a dose of tranquilizer before they could be persuaded docilely to climb the steep steps to the altar.

The Aztec innovation was the work of a member of the royal family, Tlacallel, kingmaker and adviser to a series of emperors. This prince of darkness thought to impose and substitute for other, milder gods the Aztec tribal god Huitzilopochtli, the hummingbird of the south, a bloodthirsty divinity all wings and claws; and behind those beating wings, to make of the sacrificial cult a weapon of intimidation. Where once the sacrifice touched a handful, Tlacallel instituted blood orgies that lasted days and brought hundreds, then thousands, of victims to the stone, their hearts ripped out while still beating, their blood spattered and sprinkled on the idols, their bodies rolled down the steps and butchered to furnish culinary delicacies to the Aztec aristocracy.

This last practice embarrasses politically correct ethnologists, who see in such descriptions of cannibalism a justification for foreign contempt and oppression.[4] (It was certainly that for the conquistadors, who were disgusted when their Mexican hosts showed hospitality by saucing their guests' food with the blood of victims sacrificed right before their eyes.) Some have tried to argue that the whole business of cannibalism is a myth, a Spanish invention. Others, ready to concede the anthropophagy, have pointed to occasional Spanish lapses—as though measures of desperation are comparable to institutionalized behavior;[5] or have tried to argue that this was the only way for the Aztecs (or at least the aristocracy, who had a quasi-monopoly of human flesh) to get enough protein in their diet. The best one can say for such nonsense, especially as applied to the privileged members of Aztec society, is that it shows imagination.*

(Ironically enough, the Europeans would later find themselves accused of cannibalism by the Chinese, who preferred to think of foreigners as barbarians anyway.[6] In China, such rumors served as a barrier to contact between natives and foreigners. In Africa, where cannibalism was not unknown, the Portuguese warned the locals against an alleged English appetite for human flesh, in the hope the natives would send these interlopers packing, or perhaps do worse. And the Chinese, undiscriminating in their superiority, said as much of the Portuguese. Barbarians are barbarians.)

These mass sacrifices had precisely the effect desired by our Mexican Darth Vader: they sharply lowered Aztec enemies' will to resist. But the losers naturally nursed their hate. Aztec ceremonies also created a supply problem: where to get enough victims. In war? But that meant incessant fighting. In the prisons or among the slaves? But that meant an intensification of oppression and potential instability. With the connivance of the rulers of allied/subject peoples? This was the device of the so-called flower wars, where aristocratic collaborators from other nations watched behind flower screens as the Aztecs staged simulated

---

* It would seem, however, that the Mexicans were astonishingly inclusive in their diet, finding animal protein in dogs, guinea pigs, and worms, among other fauna. The worms have become something of a cult item for aficionados of pre-Columbian American cuisine, if we are to believe an article on the subject published in 1990 in the magazine of American Airlines. As a kindness, I shall not cite the name of the author, who brags that he tried some of his worms live and was bitten on the tongue for his temerity.

war games and jousts designed to produce prisoners for sacrifice before the hidden eyes of their own chiefs.

For all its seeming power and glory, then, the Aztec empire was a house of feathers. Detested for its tyranny and riven with dissension, it was already in breakup when the Spanish arrived. Such was the hatred that Cortés had no trouble finding allies, who gave him valuable intelligence and precious help with his transport. Without this he could never have brought his small force up from the coast, guns and all, over the sierra, and into the valley of Mexico.

Once there, the invaders enjoyed an enormous advantage. They had superior weapons—not so much guns and cannon, although these proved terrifying initially and Cortés used well-timed salvos to impress and intimidate—but their steel swords and daggers. The Aztec sticks and slings and obsidian-spiked clubs wounded more than killed, and this indeed was what they were made for. The purpose of warfare was to disable and capture, the better to immolate. By Aztec standards, the Spanish did not fight fair: they thrust at the body rather than at arms and legs, because a belly wound stopped an opponent if it did not kill him outright. The Aztec tactic of crowding round and smothering the adversary by weight of numbers ironically worked against them: every Spanish thrust went home. On the edges of the fray, Spanish lancers and swordsmen on horse were a nightmare with their swift slashing movements. The Aztec thought them at first a single, two-headed animal.*

All of this testifies to the fundamental advantage of ferrous metallurgy. Weapons were only part of the story. The Spanish depended completely on such iron objects as shovels, picks, axes, hammers, anvils, tools. They needed to make horseshoes and affix them, to repair weapons, to replace things broken. Every nail, every piece of iron was precious, because it had to come from Spain. A horseshoe cost 30 pesos; nails, 80 pesos the hundred. Many a horseman found it cheaper to have his animal shod with gold.[7]

The Aztec response to these tactics was drastically weakened by uncertain, wavering leadership. The emperor Moctezuma, on learning of these strangers, of their tall ships, their sometimes fair hair and light skin, their bearded faces, their gleaming garments, did not know

---

* The battle dogs were also terrible—rippers and killers against which Aztec weapons were almost unavailing—but their tenacity limited the damage. The Spanish used them primarily in reconnaissance and against prisoners and passersby, instruments of terror and entertainment. Cf. Todorov, *La conquête de l'Amérique*, p. 146.

whether to think them gods or men. Mexican legend had it that the great god Quetzlcoatl, highest of the pantheon but long ago entrapped by his all-too-human appetite for drink and driven into exile by a rival deity, would one day return from the east and the sea. Was this the promised return?

Moctezuma's spies reported that these strangers behaved more like men than gods. For one thing, they enjoyed eating. This could be interpreted both ways, because they would not partake of blood or human flesh, and that accorded with the legend of Quetzlcoatl's humane disposition and his opposition to human sacrifice. For another, they had a marked fondness for women, especially pretty women. Did gods like or need sex? Hard to say. The question, of course, would have posed no problem to a European. Had the Aztecs known their Greek mythology, they would have recognized these carnal appetites as a sign of divinity. Torn between the impulse to fight and acceptance of dismissal, Moctezuma tried to bribe Cortés to go away while inviting him to receive his kingdom.

For all this, the Spanish found themselves in perilous plight. They were there to stay: Cortés had burned his vessels, which told his men that they could not run. They had to fight or die. Or worse than die: the Aztecs made sure the Spanish knew the fate of Mexican prisoners, displaying bloody, flayed bodies on their walls. Another mistake in tactics. Nothing was better calculated to make the Spanish brave and resolute.

Even so, despite reinforcements (originally sent to arrest Cortés) and some success in hand-to-hand combat, the Spanish, so grievously outnumbered, suffered disproportionately heavy losses. Moctezuma may have vacillated, but other Aztecs, born and trained warriors, knew men when they saw them and had no intention of yielding to a handful of arrogant invaders. The Spanish were driven out of the capital city. They made a nightmarish retreat, along the causeways, in the water (the Aztecs had cut the bridges), enemies on all sides. Numbers of Spanish were pulled to the bottom by the weight of their gold, which they could not bear to abandon. Something between half and three quarters of their small force died.

*Noche trista,* the Spanish called it, and yet it was a miraculous escape. The Mexicans, moreover, could not pursue their advantage and finish them off, in large part because they were tragically weakened by the most subtle and secret of the Spanish weapons, one the invaders did not even know they possessed. These were the Old World pathogens, invisible carriers of death to a population never exposed to these diseases. They had already done terrible work in the Caribbean. Now they laid hundreds of Aztec warriors low at the very moment of their victory.

Cortés got his respite. Months passed. New fleets brought new forces. His Indian allies helped build the components of ships and move them across the sierra into the valley of Mexico, where they were assembled and launched against the Aztec island capital. This time, the war was over; the Aztec empire beaten; their temples destroyed; their idols overthrown. They could hardly be surprised: the Aztec glyph for a conquered city was a burning temple. Winner's god takes all.

The conquest of the Inca empire was essentially similar: again, a far-flung tributary empire, centralized and ingenious in its administrative structures; but again, internal divisions and hatreds, setting Incas not only against subject tribes but against one another; and again, European disease as a silent partner of European conquest. When Francisco Pizarro arrived with his small war party, the country was just coming off seven years of civil war (the Inca had apparently died of smallpox) and much the weaker for it.

Here, too, the first contacts were appetizing: the smallest coastal villages seemed to abound in gold. Again, mistaken dispositions facilitated the Spanish advance. The Incas did not mistake them for gods, but they sorely underestimated the possibilities of so small a force and they had an immemorial contempt for the people of the coast. How could these possibly prevail against the harder warriors of the highlands? Again, the Spanish knew to make the most of these divisions to get help from locals. They went up to the highland town of Cajamarca, there to meet the Inca, whom Pizarro, with sublime assurance, promised to receive as friend and brother. Then most of them hid and lay in wait. The Incas took this as a sign of fear, and indeed, many of the Spaniards were literally peeing in their pants.

The Inca party of thousands marched in, brilliantly clad but unarmed. They filled the square, the greatest nobles in the kingdom bearing Inca Atahualpa on his royal litter. Now a Spanish priest advanced to offer the Inca a holy bible. Atahualpa opened it, looked, and threw it on the ground. That did it. The friar ran back to Pizarro: "Come out! Come out, Christians! Come at these enemy dogs who reject the things of God." The slaughter that followed left some seven thousand Indians dead on the spot, plus numerous wounded. Spanish horsemen pursued the rest, spearing them at will, targeting those with fancy clothes, presumably leaders. "If night had not come on, few out of the more than 40,000 Indian troops would have been left alive."

Atahualpa was taken prisoner, naked but unharmed. The Spanish demanded and obtained a ransom greater than any European monarch could have paid—enough gold to fill a good-sized room to the ceiling. So the Indians paid, and now the Spanish had to free their hostage; a deal is a deal. But they immediately rearrested him on a charge of treason to the Spanish crown (sic!); and after bestowing the last rites (salvation first), figuratively and literally decapitated the kingdom.*

It is a bloody story, full of cruelty and bad faith, condescension and sanctimony; but one must not judge these events in terms of the good, the bad, and the ugly. They all deserved one another. Before Pizarro arrived on the scene, Huayna Capac, emperor and father of Atahualpa, set the terms for defeat when he decapitated the members of a rebel tribe and threw their bodies into a lake: "Now you're just a bunch of little boys!"[8] We are told that the victims numbered twenty thousand, that this "was probably the bloodiest encounter in the history of the pre-Hispanic New World."[9] The place is known to this day as the Lake of Blood.[10]

In a penetrating analysis, the biologist-historian Jared Diamond asks why the Incas behaved so naively—by our standards, stupidly. His explanation: the difference in cunning and experience between a literate people and an illiterate. The Spanish were "heirs to a huge body of knowledge about human behavior and history"; the Incas had "no personal experience of any other invaders from overseas . . . had not even heard (or read) of similar threats to anyone else, anywhere else, anytime previously in history."[11]

But the Incas should have known themselves.

The peoples of Peru resisted longer and better than the Mexicans; indeed, some would say that this insurgency is not yet ended. Pizarro seized Atahualpa in 1532, but not until 1539, when the Inca army of Charcas surrendered and Manco Inca took refuge at Vilcabamba, was Spanish control reasonably secure. Even then, the Inca government-in-exile promoted rebellion from the mountains, and not until 1572 could Viceroy Francisco de Toledo put an end to this resistance. Inca

---

* They persuaded the Inca Atahualpa to embrace Christianity by telling him that if he died a Christian, his body would not be burned; which meant, by Inca belief, that he might yet return to lead his people.

tenacity reflected in part the lesser effect of European diseases on the Peruvian population. The reason is not clear, but where Mexican population fell by over 90 percent in the century after arrival of the Spanish, from about 25 million to between 1 and 2 million, Peruvian numbers shrank by about one fifth.[12]

In spite of occasional successes, these efforts to throw out the invader were unavailing. The Spanish had technology, discipline, and organization on their side, an experience of war that made the natives look like amateurs. They had the help of collaborators, among them numerous converts to a Christianity elastic in its tolerance for nonsanguinary pagan practices but uncompromising in its commitment to Spanish rule.[13] They were backed by the resources of a distant but powerful empire and by a seemingly endless flow of soldiers of fortune. And they wisely turned older structures of authority to their service. The heirs of the Inca became a hereditary, idle noble caste, increasingly intermarried with Spanish dignitaries. Their descendants, some of them active in business and government, constitute today the high society of Lima and Quito. The former tribal headmen *(caciques)* continued to administer locally. They were given special status and exemptions from labor burdens and taxes; from 1619, their children were educated in special Jesuit schools. Some of these children would become nostalgic annalists of an old regime seen through tears of regret and sympathy; some became eloquent spokesmen for a grossly exploited population. (Such memorials for a lost world found more resonance among Europeans than with the largely illiterate native population.) Any lingering protest usually took the form of petitions, duly submitted within the rules and hierarchy of Spanish ascendancy. The Inca empire was history.[14]

〰

# "He Who Sees All":
## The Incas before Pizarro

The Incas left no written records—they did not know writing. We must rely, then, on archeological remains, substantially reduced by a Spanish fury for gold and silver that spared little, and on the romanticized accounts collected from the conquered, or written by their descendants, or by some of the early Spanish visitors to the area.[15] On the whole, these sources agree on the essentials.

The Inca empire was the biggest ever established in the New World. It stretched from what is now Colombia in the north (2°N.) to the area around today's Santiago in the south (35°S.), over 4,000 kilometers; and from the coast to the eastern side of the Andean watershed and what is now the Bolivian plateau. Its limits, as for the Aztecs in Mexico, were set partly by nature—the Incas were never comfortable in heavy forest—and partly by the opposition of such recalcitrant tribes as the Araucanians. These last long made humiliating resistance to the Spanish and yielded only to repeating weapons in the nineteenth century.[16]

The size of the Inca empire astonishes for the barriers to land travel and communication. South American valleys and hills run from the mountains down to the ocean, cutting the routes from north to south; and these natural obstacles were aggravated by the absence of the wheel (all porterage was by llamas or humans) and a failure to develop coastal shipping.* The secret lay in communication by runners and porters. All along the routes of the empire, about 1.5 Spanish leagues (about 4.5 miles) apart, were pairs of small hutments, shelters for couriers, one on each side of the road. Each runner looked only one way, waiting to relay to the next stage the messages and packages that might come at any moment. The couriers were trained from early age to do this work, and by running around the clock, managed to average about 50 leagues a day (some 150 miles!). The chronicler Bernabe Cobo tells us that from Lima to Cuzco, some 140 leagues of bad road, took three days.[17] About a century later, the horse-drawn Spanish mail took twelve to thirteen days.† In the eighteenth century, coach service New York to Boston, over two hundred miles of flat terrain, took a week. (Of course wagons carry far more than pack animals and porters.)

The Inca emperor, then, could remain in close and rapid touch

---

* The peoples of the empire knew how to make boats, or rather rafts, of balsa wood; also small barks and floats made buoyant by the use of inflated skins and the like and propelled by swimmers. But however unsinkable the bigger rafts, they were small, unstable craft, easily waterlogged, unsuited to the open sea. Cf. Rowe, "Inca Culture," p. 240: "The real limitation to Peruvian navigation was not lack of ingenuity but lack of convenient supplies of suitable lumber." Which raises the question, why not bring timber down from the mountains? The answer probably lies in the lack of iron or steel cutting tools and hard transport.

† These runners, to be sure, relied on more than their own juices; the coca leaf was there to stimulate and impart an artificial stamina. Indeed, it was not uncommon to measure tasks by the amount of coca required (*cocadas*), just as the Chinese were wont to measure in bowls of rice.

with the farthest reaches of the kingdom and impose his absolute, uniform rule over a highly diverse society. He was seen as divine. All land was in principle his, and he in turn graciously lent it to communal groups in return for tribute in kind and, above all, labor, the so-called *mita*. This forced labor did road and water work, served in the army and in the courier post, hauled goods and built official structures (palaces to storehouses), collected and gave out the things owed and bestowed. All garments were Inca issue. The ordinary commoner, on the occasion of his marriage, would draw one garment for everyday wear, another for holidays, and a working cape for inclement weather. When these became worn, he could go back for more. Aside from corvée labor, people had their own tasks. Inca society was something like an anthill: everyone worked, even the little children, from the age of five on. The women spun thread while walking, and the story has it that the roads were built smooth to keep them from tripping; they were too busy to watch their feet. Except for local barter, trade was reserved to the authorities.

Some scholars have called the system socialist, in that so much of the social product was delivered to the center for ultimate redistribution, and that may be a reasonable appellation; but the system was in form and effect not different from those prevailing in other aristocratic despotisms, with their "prime divider" separating a small elite from the large, relatively undifferentiated mass. Like these, Inca society had its leveling, homogenizing aspects: rough and humble in subsistence and appearance, just about everyone learned to eat and wait by squatting on haunches. The rulers were set apart by dress and furniture and diet—among other things, the right to "turn on" by chewing coca. Common folk, to be sure, managed to get hold of this reserved substance; they could not have performed their toilsome tasks without it. But pure pleasure was something else again, and informers and inspectors swarmed, ready to follow their noses into houses and pots at any hour of day or night and enforce the exclusivity of these privileges. What is a privilege after all, if everyone can enjoy it?

The eyes of the Inca were everywhere. The word for governor was *tukrikuk*, he who sees all.

In the short century of its existence, the Inca empire did much to unify the peoples under its rule and to establish a common language, *quechua*, still spoken by the Andean population—as Che Guevara learned when he tried to mobilize them in Spanish for the revolutionary cause. Under this Inca "peace," however, all was not order and harmony. The Indians seem to have been patient and obedient, but recourse to alcoholic beverages and drugs is always a bad sign. Some of this may be blamed on what we would see as loveless child rearing: the baby was never held, even for nursing. In any event, the culture deprived the ordinary person of initiative, autonomy, and personality.

# ∼ 8 ∼

# Bittersweet Isles

Once the Spanish conquistadors found the mainland empires with their treasures and people, they lost interest in the Caribbean. They stayed long enough in those islands to sweep up what gold they could, whether accumulated ornaments or placer tailings, and wiped out most of the natives in the process. They needed food and found the local starch staple, manioc, noxious and inedible.* Grain cultivation never entered their mind: the Indians were wanted for mining, and the Spanish had not come to be farmers. So they imported food from Europe—very expensive—and brought in cattle to pasture where men had once hunted and fished. In those early years, the conquistadors went hungry; "on the edge of famine," says Pierre Chaunu. In the next stage they became the biggest meat eaters in history.†

---

* Chaunu speaks of "manioc, the mediocre, the dangerous *pan cazabe* ou *cazabi*. The shift from the traditional bread to manioc flour proved catastrophic"—*L'Amérique*, p. 86. Manioc, or cassava, contains a cyanide-developing sugar that primitive peoples have learned to eliminate by a complex process of grating, pressing, and heating. Presumably the Caribbean Indians were not telling the Spanish how to do this.

† *Ibid.* Many of these cattle ran wild and offered the prospect of easy game to interlopers and buccaneers. The buccaneers got their name from the grill *(bocan)* they used to smoke meat, both for themselves and for sale to passing vessels. (My French

The Spanish posted small garrisons and maintained naval stations to protect the treasure that moved through these islands from the continent to Europe. But aside from a few administrators in Cuba, Santo Domingo (Hispaniola), Jamaica, and Puerto Rico (the Greater Antilles), they went on to settle the mainland, to live like dons and hidalgos of Castile. Thereafter they gave little thought to the economic possibilities of these sun-drenched pieces of paradise. To quote Chaunu again: "Spanish colonization is premised on the Indian." With the Arawaks wiped out and the Caribs unwilling, *que d'îles inutiles!* What useless islands![1]

In retrospect, the Spanish passion for gold was a big mistake. The islands were there for the using, and Spain's failure was Europe's opportunity. Columbus had understood. When he did not find the gold he had hoped for, he wrote his sovereigns that these islands were made for sugar. At the time, he was trying to hold their interest, to justify his voyage. And he was right. Columbus had learned about sugar cane in the Madeiras and Canaries. He was in effect recommending the continuation of a plant migration, and the agriculture that went with it, that had begun centuries before in South Asia and was as much driven by soil exhaustion as drawn by consumer demand.

The sugar leap from the African-Atlantic islands to the New World came not with the Spanish but with the Portuguese, who early on planted cane in Brazil, and the Dutch, who served as merchants, refiners,[2] and financiers of the Brazilian crop. The Dutch seized the northeast coast (Pernambuco) for some years (1630–43) during the period of Luso-Hispanic union, and learned about soil and cane; even before they were expelled, they were looking for fresh cane fields. This search turned them north to the nearest weak point in the enemy armor, the Lesser Antilles. There they seized a few islands (Aruba, St. Martin, Curaçao, Santa Lucia), "mere crumbs of land." They also planted themselves on the South American mainland (Surinam), where they established a few plantations on virgin soil. These did poorly. The Dutch proved better at moving sugar and slaves than growing the one and working the other.

Meanwhile the English were already jostling them, occupying St. Christopher (St. Kitts) in 1624, Nevis in 1628, and other tiny isles. The best of these early prizes was Barbados (1627), because it was essen-

---

dictionary, *le Robert*, says the word meant the smoked meat, and by extension the grill.) But hides came to be the big staple, and once the freebooters began to supply these, the herds were not long for this world.

tially uninhabited—theirs for taking and making. Upwind and well to
the east of the other Antilles, it was rarely visited by either Caribs or
Spanish. Jamaica, far bigger than any of these, came later (1655). It had
been turned over by the Spanish crown to eight noble families, who
were unwilling to share it and unable to develop it; so that when the
English took the island, whites and blacks together counted no more
than 3,000.[3] In fact, Jamaica was a hellhole of sandflies, gnats, cock-
roaches, and malarial mosquitoes; but then, bugs were everywhere in
the Caribbean, either too big to be believed or too small to be seen.
Even the smallest were maddeningly audible and excruciatingly ven-
omous. Gentlefolk put the legs of their tables and beds in bowls of
water to keep the crawlers grounded.[4]

The English initially saw these Caribbean islands as settler colonies,
like the east coast of North America. Homesteaders came in number,
attracted by cheap and fertile land, and grew tobacco, indigo, cotton.
(The tobacco, singularly poor, made the lowest prices on the London
market.) Indentured servants came with them, ready to work a few
years for someone else until they could farm on their own. By 1640,
little more than a decade after first occupation, the population of Barbados was said to be over 30,000, equal to that of Massachusetts and
Virginia combined, 200 to the square mile.[5]

After them, however, came the sugar planters, inspired by Dutch example and even financed in part by Hollanders; and sugar swallowed
all the rest. No commercial crop paid more. And no commercial crop
cost more: heavy capital expenditure for crushing mills, boilers, tanks,
and stills (for rum), and a large estate to match. The biggest items of
expenditure were livestock, which might multiply, and slave labor,
which typically did not. The slave population of the Caribbean could
be maintained only by continuing imports.

The success of the sugar plantations was the ruin of the small and
middling tobacco and cotton farms. The resulting concentration of
landholding made indenture less attractive: what was the point of la-
boring for years if one could not count on a homestead at expiration
of contract? Besides, sugar work was uniquely demanding and disagreeable, and too often the planters treated their servants like curs,
beating them until the blood ran. Many jumped their indenture and
ran away, to try their luck on other islands or join the buccaneers.
Many "died of hunger and hardship in this pitiful dispersal."[6]

The French followed close behind the English. They concentrated
at first on Guadeloupe and Martinique (1635), which had not attracted
the English because they were full of those nasty Caribs, who sprang

ambushes and used poisoned arrows. Unlike the Aztecs, the Caribs tried to kill their adversaries. The French paid dearly for their temerity, but in the end they got two of the largest islands in the Lesser Antilles, with fertile soil and good harbors, and these are still French today, *départements d'outre-mer.* (Sometimes these tiny islands were shared, as is St. Martin to this day. Make room for me too. Even those traditional enemies the English and French lived at times side by side, joining forces to defend against the common Spanish foe.)

The big French prize, however, like Jamaica for the English, was the western end of Hispaniola (Saint-Domingue for the French, now Haiti). The eastern half remained Spanish. The island lends itself to this division: the two ends are separated by a high mountain barrier. Over the years Saint-Domingue had become a favorite hideout of *flibustiers* (freebooters) and maroons (runaway slaves). Their very presence was a bad example and their predatory habits—Chaunu calls them "an international crime association of French origin"—had drawn several Spanish punitive expeditions, to no avail.[7] (These people could shoot back.) The French made allies of these troublemakers and with them simply took over that part of the island. The Spanish stayed far away.

Saint-Domingue was the last of the great sugar isles to come into production, and being last, was the most fertile and profitable. Sugar spawned enormous fortunes, in France and on the island; paid for high living, beautiful estates, handsome coaches, and gaudily liveried (though generally barefoot) black servants. (The French peasantry also went around barefoot.) So profitable was this plantation enterprise that Adam Smith, who knew the English Indies better than the French, took it to be evidence of French superiority: " . . . the genius of their government," he wrote, "naturally introduces a better management of their negro slaves."[8] He could not have been more wrong. In 1790 the slaves of Saint-Domingue, encouraged by revolutionary doctrines from France, rose in revolt and established the second new nation of the New World. The French tried to return and failed, defeated more by disease than by bullets. By the time the guns were laid down and the steel sheathed, every white person in Haiti was dead, from the old in bed to the suckling babe. Exception was made for a handful of doctors.

It took a lot of work to grow sugar cane, cut it, crush it, and refine the juice: gang labor under a hot sky; dangerous, hurried round-the-clock pressing, boiling, and skimming before the crop spoiled. In the fields, men and women did the work of animals. No plows, few tools, everything by hand. The idea was to make work and keep the hands busy, because idleness invited trouble. In the sugar mill, the workers fed the stalks into rollers; the smallest inattention, catch a hand, a finger, and the rest would follow. The boilers had their own small hell. Stir carefully: a splash of syrup, and the pain was excruciating. "If a Boyler get any part into the scalding sugar, it sticks like Glew, or Birdlime, and 'tis hard to save either Limb or Life."[9]

The sugar planters wanted to hire white men, but white men, that is, free men, would not do such work—at least not at wages that the planter could afford to pay. The Spanish would have compelled Indians to the task, but in the Caribbean the Indians were gone. In Mexico and Peru, Indians were bound to *encomenderos;* they were not for hire on the open market. Insofar as they were forced to labor, they were wanted above all in the mines. Even so, some Indians were pressed into service on the sugar plantations of Vera Cruz. They did not do well. Their masters worked them to death—when they did not die of disease.

The answer to labor needs, in the islands as on the mainland, was to bring in African slaves, by the tens of thousands. Even Bartolomé de Las Casas, that paragon of clerical humanism, distinguished between Indians and Africans in this regard. He wanted to encourage white immigration while protecting the natives, who were already dying in large numbers and whom he saw as a special responsibility: he wanted to save their souls, because they had souls. He was apparently not sure that blacks did. Each settler, he proposed, should be allowed to bring in a dozen black slaves, that the Indians might be spared.[10] Needless to say, such a modest proposal soon proved grossly inadequate. For one thing, Africans also died of disease and mistreatment.

How many Africans were imported into the New World? Estimates have grown over the years by way of aggravating the crime, but it is not unreasonable to speak of some 10 million over the course of three centuries. And these are just the survivors of a deadly traffic. The track from point of capture or sale in the interior to port of embarkation was marked by the bones and shackles of those who died along the way—up to half, guesses a leading student of the subject.[11] That was just the beginning. On the coast, the captives were kept under conditions that would undermine the strongest constitution. Then, because it took time for slavers to select a full cargo of apparently healthy bodies, large numbers were held on board and died before the ship even set sail. The so-called middle passage, a transoceanic swim in tight-packed filth, mucous, vomit, and diarrheic excrement, was a killer. Yet the trader was afraid to allow his cargo to leave their fetid quarters and come above deck—they might jump overboard. To lose one in seven was considered normal; one in three or four, excessive but pardonable.

Every day's sail cost lives—no slave ship without its escort of sharks. So slavers preferred to land and sell their cargo in the eastern islands—the sooner the better—and charged a premium in the Greater Antilles. Slave ships announced themselves for miles downwind by their stench, which never left them, even after the slaves were unloaded, even after the ship had left the trade. Survivors arrived so sick, weak, terrified, and disheartened ("fixed melancholy")—the blacks were convinced that the white man wanted to eat them—that many succumbed shortly after in the course of the "seasoning" process.

Only commercial interest protected the slaves: the trader did not want to lose valuable stock. The crew, whose own mortality rates were about as high as the slaves', had every reason, olfactory to begin with, to keep the vessel shipshape and clean. We hear of some vessels that made the trip without losing anyone, so it could be done. We are also told that some countries shipped better than others. The Dutch were said to be the best, with specially built vessels that had more spacious quarters below deck and even cowls to draw in air for ventilation. Some slavers packed tight, knowing that more would die but figuring to maximize the number delivered. Others packed loose (less tight), on the theory that it paid to buy fewer slaves but bring more of them to port. But it was hard to deal kindly, if only because a slave ship's atmosphere reeked of fear and hate.

Once on land, the slave was sold and, after a period of "seasoning," set to labor. The seasoning, a selection process, weeded out the weak and tamed the rebellious. Flogging did for persistent offenders, expendable as labor and useful as bad examples. Those who ran away were often pursued and returned by their fellows, who otherwise had to make up for labor lost and stood to gain by collaboration. Like other such oppressive systems, slavery rested in part on cooperation from the victims.

The work itself, toilsome and tiresome, was designed for some efficiency (coordinated gang labor), but also for monotony and stultification. The aim was to not stimulate the mind and hand, but rather to keep these creatures dull and docile. When speed mattered, as at harvest time, the slaves were whipped to the task. Master and overseers thought the blacks no better than brutes, and used stick and lash freely, sometimes so freely as to maim and kill. For good material reasons, pregnant women were exempted from beating until after delivery; the mother was then expected to work in the field with the baby on her back. The law stipulated fines for killing a slave, greater of course for someone else's slave than one's own, but since correction was always legitimate, a brutal master had little difficulty escaping penalty.

And so on and on in a ceaseless round of torment and humiliation. The occasional humanitarian masters were far outnumbered by others who saw them as a danger to society and wealth. Nor did good masters last forever: death, departure, a change of manager, and the bearable could become unbearable. Slave societies could not afford to encourage kindness and leniency. On Barbados, Quakers were fined heavily for bringing blacks into their churches, thereby according them a measure of humanity and an unwarranted sense of sabbath. Rest? Rest was for people who did not have to work.

The demographic data tell the story. Caribbean slaves died faster than they reproduced.

The significance of sugar cultivation for the development of an Atlantic (intercontinental) economy and the industrialization of Europe has long been debated. At the simplest level, some have argued—most prominently Eric Williams—that slave trade profits and the exploitation of slave labor watered the garden of a nascent capitalism, or, to use another metaphor, "fertilized the entire productive system of the country."[12] On a more complex level, the reasoning is Adam Smithian: "The slave-based Atlantic system provided England with opportunities for the division of labor and for the transformation of economic and social structures. . . . "[13]

The Williams thesis has drawn fire and praise, for good and bad reasons. Initial response was largely negative, as might have been expected; but this "almost monolithic opposition has been challenged in recent years by new research, analysis, and interpretation." Some of this reaction reflects "the intellectual and moral ferment generated by the revolt against colonialism and the rise of new nations and the civil rights crusade, together with the bitter memory of the slave trade and slavery."[14] The aim, as for Williams himself, is to remind complacent, empire-proud Britons of their debt to Africa. If Britain made of itself the "first industrial nation," it did so on the whiplashed backs of its black slaves.[15]

Critics of Eric Williams have been put off by his materialist (Marxist) premises: he reduces everything, they say, to economic motives and interests.[16] True enough; but after all, the planters were in it for the money. More cogent have been the empirical attacks on Williams: historians have tried to calculate the gains from slaving and find it far from a bonanza. Some voyages did prove extremely profitable; others were a dead loss, including the ship. One estimate gives the rate of return as comparable to that in other trades, averaging less than 10 percent. Variance (risk) was greater, but this was presumably encouragement as well as discouragement.[17] Not everyone would agree. One critic finds this 10 percent figure low because it counts too few slaves transported and prices them down by more than a quarter.[18] Even so, these gains were simply not big enough in total, let alone that part that went back into trade and industry, to alter the path of British development. As the same critic recognizes.

But the slave trade was only part of a larger complex—what used to be known as the triangular trade(s) and is now called the Atlantic system. Slave labor made high-intensity sugar cultivation and refining possible. The sugar (and such derivatives as rum and molasses) generated in turn its own profits, nourishing both planters and the merchants who sold the sugar and financed the plantations, while providing tea and coffee drinkers and other caffeine addicts with the illusion of nourishment.[19] The planters in turn bought food for themselves and their slaves (because they were unwilling to sacrifice to food cropland that could be used for cane). Some of this food came from Europe; an increasing proportion from the settler colonies of North America. They also bought manufactures: cheap cotton textiles and high-fashion silks; copper vessels for boiling shed and still; iron, nails, guns; and machines and parts for the mill. Meanwhile British producers were turning out trade goods to exchange for slaves in Africa. All of this was a whole, and slavery a crucial part. The effect was to stimulate both agriculture and industry, increase wages and incomes in Britain, promote the division of labor, and encourage the invention of labor-saving devices.[20]

From this holistic perspective one does not have to rest the argument (for the importance of slavery to industrialization) on the profits (not nearly so great as popularly believed) and spending of those who bought, sold, and used slaves. To be sure, much of this money did accrue to Britain, and some of it found its way indirectly into manufacturing. Yet it constituted a minor addition to industrial capital. Absentee planters tended to put their fortunes into land, status, and country living. (Their incomes also suffered badly by their absence from production and management.) Merchants were another matter, and some of them did invest in industry; but they were the exception among merchants and more so among industrialists.

On the other hand, the increase in the size of the market made a difference. (We are not talking profit here but volume.) Africans and Americans wanted products made by repetitious techniques that lent themselves to mechanization. Take cotton. An infant industry at the beginning of the eighteenth century, British cotton was inadvertently protected by the so-called calico arts, directed against Indian goods; and although it was still far behind wool in the middle of the century when inventors first tried to mechanize spinning, it was much bigger than before and rising fast, in part on the strength of sales to the plantations. So, when wool proved difficult, the inventors tried cotton; and they succeeded.

The question still remains whether the Atlantic system played a *decisive* role in stimulating this revolutionary change; or to put it in the contrafactual terms currently popular among economic historians, whether the Industrial Revolution would have taken place without it. The answer, I think, is clearly, yes, it would have. The crucial changes in energy (coal and the steam engine) and metallurgy (coke-smelted iron) were largely independent of the Atlantic system; so was the attempt initially to mechanize wool spinning.

But without slavery, industry would have developed more slowly. That in itself is not a strong statement. One could say that of any increment of demand: more is better than less. The operative question is, how much more slowly? Here one has to look at industrial exports as a component of demand and Atlantic exports as part of all. Viewed statically, that is, as a series of still photos, the export market was substantially smaller than the home market; and sales to America, an even smaller part of home market plus the traditional export markets in Continental Europe. Viewed dynamically, however, like a motion picture, exports were growing faster than home demand, and Atlantic exports much faster than those to European buyers. They mattered. In the words of Barbara Solow and Stanley Engerman: "It would be hard to claim that [widening of the market owing to plantation profits was] either necessary or sufficient for an Industrial Revolution, and equally hard to deny that [it] affected its magnitude and timing. . . . Had all emigration to the Western Hemisphere been voluntary and none coerced, the British economy and its North American colonies would have developed more slowly."[21]

The question remains, then, how much more slowly? But that's about it.

(Of course, that will not be the end of the story, because other ideological positions are riding on this kind of historical debate. Third

World countries and their sympathizers want to enhance the bill of charges against the rich, imperialist countries, the better to justify not only recriminations but claims for indemnity. For the rich, imperialist countries, honor and self-esteem demand denial. This argument about the effects of slavery will go on indefinitely, because it is not susceptible of factual settlement and is a proxy for other issues.)

## The Sugar Plantation as Hacienda[22]

The Spanish were never important players in the sugar trade. They had quicker ways to get rich, and when they did turn to sugar, they saw it essentially as a material basis of status and lifestyle. They never understood, as the English planters did, the advantages of specialization and division of labor, of the integration of sugar plantations as production units into a larger economic system.

Sugar cane came early to New Spain. Already in 1524, just a few years after the capture of Tenochtitlan and overthrow of the Aztecs, Hernan Cortés was growing cane and building a mill *(ingenio)* near Vera Cruz. (In that sultry sea-level plain, wheat and maize grew poorly, and the Spanish were quick to see the potential for semitropical crops.) Others followed suit, and soon Indians were growing cane to sell to the mills. In 1550, the Spanish crown recognized the possibilities and ordered the viceroy of New Spain to grant land to would-be sugar cultivators and mill operators. By 1600, there were over forty mills in the country, representing a substantial industrial as well as agricultural investment. These mills were small units *(trapiches)*, using animal power and even manpower *(trapichillos a mano);* or larger, water-driven *ingenios*, which accounted for by far the greater part of output. One of the largest of the mills, Santisima Trinidad in Jalapa, had seven boilers and two purging houses. It employed more than two hundred African slaves, was valued at 700,000 pesos, and netted 40,000 gold pesos a year.

In the beginning, the sugar estates tried to use Indian labor, and the fact that some Indians voluntarily cultivated cane on their own lands would indicate that they had no distaste for this crop; on the contrary. But there is cultivation and cultivation, and the whole point of the plantation economy was to extract a maximum of output by the imposition of long hours and infernal rhythms, driving labor to the point of exhaustion. For a time Indians and blacks were used indifferently in field work and the mill, but the African proved far more productive because more resistant. Trade wisdom had it that one black equaled four Indians. Many Indians simply collapsed and died, so many that the Spanish crown issued decrees in 1596 and 1599 prohibiting the use of Indians in the mills. This created problems at harvest time, and planters petitioned for emergency exemptions to press *indios de socorro* into service, but in November 1601 Philip III prohibited the use of Indians in any plantation activity. From then on, Mexican sugar was a slave industry.

The brutalities perpetrated by these plantations and *ingenios* can only be explained by the assumption that blacks were seen as no better than inanimate pieces of equipment, to be used up and replaced as needed, or as fuel to be consumed in the fires. Work during the grinding season ran around the clock. Overseers and drivers imposed near-continuous toil; adult males worked twenty hours a day. Food was typically provided by the master, but some masters felt no obligation to feed their hands. Some gave the slaves a free day on Sunday to work their plots and gather food for the week; others simply left their slaves to fend for themselves. In general the masters had more care for their animals than for their slaves, resting them as needed—not presumably because of love for animals, but because these dumb creatures would simply stop where a slave, who had the mind and imagination to fear worse, would work on.

It goes without saying that such mistreatment aroused resistance, both passive (suicide, abortions, and infanticide) and active (sabotage, murder, flight to a life of brigandage). Suicide took a variety of forms, but one of the more common was eating dirt instead of food. The whites took most sabotage for accident; they thought the black too dull to imagine such tricks. This did not deter masters from making slaves pay for mistakes, or others pay, in flesh and blood. How else teach these brutes to be careful? In the meantime, fugitives *(cimarrones)* were as ferocious and cruel as their masters had taught them and as reasonable expectations of white punishment led them to apprehend, to the dismay of the white population. Not good for industry.

The largest Spanish sugar plantations were self-sufficient domains, very much like medieval manors. They grew food, kept herds, built chapels for the cultivation of piety and pursuit of salvation, sometimes even wove their own clothing for slaves and tenants. The master and family lived a life of flamboyant luxury, as though to shut out the pain and misery around them with a silk and lace curtain. Contrast the single-minded specialization of the English sugar islands, which left so little land for food production that it had to come from the North American mainland or even Europe. Textile manufacture would have been out of the question. And by the eighteenth century, the last thing most British planters wanted was to spend their days on the plantation. That was for attorneys and stewards. One lived and enjoyed life in England. Call it division of labor, of an inefficient kind.

Meanwhile the attorneys and stewards got rich, but they lived shorter lives.

# 9

# Empire in the East

Portugal is a small country of moderate fertility. In the fifteenth century its population numbered about 1 million and its chief products and exports consisted of wine (port and, increasingly, madeira—rich, head-turning beverages) and, rising fast, cane sugar. Had the Portuguese of that era been able to anticipate the now classical analysis of comparative advantage by David Ricardo, they would have continued on this sensible path, minding their own business and trading their natural produce for the manufactures of other lands. Instead, they jumped the traces of rationality and turned their land into a platform for empire. Portugal's far-flung network of dominion would come to stretch three quarters of the way around the world, from Brazil in the west to the Spice Islands and Japan in the Far East.

Such a leap beyond sense and sensibility is not unknown in history. We shall see several examples later on; and indeed it is precisely this kind of unreasonable initiative that endows history with uncertainty and defeats prediction. But the Portuguese expansion is particularly surprising, for Portugal had neither people nor means. Its population was too small to send large numbers abroad; indeed one reason why Portugal was so quick and eager to import slaves from Africa was to make up for labor scarcity at home. Its material resources, specifically its ability to build and arm oceangoing vessels, were limited. This was a lightweight going up against heavies.

The Portuguese achievement testifies to their enterprise and toughness; to their religious faith and enthusiasm; to their ability to mobilize and exploit the latest knowledge and techniques. No silly chauvinism; pragmatism first. They drew in outsiders for their money, know-how, and labor; used slaves as workers and occasionally as fighters; married women of every race and more than one at a time. They had no room for Portuguese women on these long voyages, although sometimes they sent out a few orphans, who could not say no. Like the men, these few white women did not do well in pestilential climes: childbirth, for example, was typically a death sentence for both mother and babe. Miscegenation worked better: the men bought and enjoyed female slaves of color by the dozen—as though to beget a new nation from their loins.

Their one emotional outlay was piety. The Portuguese took priests and friars with them on every vessel, for their own safety and salvation (the power of prayer and sacrament); for the propagation of the faith among infidels and pagans; and as salve to their own conscience. These men of God legitimated and sanctified greed.

Religious commitment entailed a serious commercial disadvantage: it introduced an element of irreconcilability into what might have been an easier, more profitable encounter. For the Portuguese, the Muslims were infidels and enemies of the true faith. No brutality was too much. All Muslim shipping was fair game; all Muslim kingdoms were defined as foes. On his second voyage of 1502, Vasco da Gama capped a victory over a Muslim flotilla before Calicut by cutting off the ears, noses, and hands of some eight hundred "Moors" and sending them ashore to the local ruler with the facetious suggestion that he make curry of them. And one of his captains, his maternal uncle Vincente Sodre (whose name deserves to be remembered *ad opprobrium*), flogged the chief Muslim merchant at Cannanore (Malabar coast) until he fainted, then stuffed his mouth with excrement and covered it with a slab of pork to make sure he ate the filth.[1]

Such actions led to war with the many lands bordering the Indian Ocean: East Africa, Arabia and Persia, much of India, the greater part of the Indonesian archipelago. In the words of a sixteenth-century essay on the *Excellency and Honourableness of a Military Life in India*: "Nor is this to be wondered at, since we are the sworn foes of all unbelievers, so it is hardly surprising if they pay us back in the same coin. . . . We cannot live in these regions without weapons in our hands, nor trade with the natives except in the same manner, standing always upon our guard."[2]

Did ever newcomers try harder to make trouble for themselves?

Even so, Portuguese political strategy necessarily diverged sharply from the opportunistic Spanish conquests. For one thing, the locals were far more numerous, and their familiarity with metal and war made them serious adversaries. For another, they were not vulnerable to Portuguese-imported diseases. On the contrary, the Portuguese had cause to fear local contagion and parasites. As a result, they had to limit their craving so as not to dissipate their forces. The Portuguese looked for choice places of strategic import, key points controlling key passages—Malindi and Mombasa on the African coast (jump-off points for voyages to India), Ormuz at the mouth of the Persian Gulf, Malacca (between Sumatra and Malaysia, on the strait connecting the Indian Ocean and Gulf of Ceylon to the South China Sea and the Spice Islands), Macao near the mouth of the Pearl River (entry to southeast China). They wanted Aden (access to the Red Sea), but could never take it. The most important base of all was Goa, pearl of the Malabar coast—entrepôt for pepper, port of entry for Arabian horses into South India (the climate made it impracticable to breed horses locally), defended by sea and, on the landward side, by a channel stocked with crocodiles.

In the end, the native rulers of these regions learned to live and do business with these Portuguese enclaves, as they had with other outsiders since time immemorial. When they did attack Europeans, they were thwarted as often as not by their own local enemies. The Portuguese played the balance of power to a fare-thee-well, and it saved them more than once.

But more serious adversaries were on their way. Everything changed once the Dutch and English entered the arena. In 1605, the Dutch took Amboina and drove the Portuguese from other bases in the Moluccas (Spice Islands). In 1622, the Portuguese lost Ormuz to the Persians, who were decisively assisted by English ships and gunners. In 1638, the Dutch took Elmina, that first Portuguese fort on the Guinea coast, symbol of their pioneer voyages and market for African gold and slaves. In 1641, it was Malacca's turn, again to the Dutch; in 1665–67, Macassar's. In the course of all this, the Dutch simply threw the Portuguese out of the Spice Islands, the original point of the exercise. Portugal's day had come and gone, but pride thrives on reverses, and they clung to what they could. Thus they held Goa until 1961 (long after it had lost wealth and commercial importance), when

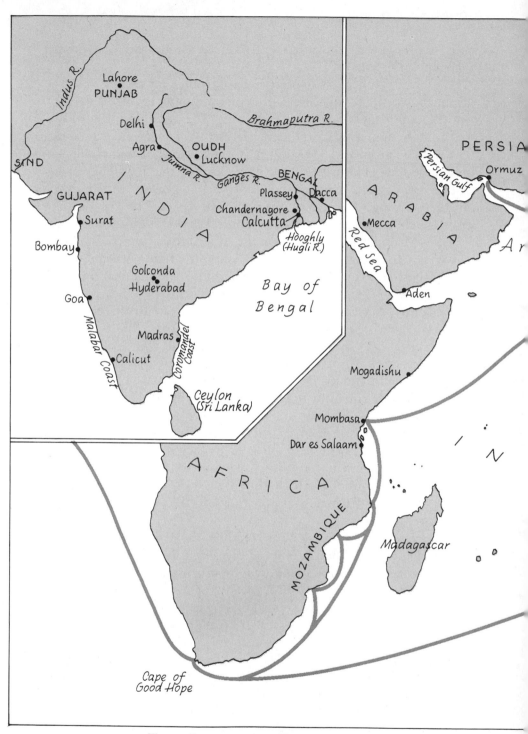

TRADE ROUTES IN THE EASTERN SEAS
This regional (country) trade flourished well before the Europeans arrived
in the sixteenth century.

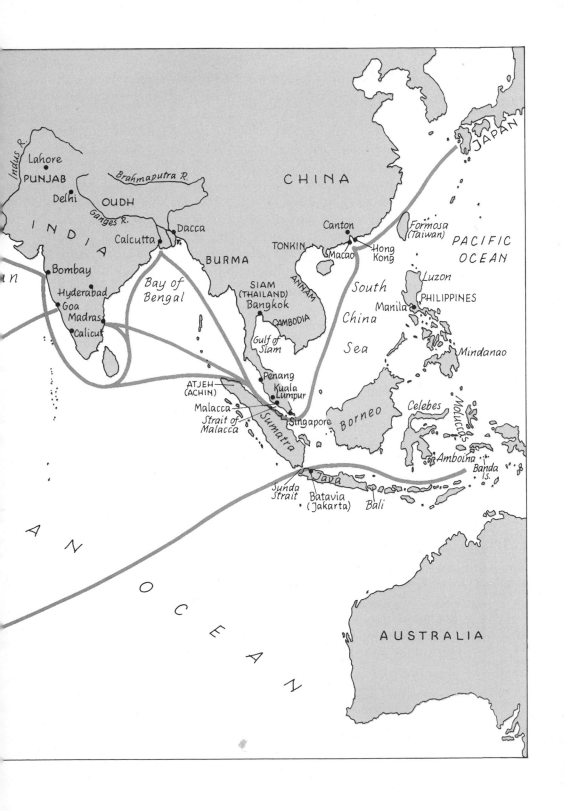

Indus R.
Lahore
PUNJAB
Delhi
OUDH
Ganges R.
Brahmaputra R.
INDIA
Dacca
Calcutta
BURMA
Bombay
Hyderabad
Goa
Madras
Calicut
Bay of
Bengal

CHINA

Canton
TONKIN
Macao
Hong
Kong
Formosa
(Taiwan)

PACIFIC
OCEAN

SIAM
(THAILAND)
Bangkok
CAMBODIA
Gulf of
Siam
ANNAM

South
China
Sea

Luzon
PHILIPPINES
Manila

Mindanao

ATJEH
(ACHIN)
Penang
Kuala
Lumpur
Malacca
Strait of
Malacca
Sumatra
Singapore

Borneo

Celebes
Moluccas

Amboina
Banda
Is.

Sunda
Strait
Batavia
(Jakarta)
Java
Bali

AUSTRALIA

OCEAN

a far stronger Indian government marched in and took it over, without provocation or pretext. No self-respecting independent country could live with such a colonial boil on its flank.

Portugal's primary commercial objective in the East was to obtain pepper and other spices and ship these directly to Europe, bypassing the intermediaries that encumbered the traditional traffic across Asia and into the Mediterranean.* This the Portuguese did by purchase or seizure, compensating by force for the obstacles that Muslim merchants put in their way. In the early decades, these measures garnered a large share of the trade. At the peak, some 40 percent of the pepper imported into Europe was going around the Cape of Good Hope, and the Venetians were hurting. But with time, the older trade routes reasserted themselves. The direct Portuguese share fell back to about 20 percent, still important but no longer dominant. In 1570, the Portuguese crown gave up its monopoly of the trade between Lisbon and the east (Goa). The king ceased to be a merchant and instead sold concessions, frequently to foreign traders. In 1586, the German merchant house of Welser leased the exclusive rights to purchase pepper in the Indies. The sale marked ebbtide. The Portuguese were selling an empty hand.[3]

(These figures of market share are grossly approximate. We have no aggregate data.[4] But we do know that Venice, drawing on overland shipments to the Levant, once again found itself Europe's key pepper emporium in the latter part of the sixteenth century. When the news came of the first successful Dutch voyages to the East Indies [Cornelis Houtman, 1595], Venice, as well as Portugal, could see the imminent, "utter overthrow" of the older trade.[5] By 1625, the Venetian customs classified spices as "western commodities": they now came from the Atlantic rather than the Near East.)

To make up for the shrinking spice trade, the Portuguese got into intra-Asian exchange. This had flourished well before the Europeans came: Gujrati, Javanese, and Chinese merchants trading pepper and spices for Indian and Chinese textiles and Chinese porcelain; Arab merchants walking and shipping slaves from Africa throughout the Mus-

---

* The potential margins of profit were substantial. The one ship that survived Magellan's circumnavigation of the globe brought back 26 tons of cloves, which were sold for 10,000 times cost, just about enough to cover the cost of the expedition—Humble, *The Explorers*, p. 162. (Note that cloves were probably the most valuable spice of all in proportion to weight: a small bag constituted a fair bounty for a seaman over and above wages.) Needless to say, such fabulous differentials rapidly narrowed as other sources of supply responded to the competition.

lim world; ships from everywhere moving teak, sandalwood, and other fine woods; ivory and rhinoceros horn, valued as an aphrodisiac; also rare and not-so-rare animals, including monkeys, tigers, and above all horses and elephants, for use in war and ceremony; and everyone bringing precious metals to balance accounts (silver from the New World to India and China, gold from East Africa and Japan). Much of this Asian trade was spontaneous and improvisational—a kind of Brownian movement. One went where the cargoes were, bouncing from port to port. This is the way of what later came to be known as tramp steamers; these were tramp sailing ships.[6]

Along with this went a shift out of trade into what the economist would call rent-seeking activities. In particular, the Portuguese sought to use their power to batten on the trade of others. They became the robber barons of the Indian Ocean. All merchant vessels were required to purchase a Portuguese trading license. Those that did not were liable to seizure. The shift to racketeering and local trade made possible important economies: many fewer ships went out from Europe to Asia. In their stead, the Portuguese used Indian-built vessels. Hardwood was readily available, and Indian carpenters quickly learned to work to European specifications—and for much lower wages. Crews also went native. Sometimes, except for fifteen or twenty European (or Eurasian) soldiers, gunners, and officers, the entire ship's complement would be Asians or African slaves. Given the size of the Indian Ocean, one might have thought the need for patrol ships endless, to ensure obedience to Portuguese controls. Here the topography helped: the narrow trade routes and passages made for easy surveillance. Besides, one did not have to be everywhere; a few exemplary boardings and seizures made the point.

The trouble is, two and more can play the game. The European newcomers fought harder and sailed better. Accounts of early Dutch and English voyages to the area (early seventeenth century) are full of waiting and skulking, of traps and perfidy, of attacks and captures. One side's knave was another's hero. James Lancaster, a bold and skillful English captain, could not get enough by trade on his second voyage to the Indies (1601)? No problem. When Lancaster returned to England two years later, his ships laden with booty, King James knighted him for his efforts. The surface of the Indian Ocean mimicked the waters below, full of predators feeding on one another. All of this amounted to legalized piracy, legitimized for the Dutch and English by a state of war with Spain, which war extended to Portugal once the two Iberian kingdoms were joined in 1580 by common rule. So profitable was this game that even after the two Iberian kingdoms separated in 1640, the Dutch and English were loath to return to peace. What could be better than

> *The good old rule, the simple plan,*
> *That they should take who have the power,*
> *And they should keep who can?*[7]

The land powers of the Indies watched this intra-European contest and kept clear. They preferred to take their share of monopolistic trade or even to use the foreigner as an ally in their own wars. Besides, the Asians were largely indifferent to maritime power and naval prowess— "Wars by sea," said Bahadur Shah, ruler of Gujarat and neighbor of the Portuguese, "are merchants' affairs and of no concern to the prestige of kings." That was not far from the Chinese attitude. Another bad mistake.

Meanwhile Portuguese power shriveled: one historian speaks of "the inherently brittle superstructure of their maritime dominance."[8] And, he might have added, the sandy infrastructure. Soon, only the great memories remained, enshrined in the poetry of Luis da Camoëns *(The Lusiads)*, who sang of invisible tracks through "oceans none had sailed before."[9] All pride. As the English governor of Bombay observed in 1737: "The Crown of Portugal hath long maintained the possession of its territories in India at a certain annual expense, not inconsiderable; purely as it seems from a point of Honour and Religion."[10]

⁀ ⁀

## The Spice of Life

People of our day may wonder why pepper and other condiments were worth so much to Europeans of long ago. The reason lay in the problem of food preservation in a world of marginal subsistence. Food supply in the form of cereals barely sufficed, and it was not possible to devote large quantities of grain to animals during long winters, excepting of course breeding stock, draft animals, and horses. Hence the traditional autumnal slaughter. To keep this meat around the calendar, through hot and cold, in a world without artificial refrigeration, it was smoked, corned, spiced, and otherwise preserved; when cooked, the meat was heavily seasoned, the better to hide the taste and odor of spoilage. Hence the paradox that the cuisine of warmer countries is typically "hotter" than that of colder lands—there is more to hide.

Condiments brought a further dividend. The people of that day could not know this, but the stronger spices worked to kill or weaken the bacteria and viruses that promoted and fed on decay. Tabasco and other hot sauces, for instance, will render infected oysters safer for human consumption; at least they kill microorganisms in the test tube. Spices, then, were not merely a luxury in medieval Europe but also a necessity, as their market value testified.

⌣ ⌣

## *"Os Cafres da Europa"*— The "Kaffirs of Europe"[11]

To understand the rise and fall of empires, one must always look as much at the forces and circumstances of the home country as at conditions in the field. When the Portuguese conquered the South Atlantic, they were in the van of navigational technique. A readiness to learn from foreign savants, many of them Jewish, had brought knowledge that translated directly into application; and when, in 1492, the Spanish decided to compel their Jews to profess Christianity or leave, many found refuge in Portugal, then more relaxed in its anti-Jewish sentiments. But in 1497, pressure from the Roman Church and Spain led the Portuguese crown to abandon this tolerance. Some seventy thousand Jews were forced into a bogus but nevertheless sacramentally valid baptism. In 1506, Lisbon saw its first pogrom, which left two thousand "converted" Jews dead. (Spain had been doing as much for two hundred years.) From then on, the intellectual and scientific life of Portugal descended into an abyss of bigotry, fanaticism, and purity of blood.*

The descent was gradual. The Portuguese Inquisition was installed only in the 1540s and burned its first heretic in 1543; but it did not become grimly unrelenting until the 1580s, after the union of the Portuguese and Spanish crowns in the person of Philip II. In the

---

* The Portuguese "old Christians" eventually came to call themselves *puritanos*.

meantime, the crypto-Jews, including Abraham Zacut and other astronomers, found life in Portugal dangerous enough to leave in droves. They took with them money, commercial know-how, connections, knowledge, and—even more serious—those immeasurable qualities of curiosity and dissent that are the leaven of thought.

That was a loss, but in matters of intolerance, the persecutor's greatest loss is self-inflicted. It is this process of self-diminution that gives persecution its durability, that makes it, not the event of the moment, or of the reign, but of lifetimes and centuries. By 1513, Portugal wanted for astronomers; by the 1520s, scientific leadership had gone. The country tried to create a new Christian astronomical and mathematical tradition but failed, not least because good astronomers found themselves suspected of Judaism.[12] (Compare the suspicious response to doctors in Inquisition Spain.)

As in Spain, the Portuguese did their best to close themselves off from foreign and heretical influences. Education was controlled by the Church, which maintained a medieval curriculum focused on grammar, rhetoric, and scholastic argument. Featured were exhibitionism and hair-splitting (some 247 rhymed, learn-by-heart rules on the syntax of Latin nouns). The only science at the higher level was to be found in the one faculty of medicine at Coimbra. Even there, few instructors were ready to abandon Galen for Harvey or teach the yet more dangerous ideas of Copernicus, Galileo, and Newton, all banned by the Jesuits as late as 1746.[13]

Meanwhile no more Portuguese students went to study abroad, and the import of books was strenuously controlled by inspectors sent by the Holy Office to meet incoming ships and visit bookshops and libraries. An index of prohibited works was first prepared in 1547; successive expansions culminated in the huge list of 1624— the better to save Portuguese souls.

Within the kingdom and overseas, a triple censorial barrier begrudged imprimaturs and discouraged originality. Such printing presses as were allowed (in Goa, none in Brazil) were in the hands of clerics, generally Jesuits, who limited their publications to dictionaries and religious matter.* From Brazil and Angola, even these safe materials had to be sent to Portugal for prior censorship.

* The printing press was not brought to Brazil until 1807, when the Portuguese court fled there. Modern bureaucracies keep records and issue decrees and regulations, and a printing press was indispensable—Lang, *Portuguese Brazil,* p. 195.

Small wonder that the life of science and speculation decayed. A privileged few were eventually exempted from controls—thus the noble and clerical members of the royal historical academy (founded 1720), amateurs all, who were permitted to import otherwise forbidden books, but found it easier to write fawning eulogies of the royal family.

To be sure, it was impossible to isolate a country caught up in the concert of Europe and the course for empire. Portugal diplomats and agents abroad came back with the message that the rest of the world was moving on while Portugal stood still. These *estrangeirados*—their pejorative nickname—attracted deep suspicion, for they were tainted. Their dismissal was implicit in Portuguese pride. Most unfortunate. They saw what few Portuguese could or would see: that the pursuit of Christian uniformity was stupid; that the Holy Office of the Inquisition was a national disaster; that the Church was swallowing the wealth of the country; that the government's failure to promote agriculture and industry had reduced Portugal to the role of "the best and most profitable colony of England."[14] (British classical economists would put it differently. Portugal was Ricardo's chosen example of the gains from trade and pursuit of comparative advantage.)

Portuguese intellectual shortcomings soon became a byword: thus Diogo do Couto, referring in 1603 to "the meanness and lack of curiosity of this our Portuguese nation"; and Francis Parry, the English envoy at Lisbon in 1670, observing that "the people are so little curious that no man knows more than what is merely necessary for him"; and the eighteenth-century English visitor Mary Brearley who remarked that "the bulk of the people were disinclined to independence of thought and, in all but a few instances, too much averse from intellectual activity to question what they had learned."[15]

Through this self-imposed closure, the Portuguese lost competence even in those areas they had once dominated. "From being leaders in the van of navigational theory and practice, [they] dropped to being stragglers in the rear."[16] By the end of the seventeenth century, several of the pilots in the *carreira da India* (the Indian trade) were foreigners. Gone the days of top-secret navigational charts; the Dutch had better ones. And when the chief engineer persuaded King John (João) V (reigned 1706–50) to renew the teaching of mathematics, military engineering, and astronomy, the instruments required came from abroad.

By 1600, even more by 1700, Portugal had become a backward,

weak country. The crypto-Jewish scientists, mathematicians, and physicians of yesteryear were fled; no dissenters appeared to take their place. In 1736, Dom Luis da Cunha deplored the absence of a Reformist (Calvinist) community in Portugal. He noted that the Huguenot challenge had kept the French Catholic clergy from sinking to the "sordid" level of their Portuguese brethren.[17] Very provocative words, but right on the mark: if the gains from trade in commodities are substantial, they are small compared to trade in ideas.

# ～ 10 ～

# For Love of Gain

... We Amsterdammers journey ...
Wherever profit leads us, to every sea and shore,
For love of gain the wide world's harbors we explore.
—JOOST VON DEN VONDEL[1]

As countries go, Holland is small—almost as small as Portugal, and hardly big enough to play the grand imperialist. In 1500, the Dutch numbered about 1 million; 150 years later, twice that. Small, but potent: in the seventeenth century, half the people lived in cities, a higher percentage than anywhere else in Europe. And active: an observer of 1627 noted that Dutch roads and waterways were crowded, "that there are not so many carriages (and heaven knows there are) in Rome than there are wagons here, filled with travelers, while the canals, which crisscross the country in all directions, are covered by innumerable boats."[2] Even more impressive were the ports large and small, hives of shipping. By the 1560s the province of Holland alone possessed some one thousand eight hundred seagoing ships—six times those floated by Venice at the height of its prosperity a century earlier. About five hundred of these were attached to Amsterdam, but in fact the whole seaboard was a pincushion of masts: over five hundred busses for the herring trade alone, sited for the most part in small ports long forgotten—Hoorn, Enkhuizen, Medemblik.[3]

Once again, a small European nation surpassed itself, and this achievement reflected both intrinsic capabilities and the highly competitive character of European nation building. Above all, Dutch success reflected an attitude toward work and trade best exemplified by the fable of the Tortoise and the Hare. Loot and prizes were well and good, but what mattered in the long run (never forget the long run) were those small, low-risk gains that add up and do not disappoint.[4]

We call it Holland, but the Dutch knew it as the United Provinces of the Netherlands. It was a confederation, the northern half of a collection of cities, counties, and duchies once northern Europe's most vital and precociously urban civilization, only to become the pawn and prize of feudal bargains and matrimonial accident. In the early seventeenth century, Charles V, Holy Roman Emperor, also became king of Spain through the marriage of his father Philip to Juana, daughter of Ferdinand and Isabella. Charles brought along in his basket of titles and sovereignties the duchy of Burgundy (fruit of another happy alliance). Burgundy, in turn, held sway over the Low Countries. In this roundabout way, one of the wealthiest and most cosmopolitan areas of Europe—hub of industry, trade, and ideas, long free of seigneurial servitudes and accustomed to economic, intellectual, and spiritual diversity—got tied to the short leash of the Spanish Habsburgs. One source of irreconcilable conflict: the ruler of Spain, bound by his country's past, could never tolerate open Protestant worship in his dominions.[5]

It is an irony of history that Dutch and Spanish should do battle. The Low Countries (north and south) had better things to do. These doughty burghers, seamen, fishers, and peasants had become the middlemen of northern Europe. They imported and reexported the primary products of the North Sea, Scandinavia, and eastern Europe: grain, timber, fish, tallow, tar, hides. They manufactured woolen and mixed fabrics and were masters of commercial credit and international finance. Antwerp, great port on the Scheldt, dominated the new maritime economy. It linked an enormous European hinterland to the Atlantic and beyond, sweeping past older centers such as Venice and Genoa to become the ultimate destination of cargoes from new worlds overseas. These might stop first in Lisbon and Seville, but they finished in the Netherlands, there to be absorbed, processed, and redistributed throughout the world.

On the other hand, this was Spain's moment on the world stage. The immense inflow of colonial treasure gave the Spanish crown unheard-of sway. Spain was now the greatest power in Europe, and nothing must thwart its claims and ambitions. So when these pesky wool-clad Lowlanders dared to stand up to Spain's silky representatives, they were dismissed as a bunch of bums *(tas de gueux)*. Spain would spare neither money nor men to show them who was boss.

That was the world of wealth and guns. But in the realm of belief, two things sharpened the conflict and shaped the fate of this region. First fanaticism and intolerance triumphed in Spain, leading in 1492 to the expulsion of the Jews (later on to a similar expulsion of Muslims). Many of the Jews sought peace and dignity in the Low Countries, which had a reputation for tolerance.

The second great religious event was the rise of Protestant Christianity as a system of organized worship and belief. Dissent and heresy were an old story, but in 1517, when Martin Luther nailed his "Ninety-five Theses" to the church door in Wittenberg, he struck the first blow for secession. Christendom was headed for breakup. In the decades that followed, Protestants in several countries (the English Lollards had preceded them) translated the Bible into the vernacular. People read and started thinking for themselves, and laymen joined divines in rebellion. Among the areas that took smartly to the new dispensations: the Low Countries, particularly the northern provinces, where dissenters had long been indulged in matters of personal conscience.

So it was that when Spanish administrators and clerics went north, they found a spiritual diversity and anarchy long since uprooted in Spain. Intolerable. Their response was to punish and suppress, in the face of outrage and against an abundance of good advice. After all, right is right, and one must not sacrifice God to Mammon (except of course in colonial areas). So the Spanish brought in the spies and thought police and soldiery; introduced the Holy Office of the Inquisition into a land that had never known it (1522–23); and ordered a number of exemplary executions that enraged the public and mobilized resistance.

The inevitable rebellion was led by the Calvinists of the northern provinces, the so-called sea-beggars; the southern provinces, overwhelmingly Catholic, remained more submissive. Even there, however, martial law and an all-intrusive surveillance did violence to an open and free market. In 1576, the southern provinces joined with their Protestant brethren to make war against the intruders. In return the intruders took some important cities—Antwerp and Ghent among them—and put them to the sack in the time-honored mode of sixteenth-century warfare. In a matter of years, the Spanish destroyed Antwerp's prosperity and provoked a new exodus. Merchants, weavers (who brought the valuable secrets of the "new draperies" to England),

Jews, Calvinists—all left. Also Catholics, who understood that even the faithful had no business future in a world of arrogant caballeros and prying friars.

The southern counties yielded; the northern persisted, and by 1609 effectively won their independence. They were not yet Calvinist in their majority, but the Protestants had led the revolt. In the beginning, the Spanish put down these insolent rebels with a sword swipe and a few cannonades. But in those days the Dutch were made of tough metal. They bent but did not break, and they learned the art of war. And like the Flemish burghers of medieval Courtrai and the Swiss peasantry at Morgarten, Sempach, Murat, Dornach, and other battle venues; like the English longbowmen of Agincourt and the Japanese peasantry against the *samurai* of Satsuma, they taught the prideful heirs of martial tradition that little people too can fight.

Amsterdam brought up the rear—cautious, collaborationist. Not until the war was won did it come over to the side of independence. For all its prudence, however, and perhaps because of it, Amsterdam straightway became the capital of the confederation, the business center. What it lacked in virtue, it made up in good sense. Sometimes lack of principle pays.

The same for colonial adventure. The Dutch would have preferred to let the Portuguese and Spanish have the blood and glory, while they served as middlemen, agents, processors, distributors, and the like. But when Spain virtually annexed Portugal and closed the ports of Seville and Lisbon to Dutch vessels in 1585, it forced these sober flatlanders to become fighting seamen in alien seas.

The Hollanders learned by espionage. The key figures were Cornelis de Houtman, seaman and captain, and Jan Huyghen van Linschoten, clerk, traveler, and geographer. Both men spent some years in Portuguese service, because the Portuguese needed all the help they could get and did not understand that Dutchmen were a security risk. When our expatriates returned to Holland, they brought precious information about eastern lands and seas: the shores, rocks, and reefs; the islands and harbors; the routes, winds, and currents; seasonal storms and calms; latitudes and compass bearings; the birds that fly and signal the land; the friends and enemies; the strengths and weaknesses of the Portuguese.

Then the Dutch set sail. A half-dozen ships went out and came back, some empty, some laden. The main point—it could be done. A half-dozen companies, then four more, were formed, all determined to take the spices and treasures of the Indies. That clearly would not do.

They were persuaded to merge. Like the Confederation: in union, strength. So was born in 1602 the Vereenigde Oost-indische Compagnie (VOC), alias Jan Compagnie.

The Dutch set out to make money by commerce. They found a world where trade was bound to force. No spice could be bought without the benevolence of the local ruler or his agent, who had his own living to worry about. No buy was sure: local rulers would sell the same crop twice. The political rivalries of the region were complex and ephemeral—Muslims vs. infidels, petty chiefs who would be king or sultan, loyalists vs. rebels, with the one becoming the other and then back again. And all of this was complicated and exacerbated by the actions of other Europeans. The Portuguese, already installed, were ready to bribe, lie, steal, even kill to thwart the Dutch. Likewise the Spanish, coming in through their Philippine back door. And hot on their heels, the English, too few yet to compete for market or territory, but making up for numbers with seamanship and gunnery.

Everyone in these Eastern waters was half bandit, including the local sea jackals who ambushed the small boats and still in our time prey on defenseless refugees. But the English were the big guns, the pirates' pirates. No vessel too big for the taking. Not a bad strategy: if you can't make money in business, you grab from those who do. And moving and maneuvering among these were the locals: Gujrati merchants from India, Arabs from the Red Sea and the Gulf, Malaysians and Indonesians; above all, the Chinese. These last had their hands tied by government interference and corruption back home, but once abroad showed a spirit of enterprise that left rivals far behind.

So the Dutch learned to fight. Their seamen may have left the Texel as landlubbers, but in the months it took to reach the Indies, they drilled every day, clearing the decks, running the guns into position, hauling ammunition, testing their marksmanship, working the firefighting apparatus, getting ready for combat at sea. They would need these skills, if they were fortunate enough to survive the normal hazards of a long sea journey.

Back in Amsterdam, company directors had little stomach for these costs and risks, which ate up most of the price differential between purchase and sale. Spices, for example, were then worth ten and twelve times in Europe what they brought in the Indies; but once the overhead was factored in, profits fell to less than 100 percent—still substantial, but a far cry from the mirage of expectation.

To be sure, it was precisely the trammels of this market that accounted for the huge difference in price between origin and con-

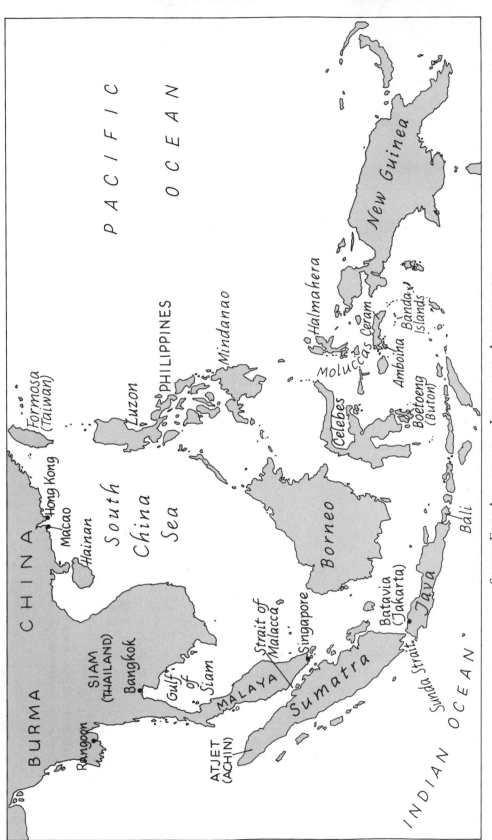

SOUTH EAST ASIA AND THE INDONESIAN ARCHIPELAGO

For the Dutch, the great source of treasure was the "Spice Islands"—the Moluccas and Banda islands. That was where the rarest condiments came from—cloves, nutmeg, cinnamon—and laid the basis of monopoly.

sumption. A free, efficient market would have reduced profit margins per unit of merchandise, even while it increased the return to capital. But the VOC would not have liked that either. What Jan Compagnie wanted was to exclude competitors, impose prices in the Indies, and maintain wide differentials between buy and sell. There lay maximum profits. That was not business; that was power and its uses—what the economist calls rent-seeking.

Besides, these men of the VOC were pragmatists. They cheered the prospect of peace with Spain in 1609—finally, after some eighty years of cold and hot war. The peace accord called for a division of turf on the basis of the status quo, and the company wanted to alter the status quo in anticipation. So the directors sent a fast yacht to the Indies to get the word to its agents ahead of the Spanish in the Philippines: Plant factories and agencies wherever possible, by way of posing a claim. Such aggressive spoor-planting was bound to invite clashes, but this was no time to be timid. The VOC wanted above all to establish itself in the Spice Islands, the world's only source of nutmeg, cloves, and mace. Delivered in India, these spices brought profits ten and fifteen times cost. "The Islands of Banda and the Moluccas are our main target. We recommend most strongly that you tie these islands to the Company, if not by treaty then by force!"[6]

Those were the early years, the years of dirty diapers. Once the company had stabilized its position, it came to disapprove of muscular enterprise. But then its agents in the field were there to remind it of the facts of Asian life, at least as they saw them. Here is Jan Pieterszoon Coen, the VOC's young and forceful proconsul in Batavia, now Jakarta—a city he founded to serve as company headquarters in the Indies (the Dutch Goa) and to control the narrow gateway to the Moluccas known as the Sunda Strait:

> Your Honors should know by experience that trade in Asia must be driven and maintained under the protection and favor of Your Honors' own weapons, and that the weapons must be paid for by the profits from the trade; so that we cannot carry on trade without war nor war without trade.[7]

A generation later, it was the same story. The Delft Chamber of the company deplored the cost in lives and money of the campaigns for Malacca and Ceylon. "A merchant," they observed, "would do better honorably to increase his talent and send rich cargoes from Asia to the Netherlands, instead of carrying out costly territorial conquests, which are more suitable to crowned heads and mighty monarchs than to mer-

chants greedy of gain." To which Antonio van Diemen, writing from
the Indies, made reply: "There is a great deal of difference between the
general and the particular, and between one kind of trade and another.
We are taught by daily experience that the Company's trade in Asia
cannot subsist without territorial conquests."[8]

Over the years, the men in the field made like monarchs and the
burghers back home wrung their hands. How could the directors make
the decisions? It generally took two to three years for instructions to
go from Amsterdam to the Indies and for replies to come back. By that
time, done was done. The history of overseas empire, and not only for
Holland, is largely a story of faits accomplis.

It would take too long to review the history of these done deeds—
of Dutch attacks on the Portuguese (often in connivance with local
Muslim rulers), of sallies into Spanish territory, of fights with the English, of pursuit of pirates and practice of piracy (one country's piracy is
another's police), of punitive expeditions and preemptive strikes against
local rulers, of promises and treaties, cross and double cross. Suffice it
to say that the Dutch came to "own" the Moluccas (the Spice Islands)
and Java while establishing an effective sphere of influence over the rest
of the Indonesian archipelago. They also took Ceylon and Formosa
(Taiwan) and planted factories along the east coast of India (Coromandel and as far north as Bengal). They did less well on the western
side (Malabar)—too close to the Portuguese, who could still defend
their own turf. The Dutch tried and failed to snatch Macao too, but
eventually got permission (along with others) to trade at Canton; and
in Japan they were the only Europeans allowed, on condition that they
accept confinement to a tiny island in Nagasaki harbor and submit to
condign humiliation. Profit goeth before pride.

From this experience of combat and commerce, the Dutch drew
certain lessons: no one could be trusted, not even one's fellow Christians (they had good reason to know); and Asians in general and Muslims in particular were lying, thieving scoundrels. In return, other
Europeans came to think of the Dutch as avaricious, sanctimonious
hypocrites; while the Muslims and other natives were convinced by
faith, fear, and contact that no stratagem was too duplicitous for such
infidels as these. None of these stereotypes was wholly true or wholly
false. Life and work in the Indies did not bring out the best in people.
Besides, although the Asians could not know it, they rarely met the best
of the Dutch. The VOC recruited to its lower ranks the dregs of Dutch
and German society; at the higher levels, the company got the greed-
iest of the greedy. Batavia had a murderous reputation, and no one

with a modicum of survivor instinct cared to stay long in these pestilential lands whence few returned. These men had to get rich fast.

How to tame this understandable voracity? The company thought to inculcate habits of modesty by the exercise of parsimony. It paid niggardly wages. This, needless to say, proved a bad tactic. Greed elicits greed, and the meanness of the company's directors brought out the worst in its representatives. In the end, these were far more concerned with their own enrichment than with serving their masters back in Amsterdam. A good lawyer would say in their defense that they had no choice. They had to find ways to make money; they had to steal if necessary.

And so they did. The greater volume of Dutch business in the Indies was not the company's shipments to and from the Netherlands, but rather the so-called country trade, the movement of cargoes from one Asian point to another: cottons from Coromandel to Indonesia and China, silks from China, Tonkin, India, and Persia to Manila and on to New Spain (Mexico), bullion and specie from Japan and the Philippines (out of Mexico), tea and gold from China, coffee from Mocha and later Java, slaves from Arakan, Buton, and Bali. And so on. A host of middling and small ships and junks (the Chinese were very busy) tramped the eastern seas, going from port to port as supply and demand suggested. Along with these cargoes went the treasures, purchased and pilfered, that individual sailors carried in their sea chests or hung over gunwales on company and private vessels. These rascals lived like dogs and were treated like dogs (slaves got better care, because slaves were worth money).[9] So they traded. Everyone on shipboard was a dealer, and captains and supercargoes had to defend their space from the trespass of private merchandise. They had their own saleables to move.

One truism of historical evidence: rules that constantly have to be repeated and strengthened are no rules. So here: the VOC was always redefining the quality and quantity of goods that could be shipped back to Holland duty-free and tried to reserve the most valuable commodities to the company. To little avail. As a British historian wrote of similar regulations for the English East India Company, "What came of this egregious arrangement might have been foreseen by the intellect of a moderate-sized rabbit."[10] In spite of occasional seizures and punishments, everyone got away with this illicit trade, if only because everyone, right up to the top, was doing it.

The big shots had even more incentive than the small fry—their sea chests were bigger. Even the so-called inspectors could make far more money by averting their eyes. A governor-general, nominal salary 700 florins a month, could take home a fortune of 10 million florins; a junior merchant was ready to pay 3,500 florins to the Appointments Board for a post that paid 40 a month but yielded 40,000. In the end, the company began to tax its officers on their presumed gains, which only encouraged them to attend more assiduously to their own business. Small wonder that after the VOC's demise, its logo came to be read as *Vergaan onder Corruptie* (Perished by corruption).[11]

Even so, the company made money. It paid dividends that averaged 18 percent per year from the time of its founding. Most of the VOC's earnings came from its monopolies of agricultural products: spices from the Spice Islands to begin with; then rice from Java, because one could not allow these specialized islands to waste spice land on food; then coffee and sugar, which the company introduced into Java. (Coffee came originally from the Mocha area in the Arabian peninsula, but the Dutch did so well acclimating it in Java that they gave us a new generic term for the beverage.) The other profits came from purchases in the open market: porcelain, silks, and tea in China; silks and cotton in India; and so on. But here the company had to compete with other buyers, including its own agents. No wonder the directors preferred monopolies.

Yet in the long run the monopolies were precarious. To maintain them against native and outsiders required the use of force so expensive that only a sovereign with taxing power could hope to pay the bill.[12] Inevitably, the VOC was led to substitute its own governance for that of native princes. The VOC thereby incurred the kind of non-business expenses that are open-ended and unpredictable; that do not show up in the books because they are so easily spread about; that grow insensibly until too late. (Compare the budgetary deficits that afflict modern nation-states.)

This governance, moreover, led the company to impose a command economy. In J.S. Furnivall's words, "the archipelago became one vast estate, literally, a plantation."[13] This strategy may have enhanced on occasion the direct revenues of the company, but only at the expense of native cultivators and tax revenues; so that in the long run the VOC earned less than it could have in a free market.[14]

In the long run: in the absence of force (and force has its own costs), people will not allow themselves to be done to. At some level they would rather sit on their hands or resort to "crime."

Take cloves. The clove tree, which grows to some forty feet at maturity, was found only on Amboina (Ambon) and a few lesser islands. The Dutch, seeking monopoly, moved people from the other clove islands to Amboina, destroying their trees beforehand, the better to control them and prevent them from selling to non-Dutch buyers. In the language of the VOC, only the Amboinese were "privileged" to grow cloves.

This privilege entailed the obligation to cut down trees on demand; also to buy all foodstuffs from the company at company (that is, high) prices. On the company side, the VOC was free to set the price for the clove crop. The aim presumably was to give the grower as little as possible, but not so little as to drive him out of business. Needless to say, the VOC, in its instinctive greed, did not pay enough, and the "privileged" Amboinese lost interest in their privilege. When the Dutch found clove output lagging demand in 1656, they made the people of the island plant more trees. But then in 1667 further planting was forbidden, and in 1692 and 1697 the growers were made to cut trees down. In the mid-eighteenth century demand picked up again, so the company imposed new planting, only to follow that a few years later by more cutting. By this time, growers were impoverished and disgusted, and the population of Amboina had fallen by a third. Meanwhile the British and French had started cultivating cloves in their own territories. The Dutch monopoly was broken, and spices in general faded as a precious commodity.[15]

Coffee is another, more egregious example of what Adam Smith called "so perfectly destructive a system."[16] Coffee was first brought to Holland in 1661, and from 1696 attempts were made to cultivate the coffee tree in Java. Native growers were paid some 10 stuiver a pound, and at that price took eagerly to the new crop. So the company, always on the alert for economies, reduced the price to 2.5 stuiver, whereupon the natives began cutting coffee trees down, even in the face of punishment. So the company introduced compulsory cultivation and delivery, while raising the price; but later, when pepper gained in value, the company told the growers to cut down the coffee trees and substitute pepper. In 1738 it was decided to reduce the area under coffee by half, and the next year the company fixed the purchase quota at 2.7 million pounds. But when it became clear that the Netherlands alone would take 6 million, the company raised its quota to 4 million—always playing it safe. Yet it paid the Javanese grower so little that in 1751, it was able to buy less than 1 million pounds. Coffee trees take four years to mature, and these alternate plantings and cuttings precluded a flexible, rational response to changing demand.

Over the course of the eighteenth century the Dutch East India Company saw trade volume fall (spices were down) and profits with it;

but it continued to pay generous dividends, even borrowing the sums required. A very bad sign. Was it making money? Our records are incomplete, and the methods of accounting make calculations difficult. The profits and losses of governance, for example, are not included with the commercial results, indeed are not available. Even Fernand Braudel, who had at his disposal a large squad of research assistants, had to give up: " . . . the very system of accountability prevents drawing up a general balance sheet and thus any exact calculation of real profits."[17] Who is to say that even the directors, the Heeren XVII, knew the real state of affairs? We assume that big business enterprises are rational and that rationality entails awareness. The annals of business make it clear, though, that much decision making is guesswork and improvisation. Otherwise, how do these enterprises manage to dig themselves so deep a hole?[18]

Toward the end of the century the hazards of politics made matters much more difficult. Holland got caught up in war with England in 1781–84, and the VOC found it hard to move goods between the Low Countries and the Indies. It had to ask for moratoria on its debt while borrowing afresh. The state was now the company's only creditor (bankers knew better), and its fate was bound up with that of the United Provinces. Then came the French Revolution, which boosted radical politics in the Netherlands and set up a puppet Batavian Republic (1795), much less sympathetic to the big business interests of the old regime. When the renewal of war with Britain drove sales down by almost two thirds, the outcome was inevitable. The Dutch state took over the company—assets, debt, and empire.

This empire remained; indeed, the governments of a restored Holland (1814– ) worked well into the nineteenth century to round it out. Costs of administration were covered by imposing delivery quotas on selected plantation crops (coffee, tea, sugar), and by lucrative monopolies of salt and opium. From 1870 on, the Dutch abandoned the plantation "Culture System," partly owing to the conviction that a free market would work better, partly owing to a bad conscience about forced labor. Two new, high-growth products eased the transition to liberalism: the transplantation of Brazilian rubber in 1883, and the discovery and exploitation of oil deposits in Borneo and Sumatra in the late 1880s (foundation of Royal Dutch, 1890). But little time remained to redeem the errors of an earlier age before World War II allowed the Japanese to seize these Dutch possessions. The Japanese occupation lasted only a few years, yet that was more than enough. The change in regime fed aspirations for freedom. It taught the Indonesians

that Asians could beat Europeans, that the Europeans were not invincible.

Japan's surrender returned the archipelago to the Dutch, but only
for a moment. In 1949, the Netherlands granted the islands independence, the more readily because Dutch public opinion had been prepared by several generations of penitent self-criticism. A new
Indonesian republic took command. It too was an empire, claiming
sovereignty over all the lands received from the Dutch, plus extra pieces
like East Timor, regardless of local identity and aspirations. Unhappy
dissenters from Indonesian dominion could seek shelter in the Netherlands—the Dutch would treat them better. Ironically, thanks to the
VOC and Western imperialism, the dream of the old sultans of Sumatra and Java was finally realized by the new sultans of "popular democracy."

# ~ 11 ~

# Golconda*

The British are like the strong rapid current of water, they are persevering, energetic, and irresistible in their courage. If they really want to obtain something they will use violence to get it. The Dutch are very able, clever, patient, and calm. If possible they try to reach their goal by persuasion than by force of arms. It may well happen that Java will be conquered by the British.
—A Javanese prince, c. 1780[†]

T he Romans had a saying, *Pecunia non olet*—Money does not smell. People may not like the way it was made or the person who made it, but they like, and will take, the money.

In another sense, though, money does smell, powerfully, and its odor will draw people from far and near.

In 1592, England was at war with Spain and Portugal, which we saw had been joined to the Spanish crown by the play of marriage and inheritance. Some four years before, the English had repelled and destroyed a Spanish seaborne invasion (the self-styled Invincible Armada). Now an English naval squadron was waiting off the Azores to intercept and capture Spanish ships coming from the New World and perhaps laden with the treasure of Mexico or Peru, when along came a Portuguese carrack. This was the *Madre de Deus,* back from the East Indies,

---

* Golconda: (1) A ruined city of western Andhra Pradesh, Republic of India, the capital (1512–1687) of a former Muslim kingdom. (2) A source of great riches, as a mine—*The American Heritage Dictionary of the English Language,* 1978.

† The prince had returned from some years of exile in Ceylon. Cited by Vlekke, *Nusantara,* pp. 225–26.

headed for Lisbon.* She was bigger than any vessel the English had ever seen: 165 feet long, 47 feet of beam, 1,600 tons, three times the size of the biggest ship in England; seven decks, thirty-two guns plus other arms, gilded superstructure; and her hold was filled with treasure.

Here was the stuff of dreams—chests bulging with jewels and pearls, gold and silver coins, amber older than England, bolts of the finest cloth, tapestries fit for a palace, 425 tons of pepper, 45 tons of cloves, 35 tons of cinnamon, 3 of mace, 3 of nutmeg, 2.5 tons of benjamin (a highly aromatic balsamic resin used as base in perfumes and pharmaceuticals), 25 tons of cochineal (a dyestuff made from the dried bodies of the female of an insect found in semitropical climes), 15 tons of ebony. Even before the English squadron commander could take charge of the prize, his rampaging crewmen had stuffed their pockets with everything they could carry.

When the prize came into Dartmouth Harbor, it towered over the other ships and the small houses at quayside. Traders, dealers, cutpurses, and thieves came from miles around, from London and beyond, like bees to honey—to visit the ship (the local fishermen plied ceaselessly and expensively between vessel and shore) and seek out drunken sailors in the taverns and dives, the better to buy, steal, pilfer, and fence the loot. By English law, a large share of this catch was owed to the queen; and when Elizabeth learned what was going on, she sent Sir Walter Raleigh down there to get her money back and punish the looters. "I mean to strip them as naked as ever they were born," swore the valiant Sir Walter, "for Her Majesty has been robbed and that of the most rare things."

By the time Sir Walter took things in hand, a cargo estimated at half a million pounds—nearly half of all the monies in the Exchequer—had been reduced to £140,000. Even so, it took ten freighters to carry the treasure around the coast and up the Thames to London. Next to the ransom of Atahualpa, it was perhaps the greatest haul in history. And like the ransom of Atahualpa, it was an immensely potent appetizer. This whiff of wealth, this foretaste of the riches of the East, galvanized English interest in these distant lands and set the country (and the world) on a new course.

---

* Because of the westerlies (winds are named for their source) and the easting Gulf Stream, the Azores were in effect the gullet for vessels returning from the West and East Indies alike. On their role in the American trade, see Landes, "Finding the Point at Sea"; also Broad, "Watery Grave of the Azores."

The English learned another lesson from the *"Mother of God."* When, some years later, a rich prize vessel was brought into the Thames for unloading, the men who did the job were given as work clothes "suits of canvas doublet without pockets."[1]

The English came into the Indian Ocean, like the Hollanders, at the end of the sixteenth century. They came as interlopers and plunderers, better at fighting than trading. Only later, and then cautiously, did they shift to commerce.

The Dutch formed their VOC by merger of independent companies, and moved vessels and armaments into the area on a substantial scale, with a view to booting the Portuguese and other pretenders from the Indonesian archipelago. The English, by contrast, acted piecemeal, treating each voyage as a separate venture and requiring participating merchants to reassemble their capital each time. When the English and Dutch clashed in those early days, the English sometimes won but lacked the muscle to mount a real challenge; and so, looking for alternative trade opportunities, they turned north to India. This would prove a lucky strike.

Like the Dutch, the English preferred to avoid the Portuguese. They set up at first on the eastern or Coromandel coast, well away from Malabar. On the western side of India they leapfrogged Goa to obtain trading privileges in Surat, the major port of the Moghul empire, gateway to the riches of the Indian interior and the trade with Persia and Arabia. Later on (1661) they got permission to set up in Bombay, then an almost uninhabited island. This was reasonably safe from landside aggression (compare Goa), and the English developed it into a factory-base and the major commercial center of the west coast.

On the other side of the peninsula, after planting themselves at Madras, the English moved north into the Bay of Bengal and the valley of the Hugli River. There, beginning in 1690, they built their own commercial city on the territory of a tiny village called Calcutta. The key was the purchase in 1698 of a kind of "feudal" privilege (*zamindari* rights of tax collection). These rights, though flouted at first by local authorities resentful of European intrusion, were increasingly honored as Indian merchants and officials came to depend on English trade, assistance, and goodwill.[2]

In all of this, the name of the game was buying interested friendship and collaboration. Begin with the big merchants and the courtiers of the Great Moghul. Go on to local agents and feudatories, who looked to the English for gifts (bribes) and stipends, shipped export goods in their vessels, and in some instances even invested with them. Thomas Roe, ambassador to the Court of the Great Moghul in Agra, defined the task: "Let this be received as a rule, that if you will profit, seek it at sea and in quiet trading, for without controversy it is an error to seek garrisons and land wars in India."[3]

The Dutch also tried to play this game in India, but fell short of English success. For the Dutch, Indonesia had priority, and India got the leavings of their attention and resources. In the islands, Dutch firepower extruded competitors, made violence easier. They got off on their strong foot, and the aggressive temperament of such proconsuls as Coen set the pattern. Dutch preferences also reflected material opportunities. They aimed at monopoly in Indonesia, against the interest of the locals. That was not feasible in India, where home rulers were stronger and where other players, already established, disputed the marketplace.

Yet all businessmen prefer monopoly to competition. Once English strength increased, they too resorted to force: threats of naval blockade that would have hurt Indian trade to other countries and interrupted the pilgrimage to Mecca; construction and garrisoning of forts; seizure and ransom of Indian vessels. In 1677, Gerald Aungier, the East India Company's president at Surat and governor at Bombay, wrote the directors in London to spell out the new conditions of business. He recommended a "severe and vigorous" policy: "Justice and necessity of your estate now require you to manage your general commerce with your sword in your hands." This advice found favor in London, where Josiah Child headed the company and was determined to surmount the vagaries of Indian politics. In 1687, instructions went out to Fort St. George (outside Madras): use power to ensure a large and continuing revenue, such as might lay "the foundation of a large, well-grounded, sure English dominion in India for all time to come."[4] Here was a ticket to involvement in Indian politics and government. Already the breakup of the Moghul empire loomed, leading Indian pretenders to power to seek allies among the foreign companies.

Meanwhile the nature of hereditary rule is to produce fools as well as statesmen, and the Moghuls mistakenly nourished the conviction that merchants like the British could only submit to the warrior children of Timur and Babar. The Nawab of Bengal squeezed and mulcted them in time-honored fashion—after all, what are sponges good for?

For a time, the British stood still and complied. But these were not ordinary merchants. Arbitrary levies turned the intruders to thoughts of violence. One vexed Englishman said it straight in 1752: "Clive, 'twould be a good thing to swinge the old dog [the Nawab] . . . the Company must think seriously of it, or twill not be worth their while to trade in Bengal."[5] And Clive thought seriously.

In India the English learned that Asia had more and better to trade than spices. In particular, India produced the world's finest cotton yarn and textiles, and the English were quick to seize the opportunity. Here they left their rivals behind. The Portuguese had shown little interest in these products, and even the Dutch were slow to catch on. But the East India Company (EIC) decided to push cotton fabrics and make a market: "calicoes are a commodity whereof the use is not generally known, the vent must be forced and trial made into all ports."[6]

This vent had traditionally been directed toward regional buyers in Indonesia and Southeast Asia, who exchanged spices and other local goods for Indian cloth. Like the Dutch, the English continued this pattern, for they had little of their own to sell and cottons thus furnished vital means of payment. (England's woolens had little appeal in climates where the problem was to stay cool rather than keep warm.) But the EIC's momentous innovation lay in introducing these cottons to Europe. In 1619–21 the VOC was shipping some 12,000 pieces of calico to the Netherlands; the EIC was up to 221,500 pieces by 1625. Then, after a slow period of digestion and retrenchment, the trade took off toward the end of the century: some 200,000 pieces a year in the late 1660s; 578,000 in the 1670s; 707,000 in the 1680s. The Dutch followed suit, but remained at half or less of English levels.[7]

Indian cottons transformed the dress of Europe and its overseas offshoots. Lighter and cheaper than woolens, more decorative (by dyeing or printing), easier to clean and change, cotton was made for a new wide world. Even in cold climes, the suitability of cotton for underwear transformed the standards of cleanliness, comfort, and health. In the American plantations, it answered perfectly; as some Jamaica traders put it (1704): " . . . the said island being situated in a hot climate, much of the clothing of the inhabitants is stained callicoes, which being light and cheap and capable of often washing contributes very much to the keeping them clean and in health."[8] Here was a commodity of such broad and elastic demand that it could drive an industrial revolution.

So the English bought cotton piece goods and to a lesser extent raw silk (from Bengal), indigo, and saltpeter;* also pepper, while conceding the costlier, rarer spices to the Dutch. But pepper, once the lodestone of European exploration and expansion, was in decline. New areas of cultivation had opened up; supply exceeded demand. The price of pepper sank so far that this once noble spice had to earn its way to Europe as ballast on certain routes.**

India led to China. When Europeans entered the Indian Ocean, they found a flourishing network of trade linking Asia from east to west, from China, Japan, and the Philippines to the caravan stations and ports of the Levant and East Africa. The intruders forced their way in. In the eighteenth century, European appetite for Chinese goods grew rapidly: porcelains, which Europe did not learn to manufacture until the 1720s; raw silk; and tea, an addictive substance complementary to West Indian sugar.

These purchases posed a payments problem. The Europeans would have liked to pay with their own manufactures, but the Chinese wanted almost nothing they made (clocks and watches were a great exception). So the Europeans paid in bullion and specie, but that only shifted the problem: what could they sell for Spanish silver, Japanese or Brazilian gold? Not easy.

The answer, of course, was to find something the Chinese wanted. This turned out to be opium, grown in Bengal and market-making as well as habit-forming. Here the British had a big advantage over the Dutch. In principle the traders of both nations had the right to compete for this commodity, but the British used their growing political power in the region to squeeze the Dutch out—a major blow.

The English, then, after starting with the Dutch, now moved well

---

* Saltpeter (potassium nitrate, $KNO_3$) was an essential ingredient of gunpowder, hence a raw material of unusual political as well as economic potency. The nitrogen was recovered from soil deposits of urine, which contains urea $(CO(NH_2)_2)$; and India, with a population as large as that of western Europe, produced a lot of urine while possessing singularly favorable soil conditions. Compounds of nitrogen are an essential ingredient of all manner of explosives (thus nitrocellulose and nitroglycerine), and as early as the fifteenth century, Henry V ordered that gunpowder not be exported from England without a license. Such countries as France and Germany tried to give nature a helping hand by creating saltpeter farms or nitriaries. The opening of a large Indian supply provided an important strategic advantage.

** As ballast, it made some East India ships smell better than most vessels on the long oceanic reaches, but it had one inconvenience. Its overpowering odor altered the flavor of goods in transport, in particular coffee. The English had to reconcile themselves to lower prices for coffee moved on pepper. But they needed that ballast. It made all the difference to stability in stormy waters—Chaudhuri, *Trading World of Asia*, p. 313.

beyond them. More, they found themselves well placed to penetrate and pillage a far richer place than Indonesia. India, next to China, was the most populous country in Asia. We have no censuses, but one estimate gives the figure of 100 million for the late sixteenth century, and this may well be low.[9] India possessed large fertile territories, notably the great river valleys of the northern plains—the Indus, Ganges, Brahmaputra—and was far from densely settled. One Indian scholar describes it as land-abundant and assumes that in the seventeenth century, it was still able to confine agriculture to the most productive areas; also to profit from pasture and waste to keep large numbers of livestock.[10] (On the other hand, India got far less from its cattle than it might have, even less than nothing, because of religious taboos.) India also—far more than Indonesia—had a large and skilled industrial workforce, whose products circulated throughout the region. As a result, the Indian economy yielded a substantial surplus that supported rulers and courts of legendary opulence:

> The annual revenues of the Mogul emperor Aurangzeb (1658–1701) are said to have amounted to $450,000,000, more than ten times those of [his contemporary] Louis XIV. According to an estimate of 1638, the Mogul court of India is supposed to have accumulated a treasure equivalent to one and one-half billion dollars.[11]

India's reputation for wealth in palaces and temples attracted one invader after another—in particular, Turkic nomads, horse-mounted warriors, who rode from the plains of central Asia to plunder the sedentary societies on their periphery. The last of these Turkic rulers of India were Moghuls (Mughals), the dynasty of Babar (1483–1530), a descendant of the terrifying Timur (Tamerlane), driver of human cattle, heaper of skulls. It was Babar's grandson Akbar (reigned 1556–1605) and great-grandson Jahangir (reigned 1605–27) whom the English found on the throne when they first came to India.

The Moghuls were Sunni Muslims, different then from their neighbors to the west in Shiite Persia. They generally tolerated and even depended on the Hindu majority, but gave northern India a Muslim cast that marked it off from the south. The Moghuls, of course, held the land as a despotic occupier and commanded no loyalty. Their rule was repeatedly challenged by the indigenous Hindu states and subverted by rebellions and palace conspiracies. Brothers killed brothers; children, fathers; fathers, children. In a world of competing claims to legitimacy, one could trust strangers little, though more than relatives.[12]

The tyranny of these Muslim rulers—no better or worse than that of Hindu despots—was aggravated by the measures taken to prevent sedition. This is a classic problem of autocracies: how to prevent lieutenants from taking root and creating rival centers of power. In medieval Europe, the grant of landed fiefs was originally personal, not heritable, but over time local lords tended to stay put and pass domains down to their heirs, bonding with the landed elites of the area and creating the fragmented authority we know as feudalism. In Moghul India, as in other Turkic states, agents of the ruler were moved about. This limited local power, but also destroyed the official's commitment to his territory. His aim became to make and take as much as possible as fast as possible, spending little on social capital.[13] All take and no give. In those regions dependent on irrigation, this neglect of communal equipment could be disastrous, as the annals of Indian famines testify.

For similar reasons, the peasant (and indeed all subjects) had no reason to improve the land, holding it as he did at the pleasure of the ruler. There is in this country, wrote François Bernier, a French physician who spent a dozen years in India in the seventeenth century, no *mien et tien* (no mine and yours), that is, no right or sense of property. No one, he wrote, dares to show his wealth, for fear of extortion or seizure. No one cares to improve ways or tools of production. Hence, wrote Bernier, the appalling contrast between the opulent few and the impoverished many; the decrepitude of the houses; the humiliation of the mass; the absence of incentives to learning and self-improvement.

Hence also severe constraints on credit and on the commercial possibilities that credit makes possible. Much has been made of the beehive of trade in the Indian ocean when the Europeans arrived;[14] also of the wealth of the *sarafs,* who lent at high rates to peasants and merchants alike. But high rates mean high risk. What security could the borrower offer? How much can a lender afford to lend when the need to hide assets severely reduces information?[15] India's commercial activity languished well below its potential.

How, then, did some Indian traders, bankers, and lenders manage to get rich? The answer is, they laid golden eggs. They paid and bribed, hoarded and shared; and when they died, the family hid as much wealth as it could. Here are the observations of an Englishman in 1689:

> Their [merchants'] Wealth consists only in Cash and Jewels, the distinction of personal and real Estate is not heard in India and that they preserve

as close and private as they can, lest the Moghul's Exchequer shou'd be made their Treasury. This curbs them in their Expences, and awes them to great secresie in their Commerce. . . .[16]

Tension thus abided throughout—for rulers between seizing and nursing, for subjects between hiding and enjoying. But in the last analysis, the despot and his agents controlled. Here the European visitors held an enormous advantage. They could not be maltreated in this manner, and they could even take native businessmen and workers under their protection. In the long run, this constituted an appropriation of sovereignty. Some might say a usurpation, but in despotisms all transfers of power are usurpations.

And what of the *ryots* and untouchables, the lowest of the low? They fell back on patience, stubbornness, resilience—the resources of an oppressed population. They also fled their abusers more often than one would expect in a society of communitarian villages and uncertain improvement. In medieval Europe, exit or the threat of exit deterred abuse, especially in urbanized and frontier areas. Exit paid. In India, flight probably exchanged one unhappiness for another; even so, it could encourage moderation, for no predator likes to lose his prey.

That still left a fortune for the taking—one scholar estimates India's surplus at half the agricultural product. This "bundle" was bound to turn the East India Company toward political as against commercial activity, for more money could be had by taking than by earning. Endemic conflict and violence, moreover, incited (compelled) the company to look to its defenses by mobilizing military power, and power encouraged intervention in local disputes.

Sage advice from London could not deter the EIC's men in the field from taking this slippery slope. The proconsuls had the Dutch example in Indonesia to instruct and justify them, and they won the argument. London came around. In 1689, when the company's activities in India had been reorganized under three "presidencies," the London directors passed a resolution that redefined the company's mission in the Dutch image:

> The increase of our revenue is the subject of our care, as much as our trade; 'tis that must maintain our force when twenty accidents may interrupt our trade; 'tis that must make us a nation in India; without that we are but a great number of interlopers, united by His Majesty's royal charter, fit only to trade where nobody of power thinks it their interest to prevent us. . . .

This broader purpose did not aim at monopoly as in Indonesia. The EIC was ready to let others into the Indian market—except perhaps the French, who chose to challenge them politically. Still, the EIC's power and privilege gave it a decisive advantage in an ostensibly level field. Employees of the company were quick to seize the opportunity, not only trading on their own account but lending their name and virtual authority to native servants and business associates ready to pay for the favor.

In a world of Muslim pride and xenophobia, this British assertion brought humiliation high and low, for the turnpike man at the customs station as much as for the prince in his palace. These infidel pretensions undermined the dignity and legitimacy of the viceroyal authorities and led to war between the Nawab of Bengal and the company; and war will always provide grounds for grievance and hate. So here: the young prince Suraj-ud-Dowlah (Sirajuddaullah) decided to teach the British a lesson and in 1756 took Calcutta against the merest shadow of resistance. He then perpetrated "that great crime, memorable for its singular atrocity, memorable for the tremendous retribution by which it was followed."[17] This was the massacre of the "Black Hole," a chamber 18 by 15 feet with only two small, barred windows. Into this box the nawab's men jammed one hundred forty-six prisoners on a steamy-stifling June night—civilians as well as soldiers, including a few women. Pleas and protests went up, but the nawab had retired to sleep and could not to be disturbed. The cries ebbed. In the morning only twenty-three prisoners were still alive.

The crime demanded reprisal, and local representatives of John Company were only too pleased to have a go at it.[18] As soon as a fleet could be armed, it sailed up from Madras with a small detachment of British and sepoy troops under the command of Robert Clive, a young civil servant of the company, a desk man with a genius for war. Because of adverse winds, the ships took some two months to sail up the Bay of Bengal and enter the Hugli River. There the British easily recaptured Calcutta, imposed a huge indemnity on ud-Dowlah, and compelled restoration of all company privileges. For the nawab, an expensive night's sleep.

But that was not the end of the story. The war in Europe between Britain and France had its echo in Bengal, where the nawab courted the French for the best of reasons—revenge and the opportunity to escape from his engagements. Another Moghul miscalculation. Apprised of these maneuvers, the British under Clive attacked and captured the French trading station at Chandernagore (Chandarnagar), a festering sore of commercial competition. The nawab took badly to this: Who were these British merchants to engage in war against other merchants within his dominions? Besides, like Pharaoh, he had repented himself of his weakness and felt he could do better a second time; after all, his army far outnumbered British forces.

This time the British decided to be rid of ud-Dowlah. Seeking allies among disaffected members of the Indian court—"How glorious it would be for the Company to have a Nabob devoted to them!"—they found Mir Jafar, the nawab's uncle by marriage and a commander of his armed forces.[19] Local officials and traders were there to be bought and sold, crossed and double-crossed. Using a shrewd Hindu merchant named Omichund (Umichand or Amin Chand) as intermediary, the British bought Mir Jafar's treason with the promise to name him nawab. Mir Jafar in turn committed himself to pay an elephantine fortune for his elevation.

In the end, on 23 June 1757, the issue came down to a battle, at Plassey (Placis, Palasi), a village ninety miles north of Calcutta—British and allies on one side, nawab and minions on the other. The British won, and winning, changed Indian history. The bards of imperial greatness sing of Robert Clive, accountant-turned-commander. They tell of generalship and treason and small but decisive precautions—like covering the guns in a monsoon rain. The anti-imperialist iconoclasts dismiss narrative, play down heroism (everyone is brave), and deplore the readiness of local officials and magnates to be bought, their want of loyalty.[20]

But, of course, that is the Achilles heel of aristocratic empires like the Moghul and its parts: What loyalty? The nawab began the battle with fifty thousand troops, against three thousand for the British. Of the fifty thousand, only twelve thousand actually fought for him, and these withdrew so quickly that they suffered only five hundred casualties. British losses numbered four Europeans and fourteen sepoys. And this was one of history's decisive battles.[21]

After victory came the counting. The sums eventually arrived at were 10 million rupees ( = £1.4 m. at an exchange of 7.14285 rupees to the pound) to the company as compensation for losses; indemnities and bribes for the resident merchants of Calcutta (5 m. rupees for the British; 2 m. for the Armenians; 1 m. for the Indians); 5 million rupees for the British naval squadron and army detachment; plus large personal fees to members of the company council, of the order of over a quarter-million rupees each.

The whole amounted to £2,340,000, five times the loot captured on

the *Madre de Deus*—a sum that would amount nowadays to more than
$1 billion.* Mir Jafar hardly cared. The money would not come from
his pocket. Even so, the Bengali treasury could not satisfy these extravagant demands. In the end, about half the sum was paid, in specie
and jewels. The rest was rescheduled, then rescheduled again; and with
each postponement, the company received compensation in the form
of privileges, territory, and revenues. The EIC Council members, however, got their money in full—a lesson in priorities.**

Attached to these extortions was a quiet codicil, granting the company *zamindari* rights over a large tract of land around Calcutta. This
land paid a quit-rent to the nawab of some £23,000 but yielded a
gross rental of £53,000—a net gift, then, of some £30,000. And as
Calcutta grew, so did the value of land around it, so that by the end of
a decade, rentals rose to £146,000. Meanwhile the nawab had turned
his right to the quit-rent over to Clive, since named governor of the
company's settlements in Bengal: the employee was now his employer's
landlord. Clive also received a *jagir*, a feudal right of command over
some six thousand foot and five thousand horse in the army of the
Moghul emperor. The confusion of political and commercial within the
company was duplicated in the identity of its agents.

In India, then, as in Indonesia, power was money, and money was
power. India's surplus, once creamed off by the Moghul state and its
feudal dependencies, now shifted to the East India Company and its officers and agents. Merchants and civil servants welcomed their inadequate salaries as a pretext for private enterprise and public venality.
Young, ambitious men paid money for appointment to company service. Members of Parliament and people of influence sought jobs for
friends and relations and paid for them in their own way. The India
House was a "lottery-office, which invited every body to take a chance

* The conversion is based on the then prevailing wage of a skilled worker (£50 a year)
into the equivalent modern wage of $25,000. In conversions of this kind, covering
long periods, the best standard of comparison is the price of labor.
** Clive's cash reward was the equivalent of some $140 million in our money. Some
regarded this fabulous sum as extortionate, but Macaulay says that Clive could as easily have had twice that for the asking: "He accepted twenty lacs of rupees [2 m. ru-
pees]. It would have cost him only a word to make the twenty forty"—Macaulay,
"Clive," p. 243. This is certainly what Clive gave the world to understand. Cf. Keay,
*Honourable Company,* pp. 320 ff. Macaulay does raise the question, however, whether
it was appropriate for a British subject to accept a large gift from a foreign ruler. True,
it was not against the law; but what would people have said, he asks, if Wellington had
accepted such a gift from Louis XVIII of France?

and held out ducal fortunes . . . for the lucky few."[22] Luck, obviously, was only part of the story.

To be sure, India was a disease-ridden place. Many of these new rich never made it back to England. Even healthy and competent survivors had problems cashing in their assets; the dead had to rely on agents with their own interests to nourish and often no one to answer to. The crumbs that fell in this way from the Indian table fattened a small army of dealers, lawyers, scrivenors, jewelers, bill brokers, smugglers, confidence men, and profiteers.

Lord Clive (he had received an Irish peerage and hoped soon for an English title) had a bigger problem than most; he had so much more to take back. He sent £180,000 in bills of exchange on the VOC in Amsterdam, which then had to be discounted and used to buy sterling remittances. More than £40,000 went through the English East India Company, and considerable though unknown amounts through private merchants. He also invested hugely in jewels—£25,000 in diamonds bought in Madras alone—and carried these back for resale in England. "We may safely affirm," wrote Macaulay, "that no Englishman who started with nothing has ever, in any line of life, created such a fortune at the early age of thirty-four."[23]

When Clive returned to England, he put his fortune to "creditable" use. He gave large sums to sisters, other relations, impecunious friends; arranged an income of £800 a year for his parents, say $400,000 of today's money, while insisting that they keep a carriage; and settled £500 a year on his old commanding officer, "whose means were very slender." After devoting some £50,000 to these generosities, he bought land with a view to securing seats in the Commons for himself and a small coterie of clients. He also bought a substantial packet of shares (£100,000) in the East India Company, which he assigned to strawmen so as to make a small voting bloc. In those days, the meetings of the court of proprietors, as it was called, were "large, stormy, even riotous. . . . Fictitious votes were manufactured on a gigantic scale." Robert Clive was someone to be reckoned with.

In the short run, this transfer of wealth and political power from the mysterious East to the country shires and parliamentary halls of England proved unpalatable—too fast, too new. Who were these nabobs (the then current version of the Indian title of nawab), to buy large estates, pretend to social eminence, corrupt English politics? Inevitably, a cry went up for official investigation and parliamentary inquiries. These led to scandalous trials (Warren Hastings) and provoked important changes in the constitution of the East India Company. The new arrangements, which entailed closer state oversight of the governance of Bengal, did make it harder to get "filthy rich" fast; but one could still make more in India in a few years than in a British lifetime.

In the long run, the British assumption of empire in India posed grave problems of political strategy and ethics. The EIC saw its acquisitions as permanent—"as permanent as human wisdom can make them" (1766). Therefore it had to "protect and cherish the inhabitants . . . whose interest and welfare are now become our primary care"— for the company's sake. India was compared to a landed estate where the interests of tenant and landlord were the same.[24]

Very wise, and very British; but not simple. Even after reform, the task of development remained, complicated by a prudent reluctance to tamper with Indian social and cultural institutions. The Indian economy changed and grew as new technologies, the railway in particular, came in from abroad. But it was slow to respond to the Industrial Revolution, except as supplier of raw cotton; and the Indian cotton manufacture, once the world's greatest, shrank almost to vanishing. Indian historians blame this on their colonial oppressor, who not only vetoed protective tariffs (long live free trade!) but taxed the Indian product to equalize access for British yarn and cloth. But that was not the problem. Both Indian and British entrepreneurs were free to undertake modern forms of manufacture in India, as they did beginning in the 1850s. If they refrained earlier, they presumably had good reason.

෭ ෮

# How Do We Know?
## The Nature of the Evidence

Some of the most important work on Indian history has been done by Indian scholars, yet these, ironically, have had to rely almost exclusively on European records and accounts. Almost no written documentation comes down to us from the Indian side. What we know, for example, of Indian Ocean trade in the sixteenth to eighteenth centuries, and of the textile manufacture in particular, is drawn almost exclusively from the archives of the chartered trading companies and their home governments; also from travel accounts and correspondence to and from Europe.[25] These records tell therefore only the outside of the story. They are, however, rich and suggestive—including a certain amount of indigenous material—and have provided evidence for a lot of good history.

Why this asymmetry is an interesting question in cultural history. The Indians were literate (though they lacked printing), and no empire like the Moghul could operate without records and correspondence. Nor could Indian merchants, active in international trade, have done without similar aids to memory and communication. Was there a problem of preservation? If so, how have East India Company records survived in Madras, Bombay, and Calcutta? Was there a crucial difference in forms of commercial organization? Chartered companies depended on an elaborate bureaucratic apparatus, and bureaucracy means paper. Perhaps the problem is one of continuity and custodianship. The Indian political units were ephemeral, and their papers with them. Perhaps they should have written on clay tablets or stone.

One thing is clear: the Europeans of that day were already interested in records. Mark here the difference between *hieratically* literate and *generally* literate societies. The Europeans, for all the analphabetism of the populace, were of the latter category. From middling on up, they read, but also wrote and published—not only the officials but private citizens. The nearest equivalents in the non-European world would be the Japanese and the Jews. Europeans also were passionately curious about other peoples and societies: the overwhelming majority of travel accounts of that day were written by and for them.

This curiosity quotient was an important and characteristic aspect of European expansion and dominion. Whether deliberate or unconscious (and it was both), it prepared the way for reconnaissance and exploitation. In recent years, anticolonialist critics have made much of the alleged misdeeds of Western curiosity, putting scholars, spies, and diplomatic agents in the same knaves' basket. The best known elaboration of these charges is Edward Said's much-discussed *Orientalism* (1978). (More on this powerful and influential book in chapter 24, pp. 415–18.) Insofar as the critique holds that only insiders can know the truth about their societies, it is wrong. Insofar as one uses this claim to discredit the work of intellectual adversaries, it is polemical and antiscientific. But insofar as it points to the instrumental value and power of information, for good and for bad, it makes an important point.

≈ ≈

# Food, Income,
# and Standard of Living

What was the condition of the "mass" in pre–British India?
European travelers and visitors reported general poverty, even
misery, and Indian interlocutors agreed. Why so many temples in
South India? " . . . the soil is immensely productive while the
subsistence needs of the inhabitants are so few." An English traveler
visits a local king who speaks of his peasants as "Naked, Starved
Rascals." Their needs? "Money is inconvenient for them: give them
Victuals and an Arse-Clout, it is enough."[26]

Some historians would argue that these strangers saw and
understood less than they thought, or that they blackened the Indian
picture by way of brightening the European. A few have even
asserted—on the strength of estimates of food intake—that the
Indian *ryot* lived better than the English farm laborer.[27]

Such calorimetric cliometrics seem to me implausible in the light
of the gulf between European and Asian techniques. Nor am I
persuaded by efforts to project twentieth-century comparative
income estimates back to the eighteenth century.[28] The
opportunities to distort the result are endless, and the leverage of
even a small mistake extended over two hundred years is enormous.

In these speculative exercises, the numbers deserve credence only
if they accord with the historical context. That context, for India,
was one of limited property rights and technological backwardness.
Western Europe, well on its way to the Industrial Revolution, was
inventing and improving ingenious, labor-saving devices, in
particular, both hand- and power-driven machines. It had long since
passed Asia by. It's as simple as that: more productive techniques
translate into higher incomes.

≈ ≈

# And What Happened to Omichund?

The negotiations between the British and Mir Jafar were carried out
by two agents, one of them Omichund, a merchant of Bengal who

had taken up residence in Calcutta to benefit from the company's protection and had suffered heavy losses in the course of the nawab's seizure and occupation of the city. This Omichund, the historian Macaulay tells us with the candor of an age that did not know political correctness, was well equipped by his business experience to mediate between the English and the nawab's court. "He possessed great influence with his own race, and had in large measure the Hindoo talents, quick observation, tact, dexterity, perseverance, and the Hindoo vices, servility, greediness, and treachery."

It was Omichund's task to lull and gull the nawab. This he did. Thanks to his inventions and fictions, the planning proceeded apace; but the more it advanced, the more everything depended on the discretion of Omichund. A word from him could destroy the conspiracy. And just at this point Clive began to hear disquieting news, that Omichund was hinting at betrayal unless he got a huge compensation. Huge? He asked for 300,000 pounds sterling (say 150 million of today's dollars), and what's more, he wanted this commitment written into the treaty that would seal the installation of Mir Jafar on the throne of Bengal.

Clive was outraged. This was blatant dishonesty. It was also greedy. He decided to repay cross with double cross and had two treaties drawn up—one real, on white paper, making no mention of Omichund; the other false, on red paper, with a clause in the merchant's favor. Not all Englishmen were ready to connive at this fraud: Admiral Watson refused to sign the red version, an omission that would surely arouse Omichund's suspicions. So Clive—as much be hanged for a cow as a sheep—forged the admiral's signature.

Now it was time for action. The confident nawab took up arms. Clive and his English troops—the kind of men, as he put it, who had never turned their back—routed him at Plassey (1757). The nawab fled the field and then his throne. The winners met to divide the spoils. Omichund came to the conference full of expectation, for Clive had treated him up to the last minute with unfailing consideration. The white treaty was then read. No mention of Omichund. Turning to Clive, he had his answer: "The red treaty is a trick. You are to receive nothing." The poor man swooned, was revived, but never regained his senses. Gradually he sank into lethargy and bewilderment. Once a man of sharp reasoning and simple dress, he now walked pointlessly about in lavish, bejeweled accouterments. Within a few months he was dead.

Macaulay, normally sympathetic to Clive, draws the line at this deceit: " . . . this man, in the other parts of his life an honourable English gentleman and soldier, was no sooner matched against an Indian intriguer, than he became himself an Indian intriguer, and descended, without scruple, to hypocritical caresses, to the substitution of documents, and to the counterfeiting of hands."[29] But this was not the gravamen of Macaulay's condemnation. While pointing to Clive's moral shortcomings, Macaulay prefers to argue his case on grounds of expediency "such as Machiavelli might have employed."

The point was that Clive had committed "not merely a crime, but a blunder." Individuals, Macaulay points out, may get rich by perfidy, but not states. In the public domain, a reputation for veracity is worth more than valor and intelligence, and this especially in a world of ubiquitous guile and duplicity. Nothing other than a reputation for unconditional honesty could have enabled Britain to maintain its empire in India at so little expense; nothing else could have brought out the wealth of the nation from its hiding and hoarding places. The mightiest princes of the East, he notes, cannot persuade their subjects to part with their wealth for usurious returns; the British can bring forth tens of millions of rupees at 4 percent.

This is Macaulay's judgment. He has a point. But were Clive's successors more scrupulous than he? Or have imperialists and statesmen simply learned to lie better? Or to lie in some things and not in others? Pursue honesty in money matters, and Devil take the rest? That would be an irony. The fact is that even in Macaulay's righteous time, veracity was a function of *raison d'état*. Even in money matters—especially in money matters. It is true that investors trusted the word of Britain and bought consols at 4 percent, and Britain never let them down . . . until the twentieth century, when war and deficits undermined the purchasing power of the pound and killed the gold standard. Is inflation a kind of impersonal lie?

# ~ 12 ~

# Winners and Losers:
# The Balance Sheet
# of Empire

The discovery of America, the rounding of the Cape, opened up fresh ground
for the rising bourgeoisie. The East-Indian and Chinese markets, the colonisation of America, trade with the colonies, the increase in the means of exchange and in commodities generally, gave to commerce, to navigation, to
industry, an impulse never before known, and thereby, to the revolutionary
element in the tottering feudal society, a rapid development.
—MARX and ENGELS, *Manifesto of the Communist Party*

The turn of the eighteenth century was both end and beginning.
It saw the liquidation of the Dutch East India Company; the prohibition of the British Atlantic slave trade (but not the end of slavery);*
the peak and decline of the sugar bonanza (including revolution and
the fall of planters and plantations in Saint-Domingue [now Haiti]); an
end to the Old Regime in France; an end to the period of Old Empire.
The new era would see Europe lose formal control of territory overseas
(Spain would be the big loser) but gain wider economic dominance.
Europe would also force its way into territories previously seen as inaccessible and untouchable (China, Japan), while creating in others
(India, Indonesia) a new kind of imperium in its own image.

The hinge of this metamorphosis was the Industrial Revolution,
begun in Britain in the eighteenth century and emulated around the
world. The Industrial Revolution made some countries richer and others (relatively) poorer; or more accurately, some countries made an industrial revolution and became rich; and others did not and stayed

---

* In places such as the Caribbean, however, where the pool of slaves could not maintain itself by natural reproduction, the interdiction of fresh supplies would kill the old
plantation system.

poor. This process of selection actually began much earlier, during the age of discovery.

For some nations, Spain for example, the Opening of the World was an invitation to wealth, pomp, and pretension—an older way of doing things, but on a bigger scale. For others, Holland and England, it was a chance to do new things in new ways, to catch the wave of technological progress. And for still others, such as the Amerindians or Tasmanians, it was apocalypse, a terrible fate imposed from without.

The Opening brought first an exchange—the so-called Columbian exchange—of the life forms of two biospheres. The Europeans found in the New World new peoples and animals, but above all, new plants— some nutritive (maize [Indian corn], cocoa [cacao], potato, sweet potato), some addictive and harmful (tobacco, coca), some industrially useful (new hardwoods, rubber). These products were adapted diversely into Old World contexts, some early, some late (rubber does not become important until the nineteenth century).

The new foods altered diets around the world. Corn, for example, became a staple of Italian (polenta) and Balkan (mamaliga) cuisines; while potatoes became the main starch of Europe north of the Alps and Pyrenees, even replacing bread in some places (Ireland, Flanders). So important was the potato that some historians have seen it as the source and secret of the European population "explosion" of the nineteenth century.[1] But not only in Europe. Grown on poor, hilly soils, the potato, along with peanuts, sweet potatoes, and yams, provided a valuable dietary supplement for a Chinese population that in the eighteenth century began to outstrip the nourishment provided by rice.

In return, Europe brought to the New World new plants—sugar, cereals; and new fauna—the horse, horned cattle, sheep, and new breeds of dog. Some of these served as weapons of conquest; or like the cattle and sheep, took over much of the land from its inhabitants. Worse yet by far, the Europeans and the black slaves they brought with them from Africa carried nasty, microscopic baggage: the viruses of smallpox, measles, and yellow fever; the protozoan parasite of malaria; the bacillus of diphtheria; the rickettsia of typhus; the spirochete of yaws; the bacterium of tuberculosis. To these pathogens, the residents of the Old World had grown diversely resistant. Centuries of exposure within Eurasia had selected human strains that stood up to such maladies. The Amerindians, on the other hand, died in huge numbers, in some places all of them, to the point where only the sparsity of survivors and some happy strains of resistance enabled a few to pull through.

Why the Eurasian biosphere was so much more virulent than the

American is hard to say. Greater population densities and frequency of contagion? The chance distribution of pathogens? Where were the Amerindian diseases? Only one has come down to us—syphilis, which the French called the Italian disease, the Germans the French disease, and so on as it made its way from seaports to the rest of Europe.*

Yet the invaders had their own weaknesses. American visitors to Mexico call travelers' diarrhea "Montezuma's revenge"; those to India speak of "Delhi belly." Such tags are supposed to be funny, but in fact, Europeans migrating to these strange lands in the early centuries fell easy victim to local pathogens and infections and died "like flies."[2] Depending on place. Climate and hygiene—modes of evacuation and waste disposal, water supply and run-off, personal habits, social customs—could make all the difference. Thus the Indian Ocean area was three to four times more virulent than the temperate zones; the West Indies and American tropics up to ten times more; and West Africa was a one-way door to death. Mortality rates there ran fifty times higher.[3] Within these larger regions, higher densities made for festering pestholes: Bombay in India, Batavia in Indonesia. A jacket illustration of Fernand Braudel's trilogy ( *Civilisation matérielle,* etc.) shows a well-to-do Portuguese family in Goa dining in a water-covered room: the table stands in water; their feet rest in water. This no doubt kept crawlers from joining the repast, but it was an invitation to enemy swimmers. Forget about flyers.

Oceanic migrations, then, voluntary and involuntary (slaves), brought much death into the world and much woe. But also riches and opportunity for the Europeans, whether leavers or stayers. That is the law of migration in market societies: people go to improve their situation, and so doing, enhance the bargaining power of those left behind; while in their new home they create or seize wealth (food, timber, minerals, or manufactures) to ship or take back to the old country.

These gains were realized only slowly. Not until the nineteenth century did improvements in transport open the American Midwest to commercial agriculture. These same advances made immigration much cheaper and easier, just in time to tap an unprecedented upswing in European population. But even the smaller movements of the earlier pe-

---

* Some medical ethnologists question the American origin of syphilis, pointing to evidence of pre-Columbian veneral disease in Europe of somewhat similar course and effects. But similar is not identical, and there is no question that syphilis became an epidemic phenomenon only in the sixteenth century. Compare AIDS, which may be older than we know but surfaced as an epidemic disease only in the 1980s.

riod made possible a substantial North American contribution to the food supply of the colonial plantations and the mother countries; and all the rest was there in prospect. European economic and demographic growth in the eighteenth and nineteenth centuries had its strains and pains; but no continent ever modernized more easily. Much of that was due to the New World—was done on the backs of Amerindians, African slaves, indentured servants.

> If Spain has neither money nor gold nor silver, it is because it has these things, and if it is poor, it is because it is rich. . . . One would think that one wanted to make of this republic a republic of enchanted people living outside the natural order.
> —Martin Gonzales de Cellorigo, 1600[4]

Well before the agriculture and manufactures came the loot and booty. The Columbian exchange redistributed wealth as well as flora and fauna—a one-stage transfer from old rich to new. The primary economic significance of the influx of wealth from overseas, however, lay in its uneven effects. Some people got rich only to spend; others to save and invest. The same with countries: some were little richer in the end than at the beginning, while others used their new fortune to grow more money.

Ironically, the nations that had started it all, Spain and Portugal, ended up losers. Here lies one of the great themes of economic history and theory. All models of growth, after all, stress the necessity and power of capital—capital as substitute for labor, easer of credit, balm of hurt projects, redeemer of mistakes, great enterprise's second chance, chief nourisher of economic development. Given capital, the rest should follow. And thanks to empire, Spain and Portugal had the capital.

Spain particularly. Its new wealth came in raw, as money to invest or spend. Spain chose to spend—on luxury and war. War is the most wasteful of uses: it destroys rather than builds; it knows no reason or constraints; and the inevitable unevenness and shortage of resources lead to ruthless irrationality, which simply increases costs. Spain spent all the more freely because its wealth was unexpected and unearned. *It is always easier to throw away windfall wealth.*

Who got the money? Short of hoarding, money will be used somehow, go round and come round, for better or worse. Spain wasted much of its wealth on the fields of Italy and Flanders. It went to pay for soldiers and arms, including iron cannon from the English intermittent enemy; for provisions, many of them bought from the Dutch and Flemish intermittent enemy; and for horses and ships.

In the meantime, the wealth of the Indies went less and less to Spanish industry because the Spanish did not have to make things any more; they could buy them.[5] In 1545, Spanish manufacturers had a six-year backlog of orders from the New World. At that time, in principle, the overseas empire was required to buy from Spanish producers only. But customers and profits were waiting, and Spanish merchants turned to foreign suppliers while using their own names to cover the transactions. So much for rules. Nor did the American treasure go to Spanish agriculture; Spain could buy food. As one happy Spaniard put it in 1675, the whole world is working for us:

> Let London manufacture those fabrics of hers to her heart's content; Holland her chambrays; Florence her cloth; the Indies their beaver and vicuna; Milan her brocades; Italy and Flanders their linens, so long as our capital can enjoy them. The only thing it proves is that all nations train journeymen for Madrid and that Madrid is the queen of Parliaments, for all the world serves her and she serves nobody.[6]

Such foolishness is still heard today, in the guise of comparative advantage and neoclassical trade theory. I have heard serious scholars say that the United States need not worry about its huge trade deficit with Japan. After all, the Japanese are giving us useful things in exchange for paper printed with the portrait of George Washington. That sounds good, but it's bad. Wealth is not so good as work, nor riches so good as earnings. A Moroccan ambassador to Madrid in 1690–91 saw the problem clearly:

> . . . the Spanish nation today possesses the greatest wealth and the largest income of all the Christians. But the love of luxury and the comforts of civilization have overcome them, and you will rarely find one of this nation who engages in trade or travels abroad for commerce as do the other Christian nations such as the Dutch, the English, the French, the Genoese and their like. Similarly, the handicrafts practiced by the lower classes and common people are despised by this nation, which regards itself as superior to the other Christian nations. Most of those who practice these crafts in Spain are Frenchmen [who] flock to Spain to look for work . . . [and] in a short time make great fortunes.[7]

Reliance on metics (outsiders) testifies to the inability to mobilize skills or enterprise.

Spain, in other words, became (or stayed) poor because it had too much money. The nations that did the work learned and kept good habits, while seeking new ways to do the job faster and better. The Spanish, on the other hand, indulged their penchant for status, leisure, and enjoyment—what Carlo Cipolla calls "the prevalent *hidalgo* mentality." They were not alone. Everywhere in Europe, genteel living was honored and manual labor scorned; in Spain, however, more so, partly because a frontier, combative society is a poor school for patience and hard work, partly because the crafts and tasks of industry and agriculture were long especially associated with despised minorities such as Jews and Muslims. As the chronicler Bernaldez put it, writing of the Jews at the end of the fifteenth century:

> . . . all of them were merchants, dealers, tax farmers; they were stewards of the nobility and skilled shearers *(oficiales tondadores),* they were tailors, shoemakers, tanners, beltmakers, weavers, grocers, peddlers, silkmakers, smiths, goldsmiths, and other like professions. None of them cultivated the land; none was a farm worker, carpenter, or mason. All of them looked for easy trades and for ways to make a living with little work.

What is accursed is left to pariahs; and what the pariahs do is accursed.[8] Better to be poor and unemployed. The poor in Spain played a most important role: they helped the rich buy salvation.[9]

By the time the great bullion inflow had ended in the mid-seventeenth century, the Spanish crown was deep in debt, with bankruptcies in 1557, 1575, and 1597. The country entered upon a long decline. Reading this story, one might draw a moral: Easy money is bad for you. It represents short-run gain that will be paid for in immediate distortions and later regrets.*

The nations of northern Europe would have agreed. They throve on the opening of the world. They caught fish, tapped and refined whale oil, grew and bought and resold cereals, wove cloth, cast and forged iron, cut timber and mined coal.[10] They won their own empires, fortunately not endowed with gold and silver. Looting and pillaging when the opportunity offered, they nonetheless built largely on renewable harvests and continuing industry (including the industry of slaves, but

---

* Ironically, the economists of today have adopted the term "Dutch disease" to describe this syndrome, from the response of the economy of Holland to the discovery and exploitation of natural gas under the North Sea. As though the Dutch did not know how to make the most of these new resources.

that was a negative) rather than on depletable minerals. They built on work.

Europe's shift in economic gravity northward obviously transcends the inglorious Spanish fiasco. The great old mercantile and industrial city-states of Italy—Venice, Florence, Genoa—also lost out. Italy had been at the forefront of the medieval commercial revolution and had led the way out of autarky into international trade and division of labor. As late as the sixteenth century, Italy was a major player, splendid in its manufactures, preeminent in the commercial and banking services rendered to Spain and northern Europe. Yet Italy never really seized the opportunities offered by the Great Opening: one does not find Italian ships in the Indian ocean or crossing the Atlantic. Italy was centered in, caught in, the great Inland Sea. Caught also by old structures: guild controls fettered industry, made it hard to adapt to changing tastes. Labor costs stayed high because manufacture was largely confined to urban, corporate workshops employing adult male craftsmen who had done their years of apprenticeship.[11]

The advance of North over South attracted notice. In the eighteenth century already, observers commented on the difference in psychological terms. Northerners were said to be dour, dull, and diligent. They worked hard and well but had no time to enjoy life. In contrast, the southerners were seen as easygoing and happy, passionate to the point of needing close watching, and given to leisure rather than labor. This contrast was linked to geography and climate: cloudy vs. sunny skies, cold vs. warmth. Some people even found analogous differences within countries: between Lombards and Neapolitans, Catalans and Castilians, Flemings and the *gens du midi,* Scots and Kentishmen.

These stereotypes held an ounce of truth and a pound of lazy thinking. It is easy to dismiss them. But that still leaves the question, why do some fall from high estate and others rise? The "decline and fall" of Spain is like that of Rome: it poses the fascinating problem of success vs. failure, and scholars will never get tired of it.

Probably the most provocative explanation is the one offered by the German social scientist Max Weber. Weber, who began as a historian of the ancient world but grew into a wonder of diversified social science, published in 1904–05 one of the most influential and provocative essays ever written: "The Protestant Ethic and the Spirit of Capitalism." His thesis: that Protestantism—more specifically, its Calvinist branches—promoted the rise of modern capitalism, that is, the industrial capitalism that he knew from his native Germany. Protestantism did this, he said, not by easing or abolishing those aspects of the Roman faith that had deterred or hindered free economic activity (the prohibition of usury, for example); nor by encouraging, let alone inventing, the pursuit of wealth; but by defining and sanctioning an ethic of everyday behavior that conduced to business success.

Calvinistic Protestantism, said Weber, did this initially by affirming the doctrine of predestination. This held that one could not gain salvation by faith or deeds; that question had been decided for everyone from the beginning of time, and nothing could alter one's fate.

Such a belief could easily have encouraged a fatalistic attitude. If behavior and faith make no difference, why not live it up? Why be good? Because, according to Calvinism, goodness was a plausible sign of election. Anyone could be chosen, but it was only reasonable to suppose that most of those chosen would show by their character and ways the quality of their souls and the nature of their destiny. This implicit reassurance was a powerful incentive to proper thoughts and behavior. As the Englishwoman Elizabeth Walker wrote her grandson in 1689, alluding to one of the less important but more important signs of grace, "All cleanly people are not good, but there are few good people but are cleanly."[12] And while hard belief in predestination did not last more than a generation or two (it is not the kind of dogma that has lasting appeal), it was eventually converted into a secular code of behavior: hard work, honesty, seriousness, the thrifty use of money and time (both lent us by God).* *"Time is short,"* admonished the Puritan divine Richard Baxter (1615–1691), "and *work is long.*"[13]

All of these values help business and capital accumulation, but Weber stressed that the good Calvinist did not aim at riches. (He might easily believe, however, that honest riches are a sign of divine favor.) Europe did not have to wait for the Protestant Reformation to find people who wanted to be rich. Weber's point is that Protestantism produced a new kind of businessman, a different kind of person, one who aimed to live and work a certain way. It was the *way* that mattered, and riches were at best a by-product.

A good Calvinist would say, that was what was wrong with Spain: easy riches, unearned wealth. Compare the Protestant and Catholic

---

* The best analysis of the Weberian model is still Talcott Parsons's *Structure of Social Action*. Elaborating the paradigm, Parsons divides action into three categories: rational (appropriate to ends), irrational (unrelated to ends), and nonrational (action as an end in itself). A good example of this last: "Father, I cannot tell a lie; it was I cut down the cherry tree." Weber's Calvinist ethic falls in the realm of the nonrational.

attitudes toward gambling in the early modern period. Both condemned it, but Catholics condemned it because one might (would) lose, and no responsible person would jeopardize his well-being and that of others in that manner. The Protestants, on the other hand, condemned it because one might win, and that would be bad for character. It was only much later that the Protestant ethic degenerated into a set of maxims for material success and smug, smarmy sermons on the virtues of wealth.

The Weber thesis gave rise to all manner of rebuttal. Roman Catholics did not know whether to accept it as praise or denounce it as criticism. Materialist historians rejected the notion that abstractions such as values and attitudes, let alone those inspired by religion, could motivate and shape the mode of production. This refusal was the stronger for Max Weber's explicit and sacrilegious intention to rebut Marx on this score. To get cart and horse in proper order, some argued that the rise of capitalism had generated Protestantism; or that Protestantism appealed to the kinds of people—tradesmen, craftsmen—whose personal values already led to hard work and business success.[14]

In an influential study called *Religion and the Rise of Capitalism,* the English social historian R. H. ("Harry") Tawney rejected the link between Protestantism and economic growth. The English economy, he said, took off in the sixteenth century only when religious influence diminished, to be replaced by secular attitudes. One thing he did grant to the Puritan-Dissenter ethic: it shielded tradesmen and manufacturers against the slings and arrows of genteel contempt. It gave them a sense of dignity and righteousness, armor in a world of anticommercial prejudices. And so, not yielding to the temptation of a higher leisure, good Calvinists kept at their task from generation to generation, accumulating wealth and experience along the way.[15]

The same kind of controversy has swirled around the derivative thesis of the sociologist Robert K. Merton, who argued that there was a direct link between Protestantism and the rise of modern science. He was not the first to make this point. In the nineteenth century Alphonse de Candolle, from a Huguenot family of Geneva, counted that of ninety-two foreign members elected to the French Académie des Sciences in the period 1666–1866, some seventy-one were Protestant, sixteen Catholic, and the remaining five Jewish or of indeterminate religious affiliation—this from a population pool outside of France of 107 million Catholics, 68 million Protestants. A similar count of foreign fellows of the Royal Society in London in 1829 and 1869 showed equal numbers of Catholics and Protestants out of a pool in which

Catholics outnumbered Protestants by more than three to one.[16]

Much of this no doubt reflected the greater access of Catholics in Catholic countries to the older liberal professions and the governing bureaucracy, and hence their preference for a different kind of schooling. But much was dictated by the fears of the clerical hierarchy, by their distaste for the findings and paradigms of a science that negated religious doctrine. As the English chemist and Unitarian minister Joseph Priestley put it, the pope, in patronizing science, "was cherishing an enemy in disguise," for he had "reason to tremble even at an air pump, or an electrical machine."[17]

Against all of this, one scholar has categorically asserted that there is no empirical basis for the alleged link;[18] that Weber's data on differential education of Catholics and Protestants in the Germany of the turn of the century (Protestants more inclined to commercial and scientific programs) are badly calculated; that Catholic and non-Calvinist businessmen did as well as Weber's ideal Calvinist types; that one might as well explain the differences between northern and southern Europe by geography or race; and that Max Weber is like the tailors who clothed the Chinese emperor, and his Protestant connection much ado about nothing.

Indeed, it is fair to say that most historians today would look upon the Weber thesis as implausible and unacceptable: it had its moment and it is gone.

I do not agree. Not on the empirical level, where records show that Protestant merchants and manufacturers played a leading role in trade, banking, and industry.[19] In manufacturing centers (*fabriques*) in France and western Germany, Protestants were typically the employers, Catholics the employed. In Switzerland, the Protestant cantons were the centers of export manufacturing industry (watches, machinery, textiles); the Catholic ones were primarily agricultural. In England, which by the end of the sixteenth century was overwhelmingly Protestant, the Dissenters (read Calvinists) were disproportionately active and influential in the factories and forges of the nascent Industrial Revolution.

Nor on the theoretical. The heart of the matter lay indeed in the making of a new kind of man—rational, ordered, diligent, productive. These virtues, while not new, were hardly commonplace. Protestantism generalized them among its adherents, who judged one another by conformity to these standards. This is a story in itself, one that Weber did surprisingly little with: the role of group pressure and mutual scrutiny in assuring performance—everybody looking at everyone else and minding one another's business.

Two special characteristics of the Protestants reflect and confirm this link. The first was stress on instruction and literacy, for girls as well as boys. This was a by-product of Bible reading. Good Protestants were expected to read the holy scriptures for themselves. (By way of contrast, Catholics were catechized but did not have to read, and they were explicitly discouraged from reading the Bible.) The result: greater literacy and a larger pool of candidates for advanced schooling; also greater assurance of continuity of literacy from generation to generation. *Literate mothers matter.*

The second was the importance accorded to time. Here we have what the sociologist would call unobtrusive evidence: the making and buying of clocks and watches. Even in Catholic areas such as France and Bavaria, most clockmakers were Protestant; and the use of these instruments of time measurement and their diffusion to rural areas was far more advanced in Britain and Holland than in Catholic countries.[20] Nothing testifies so much as time sensibility to the "urbanization" of rural society, with all that that implies for rapid diffusion of values and tastes.

This is not to say that Weber's "ideal type" of capitalist could be found only among Calvinists and their later sectarian avatars. People of all faiths and no faith can grow up to be rational, diligent, orderly, productive, clean, and humorless. Nor do they have to be businessmen. One can show and profit by these qualities in all walks of life. Weber's argument, as I see it, is that in that place and time (northern Europe, sixteenth to eighteenth centuries), religion encouraged the appearance in numbers of a personality type that had been exceptional and adventitious before; and that this type created a new economy (a new mode of production) that we know as (industrial) capitalism.

Add to this the growing need for fixed capital (equipment and plant) in the industrial sector. This made continuity crucial—for the sake of continued maintenance and improvement and the accumulation of knowledge and experience. These manufacturing enterprises were very different in this regard from mercantile ones, which often took the form of ad hoc mobilizations of capital and labor, brought together for a voyage or venture and subsequently dissolved. (Recall that the English East India Company operated in this way in the early years, although there too it was soon apparent that a continuing mobilization would be necessary.)

For these requirements of a new kind of economy, the Weberian entrepreneur was specially suited by temperament and habit; and here the Tawney emphasis on the link between self-respect and continuity is especially pertinent. It is no coincidence that the French crown, always ready and willing to honor socially ambitious bourgeois (typically men of law) with patents of nobility—for a price, of course—began in the seventeenth century to permit noblemen to engage in wholesale (as opposed to retail) trade; and in the eighteenth century to impose on aspirants from industry a condition of continuity. The newly ennobled *négociant* or *fabricant* was required to remain "in trade"—a condition that would once have been perceived as inherently *déshonorante*, incompatible with such exalted status.[21] The problem, as a good Calvinist would have seen it, was that honors and pretensions ill became men of the countinghouse and *fabrique*. They worked better and harder dressed in dark woolen cloth, without silk, lace, and wig.

However important this proliferation of a new business breed, it was only one aspect of shifting economic power and wealth from South to North. Not only money moved, but knowledge as well; and it was knowledge, specifically scientific knowledge, that dictated economic possibilities. In the centuries before the Reformation, southern Europe was a center of learning and intellectual inquiry: Spain and Portugal, because they were on the frontier of Christian and Islamic civilization and had the benefit of Jewish intermediaries; and Italy, which had its own contacts. Spain and Portugal lost out early, because religious passion and military crusade drove away the outsiders (Jews and then the *conversos*) and discouraged the pursuit of the strange and potentially heretical; but Italy continued to produce some of Europe's leading mathematicians and scientists. It was not an accident that the first learned society (the Accadémia dei Lincei, Rome, 1603) was founded there.*

The Protestant Reformation, however, changed the rules. It gave a big boost to literacy, spawned dissents and heresies, and promoted the skepticism and refusal of authority that is at the heart of the scientific endeavor. The Catholic countries, instead of meeting the challenge, responded by closure and censure. The reaction in the Habsburg dominions, which included the Low Countries, followed hard on the heels of Luther's denunciation. The presence there of Marrano refugees, feared and hated as enemies of the true Church and accused of deliberately propagating the new doctrines, aggravated the hysteria.

A rain of interdictions followed (from 1521 on), not only of publishing but of reading heresy, in any language. The Spanish authorities,

---

* Lincei = lynxes. The animal was chosen for its reputedly keen sight.

both lay and clerical, viewed Lutherans (all Protestants were then seen as Lutherans), not as dissenters, but as non-Christians, like Jews and Muslims enemies of the faith.[22] Any thoughts of ending the Inquisition were shelved, and Church and civil authorities joined to control thought, knowledge, and belief. In 1558, the death penalty was introduced for importing foreign books without permission and for unlicensed printing. Universities reduced to centers of indoctrination; unorthodox and dangerous books were placed on an *Index Librorum Prohibitorum* (1557 in Rome, 1559 in Spain), and safe books appeared with an official *imprimatur* ("let it be printed"). Among the books on the Spanish list: scientific works banned because their authors were Protestant. Despite smuggling, hazardous to the health, the diffusion of new ideas to society at large slowed to a trickle. (Recall the book review and purge at the beginning of *Don Quixote*. The point is not only the role of whim, but the absurd reasons—the trivia that brought risk in a fantasy-ridden, knowledge-starved society.)

Nor were Spaniards allowed to study abroad, lest they ingest subversive doctrine. That same year (1559), the crown forbade attendance at foreign universities except for such safe centers as Rome, Bologna, and Naples. The effect was drastic. Spanish students had long gone to the University of Montpellier for medical training; they just about stopped going—248 students from 1510 to 1559; 12 from 1560 to 1599.[23] (One wonders about those dozen mavericks.) Subversive scientists were silenced and forced to denounce themselves. Regimes that exercise thought control and enforce orthodoxy are never satisfied with prohibitions and punishments. The guilty must confess and repent—both for their own and for others' salvation.

Persecution led to an interminable "witch hunt," complete with paid snitches, prying neighbors, and a racist blood mania *(limpieza de sangre)*. Judaizing conversos were caught by telltale vestiges of Mosaic practice: refusal of pork, fresh linen on Friday, an overheard prayer, irregular church attendance, a misplaced word. Cleanliness especially was cause for suspicion, and bathing was seen as evidence of apostasy, for Marranos and Moriscos alike. "The phrase 'the accused was known to take baths . . . ' is a common one in the records of the Inquisition."[24] Inherited dirt: clean people don't have to wash. In all this, the Spanish and Portuguese demeaned and diminished themselves. Intolerance can harm the persecutor more than the victim.

So Iberia and indeed Mediterranean Europe as a whole missed the train of the so-called scientific revolution. In the 1680s Juan de Cabriada, a Valencian physician, was conducting a running war with doctors in Madrid, trying vainly to persuade them to accept Harvey's discovery of the circulation of the blood in the face of antique Galenist tradition. What, he asked, was wrong with Spain? It is "as if we were Indians, always the last" to learn of new knowledge.[25]

The British historian Hugh Trevor-Roper has argued that this reactionary, anti-Protestant backlash, more than Protestantism itself, sealed the fate of southern Europe for the next three hundred years.[26] Such retreat was neither predestined nor required by doctrine. But this path once taken, the Church, repository and guardian of truth, found it hard to admit error and change course. How hard? One hears nowadays that Rome has finally, almost, rehabilitated Galileo after almost four hundred years. That's how hard.

⁊ ⁏

## The Condemnation of Galileo

Galileo Galilei was not a saint, but he was a genius and a treasure— for Florence, Italy, Europe, and the world. He was a pioneer of experimental science, a keen observer (as befit a member of the Academy of Lynxes), a sharp thinker, and a powerful polemicist and debater. Yet in 1633 he was condemned by the Roman Church for contumacy and heresy: "The opinion that the Sun is at the center of the world and immobile is absurd, false in philosophy, and formally heretical, because it is expressly contrary to Holy Scripture."

(Galileo was not the first; or the last. Equally momentous, if less remembered, was the burning in Rome in February 1600 of Giordano Bruno, ex-Dominican, a philosopher whose imaginary concept of the universe came far closer to what we now think than that of Copernicus or Galileo: infinite space, billions of burning stars, rotating earth revolving around the sun, matter composed of atoms, and so on. All heresies, linked to mysteries and magic. In effect, by burning Bruno, the Church proclaimed its intention of taking science and imagination in hand and leashing them to Rome.[27] But while Galileo worked and spoke, freedom still had room.)

That was the sentence. The confession of error by Galileo was some fourteen times as long. The point was not to pronounce dogma, but to denounce heresy and to display for all, in great detail, the admission of the sinner, his recognition and acceptance of the authority of the Holy Church, and his sincere promise of repentance.

Never again. That is the nature of thought control in infallible systems: these aim not so much to convict as to convince—both the guilty one and all other members of the system.

Why the Church chose to make an issue of geocentrism remains a puzzle. Nothing in holy scripture seems to require such belief. To be sure, the Bible does use images of the sun crossing the sky or stopping in its course, but it is not hard to treat those as expressions, sometimes metaphorical, of what the eye on earth perceives. The Roman Curia could have ignored the matter without rending the tissue of faith and obedience. Yet any church is tempted to rest its authority on doctrine and dogma, for these are the sign and instrument of rule, especially in troublous times.

Meanwhile Galileo, for reasons as much of temperament as of intellectual integrity, enjoyed doing battle. A redoubtable debater, he would not suffer fools and found them aplenty in clerical circles. This was a dangerous game in a Roman world of virtually unlimited authority, intrigue and ambition, slander and treachery. Byzantium on the Tiber: nothing in Rome made contenders happier than the early demise of the Holy Father, for every change of pope entailed a reshuffling of power and place. Here today, gone tomorrow; friend now, foe later. Galileo could count on no one.

Even worse, perhaps, Galileo's response to hints and warnings of disapproval was to "go public"—to publish in Italian rather than in Latin—and thereby go over the head of the insiders and appeal to a larger audience. In effect he was popularizing (vulgarizing) heresy, and that was intolerable.*

So Galileo confessed; and although he is said to have made one last, stubborn demurrer ( *"Eppure si muove"* [Say what you will, it moves]), he went into a stultifying house arrest that ended his career as an effective, innovating scientist. And that was a catastrophic loss to Italian science, which, so long as the great man worked and thrived, had stood up to the growing constraint implicit in the Counter-Reformation.

And what about science in other lands? In the Protestant countries, the condemnation meant little. If anything, it confirmed

---

* Compare the long-standing Italian rule about publication of pornography: so long as the book was costly and appeared in a limited edition, it was tolerable; but no cheap editions could be allowed, for fear of corrupting those simple folk who did not have the cultural resources to resist temptation and sin. On the Church's fear of the vernacular, cf. the troubles of Giambattista della Porta in the 1580s. Eamon, "From the Secrets of Nature," p. 361, n. 41.

these rebels against Church authority in their scorn for the superstitions of Rome. Father Gassendi, professor at Aix-en-Provence and excellent observer of astronomical phenomena, went to Holland in 1632 and wrote back to a French colleague about attitudes toward the Copernican paradigm: "All those people there are for it."[28] That may have been an exaggeration, but it captures the contrast with what he had known at home. Holland, England, and the Protestant countries in general were a different state of mind.

In France, the savants swung between sense and sensibility, integrity and obedience. The same Gassendi, writing to Galileo, pleaded with him to make peace with Rome and his conscience—and both at the same time: "I am in the greatest anxiety about the fate that awaits you, O you, the great glory of the century! If the Holy See has decided something against your opinion, bear with it as suits a wise man. Let it suffice you to live with the conviction that you have sought only the truth."[29]

Only the truth. But what was truth? Within the knowledge available at that time, Copernicus alone left much to be desired. The Copernican-Keplerian paradigm fitted the observations better, but did that prove that the earth went around the sun? Better and safer to stick to experiment and not ask why. Here lay a way of continuing observation while denying consequences, and this evasion found a welcome with some of the leading French scientists of the day.* Thus Mersenne, prime communicator among European savants, wrote in 1634 that everything anyone had said about the movement of the earth did not prove the point; and he dropped plans to do a book on heliocentrism. Gassendi, the same. Descartes, the same. The great Descartes came up with his own twist: the heavenly bodies were not governed in their movements by some kind of pull, an invisible, magical attraction, but by whirling pools of force that bore them along. Attraction smacked of superstition, whereas whirlpools were somehow scientific. In the event, said Descartes, the earth was carried in its field of force like a passenger on a boat. The boat moved, but the passenger did not. So the earth did not move. *Q.E.D.*

* As it did in Italy. Compare the short-lived Accadémia del Cimento, organized and patronized by Duke Leopold of Tuscany, summoned at his beck and call and dissolved after his departure for Rome to pursue higher callings. No intellectual autonomy: the members reported on their experiments, but that was all—science, in other words, without *scientia*.

Even with such cleverness, Descartes found it hard to live in a France of Jesuitical subtleties. He moved to Holland and left no forwarding address, except with Mersenne. Meanwhile the French slowly, reluctantly, came around to his cosmology, and once there, clung to the Cartesian system by way of refusing Newtonian theories of motion and gravity. Better push than pull. For Newton was English, and the French, then as now, found it hard to learn from others *(nous n'avons pas de leçons à recevoir . . . )*, especially from their traditional enemy of Agincourt and Crécy. An outrageous instance of this intellectual chauvinism came in the 1980s, when French health authorities insisted on distributing contaminated blood rather than purchase American tests and decontaminating equipment. (The United States has replaced Britain as the Gallic *bête noire,* the worse for having helped in two world wars.) French authorities thereby condemned hundreds, maybe thousands, to AIDS and death.

When the French finally did reconcile themselves to Newtonian mathematics and physics, they did very well. They had talent and genius in abundance. But they lost several generations to pride.

~ ~

## The Tenacity of Intolerance and Prejudice[30]

Fifteenth-century Sicily had the misfortune to owe allegiance to the crown of Castile; so when Ferdinand and Isabella in 1492 ordered the expulsion or conversion of the Jews of Spain, Sicily had to go along. Not that the island lacked anti-Jewish sentiment, as a number of earlier pogroms showed. But Jews had lived there for centuries and played a disproportionate role in Sicily's trade, to say nothing of their place as doctors and apothecaries. The Sicilian viceroy dithered, reluctant to issue the fateful decree; but a series of orders prepared the way by prohibiting Jews from selling their assets, compelling them to pay all debts outstanding, and—most ominous—barring them from bearing arms.

One need not go into detail. The Jews of the island won a short delay; they were also granted benevolent permission to take with them the clothes on their back, a mattress, a wool or serge blanket, a pair of sheets, and some small change, plus some food for the way.

We are told that many Sicilians were sorry to see them go. With reason. What was left of trade shrank almost to nothing; houses and even neighborhoods were left desolate; and we must assume that some people had the decency to feel ashamed.

Much later, toward the end of the seventeenth century, some Sicilians urged the king to do something to promote trade. Charles II granted Messina the privilege of a free port and gave Jews the right to trade there—on condition that they sleep outside the city and wear a distinctive sign on their clothing. Such ambiguous hospitality did not encourage Jews to come, so in 1728 the Jews were granted the right to trade anywhere on the island, to reside in Messina, to have a synagogue and cemetery, to own and dispose of property. Even this did not help, so in 1740 the king explicitly invited the Jews to return. A number of families accepted, but found themselves mistreated by a prejudiced populace. Then it happened that the queen had not succeeded in bearing a male heir to the throne, and the royal couple were persuaded by clerics that they would not have a son so long as they allowed the Jews to stay. So, after seven years, another expulsion.

Intolerance, superstition, ignorance—these are easier to acquire and cultivate than to uproot. The same iniquities and vices, perpetrated long ago by foreign (Spanish) rulers, have contributed to this day to Sicily's persistent backwardness.

# ~ 13 ~

# The Nature of
# Industrial Revolution

In the eighteenth century, a series of inventions transformed the British cotton manufacture and gave birth to a new mode of production—the factory system.* At the same time, other branches of industry made comparable and often related advances, and all of these together, mutually reinforcing, drove further gains on an ever-widening front. The abundance and variety of these innovations almost defy compilation, but they fall under three principles: (1) the substitution of machines—rapid, regular, precise, tireless—for human skill and effort; (2) the substitution of inanimate for animate sources of power, in particular, the invention of engines for converting heat into work, thereby opening an almost unlimited supply of energy; and (3) the use of new and far more abundant raw materials, in particular, the substitution of mineral, and eventually artificial, materials for vegetable or animal substances.

These substitutions made the Industrial Revolution. They yielded a rapid rise in productivity and, with it, in income per head. This growth,

---

* By *factory* is meant a unified unit of production (workers brought together under supervision), using a central, typically inanimate source of power. Without the central power, we have a *manufactory*.

moreover, was self-sustaining. In ages past, better living standards had always been followed by a rise in population that eventually consumed the gains. Now, for the first time in history, both the economy and knowledge were growing fast enough to generate a continuing flow of improvements. Gone, Malthus's positive checks and the stagnationist predictions of the "dismal science"; instead, one had an age of promise and great expectations. The Industrial Revolution also transformed the balance of political power—within nations, between nations, and between civilizations; revolutionized the social order; and as much changed ways of thinking as ways of doing.

The word "revolution" has many faces. It conjures up visions of quick, even brutal or violent change. It can also mean fundamental or profound transformation. For some, it has progressive connotations (in the political sense): revolutions are good, and the very notion of a reactionary revolution, one that turns the clock back, is seen as a contradiction in terms. Others see revolutions as intrinsically destructive of things of value, hence bad.

All of these and other meanings hang on a word that once meant simply a turning, in the literal sense. Let me be clear, then, about the way I use the term here. I am using it in its oldest metaphorical sense, to denote an "instance of great change or alteration in affairs or some particular thing"—a sense that goes back to the 1400s and antedates by a century and a half the use of "revolution" to denote abrupt political change.[1] It is in this sense that knowing students of the Industrial Revolution have always used it, just as others speak of a medieval "commercial revolution" or a seventeenth-century "scientific revolution" or a twentieth-century "sexual revolution."

The emphasis, then, is on deep rather than fast. It will surprise no one that the extraordinary technological advances of the great Industrial Revolution (with capital I and capital R) were not achieved overnight. Few inventions spring mature into the world. On the contrary: it takes a lot of small and large improvements to turn an idea into a technique.

Take steampower. The first device to use steam to create a vacuum and work a pump was patented in England by Thomas Savery in 1698; the first steam engine proper (with piston) by Thomas Newcomen in 1705. Newcomen's atmospheric engine (so called becuase it relied simply on atmospheric pressure) in turn was grossly wasteful of energy because the cylinder cooled and had to be reheated with every stroke. The machine therefore worked best pumping water out of coal mines, where fuel was almost a free good.

A long time—sixty years—passed before James Watt invented an engine with separate condenser (1768) whose fuel efficiency was good enough to make steam profitable away from the mines, in the new industrial cities; and it took another fifteen years to adapt the machine to rotary motion, so that it could drive the wheels of industry. In between, engineers and mechanics had to solve an infinitude of small and large problems of manufacture and maintenance. The task, for example, of making cylinders of smooth and circular cross section, so that the piston would run tight and air not leak to the vacuum side, required care, patience, and ingenuity.* In matters of fuel economy, every shortcoming cost, and good enough was not good enough.

That was not all. Another line remained to be explored: high-pressure engines (more than atmospheric), which could be built more compact and used to drive ships and land vehicles. This took another quarter century. Such uses put a premium on fuel economy: space was limited, and one wanted room for cargo rather than for coal. The answer was found in compounding—the use of high-pressure steam to drive two or more pistons successively; the steam, having done its work in a high-pressure cylinder, expanded further in a larger, lower-pressure cylinder. The principle was the same as that developed in the Middle Ages for squeezing energy out of falling water by driving a series of wheels. Compounding went back to J. C. Hornblower (1781) and Arthur Woolf (1804); but it did not come into its own until the 1850s, when it was introduced into marine engines and contributed mightily to oceanic trade.

Nor was that the end of it. The size and power of steam engines were limited by the piston's inertia. Driving back and forth, it required enormous energy to reverse direction. The solution was found (Charles A. Parsons, 1884) in converting from reciprocating to rotary motion, by replacing the piston with a steam turbine. These were introduced into central power plants at the very end of the nineteenth century; into

---

* The technique that worked for boilers (roll up a sheet, weld the seams, and cap top and bottom) would not work for an engine cylinder—too much leakage. The new method, which consisted in boring a solid casting, was the invention of John Wilkinson, c. 1776, who learned by boring cannon (patent of 1774). A year later, Wilkinson was using the steam engine to raise a 60-pound stamping hammer to forge heavy pieces. By 1783, he was up to 7.5 tons. With this he was soon building rolling mills, coining presses, drawing benches (for wire manufacture), and similar heavy machinery. "By a strange caprice of public fancy," writes Usher, "this grim and unattractive character has never secured the fame he deserves as one of the pioneers in the development of the heavy-metal trades." *History of Mechanical Inventions,* p. 372. Vulcan wasn't pretty either.

ships shortly after. In all, steam engine development took two hundred years.*

Meanwhile, waterpower, itself much improved (breast wheel [John Smeaton, 1750s] and turbine [Benoît Fourneyron, 1827]), remained a major component of manufacturing industry, as it had been since the Middle Ages.[2]

Similarly the first successful coke smelt of iron, by Abraham Darby at Coalbrookdale, went back to 1709. (I have stood inside the abandoned blast furnace at Coalbrookdale, there among the pitted bricks where the fire burned and the ore melted, and thought myself inside the womb of the Industrial Revolution. It is now part of an industrial museum, and curious visitors can look at it from outside.) But this achievement, though carefully studied and prepared, was in effect a lucky strike: Darby's coal was fortuitously suitable.[3] Others had less success, and they, as well as Darby, had to confine use of coke-smelted pig iron to castings. It took some forty years to resolve the difficulties, and coke smelting took off only at midcentury.

This technology, moreover, had serious limitations. Cast iron suited the manufacture of pots and pans, firebacks, pipes, and similar unstressed objects, but a machine technology cannot be based on castings. Moving parts require the resilience and elasticity of wrought iron (or steel) and must be shaped (forged or machined) more exactly than casting can do.† A half century and much experiment went by before ironmasters could make coke-smelted pig suited to further refining

---

* The latter part of the nineteenth century saw substantial improvement in the steam engine thanks to scientific advances in thermodynamics. Where before technology had led science in this area, now science led and gave the steam engine a new lease on life.

On the logistic (lazy-S) curve of possibilities implicit in a given technological sequence—slow gains during the experimental preparatory stage, followed by rapid advance that eventually slows down as possibilities are exhausted—see the classic essay of Simon Kuznets, "Retardation of Industrial Growth."

† Pig (cast) iron is high in carbon content (over 4 percent). It is very hard, but will crack or break under shock. It cannot be machined, which is why it is cast, that is, poured into molds to cool to shape. Wrought iron can be hammered, drilled, and otherwise worked. It will not break under shock and is highly resistant to corrosion, which makes it ideal for balcony railings and other open-air uses (cf. the Eiffel Tower). To get from pig to wrought iron, most of the carbon has to be burned off, leaving 1 percent or less. Wrought iron has long since been replaced by steel (1 to 3 percent carbon), which combines the virtues of both cast and wrought iron, that is, hardness with malleability; as a result, wrought iron is just about unobtainable today except as scrap. The difficulty with the early coke-blast iron was that, on refining, it yielded an iron that was red-short, that is, brittle when hot. Until that problem was solved, wrought iron was made using charcoal-blast pig.

and before refiners had techniques to deal with coke-smelted pig (Henry Cort, patents of 1783 and 1784). Cheap steel (Henry Bessemer, 1856) took another three quarters of a century. Cheap steel transformed industry and transportation. Where once this costly metal had been reserved for small uses—arms, razors, springs, files—it could now be used to make rails and build ships. Steel rails lasted longer, carried more; steel ships had thinner skins and carried more.

Moreover, if origins we seek, we can push both these technical sequences back to the sixteenth century, to the precocious reliance of English industry on coal as fuel and raw material, in glassmaking, brewing, dyeing, brick- and tilemaking, smithing and metallurgy. One scholar has termed this shift to fossil fuel, far earlier than in other European countries, a "first industrial revolution."[4]

Next, powered machinery. The machine itself is simply an articulated device to move a tool (or tools) in such wise as to do the work of the hand. Its purpose may be to enhance the force and speed of the operator as with a printing press, a drill press, or a spinning wheel. Or it may channel its tool so as to perform uniform, repetitive motions, as in a clock. Or it may align a battery of tools so as to multiply the work performed by a single motion. So long as machines are hand-operated, it is fairly easy to respond to the inevitable hitches and glitches: the worker has only to stop the action by ceasing to wind the crank or yank the lever. Power drive changes everything.*

The Middle Ages, we saw, were already familiar with a wide variety of machines—for grinding corn or malt, shaping metals, spinning yarn, fulling cloth, scrubbing fabrics, blowing furnaces. Many of these were power-driven, typically by water wheels. In the centuries that followed (1500– ), these devices proliferated, for the principles of mechanics were widely applicable. In textiles, some of the important innovations were the knitting frame, the "Dutch" or "engine" loom, the ribbon loom; also powered machines for throwing silk. But the most potent advances, as is often the case, were the most banal:

—the introduction of the foot treadle to drive the spinning wheel, thereby freeing the operative's hands to manipulate the thread and deal with winding; or, for the loom, to work the headles while throwing the shuttle;

---

* Power machinery was inevitably a new source of industrial accidents. On problems in the sugar mills and the greater safety of hand-operated or animal-driven devices, see Schwartz, *Sugar Plantations*, pp. 143–44. Horses were more dangerous than mules or oxen: " . . . the screams of the unfortunate slave caused the horses to run faster."

—the invention of the flyer (the Saxon wheel), which added twist by winding the yarn at the same time as it turned the spindle, but at a different speed;

—the achievement of unidirectional, continuous spinning and reeling.

These changes together quadrupled or better the spinner's productivity.[5]

The next step was to mechanize spinning by somehow replicating the gestures of the hand spinner. This required simplifying by dividing: breaking up the task into a succession of repeatable processes. That seems logical enough, but it was not easy. Not until inventors applied their devices to a tough vegetable fiber, cotton, was success achieved. That took decades of trial and error, from the 1730s to the 1760s. When power spinning came to cotton, it turned industry upside down.

In metallurgy, big gains came from substituting rotary for reciprocating motion: making sheet metal by rolling instead of pounding; making wire by drawing through a sequence of ever narrower holes; making holes by drilling instead of punching; planing and shaping by lathe rather than by chisel and hammer. Most important was the growing recourse to precision gauging and fixed settings. Here the clock- and watchmakers and instrument makers gave the lead. They were working smaller pieces and could more easily shape them to the high standards required for accuracy with special-purpose tools such as wheel dividers and tooth-cutters. These devices in turn, along with similar tools devised by machinists, could then be adapted to work in larger format, and it is no accident that cotton manufacturers, when looking for skilled craftsmen to build and maintain machines, advertised for clockmakers; or that the wheel trains of these machines were known as "clockwork." The repetitious work of these machines suggested in turn the first experiments in mass production based on interchangeable parts (clocks, guns, gun carriages, pulley blocks, locks, hardware, furniture).

All these gains, plus the invention of machines to build machines, came together in the last third of the eighteenth century—a period of contagious novelty. Some of this merging stream of innovation may have been a lucky harvest. But no. Innovation was catching because the principles that underlay a given technique could take many forms, find many uses. If one could bore cannon, one could bore the cylinders of steam engines. If one could print fabrics by means of cylinders (as against the much slower block printing), one could also print wallpaper that way; or print word text far faster than by the up-and-down strokes of a press and turn out penny tabloids and cheap novels by the tens and hundreds of thousands. Similarly, a modified cotton-spinning machine could spin wool and flax. Indeed, contemporaries argued that the mechanization of cotton manufacture forced these other branches to modernize:

> . . . had not the genius of Hargreaves and Arkwright changed entirely the modes of carding and spinning cotton, the woollen manufacture would probably have remained at this day what it was in the earliest ages. . . . That it would have been better for general society if it had so remained, we readily admit; but after the improved modes of working cotton were discovered, this was impossible.[6]

And on and on, into a brave and not-so-brave world of higher incomes and cheaper commodities, unheard-of devices and materials, insatiable appetites. New, new, new. Money, money, money. As Dr. (Samuel) Johnson, more prescient than his contemporaries, put it, "all the business of the world is to be done in a new way."[7] The world had slipped its moorings.

Can one put dates to this revolution? Not easily, because of the decades of experiment that precede a given innovation and the long run of improvement that follows. Where is beginning and where end? The core of the larger process—mechanization of industry and the adoption of the factory—lies, however, in the story of the textile manufacture.* Rapid change there began with the spinning jenny of James Hargreaves (c. 1766), followed by Thomas Arkwright's water frame (1769) and Samuel Crompton's mule (1779), so called because it was a cross between the jenny and the water frame. With the mule, one could spin fine counts as well as coarse, better and cheaper than any hand spinner.

---

* Core of the process: John Hicks, *A Theory of Economic History*, p. 147, and Carlo Cipolla, *Before the Industrial Revolution*, p. 291, would not agree. Hicks saw the early cotton machinery as "an appendage to the evolution of the old industry" rather than as the beginning of a new one. He thought that something like this might well have occurred in fifteenth-century Florence had waterpower been available (but Italy does have waterpower). "There might have been no Crompton and Arkwright, and still there would have been an Industrial Revolution." "Iron and coal," writes Cipolla, "much more than cotton stand as critical factors in the origins of the Industrial Revolution." Perhaps; it is not easy to order improvements by impact and significance. But I would still give pride of place to mechanization as a general phenomenon susceptible of the widest application and to the organization of work under supervision and discipline (the factory system).

Then in 1787 Edmund Cartwright built the first successful power loom, which gradually transformed weaving, first of coarse yarn, which stood up better to the to-and-fro of the shuttle, then of fine; and in 1830 Richard Roberts, an experienced machine builder, devised—in response to employer demand—a "self-acting" mule to free spinning from dependence on the strength and special skill of an indocile labor aristocracy. (The self-actor worked, but the aristocracy remained.)

This sequence of inventions took some sixty years and dominated completely the older technology—unlike the steam engine, which long shared the field with waterpower.* The new technique yielded a sharp fall in costs and prices, and a rapid increase in cotton output and consumption.[8] On this basis, the British Industrial Revolution ran about a century, from say 1770 to 1870, "the entire interval between the old order and the establishment of a fairly stable relationship of the different aspects of industry under the new order."[9]

Other specialists have adopted slightly different periodizations.[10] Whatever; we are talking about a process that took a century, give or take a generation. That may seem slow for something called a revolution, but economic time runs slower than political. The great economic revolutions of the past had taken far longer.

Even when one takes account of the quantitative data put forward by the practitioners of the self-proclaimed New Economic History, one still has a break in the trend of growth around 1760–70; unprecedented rates of increase; above all, the beginnings of a profound transformation of the mode of production. Technology matters. The aggregate figures show this, and elementary logic makes it clear. If one takes even the lowest estimates of increase for the latter part of the eighteenth century and extrapolates *backward,* one quickly arrives at levels of income insufficient to support life. So something had changed.

The question remains why overall growth was not faster. It is an anachronistic question that reflects the expectations of more recent

---

* One should distinguish here between the spinning and weaving sectors of the industry. In cotton spinning, machinery simply wiped out the older hand techniques. Even the Indian spinner, working for a small fraction of English wages, had to give up in the face of machine-spun yarn. In weaving, however, the power loom took decades to reach the point where it could deal with the more delicate, high-count yarn. So the handloom weavers hung on grimly, forever reducing expectations and standard of living in the effort to stay out of the mills, until death and old age eliminated them. By the second half of the nineteenth century, even those manufacturers who had special reasons to hire handloom weavers could no longer find them. Young persons were not ready to go into a dying trade.

times—of an era of quicker, more potent innovation and leapfrog catch-up. Even so, the question is worth posing. The answer is that the Industrial Revolution was uneven and protracted in its effects; that it started and flourished in some branches before others; that it left behind and even destroyed old trades while building new; that it did not, could not, replace older technologies overnight. (Even the almighty computer has not eliminated the typewriter, let alone pen-and-paper.)[11] This is why estimates for growth in those years are so sensitive to weights: give more importance to cotton and iron, and growth seems faster; give less, and it slows down. All of this, of course, was obvious to such earlier students of technological change as A. P. Usher and J. H. Clapham. The "new economic historians" who have stressed the theme of continuity have essentially revived their work without citing them, perhaps without knowing them.*

Many of the anti-Revolutionists have also committed the sin of either–or. Their point about continuity is well taken. History abhors leaps, and large changes and economic revolutions do not come out of the blue. They are invariably well and long prepared.[12] But continuity does not exclude change, even drastic change. One true believer in the cogency of economic theory and cliometrics notes that British income per head doubled between 1780 and 1860, and then multiplied by six times between 1860 and 1990 and acknowledges that we have more here than a simple continuation of older trends: "The first eighty years of growth were astonishing enough, but they were merely a prelude."[13] To which I would add that Britain was not the most impressive performer over this long period.

The consequence of these advances was a growing gap between modern industrial countries and laggards, between rich and poor. In Europe to begin with: in 1750, the difference between western Europe (excluding Britain) and eastern in income per head was perhaps 15 percent; in 1800, little more than 20. By 1860 it was up to 64 percent; by the 1900s, almost 80 percent.[14] The same polarization, only much sharper, took place between Europe and those countries that later came to be defined as a Third World—in part because modern factory industries swallowed their old-fashioned rivals, at home and abroad.

---

* Economics is a discipline that would be a science, and as everyone knows, science marches on. So away with the monographs and articles of predecessors. Hence the paradox of a discipline that would be up to date, yet is always rediscovering yesterday's discoveries—often without realizing it.

Paradox: the Industrial Revolution brought the world closer to-gether, made it smaller and more homogenous. But the same revolu-tion fragmented the globe by estranging winners and losers. It begat multiple worlds.

≈) ⊂

## When Is a Revolution Not a Revolution?

The reliance of early students of the Industrial Revolution on the output and price data for particular industries reflected the statistical limitations of that day: that was what they had and knew to work with. The data did not let them down. They represented direct and simple returns, and where the historian had to make use of proxy measures (imports of raw cotton, for example, as stand-in for the output of cotton yarn in countries that did not grow cotton), these were good and fairly stable indicators of a narrowly defined, unambiguous reality.[15]

Beginning in the late 1950s, however, numerically minded economic historians began to construct measures of aggregate growth during the eighteenth and early nineteenth centuries. This was a natural extension of historical work on national income for more recent periods, where data were fuller and more reliable.* But as one went back in time before the systematic collection of numbers by government bureaus, such reconstructions entailed a heroic exercise of imagination and ingenuity: use and fusion of disparate figures estimated or collected at different times, for different purposes, on different bases; use of proxies justified by often arbitrary and not always specified assumptions concerning the nature of the economy; assignment of weights drawn from other contexts and periods; index problems galore; use of customary or nominal rather than market prices; interpolations and extrapolations without end, thereby smoothing and blurring breaks in trend. It will not come as a surprise, then, that these constructions have varied with

---

* The model was the work done by Simon Kuznets and colleagues at the National Bu-reau of Economic Research. After working on U.S. data, Kuznets helped advise and finance similar projects in other countries from the 1960s. The pioneering work on British industrial output went back even further, to the calculations of Walther Hoff-mann, but a fresh start began with the researches of Phyllis Deane, followed after an interval by Charles Feinstein, Nick Crafts, Knick Harley, and others.

the builder and have changed over time; that the latest estimate is
not necessarily better than the one before (the estimators would not
agree); and that the appearance of precision is not an assurance of
robustness or a predictor of durability.*

Neither is the appearance of precision an unambiguous indicator
of meaning. Believe the data; the interpretation remains a problem.
Theoretical economists have long appreciated this difficulty. Here is
one "Nobéliste" who puts the matter with disarming frankness:
"Early economists were not inundated with statistics. They were
spared the burden of statistical proof. They relied on history and on
personal observations. Now we place our trust in hard data provided
they are sanctioned by theory."[16] In the light of this principle, the
least one might expect of economic historians is that they put their
trust in "hard [read: numerical] data" provided they are sanctioned
by historical evidence. Instead, their leap to judgment often beggars
credulity.

The crux of disagreement in this instance has been what has been
presented by some as an unrevolutionary ("evolutionary")
revolution. However impressive the growth of certain branches of
production, the overall performance of the British economy (or
British industry) during the century 1760–1860 that emerges from
some recent numerical exercises has appeared modest: a few percent
per year for industry; even less for aggregate product. And if one
deflates these data for growth of population (so, income or product
per head), they reduce to 1 or 2 percent a year.[17] Given the margin
of error intrinsic to this kind of statistical manipulation, that could be
something. It could also be nothing.

But why believe the estimates? Because they are more recent?
Because the authors assure us of their reliability? The methods
employed are less than convincing. One starts with the aggregate
construct (figment) and then shoehorns the component branches to
fit. One recent exercise found that after adding up British
productivity gains in a few major branches—cotton, iron, transport,
agriculture—no room was left for further gains in the other
branches: other textiles, pottery, paper, hardware, machine building,

---

* On the weaknesses and pitfalls of these quantitative elucubrations, see Hoppit,
"Counting the Industrial Revolution," who cites (p. 189) Thomas Carlyle on the subject: "There is, unfortunately, a kind of alchemy about figures which transforms the
most dubious materials into something pure and precious; hence the price of working
with historical statistics is eternal vigilance." So, mid-nineteenth century and already
disillusioned.

clocks and watches. What to do? Simple. The author decided that most British industry "experienced low levels of labor productivity and slow productivity growth—it is possible that there was virtually no advance during 1780–1860."[18] This is history cart before horse, results before data, imagination before experience. It is also wrong.

What is more, these estimates, based as they are on assumptions of homogeneity over time—iron is iron, cotton is cotton—inevitably underestimate the gain implicit in quality improvements and new products. How can one measure the significance of a new kind of steel (crucible steel) that makes possible superior timekeepers and better files for finishing and adjusting machine parts if one is simply counting tons of steel? How appreciate the production of newspapers that sell for a penny instead of a shilling thanks to rotary power presses? How measure the value of iron ships that last longer than wooden vessels and hold considerably more cargo? How count the output of light if one calculates in terms of lamps rather than the light they give off? A recent attempt to quantify the downward bias of the aggregate statistics on the basis of the price of lumens of light suggests that in that instance the difference between real and estimated gains over two hundred years is of the order of 1,000 to 1.[19]

In the meantime, the new, quantitative economic historians ("cliometricians") have triumphantly announced the demolition of doctrine received. One economic historian has called in every direction for abandonment of the misnomer "industrial revolution," while others have begun to write histories of the period without using the dread name—a considerable inconvenience for both authors and students.[20] Some, working on the border between economic and other kinds of history or simply outside the field, have leaped to the conclusion that everyone has misread the British story. Britain, they would have us believe, never was an industrial nation (whatever that means); the most important economic developments of the eighteenth century took place in agriculture and finance, while industry's role, much exaggerated, was in fact subordinate.[21] And some have sought to argue that Britain changed little during these supposedly revolutionary years (there went a century of historiography down the drain), while others, acknowledging that growth was in fact more rapid, nevertheless stressed continuity over change. They wrote of "trend growth," or "trend acceleration," and asserted that there was no "kink" in the factitious line that traced the increase in national product or income. And when some scholars refused to adopt this new dispensation, one historian dismissed them as "a dead horse that is not altogether willing to lie down."[22]

Who says the ivory tower of scholarship is a quiet place?

⇒  ⇐

## The Advantage of
## Going Round and Round

Rotary motion's great advantage over reciprocating motion lies in its energetic efficiency: it does not require the moving part to change direction with each stroke; it continues round and round. (It has of course its own constraints, arising largely from centrifugal force, which is subject to the same laws of motion.) Everything is a function of mass and velocity: work slowly enough with light equipment, and reciprocating motion will do the job, though at a cost. Step up to big pieces and higher speeds, and reciprocating motion becomes unworkable.

Nothing illustrates the principle better than the shift from reciprocating to rotary steam engines in steamships. Both merchant marines and navies were pressing designers and builders for ever larger and faster vessels. For Britain, the world's leading naval power, the definitive decision to go over to the new technology came with the building of *Dreadnought,* the first of the big-gun battleships. This was in 1905. The Royal Navy wanted a capital ship that could make 21 knots, a speed impossible with reciprocating engines. Although earlier vessels had been designed for 18 or 19 knots, they could do this only for short periods; eight hours at even 14 knots, and the engine bearings would start heating up and breaking down. A hard run could mean ten days in port to readjust—not a recipe for combat readiness.

Some of the naval officers were afraid to take chances with the new technology. It was one thing to use turbines on destroyers, but on the Navy's largest, most powerful ship!? What if the innovators were wrong? Philip Watts, Director of Naval Construction, settled the issue by pointing to the cost of old ways. Fit reciprocating engines, he said, and the *Dreadnought* would be out of date in five years.

The result more than justified his hopes. The ship's captain, Reginald Bacon, who had previously commanded the *Irresistible* (the Royal Navy likes hyperbole), marveled at the difference:

[The turbines] were noiseless. In fact, I have frequently visited the engine room of the *Dreadnought* when at sea steaming 17 knots and have been unable to tell whether the engines were revolving or not. During a full speed run, the difference between the engine room of the *Dreadnought* and that of the *Irresistible* was extraordinary. In the *Dreadnought*, there was no noise, no steam was visible, no water or oil splashing about, the officers and men were clean; in fact, the ship to all appearances might have been in harbor and the turbines stopped. In the *Irresistible*, the noise was deafening. It was impossible to make a remark plainly audible and telephones were useless. The deck plates were greasy with oil and water so that it was difficult to walk without slipping. Some gland [valve] was certain to be blowing a little which made the atmosphere murky with steam. One or more hoses would be playing on a bearing which threatened trouble. Men constantly working around the engine would be feeling the bearings to see if they were running cool or showed signs of heating; and the officers would be seen with their coats buttoned up to their throats and perhaps in oilskins, black in the face, and with their clothes wet with oil and water.[23]

The next step would be liquid fuel, which burned hotter, created higher pressures, and drove shafts and propellers faster. The older coal bins took up too much space, and the stokers ate huge amounts of bulky food—human engines also need fuel. As coal stocks fell, more men had to be called in to shovel from more distant bunkers to those closer to the engines: hundreds of men never saw the fires they fed. In contrast, refueling with oil meant simply attaching hoses and a few hours of pumping, often at sea; with coal, the ship had to put into port for days.

Incidentally, much of this improvement would not be captured by the conventional measures of output and productivity. These would sum the cost of the new equipment, but not the change in the quality of work.

# ~ 14 ~

# Why Europe? Why Then?

If we were to prophesy that in the year 1930 a population of fifty million, better fed, clad, and lodged than the English of our time, will cover these islands, that Sussex and Huntingdonshire will be wealthier than the wealthiest parts of the West Riding of Yorkshire now are . . . that machines constructed on principles yet undiscovered will be in every house . . . many people would think us insane.
                    —MACAULAY, "Southey's Colloquies on Society" (1830)[1]

Why Industrial Revolution there and then? The question is really twofold. First, why and how did any country break through the crust of habit and conventional knowledge to this new mode of production? After all, history shows other examples of mechanization and use of inanimate power without producing an industrial revolution. One thinks of Sung China (hemp spinning, ironmaking), medieval Europe (water- and windmill technologies), of early modern Italy (silk throwing, shipbuilding), of the Holland of the "Golden Age." Why now, finally, in the eighteenth century?

Second, why did Britain do it and not some other nation?

The two questions are one. The answer to each needs the other. That is the way of history.

Turning to the first, I would stress *buildup*—the accumulation of knowledge and knowhow; and *breakthrough*—reaching and passing thresholds. We have already noted the interruption of Islamic and Chinese intellectual and technological advance, not only the cessation of improvement but the institutionalization of the stoppage. In Europe, just the other way: we have continuing accumulation. To be sure, in Europe as elsewhere, science and technology had their ups and downs, areas of strength and weakness, centers shifting with the accidents of politics and personal genius. But if I had to single out the critical, distinctively European sources of success, I would emphasize three considerations:

(1) the growing *autonomy* of intellectual inquiry;

(2) the development of unity in disunity in the form of a common, implicitly adversarial *method,* that is, the creation of a language of proof recognized, used, and understood across national and cultural boundaries; and

(3) the invention of invention, that is, the *routinization* of research and its diffusion.

*Autonomy:* The fight for intellectual autonomy went back to medieval conflicts over the validity and authority of tradition. Europe's dominant view was that of the Roman Church—a conception of nature defined by holy scripture, as reconciled with, rather than modified by, the wisdom of the ancients. Much of this found definition in Scholasticism, a system of philosophy (including natural philosophy) that fostered a sense of omnicompetence and authority.

Into this closed world, new ideas necessarily came as an insolence and a potential subversion—as they did in Islam. In Europe, however, acceptance was eased by practical usefulness and protected by rulers who sought to gain by novelty an advantage over rivals. It was not an accident, then, that Europe came to cultivate a vogue for the new and a sense of progress—a belief that, contrary to the nostalgia of antiquity for an earlier grace (Paradise Lost), the Golden Age (utopia) actually lay ahead; and that people were now better off, smarter, more capable than before. As Fra Giordano put it in a sermon in Pisa in 1306 (we should all be remembered as long): "But not all [the arts] have been found; we shall never see an end of finding them . . . and new ones are being found all the time."[2]

Of course, older attitudes hung on. (A law of historical motion holds that all innovations of thought and practice elicit an opposite if not always equal reaction.) In Europe, however, the reach of the Church was limited by the competing pretensions of secular authorities (Caesar vs. God) and by smoldering, gathering fires of religious dissent from below. These heresies may not have been enlightened in matters intellectual and scientific, but they undermined the uniqueness of dogma and, so doing, implicitly promoted novelty.

Most shattering of authority was the widening of personal experience. The ancients, for example, thought no one could live in the tropics: too hot. Portuguese navigators soon showed the error of such preconceptions. Forget the ancients, they boasted; "we found the contrary." Garcia d'Orta, son of *converso* parents and himself a loyal but of course secret Jew, learned medicine and natural philosophy in Salamanca and Lisbon, then sailed to Goa in 1534, where he served as physician to the Portuguese viceroys. In Europe, intimidated by his teachers, he never dared to question the authority of the ancient Greeks and Romans. Now, in the nonacademic environment of Portuguese India, he felt free to open his eyes. "For me," he wrote, the testimony of an eye-witness is worth more than that of all the physicians and all the fathers of medicine who wrote on false information"; and further, "you can get more knowledge now from the Portuguese in one day than was known to the Romans after a hundred years."[3]

*Method:* Seeing alone was not enough. One must understand and give nonmagical explanations for natural phenomena. No credence could be given to things unseen. No room here for unicorns, basilisks, and salamanders. Where Aristotle thought to explain phenomena by the "essential" nature of things (heavenly bodies travel in circles; terrestrial bodies move up or down), the new philosophy proposed the converse: nature was not in things; things were (and moved) in nature. Early on, moreover, these searchers came to see mathematics as immensely valuable for specifying observations and formulating results. Thus Roger Bacon at Oxford in the thirteenth century: "All categories depend on a knowledge of quantity, concerning which mathematics treats, and therefore the whole power of logic depends on mathematics."[4] This marriage of observation and precise description, in turn, made possible replication and verification. Nothing so effectively undermined authority. It mattered little who said what, but what was said; not perception but reality. Do I see what you say you saw?

Such an approach opened the way to purposeful experiment. Instead of waiting to see something happen, make it happen. This required an intellectual leap, and some have argued that it was the renewal and dissemination of magical beliefs (even Isaac Newton believed in the possibility of alchemy and the transmutation of matter) that led the scientific community to see nature as something to be acted upon as well as observed.[5] "In striking contrast to the natural philosopher," writes one historian, "the magician manipulated nature."[6]

Well, at least he tried. I am skeptical, however, of this effort to conflate personal confusions with larger causation. The leap from observation to experiment, from passive to active, was hard enough, and the temptations of magic, this "world of profit and delight, of power, of honor, of omnipotence," were diversion and obstacle. If anything, the world of magic was a parody of reality, a shrinking residual of ignorance, a kind of intellectual antimatter. Magic's occasional successes were serendipitous by-products of hocus-pocus. Its practitioners were easily seen as crazies, if not as agents of the devil, in part because of their frequently eccentric manner and occasionally criminal behavior.* Such practices went back to the dawn of time; they are still with us and always will be, because, like people who play the lottery, we want to believe. That they revived and flourished in the rush of new knowledge, of secrets uncovered, of mysteries revealed, should come as no surprise. Magic was more response than source, and insofar as it played a role, it was less as stimulant than as allergenic.[7]

Note that for some, this is cause for regret, as at a self-imposed impoverishment: " . . . the new quantitative and mechanistic approach eventually established a metaphysics which left no room for essences, animism, hope, or purpose in nature, thus making magic something 'unreal,' or supernatural in the modern sense."[8] Not to feel bad: the road to truth and progress passed there. As David Gans, an early seventeenth-century popularizer of natural science, put it, one knows that magic and divining are not science because their practitioners do not argue with one another. Without controversy, no serious pursuit of knowledge and truth.[9]

This powerful *combination* of perception with measurement, verification, and mathematized deduction—this new method—was the key to knowing. Its practical successes were the assurance that it would be protected and encouraged whatever the consequences. Nothing like it developed anywhere else.[10]

How to experiment was another matter. One first had to invent research strategies and instruments of observation and measurement, and almost four centuries would elapse before the method bore fruit in the spectacular advances of the seventeenth century. Not that knowledge stood still. The new approach found early application in astronomy and navigation, mechanics and warfare, optics and surveying—all of them practical matters. But it was not until the late sixteenth century, with Galileo Galilei, that experiment became a system. This en-

---

* Hence the poison scandal (*l'affaire des poisons*) of the 1680s in France, which saw hundreds of fortunetellers, astrologers, and their clients arrested and strenuously interrogated, and some thirty-four executed for complicity in murder. Nothing, says Grenet, *La passion des astres,* pp. 136–59, did more to discredit astrology and magic among the larger public and the political authorities. The scientists had already abandoned this nonsense.

tailed not only repeated and repeatable observation, but deliberate simplification as a window on the complex. Want to find the relations between time, speed, and distance-covered of falling objects? Slow them by rolling them down an inclined plane.

Scientists had to see better and could do so once the telescope and microscope were invented (c. 1600), opening new worlds comparable for wonder and power to the earlier geographical discoveries. They needed to measure more precisely, because the smallest shift of a pointer could make all the difference. So Pedro Nuñez, professor of astronomy and mathematics in the University of Coimbra (Portugal), invented in the early sixteenth century the *nonius* (from his latinized name), to give navigational and astronomical readings to a fraction of a degree. This was later improved by the vernier scale (Pierre Vernier, 1580–1637), and this in turn was followed by the invention of the micrometer (Gascoigne, 1639, but long ignored; and Adrien Auzout, 1666), which used fine wires for reading and a screw (rather than a slide) to achieve close control. The result was measures to the tenth and less of a millimeter that substantially enhanced astronomical accuracy.[11] (Note that just learning to make precision screws was a major achievement; also that the usefulness of these instruments depended partly on eyeglasses and magnifying lenses.)

The same pursuit of precision marked the development of time measurement. Astronomers and physicists needed to time events to the minute and second, and Christian Huygens gave that to them with the invention of the pendulum clock in 1657 and the balance spring in 1675. Scientists also needed to calculate better and faster, and here John Napier's logarithms were as important in their day as the invention of the abacus in an earlier time, or of calculators and computers later.[12] And they needed more powerful tools of mathematical analysis, which they got from René Descartes's analytic geometry and, even more, from the new calculus of Isaac Newton and Gottfried Wilhelm von Leibniz. These new maths contributed immensely to experiment and analysis.

*Routinization:* The third institutional pillar of Western science was the routinization of discovery, the invention of invention. Here was a widely dispersed population of intellectuals, working in different lands, using different vernaculars—and yet a community. What happened in one place was quickly known everywhere else, partly thanks to a common language of learning, Latin; partly to a precocious development of courier and mail services; most of all because people were moving in all directions. In the seventeenth century, these links were institutionalized, first in the person of such self-appointed human switch-boards as Marin Mersenne (1588–1648), then in the form of learned societies with their corresponding secretaries, frequent meetings, and periodical journals. The earliest societies appeared in Italy—the Accadémia dei Lincei (the Academy of Lynxes) in Rome in 1603, the short-lived Accadémia del Cimento in Florence in 1653. More important in the long run, however, were the northern academies: the Royal Society in London in 1660, the Academia Parisiensis in 1635, and the successor Académie des Sciences in 1666. Even before, informal but regular encounters in coffeehouses and salons brought people and questions together. As Mersenne put it in 1634, "the sciences have sworn inviolable friendship to one another."[13]

Cooperation, then, but enormously enhanced by fierce rivalry in the race for prestige and honor. In the pre-academy environment of the sixteenth century, this often took the form of concealment, of partial divulgence, of refusal to publish, of saving the good parts for debate and confutation.[14] Even in the late seventeenth century, one has the eccentric figure of Robert Hooke, active member of the Royal Society, whose motto might have been, "I thought of that first." If we can believe him, he put all manner of valuable creations in his cabinet drawers, only to bring them out when someone else had come up with a comparable device. In this way, he challenged Christian Huygens on the invention of the watch balance spring (1675), a major advance in the accuracy of portable timepieces. History has given the palm to Huygens, not only because his spiral spring was tried in a watch and worked, but also because he announced his invention when he made it. One cannot have these unprovable claims *ex post,* not even from so gifted a mechanical genius as Hooke.[15]

In general, fame was the spur, and even in those early days, science was a contest for priority. That was why it became so important to show-and-tell to aficionados, often in elegant salons; these ladies and gentlemen were witnesses to achievement. And that was why scientists, amateur and professional, were so keen to found journals and get dated articles published. Also to replicate experiments, verify results, correct, improve, go beyond. Here again the role of the printing press and movable type was crucial; also the shift from Latin, an invaluable means of international communication among savants of different countries, to the vernacular, the language of the larger public. Again, nothing like these arrangements and facilities for propagation was to be found outside Europe.

Scientific method and knowledge paid off in applications—most importantly in power technology. During these centuries, the older power devices—the windmill and water wheel—got continuing attention, with some gain in efficiency; but the great invention would be the conversion of heat energy into work by means of steam. No technique drew so closely on experiment—a long inquiry into vacuums and air pressure that began in the sixteenth century and reached fruition in the late seventeenth in the work of Otto von Guericke (1602–1686), Evangelista Torricelli (1608–1647), Robert Boyle (1627–1691), and Denys Papin (?1647–1712), German, Italian, English, French. To be sure, the scientists of the eighteenth century could not have explained why and how a steam engine worked. That had to wait for Sadi Carnot (1796–1832) and the laws of thermodynamics. But to say that the engine anticipated knowledge is not to say that the engine builder did not draw on earlier scientific acquisitions, both substantive and methodological. James Watt made the point. His master and mentor Joseph Black (1728–1799) did not give him the idea for the separate condenser, but working with Black gave him the practice and method to probe and resolve the issue.[16] Even at that, the heroic inventor did not give full credit. Watt was a friend of professors in Edinburgh and Glasgow, of eminent natural philosophers in England, of scientists abroad. He knew his mathematics, did systematic experiments, calculated the thermal efficiency of steam engines; in short, built on accumulated knowledge and ideas to advance technique.[17]

All of this took time, and that is why, *in the long,* the Industrial Revolution had to wait. It could not have happened in Renaissance Florence. Even less in ancient Greece. The technological basis had not yet been laid; the streams of progress had to come together.

The answer *in the short* lies in conjuncture, in the relations of supply and demand, in prices and elasticities. Technology was not enough. What was needed was technological change of mighty leverage, the kind that would resonate through the market and change the distribution of resources.

Let me illustrate. In fourteenth-century Italy, gifted mechanics (we do not know their names) found ways to throw silk, that is, to spin silk warp, by machine; and even more impressive, to drive these devices by waterpower. On the basis of this technique, the Italian silk industry prospered for centuries, to the envy of other countries. The French managed to pierce the secret in 1670, the Dutch at about the same time; and in 1716, Thomas Lombe, after some years of patient espionage, brought the technique to England and built a large water-powered mill employing hundreds of people.[18]

This was a factory, comparable in almost every way to the cotton mills of a later era. Almost . . . the difference was that the Lombe mill at Derby, along with the hand-operated throwsters' shops that had preceded it and some smaller machine imitators, was more than enough to accommodate England's demand for silk yarn. Silk, after all, was a costly raw material, and the silk manufacture catered to a small and affluent clientele. So the Lombe mill, fifty years ahead of those first cotton mills of the 1770s, was not the model for a new mode of production. One could not get an industrial revolution out of silk.[19]

Wool and cotton were something else again. When wool sneezed, all Europe caught cold; cotton, and the whole world fell ill. Wool was much the more important in Europe, and cotton's role in the Industrial Revolution was in some ways an accident. The British "calico acts" (1700 and 1721), which prohibited the import and even wearing of East Indian prints and dyestuffs, were intended to protect the native woolen and linen manufacturers, but inadvertently sheltered the still infant cotton industry; and while cotton was a lusty infant, it was still much smaller than the older branches at midcentury. The first attempts to build spinning machines aimed at wool, because that was where the profit lay. But when wool fibers proved troublesome and cotton docile, inventors turned their attention to the easier material.

Also, the encrustation of the woolen industry and the vested power of its workforce impeded change. Cotton, growing fast, recruiting new hands, found it easier to impose new ways. This is a constant of technological innovation as process: it is much easier to teach novelty to inexperienced workers than to teach old dogs new tricks.*

Why the interest in mechanization? Primarily because the growth of the textile industry was beginning to outstrip labor supply.† England

---

* On the resistance of workers in wool to mechanization, see especially Randall, *Before the Luddites,* who points out this response was also a function of organization and the sharing of gain. Where the workers were in effect independent agents, as in Yorkshire, they had little trouble adopting new ways that profited them; where they served as wage labor, as in the West Country, they fought machines that threatened employment.

† The first in the series of spinning machines that laid the foundation of the factory system was that of Lewis Paul and John Wyatt (patented in Paul's name) in 1738. The key invention here was the use of rollers turning at different speeds for drawing out the fiber—a feature that became thereafter a regular component of spinning machines fitted with a flyer or equivalent. At that time, we are told, the shortage of spinning labor was nothing like what it would become in another generation; in the words of

had jumped ahead on the strength of rural manufacture (putting-out), but the dispersion of activity across hill and dale was driving up costs of distribution and collection. Meanwhile, trying to meet demand, employers raised wages, that is, they increased the price they paid for finished work. To their dismay, however, the higher income simply permitted workers more time for leisure, and the supply of work actually diminished. Merchant-manufacturers found themselves on a treadmill. In defiance of all their natural instincts, they came to wish for higher food prices. Perhaps a rise in the cost of living would compel spinners and weavers to their task.*

The workers, however, did respond to market incentives. They were contractors as well as wage laborers, and this dual status gave them opportunity for self-enrichment at the expense of the putter-out. Spinners and weavers would take materials from one merchant and then sell the finished article to a competitor, stalling now one, now another, and juggling their obligations to a fare-thee-well. They also learned to set some of the raw material aside for their own use: no backward-bending supply curve when working for their own gain. Trying to conceal the embezzlement, weavers made thinner, poorer fabrics and filled them out by artifice or additive. The manufacturer in turn tried to discourage such theft by closely examining each piece and if necessary "abating" the price of the finished article. This conflict of interests gave rise to a costly cold war between employer and employed.

The manufacturers clamored for help from the civil authorities. They called for the right to inflict corporal punishment on laggards and deadbeats (no use trying to fine them); also the right to enter the weavers' cottages without warrant and search for embezzled materials. These demands got nowhere. An Englishman's home was his castle, sacred.

Little wonder, then, that frustrated manufacturers turned their

---

Wadsworth and Mann, hardly serious—*The Cotton Trade,* p. 414. Yet the unevenness of the yarn produced by hand spinners—both the individual's work and from one spinner to the next—meant that weavers had to buy far more yarn than they actually used in order to have enough of a given quality. The machine promised to end that—*Ibid.,* p. 416.

* These constraints were the more vexatious in a context of rising consumer demand. The growing appetite for things should have increased the supply of labor; and so it did in the long run. But in the short, demand got ahead of supply, and manufacturers got impatient. On the link between consumption and industry, see de Vries, "Industrial Revolution."

thoughts to large workshops where spinners and weavers would have to turn up on time and work the full day under supervision. That was no small matter. Cottage industry, after all, had great advantages for the merchant-manufacturer, in particular, low cost of entry and low overhead. In this mode, it was the worker who supplied plant and equipment, and if business slowed, the putter-out could simply turn off the orders. Large shops or plants, on the other hand, called for a substantial capital investment: land and buildings to start with, plus machines.

Putting-out, moreover, was popular with everybody. The workers liked the freedom from discipline, the privilege of stopping and going as they pleased. Work rhythms reflected this independence. Weavers typically rested and played long, well into the week, then worked hard toward the end in order to make delivery and collect pay on Saturday. On Fridays they might work through the night. Saturday night was for drinking, and Sunday brought more beer and ale. Monday (Saint Monday) was equally holy, and Tuesday was needed to recover from so much holiness.

Such conflict within the industry—what a Marxist might call its internal contradictions—led logically, then, to the gathering of workers under one roof, there to labor under surveillance and supervision. But manufacturers found that they had to pay to persuade people out of cottages and into mills. *So long as the equipment in the mill was the same as in the cottage, mill production cost more.* The only operations where this law did not hold was in heat-using technologies (fulling, brewing, glassmaking, ironmaking, and the like). There the savings yielded by concentration (one hearth as against many) more than compensated for the capital costs.* Efforts to concentrate labor in textile manufacture, however, which went back in England to the sixteenth century, invariably failed. They did better in Europe, where governments tried to promote industry by subsidizing and assigning labor to large hand-powered shops—"manufactories" or "protofactories." But this was an artificial prosperity, and the withdrawal of support spelled bankruptcy.

It took power machinery to make the factory competitive. Power made it possible to drive larger and more efficient machines, thus underselling the cottage product by ever bigger margins. The hand spinners went quickly; the hand weavers more slowly, but surely. In spite

---

* The Chinese Communist regime learned this later when it tried to make a go of backyard blast furnaces.

of higher wages, the mills still seemed a prison to the old-timers. Where, then, did the early millowners find their labor force? Where else but among those who could not say no? In England that meant children, often conscripted (bought) from the poorhouses, and women, especially the young unmarrieds. On the Continent, the manufacturers were able to negotiate for convict labor and military personnel.

So was born what Karl Marx called "Modern Industry," fruit of a marriage between machines and power; also between power (force and energy) and power (political).

## The Primacy of Observation: What You See Is What There Is

The great Danish astronomer Tycho Brahe (1546–1601) lived and worked before the invention of the telescope, but he was a keen observer and he knew all the stars he could see in the sky. And these were all there were supposed to be. One night in November 1572, however, he saw something new in the heavens, a point of light in the constellation Cassiopeia that should not have been there. This troubled him, so he asked his servants whether they saw what he saw, and they said yes, they did. For a moment he was satisfied, at least regarding his power of sight; but then he began to worry that his servants had merely wanted to reassure him and were reluctant or afraid to contradict their master, for he knew himself to be a man of pride and temper. (He had lost his nose in a duel as a youth and wore a copper—some say silver—prosthesis.) So he went out into the street and stopped some passing peasants and asked them the same question. They had nothing to gain or lose by telling the truth, and no one could be more matter-of-fact than a peasant. And they also said they saw the light. And then Tycho knew that there were more things in heaven than were dreamt of in his philosophy. He wrote up his observations in a pamphlet, *De nova stella,* published in Copenhagen in 1573, a monument in the history of science.

A note of caution: Tycho, for all his show-me empiricism, sought to find a middle way between Ptolemy and Copernicus by having the sun, circled by the planets, revolve around the earth. It takes good induction as well as good observation to do good science.

≈ ≈

# Masters of Precision

All studies of change and rates of change have to measure elapsed time. To do this, one needs a standard unit of measure and an instrument to count the units; we call that a clock. In the absence of a clock, one can substitute approximate equivalents. The seamen of the fifteenth and sixteenth centuries who wanted to count the time it took for a float to go from bow to stern by way of estimating the speed of the vessel, might use a sandglass; but if they did not have one, they could always recite Hail Mary's or some other conventional refrain; and today any practiced photographer knows that one can count seconds by reciting four-syllable expressions: one one thousand, two one thousand, three one thousand . . .

Needless to say, such idiosyncratic improvisations will hardly do for scientific purposes. For these one needed a good clock, but it took four centuries to make one. Still, scientists are ingenious people, and they found ways to enhance the precision of their pre-pendulum, pre-balance spring timepieces. One way was to use clocks with very large wheels with hundreds and even a thousand or more teeth. Tycho Brahe did this, and instead of reading the single hour hand of his clock (these early machines were not accurate enough to warrant the use of minute hands), he counted the number of teeth the wheel had turned and got much closer to the exact time elapsed. He did so to track star movements and locate these bodies on celestial maps (time was one of the two coordinates). Galileo needed even closer measurements for his studies of acceleration. Ever ingenious, he used small, hand-held water clocks rather than mechanical clocks, opening and closing the outflow hole with his finger at the start and end of the run. He then weighed the water released as a measure of time elapsed, for in those days, the balance scale was the most precise measuring instrument known.

The invention of the pendulum clock changed everything. This was the first horological device controlled by an oscillator with its own intrinsic frequency. Earlier clocks used a controller (swinging bar or circle) whose frequency varied with the force applied. After improvements (all inventions need improvements), a good pendulum clock kept time to a few seconds per day. Watches were less accurate, because they could not work with a pendulum. The invention of the balance spring, however, made it possible to get much closer to a regular rate, steady from hour to hour and day to day. A good pocketwatch, jeweled and with a decent balance, could keep time in the early eighteenth century to a minute or two a day. For the first time it paid to add a minute hand, and even a second hand.

These advances substantially enhanced the advantage that horological technology gave to Europe. What had long been an absolute monopoly of knowledge remained an effective monopoly of performance. No one else could make these instruments or do the kinds of work that depended on precision timekeeping. The most important of these, politically as well as economically: finding the longitude at sea.

# ~ 15 ~

# Britain and the Others

And in Europe, why Britain? Why not some other country?

On one level, the question is not hard to answer. By the early eighteenth century, Britain was well ahead—in cottage manufacture (putting-out), seedbed of growth; in recourse to fossil fuel; in the technology of those crucial branches that would make the core of the Industrial Revolution: textiles, iron, energy and power. To these should be added the efficiency of British commercial agriculture and transport.

The advantages of increasing efficiency in agriculture are obvious. For one thing, rising productivity in food production releases labor for other activities—industrial manufacture, services, and the like. For another, this burgeoning workforce needs ever more food. If this cannot be obtained at home, income and wealth must be diverted to the purpose. (To be sure, the need to import nourishment may promote the development of exports that can be exchanged for food, may encourage industry; but necessity does not assure performance. Some of the poorest countries in the world once fed themselves. Today they rely heavily on food imports that drain resources and leave them indebted, while the merest change in rainfall or impediment to trade spells disaster. At worst, they stagger from one famine to the next, each one leaving a legacy of enfeeblement, disease, and increased dependency.)

So one can hardly exaggerate the contribution of agricultural improvement to Britain's industrialization.[1] The process began in the Middle Ages, with the precocious emancipation of serfs and the commercialization of both cultivation and distribution. The spread of market gardening (fruits and vegetables) around London in the sixteenth century and the pursuit of mixed farming (grain and livestock and grain-fed livestock) testify to the responsiveness of both landowners and tenants. This development made for richer and more varied diets, with an exceptionally high proportion of animal protein.[2] Further contributing was the adoption of new techniques of watering, fertilizing, and crop rotation—many of them brought by immigrants from the Low Countries. The Netherlands were then the seat of European agricultural improvement, a land that man had created (won from the sea) by effort and ingenuity and had cherished accordingly. Dutchmen were already teaching farming in the Middle Ages—to the Slavic frontier. In the sixteenth and seventeenth centuries, the English were among the principal beneficiaries. Initiative followed initiative. In eighteenth-century England, it was enclosures that held center stage—the shift from the collective constraints of open fields to the freedom of concentrated, fenced or hedged holdings. Historians have debated the contribution of the enclosure movement; but logic suggests that, given the costs, it must have paid.

Unlike most other countries, then, British agriculture was not conservatism's power base. It was a force for economic change—as much as any other sector. Agriculture paid, and because it paid well, it became something of a passion, not only for farmers but for wealthy, aristocratic landowners who were not above getting their boots muddy and mingling with anyone and everyone at cattle shows and sales. Inevitably, in this money- and market-conscious society, agricultural societies made their appearance, where "improving" farmers could meet and learn from one another, and agronomic literature proliferated, the better to propagate best practice. This commercialism promoted an integrated approach to estate management: all resources counted, below as well as above ground; and in Britain, unlike the Continental countries, mineral resources belonged to the owner of the land, not to the crown. More opportunity for enterprise.

At the same time, the British were making major gains in land and water transport. New turnpike roads and canals, intended primarily to serve industry and mining, opened the way to valuable resources, linked production to markets, facilitated the division of labor. Other

European countries were trying to do the same, but nowhere were these improvements so widespread and effective as in Britain. For a simple reason: nowhere else were roads and canals typically the work of private enterprise, hence responsive to need (rather than to prestige and military concerns) and profitable to users. This was why Arthur Young, agronomist and traveler, could marvel at some of the broad, well-drawn French roads but deplore the lodging and eating facilities. The French crown had built a few admirable king's highways, as much to facilitate control as to promote trade, and Young found them empty. British investors had built many more, for the best business reasons, and inns to feed and sleep the users.

These roads (and canals) hastened growth and specialization. This was perhaps what most impressed Daniel Defoe is his masterly *Tour Through the Whole Island of Great Britain* (1724–26): the local crops (hops for beer, sheep for wool, livestock for breeding) and the regional specialties (metal goods in Sheffield, Birmingham, and the Black Country; woolens in East Anglia and the West Country; worsteds around Bradford, woolens around Leeds; cottons around Manchester; potteries in Cheshire; and on and on). No wonder that Adam Smith emphasized size of market and division of labor: his own country gave him the best example.

Yet to say that is just to tell *what* and *how*, not *why;* to describe rather than to explain.[3] This advance *cum* transformation, this revolution, was not a matter of chance, of "things simply coming together." One can find reasons, and reasons behind the reasons. (In big things, history abhors accident.)[4] The early technological superiority of Britain in these key branches was itself an achievement—not God-given, not happenstance, but the result of work, ingenuity, imagination, and enterprise.

The point is that Britain had the makings; but then Britain made itself. To understand this, consider not only material advantages (other societies were also favorably endowed for industry but took ages to follow the British initiative), but also the nonmaterial values (culture) and institutions.*

These values and institutions are so familiar to us (that is why we call

---

* Such terms as "values" and "culture" are not popular with economists, who prefer to deal with quantifiable (more precisely definable) factors. Still, life being what it is, one must talk about these things, so we have Walt Rostow's "propensities" and Moses Abramowitz's "social capability." A rose by any other name.

········· Canals

NORTH
SEA

IRISH SEA

*Pennine Mts.*

Tyne R.

Glasgow
Edinburgh
Newcastle
Bradford
Leeds
Preston
Prescot
Liverpool
Manchester
Sheffield
Nottingham
Derby
Birmingham
Coventry
South
Wales
Black
Country
Cardiff
Bristol
Thames R.
London
Dover

ENGLISH CHANNEL

BRITAIN ON THE WAY TO INDUSTRIAL REVOLUTION
These canals responded to the need for cheap transport from mines to urban
centers and seaports. The real commodity was coal—fuel and source of carbon.

them modern) that we take them for granted. They represent, however, a big departure from older norms and have been accepted and adopted, over time and in different places, only in the face of tenacious resistance. Even now, the older order has by no means vanished.

Let us begin by delineating the ideal case, the society theoretically best suited to pursue material progress and general enrichment. Keep in mind that this is not necessarily a "better" or a "superior" society (words to be avoided), simply one fitter to produce goods and services. This ideal growth-and-development society would be one that

1. Knew how to operate, manage, and build the instruments of production and to create, adapt, and master new techniques on the technological frontier.
2. Was able to impart this knowledge and know-how to the young, whether by formal education or apprenticeship training.
3. Chose people for jobs by competence and relative merit; promoted and demoted on the basis of performance.
4. Afforded opportunity to individual or collective enterprise; encouraged initiative, competition, and emulation.[5]
5. Allowed people to enjoy and employ the fruits of their labor and enterprise.

These standards imply corollaries: gender equality (thereby doubling the pool of talent); no discrimination on the basis of irrelevant criteria (race, sex, religion, etc.); also a preference for scientific (means-end) rationality over magic and superstition (irrationality).*

Such a society would also possess the kind of political and social institutions that favor the achievement of these larger goals; that would, for example,

1. Secure rights of private property, the better to encourage saving and investment.

---

* The tenacity of superstition in an age of science and rationalism may surprise at first, but insofar as it aims at controlling fate, it beats fatalism. It is a resort of the hapless and incapable in the pursuit of good fortune and the avoidance of bad; also a psychological support for the insecure. Hence persistent recourse to horoscopic readings and fortunetelling, even in our own day. Still, one does not expect to find magic used as a tool of business, to learn for example that exploration of coal deposits along the French northern border (the Hainaut) and in the center of the country (Rive-de-Gier) in the eighteenth century was misguided and delayed by reliance on dowsers (*tourneurs de baguettes*)—Gillet, *Les charbonnages*, p. 29.

2. Secure rights of personal liberty—secure them against both the abuses of tyranny and private disorder (crime and corruption).
3. Enforce rights of contract, explicit and implicit.
4. Provide stable government, not necessarily democratic, but itself governed by publicly known rules (a government of laws rather than men). If democratic, that is, based on periodic elections, the majority wins but does not violate the rights of the losers; while the losers accept their loss and look forward to another turn at the polls.
5. Provide responsive government, one that will hear complaint and make redress.
6. Provide honest government, such that economic actors are not moved to seek advantage and privilege inside or outside the marketplace. In economic jargon, there should be no rents to favor and position.
7. Provide moderate, efficient, ungreedy government. The effect should be to hold taxes down, reduce the government's claim on the social surplus, and avoid privilege.

This ideal society would also be honest. Such honesty would be enforced by law, but ideally, the law would not be needed. People would believe that honesty is right (also that it pays) and would live and act accordingly.

More corollaries: this society would be marked by geographical and social mobility. People would move about as they sought opportunity, and would rise and fall as they made something or nothing of themselves. This society would value new as against old, youth as against experience, change and risk as against safety. It would not be a society of equal shares, because talents are not equal; but it would tend to a more even distribution of income than is found with privilege and favor. It would have a relatively large middle class. This greater equality would show in more homogeneous dress and easier manners across class lines.

No society on earth has ever matched this ideal. Leaving ignorance aside (how does one know who is better or more meritorious?), this is the machine at 100 percent efficiency, designed without regard to the vagaries of history and fate and the passions of human nature. The most efficient, development-oriented societies of today, say those of East Asia and the industrial nations of the West, are marred by all manner of corruption, failures of government, private rent-seeking. This paradigm nevertheless highlights the direction of history. These are the virtues that have promoted economic and material progress. They represent a marked deviation from earlier social and political arrangements; and it is not a coincidence that the first industrial nation came closest earliest to this new kind of social order.

To begin with, Britain had the early advantage of being a *nation*. By that I mean not simply the realm of a ruler, not simply a state or political entity, but a self-conscious, self-aware unit characterized by common identity and loyalty and by equality of civil status.[6] Nations can reconcile social purpose with individual aspirations and initiatives and enhance performance by their collective synergy. The whole is more than the sum of the parts. Citizens of a nation will respond better to state encouragement and initiatives; conversely, the state will know better what to do and how, in accord with active social forces.[7] Nations can compete.

Britain, moreover, was not just any nation. This was a precociously modern, industrial nation. Remember that the salient characteristic of such a society is the ability to transform itself and adapt to new things and ways, so that the content of "modern" and "industrial" is always changing. One key area of change: the increasing freedom and security of the people. To this day, ironically, the British term themselves *subjects* of the crown, although they have long—longer than anywhere— been *citizens*. Nothing did more for enterprise. Here is Adam Smith:

> The natural effort of every individual to better his own condition, when suffered to exert itself with freedom and security, is so powerful a principle, that it is alone, and without any assistance, not only capable of carrying on the society to wealth and prosperity, but of surmounting a hundred impertinent obstructions with which the folly of human laws too often incumbers its operations; though the effect of these obstructions is always more or less either to encroach upon its freedom, or to diminish its security. In Great Britain industry is perfectly secure; and though it is far from being perfectly free, it is as free or freer than in any other part of Europe.[8]

How far to push back the origins of English social precocity is a matter of historical dispute. One scholar would go back to the Middle Ages (pre-1500) and what he calls the rise of individualism. This was a society that shed the burdens of serfdom, developed a population of cultivators rather than peasants, imported industry and trade into the countryside, sacrificed custom to profit and tradition to comparative advantage. With mixed effect. Some found themselves impoverished, but on balance, incomes went up. Many found themselves landless, but mobility was enhanced and consciousness enlarged.[9]

England gave people elbow room. Political and civil freedoms won first for the nobles (Magna Carta, 1215) were extended by war, usage, and law to the common folk. To all of these gains one can oppose exceptions: England was far from perfect. It had its poor (always with us)—many more of them than of the rich. It knew abuses of privilege as well as enjoyment of freedom, distinctions of class and status, concentrations of wealth and power, marks of preference and favor. But everything is relative, and by comparison with populations across the Channel, Englishmen were free and fortunate.

They knew who they were. Their first mass experience of life in other lands came with the Hundred Years War (fourteenth and fifteenth centuries) in France, where English yeomen more than held their own against the flower of French chivalry. Among those who campaigned there: John Fortescue, later Sir John and chief justice of the Court of King's Bench. In the 1470s Sir John wrote a book on *The Governance of England,* where he spoke of French misgovernment and misery. The French king, he wrote, does as he pleases and has so impoverished his people that they can scarcely live. They drink water (rather than beer and ale); they eat apples with brown (as against white) bread; they get no meat but maybe some lard or tripe—what's left over from the animals slaughtered for the nobles and merchants. They wear no wool, but rather a canvas frock; their hose, of canvas too and do not go past the knee, so that they go about with bare thighs. Their wives and children go barefoot. They have to watch, labor, and grub in the ground. They "go crooked and be feeble, not able to fight nor to defend the realm." They have no arms, or money to buy arms. "But verily they live in the most extreme poverty and miserie, and yet dwell they in the most fertile realm of the world."[10]

To be sure, this is an Englishmen talking (but oh, how early!), and he may be forgiven if he rhapsodizes about the superiority of his country. That is the nature of nationalism, a feeling of identity and superiority, and England was one of the first countries to nurse this new sentiment (read Shakespeare), which differed sharply from the local identification of the medieval serf in his narrow *pays,* or for that matter, the dumb submission of the Asian *ryot.*[11]

But the English were not the only ones to praise England. Foreign visitors to the island chorused respect and admiration. For some Asians, all westerners may have looked alike, but Europeans saw the differences. Visitors exclaimed about the high standard of living of the English countryman: brick cottages, tile roofs, woolen clothing, leather shoes, white bread (one can follow the rising incomes of industrializing Europe by the white bread frontier). They saw women in cotton prints and wearing hats; servant girls who so resembled their mistresses that the foreign caller wondered how to address the person answering the door. They saw poor people, they tell us, but no *misérables;* no starved, pinched faces; beggars, but no beggar "without both a shirt, and shoes and stockings." (The English seem to have been proud of their beggars, whom they saw as plying a trade.)[12]

To the purchasing power of the lower classes, to their ability to buy beyond the necessities, must be added the wealth—remarkable for its time—of the great English middle class: the merchants and shopkeepers, manufacturers and bankers, men of law and other professions. Daniel Defoe, best known as a writer of imaginative fiction, also wrote delicious travel accounts and economic tracts of remarkable perspicuity. He saw what was happening around him, and when he wrote of the English consumer, he told us more than any dusty functionary could:

> It is upon these two classes of People, the Manufacturers [not the employers but rather those who labor in industry] and the Shopkeepers, that I build the hypothesis which I have taken upon me to offer to the Public, 'tis upon the Gain they make either by their Labour, or their Industry in Trade, and upon their inconceivable Numbers, that the Home Consumption of our own Produce, and of the Produce of foreign Nations imported here is so exceeding great, that our Trade is raised up to such a Prodigy of Magnitude, as I shall shew it is. . . .
> . . . These are the People that carry off the Gross of your Consumption; 'its for these your Markets are kept open late on *Saturday* Nights; because they usually receive their Week's Wages late. . . . Their Numbers are not Hundreds or Thousands, or Hundreds of Thousands, but Millions; 'tis by their Multitude, I say, that all the Wheels of Trade are set on Foot, the Manufacture and the Produce of the Land and Sea, finished, cur'd, and fitted for the Markets Abroad; 'tis by the Largeness of their Gettings, that they are supported, and by the Largeness of their Number the whole Country is supported; by their Wages they are able to live plentifully, and it is by their expensive, generous, free way of living, that the Home Consumption is rais'd to such a Bulk, as well of our own, as of foreign Production. . . .[13]

The contribution of high consumption to technological progress struck contemporaries, and more of them as the British advance grew. Without taking a course in Keynesian economics, French merchants understood that mechanization made for high wages, that high wages made for increased demand for manufactures, and that effective demand made for increased prosperity. "Thus, by the working of a system that seems paradoxical, the English have grown rich by consuming."[14] Paradoxical indeed: such dispendious habits ran against the folk wisdom that counseled thrift and abstemiousness, habits congenial to French peasants compelled to avarice. One result was a manufacture that aimed at a large national and international market and focused on standardized goods of moderate price—just the kind that lent themselves to machine production. "The English," wrote Charles marquis de Biencourt, "have the wit to make things for the people, rather than for the rich," which gave them a large and steady custom.[15]

This custom has recently attracted much attention, not only for its own sake but as a window on technological change and on larger social changes, in particular the growing importance of women as consumers.[16] What these studies show is a lively market for all manner of fabrics, clothing, clocks and watches, hardware, pins and needles, and above all notions—a catchall term for those personal accessories (combs, buckles, buttons, adornments) that go beyond the necessities and cater to appearance and vanity. Many of these were semidurables and were passed on in wills and as gifts. Their increased volume reflected not just rising incomes, but quicker distribution and new techniques of manufacture (division of labor, repetitious machines, superior files) that yielded lower costs and prices.

This production, needless to say, though largely directed to home demand, also sold to plantations and colonies and kingdoms abroad. (Small objects of high value in proportion to weight and volume are ideally suited to smuggling. The best example is watches.) Small-town, relatively isolated markets on the European Continent, once reserved for local craftsmen, were now visited by tireless peddlers, bringing with them the outside world. Conservatives resented these intruders, not only for their competition and their foreignness (many peddlers were Jews) but for their threat to order and virtue. The German moralist Justus Möser, writing in the latter eighteenth century of the Osnabrück area in northern Westphalia, denounced the brass of these itinerants. They came to the cottage door while the husband was away (alas for patriarchal authority), tempting the wife with kerchiefs, combs, and mirrors, the instruments of vanity and waste. A Snow White story: the wicked stepmother is now a cunning peddler (as she becomes in the tale), and the princess is an adult, but as susceptible as a child.[17]

≈ ⌒

## Some Good Deeds Go Rewarded

Britain was largely free of the irrational constraints on entry that dogged most Continental societies. The stupidest of these were religious:* the persecution and expulsion of Protestants from France (revocation in 1685 of the Edict of Toleration of Henri IV); and the widespread exclusion of Jews from all manner of trades, partly (psychologically) out of fear and hatred, partly (institutionally) by virtue of the Christian character of craft guilds and the lingering effects of earlier expulsions. Religion, moreover, was not the sole criterion of admission to craft and trade guilds. In parts of Germany, for example, only men "conceived by honorable parents under pure circumstances" (the German is better—*von ehrliche Eltern aus reinem Bett erzeuget*) were eligible.[18] (Some scholars have tried to trivialize the economic consequences of these discriminations, as though for every person excluded, someone just as good or smart or experienced was waiting to step in; or as though these victims of prejudice and hatred were not precious carriers of knowledge and skills to eager competitors.[19] We need not take these clevernesses seriously; they fail in logic and in fact.)

England profited here from other nations' self-inflicted wounds. In the sixteenth century, weavers from the southern Netherlands sought refuge and brought with them the secrets of the "new draperies," and Dutch peasants imported arts of drainage and a more intensive agriculture. In the seventeenth century, Jews and crypto-Jews, many of them third- and fourth-stage Marrano victims of Spanish and other persecutions, brought to England an experience of public and private finance;[20] and Huguenots, merchants and craftsmen, old hands of trade and finance, came with their network of religious and family connections.[21]

* The British also had their constraints on participation of religious outsiders in political life and admission to the universities; but these paradoxically steered these "minorities" into business and saved them from the seductions of genteel status.

# The Value of Time

The Britain of the Industrial Revolution had preserved the structures and institutions of an older time—the monarchy, the guilds, the ceremonies, the costumes—but over a long period had sidetracked these and reduced them to vanities and appearances. Insofar as they retained influence and prestige, they were a drag. They gave us the nostalgic world (our nostalgia) of Jane Austen: a world of rural gentility and idleness, of heirs, nonheirs, and poor intriguers—pretenders to unearned wealth. It was a world that possessed considerable appeal, quietly lying in wait to draw the tired and incapable and handsome seekers of social rent into the nirvana of triviality.

But the action was elsewhere; with new men, improving landlords, aristocrats turned entrepreneurs, immigrants from within and without. The energy and busyness of this society could be measured by its material achievements, but also by its values. I would stress here the importance it gave to time and to saving time, because nothing better sums up the priorities. Two pieces of "unobtrusive" evidence: (1) the passionate interest in knowing the time; and (2) the emphasis on speed of transport.

The British were in the eighteenth century the world's leading producers and consumers of timekeepers, in the country as in the city (very different here from other European societies). They made them well and pricey; they also batch-produced them and sold them cheap, if necessary on the installment plan. They stole them and resold them: if you couldn't afford a new watch, you could buy an old one from a fence. Impecunious (and honest) would-be watch owners formed pools to buy one and drew for the right to get it.

The coaching services reflected this temporal sensibility: schedules to the minute, widely advertised; closely calculated arrival times and transfers; drivers checked by sealed clocks; speed over comfort; lots of dead horses. Note here the contrast with France. Across the Channel the government set speed limits and, to save the roads, required broad-rimmed wheels that rode heavy and slow. The passengers apparently did not mind. They preferred economy over time and quite correctly found that speed clashed with comfort. But

France too was changing. As one coaching service put it in 1834 (on the eve of the railway age): "greater speed is incompatible with certain needs which, on grounds of convenience and sometimes health, are not dispensable. One no longer stops to take meals, even far apart; one can't get off, even at the relay stations, and so on." In short, no pit stops. Where is modesty? "Women, children, older men can't take this regimen."[22]

## Why Not India?

Why no industrial revolution in India? After all, India had the world's premier cotton industry in the seventeenth and eighteenth centuries, unbeatable for quality, variety, and cost. This industry not only satisfied the large domestic demand but exported roughly half its output throughout the Indian Ocean and indirectly to Southeast Asia and China. To this huge market, beginning in the seventeenth century, came the stimulus of European demand—a huge shot in the arm that inevitably aggravated old and created new supply problems. Why, then, was there no interest in easing these difficulties by substituting capital (machines) for labor?

Indian historians have tended to overlook or reject this omission. Some, especially Indian nationalists, blame it on the Europeans, and most particularly the British. India had been prosperous and resourceful until these intruders burst on the scene, mixing into Indian politics and fomenting conflict. Some of this speculation is fantasy, and misdirected at that. One historian, for example, looks at the royal workshops (the *karkhanas*) of seventeenth-century India and dreams wistfully of a technological revolution: "One is tempted to speculate if [they] might not have moved in the direction of mechanization and become the state model factories for the modern industrialization of India, had they not been terminated by the British conquest of the country."[23] This, of an institution that could buy or command labor at will!

One useful way to approach the problem is to ask, *cui bono*, who benefits? Who would have gained from mechanization and transformation? Three groups or interests were involved: the workers (spinners and weavers); the middlemen, who typically advanced capital to the weavers against the promise of delivery; and the European traders and chartered companies, who wanted to buy for both the country (intra-Asian) trade and their European clientele.

It would be unreasonable to expect capital-using technological innovations from the first group. Workers had an obvious interest in getting materials (cotton fiber for spinners, yarn for weavers), but here they simply counted on merchant intermediaries. They had neither means nor the habit of command. A leading Indian economic historian cites as exceptional a "mutiny" of weavers in 1630 to protest against English competition for cotton yarn, and goes on: "Such instances of resistance were rare and have to be read together with the fact that the use of the horsewhip by the merchants' servants was accepted as a normal fact of life by most artisans."[24]

If there was to be a move to technological change, then, it would have to come from the Indian middlemen, who had both interest and, some of them, means; or from the European chartered companies. Yet neither budged.

Why not? Some explanations have been based on an implicit law of conservation of energy. The supply of labor was elastic, so it was easier and more economical to hire additional workers, from among untouchables and poor women for spinning, from agricultural laborers for weaving, than to look to change in technology; and that may well be the whole of the story.[25] Also, any unanticipated surge in demand (demand was segmented and different markets wanted different fabrics) could be met by shifting goods among markets, from domestic to foreign and from one foreign to another.

It was even possible, though very difficult, to assemble large numbers of workers "under one roof" (in one place), to toil under supervision. This was the sort of thing the foreign trading companies tried to do, by way of ensuring prompt completion of tasks. In some instances such concentration yielded economies of scale and materials—in fuel-using branches, for example, or in assembly work such as shipbuilding. Technological change, then, in the form of organizational innovation, was not unknown. Such enterprises, however, remained the exception; "the small-scale family-based unit [retained] its position of primacy."[26]

Hardware—instruments, equipment, machines—was another matter. This is what it took to make an industrial revolution, and India was not ready. "In India it is seldom that an attempt is made to accomplish anything by machinery that can be performed by human labour."[27] One reason for this "general indifference": no one seems to have had a passionate interest in simplifying and easing tasks. Both worker and employer saw hard labor as the worker's lot—and as appropriate. Indifference, moreover, was promoted by segmentation: it was not the cloth merchant's job to find, assemble, and deliver the raw materials. He advanced capital, and it was up to weaver and spinner to do the rest. This was significantly different from putting-out as practiced in Europe, where the merchant took part in the production process.

In India, then, the final buyer was cut off from the means of remedy. The worker did what he had always done, and so did the merchant. Dutch records tell us that merchants kept weavers "on a short leash," paying them by the day so that they could not get ahead and run off, presumably with the goods.[28] Some merchants hired agents to keep an eye on the weavers and check their progress. The aim here was to prevent the weaver, who invariably consumed his advance by the time he finished the work, from selling his finished piece to another buyer. We hear of agents who would enter the weaver's house and cut the cloth from the loom, even though not completely done. Come back a day later, and it might be gone, and nine tenths of a piece was better than none.

The European companies in turn learned to accommodate these irregularities. Markets failed at times, but both Indians and Europeans seem to have viewed these lapses as a fact of life. Like famine: This too shall pass. The industry seems to have followed its own leisurely pace, which was not irrational. (It is ends that determine which means are rational.) In the Coromandel (southeast coast), for example, the raw cotton was moved from the interior to the spinning and weaving villages on and near the coast by huge bullock trains numbering in the thousands and tens of thousands, the whole shapeless mass feeding while shambling along at a rate of a few miles a day. Since the trek covered some three hundred or more miles, it took about half a year to deliver the goods.[29]

Meanwhile the European companies' own rhythm of purchases and shipments reflected the irregularities of shipping and of capital availability, to say nothing of fluctuations in supply. Data, for example, on shipments by the East India Company of textiles from Bombay show a high variance, ranging from a few thousand (zero in one year) to almost a million pieces.[30] The companies' remedy was to keep large stocks and time their auction sales to match fluctations in European demand. (Their agents and purveyors in India did their best meanwhile to "shortstop" shipments normally destined to Asian markets.) All of this was costly, but cheaper than trying to transform technology.

Besides, it was not obvious to the East India Company that direct assistance to the Indian cotton industry was politically wise. British manufacturing interests would have seen that as treason. Toward the end of the seventeenth century a pamphleteer denounced the prospect that merchants would send over to India "Cloth-Weavers, and Dyers, and Throwsters, as well as Silk." Do that, he warned, and "I question not but we shall have Cotton-Cloth and Knaves enough to make it a fashion and Fools enough to wear it." The company made haste to deny the charge.[31] The EIC was under constant attack as an exporter of specie and bullion; it did not want the additional onus of exporting jobs.

Finally, where were India's ideas of mechanization to come from? Indian society did know technological change: the most important in the textile manufacture came with the substitution of the wheel for the distaff (though not for the finest muslin yarn). But innovation took place within the conventional manual context, and a big conceptual and social difference separates machines and hand tools. One must distinguish further between all-purpose tools and specialized: Indian artisans, however skilled, had scarcely started on the path to instrumentation. Here is Major Rennell, the first surveyor-general of Bengal, on a visit in 1761 to the Bombay shipyard: " . . . the work is performed by Indian artificers, who are observed to use but two kinds of edged tools, tho' their work is durable and neat."[32] The skill was all in the hand, and not so much in the eye as in the feel; not surprising in a society without corrective lenses.

Worse yet, Indian craftsmen avoided using iron, and iron (and steel) is indispensable to precision work. This was not a ferruginous society. One Indian historian contrasts here Persian irrigation technique, which used iron wheels and gearing, and the Indian system, using wood, rope, and earthen pots; and like a good believer in substitutability, he explains the difference in economic terms: " . . . a tool of lower efficiency can be used to manufacture the same commodity by employment of cheap skilled labor."[33] He might also have noted that India had no screws: the metalworkers could not cut a proper thread; and that iron nails were rare. Their absence made a difference in shipbuilding. European ships were nailed and spiked; Indian vessels tied the planking to the hull with cords and ropes and rabbeted and glued the boards end to end.[34]

This manual mode explains as much as anything the failure of non-European craftsmen to make clocks and watches as good as Europe's. They had the hands, the "matchless ingenuity," but not the tools. They did extraordinary work, in musket making for example. "Even today, 1786," wrote a French convert to Islam named Haji Mustafa, "Colonel Martin, a Frenchman, who has greatly distinguished himself these twenty-two years in the English service, has at Lucknow a manufactory where he makes pistols and fuzils better, both as to lock and barrel, than the best arms that come from Europe."[35] But these gifted craftsmen made each piece differently, because they could not or would not work by instruments. When the aforesaid Colonel Claude Martin, one of the most enterprising agents of the East India Company, wanted to buy a watch for himself, he sent to Paris and bought it from Louis Berthoud, the finest *chronométrier* in France; and when, as often, he sold clocks and watches to the court of Aoudh and other Indian clients, he got them too from Europe. Where else? The Indians, like the Chinese, were not doing anything in this area.[36]

Under the circumstances, the move to machinery in India was not to be envisaged. Such a leap would have entailed a shift from hand skills nurtured from childhood, linked to caste identity and division of labor by sex and age. It would also have required imagination outside the Indian cultural and intellectual experience. As Chaudhuri puts it: "In eighteenth-century India the empirical basis for an Industrial Revolution was conspicuously lacking. There had been no marked progress in scientific knowledge for many centuries, and the intellectual apparatus for a diffusion and systematic recording of the inherited skills was seriously defective."[37]

And still in the nineteenth century: the British engineers who built the Indian railways understood that Indian labor, cheap as it was, would move earth and rock by hand; but they also took for granted that the Indians would use wheelbarrows. Not at all: the Indians were used to moving heavy burdens in a basket on their head and refused to change. We even have one report of Indian laborers placing barrows on their head rather than wheel them. Presumably such resistance reflected a desire to spread the work and increase employment, especially to women and children.[38] All the same, European workers, very different, would have been happy to gain higher pay through greater productivity; to say nothing of easier labor.*

* Part of the explanation lies in the assignment of such tasks in Asia to women and children, that is, to people who could not say no. One finds similar patterns elsewhere, for example, in Southeast Asia, where women harvested rice with a finger-knife, one stalk at a time, rather than with a sickle. This was said to honor the rice spirit; but then, it is not uncommon to sanctify women's toil with pious myths. Had men done the cutting, the rice spirit would have been honored by a quick sickle and a symbolic handful of the harvest. On finger-knife harvesting, see Reid, *Southeast Asia,* I, 5.

# ～ 16 ～

# Pursuit of Albion

When I was a student I learned that *homo sapiens* is an animal species of single origin: all humans today, of whatever color or size, are descended from a common ancestor, split off from a larger hominid genus some millions of years ago. The same is true of the species *industrial society*. All examples, however different, are descended from the common British predecessor.

The Industrial Revolution in England changed the world and the relations of nations and states to one another. For reasons of power, if not of wealth, the goals and tasks of political economy were transformed. The world was now divided between one front-runner and a highly diverse array of pursuers. It took the quickest of the European "follower countries" something more than a century to catch up (see Table 16.1).

Some practitioners of the "New Economic History," beguiled by measurement and impressed by puffish numbers of French commercial and industrial growth during the eighteenth century, have argued that British priority in industrialization was something of an accident and that the Industrial Revolution might as easily have occurred across the Channel. France, after all, was a bigger, more populous country, with a greater product in the aggregate, and it was *overall* equal to Britain

Table 16.1. Estimates of Real GNP per Capita
for Selected Countries (in 1960 $ U.S.)

|  | 1830 | 1860 | 1913 | 1929 | 1950 | 1960 | 1970 |
|---|---|---|---|---|---|---|---|
| Belgium | 240 | 400 | 815 | 1020 | 1245 | 1520 | 2385 |
| Canada | 280 | 405 | 1110 | 1220 | 1785 | 2205 | 3005 |
| Czechoslovakia | — | — | 500 | 650* | 810 | 1340 | 1980 |
| Denmark | 225 | 320 | 885 | 955 | 1320 | 1710 | 2555 |
| France | 275 | 380 | 670 | 890 | 1055 | 1500 | 2535 |
| West Germany | 240 | 345 | 775 | 900 | 995 | 1790 | 2705 |
| Italy | 240 | 280 | 455 | 525 | 600 | 985 | 1670 |
| Japan | 180 | 175 | 310 | 425 | 405 | 855 | 2130 |
| Netherlands | 270 | 410 | 740 | 980 | 1115 | 1490 | 2385 |
| Norway | 225 | 325 | 615 | 845 | 1225 | 1640 | 2405 |
| Portugal | 250 | 290 | 335 | 380 | 440 | 550 | 985 |
| Russia/Soviet Union | 180 | 200 | 345 | 350 | 600 | 925 | 1640 |
| Spain | — | 325 | 400 | 520 | 430 | 640 | 1400 |
| Sweden | 235 | 300 | 705 | 875 | 1640 | 2155 | 2965 |
| Switzerland | 240 | 415 | 895 | 1150 | 1590 | 2135 | 2785 |
| United Kingdom | 370 | 600 | 1070 | 1160 | 1400 | 1780 | 2225 |
| United States | 240 | 550 | 1350 | 1775 | 2415 | 2800 | 3605 |

*As corrected by Professor Bairoch
SOURCE: Bairoch, "Main Trends in National Economic Disparities," in Bairoch and Lévy-Leboyer, eds., *Disparities in Economic Development*, p. 10.

in scientific and technological knowledge and capability. Still others, following the a priori reasoning of classical economic theory, have argued that it really made no difference to other countries that Britain had moved ahead in industrial technology and productivity. Each nation, after all, could and would follow its own comparative advantage, could and would buy what it needed on the most favorable terms.* So what if Britain made better and cheaper iron and steel? One could

* A word about the term *comparative advantage*, which we shall use again on other occasions. Contrary to appearance, it does not mean the ability to produce something at lower cost than some other producer. It means the ability to make more money doing one thing than another. A country that follows its comparative advantage, then, will make those things that earn it most, and not just anything that it can sell for less than competitors can.

trade Lyons silks and Bordeaux wines and come out the better for the trade.[1]

That is the theory. The statesmen who guided the destinies of European nations did not have access to this logic; and if they had, they would have paid it little mind. They linked industrial advance to power.

The material and social advance of England could not fail to draw the attention of commercial and political rivals: Spain, to begin with, which came a cropper in its project to invade and dominate this sassy island; then Holland, which saw the little pretender pass it in trade and drub it on the high seas; and finally and persistently, France, immemorial enemy, bigger and more populous, pretender to European hegemony and yet repeatedly loser to Britain's naval strength, financial sinew, and commercial enterprise. Some French wrote of England in admiration, by way of holding an example to their own government. "England does not make the quarter of France," observed Pierre Le Pesant, seigneur de Boisguillebert (1656–1714), French magistrate and economist, toward the end of the seventeenth century, "neither in number nor the fertility of its land. . . . Yet England has been able to yield the Prince of Orange for the last three or four years revenues of 80 million livres [say 3 million pounds sterling], and do it without reducing the population to begging or forcing them to abandon their land."[2]

Others wrote in fear, seeing England not only as their country's enemy but as a commercial power of unlimited potential. Thus the first secretary (*premier commis*) of the Ministry of Foreign Affairs, preparing for the negotiations that led to the Treaty of Utrecht (1713), warned his superiors against letting England obtain a foothold in the Pacific. If, for example, one were to let them have a small island in the Juan Fernandez group off the coast of Chile—a place whose sempiternal solitude recommended it to Defoe as the locale of *Robinson Crusoe*—

one can be sure that, however deserted it may be today . . . if it came into English hands, one would see there, in a few years, a large number of inhabitants, built-up ports, and the greatest entrepot in the world of European and Asian manufactures, which the English would then purvey to the kingdoms of Peru and Mexico. . . . Sixty millions in gold and silver coming from the mines of those countries would be the object and reward of their industry. What efforts would this nation, so skillful in trade and rich in vessels not be ready to make to get for itself this immense revenue from America! . . . and what a loss for France to lose this market for its gildings [*dorures*], its silks, its linens; because, since the English don't make these things, they'd go buy them in China and the East, and while these islanders got rich, indeed became the strongest European nation, France would grow weak.[3]

Perfidious Albion as superpower. To this day, and in spite of two world wars, the average Frenchman thinks of Britain as his country's chief rival and adversary in Europe. One does not forget Agincourt and Joan of Arc that quickly.

These animadversions, of course, were unconscious salutes to English success. The French, as we have seen, were particularly vexed to watch the British pull ahead. They viewed economic growth and the accumulation of wealth as the keys to political power, and they correctly associated the succession of British victories in European and overseas combat with the resources the British could mobilize: the numerous ships (over a hundred thousand of theirs, only twenty thousand of ours), the countless seamen. Some French even imagined that England was an island without an interior, all coasts and harbors, a land without cultivators, composed entirely of sailors and city dwellers. Others, like Boisguillebert, were overawed by British wealth, the revenues of the crown, the ability to borrow both at home and abroad.

In all this the link to trade was self-evident; Voltaire expressed it with characteristic abandon:

> What has made England powerful is the fact that from the time of Elizabeth, all parties have agreed on the necessity of favoring commerce. The same parliament that had the king beheaded was busy with overseas trading posts as though nothing were happening. The blood of Charles I was still steaming when this parliament, composed almost entirely of fanatics, passed the Navigation Act of 1650.[4]

Contrary to French adage, to understand is not necessarily to forgive. English commercial protectionism, and even more English success, aroused more resentment than admiration. In 1698, Louis XIV gave advice to his ambassador in London: "Nowhere in the world are the rules of Equality, so right and necessary for trade, more flouted than in England."[5] Other Frenchmen felt the same. One even complained that, so far did the British push their contempt for fair play, they tried to stop foreigners from smuggling in contraband.[6]

In general, the critical foreigner condemned the English for their greed and materialism. "The notorious avarice of the Dutchman," wrote a German traveler circa 1800, pales before that of the Briton, as the shadow before the light."[7] And a French visitor, the comte de Mirabeau: "Accustomed as [the British] are to *calculate* everything, they calculate talents and friendship. . . . "

(To this day, the French like to think and pretend to others that they do not care for money. They are not alone: idealism is the affectation of those who feel they have less than they deserve in the presence of those who have more. In the eighteenth century, Continental observers saw the English as great materialists. A hundred years later, the Americans became the new target of obloquy, the British now joining their erstwhile critics in scorning these *nouveaux riches*.)

In short, you couldn't trust these Brits.[8] Some French took comfort in antique precedent: Britain was the "modern Carthage"; France, the heir of Rome. In the last analysis, an island-nation of rootless traders (shopkeepers) could not hold its own with a solid, *terra firma* kingdom. Another big mistake.

In the European world of competition for power and wealth, then, Britain became the principal target of emulation from the beginning of the eighteenth century. Other countries sent emissaries and spies to learn what they could of British techniques. Merchants and industrialists visited the island to see what they could. Governments did their best to stimulate enterprise by the usual array of incentives: subsidies, monopoly privileges, exemptions from taxes, assignment of labor, bribes. Such efforts had mixed results, partly because these very encouragements, by their partiality, prevented or retarded the diffusion of techniques; but even more because the follower countries were not yet ready to learn and adopt the new mode of production. What's more, just about the time when the Continental countries became aware of the extent of the British lead and were making their first, tentative gains in the crucial cotton manufacture, the French Revolution brought political turmoil, interrupted communications, and imposed a time-out. Not absolute: intervals of peace, partial or general, permitted British expats and Continental competitors to get on with the task—to introduce machine spinning, for example, in the southern Netherlands (Ghent and Verviers) and northern France. Innovation was necessarily spotty, however, and the technologies were already out of date. Not until the defeat of Napoleon at Waterloo in 1815 brought a definitive end to the fighting could Europe get on with the process of catch-up. (There is no street named Waterloo in Paris, nor Napoléon, for that matter.)

Karl Marx saw the British experience as an expression of historical logic. Capitalist production had its laws: "It is a question of these laws themselves, of these tendencies working with iron necessity towards inevitable results. The country that is more developed industrially only shows to the less developed, the image of its own future."[9]

Yes and no. On a larger, metaphorical level—Adam Smith's "natural progress of opulence"—Marx was right. But in detail—timing, composition, direction of change—he was wrong. Every country has its own resources and capabilities, and if it permits reason and the market to rule, its economic development will follow those paths that make the most of its means. Thus a country rich in coal will engage in fuel-intensive branches of industry and adopt techniques that a coalless country would eschew. A country short of coal but rich in running streams will rely, when possible, on waterpower rather than steam engines.

(To be sure, the force of these material constraints will vary with technique: a lack of coal, for example, will be far more constraining if costly transport makes it impractical to bring in fuel from outside. In the eighteenth and early nineteenth centuries, the French iron industry was severely handicapped by the high cost of fossil fuel, and it was not until canals and railways were built that this constraint was eased, at least partially. Two hundred years later, it paid South Korean iron-makers to move coking coal from western Pennsylvania to the Great Lakes, ship it down the St. Lawrence to the Atlantic, and move it by ship through the Panama Canal and across the Pacific. Different times, different means, different possibilities. Meanwhile, a few miles away, Pittsburgh steel was dying. It takes more than cheap raw materials to make a successful industry.)

So we have no uniformity of sequence, no single way, no law of development. Each of the would-be industrializers, the so-called follower countries, however much influenced by the British experience—to some extent inspired, to some extent frightened or appalled—developed its own path to modernity. And if this was true of the early industrializers, how much more is it true today. Everything depends on timing. The content of modern technology is ever-changing and the task and means of emulation change with it. Developing countries today will necessarily skip stages and processes that occupied the British for decades: why should they repeat what they don't have to?[10]

All of which does not make the British experience irrelevant. One must distinguish between objective and process. The nineteenth-century statesmen who tried to move their countries toward industrialization kept the British example before them, whether as model or countermodel. To understand them and the process, one has to know the point of departure and the goal. And of course historians have their own special needs: an ideal type has heuristic value, if only as measuring stick and counterexample, so long as one keeps in mind what one is doing.[11]

A map of the Europe of 1815 in terms of machine readiness would give the highest grades to those countries and regions already engaged in manufacture for the larger world economy. I say "regions," because some of these industrial areas overlapped national boundaries, themselves unsettled and ephemeral; and because all these countries were socially and culturally heterogeneous.* Indeed, this temporal diversity (as though they were living in different times) was a critical aspect of economic preparedness. The lowest grades would go to those that had long lived in isolation from the currents of exchange, whether of commodities or ideas, the places were older agrarian structures of status and power were largely intact.

The machine-readiest societies lay in the northwest quadrant of the Continent: France, the Low Countries, the Rhineland, the Protestant cantons of Switzerland, and outliers in the northeast corner of Spain (Catalonia) and in Bohemia. Readiness fell, often precipitately, as one moved east across the Elbe to eastern Germany, Austria, Poland, and Russia and southeast into old Ottoman lands; also south to the Mediterranean (most of Iberia and the Kingdom of Naples). One economic historian speaks of a "developmental gradient," a downward slope, and quotes from another who does not mince words: "To move east was likewise to go back in time, or in levels of economic development; in eastern Europe and Russia the industrial centers were oases in a sea of peasant sloth and bureaucratic inertia."[12]

---

* The importance of the region as a unit of production has long been noted. See, for example, the monographs of N. J. G. Pounds in the 1950s; Pounds and Parker, *Coal and Steel*; Wrigley, *Industrial Growth* (on what was once called Neustria, in Charlemagne's time); and a long series of French studies of human geography going back to the beginning of the century. To argue from this, however, to a rejection of the nation-state as a useful, nay indispensable, unit of study is to throw the baby out with the bathwater. The one does not exclude the other. So long as economic activity is shaped by national concerns and policy, and so long as it is the nation that is the principal source and frame of our numbers—'twas ever thus, and I see no change in prospect— national studies and comparisons will be the heart of the matter. Cf. on this point John Davis's discussion of Pollard, *Peaceful Conquest*, in Davis, "Industrialization in Britain and Europe, p. 55.

What our critic alludes to here is what I shall call "the medieval legacy"—what European (as opposed to British or American) historians would call "feudalism," which they see as persisting to the French Revolution and, in other countries, beyond. The Old Regime, in other words.* This was a big complex of customs, laws, practices, attitudes, and values—the work of centuries—but for the purposes of this analysis, three aspects are specially germane.

## The Status of the Peasantry

In the Middle Ages, most peasants had been reduced (or raised, for slaves) to a condition of bondage or serfdom. Typically the peasant was tied to the soil, not free to leave without the consent of his lord. Serfdom sometimes also implied a personal, "bodily" tie of serf to master, so that the lord could move the peasant about, and the peasant, even leaving with permission, continued to owe dues.

In western Europe during the high and late Middle Ages, these bonds relaxed, partly because the monetization of the economy and the growing appetite for exotic goods led landlords to commute labor services into money rents, even more because the rise of cities provided points of exit from the seignorial system. By 1500, England, France, the Low Countries, and western Germany had few serfs in the old sense. The process had proceeded farthest in England, where land was farmed either by yeomen or by free tenants; agricultural laborers, themselves often owners of small plots inadequate to their sustenance, were hired as needed. France and the others were not far behind, except for local vestiges and the widespread persistence of seignorial dues over and above commercial rents. The French Revolution simply abolished these remnants in France and areas annexed. This did not mean the peasant stopped paying; he just acquired a new lord, the state, and his dues became taxes. The lords got no compensation for their loss, which was seen as overdue justice.

In the diversity that was Germany, the nature of serfdom varied. West of the Elbe River, it resembled the French arrangement: generally money rents plus seignorial dues, little or no payment in labor, and

---

* In Anglo-American historiographical usage, the word "feudal" (from the word *feudum* or fief) is reserved to relations among lords or between lord and vassals—rules and practice above the line. Rules and practice between lord and peasants (across the line) are typically denoted as "seigneurial" or "manorial." Continental practice is to use "feudal" for those aspects of the society and economy that hark back to medieval usage—in effect, the Old Regime.

freedom of movement. Eastward lay the lands of estate bondage (*Gutsuntertänigkeit*) and personal (bodily) servitude (*Leibeigenschaft*); so, no movement except at the pleasure or order of the lord.

Political events accentuated the difference. The lands west of the Rhine were absorbed for a moment (until 1815) into Revolutionary France, and came and stayed under the new emancipatory dispensation. East of the Rhine, however, the French came and went. They left a memory of foreign oppression that served as justification for the later reimposition of servile obligations. Even so, war and the pursuit of power had their own surprising logic. The most important German political unit east of the Rhine was the kingdom of Prussia, a modern Sparta, an overmilitarized kingdom not given to romantic ideals. Yet Prussia emancipated the serfs in 1809—not because of enlightened attitudes, but rather because it had suffered grievous defeats at the hands of the French army and recognized that serfs will not fight so hard and well as free men.

In other German states, the taste of freedom had created an instant addiction; reactionaries found little support. The solution, which tried to please everybody, was to free the peasants and buy the landowners off; nothing like cash in the hand to overcome scruples and regrets. Where to find the money? The landowners were generally indemnified by state bonds, which the state then amortized by levies on the peasants over a period of years. (The one issue where reaction was acceptable, even popular, was the status of Jews. There disabilities were restored, and decades were to pass before full emancipation was grudgingly conceded. Even then, public gains were spoiled by private hatred.)

The other great barrier to mobility in German lands was the division of society into status groups (*Stände*) of reserved vocation and privilege. The lords had their land, ruled over their serfs and tenants, administered low if not high justice, led soldiers into battle. Merchants held a monopoly of trade but were not permitted to own rural land. The industrial crafts were reserved to properly trained journeymen and masters in the cities and towns. The countryside was peasant and seigneurial turf. The relationship of all this to medieval concepts of the three orders (lords, peasants, clergy), now with urban traders and artisans thrown in, will not have escaped the reader.*

---

* One finds similar social schemas in India: brahmins, warriors, merchants, peasants; and in Tokugawa Japan: *samurai*, peasants, merchants. These are attempts to give functional order and stability to society, thus protecting elites from change. The

Much of this was already breaking down in the eighteenth century. Still, one found persistent vestiges into the twentieth, especially in areas where German noblemen could lord it over a Slavic peasantry. In East Elbean Germany in general, lords continued to administer justice and collect fees and fines for their trouble; as the saying had it, the power of the state stopped at the gate to the estate. To be sure, some concessions had been made to the appearances of parliamentary democracy; but much of this was sham. In Prussia, for example, the most important of the German states, elections were held in tripartite colleges that gave hugely disproportionate clout to wealth.

Farther east, in Poland and Russia, the old ways held on longer, indeed were reinforced by the logic of commercial agriculture and comparative advantage. From the sixteenth century, the open plains of East Elbean Europe became a granary and livestock breeder for the urban centers of the west. The resulting exports (cereals, hides, tallow) stimulated land settlement; with one major hitch: scarcity of labor. Land was far more abundant than people.

Over a hundred years ago, Russian agrarian scholars pointed out that such disparity was incompatible with large holdings; or as one theoretical economist, picking up on this tradition, put it, three things cannot coexist: free land, free labor, and large estates. Why should peasants sign or stay on as hired labor when they can go off to the frontier and farm their own land?[13]

This meant that lords in Russia who wanted to cultivate on a large scale had to fix their workers to the soil. Hence the phenomenon known as the second serfdom—a progressive reinforcement of the peasant's obligations, reducing him to near-slave status. This policy can be tracked through a succession of decrees, each stronger than the one before, from the sixteenth to the eighteenth century. These deepened the social and political gulf between West and East—the one moving steadily toward greater freedom, the other to petrified servitude. Russia became in effect a huge prison, and with the exception of some months in 1917 and the few years since 1990, it has remained a prison ever since. (It remains to be seen whether the current experiment in democracy will last.)

Such a system could not work unless no exit. The absence of urban

---

French, while not enforcing vocational barriers, still used these divisions to determine political representation in the Estates-General on the eve of 1789. The English had their own political version, even more summary, in the division of the Parliament into Lords and Commons.

communes with the right to define the status of their inhabitants made
all the difference. Such cities and towns as existed were far sparser than
in the West and enjoyed neither liberties nor immunities. Emigration
was prohibited, except to Jews and other non-Russians. Meanwhile
the state and the aristocracy cooperated in catching and returning runaway serfs. (One significant exception: in the eighteenth century, the
mining and metallurgical enterprises of the Urals grabbed and kept
any loose, breathing male they could lay their hands on. No room for
altruism.)

In general, whenever industry located in empty places, usually to
minimize transport costs (also in connection with canal and road projects), the only solution was to move in forced labor. This was Russia's
school for wastage, an anticipation of the gulag. Even in more densely
settled areas, where casual layabouts and "street people" could be had
for food and booze to do loading, unloading, carting and hauling,
steady work called for servile labor assigned to the job. Entire villages,
often belonging to the state, were moved about in this way.

In the long run, of course, the system failed. Unfree labor would not
work well or honestly. In the words of a report on the Tula Armory in
1861: "It would seem to be generally indisputable that only free men
are capable of honest work. He who from childhood has been forced
to work is incapable of assuming responsibility as long as his social
condition remains unchanged."[14]

This, more than scale of production, explains the giantism of some
of these early enterprises: they needed lots of people because productivity was so low. A better solution was eventually found in the institution of *obrok,* personal dues paid by serfs detached from the estate to
earn a living elsewhere.* This arrangement allowed the serf to keep
what he made above the *obrok,* hence encouraged initiative and diligence. Some even became entrepreneurs, and the best of these could
become quite wealthy—thus the Elisseeffs, owners of St. Petersburg's
most luxurious delicatessen, later reduced to "Gastronom No. 1" after
confiscation by the Soviets. One of the descendants fled to the United
States, became professor of Japanese language and literature at Harvard. Many of these successful serfs paid fortunes to buy their freedom
and that of their family, although cunning estate owners often held one
or two children back, just in case the serf became even richer.

The system of servitude, then, was not without its expedients, as the

---

* The word means a money payment. Sometimes it was used to designate tax payment, sometimes rent.

rise of a private factory sector shows. By 1860 an estimated 4 million people were working for wages, plus an indeterminate number of peasant households engaged in industry on a seasonal or part-time basis.[15] In effect, the jobs found the workers and bent them to the task and, in some instances, to the lash. Whether the jobs got the skills needed was another matter.

It is not clear, then, that general emancipation of the serfs in Russia in 1861–66, usually seen as the great economic watershed, made much difference to the supply of bodies; but by obliging enterprises to hire free wage labor (or keep the labor they had), it compelled better treatment and more careful recruitment and opened the way to new technologies and higher standards.[16] Opened the way . . . The way was tortuous and thorny, especially in those branches and enterprises that had long been managed by the state and its agents. Emancipation here was initially partial and halfhearted. Some workers were freed; others kept on. Managers found consolation in illusions: if the best workers left, they were too old anyway and were not interested in making and doing; if the worst drifted away, well, where was the loss? The country was suffering from a massive institutional hangover, caught between new and old, anticipating by its dualism the schizophrenia of much Third World development in the twentieth century.

## The Organization of Manufacture

A second medieval legacy was the organization of industry into guilds or corporations. These were bodies of masters and workers, organized perhaps for social or fraternal reasons, but quickly transformed into business associations and collective monopolies.

Guilds were to be found all over the world—in Europe, but also in Islamic lands, India, China, and Japan. The economic objectives were to control entry, typically via obligatory apprenticeship and limitations on mastership; to uphold quality standards (no amateurs or "botchers" (bunglers) allowed); and to restrict competition both within (limitations on size of workshop and numbers employed) and without (prohibition of nonguild manufacture within the jurisdiction and exclusion of all imports from outside).

Behind this array of rules lay a set of moral principles, themselves derived from the values of the rural village community and transposed to the urban context. Two considerations dominated: first, the sense of limited resources, whether in land or custom (market demand), hence of a zero-sum game (one person's gain is someone else's loss); and second, the priority of moral criteria over commercial. So long as a crafts-man did his work conscientiously and to standard, he was entitled to a living.

Against this good worker ethic, however, beat the forces of greed and ambition—the morality of market and money. As we have seen in our discussion of putting-out, merchants learned to bypass guild re-strictions by finding workers in the countryside; or when, as in clock- and watchmaking, the work called for skills not found in cottages, by hiring journeymen (once apprentices, not yet masters) to work in their own rooms or in suburbs outside guild jurisdiction. That was a great weakness of these corporate monopolists: they were closely bound with municipalities and ill-equipped to impose themselves on a changing turf.

Not that they did not try. In Italy, industrial centers typically annexed the surrounding countryside, and guild controls extended beyond city limits. In the Low Countries (the other great manufacturing center of medieval Europe), urban masters and their henchmen sallied forth into the countryside to break looms and terrorize their rural competition. Such expeditions succeeded only until the country weavers learned to defend themselves, giving blow for blow, and from the seventeenth century on, rural manufacture was tolerated if not recognized. In Ger-many, the complication of political boundaries was such that every ex-clusive center had a potential rival next door, only too happy to welcome interlopers, "botchers," Jews, and similar fee- and taxpaying outlaws.

In France, on the other hand, the guilds were well placed to defend their interests because they were sanctioned and defended by the crown, partly for fiscal reasons, partly as instruments of social control. The crown's writ extended almost everywhere.* Even so, maverick masters found ways to bypass constraints. Some of them, for example, enjoyed the kind of reputation that created demand beyond their shop's capacity. So they hired others to do their work and signed it with their own name. Such outsourcing was strictly forbidden, and occa-sionally guild representatives came searching, accompanied by bailiffs, confiscated the contraband, fined the culprit. For every master turned in and caught, dozens got away with it.

---

* There were exceptional jurisdictions: Alsace, much of it acquired in 1648 (Stras-bourg in 1681); the Franche-Comté of Burgundy, won from Spain in 1678; Lorraine, annexed in 1766; and recent conquests in Flanders—all in part subject to their own laws and customs. European nation-states were still in the making.

Toward the end of the Old Regime, in 1762, the French government formally recognized the status quo and legitimized rural manufacture, while a succession of functionaries tried vainly to abolish corporate privileges or the corporations themselves. In vain; but here again the revolution accomplished what an inept monarchy could not. In 1791, the momentarily laissez-faire government abolished trade and craft corporations—not only workers' guilds but associations of employers. It was all very progressive and impartial, but over the next three quarters of a century, the law was applied much more strictly against labor unions than against employers' associations. Not surprising: the first priority was order, which meant keeping those above on top and those below in their place.*

In Germany, where the guilds had long been bypassed by employers and interlopers, they remained a force in the cities and in divers principalities and kingdoms, and it was not until the formation of the empire in 1870 that they finally gave up the ghost. The issue of their legitimacy was subsumed in a general debate concerning "industrial freedom." On one side were the liberals and big business, which felt that Germany could not hold its own with modern competitors unless people were free to work, move, and reside where they pleased. What was the point of a German customs union where goods could pass and people not? What good the right to establish mills if there were no hands to hire? On the other side were conservatives and small tradesmen and artisans, fearful of such new forms of enterprise as factories and now department stores. The modern men (among them, the Jews), the free market, open competition, new wealth . . . these were the enemy.

These attempts to hold back the future were doomed in a Germany still pursuing power. Power meant engines, machines, modern technologies and the rules to go with them. The balance tilted inexorably toward the apostles of change. The guildsmen had a moment of revival in 1848–49, when revolutionary disturbances gave them an opportunity to make their local power felt. They attempted to reimpose long abandoned or neglected constraints on entry and movement, but failed, essentially because this reactionary move was seen as a blow to

---

* An exception was made for fraternities of journeymen, many of whom did a tour of the country by way of professional preparation and found hospitality at every stop. These *compagnonnages,* as they were called, did networking and supplied intelligence about jobs and employers, but did not play much of a role in labor conflict. Their secret greetings and their peripatetic, often literate membership inspired romantic images. Yet they gave no trouble and got no trouble.

order. Besides, the rising commercial and industrial bourgeoisie was in no mood to return to the Middle Ages.

The dam broke first in relatively backward Austria. The Ministry of Commerce put it bluntly: " . . . for Austrian industry, which since the fall of the prohibitive system has to struggle in all directions against foreign competition, the grant of complete freedom of movement is no longer a question of mere improvement and greater well-being, but a necessary condition of its ability to compete."[17] If the government still had doubts about the matter, the military defeats in northern Italy drove home the need for reform. War, especially unsuccessful war, concentrates the mind. On 20 December 1859 an imperial patent established freedom of enterprise throughout the Habsburg dominions. The move was contagious. The system of corporate industrial control began collapsing throughout the Germanies. By 1870 and unification, the battle was over.[18]

## Boundaries and Barriers

A third major medieval legacy in restraint of trade was the extraordinarily complex array of interferences with transport and travel: river and port tolls; road fees; entrance duties at city gates ("Oxen and Jews: 4 Pfennig"); customs barriers following one upon the other because of the lacework of political boundaries, including enclaves and exclaves; a multiplicity of exemptions and franchises, honored as much in the breach as in the observance.

Most of the road and river tolls went back to times of political weakness and general insecurity when higher political authority could not prevent robber barons and local jurisdictions from levying on passersby. Once there, only try to remove: the one thing everyone respected was vested interest, because everyone had one, or wanted to have one. Even where higher authority ruled and permission was needed to levy, the right to charge was seen, not as a fee for service or facilities, but as one more source of income, hence a mark of favor to be solicited or bought. We have the story of this Count of the Palatinate, impecunious and importuning, who in 1579 pulled out all the stops in his petition for toll-right: "God have mercy and help us and our six poor uneducated children and our wife with heavy belly full with child."[19]

These tolls, then, did not pay for improvements and maintenance, but were simply extortion; and so well did they return, especially on water routes, that haulers were often compelled to use roads, however poor and slow, even for bulk commodities of low value per weight.

Equally costly were the delays for inspection and sometimes transshipment—a form of job creation and a pretext for further exactions.

The maximizing strategy of these brigands-in-guise-of-officials may be inferred from their policy of deliberate uncertainty. Even where tariffs were set, the toll-takers would make it a point not to publish them, the better to levy as opportunity offered.[20] (That kind of transaction put a premium on shrewdness and separated the "slick traders" and fast talkers from the easy marks—a selection process, in effect.) The whole system was designed to encourage bribes, including rounds of food and drinks for the boys, which did not help the next boat to get through.

Needless to say, the local barons and municipal authorities who enjoyed these gains had no desire to give them up by way of easing trade and encouraging business; on the contrary, growing trade was an incentive to increase the tariffs. Such increases invariably drew howls of protest and pain, but no one was ready to crack down even on small gougers; too many glass houses to start throwing stones. The initial result of industrial development, then, was to raise the barriers.

From the seventeenth century on, the centralizing tendency of European monarchies worked against this racket. One of the primary goals of the new bureaucracies was to erase these levies and interferences, seen not only as restraints of trade, hence tax-eaters, but also as poaching, as *lèse-majesté*. The British had little to do along these lines: their local tolls had largely disappeared by the fifteenth century; as a result they had the largest national market in Europe. The French needed much more, and the great minister Colbert issued order upon order banning and abolishing this legacy of disorder; to little avail. Once again, it was the revolution that did the job, one hundred years later, clearing the debris of an outworn regime.

Germany, whose proliferation of tolls was a byword for madness—*furiosa Teutonicorum insania*—was much slower to clear the way, partly because of the very size of the task, partly because of the extraordinary territorial fragmentation: thirty-eight separate tariff systems in 1815, plus thousands of local autonomies, down to small towns and landed estates. Only power politics—Prussian screws—and chauvinist ideology could do the job, and then painfully. Die-hards had to be shown that it cost more to stay out than to come in. Treaties and negotiations following the Napoleonic wars freed up transport along the Rhine, and a series of ever bigger customs unions culminating in the *Zollverein* of 1834 opened most of the country to relatively untrammeled trade. I say "relatively," because even then much remained to be done. Some states were not brought in, heels dragging, until the 1860s and in 1870. The old Hanseatic cities of Frankfurt and Hamburg, rich in history and pride, yelped with pain, but in such matters, La Fontaine's dictum applies: *La raison du plus fort est toujours la meilleure,* or might makes right.

The tenacity of the enemies of other people's trade fairly beggars the imagination. Take the river Scheldt. It rises in northern France and flows through one of the most prosperous industrial regions in the world on its way past Tournai, Ghent, and Antwerp to the sea. Some distance below Antwerp, by the accidents of history, the mouth of the river passes into Holland, which by the Treaty of Munster in 1648 obtained the right to close it to navigation. This Holland did, for over two hundred years, for the aim was to kill Antwerp as seaport in favor of Rotterdam—no small matter. For fifteen years, however, from 1815 to 1830, Antwerp and Rotterdam were both part of the Netherlands, so in theory, these rights should have lapsed. Not at all: in 1830, when Belgium seceded, Holland reaffirmed its right and got the other interested powers to accept this levy on international trade. Not until 1863 could Belgium, after long negotiations, buy in this outrageous toll, with each of the powers interested in the trade paying its quota.

The sole exception to this process of rationalization and unification was the persistence of customs barriers at the entrance of cities, what the French call the *octroi.* These survived into the twentieth century; even the railway had not managed to kill them (one could always inspect baggage on arrival). It was the automobile that did the job: as the number of vehicles increased, it became impossible to halt them at city boundaries for inspection of contents; or to compel Paris autos, for example, to submit as in the 1920s to a dipstick measurement of the fuel in the gas tank upon leaving and returning. Even so, as late as the 1960s, road signs advised drivers entering Florence from the surrounding countryside to declare such commodities as wine and cigarettes. So far as I could tell, no one stopped or was stopped; but I was a short-term visitor.

Russia was a different story. Transport was difficult, to begin with, and tolls were not a problem. Nature was. On land, it was easier to move goods in winter than in summer. Snow and ice were smooth; the roads were not. Water was better for bulky commodities (grain, timber). But Russian rivers run north-south, and most traffic moved east-west. Here cold was the enemy: in the south, waterways remained open nine months of the year; in the north, only six weeks. Miss the cut-off, and goods would perish; machines, rust; idleness, turn into oblivion.

The significance of institutional and cultural impediments to development shows well in the contrasting experience of Europe's periphery—the lands around the edge, outside the core of industrialization in western and central Europe; and, within this periphery, between those countries and regions that learned to catch up and those that still lag.

Start in the north. Scandinavia, desperately poor in the eighteenth century yet intellectually and politically rich, was late in learning the ways of modern industry, but, once started, quick to pick them up. The implications for wages and income show in the statistical estimates (see Table 16.2).

This impressive performance owes everything to cultural preparation. The Scandinavian countries, equal partners in Europe's intellectual and scientific community, enjoyed high levels of literacy and offered a first-class education at higher levels.[21] They also operated in an atmosphere of political stability and public order. Once among the most warlike populations in Europe—one thinks of the Viking raiders of the Middle Ages or of the imperial ambitions of seventeenth-century Sweden—now they were the most peaceable, even stolid by comparison with peoples to the south. Property rights were secure; the peasantry was largely free; and life was a long stretch of somber hard work broken intermittently by huge bouts of drinking and seasonal sunshine.

Table 16.2: Estimates of Real GNP per Capita in Groups of
European Countries, 1830–1913 (U.S.$ of 1960;
unweighted averages within each group)

|  | 1830 | 1860 | 1913 |
|---|---|---|---|
| Industrial core | 268 | 402 | 765 |
| Scandinavia | 219 | 297 | 682 |
| Scandinavia without Finland | 228 | 315 | 735 |
| Rest of periphery | 215 | 244 | 343 |

*Industrial core:* Austria (except 1830), France, Germany, Italy, Netherlands, Switzerland, U.K.
*Scandinavia:* Denmark, Finland, Norway, Sweden
*Rest of periphery:* Bulgaria, Greece, Hungary (except 1860), Portugal, Romania, Spain, Russia, Serbia. The 1830 figure refers to Portugal and Russia only
SOURCE: Pollard, "The Peripheral European Countries," as from Bairoch, "Main Trends in National Economic Disparities."

Scandinavia was ready. Even in the eighteenth century, one sees the promise of later enterprise: the machine works and ingenious equipment of Polhem in Sweden; the Norwegian cobalt mines and refinery, which supplied brilliant blue colorants to the glass and porcelain works of Europe, from Wedgwood to Meissen. Much of the craftwork was crude and dowdy by comparison with that of nations to the south, but Scandinavia was fast catching up in tools, instruments, and technique. No better clue than horology: by the end of the eighteenth century, the best Danish and Swedish clock- and watchmakers were making machines equal to those of London and Geneva; and these were local artists, not the West European expats of Constantinople, Moscow, and Peking.

Scandinavia built on free enterprise and quick response, on the export of staples to more advanced industrial countries, on the investment of these gains in more diversified production. The big export commodities were timber, copper, later on, iron ore; for Denmark, agricultural products. In all cases, development proceeded by moving from the raw to the processed—from logs to boards, and then to pulp; from iron ore to pig iron to wrought iron; from raw fish to canned and jarred; from milk to cream, butter, and cheese. Much of this was fostered by improvements in transportation and banking institutions, and here the state and foreign capital played a role. But very early on, Scandinavia was exporting know-how in the form of its own émigrés, toward tsarist Russia for example, where Alfred Nobel was one of the pioneers of the infant petroleum industry. The Russian state had been pushing industrial development on and off for hundreds of years, huffing and puffing and squeezing the population as it went; the Scandinavians eased into the process and glided away.

Compare the late industrial development of Mediterranean Europe, in particular of Italy, Spain, and Portugal. All of these were hurt by religious and intellectual intolerance, and all were plagued by political instability. Spain, though nominally united, was divided as before by regional autonomies, and the weakness of central authority invited foreign intrusion and dynastic pretensions, with intermittent revolution and civil war. Portugal, better knit, was politically much the same, with the exception that the monarchy could flee to Brazil and wait for better times. Italy remained fragmented, with Lombardy still in Habsburg (Austrian) hands as late as 1860 and Venetia to 1866; the Kingdom of the Two Sicilies (Naples and the south) under Bourbon rule until 1861; the papal states and Rome under clerical government until 1870.

All these countries were poor, handicapped by meager, highly variable rainfall that reduced agricultural yields far below those of well-watered northern Europe. Spain was the least favored. A notional line between wet northern Europe and dry southern (above and below 750 mm. [30 in.] of rain a year) divides Portugal and Italy approximately in half; but 90 percent of Spain lies on the dry side, and much of the wetter land above the line is mountainous and not arable. Add in Spain's high average altitude and hence extremes of temperature, and we have a bad country for cereals.[22]

One might have thought such poor lands good candidates for cottage industry, *à la suisse*, but Iberia particularly wanted for enterprise and skills, including the ability to read. These failings went back centuries—to religious zealotry and Counter-Reformation cultivation of ignorance—and ruled out the kind of diversification that would have compensated for agricultural infertility and poverty.[23] Comparative literacy rates are not exact, in large part because definitions and judgments varied from one country to another. Even so, the contrast between Mediterranean and northern Europe is undeniably large. Around 1900, for example, when only 3 percent of the population of Great Britain was illiterate, the figure for Italy was 48 percent, for Spain 56 percent, for Portugal 78 percent.[24] The religious persecutions of old—the massacres, hunts, expulsions, forced conversions, and self-imposed intellectual closure—proved to be a kind of original sin. Their effects would not wear off until the twentieth century . . . and not always even then.[25]

(Needless to say, this indictment has not been to the taste of Spanish elites, political and intellectual. No one likes to be told [reminded] that his failures are due to his failings; or that his sources of pride are vices rather than virtues. Hence a protracted effort by Spanish and hispanophile scholars to dismiss the historical indictment as a "black legend"—a slander by people of bad faith. Yet the fact of "decadence" remains and calls for explanation: more than three centuries of backwardness exacted a high price in income and achievement.)

A few centers of exceptional (if modest) adaptability escaped the general fate. In Spain, Catalonia diverged from the rest and as early as the eighteenth century began mechanizing textile manufacture. Later on, the exploitation of mineral resources, especially of iron ore in the later nineteenth century, drew money and trade to the Basque country. Most of this ore, however, went to ironmaking centers abroad; Spanish industry made little use of it.

Italy moved ahead faster, especially in the Po Valley (Lombardy, under Habsburg rule) and in and around Genoa. Venice and Florence, once flourishing industrial as well as commercial centers, were well on the way to becoming pure tourist attractions—clusters of shops and hotels and living museums. No traveler could afford to miss them. (The process continues, and Venice has already had to restrict access.) Italian unification (1870) changed little of the earlier division of labor and wealth. The north, especially Lombardy and the Piedmont, mixed agricultural and industrial, riverbottom and plain. The south (*il mezzogiorno,* the land of noon) remained a wilderness of hardscrabble landscratching on barren uplands and broad latifundia. Illiterate peasants, most of them sharecroppers and landless laborers, deferred to local notables—old and new rich, who cultivated pride ("respect") and a style of living that evoked the Old Regime.* The biggest export of the Mezzogiorno was people: emigrants to the New World, especially to the United States and Argentina, and after World War II, to the northern half of the country. Even the north sent its children abroad, generally to the richer industrial areas north of the Alps. The French, for example, relied heavily on Italian immigrants to work the newly opened (1880s) iron mines and mills of Lorraine.

The south has remained backward, in spite of huge development subsidies from the Italian government and, in our time, from the European Community. The landscape is dotted with idle factories, unfinished housing developments, roads that go nowhere. This slough of failure and despond testifies to deep failings: ignorance, bias, want of community, organized criminality. The Mezzogiorno continues to pay for the sins of yesteryear. Many northerners are disgusted to the point of talking secession. Read: expulsion. It won't happen. It takes matter-of-fact Czechs to let Slovakia go.

Eastern Europe was like another world. In Slavic lands—Russia particularly—serfdom persisted in its worst form. So much wealth in the hands of a spendthrift nobility meant reduced consumer demand for those basic manufactures that might lead to modern industry. Under ordinary circumstances, autocratic Russia might simply have taken its time about emulating the West: the people were used to poverty and ignorant of the outside world. But Russia was a power, with big territorial ambitions. It had tried very early (sixteenth century) to learn from the West, if only to gain autonomy in such strategic branches as gunmaking. Russia as a power needed industry, and the tsarist gov-

---

* The best, certainly the most accessible, source is a novel, Lampedusa's *Il Gattopardo—The Leopard.*

ernment wooed foreigners, paying them to set up factories or to settle and work in Russia. Individual landowners allowed enterprising serfs to engage in trade and industry in return for money dues. The result was a spotty, stunted industrialization.

Nor did Russian enterprises operate in the same world as those of western Europe. They sold to the national market, exported little or nothing. They were simply not competitive—not then, not later—especially not during the Soviet years. The only sales of manufactures outside the USSR went to satellite countries and dependencies in the Third World. Meanwhile the production data piled up, and many believed. Are you going to trust the numbers or the lying evidence? The statisticians would have come far closer to the truth had they deflated output for true market price and quality.

Poorer and more backward than Russia were the Balkan lands, most of them suffering under the inefficient Ottoman yoke, the tyranny of a society more primitive than theirs. Long quiescent, they caught the nationalist virus in the eighteenth and nineteenth centuries and got tangled in an endless struggle for freedom, first with the Turks and then with other Balkan nationalities. This could be a noble cause, but because identity rested on uncompromising religion, it easily conduced to hatred and unreason. Not good for business or development.

These were societies that did not generate enterprise from within. Trade and money were for Greeks, Jews, Armenians, Germans. These outsiders were not popular—not only because they got rich by buying and selling (so, not by hard work) and did so at the expense of peasants and landowners, but also because they were different in manners, dress, appearance, religion. (The outsiders returned the scorn, in spades.) When independence and modern politics came to the Balkans, the natives did their best to drive out the strangers, that is, to expel the most active elements in the economy. And they succeeded, in the face of the outsiders' natural reluctance to leave. (These inhospitable and hostile places offered so many chances to make money.)

The Balkans remain poor today. In the absence of metics, they war on one another and blame their misery on exploitation by richer economies in western Europe. It feels better that way.

Leftist political economists and economic historians like such explanations. They think in terms of core and periphery: the rich center vs. the surrounding dependencies. But that is not the relevant metaphor or image: Europe's development gradient ran from west to east and north to south, from educated to illiterate populations, from representative to despotic institutions, from equality to hierarchy, and so on.

It was not resources or money that made the difference; nor mistreatment by outsiders. It was what lay inside—culture, values, initiative. These peoples came to have freedom enough. They just didn't know what to do with it.

≈ ≈

## "The Bayonet Is a Fine Lad"

During the first half of the nineteenth century, the standard Russian infantry weapon was a smoothbore, muzzle-loading, flintlock musket rather like the weapons used in the previous century. (Daniel Boone, with his Kentucky long rifle, had better.) The 1828 Russian model, like those before, used round balls and was not accurate beyond 200 yards. The breechloaders used in West European armies were not deemed suitable—too complicated and not sturdy enough for field combat. Also too difficult for Russian armory production techniques.

Russia's army as a whole was reconciled to this backwardness. For one thing, procurement was a regimental matter, and officers preferred to spend their money on food and drink. (Drink, more than combat, was the favorite test of an officer's manliness.) "Regiments tried to pay as little as possible for weapons, and the regimental suppliers regarded periodic trips to grimy government arsenals and to distant small arms factories as punishment."[26] The arms makers in turn gave the buyers what they were looking for—so and so many pieces, good, bad, and indifferent. The government tried to prevent shoddiness by assigning inspectors to examine the arms. To little avail; the inspectors were part of the system and were not going to bite the hands that fed them. (A similar attitude toward production would flourish under various Soviet five-year plans. Fulfill the plan, turn out the units, pay the inspectors, and devil take the quality.)

The result was bad screws and rivets, misfit barrels, rotten stocks, mismatched lock parts. In 1853, just before fighting began in the Crimea, the tsarist army had only half the muskets that were authorized. And as bad as the arms were, the Russian soldier made them worse. Like the serf on the land, the twenty-five-year conscript—military duty was a life sentence—had no care of his tools. Guns ("a machine for presentation") were polished for parade, but the soldier had to pay out of pocket for grease; so, little or no grease. Bullets were costly—they were not the sort of thing that Russia could produce in large quantities—so clay bullets were used for target practice and damaged the barrels. Even officers took little care of their sidearms, to the point where the Ministry of War advised issuing pistols rather than revolvers. Regimental gunsmiths lacked training and proper equipment and had to shoe horses, fix wheels, and repair guns with the same chisels, hammers, and saws.

Rules follow practice. Confronted with these shortcomings, Russian military strategists systematically underestimated the value of firepower. Bodies were seen as more important than arms—bodies and "moral force"—and the bayonet was preferred to guns. "The bullet is a fool," opined Marshal Suvarov, "but the bayonet is a fine lad."* The bayonet was surer, and reliance on guns could only weaken resolve and fighting spirit. It would be a mistake, therefore, to change from muzzleloaders to breechloaders. The soldier would only waste a lot of ammunition and forget how to charge. As firepower in other armies shot up, the Russian soldier was being schooled in thrift. The regimental economy mirrored the larger society: dragged down by inefficiency; wasting time and labor in accessory activities (agriculture, gathering wood and hay, construction, haulage); afraid of change.†

The Crimean War (1854–56) was a disaster. The Russians lost what they could afford to lose most—people, six hundred thousand of them. The trivial losses in territory hurt the generals and the tsar more. Some Russians were still using muzzle-loading flintlocks, while the British and French picked them off with percussion rifles that had three and five times the range. Even the Russian generals

---

* Remember the Portuguese instructions to their second Indies fleet (see chapter VI): stand off and blow them out of the water. A preference for steel over guns signals technological inferiority.

† Cf. Bradley, *Guns for the Tsar*. The similarity to Japanese attitudes is striking. One normally thinks of Japanese industry as exceptionally effective, but as late as World War II, Japanese armaments manufacture was extremely spotty, and the army-issue rifles, sidearms, and ammunition left much to be desired. Soldiers sought compensation in the bayonet, which was often left permanently fixed, and cultivated the mystique of personal bravery in close combat: "The fixing of bayonet is more than a fixing of steel to the rifle since it puts iron into the soul of the soldier doing the fixing." Similarly, officers relied more on sword than revolver, abandoning whenever possible standard issue for *samurai* blades. A favorite test of prowess: decapitation or cleavage, often of prisoners, at one stroke. Cf. M. and S. Harries, *Soldiers of the Sun*, ch. 35, " 'My Sword Is My Soul.' "

were sitting ducks. Not that the allies were models of homicidal efficiency. They had their own failures of supply and hygiene (their greatest enemy was disease) and their share of stupidities of command (in those days the British army was still selling commissions), fondly immortalized in Tennyson's "Charge of the Light Brigade."

But the Russians were worse.

# ~ 17 ~

# You Need Money
# to Make Money

One knows how the "first industrial nation" did it. Slow and easy. Britain trained a factory labor force and accumulated capital as it went. In those early days, machines were typically small and cheap. Scale was small. Older buildings could be converted to industrial use. In short, threshold requirements were modest. So British enterprise could grow by plowing back earnings, by pooling personal resources, by borrowing from relatives, by renting facilities. Financial intermediaries, except for such loan brokers as attorney/solicitors, played a very small role. Banks confined themselves to supplying short-term or demand loans to facilitate real transactions. Some of this took the form of lines of credit, renewed as paid down. In good times, such lines were the equivalent of medium- or even long-term credit. In good times. In bad, they could be called in, or maturities could be shortened.

With the passing years, all of this changed: machines got bigger and heavier, required buildings to their measure. Scale economies and throughput grew as transport facilities improved. Still, British enterprise was rich enough to finance these outlays from within; if internal funds fell short, one typically brought in additional partners.* But even

---

* Some industrial firms founded their own banks, partly to facilitate their commer-

Britain had to find special ways to pay for public and quasi-public undertakings like docks, canals, and railways. Because the Bubble Act of 1720, passed in the wake of the notorious South Sea speculation and crash, prevented the creation of a joint stock with freely transferable shares, big projects typically went to large partnerships with assets vested in trustees. Not a happy solution in a commercial world of unlimited liability "to the last shilling and acre." Yet the absence of serious legal change for a century testifies to the solidity of these undertakings and the general vitality of the British economy. (I am assuming here that if a need for bank financing had existed, a society so responsive to business interests would have changed the rules.)

In the nineteenth century, when things got costlier and risks greater, the most effective device for mobilizing capital was the chartered joint-stock company with limited liability—chartered because limited liability could be conferred only by the crown or Parliament. These large, semipublic enterprises never made much use of long-term bank financing, because no bank was big enough. The charter of the Bank of England provided that no other bank could have more than six partners. Not until 1826, and then only outside a sixty-five-mile radius from London, were joint-stock banks permitted; and only in 1833 were non-note-issuing joint-stock banks permitted inside that radius. Yet these new banks were little different in size and policy from their private counterparts, and even the railway builders didn't need their help.

That was Britain. By the time Europe's first follower countries got going (post-1815), Britain had known two human generations of growth and industrial development. That delay was in part an accident of political history, which has a nasty way of interfering with the best-laid plans. Twenty-five years of revolution and war from 1789 to 1815 diverted Continental resources from building to destruction, played havoc with enterprise and trade, generated some invention but delayed much application, inspired projects but then inhibited them—in effect, delayed industrial emulation of Britain an extra generation.

Not that the balance sheet was exclusively negative. The turmoil also promoted social and institutional changes favorable to industrial development. In particular, the French abolition of "feudal" dues and

---

cial transactions, partly to pull in capital from local depositors. Insofar as such firms immobilized (invested) funds payable to depositors on demand, they were highly vulnerable to contractions and crises. In any event, the direction of the initiative, from industry to banking, testifies to the wealth of British industrial resources.

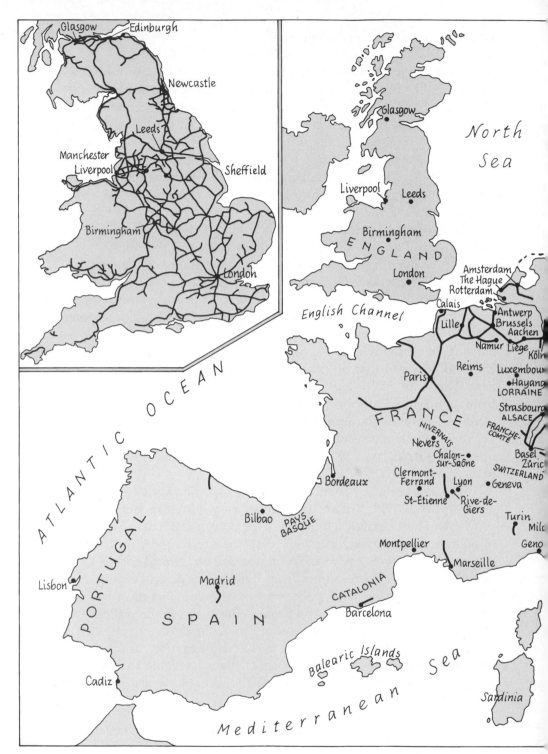

INDUSTRIALIZING EUROPE, c. 1850

The density of the railway networks is the best physical marker of the location
and pattern of European industrial development. The earliest industrializers
were those nations and regions already experienced in manufacturing: Benelux,
northern and eastern France, Rhineland and Ruhr, and Protestant Switzerland.

FINLAND

St. Petersburg

SWEDEN

Stockholm

DENMARK

Copenhagen

Baltic Sea

RUSSIA

remen

Hamburg

GERMANY

Hannover

ortmund

Berlin

Leipzig

Elbe R.

Oder R.

Warsaw

rankfurt

SAXONY

Dresden

SILESIA

Breslau

POLAND

Prague

BOHEMIA

Stuttgart

Brünn
(Brno)

MORAVIA

Lemberg

Munich

BAVARIA

Vienna

AUSTRIA

HABSBURG
LANDS

Budapest

HUNGARY

Venice

Trieste

Bologna

ITALY

Rome

Haarlem
Leiden
The Hague
Rotterdam

Amsterdam

Utrecht

Arnhem

HOLLAND

G
E
R
M
A
N
Y

to Hannover

Bruges

Ghent

Antwerp

Duisburg

Essen

Hamm

Dortmund

Hagen

Düsseldorf

Köln (Cologne)

Calais

Boulogne

Brussels

Schelde R.

BELGIUM

Liège

Aachen

Bonn

Lille

HAINAUT

Verviers

RHINELAND

Rhine R.

Frankfurt

Mons

Charleroi

Namur

Mainz

Amiens

Luxembourg

Meuse R.

Mannheim

FRANCE

Hayange

Metz

LORRAINE

Karlsruhe

to Paris

bonds led (obliged) other countries to do the same, freeing people to move in space and across outworn status lines. The economic payoff to these changes did not come until after the peace. By that time, the task of catching up was bigger, but the potential gain as well.

For this reason, some have argued that it pays to be late: you can skip the mistakes, begin with the latest techniques and equipment.* On the other hand, the time lost lagging also costs. It pays to get started as soon as possible.

So the Continental follower countries felt that they had neither means nor time to grow as Britain had. They were competing in the same arena. Why wait fifty years to catch up with 1815? They needed more capital than Britain had needed, and they wanted it now. They wanted up-to-date factories, machines, engines. From about 1830 on, they wanted railways, canals, roads, and bridges. Where would they get the money?

Four places: (1) personal investment; (2) financial intermediaries and private credit; (3) government assistance; (4) international capital flows.

First, the Continent had its share of rich people. Unfortunately, most of these were landowners who scorned the ungenteel activities of trade and industry. Indeed, many of them had a distaste even for agriculture (they preferred to feel the earth through horses' hoofs) and hired stewards to manage their estates. The owners lived on rents and produce; sometimes on capital. The stewards got rich.

Yet some gentry and aristocrats did gravitate to industry, partly because they hoped to make money, partly because industry was a logical by-product of estate management and regalian rights. Their land held valuable mineral resources or forests that could provide timber for ships, buildings, or pit props in mines. In central and eastern Europe, their control over a resident serf population provided them with a ready-made factory (or protofactory) labor force. Some of these noblemen actually became industrialists and merchants themselves. One thinks of such families as the Desandrouin and the Arenberg in the Hainaut (in later Belgium), the Fürstenberg and Schwarzenberg in Austria, the Wendel in Lorraine (become French in 1766), the

---

* These may or may not be appropriate to relative factor costs. The choice of technique is a complicated matter. Take equipment: new machines may be available only in the latest version, because that is what manufacturers are making. But second-hand equipment may offer significant economies—for those who know how to use it. Not simple, though; older machines may be harder to maintain; and where to get replacement parts—cannibalize?

Stroganoff and Demidoff in Russia; or of rulers such as Prince Wilhelm
Heinrich of Nassau-Saarbrücken (ruled 1740–68).*

Normally such aristocratic entrepreneurs worked with bourgeois
partners, better suited by status and values to do the dirty work—that
is, make the money. (Noblemen are better at spending it.) Sometimes
these commoners profited from business connections to gild their es-
cutcheon. Take the rules of aristocratic alliance. In theory, noble married noble. But what if a commoner was very rich? Well, then, noble
might marry commoner; the higher the noble rank, the more comfortable the misalliance. (Petty noble families had to be careful about
that kind of thing.) Luck helped, as when a prince Schwarzenberg
(good name), aged thirty-one, married the eighty-two-year-old sole
heiress to a merchant fortune. The lady obligingly died soon after, but
then the young prince died too—"without descendants," of course. So
the estate fell to the main branch of the Schwarzenberg clan, which
went on to prove its spirit of enterprise, not only by its choice of marriage partners but by setting up industrial ventures, reclaiming land,
founding an investment bank.[1]

Such examples, however striking, fell short of an industrial revolution.
That needed a wider range of sources, including banks and other financial intermediaries.

Here commercial experience proved a major asset. After centuries of
more or less profitable activity, a network of private banks was in place
(personal firms or partnerships), collectively rich and capable of financing medium- and long-term investments in industry and choosing
customers not so much by price and terms as by probity, resourcefulness, above all connections. These groups typically hung on religious
and cultural affinities: the Huguenot-Calvinist, Sephardic-Jewish,
German-Jewish, Greek-Orthodox commercial "families" knew their
own kind—whom to trust and whom to worry about, whom to ask
and whom to work with.[2]

These small firms had more scope and surface than met the eye. As
in Britain, bank finance on the Continent typically took the form of

---

* Some of these families began as commoners (the Demidoff as serfs), built their fortune in industry, obtained nobility for their services, stayed in industry, and enhanced
their status by a policy of well-chosen marriages. Thus the Wendel iron dynasty became
*de* Wendel, and while not marrying into the high nobility, found a large reservoir of
talent and pride among very old families of modest means. As one *grande dame* of medieval line, Wendel by marriage, liked to remind listeners (smiling the while, of course),
her people knew her husband as *le gros quincailler*—the big hardware dealer.

lines of credit, extended in support of real commercial transactions and covered by discountable commercial paper. But we also have examples of direct long-term funding and participation in company formation: thus the Paris Rothschilds financed French railways and French and Belgian coal mines and forges; the Vienna branch of the bank promoted railways and invested in ironworks and coal mines in Habsburg territory; and the Banque Seillière in Paris joined the merchant house of Boigues to relaunch the ironworks at Le Creusot in 1836.[3]

One should not underestimate the resourcefulness of these old trading houses. They could fairly smell profit and had built their fortunes on opportunism and variety. To this we should add a flair for profitable marital alliances, which could provide both funds and business contacts.[4] Any effort to understand the Industrial Revolution in Europe before the age of public joint-stock companies and stock exchanges must take family and personal connections into account.

In good times, short-term and demand loans could turn into long credit; in bad times, failure to renew such support could push a desperate company into liquidation. Much depended on the robustness and loyalty of one's creditor, but even the most trusting and determined lender could find his hand forced as other banks began calling in their loans. That is the trouble with a network system: when it is strong, it is stronger than the sum of the parts; but when it weakens, the weakness spreads easily from one link to the next.

This collective danger, and the need for long-term investment, led to the invention of a new financial intermediary, the joint-stock investment bank, or as the French came to call it, the *crédit mobilier*. The first inspiration for such institutions came from bureaucrats as well as business interests: even before 1820, officials and merchants in Bavaria were calling for a special bank to promote industry. The earliest working examples were quasipublic institutions—the Société Générale in Brussels and the Seehandlung in Berlin. The new form gained considerably in importance with the coming of the railway—a capital-eater if ever there was one, both in itself and for the large-scale industrial enterprises it encouraged. So it was that in the 1830s the Société Générale, until then a quiet commercial bank, turned into a development bank; and that France spawned a gaggle of *caisses*—joint-stock limited partnerships *(commandites par actions)* created to finance industry at medium and long term.* Why *caisses*? The Bank of France

* French company law distinguished among (1) ordinary partnerships *(sociétés en nom collectif)*, where all partners had unlimited personal liability for the firm's debts;

was opposed to the use of the word *banque* for such intrinsically risky ventures. This was also why the brothers Pereire later baptized their bank the Société Générale du Crédit Mobilier and thereby gave birth to a generic. If you can't call a bank a bank, you have to think of something else that will smell as rich.

It was once thought that these new financial institutions came into being over the opposition of the older private banks, which had their own industrial interests. In fact, the private banks actively promoted the *crédits mobiliers,* for the best of reasons. Long-term investments put them at great risk, and the losses and bankruptcies of the business crises of 1837–39 and 1848 convinced them that discretion was the better part of valor. Shift the risk to shareholders of separate firms and if possible get permission to incorporate with limited liability.

After the panic of 1848–49, the Crédit Mobilier of Emile and Isaac Pereire seemed a new departure and quickly found imitators.[5] Its approval by the regime signaled explicit encouragement for industrial development; also for the arrival of new men. President Louis Napoléon, nephew of the great Napoléon, soon to be Napoléon III, alias *"le Petit,"* wanted to make his place in history; also to create a counterweight to the older network of top-drawer private banks—the so-called *haute banque*—which had been thick with the late Orléanist regime. In the same spirit, the regime relaxed the constraints that favored old wealth. In 1867, in a belated response to general incorporation in Great Britain in 1856, the French went over to routine registration of public companies.[6]

French investors could create and pay for development banks because the country already held a lot of private capital. At that point, in fact—and contrary to historical myth—the Crédit Mobilier and its imitators in France were not much needed. The best of the railway lines had already been conceded to syndicates of the older financial powers;

---

(2) limited partnerships *(sociétés en commandite),* where the general partners had unlimited liability and the limited partners liability only to the extent of their share in the capital; (3) share limited partnerships *(commandites par actions),* where the limited partners owned transferable shares; and (4) true corporations *(sociétés anonymes),* where everyone enjoyed limited liability and all ownership parts took the form of transferable shares. Until general limited liability was introduced in 1867, all such companies required a charter from the legislature. This requirement rendered company formation costly and difficult (political connections helped), but the general assumption was that limited liability was a violation of commercial morality and usage (creditors were deemed entitled to better protection), to be granted only in exceptional circumstances.

the Crédit Mobilier got the leavings. Nor did French industrial firms turn to the new investment banks, preferring the discretion of the old-style merchant houses. A company that resorted to long-term bank financing, with its concomitant surveillance and interference, was probably in deep trouble.* None of this helped the new-model institutions; the great Crédit Mobilier went bust in 1867.

In Germany and farther east, the development bank came into its own, founding and financing industry, supervising performance, promoting innovation. These new institutions combined investment, commercial, and deposit banking (hence the appelation "universal banks"). The best of them gathered technical intelligence and served as consulting bureaus. Such a mix of functions struck British bankers as a violation of sacred writ. How could one safely combine short-term, even demand, liabilities with long-term immobilization of funds? Surely a recipe for disaster.

The answer lay, first, in the rapid growth of the German economy from the 1830s on—the kind of thing that makes everyone look good; and second, in the preference of these banks for "well-heeled" customers. (The two essentials of successful banking are, first, other people's money, and second, lending to the rich.)[7] The ability of these universal banks to find well-heeled customers and offset risks became legendary. The best and biggest were the famous *D-Banken* (so-called because their names all began with the same letter): the Darmstädter Bank, Discontogesellschaft, Deutsche Bank, Dresdner Bank. Two of these (Darmstädter and Dresdner) started in provincial centers and moved to Berlin; one finds similar transfers in Britain and France. They signal the strength of local enterprise and capital. Between 1870 and 1913, book value of assets of these mixed banks rose from about 600 million to over 17.5 billion marks—from 6 to over 20 percent of the stock of industrial capital.[8] Most of the shares were in heavy industry. Smaller enterprises found help elsewhere; the business of big banks was big business.

But what if the country was too poor to finance the banks needed to finance industry? Well, then the state might step in, either by promoting financial intermediaries or by direct investment and participation. Here the west-east gradient took the form of increasing intervention. At one end, in Britain, enterprise got nothing from the

---

* Yet even now much of the literature, echoing a theme that goes back almost a century, continues to stress the critical contribution of the Crédit Mobilier. It did serve as example, but not in France, where it was if anything a counterexample.

state; even the canals and railways were financed by private investment. Across the Channel in France, manufacturing enterprise got no further direct assistance after 1830; as for railways, a thrifty bourgeois regime—symbolized by a portly Louis-Philippe and his prudent black umbrella—resisted calls for help from promoters and banks. The days of direction and sponsorship were past. The French state sought private enterprise to build the railroads and refused to purchase shares. On the other hand, it agreed to pay for the land and roadbed (including tunnels and bridges), justifying this substantial aid—about 18 percent of total cost as of early 1848—on the ground that the road was going to come back to the state anyway at the end of the concession period. All in all, and counting a few state loans, the French government paid slightly over 25 percent of the cost of railway lines to that date.

In the Germanies, political fragmentation made for a variety of policies. Some regimes continued to subsidize industry, partly because of its technological or strategic interest, partly in the cause of social order; while railway financing varied from purely private to state purchase of shares, to public construction, ownership, and operation. In the United States, too, home rule meant that policy varied from one state to another. Insofar as the individual states wanted to encourage public works, subsidy was the rule, often in the form of land grants along the railroad right of way. In Russia, the state assisted banking and industry, and the railroads were state-built, owned, and operated. Commerce and topography be damned. The emblematic example: the construction of the first important line, from Moscow to St. Petersburg. The tsar was asked to select the route. He took a ruler and drew a straight line between the two cities. But the tip of one finger stuck out, so the line was built with one curved section.

Direct subsidies and aids are only part of the story. The state's hand lay everywhere, even where not directly manifest. Even in Britain, government supported and protected overseas trade: the country as a whole paid the associated security costs of private venturers and adventurers in distant seas. Such indirect subsidy, easy to overlook, was crucial.

In Britain again, as elsewhere, industrial promotion also took the form of defense against outside competition. The later record of British commitment to free trade (more or less mid-nineteenth century to 1930) has tended to obscure the earlier and much longer practice of economic nationalism, whether by tariff protection or discriminatory shipping rules (navigation acts). Economic theorists have argued forcibly, even passionately, that such interferences with the market hurt everyone. The fact remains that history's strongest advocates of free trade—Victorian Britain, post–World War II United States—were strongly protectionist during their own growing stage. Don't do as I did; do as I can afford to do now. The advice does not always sit well.

In France, the old monarchy assisted new industries and technologies—by subsidy and stipend, fiscal exemption and privilege, or so-called loans that remained unpaid. Because of these helps, ambitious businessmen had reason to court people of influence, and the court, like an overripe cheese, invited corruption. The only real constraint was the increasing penury of the French treasury; by the 1780s, the money had run out. Meanwhile, as in England, enterprise found a silent ally in tariff protection, against the world without and other parts of the kingdom within. (Commercial barriers reflected France's history of piecemeal territorial accretion.) This long-standing policy stood inviolate until 1786, when a bureaucrats' treaty traded easier access for French wines and silks to Britain for admission of British cottons, woolens, and iron into France.* Such an opening would have had drastic consequences for French industry, unprepared as yet for the new machine technologies. But revolution in 1789 and war with Britain in 1792 put an end to the experiment.

The French Revolution reinforced the role of the state. Authority was harder, more peremptory; control, more centralized. War needs made production an urgent priority. Yet the regime lacked resources (wars eat up money), and military orders only hardened old technologies. Aid to industry consisted primarily of transfers of wealth—Church properties, for example, confiscated by a militantly anticlerical regime and granted to industrial enterprises or sold on concessionary terms.

After the revolution (1798 on), the Bonapartist (later Napoleonic) regime undertook a modest program of economic development. Once again wealth (including fine art) changed hands, both within conquered territories and from conquered lands to France. The greatest contribution to industry, however—for better or worse—took the disguised form of an imperial market closed to British imports. Then, for a brief moment after 1815, defeated France went over to laissez-faire and free trade, if only by concession to the British victors and reaction

---

* European tariff history tells a story of popular, almost instinctive, protection punctuated by episodes of administrative, elitist moves in the direction of freer trade. So with the Eden Treaty of 1786, the Cobden-Chevalier Anglo-French Treaty of 1860, the post–World War II common market, and GATT. The contest lies between lowbrow vested interests on the one hand, highbrow economic reasoning on the other.

against imperial authoritarianism. The protectionist wall fell. But very quickly a cold shower of foreign manufactures (textiles particularly) revived the national instinct. French manufacturers cried havoc, and the Chamber of Deputies promptly voted a series of tariffs, each higher than the one before. Import of key commodities such as cotton yarn and cloth was prohibited outright. Whether this kind of wall was good for French industry is a matter of debate. It raised prices for French consumers, reduced demand, and sheltered obsolete technologies. But it increased the *rate* of profit for those more efficient firms that flourished inside the price envelope.* There is more than one way to fatten enterprise.

Meanwhile French economists, inspired by their English counterparts, argued the advantages of liberalization. With the revolution of 1848, the political pendulum swung back, away from high protection and its Orléanist beneficiaries. No sooner had Louis Napoléon settled in than pressure increased for an end to prohibitions and an easing of duties. The economists at least were not afraid of Big Bad Britain. In the face of strenuous resistance by manufacturers, who wept tears for their employees, the imperial regime lowered tariff barriers significantly, first by opportunistic decrees, then by an Anglo-French commercial accord (Cobden-Chevalier Treaty, 1860) that was put to public discussion only after it was concluded. (That's the best time, of course.) The testimony of witnesses was published in seven large quarto volumes and provides an extraordinary insight into a split French "establishment." So finally ended the regime of prohibitions on key industrial products (cotton textiles, ships). If France, moreover, could afford to take on British competition, it could certainly compete with less developed countries. In subsequent years, the new low tariff regime was extended to others (thus the German Zollverein in 1865) on the most-favored-nation principle.[9]

* In theory, competition on the domestic market should have pushed prices (and profits) down, even in the presence of tariff walls. But the more efficient producers were only too happy to set prices by (hide behind) their backward competitors and enjoy monopolistic gains. Cf. Guy Thuillier, *Aspects,* p. 255: "The survival [of small, old-fashioned charcoal iron works], the inertia of the economic milieu and the protection of vested interests, assure a supplementary rent to the new forges; not only do tariff duties protect them from the competition of foreign iron, but the rent of protection is doubled by a technological rent due to the survival of small, archaic forges producing at a very high price." Also pp. 249–50, on the delayed dominance of rolled as against hammered gun barrels: the rolled cost much less to make, but the makers wanted to charge the same price as for the others. The goal was not market share but rate of profit. But since the buyer was the state, why not?

Russia, poor Russia, was the epitome of state-driven development. The push, from the sixteenth century, was to catch up with the West by adoption of Western ways. The push was fitful, partly because it was motivated from above and not every tsar was so inclined, partly because each effort was so exhausting. Who paid the bill? The serf—who else? Modernization from above rested on forced labor. In the long run, however, the whole country paid. Serfdom fostered stupid arrogance above; greed and envy, resentment and gall below. Even after emancipation, these attitudes remained to pose the biggest obstacle to Russian development.

Just as the big banks in Germany preferred to put their money into the capital-intensive branches of heavy industry, so in Russia the state gave its support above all to mining and metallurgy, encouraging the formation of huge enterprises—the megalomaniac pursuit of giantism. Russian blast furnaces, we are told, were larger than the German (a few were), illustrating what for some was a law of backwardness: the later, the bigger and faster. (Economists today speak of leapfrogging—every generation needs its key words and jargon.) And once state-sponsored industrialization had made enough progress, the accumulated capital financed investment banks comparable in function and strategy to their German predecessors.

The result was considerable but fragile. Russian industrial product rose 5 to 6 percent a year between 1885 and 1900, and again between 1909 and 1912. Railroad mileage doubled between 1890 and 1904, and iron and steel output increased ten times from 1880 to 1900. Between 1860 and 1914, Russia went from the seventh to the fifth largest industrial power in the world. No small achievement, but long forgotten, because later, after the revolutions of 1917, Communist spokesmen and their foreign adulators rewrote history so as to blacken the reputation of the tsarist regime, while throwing favorable testimonies down the memory hole.

They need not have worked so hard at vilification. Tsarist Russia had an abundance of flaws. The country was schizophrenic in its contrasts and contradictions: a poorly educated, largely illiterate population with spots of intellectual and scientific brilliance; a privileged, self-indulgent aristocracy contemptuously resisting modernization; a rabidly radical revolutionary movement—sables and rags, vintage brandy and cheap vodka, broken crystal in the officers' mess, broken earthenware in the isbas. The push to economic development awakened a sleeping giant, brought it into contact with more advanced countries, imported strange and disturbing technologies, poisoned it with alien dreams.

The dreams caught on faster than the technologies and wrenched the country out of sync. Three wars destroyed the regime by exposing the gap between east and west, backward and advanced, fantasy and reality. The first was the Crimean War (1854–56), which underlined the difference between citizen and servile armies; the emancipation of the serfs followed shortly thereafter. The second was the humiliating defeat by Japan (1904–05), the first time Russia had known a setback in its *Drang nach Osten*. This was followed by the installation of a parliament (the Duma) and popular elections—a good idea in principle but bad for autocracy. The third was World War I, the Great War, when millions of Russian peasants were ordered into clouds of bullets and shrapnel. With that, an incompetent government and military establishment deservedly lost legitimacy, and the regime was overthrown. The whole sequence was a repeat in its way of Spain's long decline: a great *pre*industrial power could not cope with the demands and pretensions of better-equipped nations. And like Spain, Russia knew what was happening, but responded with too little, too late.

The last of our four sources of funds was international capital flows. Here again, one sees the east-west gradient at work. England invested in French railways; France and Belgium in Prussian ironworks and Austrian banks; Germany in Italian banks and Balkan railways; everybody in Russian mining and industry. In general, money a-plenty followed opportunity a-plenty, with no lack of promoters and pied pipers.

Some students of economic development, specialists in Third World backwardness, seek to explain retardation by the unwillingness of rich countries to invest in the poor. The charge does not stand up in history or logic. Businessmen have always been "in it for the money" and will make it and take it where they can. To be sure, they have their preferences. They have always sought to minimize risk and maximize comfort; also have preferred kind climates to unkind, close places to far, familiar cultures to strange.

They sometimes make big mistakes. In spite of the greatest care and forethought, not every investment pays off. But this has not stopped businessmen and investors from trying again. It is not want of money that holds back development. The biggest impediment is social, cultural, and technological unreadiness—want of knowledge and knowhow. In other words, want of the ability to use money.

ᵔᶜ ᶜᵔ

# Le Creusot: The Tales
# That Business History Can Tell

In the decades following the Peace of 1815, the French iron industry entered the world of modern technology. Three factors were decisive: (1) the backlog of technique waiting to be learned, in particular, the adoption of coke smelting and coal-fueled puddling-rolling, where France was more than half a century behind; (2) improvements in transportation, which made it profitable to bring coal to the iron ore or vice versa; and (3) a huge demand for wrought iron as a result of railway construction.

These circumstances changed the opportunity of Le Creusot, the enterprise that, largely owing to fortuitous natural advantages (coal and iron ore in proximity) and royal support, initiated coke smelting in France in the 1780s. But Le Creusot suffered from a variety of handicaps, most seriously its poor access to iron-using markets.* These, plus poor management and the perturbations of revolution and war, had brought it low. In 1835, it lay fallow in bankruptcy while much of its equipment rusted.

At this point a team of experienced technicians and merchants pooled knowledge, money, and connections to buy up the debris of earlier firms and relaunch the enterprise. The makeup of the team says a lot about the needs of business and the character of the French bourgeoisie.

The point men in the venture were the brothers Adolphe and Eugène Schneider, merchants, bankers, technicians, and forgemasters. Their father Antoine Schneider was a notary (something like an English solicitor) and local notable in Lorraine. A nephew was an early graduate of the Ecole Polytechnique and rose in the army to become a general and for a brief period minister of war—a useful career for cousins who would be making and selling iron and steel.

Of the two brothers, Adolphe married Valerie Aignan, stepdaughter of Louis Boigues, a wealthy Paris merchant specializing in metallurgical products—again a most useful industrial connection.

---

* The town of Le Creusot is located in the region known as the Nivernais, 370 kilometers south-southeast of Paris.

Boigues had already invested in foundries and forges, most notably in a large plant at Fourchambault that was one of the pioneers of coke-blast smelting when the method was reintroduced in France in the 1820s.* The Boigues family, apparently of Catalan origin, had settled in central France in the seventeenth century and established a firm base in land ownership and strategic alliances. Their sons and daughters had married into the moneyed aristocracy—new but the more influential for that—people who bore titles of baron and count or at the least had names with the telltale particule *de*. Thus Louis Boigues's sister Marie married the comte Hippolyte Jaubert, nephew and adopted son and heir of the rich and powerful comte François Jaubert, a regent of the Banque de France.

This Fourchambault ironworks was itself the product of a marriage between Boigues's money and commercial connections (Louis Boigues was not a passive investor) and the technical knowledge of Georges Dufaud, son of an ironmaster of the Old Regime. Dufaud was one of the first graduates of the Ecole Polytechnique and a pioneer of the new coal-based iron technologies. He had gone through the fires of bankruptcy and returned—no mean feat in France, where bankruptcy was almost invariably a stain for life. Now he would be managing a multi-million-franc enterprise. His success in this task (to say nothing of personal relations) would bring him invitations to serve in high office and to take over other business enterprises, all of which he refused. His heart and head belonged to those forges and foundries and machine shops in the Nivernais.

His son Achille took over after him, while his daughters got married, the first to George Crawshay, descendant of one of the oldest and most important dynasties of British ironmasters, and the second to Emile Martin, metallurgical entrepreneur in his own right and later immortalized by his contribution to the Siemens-Martin process for making open-hearth steel. All of this paid off in valuable exchanges of knowledge and know-how. When Georges Dufaud made one of his prospecting trips to Britain in 1826 (almost two weeks to get from Fourchambault to London, but he may have stopped in Paris along the way), he took the occasion to order a steam engine and power bellows for Martin; recruited a top-notch British engineer, also for Martin; and visited numerous British plants and public works (Crawshay's introduction presumably helped),

* The factory was located just north of Nevers on the Loire River, about 230 kilometers south of Paris.

bringing home all kinds of sample products that the British, unlike the French, were making of metal. So diligently did he buy that Dufaud had to freight a ship to haul his loot across the Channel.[10]

But back to Le Creusot. In 1821, aged only nineteen, Adolphe Schneider entered the Seillière bank. The Seillière had started as merchant-manufacturers of woolens, but like a number of such putters-out, had branched into related commercial transactions. From there they had gone into banking, moving from their ancestral Lorraine to Paris.[11] They were among the few leading Catholic families in a field dominated in France by Protestant firms with strong connections to co-religionists in Switzerland. Among their special business interests were ironmaking and metallurgy. The Seillière were strong backers of their fellow Lorrain Ignace-François de Wendel, artillery officer turned ironmaster in the Wendel family tradition, probably the single most enterprising and influential pioneer of iron-cum-coal technology in the France of the Old Regime. When the Wendel lost their forge and foundry of Hayange as a result of the revolution, Florentin Seillière helped them buy the plant back in 1804, then again the nearby forge of Moyeuvre in 1811.[12]

In 1830, the Seillière bank won the contract to provide equipment for the French expeditionary force to Algiers (the start of French imperialism in North Africa). Adolphe Schneider was sent to be their agent on the scene and received a lucrative commission of 2 percent on the total value of the merchandise. Much enriched, he then set up on his own as a cloth merchant in Paris. It was in this capacity, we are told, that he entered into business relations with the current owners of Le Creusot, a pair of expatriate Englishmen, and became their creditor. This put him in a good position to bid for the enterprise when it failed shortly thereafter.

Meanwhile the younger brother, Eugène, was busily making his own way. He started as a clerk in Reims, a center of wool manufacture, and from there rejoined his brother in the Seillière bank. In 1827, however, all of twenty-two years old, he was engaged by the baron de Neuflize, descendant of an old Protestant wool dynasty of Sedan, the Poupart, to run a nearby forge for them. (One feels that all kinds of people, especially young people, were going into iron.)

Eugène ran the forge for almost a decade. Meanwhile Adolphe was pursuing the matter of Le Creusot, then languishing in bankruptcy. In 1835, the works was sold at auction for 1.85 million francs to an ironmaster of Chalon-sur-Saône named Coste; but Adolphe was determined to have it, and drawing on his connections (Louis Boigues and François Seillière), he bought the firm for an additional million. Not bad for M. Coste. Not bad for Adolphe Schneider.

Adolphe brought his brother in to help him: he would handle trade and finances; Eugène would direct exploitation and production. Shortly thereafter Eugène married Constance Le Moine des Mares, granddaughter of the baron de Neuflize and daughter of a *receveur des finances*. (These were tax collectors who held and invested the proceeds for considerable periods before they had to turn them over to the state treasury. This made them in effect important private bankers.) To improve his technical knowledge, Eugène took courses at the Conservatoire des Arts et Métiers in Paris and in the time-honored French tradition visited England to learn what his competitors were up to. So, Catholic enterprise and money married Protestant enterprise and money, and all together built on ties to political power to make Le Creusot a major supplier of rails and forgings, a builder of steam engines, locomotives, steamboats, boilers, and presses, and eventually France's greatest armsmaker.

Bread upon the waters. In 1848, a year of omnivorous crisis, Fourchambault got into deep financial trouble. The Wendel (Hayange) and Schneider (Le Creusot) saved it by co-signing a huge bank loan: we ironmasters have to stick together. And when, a century later, Maurice de Wendel had four daughters to marry (and no sons), one of them wedded a Seillière.

None of this was accidental, not even the romance.

꙰ ꙰

## Making a Virtue of Lateness

It was almost half a century ago, in 1951, that Alexander Gerschenkron wrote his seminal essay on "Economic Backwardness in Historical Perspective." In it he posed the question, what does it take for a follower country to undertake industrialization and emulate its predecessors? Or, to put it differently, does it make any difference to come along later?

What does it take? Gerschenkron answered metaphorically: an ability to leap the gap of knowledge and practice separating the backward economy from the advanced. Gerschenkron made no effort to ask why anyone should want to leap the gap. The advantages were obvious. Rather, he saw the gap as an incentive in itself, an invitation to effort—like a gap in potential that, when sufficiently great, is crossed by electrical energy in the form of a spark. (That is my metaphor, but it is not unjustified. Gerschenkron speaks explicitly of "tension" between "potential" and actual.)

In Gerschenkron's model, then, it pays to be late. Not before the leap, but after. (He makes no effort to estimate the cost of relative poverty before industrialization, but he doesn't have to. It's high.) The greater the gap, the greater the gain for those who leap it. Why? Because there's so much more to learn—including mistakes to be avoided. As a result, follower countries grow faster than their predecessors. Their growth is characterized by what Gerschenkron calls a spurt (or spurts), a period (or periods) of exceptional rates of increase.

Late growth, says Gerschenkron, also tends to be based on "the most modern and efficient techniques," because they pay the most and nothing less can compete with more advanced nations. These techniques are typically capital-intensive, which would seem to be irrational for countries that abound in cheap labor.* Gerschenkron recognizes the paradox, but explains it by the quality of the workforce. Good, well-disciplined labor is in fact scarce, he says, scarcer than in richer, more advanced countries. So it pays to substitute capital for labor.

That, for Gerschenkron, is half the story. The second half concerns the how: How did backward countries, poor in capital and good labor, manage to create modern, capital-intensive industry? And (although Gerschenkron does little with this part of the story) how did they manage to acquire the knowledge and know-how? Finally, how did they overcome social, cultural, and institutional barriers to industrial enterprise? How did they create appropriate arrangements and institutions? How did they cope with the strains of change?

In his exploration of the conditions and constraints of backwardness, Gerschenkron laid particular stress on the

---

* This was partly because that was the direction of technological advance—the substitution of capital for labor; but also because Gerschenkron thought the way to rapid growth and catch-up was via heavy industry. This was what he saw in Germany and Russia, and he turned it into a paradigm. Ironically (for Gerschenkron was anything but a Marxist), Marxist economic thinking had followed similar lines.

mobilization of capital. He distinguished three levels: (1) a country with lots of private wealth and well-funded merchant banks, able to finance enterprise with family resources, small loans, and reinvestment of profits; (2) a poorer country with fewer and smaller private fortunes, but enough to finance industry if (investment) banks could be created to mobilize these dispersed funds; and (3) a country poorer still, where private wealth was insufficient and only the state could do the job, whether by financing investment banks or by direct subvention. Britain was clearly in the first category; Germany, Austria, and Italy in the second. The United States, Belgium, Switzerland, France came in between. Russia fell in the third group.

   Gerschenkron's work in this area has been criticized because of his heavy reliance on the scholarship of an earlier generation and the refusal of complex historical arrangements to fit neat schemas. Every new series of numerical estimates calls for adjustments in perspective. Even so, Gerschenkron has continued to influence students of development, in large part because of his central points: that latecomers need to make special arrangements to compensate for their backwardness and for changes elsewhere; and that with intelligence and will, they can find ways to do so.[13]

# ~ 18 ~

# The Wealth
# of Knowledge

Institutions and culture first; money next; but from the beginning
and increasingly, the payoff was to knowledge.

The first move to acquire the "secrets" of the new British technologies was to send out explorers—trained agents to observe, report, and
hire away skilled artisans. Thus in 1718–20, at the instigation of a
Scottish expatriate, John Law, France launched a systematic pursuit of
British technicians: clock- and watchmakers, woolen workers, metallurgists, glassmakers, shipbuilders—some two or three hundred people.
This campaign so troubled the British that they passed a law prohibiting the emigration of certain skilled craftsmen, the first of a series of
such measures covering more than a century and a widening array of
trades.[1]

This legislation, however, did not constitute an hermetic barrier. In
a world of high protectionism, not everyone was alert as yet to the potential of international competition. Take metalmaking skills—a special
treasure because of their tie to armament and machinery. (People will
kill to be able to kill better.). In 1764–65, the French monarchy dispatched Gabriel-Jean Jars to visit mining and metallurgical installations in England. So insensible were the British to the value of such
intelligence that he was well received at foundries and forges in

Sheffield and the Northeast. His memoranda, later published, still make a valuable source of information on the techniques of his time.* The same was true of the British advances in chronometry, the key to superior navigation: in 1769, the Board of Longitude allowed French visitors to open and examine the revolutionary marine clocks of John Harrison on the assumption that these should contribute to all of mankind. (Harrison, when he learned of this, threw a fit.)[2]

Some places and trades were not so welcoming. In Birmingham, a center of metal trades, every maker had his knacks and tricks. Craftsmen there were rationally paranoiac in their conviction that every stranger was an enemy. Not only foreigners; Englishmen as well. Arthur Young, traveler and observer extraordinary, wrote of his hostile reception in that busy town.

> I was no where more disappointed than at Birmingham; where I could not gain any intelligence even of the most common nature, through the excessive jealousy of the manufacturers. It seems the *French* have carried off several of their fabricks, and thereby injured the town not a little: This makes them so cautious, that they will shew strangers scarce anything. . . .[3]

All of which did not stop the manufacturers of Birmingham from engaging in their own spying. Britain was not the only country with techniques worth learning or stealing (although by now it had the lion's share of the potential loot), and British manufacturers had no more scruples than their Continental rivals. Besides, it takes two to tango, and skilled craftsmen, like savants and artists, took all of Europe as their home.[4] One of the most valuable secrets of French metalworkers, for example, was the gilding, usually on brass or bronze, known as *ormolu (or moulu)*—bright, shiny, phony, hence immensely profitable. Matthew Boulton gained fame as James Watt's partner in the manufacture of steam engines, but he began as master maker of buttons, buckles, watch chains, candlesticks, and all manner of metal objects. Boulton put money and men out in every direction to learn this French technique; also to seduce French craftsmen and artists, with their tools

---

* Jars also visited metallurgical installations in Styria, Bohemia, the Liège district (now Belgium), and Sweden. Although he died shortly after his final trip, to ironworks in eastern and central France (1768–69), he was able to communicate his findings personally to a number of ironmasters and technicians, among them Ignace de Wendel. Part of his reports was published by his brother, also named Gabriel, as *Voyages métallurgiques* (1774–81)—Woronoff, *L'industrie sidérurgique*, p. 16. Also Harris, *Essays in Industry*, pp. 87–88.

if possible. Eventually he succeeded and thought himself the patriot as well as the smart businessman.[5] In the meantime, Boulton himself was the target of numerous attempts at seduction. Sweden was particularly pressing, and he may even have solicited an offer from there.[6]

One cannot always discern the boundaries between curiosity, exploration, and outright spying. A leading student of the subject writes that "many foreigners . . . gathered useful intelligence . . . without ever doing anything underhand."[7] But he also notes that many "visitors" were themselves ironmasters, manufacturers, chemists, inspectors of industry, or some kind of informed observer. They had not come to England to see the monuments and the landscape. Here is Ignace de Wendel, nominally an artillery officer, more pertinently the scion of a dynasty of ironmasters and a chosen instrument of the French government. He thought himself well endowed with nose, eyes, tongue, and guile, and thought all of these necessary:

> . . . we found that there was nothing difficult in getting a good view of English Manufactures, one needs to know the language with facility, not show any curiosity, and wait till the hour when punch is served to instruct oneself and acquire the confidence of the manufacturers and their foremen, one must avoid recommendations from Ministers and Lords which will do little good . . . young men are little suited to such a mission . . . to view things usefully it is important to have at least some idea about machines, because one does not take a step without seeing them, which all tends to abridge the process of manufacture.[8]

Even more important was the flow of technological talent from Britain to the Continent: why take a quick look if you can hire someone with years of firsthand experience? Only people with hands-on knowledge could pass it on. Even in later ages of scientific diffusion and transparency, even with sample products and equipment, even with blueprints and explicit instructions, some know-how can be learned only by experience.* In 1916, in the hot middle of World War I, the French had lost some of their major centers of arms manufacture and desperately needed an additional supply of their 75-mm field guns. This was their key artillery piece, the pride of their arsenal, a machine so exquisitely designed that a glass of water perched on the carriage would not spill when the gun was fired. Violating all their rules of se-

---

* This is what Michael Polanyi called tacit knowledge. Kenneth Arrow speaks of learning-by-doing. See Polanyi, *The Tacit Dimension;* Arrow, "The Economic Implications of Learning by Doing"; J. Howells, "Tacit Knowledge."

crecy, they sent the blueprints to the United States—to no avail. Not until a team of workmen went over to show the Americans how, could they get pieces of comparable firepower and stability.)

Here, however, the eighteenth-century agent-recruiter ran up against a salient characteristic of British industry: the division of labor. No worker knew more than a small part of the production process. One French agent, by name Le Turc, alias Johnson in England, complained:

> No worker can explain to you the chain of operations, being perpetually occupied only with a small part; listen to him on anything outside that and you will be burdened with error. However it is this little understood division that results in the cheapness of labor, the perfection of the work and the greater security of the property of the manufacturer.[9]

Although specialization made the task more difficult and costly, the game was well worth the candle. Some of this emigration was solicited: foreign governments paid people to come and helped them set up in business. But some of the expats moved out of sentiment—like one John Holker, a disaffected Jacobite who was recruited to France by Directeur de Commerce Daniel Trudaine and became a manufacturer of woolens and textile machinery and Inspector-General of Foreign Manufactures. Others had strong personal reasons, like Michael Alcock, who in 1755–56 wanted to take off with his mistress, plus a little embezzled money, leaving wife and partner to face bankruptcy. The wife eventually rejoined him, and maybe she was part of the scheme in the first place. In the event, Alcock and his two women apparently managed to live together in a *ménage à trois* at La Charité, on the upper reaches of the Loire River, where Alcock made forgings and hardware and tried to teach the French something about fine steel.[10]

Most expatriates, however, had no urgent reasons to settle abroad. They did it for the money. The best of them became entrepreneurs of international scope. Take the Cockerills. The father William, a machinist, was brought over around 1800 to Verviers (then France, now Belgium), a center of woolen manufacture, by a firm of putters-out seeking to go over to factory industry. Cockerill was to supply them with the machine combinations *(assortiments)* that would take them from fiber to yarn (doing this by machinery entailed breaking the task into a sequence of processes). William, who had his own ambitions, would have happily supplied the whole industry (remember that we are talking about imperial France), but he was bound by contract to his new employers. No matter. His son-in-law set up as a machine builder, and when in 1807 William's contract expired, he opened his own shop in Liège, an age-old center of metallurgical crafts.

In 1813, William Cockerill turned the business over to his youngest son John, who diversified into heavy equipment: hydraulic presses, steam engines, pumps. By this time Belgium had been annexed to Holland, whose king looked upon the Cockerill firm as a jewel in his crown: "Continue your grand enterprises without fear and remember that the king of the Netherlands always has money at industry's service." With this and other, more material encouragements, John Cockerill went on to wider achievements—iron smelting, construction of steamboats and locomotives, a zinc mine near Aachen (nearby in Germany), woolen mills in Prussia, a cotton mill in Barcelona, a sugar refinery in Surinam, blast furnaces in southern France, shops, factories, and railway projects in far-off Russia. The trouble with this global entrepreneur, though—a Frenchman called him "a Liégeois of English descent better described as a tremendous mind without a country"— was that his eyes were too big for his means. In spite of substantial bank support, he went bust in the crisis of 1839–40 and died soon after. The firm was then reorganized—a monument more enduring than bronze and the lives of its creators.[11]

Like the Cockerills, but anonymously ordinary, most British expatriates were workmen drawn by wages that ran twice and three times higher than at home. (British wages were ordinarily considerably higher than those across the Channel, but these experienced craftsmen and mechanics were scarce commodities in follower countries.) Some of them had actually been sent on mission by manufacturers and exporters, to accompany engines and keep them working, and then found themselves more cherished abroad than at home. Many more were lured by old shop comrades, come back to recruit.

Most of this, remember, violated British law. In an effort to discourage foreign competition, Britain had prohibited the export of most machinery (though not steam engines) and the emigration of skilled artisans. In this, Britain was following an immemorial tradition. In medieval Italy, for example, the glassworkers of Murano and the shipwrights of the Arsenal in Venice emigrated only on pain of death. Such constraints delayed the diffusion of knowledge, but in a world of rudimentary surveillance, could not prevent it. So with Britain: hundreds, even thousands, of craftsmen emigrated during those early decades of the nineteenth century, most of them voluntarily. A few were captured in war.

British expats were not alone. The French imported Germans with metallurgical skills; the Russians brought in Dutch, Germans, and Swedes. The French crabbed about the Germans—their misbehavior, their ingratitude. (To some extent, these were the kinds of people who left home and moved to new jobs.) Here is a manufacturer of scythes griping about his Germans: in spite of all the advantages accorded them, he says, in spite of the better treatment, the absence of the military discipline they knew back home, they work as and when they please, and "just look for ways to get fired." Not everyone was so negative. One engineer pointed out that the availability of foreign workers had a salutary effect on French craftsmen, curing them totally of "the false principles of independence that too long have led them to regard themselves as masters of those who give them their living."[12] (This is a recurrent theme. Employers dislike being dependent on their workers, and the substitution of capital for labor—thus the original mechanization of cotton spinning and the imposition of the factory—was often motivated by considerations of power as well as of money.)*

But money too. Division of *labor* made it hard for expatriate workers to spill all the beans, but division of *capital* moved some employers to sell their product abroad and educate foreigners in its use. In particular, the new specialist machine-building industry sought markets wherever it could find them. British users of these devices understandably preferred to keep them secret; hence the general ban on exporting machinery. (Not steam engines, however, because originally they were not suited to manufacture. And when, in the 1780s, they found use in mills, you could not get an export prohibition past Boulton & Watt.) This push to sell made a huge difference when comfortable local producers were not ready to buy but foreign rivals were. The machine builders, then, were implicitly "subversives," promoting competition abroad and undermining their countrymen in third markets: "technological self-reliance [by machine users] combined with secrecy could be an unspoken suicide pact. . . . "[13]

---

* The classic example is the request made of Richard Roberts, partner in the machine-making firm of Sharp, Roberts, by a group of Lancashire spinners to build a self-acting mule, that is, a machine that would bring the spindle carriage back to begin a new stretch-and-wind cycle. The idea was to tame the mule spinners, the labor aristocracy of the industry—proud, umbrageous, and difficult in wage negotiations. When a trade contraction combined with this threat of innovation to curb the workers' pretensions, the spinners decided they did not need the new machine after all—cheaper that way. It took ten years for Roberts to make money from his invention. See MacLeod, "Strategies for Innovation," p. 291.

So much for diffusion. More important for follower countries in the long run were schools of science and technology. Pitched at the secondary or higher level, these aimed to train a higher order of technicians and supervisory personnel and laid the basis of intellectual autonomy. The French led here with the Ecole Polytechnique (originally named the Ecole Central des Travaux Publics) in 1794. This was initially designed as a military school for officers in engineering and artillery—branches where technical knowledge mattered. (Any brave fool could wave a cavalry saber about.) But from the start, the Revolutionary government appointed a faculty of top scientists and mathematicians, and these turned the Ecole in the long run from military lessons and discipline to the inculcation of maths, basic science, and technical capability. The competitive character of the institution—exam for admission, public ranking on entry, ranking on partial completion, ranking on graduation—drew France's best and brightest; so that although the school continued to furnish officers to the army, these were not the top students. The strongest "X"—as the French call them, after the algebraic unknown—went into business, private and public, and formed the cream of French engineering and technocracy. They led in building and managing the French railways; learned and adapted the latest British metallurgical techniques; directed public works abroad; and by the twentieth century, came to head some of France's biggest high-tech corporations.

The Polytechnique was if anything too rarefied and theoretical in its training. Those graduates who wanted to go on to industry usually took postgraduate instruction in the Ecole des Mines or the Ponts-et-Chaussées—both founded under the Old Regime. There they learned applied science and technology and did on-the-job training. Meanwhile French business came to feel that another school was needed, like the Polytechnique but more practical in its concerns. This was the Ecole Centrale des Arts et Manufactures, founded privately in 1829, incorporated into the state system in 1856, which served as a training ground for engineers and business managers. Students of Centrale had less prestige than the "X" of Polytechnique: the school was younger and the competition for admission was less keen; but its greater openness meant that its graduates did better than the "X" in newer branches such as motor cars and aviation.

Alongside these two pivotal, general institutions, local schools sprang up, the vocational *écoles d'arts et métiers;* and specialized industrial schools, often founded by employers, for training in particular branches: chemicals in Lyons, watchmaking in Besançon, textiles in Mulhouse. Some of this aimed to make up for the disappearance of the older apprenticeship system. Finally, such older technical institutions as the Conservatoire des Arts et Métiers—a museum to start—took to giving courses, often directed to adults who had passed beyond the normal sequence but wanted to bring themselves up to date.

The French initiatives were a beacon to countries farther east. The Polytechnique in particular sparked emulation in Prague, Vienna, Zurich, places as far off as Moscow. In addition, each country had its own combination of associated schools. The Germans, for example, developed a network of trade schools *(Gewerbeschulen)* that fed middle technological management; and a growing array of technical higher schools *(technische Hochschulen)*—the first in Karlsruhe in 1825—that taught at university level and formed generations of chemists and engineers. Finally, the Germans pushed scientific instruction and research in the universities. This was the cutting edge of experiment and inquiry, and the invention of the teaching laboratory (Justus Liebig, 1830s) capped an educational system that became by the end of the century the world's envy and model.

The reliance on formal education for the diffusion of technical and scientific knowledge had momentous consequences. First, it almost always entailed instruction in abstract and theoretical matters that lent themselves to a variety of applications, old and new. I would emphasize the new. Secondly, it opened the way to new branches of knowledge of great economic potential.

Compare such schooling with the British strategy of learning by doing—the strategy that had driven the Industrial Revolution. This had worked well enough so long as technology remained an accretion of improvements and invention a recombination of known techniques. (Even so, one can only marvel at Britain's continuing ability to generate appropriate genius and talent, much of it autodidact.) But from the late eighteenth century on, as the frontiers of technological possibility and inquiry moved outward, exploration went beyond the lessons of sensory experience.

These new directions found their biggest return in two areas, chemicals and electricity—in both, thanks to advances in scientific knowledge. The older chemical branches remained a kind of industrial cookery: mix, heat, stir, keep the good and dump the waste. They did not stand still. They gained especially from mechanization—bigger and faster kilns, mixers, grinders, and the like—as producers went after economies of scale. Another source of progress was the invention of uses for waste products (thus coal gas for illumination), sometimes in response to laws penalizing pollution. (Better to use the waste than be sued or fined.) But the revolutionary advances came in the new field of organic chemistry and derived directly from studies of carbon-based molecules. These opened the door to a multitude of applications, first in the field of dyestuffs (crucial to textile manufacture), then in pharmaceuticals and photography, and finally, toward the end of the century, in artificial matter—what we loosely call plastics.

Electricity was known, but not understood, by the ancients, and curious savants played with it, almost as with a toy, from the eighteenth century on. Such experiments could have practical consequences; hence Benjamin Franklin's invention of the lightning rod. But the systematic use of electricity as a form of energy and its application to industrial processes had to wait for the nineteenth century, after research by such people as Volta, Ampère, and Faraday, whose names have been immortalized in scientific terminology. The first industrial applications were small though impressive: batteries (Voltaic piles), which could drive telegraphs and clocks; and electrolytic techniques, used especially to plate metals and cutlery. Both of these were pre-1850. But electricity's flowering came with the invention of generators and dynamos to produce current in quantity and the building of a system of distribution. The biggest stimuli were Thomas Edison's incandescent lighting (1879) and electric motors, which justified the outlay for overhead capital.

In both chemicals and electricals, learning and competence depended on formal instruction. These phenomena are not apprehensible by sensory perception; it takes diagrams and schemas to explain them, and the underlying principles are best learned in the classroom and laboratory. Here Continental reliance on schooling paid off, generating and imparting new technologies. Catching up turned into a leap ahead, while Britain, caught in the net of habit, fell behind.

In British electricity, moreover, local autonomies exacerbated the difficulty. In some places, municipal gas networks successfully opposed electrification; elsewhere Britain built a multiplicity of power networks, each with its own voltage arrangements and hardware. Later improvements only added to the menu. To this day, British buyers of electrical appliances must deal with a diversity of plugs and outlets, and customers pay shopkeepers to ready equipment for use. The British economy grew in these new branches as it had in the old—like Topsy.

This marriage of science and technique opened an era that Simon Kuznets called "modern economic growth."[14] It was not only the extraordinary cluster of innovations that made the Second Industrial Revolution so important—the use of liquid and gaseous fuels in internal combustion engines, the distribution of energy and power via electric current, the systematic transformation of matter, improved communications (telephone and radio), the invention of machines driven by the new sources of power (motor vehicles and domestic appliances). It was also and above all the role of formally transmitted knowledge.

The marriage of science and technique had been preceded by a number of couplings. One can take the courtship back to the Middle Ages, to the use of astronomical knowledge to transform navigation (the calculation of latitudes), the use of mathematics in ballistics, the application of the pendulum to the construction of a far more accurate timekeeper. And back to the steam engine, that classic triumph of scientific empiricism. But not until the late nineteenth century does science get ahead and precede technique. Now would-be inventors and problem solvers found it profitable to survey the literature before undertaking their projects; or for that matter, before conceiving their objective—what to do and how to do it.

So it was that the leader/innovator was caught and overtaken. And so it was that all the old advantages—resources, wealth, power—were devalued, and the mind established over matter. Henceforth the future lay open to all those with the character, the hands, and the brains.

⌒⌒

## The Secrets of Industrial Cuisine

Steel, we have seen, was always the metal of choice in the making of "white arms" (swords and daggers), knives and razors, edge tools, and files (crucial to the manufacture of precision parts). In the beginning, steel was an accidental by-product of smelting in furnaces that were not hot enough to produce a homogeneous mass and yielded some steel along with soft and hard iron. Later on, with the invention of the tall blast furnace operating at higher temperatures, one had to go through multiple processes to get from pig iron to steel. One way was to reheat the metal and burn off enough of the carbon to get down to 1.2–1.5 percent. The results were not even (it was not easy to stop at the right moment) and gave a variety of steels that were then used for different purposes. The best went for guns and fine cutlery; the poorer, for plowshares and sickles.

Another way was to remove the carbon to get wrought iron, and then add carbon to get steel. The adding was typically done by packing bars of wrought iron in carbon, heating and soaking, and then hammering. The aim was to beat the composite metal in such a way as to distribute the carbon evenly and homogenize the result— something like kneading dough. And just as kneading produces a more homogeneous dough by folding, pressing, and folding and pressing again, so the best of this cementation steel was folded upon itself, rehammered, and then again and again. The result was a layered bar of steel; the more the layers (that is, the more the folding and kneading), the nervier and stronger the metal. The finest examples of this kind of work are the famous Japanese *samurai* swords, which still hold their edge and gleam after five centuries. Layered steel, invented in Europe in Nuremberg at the beginning of the seventeenth century (Nuremberg was an old center of tool- and instrument making), was immediately picked up by the English. The French did not learn the technique until about 1770.

But even *samurai* swords cannot compare for homogeneity with crucible steel, that is, steel heated to liquid so that the carbon additive mixes completely. The inventor of crucible steel, in 1740, was an English clockmaker, Benjamin Huntsman, who had an obvious professional interest in getting better metal for springs and files. The technique would remain a British monopoly for about three quarters of a century—not for want of would-be imitators.

The French in particular spent mightily to learn the secret. France was comparatively weak in steel and understandably saw this as a serious political disability. Early in the eighteenth century that scientific jack of all trades René Antoine de Réaumur (1683–1757), best known for his thermometer, claimed to have found the secret of what he himself compared to the "philosophers' stone," established a "royal manufactory" for the purpose of turning iron into steel, and got a generous government pension for his efforts. He failed, because he thought the answer lay in adding sulfur and the right salts. The role of carbon never occurred to him. He also thought that French iron was good enough for the purpose, unlike the British, who imported the finer Swedish iron for making steel.[15] He should have looked around.

"This error of analysis and this 'patriotic choice' would long be accepted in France and would aggravate the backwardness of the national industry."[16] Others came forward subsequently and bragged that they had made steel comparable to the English and German product. No go. The biggest push came after Gabriel Jars's English trip of 1765. Jars himself set out to produce cementation steel but got mediocre results, largely because he worked with French iron *à la Réaumur;* death in 1769 interrupted his efforts. Another technician named Duhamel, traveling companion of Jars and protégé of the minister Turgot, was hired by the comte de Broglie, owner of a forge and recipient of a government subsidy of some 15,000 *livres,* to undertake similar experiments. Fifteen years later the government was obliged to recognize that Duhamel was getting nowhere. Lesser metallurgists tried on their own initiative. No question about it: France needed steel and wanted to know how to make it.

Enter the Englishman, Michael Alcock of Birmingham, whom we came to know above. He told the French that there was nothing to it: making steel was easy; the hard part was making good steel. So with the help of Director of Commerce Trudaine de Montigny (son of the man who had sent Jars and Duhamel to visit England), he set up a plant of his own and produced samples of cementation and crucible steel. He never got beyond the stage of samples.

Meanwhile two of Alcock's partners went off on their own and bought a small filemaking forge at Amboise on the Loire (better known for its royal château). The forge caught the interest of the duc de Choiseul and got the French government (again with the support of Trudaine de Montigny) to sponsor a "royal manufactory" of fine steels and subsidize it in the amount of 20,000 *livres* a year. The subsidy, however, came with a curse: the obligation to use French-made wrought iron. The enterprise invested heavily in equipment—six large furnaces, forty power hammers, eighty steel forges—and undertook experiment after experiment. To no avail. It never made crucible steel, and its cementation steel did not inspire confidence.

Other enterprises, more or less well connected but equally determined, also entered the race, aiming particularly at the manufacture of good files, which were becoming ever more important as mechanization advanced and metals replaced wood. One of them, in the Dauphiné, had the support of the *intendant* and of the financial group of the duc d'Orléans. To begin with, it set its sights low: the manufacture of blades for scythes and sundry hardware. But then it ran into trouble because of embezzlement. It was easier to take money than to make it.

Denis Woronoff, historian of the French iron industry, sums up: sixty years after Réaumur, the French steel industry was still "marking time." Announcement after announcement of success had proved false. Not that the government inspectors were gullible or complaisant, but they put more emphasis on the theoretical purity of the metal than on its performance (hardness, edge, etc.). They were also "sold" on the importance of size (*gigantisme*) in circumstances of diseconomies of scale. The result was waste, dead ends, and commercial failure.[17]

After that came the revolution and Napoleon. More marking time. Only in the 1820s did the French learn how to make crucible steel, thanks to a British expatriate named James Jackson. The Germans did it about ten years earlier, essentially without outside help. The Swiss Johann Conrad Fischer, a keenly observant and indefatigably peripatetic visitor of foreign enterprises—his nose and eyes were everywhere—learned to do it from about 1805.[18]

It takes more than recipes, blueprints, and even personal testimony to learn industrial cuisine.

≈) ⊂

## Genius Is Not Enough

In the mid-nineteenth century, the alkaloid quinine was of vital importance to British rule in India, where malaria enfeebled and killed civilian and military personnel. Quinine did not cure the disease, but it relieved the symptoms. At that time, quinine was obtained from the bark of the cinchona tree, which was native to Peru. The British government, working through the world-famous botanical gardens at Kew, was making strenuous efforts to obtain cinchona seeds in Peru, nurse them into seedlings, and then plant them in India, but the results proved disappointing. India remained dependent on high-cost imports from Java, where the Dutch had managed to obtain a better transplant. The British would have preferred their own supply.

William Henry Perkin, born in London in 1838, was the son of a builder and had no connection with India. His father wished him to be an architect (social promotion), but early on he wanted to do chemistry. In 1853, only fifteen, he entered the newly founded Royal College of Chemistry, then under the direction of a German scientist, August Wilhelm Hofmann, who liked the boy and took him on as an assistant. Hofmann put Perkin onto the importance of

finding a way to synthesize quinine, and Perkin took the problem
home with him to a little laboratory he had fitted up in his family
house. He did not find a way to make quinine, but by the by he did
obtain a precipitate from naphtha (an ingredient of coal tar), aniline
black, from which he then derived the color aniline blue, or mauve.
(Chemistry has always been a science of serendipity.)

Perkin was alert enough to recognize the value of his find. His
blue coloring matter made an excellent dye, and after patenting it,
Perkin, then only nineteen years of age, set up a plant for its
manufacture with funds provided by his father and brother. That was
the end of his training at the Royal College. From this first lucky
strike to purposeful others, Perkin soon became a millionaire. And
then, another turn: he went back to his first love, experimental and
theoretical chemistry. Besides, the German chemical industry was
leaving the British far behind.

This first artificial dye was the stuff of dreams—the beginning of
the enormously important coal-tar color industry. Once Perkin had
given the cue, chemists in England, France, Germany, and
Switzerland turned to the task and a rainbow of artificial colors came
forth—fuchsia (fuchsine), magenta (after the blood shed in the battle
of that name), a range of purples, the whole alizarin family of reds,
pinks, oranges, and yellows, and a green that caused a sensation
because it did not turn blue in gaslight.* These colors in turn
stimulated demand for fashionable fabrics and weaned the women of
the rich countries of Europe from their traditional economical and
lugubrious black. (Today, richer still, many of them have gone back
to black, even at weddings.) More important in the long run,
however, was the ramification of the new techniques to wider
chemical developments: new illuminants, pharmaceuticals (aspirin,
salvarsan, sundry barbiturates, novocain, and dozens more),
photographic materials, artificial fertilizers, and, down the line,
plastics—all of these with the usual share of unexpected and
accidental finds.

Thanks to Perkin, Britain led the new industry. Britain had
everything going for it. To begin with, it had a huge, traditionally

---

* Alizarin was derived from anthracene, another component of coal tar. The synthesis was achieved by Perkin in England, Caro, Graebe, and Liebermann in Germany in
1869. The market effect was stunning: in 1870 natural alizarin as derived from madder cost 90 marks a kilo; the synthetic, 8 marks. Madder, long a feature of the landscape of Provence, was now history—Milward and Saul, *Economic Development*, p. 229.

based heavy-chemical industry producing alkalis, acids, and salt. Then, it had all the ingredients for a carbon-based manufacture: no country produced more of the raw material coal tar; nowhere was it cheaper. Finally, it offered the world's biggest market for textile dyes. Yet within a generation the industry left British shores to settle in Germany and to a lesser extent in France and Switzerland. By 1881, Germany was making about half of the world's artificial dyestuffs; by 1900, between 80 and 90 percent. The major German producers were able to pay dividends of over 20 percent, year in and year out through good times and bad, while investing large sums in plant, research, and equipment. This was one of the biggest, most rapid industrial shifts in history.[19]

Why? Why this apparent violation of the "laws" of comparative advantage and path dependency? Because apart from Perkin and a few other sports, Britain did not have the trained and gifted chemists needed to generate invention. Certainly not so many and so well trained as could be found on the Continent. So when A. W. Hofmann, Heinrich Caro, and their German colleagues in Britain were drawn back home by attractive offers, the British organic chemical industry shriveled. In Germany, by contrast, big corporations arose and flourished: Hoechst, BASF (Badische Anilin u. Soda-Fabrik), Bayer, Agfa, built around top-flight chemists and chemical engineers, equipped with well-fitted house laboratories, and closely tied to the universities.

The significance of this pool of talent combined with enterprise and a research-oriented culture shows up well in the story of artificial indigo. Here was a logical candidate for synthesis: a major colorant, carbon compound, derived at high cost from exotic plants (woad and others). In 1880, Professor A. Baeyer synthesized it and sold the process to BASF and Hoechst, which decided there was enough to share and pooled resources. They needed each other. Seventeen years, 152 patents, and many millions of marks later, the two firms still did not have a commercially feasible technique. One dead end used a different synthesis, also by Baeyer; but it required so much toluene that the coal-tar industry could not have supplied it without flooding the market with such co-products as benzene and naphthalene. Waste products are the curse of the chemical industry and the people who live near it. They are also a powerful stimulant to new research.[20]

At this point, BASF and Hoechst turned to a method worked out at the ETH (Eidgenössische Technische Hochschule, also known as the Polytechnic) in Zurich, which took its departure from naphthalene, then an almost worthless by-product of the distillation of coal tar. But this too posed practical and commercial problems that took years to solve. BASF went one way; Hoechst, which was entitled to use their process, took another path, once again based on research at the Zurich Poly. BASF got into production earlier (1897, as against 1904), but the Hoechst technique proved the better. In chemistry as in business, there is more than one way to skin a cat.

Here as in so many other instances, the new technique spelled disaster for older methods and the people who lived by them. Within three years, BASF was producing as much indigo as could be got from 250,000 acres. The big losers in this instance were the Indians who grew and exported the natural product: 187,000 tons in 1895–96; 11,000 in 1913–14. The price of the dye had been halved.[21]

By World War I, Germany had left the rest of the world far behind in modern chemistry—so far behind that even the confiscation of German industrial patents during that war did not immediately benefit competitors overseas. The biggest American firms, with the best American chemical engineers, did not know what to do with them or how to make them work. So in the twenties, they hired away German chemists. Industrial espionage back in the saddle.

# ~ 19 ~

# Frontiers

In 1700, product per head in Mexico was worth about 450 U.S. 1985 dollars; in the colonies that would become the United States, product was somewhat larger, say $490; and in the booming sugar colony of Barbados, the figure was substantially higher, $736. One hundred years later, Mexico was still at $450, and the United States was at $807. By 1989, the United States had drawn far ahead: GDP of $3,500 for Mexico, $5350 for Barbados, $18,300 for the United States.[1]

The Industrial Revolution came to a world still relatively empty—at least by comparison with the population densities we know today. Within this world, of course, concentrations varied, from the thicker settlement of China, India, and parts of northwestern Europe, to the wide spaces of central Asia, Australia, and the Americas. The reasons for this variance were largely geographical and technological: populations moved to and multiplied best in favorable climes, on fertile soils, using techniques of cultivation that seized the natural potential. Political considerations also played a role. In Europe, for example, the potentially rich Danubian plain of the early eighteenth century lay quite open. Ending hundreds of years of misrule, the Ottomans had abruptly withdrawn after the failed second siege of Vienna (1685). Half a century later, the Russians opened the great Ukrainian breadbasket by driving back the nomadic peoples that had roamed and vaguely ruled these wide spaces since the days of the Golden Horde (mid-thirteenth century).

The biggest frontiers, however, waited overseas: the Americas above all, but also lesser spaces in Australia and southern Africa. None of these lands was empty when the Europeans arrived. Everywhere, indigenous peoples tilled the soil, raised their livestock, or just hunted and gathered. But again, densities of settlement varied, dictating the opportunity and circumstances of invasion. In the Americas, a few areas were thickly settled—the valley of Mexico, the Peruvian hill country, some Caribbean islands. Ordinarily such densities would have precluded conquest, as they did in Asia, but the technological and political weaknesses of the native American population made them vulnerable. Imported pathogens did the rest. Elsewhere in the Americas, as in the northern latitudes that became the United States and Canada, low densities gave way to superior armament and organization. For the Indians, the white man was stealing their land; for the white man, the land lay before them for the taking, a boundless, profitable frontier.

Economists see the factors of production as land, labor, and capital. Land subsumes not only surface area but the resources that lie underneath; and from the point of view of economic development, the salient characteristics of a frontier region are space, soil, and wealth of materials. These in turn set opportunities and constraints: such lands can yield abundance of primary products per head of population, but only if they can get the necessary labor. They want people, whom they often draw by offering incentives to migration: free or cheap land in particular, but also higher wages, higher status, and political rights. (This was a crucial aspect of the improvement of status and tenure in medieval Europe.) And if voluntary labor does not come, they will import people by force, paying slave traders or recruiters to do the dirty work.

Once the factors of production assembled, frontier lands typically yield crops and other primary products far in excess of the needs of the population. These surpluses then become tradables. These economies can make so much more money producing cash crops for export than by devoting themselves to subsistence farming that it pays them to trade food security for income. (Witness the sugar islands of the Caribbean, which devoted every square inch to cane and imported victuals from as far away as Europe.)

The pursuit of this strategy by a number of fledgling economies has led to a staples theory, or "vent for surplus" argument.* The idea: one starts with earnings from export of primary products, which raise incomes at home. Higher incomes in turn promote a market for manufactures while financing the development of an industrial sector and a more balanced economy. (Much depends on the distribution of income in the staples producer. The less equal, the smaller the market for manufactures. Thus a plantation economy will not generate much industrial demand: the estate owners will buy luxury goods for themselves and spend a minimum to clothe and house their slaves.)

The staples model was first put forward by Harold Innes to explain Canadian performance in terms of a succession of export staples: first furs (seventeenth and eighteenth centuries), then timber (late eighteenth and nineteenth), and finally cereals (mid- and late-nineteenth century). Similar schemas have since been put forward for Sweden (timber, copper, iron), the United States (tobacco and cotton, then wheat), Australia (wool, meat, wheat), Argentina (hides, tallow, meat, grain), Meiji Japan (silk), even medieval England (wool).[2] And one could conceive of parallel developments taking place in oil-producing nations today.

But like most good economic theories, vent for surplus models have a tautological aspect: they explain best what fits best. Just because an economy earns by export of primary products does not mean that it will then use this income well to promote development. There's the rub: invest or spend? And even if one decides to invest, who says that the money will go to the right activities? Besides, what is right? Stay with staples and maximize comparative advantage? Or aim at balanced development, that is, take less now for more later?

The history of frontier economies in the Americas and their success in industrialization is a case study in the power and weakness of staples theory. On the one hand, we have the United States and Canada—high-income, developed economies; on the other, the fragments of the old Spanish empire plus the former Portuguese colony of Brazil. In the beginning these southern countries were richer and more populous; today they lag far behind, and although they are finally beginning

---

*This should not be confused with classical doctrines of comparative advantage, which are essentially static and provide no reason for economic development. On the contrary, they were used from the start to justify the prevailing international division of labor.

to modernize, few would predict their rapid convergence with the North American republics, even with the help of such common markets as NAFTA.

The divergent story of North America (ex-British) on the one hand, Latin America (ex-Spanish and Portuguese) on the other, needs multiple explanation. Economists would not always have it so. For them, one good reason is enough, and where the Americas are concerned, the best reason is resources. These frontier lands abounded in natural wealth, but this wealth proved differentially useful in the context of the new industrial technologies. Here the United States came out best: large expanses of fertile, virgin land; a fine climate for growing a crucial industrial-entry raw material, namely, cotton; rich deposits of the key ingredients for ferrous metallurgy; plenty of wood and coal for fuel, plus generous waterpower all along the east coast; an abundance of petroleum, valuable from the mid-nineteenth century for light, as lubricant, and above all as fuel for internal combustion motors; copper ores in quantity, ready by the end of the nineteenth century for the burgeoning demands of electrical power, motors, and transmission. And along with this went relatively convenient lines of access and communication: a well-indented coastline punctuated by superb harbors, large rivers (above all, the Mississippi and its affluents), and wide plains. The only serious mountain barrier between the Atlantic and the Rockies was the Appalachians, and here a number of gaps opened to trade and travel, in particular, the breach made by the Hudson River and the flat stretch to the Great Lakes. Here man was able to improve on nature, as the Erie Canal and railroads opened the Middle West to Middle Atlantic ports.

In these respects, the United States was more favored than other parts of the New World. No other country had iron and coal, for example, in proximity; no other had comparable natural ways of transport and communication. By comparison, Mexico is a puzzle of mountains, plateaus, and deserts—not without its good places but poorly joined, as railway builders found out. Much of Brazil is tropical and subtropical, so that the awesome Amazon river basin is even now penetrated with difficulty. Argentina is the country most comparable to the United States in its natural features and accessibility; but immigration there was long impeded and the key industrial raw materials are wanting.

One could, then, argue, as numerous economists have, that American priority in development was predetermined by nature—the luck of the draw. Recently, however, scholars have advanced a more complex geographical explanation, one that links natural circumstances to culture and institutions.[3] The argument here is that geography dictates crops and the mode of cultivation, hence the nature of land tenure and the distribution of wealth; while these in turn are critical to the pace and character of development. Where society is divided between a privileged few landowners and a large mass of poor, dependent, perhaps unfree laborers—in effect, between a school for laziness (or self-indulgence) over against a slough of despond—what the incentive to change and improve? At the top, a lofty indifference; below, the resignation of despair. Now and then, resistance breaks out and gives the elites and their soldiers opportunity to practice the martial arts; while religion offers the consolation of a better world after death.

This was not the case in the northern United States, nor in Canada alongside. They had the paradoxical advantage of a climate that limited cultivation to grains and yielded little at first in the way of an exportable surplus. Economies of scale were negligible, at least before the invention of mechanical technologies, so that holdings were small, often no larger than subsistence, and more or less evenly distributed.* Such equality did not always please those of aristocratic inclinations. In 1765, a British visitor to New England, Lord Adam Gordon, frowned his disapproval: " . . . the levelling principle here, everywhere, operates strongly and takes the lead. Everybody has property, and everybody knows it."[4]

In addition, quasi-free land and scarce labor made for high wages and hard recruitment in both country and town, as Adam Smith observed:

> . . . the disproportion between the great extent of the land and the small number of the people, which commonly takes place in new colonies, makes it difficult for him [the proprietor] to get this labour. He does not, therefore, dispute about wages, but is willing to employ labour at any price. The high wages of labour encourage population. The cheapness and plenty of good land encourage improvement, and enable the proprietor to pay those high wages.[5]

* This was particularly true of New England. In the Middle Atlantic colonies—New York and Pennsylvania in particular—one found larger commercial farms, producing for distant markets. See Fischer, *Albion's Seed,* pp. 174, 377–78, 567, who points out that the differences in landholding reflected not so much geographical circumstances as the circumstances of origin in the Old World and the consequent intentions of the settlers.

Farm wages and land prices, of course, set a floor for urban wages—otherwise, how hold the labor?—while the very growth of such a frontier economy pushed wages up.* Here is Smith again:

> It is not, accordingly, in the richest countries, but in the most thriving, or in those which are growing rich the fastest, that the wages of labour are highest. England is certainly, in the present times, a much richer country than any part of North America. The wages of labour, however, are much higher in North America than in any part of England.[6]

America's society of smallholders and relatively well-paid workers was a seedbed of democracy and enterprise. Equality bred self-esteem, ambition, a readiness to enter and compete in the marketplace, a spirit of individualism and contentiousness. At the same time, smallholdings encouraged technical self-sufficiency and the handyman, fix-it mentality. Every farm had its workshop and anvil, its gadgets and cunning improvements.† Ingenuity brought not only comfort and income but also status and prestige. Good workers were the envy of their neighbors, the heroes of the community. Meanwhile high wages enhanced the incentive to substitute capital for labor, machines for men.

As a result, the new technologies of the Industrial Revolution found fertile ground in the American colonies and then the United States. Even earlier, the need for self-sufficiency in an age of slow and intermittent communication gave rise to local manufacture. Listen to a report of 1681 on the quickness of Quaker settlers to engage in industry: " . . . they have also coopers, smiths, bricklayers, wheelwrights, plowrights and millwrights, ship carpenters and other trades, which work upon what the country produces for manufactories. . . . There are iron-houses, and a Furnace and Forging Mill already set up in East-Jersey, where they make iron." Another report of 1698 speaks of cloth manufacture: in the Quaker communities of Burlington and Salem, "cloth workers were making very good serges, druggets, crapes, camblets, plushes and other woolen cloths. Entire families engaged in such

---

* In an effort to protect the Indians, the British authorities tried to limit westward expansion to the Appalachians. In vain: all the redcoats on the continent could not have guarded that frontier, any more than the United States today seems able to close the Mexican border.

† The best similar example of a handyman culture that comes to mind is that of the Swiss Jura, where cottage workers laid the basis for the world's most successful watch industry—Landes, *Revolution in Time,* ch. xvi: "Notwithstanding the Barrenness of the Soil."

manufactures, using wool and linen of their own raising."[7]

New England and the middle colonies of Pennsylvania and New Jersey became the "industrial heartlands" of the new nation. Iron-making got its start in the 1640s (bog iron on the Saugus [at Lynn] in Massachusetts), only two decades after the Pilgrims' landing at Plymouth.[8] By the time of the revolution (1770s), some two hundred iron forges were in operation in Britain's American colonies, and the annual make was some 30,000 tons. Only Britain, France, Sweden, and Russia made more. Along with smelting went refining, hammering, cutting, slitting, rolling, and the sundry other operations that turn iron into tools and objects. Inevitably, the demand for British metallurgical products fell sharply, leading British manufacturers to petition Parliament for laws prohibiting colonial manufacture. As much command the tides. Such laws only sensitized the colonists to the injustice of their subordinate status and of government without representation; also to the importance of economic autonomy. As Benjamin Rush, doctor and civic leader in Pennsylvania, put it in 1775: "A people who are dependent on foreigners for food or clothes must always be subject to them."[9]

One focus of colonial industry was to cost the British dear. The colonials made guns—muskets to begin with, and increasingly rifles, which along with hunting from childhood, gave them a substantial edge in marksmanship, an edge that would persist into the twentieth century. Guns had their particular virtues in a frontier society, to the point where some of the colonies imposed an obligation to bear arms, even to church. (Again, one has here a strong and persistent cultural characteristic, as witness the present-day opposition to gun control.)

Demand, however, did not assure supply. Culture matters. The people of the South and of backwoods Appalachia went more heavily armed, but the guns were made in the northern colonies. The reason was simple: that was where the skills and tools were. By the time the South went to war against the Union in 1861, firearms production in the North outweighed that in the Confederacy by 32 to 1.[10]

One sees in these early gunshops a hint of things to come: so great was the demand for weapons that long before powered machine tools became available, division of labor was enhancing productivity. The later interest of the young American republic in the mass production of small arms using interchangeable parts was anticipated well before the revolution.

Thus the colonists imported and copied models of European devices and machines, and skilled machinists and craftsmen were invited, or sought on their own account, to move to high American wages. Here the North American colonies were helped by their anglophone culture: Britain boasted the most inventive society in Europe, and British immigrants felt at home in a society speaking the same language. The Germans also contributed. The Quakers of Pennsylvania had made it a point to encourage people of like faith on the European continent to join them in the New World, and these too (the so-called Pennsylvania Dutch) brought with them manual crafts and skills. By comparison, would-be-aristocratic Virginia, the nostalgic "Old Dominion," with its large plantations and indentured labor, found it hard to attract such people; and the crystallization of slavery only made matters worse.

(The technological dependency of the South persisted long after the end of the Civil War and the transplantation there of manufacturing industry from older centers in the Northeast, usually owned and financed from outside the region. These enterprises, typically marked by low output and value-added per worker, were mostly found in such low-tech branches as cotton and lumber. This tardy shift has given rise to diverse explanations, bearing mostly on natural resources, the low cost of labor, and the absence of trade unions. Some scholars have seen the process as an expression of economic colonialism or dependency, and many would account for the lag by anti-industrial values and culture inherited from a slave society. To which I would add the paucity of inventive activity and entrepreneurial talent.)[11]

The American republic was scarcely born when in 1790 Samuel Slater installed the first working spinning machines in Providence, Rhode Island. He was followed by others, and New England, with its strong streams, became a major center of cotton and woolen manufacture. Here, as on the European continent, British expatriates were the primary agents of technological diffusion.[12] Yet the character of the receiving society mattered even more. The few carriers who brought the knowledge found quick students to copy, imitate, and, most important, improve. When Francis Lowell of Boston introduced the power loom in 1814, he found a ready workforce, descendants of "many generations of farmer-mechanics in the workshops of New England."[13]

So a few machines came from England, but only a few, and Americans were soon adapting them to the needs and tastes of the home market. (They were also inventing new devices and exporting them to Britain—the best sign of technological independence.)[14] Thus British cotton spinners used the mule, which called for highly skilled, invariably masculine, labor, and concentrated on finer counts of yarn; while the Americans developed the throstle (derived from Arkwright's water frame), which used semiskilled women workers to make a tougher, coarser yarn; and then substantially increased its productivity by the invention, first of cap spinning, and then of ring spinning. Similarly, American innovations in weaving quickly (by the 1820s) made the Waltham-type cotton factory "at least 10 percent more efficient in throughput" than its British competitor.[15]

The figures tell the story. In 1788, Philadelphia's Fourth of July parade featured a hand-powered cotton carding machine and an eighty-spindle jenny—symbols of a preindustrial (pre-power) economic independence. Twenty years later, the young United States was powering almost 100,000 cotton spindles; between 1810 and 1820 the number tripled, and in the next decade more than tripled again. So, by 1831, the industry counted 1.2 million spindles and 33,500 looms, most of them power-driven by piedmont streams from New Hampshire in the North to Maryland in the south.[16]

A recent comparison of productivity in manufacturing shows America well ahead of Britain by the 1820s.[17] This was an extraordinary achievement, bringing together enlightened and often explicitly patriotic enterprise, knowledge and know-how, and an intelligent workforce. Some workers were Luddites who had fought machinery back in the old country but were ready to accept it in the New World; some, handloom weavers who had once refused to enter mills. Why the change? Like old England, New England resented the factory's strict hours and personal supervision. But whereas old England could count initially on involuntary labor—poorhouse apprentices, daughters and wives, people who could not say no—New England had to find ways to make these new jobs acceptable if not attractive. The American mills paid higher wages and gave their women and girls the kind of housing and chaste environment that reassured parents.* The paternalism of the cotton manufacturers of Lowell became legendary—the cleanly boardinghouses with their reading material and pianos, the women's own periodical (the *Lowell Offering*), the virtuous (sanctimonious) parietal rules.[18]

Some historians have called attention to less happy circumstances beneath the surface. These had to be there, they argue, for how could capitalism really spend for the benefit of employees? No doubt. The system had its own logic; business had its ups and downs, and hard

---

* Hours were long, but shorter for example than in Japanese mills at the same stage. They varied somewhat with the season, but ran to some eleven to thirteen hours per day—Montgomery, *Practical Detail of the Cotton Manufacture*, pp. 173–77.

times make hard masters. Inevitably, in spite of what economists tell us about the homogenizing effects of competition, some employers left much to be desired.[19] Even so, conditions were apparently better than in old England. To cite Charles Dickens, the contrast was "between the Good and Evil, the living light and deepest shadow."[20]

Another example of technological autonomy. The newly independent Americans also imported steam engines, at first of the atmospheric type. But then they opted for high pressure, and once again local invention played a critical role. The key figure was Oliver Evans (1755–1819), a brilliant jack-of-all-trades who made important contributions to wool carding and flour milling as well as to steampower. Evans's device went back to the 1780s, but the major applications date from the turn of the century.* These high-pressure reciprocating engines, typically smaller and cheaper, gave more power for size than the older atmospheric-vacuum type; hence were well suited not only to industry but to transport, where space counted. These smaller machines made possible the steamboat and the railway locomotive. On the other hand, high-pressure engines could explode—one reason why James Watt and many British engine builders and users stuck to the atmospheric variety. The Americans seemed ready here to trade dead and injured for cheaper power and transport.

The decisive and most distinctive American innovation, though, was not any particular device, however important, but a mode of production—what came to be called the American system of manufactures. This was a creative response to (1) a market free of the local and regional preferences and the class and status distinctions that prevailed in Europe, hence ready to accept standardized articles; and (2) the scarcity of labor relative to materials. The two were related. In a labor-scarce economy, standardization was a way of dividing, hence of simplifying, tasks and making them repetitive, thus substantially enhancing productivity. But fast work tended to waste material—no time for Old World habits of trimming and thrift. In Europe, even rich merchant bankers might write their letters down the page, then turn the sheet and continue at right angles in order to save paper.

Already in colonial times, for example, much American house con-

---

*Evans sent a copy of his plans to England in 1787, where Richard Trevithick, the engineer often assigned the invention, is said to have seen them in 1794–95—*Enc. Brit.*, 11th ed., s.v. Evans, Oliver. An early example, then, of a continuing battle for priority between mother country and daughter colony. Of course, the very fact of this contest testifies to the precocity of U.S. technological advance.

struction had turned from carpentry to millwork. Doors and windows were cut and assembled to standard size; glass, precut accordingly. (A French ship arriving in the young republic around 1815 with a cargo of window glass of various sizes was surprised to find it had to give most of it away.) Sawdust generated in the process might be recovered for other uses.[21] Then, in the 1830s, invention of the balloon-frame house normalized and deskilled the building itself. Gone were the heavy members of traditional barns and dwellings; gone the mortise-and-tenon joints; gone the masonry and plaster walls, interior and exterior, of Old World construction.* Instead, one used precut 2x4's and nailed them together, then sheathed the frame and clapped on such facade as was practical and pleasing. The new structures were not beautiful or authentically local; but they were cheap, made use of abundant materials, and were prosaically utilitarian. The balloon technique spread widely, except where wood was scarce.[22]

This reliance on wood led to a whole family of machines: power saws, lathes, millers, and planers, "machinery for boring, slotting, dovetailing, edging, grooving, etc." These worked fast—faster than similar machines for shaping metal—and they were, for that very reason, hugely wasteful of material. But that was all right: America could spare the wood, not the time or manpower.[23]

Houses and buildings were only the beginning. The idea was to make all assembled objects in such wise that the parts be similar, if not interchangeable.[24] The degree of similarity was a function of materials and tolerances: fit could be approximate for some purposes but not for others; and wood was a lot more forgiving than metal. So a carpenter could adjust pre-made doors and windows and a glazier could make window panes tight with a judicious use of putty; but the firing assembly of a musket called for greater precision than the stock, and a watch required closer tolerances than a clock. Meanwhile assembly depended on the skillful use of a file for last-minute adjustments and fitting; unless, that is, one wanted the parts to fit and work well from the start, without fitting, and that called for even more exactitude.

Such work required precision tools capable of exact repetition and the organization and siting of tasks in such manner as to gather, move, process (machine), and put together the materials and components in an efficient way—what we now call hardware and software. Hardware

---

* Fischer, *Albion's Seed*, p. 65, notes that the combination of timber framing and wood sheathing was "commonplace" in southeastern England. It made even more sense in the forested parts of the United States.

is often the focus of attention, because the machine tools invented for this purpose were spectacular achievements of the mechanician's art. But layout and synchrony were more important in operations such as meat slaughtering that called for disassembly rather than assembly; or where, as in flour milling and petroleum refining, higher throughput yielded major economies of scale.

In all these areas of manufacture, the United States was, if not the pioneer, then the great practitioner.* From the start, the adoption of machines, in textile manufacture for example, was followed by the creation of machine shops to maintain and build the equipment; and these shops, little worlds of assembled and interchangeable skills, often took to making other kinds of machinery: steam engines, furnaces and boilers, locomotives, above all, machine tools. These last in turn, dedicated originally to one or another special purpose, found application in diverse industrial branches. It was not only the craftsmen who had children and grandchildren to carry the torch; their machines proliferated as well.[25]

Unlike Europe, America made little resistance to this advance of deskilling and routinizing technique. In a country of continuing revolution, old ways had little leverage. Listen to an official visitor to the Springfield Armory in 1841:

> . . . the skill of the armorer is but little needed: his "occupation's gone." A boy does just as well as a man. Indeed, from possessing greater activity of body, he does better.

---

* In matter of organization, one thinks of the naval arsenal in medieval Venice; in matter of production techniques, of Henry Maudslay's manufacture of Joseph Bramah's lock in 1790–91 and Marc Isambard Brunel's famous pulley blocks (machine tools by Maudslay) in the Portsmouth naval shipyard around 1803. But locks and pulley blocks are nowhere near so intolerant of variance as guns or clocks. Note also French precedents in arms manufacture: thus Gribeauval in the manufacture of gun carriages toward the end of the Old Regime and the plans of Honoré Blanc for mass production of muskets in the 1780s and '90s. The latter were sensible and rational but were never carried out. That is the difference between imagining and doing, logic and culture. See Landes, *Revolution in Time,* pp. 309, 459, n. 2; Cohen, "Inventivité," p. 54 and n. 5. See also, on the "failure" of Blanc, the work of Ken Alder, "Innovation and Amnesia" and *Engineering the Revolution.* Alder, whose analysis gains but also loses by his focus on arms manufacture, sees engineering interests as motivating the pursuit of uniformity in France—a mix of power and aesthetic considerations, a desire "above all . . . to decouple the nation's security from the activities of unruly and money-minded artisans and merchants" ("Innovation," p. 310). This sequence from theoretical and schematic to practical was very French. It contrasted sharply with American practice, where money and market drove the pursuit of interchangeability and where progress took place in a whole range of industries.

The difficulty of finding good armorers no longer exists; they abound in every machine shop and manufactory throughout the country. The skill of the eye and the hand, acquired by practice alone, is no longer indispensable; and if every operative were at once discharged from the Springfield armory, their places could be supplied with competent hands within a week.[26]

Small wonder that when the British, with all their industrial achievements, belatedly (mid-nineteenth century) wanted to make good and cheap muskets for military use, they sent their people to the United States to study American arsenal methods.[27]

That did not mean that the British simply junked old ways. Knowing is not doing, and Europeans in general found it harder than Americans to accept the ruthless logic of productivity. Take the doctrine of sunk costs, which says that spent money is spent, obsolete is obsolete; that just because machines will work is no reason to work them. This kind of reasoning goes against the grain, but the open frontier (robber baron) mentality accommodated it. The standard examples are Andrew Carnegie and Henry Clay Frick (the big mean): when they decided to go over from Bessemer to open-hearth steel, they just scrapped the old plant. But listen also to this account of a cotton mill superintendent at the turn of the century:

> The mule spinners are a tough crowd to deal with. A few years ago they were giving trouble at this mill, so one Saturday afternoon, after they had gone home, we started right in and smashed up a room-full of mules with sledge hammers. When the men came back on Monday morning, they were astonished to find that there was no work for them. That room is now full of ring frames run by girls.[28]

The "American system" set standards of productivity for the rest of the industrial world. Each technology became a stepping stone to others. Clocks and guns prepared the way for watches and sewing machines. Mowers and harvesters led to sowers (planters and drills), reapers, binders, threshers, and eventually combines; bicycles, to automobiles; cash registers, to typewriters and calculators. And machines invented for one purpose slid easily to others: a sewing machine could be used on leather and canvas as well as fabric, could make boots and shoes and sails and tents as well as cloth garments.

This was a mechanic's wonderland, in agriculture as in industry. A letterwriter to the *Scientific American* of July 1900 exulted: "Indeed there is scarcely a thing done on the farm today in which patented ma-

chinery does not perform the greater part of the labor."[29] So agriculture became an industry too, with economies of scale, division of labor,
attention to labor productivity. And to land productivity as well,
though to a smaller degree: the accident of geography, the character of
the new land to the west—virgin prairie, deep topsoil, water for farming, open range for animals—all ensured abundant return and meant
that every movement of the frontier added substantially to the national
income. Holdings were family-size, and the system of land grants and
concessionary sales was designed to promote family farming. But family size could be very large and grew with the machinery; also with the
appearance of specialized, itinerant teams of machine operators.

All of this meant that the indigenous population was uprooted repeatedly to make way for land-hungry newcomers. The Indians fought
back, the more so as settler expansion entailed repeated violations of
ostensibly sacred and eternal agreements—as long as the sun would
shine and the waters run. The white man broke faith at will, while the
natives were slandered as "Indian givers." Here, too, technology made
the difference. Repeating weapons, batch- or mass-produced with
roughly interchangeable parts, multiplied the firepower of even small
numbers and made Indian resistance hopeless.

Of course, many Americans are sorry now, while Europeans invite
Indian chiefs to Paris and Zurich to recount the litany of white wrong-
doing. Hollywood films, once cowboy-and-Indian clichés, now remind us and others of the misdeeds of the invaders. Meanwhile the
American government has fitfully tried to recompense the descendants
of the dispossessed, hiring economic historians to calculate the value of
native land at the time it was taken; and well-meaning people offer help
with the preservation and reinvention of "Native American" culture.
Some of these compensations have proved astonishingly lucrative: thus
newfound Indian rights to engage in gambling operations, often in
partnership with white businessmen. Casino revenge.

The Indian tragedy illustrates the larger dilemma of modernization:
change or lose; change *and* lose. What is a man profited, if he shall gain
the world and lose his soul? The new ways of today tear at indigenous
peoples and ancient cultures everywhere. In the meantime, the people
of the United States are not about to give the country back and return
to the lands of their ancestors. History, like time, has an arrow; but unlike time, it moves at an uneven pace: it can only stutter forward.

And so, during those frontier days of the eighteenth and nineteenth
centuries, the technological possibilities were almost endless, and
American industry went on from one success to another. Other coun-

tries could copy; some indeed made forays along similar lines. But these older societies did not have the *tabula rasa* and the optimistic, open culture that eased the task of the American farmer and manufacturer. They had to work with cramped systems of land tenure, peasants (no peasants in the United States) who scrimped on equipment to add to their holdings, great landlords who saw land more as the foundation of status and style than as capital;* and with craftsmen who saw mechanization as a personal diminution, an offense to status, a threat to jobs. The older countries had their machine-breakers; America did not.

European countries also had a consumption problem. Class structures and segmented tastes made it harder there to adopt standardized products. Even so, I would stress supply rather than demand, the attitudes of producers rather than consumers. When Europeans belatedly adopted techniques of mass production, they had no trouble selling cheaper goods.

To get a sense of what was involved, look at the great European industrial spurt after World War II. This mirrored earlier American advances and implicitly testified to previous class-based failure. Europe had a pent-up demand for consumer durables, whetted by film images and the American presence. Few Europeans before had thought that just about everyone might want, even need, a car or a telephone.† As late as the 1970s, many French people were still going to cafés or to the post office (but only during office hours) to make their phone calls, either because they could not afford a phone at home or were waiting two or three years to get a line. Getting a dial tone could take a half-hour and more. People still reserved ahead for international calls. Business suffered and the complaints mounted to heaven: no point directing them to human beings because the authorities were imperturbably indifferent. After all, telephones were part of the postal system, and the post office thought them an extravagance, a plaything for rich people. What was wrong with writing letters and buying stamps?**

---

* One should not exaggerate. The use of land for parks and hunting was not unrelated to its productivity. In wine country, the Bordelais for example, even the richest owners planted vineyards, especially of the *premiers crus,* right up to the house.
† An exception was the German vision of a "people's car" *(Volkswagen)* in the 1930s. It did not come to fruition, however, until after the war.
** The meanness of the French Post Office was notorious. Until the 1990s, airmail letters overseas paid a surcharge above a weight of 5 grams, stamps included. That meant using specially thin and pricey paper—a boon to the stationery industry. Even so, the post office would not always have a single stamp for the postage required and would combine two or three to make the amount, and then these would tip the scale. One had to experience these exercises in petty tyranny to understand the retardative effects

In 1870, the United States had the largest economy in the world, and its best years still lay ahead. By 1913, American output was two and a half times that of the United Kingdom or Germany, four times that of France. Measured per person, American GDP surpassed that of the United Kingdom by 20 percent, France by 77, Germany by 86.[30] This American system of manufacture had created, for better or worse, a new world of insatiable consumerism, much decried by critics who feared for the souls and manners of common people. The world had long learned to live with the lavishness and indulgences of the rich and genteel; but now, for the first time in history, even ordinary folk could aspire to ownership of those hard goods—watches, clocks, bicycles, telephones, radios, domestic machines, above all, the automobile—that were seen in traditional societies as the appropriate privilege of the few. All of this was facilitated in turn by innovations in marketing: installment buying, consumer credit, catalogue sales of big as well as small items; rights of return and exchange. These were not unknown in Europe, which pioneered in some of these areas. It was the synergy that made America so productive. Mass consumption made mass production feasible and profitable; and vice versa.

⋍ ⌒

## On the Shortcomings of Economic Logic

Adam Smith took note of the absolute prohibition that Britain had imposed on its North America colonies not to build steel furnaces or slit mills; nor to make finished iron and steel articles even for their own consumption. In addition, Britain had banned commerce between colonies in fur hats or woolen goods,

> . . . a regulation which effectually prevents the establishment of any manufacture of such commodities for distant sale, and confines the industry of her colonists in this way to such coarse and household manufactures, as a private family commonly makes for its own use, or for that of some of its neighbours in the same province.[31]

---

of bureaucratic constipation. Fortunately for the French, the European Community has imposed new standards.

Conscious of the injustice here, Smith condemned it as "a manifest violation of the most sacred rights of mankind." But in view of the economic circumstances of the colonies, he found these measures not "very hurtful." "Land is still so cheap, and, consequently, labour so dear among them, that they can import from the mother country, almost all the more refined or more advanced manufactures cheaper than they could make them for themselves." The prohibitions, then, did not make that much difference. Even before these prohibitions had been instituted, he argues,

> . . . a regard to their own interest would, probably, have prevented them from doing so. In their present state of improvement, those prohibitions, perhaps, without cramping their industry, or restraining it from any employment to which it would have gone of its own accord, are only impertinent badges of slavery imposed upon them, without any sufficient reason, by the groundless jealousy of the merchants and manufacturers of the mother country. In a more advanced state they might be really oppressive and insupportable.

"Probably"; "perhaps"; "badges of slavery." Indeed. Smith should have known better. If the British could make and sell these things for less, delivered in New England, they did not need the prohibitions, and the colonists would have found better things to do. This is what they had found, said Smith, who without talking about comparative advantage understood and advocated the principle that resources should go to the most profitable employment:

> It has been the principal cause of the rapid progress of our American colonies towards wealth and greatness, that almost their whole capitals have hitherto been employed in agriculture. They have no manufactures, those household and coarser manufactures excepted which necessarily accompany the progress of agriculture, and which are the work of the women and children in every private family.[32]

Fortunately for the later United States of America, the colonists did indeed have manufactures, and Alexander Hamilton and others understood that today's comparative advantage may not be tomorrow's.

As for the supportability of these British constraints and impositions, Smith might have rested his argument better on the inefficiency of British enforcement. The whole system was a bad joke. London was trying to impose constraints on colonial trade using a handful of agents. Most of these lolled about in England while hiring underpaid subordinates overseas. They in turn found it more gainful to accept bribes from colonial merchants than to carry out their duties. Or to levy duties: Britain was paying these loafers some £8,000 a year to collect some £2,000.[33]

So, yes, these prohibitions made little difference in money.[34] But that does not mean they made little difference. When, in the 1760s, new and activist British ministers vowed to set things straight and make the colonists pay the costs of their security and administration, as good colonists should, the shock made otherwise reasonable measures intolerable. (It is astonishing how quickly neglect and tolerance become a vested right. And how quickly prospect outweighs retrospect: what will you do to me next?) The *Boston Gazette* expressed outrage: "Men of war, cutters, marines with their bayonets fixed, judges of admiralty, collectors, comptrollers, searchers, tide waiters, land waiters, and a whole catalogue of pimps are sent hither not to protect our trade but to distress it."[35]

Adam Smith's great treatise was published in 1776, in the same year that the colonists declared their independence. Even had his economic reasoning been correct, injustice perceived is injustice felt. Men are not moved by bread alone.

# 20

# The South American Way

Comparing the population of Spanish with that of British America, we shall at every step be struck with the wonderful difference in origin, in progress, and in the present situation. The conquerors from Spain, instead·of the frugal, laborious and moral description of our English settlers, partook of the ferocity and superstition of an earlier and less enlightened period. The warriors who had exterminated the Mahomedanism of Granada were readily induced to propagate their own religion by the sword. . . .
—*Quarterly Review* (London), 17, 34 (July 1817): 537.

We [Santo Domingo] became an economy of the West, not of the most developed models of Europe, but of the Spanish model. Spain transmitted to us everything it had: its language, its architecture, its religion, its dress and its food, its military tradition and its judicial and civil institutions; wheat, livestock, sugar cane, even our dogs and chickens. But we couldn't receive from Spain Western methods of production and distribution, technique, capital, and the ideas of European society, because Spain didn't have them. We knew the evangel but not the works of Erasmus.
—JUAN BOSCH, *Composicion Social Dominicana*

. . . the provinces on the Rio de la Plata . . . contain an immense extent of fertile soil, blessed with a salubrious climate, and fitted for the growth of every species of produce. Under a liberal government they must soon teem with inhabitants and wealth. They must every day abound more and more in all sorts of raw commodities, in exchange for which they must want manufactures . . .
—RODNEY and GRAHAM, *Reports of the Present State* (1818)

Latin America followed a very different pattern. It was not poorer to start with, in say the seventeenth century; on the contrary. The Spanish and Portuguese invaders thought of their English rivals as orphans of destiny: How could one compare the woods and fields of North America or the used-up or useless isles of the Lesser Antilles with the silver and gold of New Spain and Peru, or the dyewoods and diamonds and gold of Brazil? The best the English could do was lurk like jackals on the flanks of the Spanish bullion fleets while their colonists struggled to survive in a hostile environment. Even in agricultural potential, Latin America compared well, especially in its temperate parts.

But nothing stands still, and yesterday's comparisons are today's history. Gold and silver mines are wasting assets, and some two hundred years later, when the American colonists had won their freedom, North America far surpassed the lands to the south—richer in income per head, richer in its more even distribution of wealth. The only exceptions were small areas of lucrative specialty crops—specifically the sugar isles of the Caribbean; and even there only if one excludes the slave population from the data.

The change in relative wealth had deep roots. Where the English found a land lightly peopled and pushed the natives out of the way to make room for settler families—creating over time an absolute *apartheid*—the Spanish found the most densely populated parts of the New World and chose to intermarry with the inhabitants. Some see this difference as evidence of English (or Protestant) racism vs. Spanish (or Catholic) open-mindedness. Perhaps; although population distribution had its own logic.* Whereas the English migrated to the northern and central colonies in families, so that except for people over sixty, the age distribution was similar to that of England, the Spanish did not encourage the emigration of families or even women to the New World.

As the native population succumbed to violence, exhaustion, despair, and above all disease, the Spanish imported black slaves from Africa. These were worked growing sugar, panning for gold, and the like, but they never played so large a role in mainland Hispanic America as on the Caribbean islands and in the southern United States. Meanwhile immigrants from other European countries were not available. In Spain itself, locals complained bitterly of the competition and pretensions of non-Spanish and non-Catholic businessmen, traders, and craftsmen. Not so in Spanish America: the crown did its best to keep these outsiders away from its possessions in the New World. This exclusion deprived the empire of badly needed skills and knowledge, to say nothing of the cultural advantages of diversity, of those quarrelsome Protestant heresies that fostered intellectual challenge and sustained an appetite for education.[1] Everywhere in the Spanish colonies, moreover, the Inquisition pursued heresy, hunting those crypto-Jews who thought that an ocean would shield them from prying fanaticism. The aim was to complete the cleansing; the effect, to recreate the closed environment that prevailed at home. All of this proved great for purity but bad for business, knowledge, and know-how. (None of this, note,

* The record of Spanish (or Portuguese) color-consciousness in the colonial and postcolonial societies that emerged from the invasion also contradicts this reputation.

bothered Spain. As late as the beginning of the nineteenth century, the Spanish still thought their country to be the center of European civilization and the paragon of faith and virtue, equating ignorance of the Spanish language with ignorance pure and simple.)

In New Spain (Mexico), the ratio of male to female immigrants was ten to one.[2] Interracial marriage was inevitable, and indeed, in the beginning before Christian monogamy constraints took hold, some of the conquistadors collected veritable harems of Amerindian concubines. In the event, the *mestizos* of Latin America became an intermediate ethnic group, the whiter the better, few in number but more numerous than the Creoles, lower than they in status and function, but much higher than the pure natives. The mixed bloods became the overseers, the foremen, the shopkeepers, the petty officials. The Indians were assigned and conscripted to labor in fields and mines, in homes and on the roads.[3]

In this simulacrum of Iberian society, the skills, curiosity, initiatives, and civic interests of North America were wanting. Spain itself lagged in these respects, owing to its spiritual homogeneity and docility, its wealth and pursuit of vanities; and Spain exported its weaknesses overseas. How could it be otherwise? Those Spanish who came to the New World did not go there to break the mold. They went to get rich by it and even bribed people to obtain places and offices; a few years would do the trick. The road to wealth passed, not by work, but by graft and (mis)rule.

These contrasts in economic potential were matched by differences in political capability. The North American colonists came out of a society of dissent, moderately open to strangers and new ideas. I do not want to imply that England and its political culture were a liberal romance. Some of the earliest colonists, after all, refugees from religious intolerance, went on to afflict and harass in their new home. England had its share of John Bully stuffiness, of class pretension and privilege; also a tenacious legacy of older constraints, going back to medieval exclusions and anti-Puritan snobberies.[4]

But everything is relative, and when one compares English ebullience and diversity with the Counter-Reformation orthodoxy and superstitious enthusiasms of Spain and Portugal—the power of ideas and initiatives in North America as against discontents in the Spanish and Portuguese dominions—one can understand the political outcome. The British colonists *made* their revolution. They picked and defined the issues, challenged their rulers, sought the conflict; and when they had won, thanks in part to the assistance of some of Britain's rivals in

Europe, they already possessed a sense of identity, economic aspiration, and national purpose.*

In Latin America, independence came not of colonial ideology and political initiative but of the weaknesses and misfortunes of Spain (and Portugal) at home, in the context of European rivalries and wars. When Spain proved unable to rule from across the sea, New World strongmen exploited the vacuum and seized power, encountering only spotty resistance. Independence slipped in—a surprise to unformed, inchoate entities that had no aim but to change masters.[5] This kind of anarchic negativism invited *macho* warlordism *(caudillismo)*. No wonder the history of Latin America in the nineteenth century was a penny-dreadful of conspiracies, cabals, coups and countercoups—with all that these entailed in insecurity, bad government, corruption, and economic retardation.

Can any society long live in such an atmosphere? Or get anything done on a serious, continuing basis? The answer is that these were not "modern" political units. They had no direction, no identity, no symbolism of nationality; so no measure of performance, no pressure of expectations. Civil society was absent. At the top, a small group of rascals, well taught by their earlier colonial masters, looted freely. Below, the masses squatted and scraped. The new "states" of Latin America were little different, then, from Asia's autocratic despotisms, though sometimes decked with republican trappings.

In such instability and insecurity, no writ of authority went far. In the underpopulated open spaces, notables throned on their ranches and haciendas, ruling as well as employing, exercising private justice and police power. The nearest analogy would be the baronial domains of East Elbean Prussia, where the state stopped at the front gate. In the cities—usually ports where home goods crossed imports and customs duties yielded hard cash—the notables and their henchmen divided the spoils.

The one coherent institution that might have made a difference, the Catholic Church, had a vested interest in the status quo. It owned much of the land, and its wealth hung there like an apple of envy and discord. When the state got ready to seize these assets, the Church found few friends. Its clergy, literate in a sea of ignorance, held fast to legal and civil

---

* Not all colonials. Cf. Fischer, *Albion's Seed,* pp. 252 ff., on self-deprecating nostalgia in Virginia. Many of these "tories" simply left, voting with their feet against independence and for loyalty to the mother country. But that was a surrender to political death—a rejection of the spirit that otherwise filled the land and united highly diverse units into a single republic.

privileges going back to feudal times. They knew the darkest secrets of the confessional, held the keys to salvation. Not a recipe for popularity. But aside from alcohol, sex, and violence, the Church offered the only serious antidote to despair. The trouble was, it saw all intellectual and political novelty as subversive. A few liberals believed in fine slogans and sought to pull the people into the present. Much of their political energy was spent in a running war with the clergy.

As a result, newly independent Latin America saw few economic changes. As before, the key sectors were mining (gold, silver, copper), agriculture, cattle raising, forestry. The aim: to produce a surplus that could be traded for foreign manufactures. Little was done for industry, and little industry was done. As any good British classical economist would have advised, these cobbled political entities stayed with comparative advantage. Besides, manufactures were potentially antisocial. They would compete for scarce labor and generate a discontented proletariat. The Latin American countries had no program, then, no vision of economic development. Where Alexander Hamilton summoned a young America to develop industry and compete with Europe, the viscount of Cairu in Brazil "superstitiously believed in the 'invisible hand' and repeated: *'laissez faire, laissez passer, laissez vendre.'* "[6]

So the nations of South America remained, after independence as before, economic dependencies of the advanced industrial nations: Britain to begin with; then Germany toward the end of the nineteenth century, reflecting its scientific and technological gains; and from the twentieth century, the United States. Foreigners built the railways and port facilities, in large part to tap the surpluses of the interior (just as in India).[7] Foreigners lent money at high rates to poor regimes and their opponents (bad borrowers pay, and should pay, more). Foreigners built arsenals and plants and ran them. Naturally, foreigners were blamed for all the shortcomings of these economies. This cultivation of resentment, partially justified but dogmatically exaggerated, made everything worse. It ideologized economic policy, turned practical matters into issues of principle.

(The irony—but not unconnected—was that in colonial times, the Spanish and their clergy had done their utmost to keep foreigners out. Here are the comments of a ship's officer visiting Manila in 1788: "Since the Spanish make a rule of prohibiting entry to foreigners, the inns, the furnished hotels, all those amenities so necessary to hospitality are absolutely unknown, and one has to be ready to sleep in the street when all one has is money and no personal connections in the place.")[8]

One mechanized industry did gain a foothold—the textile manufacture—but only late in the nineteenth century. Brazil and Mexico led
here. In cotton, the raw fiber often had to be imported, and yielded a
coarse product for popular consumption. Mexico also boasted a
woolen industry. This went back to colonial times, took the form of
hand workshops *(obrajes),* and died in the face of imported fabrics;
then was reborn in small factories behind tariff walls, drawing fleece
from a somewhat degraded stock of merino sheep, and again supplied
popular needs. Rich folk bought their fabrics from abroad. Their skin
was more sensitive.

South America's industrial beginnings did not generate an industrial
revolution. Even the construction of railways did not do the trick.
Some things had to be done at home: the machines had to be serviced
and repaired, for example. But these shops stuck to maintenance; almost never did they move on to manufacturing on their own. Once
again, natural and social circumstances were unfavorable. Fuel and materials cost more than in Europe or the United States, and skills were
wanting. It was all very rational: comparative advantage made it easier
and cheaper to buy abroad.

The trouble with such rationality is that today's good sense may be
tomorrow's mistake. Development is long; logic, short. The economic
theory is static, based on conditions of the day. The process is dynamic, building on today's abstinence to tomorrow's abundance.*
Some things will never happen if one does not try to make them happen. If the Germans had listened to John Bowring . . . That British economic traveler extraordinary lamented that the foolish Germans
wanted to make iron and steel instead of sticking to wheat and rye and
buying their manufactures from Britain. Had they heeded him, they
would have pleased the economists and replaced Portugal, with its
wine, cork, and olive oil, as the very model of a rational economy.
They would also have ended up a lot poorer.

The Latin country with the best chances was Argentina, although no
one would have suspected this in the great days of Spanish empire.
Buenos Aires around 1600 was the end of the world. Located on open
grasslands lightly peopled, it was a way station between the silver of Potosí, high in the Andes in today's Bolivia, and the food exports of
southeastern Brazil. Commerce was in the hands of Portuguese traders.

---

* One can of course be wrong and build a house of cards. This is what happened in
the Egypt of Muhammad Ali and in the Paraguay of the dictators Lopez—see below.

An internal proletariat composed of escaped slaves from Brazil, *mestizo* deserters, and other shirtless marginals (*gente perdida*) squatted in huts and shacks on the outskirts, living on the leavings, taking cattle and horses as needed from the wild herds around (but why not—were these anyone's property?). Missing were craftsmen, tools, and industry (in both senses)—the kind of virtue that could pick up the slack as the mines played out. In colonial Buenos Aires a horseshoe cost several times the price of a horse; not surprising: the horses outnumbered the shoes. Nails were scarce throughout the Spanish empire, and wagons were held together by rawhide. People rich enough to own European clothing put it on only for special occasions and presumably hid it in between.[9] (More than three hundred years later, during World War II, things had not changed. Manufactures still had to be imported; manufacturers as well; and local industry got its biggest boost not from growth of home demand, but from wartime interference with supplies.)

In colonial times, Spanish policy aimed to truncate Argentine commerce. For reasons of control and taxation, the empire banned export of silver from Buenos Aires and tried to get all shipments out of Potosí to follow the Andean-Pacific route (over the mountains and down to the Pacific, up the west coast to the Isthmus of Panama, across to the Caribbean and on to Europe). With only partial success. Argentina's northern provinces supplied food, livestock, raw cotton, and homespun to what became for a while one of the largest cities in the Americas (160,000 people at the start of the seventeenth century), altitude 15,843 gasping feet; while the silver earned thereby paid in the Atlantic ports for iron, weapons, clothing, and other European manufactures. Needless to say, the inflated value of this contraband invited all manner of corruption; it also encouraged Spanish officials and proprietors to squeeze the Indian population to the last drop of sweat. So much for good intentions to protect the natives.

The break with Spain (1816) and fragmentation of the old Spanish empire brought an end to this trade. But the natural gifts of the Argentine remained: a wide range of climates, including a temperate core; treeless, open grasslands (the *pampas*), excellent for raising cattle and sheep; good soil for cereals; some places suited to semitropical crops such as cotton and sugar. The country had few industrial resources, however—no iron, coal, timber, petroleum, or minerals to speak of. Such waterpower as there was, along the eastern side of the cordillera, lay far from trade routes and traders. Of manufacturing, little, and most of that the remnants of domestic industry. Almost all such work fell to women—spinning and weaving, potting, soapmaking, cooking oil, candlemaking.[10] In a *macho* society with values inherited from Spain, adulthood brought males "complete independence and idleness."[11]

The improvisational character of the colonial administration combined with the unexpected collapse of Spanish rule to make the fate of this tail-land problematic. Much of post-independence Argentine politics consisted in a running battle between centralist Buenos Aires and the disjointed *federalismo* of the "provinces." Not until 1862 was the Argentine republic proclaimed; even that was premature. It took another generation of coups and killings to end sedition and secession. Some scholars dismiss this political instability by pointing to the schizophrenia of the young American republic: not until the defeat of the Confederacy in 1865 was the unity of the nation assured. I do not agree with the comparison. The United States *("E pluribus unum")* was an effective, working unit until the dispute over slavery became unmanageable. Argentina was not a working unit for half a century after independence.

Argentina, always a land of cattle and sheep, knew less of crops and men. The triumph of pastoralism and the relative neglect of agriculture were closely linked to land and immigration policies. Foreign observers saw the country as a potential magnet for settlers. So did some far-sighted natives, who called for a wider recruitment of immigrants, in particular, of settlers from Protestant Europe, whom they saw as better educated, harder working, politically mature. This would require, of course, a change in either the policy or the power of the Catholic Church; also of attitudes deep-rooted in the population:

> Respect the altar of every belief. Spanish America, limited to Catholicism to the exclusion of any other religion, resembles a solitary and silent convent of nuns. . . . To exclude different religions in South America is to exclude the English, the Germans, the Swiss, the North Americans, which is to say the very people this continent most needs. To bring them without their religion is to bring them without the agent that makes them what they are.[12]

Good advice, but hard to follow. An established population, reared in Counter-Reformation prejudice and fearful of potent strangers, was not going to welcome heretics; nor would the Church go quietly into retreat.[13]

Meanwhile immigrants could go elsewhere. Argentine land policies seem designed to keep settlers out. Most of the soil went in gigantic pieces to placemen and strongmen, often by outright gift *(emphyteusis)*, otherwise at bargain prices. Sometimes the grants or sales set conditions of settlement and cultivation, but these could not be enforced. Lacking capital and labor, the owners found it easier to leave the land idle or turn it over to cattle and sheep. Meanwhile the Argentine state expanded by driving out the Amerindians, and it paid for these campaigns by selling the new land in advance. These operations brought in money, but they meant selling the land in gobs to speculators who found their quickest return in open-range ranching.

Which came first, the chicken or the egg? Cause and effect went both ways. From time to time, the government sought to recruit abroad. It looked for volunteers in Italy especially, a seedbed of migrants in search, not of land, but of money—the better to buy a place back home. One 1880s contract with an Italian firm specified the kind of person the Argentines wanted: "field workers and artisans if possible, single and chosen among the youngest, most robust, and hard working people of the countryside."[14] These efforts ran up against social and political reality: the distribution of land and the predominance of labor-saving activities such as herding; endemic instability; religious restrictions; local prejudice. Those few areas that needed intensive labor—the sugar-growing districts, for example—had recourse to indenture and compulsion, which killed their attractiveness for free immigrants.

Compare land policy in the North American colonies and the United States. In the southern colonies, large holdings needed slave labor. The native Indians were few and unwilling, and free whites would not work for wages when land there was aplenty and one could be one's own master. So blacks were brought in from Africa until such imports were banned as of 1807. After that, the use of slaves could be maintained only by natural reproduction, which entailed a higher standard of nourishment and treatment than prevailed in the Caribbean or South America. Meanwhile Americans increasingly found slavery repugnant, and the expansion of the republic westward touched off fights over the extension of servitude and the nature of the compact that had made the Union. In the end, as everyone knows, civil war settled the matter. The slaves went free, and the large estates dissolved into family-sized units.

In former free states and new territories, the expansion of cultivation rested on the westward movement of farmers abandoning tired lands in the East for virgin soil, and of European immigrants seeking better living and land of their own. Meanwhile industry had to find its own workers.* Some branches and enterprises sent recruiters to beat the European boondocks and buy indentured labor. Not a hard task: famines, business crises, boundary changes, and persecutions gave European emigrants ample reason to leave.

Things might have gone otherwise. Nothing in material circumstances compelled the North American colonists to prefer homesteading to ranching. What mattered was culture and social purpose. Thus the New England colonies were divided from the start into family holdings, because these people had come as a community of families. The proprietary colonies of the Mid-Atlantic (New York, Pennsylvania) saw the sale of larger tracts, but here too the tendency was then to divide the land and sell it in homestead bites. While special reserves of colonial origin lasted, some very large purchases occurred—as always, linked to insider trading and graft. In the 1790s, for example, Massachusetts sold 3 million acres in Maine to Henry Knox, secretary of war, and William Duer, assistant secretary of the treasury, at 21 cents an acre. That was expensive. Massachusetts also sold the 6 million acres it had retained in western New York to Oliver Phelps and Nathaniel Gorham for $100,000—less than 2 cents an acre; but then, those lands were far away. And so on.[15] Here too, however, the proprietors saw their profit and salvation in resale to farmers; or to smaller speculators who resold to farmers. The puffery told the story: William Duer had his agent in Europe talking up the fabulous possibilities of these new territories: wheat at 60 to 80 bushels an acre; eighty-pound fish for the taking. Foreign investors were assured that population would double every twenty-five years (it almost did, at first); that fifty thousand young people were heading west every year.

Once these large tracts were gone, the holder of frontier land was the federal government, which made it policy to promote family-size units. No clearer evidence of this than the squatter dilemma. Since auction sales made acquisition uncertain, people chose to occupy first and buy later. The authorities tried to prevent this. Not only did it violate the norms of property and procedure; it also reduced prices and thwarted the intentions of rich, acquisitive people. In vain: when those squatter farmers gathered for an auction sale, rifles in hand, it took a foolhardy agent to flout their interests. So Congress passed in 1830 a law that just

---

* This was the theme of H. J. Habakkuk's classic *American and British Technology:* the high cost of unskilled labor pushed the Americans to pursue technological innovation; but then, how explain rapid growth? The answer: immigration.

about granted indemnity to squatters, which only encouraged the practice; and then in 1841 a general "pre-emption" law made squatting legal and gave the occupant the right to buy his holding at the minimum price.[16]

A big exception was made to encourage railway construction. New lines were granted land along the right-of-way, and these in turn sought generally to sell them to independent farmers. These were preferred, not because they were more lovable, but because they generated more freight than ranchers. In the last analysis, nature had its say: as one went west and rainfall diminished, more of the land went in large tracts for livestock and herding. Meanwhile towns became cities, and cities flourished, not only as markets and shipping points, but also as centers of manufacture. A good example: Cincinnati, largest city of the pre–Civil War West, center of meat processing and rendering ("Porkopolis"), pole of attraction for German immigrants, city of small factories making, among other things, jewelry, stoves, and musical instruments.[17]

These differences in policy and culture are reflected in the immigration figures. In Argentina, immigration did not pick up until the last quarter of the century, when wheat cultivation took off—about half a million hectares under cultivation in the early 1870s, still only 1.3 million in the early 1890s, and then, explosion, some 24 million on the eve of World War I.[18] One of the leading historians of Argentina writes of immigrants arriving "in enormous droves"—some 5.9 million between 1871 and 1914, of whom 3.1 million stayed, in a country of 1.7 million in 1869 (not counting Indians) and 7.8 million in 1914.[19] The flow was not even, reflecting political events, business conditions, and population pressure in the country of origin. In the 1870s, net immigration averaged 28.6 thousand per year; in the eighties it tripled, to 86.5 thousand. After that the flow diminished, to 40.6 thousand in the nineties; and then in the new century, especially from 1904 to 1913, it tripled again, to 125.9 thousand.

To be sure, the *net* figures understate the immigrant contribution to labor supply. Many of these migrants were seasonal agricultural workers, the so-called *golondrinas* (swallows), recruited largely in southern Italy, travel paid from Buenos Aires to place of work and back. Almost half of the 290 thousand immigrants per year in the decade 1904–13 turned around and left—an average of 135.7 thousand. This was an economical arrangement from the Argentine point of view: bring in harvesters and then send them away. It also suited the migrants, who could exploit the inverse harvest season north and south of the equator. But it had one serious disadvantage: it selected underemployed peasants of little skill and education, whose potential contribution to the economy was limited, even if they stayed.

The numbers alone, moreover, do not tell the whole story. Few Europeans who stayed became citizens—between 1850 and 1930, under 5 percent of immigrants took Argentine nationality because, among other reasons, as citizens they would have been liable for military service.* This was a land that needed people but, compared to the United States, found it hard to win and hold them. That was no doubt due in part to want of economic opportunity. But loyalty needs cultivation, and indifference is a weakness of accidental sovereignties. What do they stand for, and who stands for them?[20]

In contrast, immigration picked up early in the United States, rising from 14.3 thousand per year in the 1820s to 259.8 thousand in the 1850s. With the triumph of steam navigation and the opening of the West, immigration went from 281,000 per year in the 1870s, 524.7 in the 1880s, back to 368.8 thousand in the 1890s, to a peak of 879.5 thousand in the 1900s, when a number of years saw more than 1 million newcomers enter.[†] In all, some 32 million people entered the United States from 1821 to 1914, when American population went from 10 to 94 million—not so large a share of the increase as in Argentina, but far more important in aggregate.[21]

The character of the immigration also was significantly different. Most newcomers to the United States came from the British Isles and northwestern Europe, with southern and eastern Europe picking up toward the end of the nineteenth century. More of them were literate; many were trained craftsmen (classified as "skilled"); until the 1840s, more of them were farmers than laborers.[22] The immigrants were drawn by the prospect of cheap homesteads and high wages, and few of them went to the slave South. By comparison with Latin America, these newcomers brought with them greater knowledge and skills. The immigrants to Argentina would have to catch up later.** (They never did.)

---

* The earlier period saw negligible naturalization: in 1895, only 0.16 percent; in 1914, 1.4 percent—Cornblit, "European Immigrants," p. 232, Table 11.

† Immigration was much influenced by conditions in the States and in Europe, not only by business conjuncture but by war and revolution. Thus the failure of revolutions in 1830 and 1848 promoted emigration; the American Civil War discouraged it.

** Some readers may find such a comparison jarring (politically incorrect). It is, however, no more than fact; and no different in concept from the efforts of economists to weight labor inputs to productivity growth by years of schooling and other additions to human capital.

SOUTH AMERICA AFTER INDEPENDENCE
Paraguay, cut off from the sea, needed above all to live at peace with its
neighbors. Instead, ...

Historians of American immigration argue about the relative importance of push and pull, and of course both mattered, at different times. Some portray the great flood as a kind of huge kidnapping operation. (Europeans, especially, have trouble dealing with the repudiation implicit in this massive exodus.) Nonsense. For most of these newcomers, the United States was a land of hope and unlimited possibilities. Personal considerations played their part. Immigrants came because their predecessors wrote happy, if not always true, letters about life in the New World. They came because relatives, friends, and neighbors preceded them; and when they arrived, they went to stay with or lodge near their forerunners. They came to a country that in the nineteenth century offered just about no obstacle to admission. Many went back—perhaps a third. But the great majority stayed (or came back a second time), found jobs alongside their kin, moved about with a freedom they had never known in the Old World.

Back to Argentina. Its economic takeoff had to wait for the second half or even the last third of the nineteenth century. When it came, it closely fit the Ricardian trade model. The major growth sector was livestock, which yielded hides for leather and wool (often together and exported to such wool-pulling centers as Mazamet in France), tallow, and salt beef. When refrigeration came in the 1880s, it gave a big boost to the meat trade, especially to Britain. At first the process worked best with lamb and mutton, but as techniques improved and temperatures became more reliable and precise, Argentina began sending frozen beef and then much tastier chilled meat.

Agricultural development lagged, primarily because labor was scarce; but the opposition of ranchers and the depredations of the tenacious Araucanian Indians, still fighting the Europeans after three hundred years, created further impediments. (As in the American West, or for that matter in Africa, it took repeating weapons to crush native resistance.) The hostility of the Indians is understandable: they were fighting for their land. But the ranchers also: farming means fences and an end to open range. (One can't have cattle tromping the furrows and eating the crops.) Still, as in the American West, the barbed wire moved forward in Argentina, the cheapest cattle-unfriendly fencing ever devised.*

Labor remained scarce through most of the nineteenth century. Not

* Imports of barbed wire were of the order of 20,000 tons a year in the early 1890s—Rock, *Argentina 1516–1987*, p. 136.

that the pastoral, seminomadic camps of the *pampas* needed much manpower, or womanpower for that matter. (The authorities in Buenos Aires would now and then round up prostitutes and exile them to the largely male provinces by way of killing several birds with one stone.) But the tough work of transport found few volunteers. The Indians, as in the United States, would not work for wages, and Indian corvee labor was abolished, at least in principle, in 1813. The slave trade was also banned, and while slaves already there remained in servitude, their children were born free; further, any slaves imported from abroad became free on entry.[23]

The answer had to be immigration, but here, too, yesterday weighed on today. Spanish rules of exclusion had discouraged entry; and even after independence, immigration was dampened by political instability, selective recruitment, and the lack of free land. This last was one of the worst legacies of the colonial regime: vast domains had been given away, assigned to the Church and to men of respect and power, and the leftovers were grabbed up during the troubles that followed the revolution. Further territorial gains, we saw, were followed by similar distributions. Thus the 1879 campaign against the Indians (what the Argentines grandly described as *la conquista del desierto,* the conquest of the wilderness) was preceded and financed by land sales, some 8.5 million hectares going to 381 persons. The buyers needed all the land they could get, for as one moved southward, the climate became arid, the soil barren. Patagonia could support perhaps a tenth as many sheep per area as the province of Buenos Aires.

Not until the last third of the century did the flow of immigrants pick up—about a quarter of them from Spain, the traditional source, but now half from Italy, where population growth had outstripped employment, especially in the countryside, north and south. Few newcomers came from northern or eastern Europe, and of these, many subsequently left for the United States. Argentina was Mediterranean territory.

For many decades, these migrants fitted uncomfortably into this proudly backward society, full of illusions and prejudices, singularly unwelcoming. Most of them stayed in Buenos Aires, with its semicosmopolitan culture. Sensitive contemporaries despaired: "The conversion most urgently needed in this country is not that of gold for paper or paper for gold but that of the inhabitants of this land, born in Europe, into human beings with all the rights inherent in members of a civilized society: the conversion of foreign subjects into citizens."[24]

Once Argentina got into high gear, in part owing to the new, imported technologies (steam navigation, railway transport, agricultural machinery, meat refrigeration), in part to growing European demand (population growth, increased purchasing power), product and income increased substantially, to levels comparable to those of industrializing European nations. Note, however, that they were lower than those of other frontier societies (see Table 20.1). Even in the happy circumstances of Argentina, agriculture alone was not going to generate the productivity, income, and wage gains attainable in a balanced economy.[25] Farm workers, particularly hired (migrant) laborers, typically earn a fraction of industrial wages.

Meanwhile the estancieros, rancheros, professionals, officials, and the boutique trade that catered to them made money. As elsewhere, clocks and watches were both sign and instrument of a modern, time-conscious society. Swiss and American makers vied for this new market and fashioned imposing timepieces to the Latin taste.[26] At the end of the nineteenth century, Argentina was a most promising example of staples success, and optimists predicted a future like (or almost like) that of the United States. Even today, neoclassical economists gush over this case study in the benefits of comparative advantage.

But was it optimal? This country had some very rich people, yet "for reasons that have never been clear . . . has always been capital-dependent and thereby beholding [sic] to loaner [lender] nations, in ways that seriously compromise the country's ability to run its own af-

Table 20.1. Product per Head and Population of Selected Frontier Countries, 1820–1989 (1985 PPE dollars)*

|      | USA    | Argentina | Australia | Canada |
|------|--------|-----------|-----------|--------|
| 1820 | 1,219  |           | 1,250     |        |
| 1870 | 2,244  | 1,039     | 3,143     | 1,330  |
| 1890 | 3,101  | 1,515     | 3,949     | 1,846  |
| 1913 | 4,846  | 2,370     | 4,553     | 3,515  |
| 1950 | 8,605  | 3,112     | 5,970     | 6,112  |
| 1973 | 14,093 | 4,972     | 10,369    | 11,835 |
| 1989 | 18,282 | 4,080     | 13,538    | 17,236 |

*PPE = purchasing power equivalents.
SOURCE: Maddison, "Explaining the Economic Performance of Nations 1820–1989," Table 2-1.

fairs."[27] The British built Argentina's railroads—less than 1,000 kilometers in 1871, over 12,000 kilometers two decades later—but built them to British purposes: to move meat and wheat to the ports. Not to develop internal markets in Argentina, say the locals. But how does one build such a network without fostering internal markets? And if not, whose fault? What does that say about the spirit of native enterprise? The Argentines were not asking such questions. It is always easier to blame the Other. The result: a xenophobic anti-imperialism and self-defeating sense of wrong.

Withal, nature's bounty made up the difference. Economic growth continued into the twentieth century, not only in agriculture but also in the young industrial sector. This took the form of direct investment by multinationals, particularly in food processing;* and of import substitution, effected largely by small enterprises (most of them owned by foreigners and many of these, in the 1930s, by Jewish refugees) and promoted by periods of short supply (as during World War I), a few protective tariffs, bilateral agreements, and exchange controls.[28]

One should not exaggerate this late and stunted industrial sector. The data in the census of 1914—after twenty-five years, then, of mixed agriculture and heavy immigration—show that over half the "industrial" capital was in mining; a quarter in public services; and only 13.6 percent could be characterized as "basically manufacturing."[29] This production, necessarily derivative, showed little invention or adaptation. No increasing returns. It throve (survived) in primitive working conditions that recall the nightmare mills of the early British Industrial Revolution, but worse because the state didn't care. Nor did the employers, who assumed that casualties could be easily replaced by immigrant labor. They knew little of the technology of their own business and could not be expected to think of improving human capital. A few enlightened people tried to persuade these primitives that better workers and working conditions would be to their own advantage. They were dismissed as impractical utopians who knew nothing about factories and industry. The result was industry in a time warp of backwardness:[30]

---

\* Much of this was linked to the demand and tastes of the new immigration, in combination with urban growth: city dwellers need processed food. Between 1895 and 1913, the number of food-processing establishments grew by over 20 percent a year, their workforce by 221 percent, their capital by 8 percent. At the end of the period, this branch accounted for some 40 percent of all industrial shops, a third of the industrial labor force, 43 percent of all industrial investment—Lewis, *Crisis of Argentine Capitalism*, p. 32.

Each industry had its particular health hazards. In the textile, metal, match and glass factories, the air was always full of a fine dust that irritated the lungs. In leather factories, the curing process required the use of sulfuric, nitric, and muriatic acids as well as arsenic and ammonia, all of which gave off harmful vapors that filled the building. In the packinghouses, workers trod upon floors that were slippery with coagulated blood, entrails, and animal excrement. The stench was overwhelming. The men who carried meat to the freezers had to wrap their hands and faces in rags or old newspapers, being careful not to have any fresh blood on their clothes lest it freeze to their bodies. Rheumatism was a common ailment, and few packinghouse workers lasted more than five years.

Argentine industry, then, was not a driver but a passenger of growth. When a time of troubles returned after World War II, it left the vehicle. Labor, whether in industry or agriculture, was not happy and took to those ideological nostrums—anarchism before World War I, Perónism after World War II—that are the revenge of the powerless. The economist Paul Samuelson attributed this alienation to the discrepancy between economic backwardness and social indifference on the one hand, political precocity on the other.[31] The people wanted what neither economy nor state could give.

Today, Argentina is painfully finding its way back from political oppression and brutality, military adventurism, and economic depression. In particular, the tactic of "disappearing" suspected radicals, to say nothing of personal enemies, often by flying prisoners out over the ocean and pushing them out of the plane—with jailers and assassins kidnapping and "adopting" the children of the victims (a specially gruesome touch going back to Inquisition days)—all this has left a legacy of evil and horror. But also, paradoxically, sloganeering populisms have nurtured the beginnings of a national identity, witness the phenomenal success of *Evita*.

The failure of Latin American development, all the worse by contrast with North America, has been attributed by local scholars and outside sympathizers to the misdeeds of stronger, richer nations. This vulnerability has been labeled "dependency," implying a state of inferiority where one does not control one's fate; one does as others dictate. Needless to say, these others exploit their superiority to transfer product from the dependent economies, much as the earlier colonial rulers did. The pump of empire becomes the pump of capitalist imperialism.

Yet to co-opt independent, sovereign nations requires lending and investment; simple pillage is not an option. So with Argentina, which saved little and drew increasingly on foreign capital.* Some economists contend that foreign capital hurts growth; others, that it helps, but less than domestic investment. Much obviously depends on the uses. In the meantime, no one is prepared to refuse outside money on grounds of efficiency. The politicians want it and are willing to let the dependency theorists wring their hands.

One economist attributes Argentina's low rate of savings to rapid population growth and high rates of immigration—to which I would add bad habits of conspicuous consumption. In any event, foreign capital flows depended as much on supply conditions abroad as on Argentine opportunities. During World War I, the British needed money and had to liquidate foreign assets. Although remaining Argentina's biggest creditor, they no longer played the growth-promoting role of earlier decades. The United States and others picked up some of the slack, but here, too, politics and the business cycle abroad called the tune, so that Argentina found itself in intermittent but repeated difficulty both for the amount and terms of foreign investment and credit. All of this promoted conflict with creditors, which led in turn to reactive isolationism—restrictive measures that only aggravated the stringency and dependency. When Argentine economists and politicians denounced these circumstances and the misdeeds, real and imagined, of outside interests, they only compounded the problem. To be sure, cocoon economics helped shelter Argentina and other Latin American economies from the worst effects of the Great Depression. Such is the nature of cocoons. But it also cut them off from competition, stimuli, and opportunities for growth.

*Dependentista* arguments have flourished in Latin America. They have also traveled well, resonating after World War II with the economic plight and political awareness of newly liberated colonies. Cynics might even say that dependency doctrines have been Latin America's most successful export. Meanwhile they are bad for effort and morale. By fostering a morbid propensity to find fault with everyone but oneself, they promote economic impotence. *Even if they were true, it would be better to stow them.*

* Savings rates of 5 percent and under, compared to three times as much in Canada and Australia—Taylor, "Three Phases," p. 28, Table 4.

≈ ≈

## The Portuguese-Brazilian Way

Gilberto Freyre, in his classic study of Brazilian civilization, *The Masters and the Slaves,* distinguishes between Spanish and Portuguese policies of colonial settlement. Where the Spanish introduced national as well as religious restrictions, the Portuguese cared only for religion. The immigrant could come from anywhere, so long as he was Roman Catholic. In certain periods, a friar was sent abroad every vessel entering a Brazilian port to examine and verify the conscience and faith of the new arrivals.

Nothing else mattered, because this was the seal of common identity. "Whereas the Anglo-Saxon regards an individual as being of his race only when the latter is of the same physical type as himself, the Portuguese forgets race and regards as his equal the one who professes the same religion." (Such are the myths of national pride, as the very title of Freyre's book testifies.) Freyre compares the "suavity" of these controls favorably with the brusqueness of today's health inspectors and police functionaries (as though six of one, half a dozen of the other), and sums up:

> The thing that was feared so far as the Catholic immigrant was concerned was the political enemy who might be capable of shattering or weakening that solidarity which in Portugal had evolved in unison with the Catholic religion. This solidarity was splendidly maintained throughout the whole of our colonial period, serving to unite us against the French Calvinists, the Reformed Dutch, the English Protestants. To such an extent that it would, in truth, be difficult to separate the Brazilian from the Catholic: Catholicism was in reality the cement of our unity.[32]

≈ ≈

## *"Muero con Mi Patria!"*— I Die with My Country!*

In the annals of development-from-above, of industrialization by fiat, no case is more poignant and quixotic than that of Paraguay, fastness

---

* Last words of Francisco Solano Lopez, marshal-president of the republic of Paraguay, killed in the final action of the War of the Triple Alliance, 1864–70.

republic caught in the jungles and forests of South America
hundreds of miles from the sea. Some scholars, beguiled by this
experiment—one of them speaks of an economic "takeoff"[33]—see it
as one more instance of native enterprise and aspiration stifled by
European imperialists and their local henchmen.[34] This is a
misreading, however, of a not uncommon pattern of premature
development for political ends.

Paraguay was a most exceptional country, more Indian (Guarani)
than any other on the continent, for the grinding of the natives
inflicted in other parts had been prevented here by intercession of
the Jesuits. These had been allowed to establish autonomous
districts, and so far were such areas from places of treasure and traffic
that they had been largely left alone. Besides, the Spanish needed the
Guaranis: without them, they could not have held the area against
Portuguese-Brazilian incursions.

After independence, like other debris states of the great Hispanic
empire, Paraguay had fallen almost immediately under the control of
dictators. The laws said republic, but the practice was one-man
rule—a mix of benevolent despotism and populist tyranny.* The first
of these dictators (that is what he called himself), Dr. Gaspar
Rodriguez de Francia, was something special. A Jacobin ideologue,
and like many of the original French variety, a lawyer by training,
Francis was committed to a republic of equals and him more equal
than the rest. He was the "organic leader," the elitist embodying the
popular will.[35] He cultivated this image. When an Indian villager
came to see him, he received the petitioner with every courtesy, sat
down beside him, patted him on the back, radiated interest and
warmth. But let a landowner or bourgeois seek an audience, and Dr.
Francia had him cool his heels and drum his fingers, eventually to be
admitted into a disdainful, impatient presence.

This was class discrimination (affirmative action), but also racial:
the lines of division in Paraguayan society were the same for both.
The *Dictador Supremo* wanted to build on the special Guarani
character of the society, to subdue the old Spanish and Creole elite.
To this end he forbade the whites to marry among themselves,
requiring them rather to take their spouses from among Indians,
mulattoes, and blacks.[36] How strictly this rule was enforced is hard to

---

* The three dictatorial rulers and their dates were Gaspar Rodriguez Francia
(1814–40); Carlos Antonio Lopez (1840–62); and the latter's son, Francisco Solano
Lopez (1862–70).

say; but it showed an awareness of racial realities and signaled a deliberate effort to avoid the color-based segmentation that marked the rest of Latin American society.

Dr. Francia and his successors, Lopez father and son, would turn the country into an enlightened Sparta—egalitarian, literate, disciplined, and brave. Elementary schooling was to be free and compulsory from age seven, a heroic ambition. Although that was easier said than done, the system did start with 5,000 pupils, rising to 17,000 under Carlos Antonio Lopez in 1857, 25,000 in 1862— roughly half of the eligible age group. "Probably a record for the future Third World in the nineteenth century!" exults one admirer.[37] The pupils were to learn the three R's, plus a civic catechism. In this way, they would know who they were and why. Meanwhile the instructors, like good soldiers on duty, wore "government issue": two shirts, two pairs of trousers, a poncho, a hat, a scarf. Teaching materials were hard to come by, because the unfriendly Argentines were blockading river access, but in the early days the state did get hold of five thousand flutes (fifes?)—one for each child. One is reminded of the stress that Plato placed on music as part of his ideal education; also the role of music in Muhammad Ali's schools in Egypt of the same period (cf. below, chapter xxiv). But Muhammad Ali never aspired to universal schooling.

The trouble with idealized, reformist states is that they gain strength by improvement and then succumb to temptation. They threaten and subvert their neighbors, upset the balance of power and the status quo. Such actions invite reactions. So it was that the dictators of little Paraguay nursed ambitions, along with fears of danger from the bigger countries around; in short, a rational, latently irrational paranoia. (Who says paranoiacs don't have enemies?) The biggest threat came from Argentina, which saw Paraguay as a rebellious province and sought to annex it.[38] But all the neighboring countries looked unkindly on revolutionary experiments next door.

Paraguay's leaders, then, were determined to build the economy and acquire the armaments necessary to defend and attack in all directions. For this, they needed not only weapons but the tools and machines of industry. These could be had solely from Europe, and although Paraguay, with its Indian legacy, had an aversion to things European, Europeans overseas were more likely to be helpful than covetous neighbors.

Beginning with Carlos Lopez, the Paraguayan government contracted with European suppliers for steamboats, steam engines, and industrial plant (most important, an iron foundry and a forge-arsenal). The purchases were paid for with scanty natural exports (mostly yerba mate, a tealike, mildly addictive herbal) and the modest loans of a London shipbuilder and purveyor. A start was made on a railway and a telegraph network, but rail-line construction proved painfully slow, a few kilometers a year until the approach of war speeded the effort. Some two hundred European technicians were hired, but these were hardly the best. Needless to say, these rudimentary installations were not doing work of export quality; but they found outlets in the army and the native Indian population, cut off as these were from foreign imports.[39]

At the same time, the Paraguayans bought European arms, generally old, small, and discarded, and built fortresses against the likelihood of war. One in particular, located at Humaita on a U-bend in the Parana River, closed the waterway at will to foreign vessels, including those of riverine Argentina. (Turnabout is fair play.) These neighbors in turn, warned by words and incidents, began arming themselves. The Brazilians in particular began buying ironclad ships, with an eye to forcing the Parana passage if necessary.

Who started what is not easy to say. That is the way of war.[40] But certain it is that Paraguay did not hang back from combat. It had its share of *casus belli,* and boundaries in this region were dubious. Petty formalities, like having to get permission to cross neutral territory (going through Argentina to get at Brazil and Uruguay), were simply brushed aside. That was the last straw: in May 1864, Brazil, Argentina, and Uruguay joined forces to crush the pest. Paraguay, with its universal service and reserve classes, actually had far more men under arms than the three together; but the allies had a much bigger reservoir of potential conscripts, to say nothing of superior materiel. Time was on their side.

For three years, however, their efforts were blocked by the fortress of Humaita, garrisoned by thousands, bristling with cannon, equipped with its own foundry and forge—" 'that military marvel, that impregnable bastion,' that Sevastopol of the South."* Finally

---

* One must not exaggerate: one witness says that under a third of the cannon were operative; and one or two guns went back to the seventeenth century—Meyer, *The River and the People,* pp. 65–67. Meyer relies here on the publications of contemporary observers, among them Richard F. Burton (him of *The Arabian Nights*), *Letters from the Battlefields of Paraguay* (London, 1870); and on the novel *Humaita,* the second of a "historical trilogy, written in novelistic fashion" by Manuel Galvez, entitled *Escenas de la guerra del Paraguay.*

the Brazilians brought up their armored vessels, iron hulls impervious to enemy shells. Their guns broke the huge chain that had closed the river. The Paraguayans struck back by sending out boats full of boarders, who bravely climbed the enemy vessels under continuing fire from their own shore batteries. They got on board, but found everything closed, the hatches sealed, the crews below. And then the Brazilian vessels swept the decks with enfilading fire, slaughtering the intruders.

Now began the siege. The Brazilian commander wrote his Paraguayan counterpart, General Alen, to offer him a huge bribe (2.5 million gold pesos) and assurances of rank and command in the allied army if he delivered the fortress. Alen's answer deserves to be recalled: "General," he said, "I don't have that kind of money to give you, but if you surrender your squadron, I'll give you the Imperial Crown of Brazil." So the allies kept shelling and shooting, and the fortress was reduced to rubble. Alen sent news of his losses and imminent collapse to the marshal-president, but Lopez ordered him to continue resistance. Alen tried, failed, abandoned hope, and shot himself in the head. It was the easiest way to go. Eventually Lopez allowed the garrison to abandon the camp: 2,500 skeletal survivors who had to surrender a few days later when surrounded by four times their number. Furious, Lopez had the wife of Alen's successor arrested and put in chains. Who knows? Maybe she had urged her husband to quit. Lopez tortured and flogged her for a week, and when convinced that she could feel no more, had her shot.

In the end, ferocity and courage—the Paraguayan women fought as hard as the men—could not stand up to superior numbers and better materiel: white arms and muskets vs. rifled cannon and Gatling guns. Lopez led a small, scantily armed force of survivors into a swampy corner of the country. Ammunition was so scarce that executions, still free and easy, had to be done by steel. When the Paraguayans ran out of shells, they fired stones and broken glass. Lopez himself fought to the death—his death, that of his oldest son, and by this time that of the great majority of the Paraguayan male population—an overall loss (both sexes) of about 70 percent.[41] "Muero con mi patria!" Almost every Paraguayan is said to know that cry by heart. But the key word is the preposition *con:* I die *with* my country.

To celebrate their victory, the Brazilians organized at Rio one of the most extravagant concerts in history: eighteen pianos, an orchestra of six hundred fifty musicians, an infantry battalion under arms, and two field guns.[42]

Paraguay was a small country, and the madness of its rulers was paid for by hundreds of thousands of dead and many decades of impoverishment. The next century would see bigger fools and villains and far more numerous victims.

# 21

# Celestial Empire: Stasis and Retreat

Now England is paying homage.
My Ancestors' merit and virtue must have reached their distant shores.
Though their tribute is commonplace, my heart approves sincerely.
Curios and the boasted ingenuity of their devices I prize not.
Though what they bring is meager, yet,
In my kindness to men from afar I make generous return,
Wanting to preserve my good health and power.
> —Poem by the Qienlong emperor on
> the occasion of the Macartney embassy (1793)

Those sixteenth-century Europeans who sailed into the Indian Ocean and made their way to China met an unaccustomed shock of alien condescension. The Celestial Empire—the name tells everything—saw itself as the world's premier political entity: first in size and population, first in age and experience, untouchable in its cultural achievement and sense of moral, spiritual, and intellectual superiority.

The Chinese lived, they thought, at the center of the universe. Around them, lesser breeds drew on their glow, reached out to them for light, gained stature by doing obeisance and offering tribute. The Chinese emperor was the "Son of Heaven," unique, godlike representative of celestial power. Those few who entered his presence showed their awe by kowtowing—kneeling and touching their head nine times to the ground. Others kowtowed to anything emanating from him—a letter, a single handwritten ideograph. The paper he wrote on, the clothes he wore, everything he touched partook of his divine essence.*

Those who represented the emperor and administered for him were chosen by competitive examination in Confucian letters and morals.

---

* Lest one think the Chinese strange, compare the rule in early modern Spain that all kneel when the wafer and wine of the Eucharist passed in procession.

These mandarin officials embodied the higher Chinese culture—its prestige, its wholeness and sublimity. Their self-esteem and haughtiness had ample room for expression and exercise on their inferiors, and were matched only by their "stunned submissiveness" and self-abasement to superiors.[1] Nothing conveyed so well their rivalry in humility as the morning audience, when hundreds of courtiers gathered in the open from midnight on and stood about, in rain and cold and fair, to await the emperor's arrival and perform their obeisance. They were not wasting time; their time was the emperor's. No mandarin could afford to be late, and punctuality fell short: unpunctual earliness was proof of zeal.[2]

Such cultural triumphalism combined with petty downward tyranny made China a reluctant improver and a bad learner. Improvement would have challenged comfortable orthodoxies and entailed insubordination; the same for imported knowledge and ideas.[3] In effect, what was there to learn? This rejection of the foreign was the more anxious for the very arrogance that justified it. That is the paradox of the superiority complex: it is intrinsically insecure and brittle. Those who cherish it need it and fear nothing so much as contradiction. (The French today so trumpet the superiority of their language that they tremble at the prospect of a borrowed word, especially if it comes from English.)* So Ming China—convinced of its ascendancy—quaked before the challenge of Western technology, which was there for the learning.

Ironically, those first Portuguese visitors and Catholic missionaries used the wonders of Western technology to charm their way into China. The mechanical clock was the key that unlocked the gates. This, we saw, was a European mega-invention of the late thirteenth century, crucial for its contribution to discipline and productivity, but also for its susceptibility of improvement and its role at the frontier of instrumentation and mechanical technique. The water clock is a dunce by comparison.

For China's sixteenth-century officials, the mechanical clock came as a wonder machine that not only kept time but amused and entertained. Some clocks played music; others, automata, featured figurines that moved rhythmically at intervals. Clocks, then, were the sort of thing the emperor would want to see and enjoy, that had to be shown him if only to earn his favor, that a zealous courtier had to show him be-

---

* Latest move: the English CD-ROM, pronounced *say-day-rom* in French, will now be *cédérom*, pronounced *say-day-rom* in French.

fore someone else did. Not easy. This magical device had to be accompanied. Chinese instinct and practice dictated that foreigners be kept at a distance, confined to some peripheral point like Macao and rarely allowed to proceed to the center. The sixteenth-century clock, however, needed its attendant clockmaker.

No question that Chinese loved clocks and watches. They were less happy, though, with their European attendants. The problem here was the Chinese sense of the wholeness of culture, the link between things, people, and the divine. The Catholic priests who brought them these machines were salesmen of a special kind. They sought to convert the Chinese to the one true trinitarian God of the Roman Church, and the clocks served a twofold purpose: entry ticket and argument for Christian superiority. Those who could make these things, who possessed special astronomical and geographical knowledge into the bargain, were they not superior in the largest moral sense? Was not their faith truer, wiser?

The Jesuits came prepared to make this argument, stretching the while the rules and rites of the Church to fit the moment. (The Chinese ideographs for ancestor worship, for example, became the signifiers for the Christian mass.) European laymen followed suit. Here is Gottfried Wilhelm von Leibniz, co-inventor of the calculus and philosopher:

> What will these peoples say [the Persians, the Chinese], when they see this marvelous machine that you have made, which represents the true state of the heavens at any given time? I believe that they will recognize that the mind of man has something of the divine, and that this divinity communicates itself especially to Christians. The secret of the heavens, the greatness of the earth, and time measurement are the sort of thing I mean.[4]

On occasion, this argument carried. Catholic missionaries had some small success, although they had trouble persuading their open-minded "converts" to be good exclusivists (no other faith but the "true" faith) in the European tradition. But most Chinese saw these pretensions for what they were: an attack on Chinese claims to moral superiority, an assault on China's self-esteem.

The response, then, had to be a repudiation or depreciation of Western science and technology.[5] Here is the K'ang Hsi emperor, the most open-minded and curious of men in his pursuit of Western ways, the most zealous in teaching them: " . . . even though some of the Western methods are different from our own, and may even be an im-

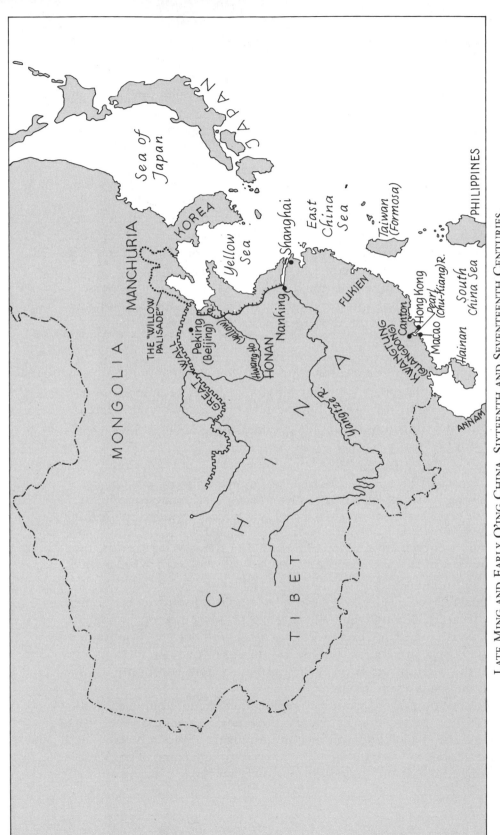

LATE MING AND EARLY Q'ING CHINA, SIXTEENTH AND SEVENTEENTH CENTURIES.
The "willow palisade" surrounded the area of Chinese settlement in Liao-tung and
cut it off from the rest of Manchuria.

provement, there is little about them that is new. The principles of mathematics all derive from the *Book of Changes,* and the Western methods are Chinese in origin. . . . "⁶

So ran the heart-warming myth. So the Chinese, who would not give up clocks, who wanted clocks, trivialized them as toys, which for many they were; or as nonfunctional symbols of status, inaccessible to *hoi pol-loi.* Premodern imperial China did not think of time knowledge as a right. Time belonged to the authorities, who sounded (proclaimed) the hour, and a personal timepiece was a rare privilege. As a result, although the imperial court set up workshops to make clocks and got their Jesuit clockmakers to train some native talent, these Chinese makers never matched Western horologists—for want of the best teachers and lack of commercial competition and emulation. Imperial China never had a clockmaking trade like Europe's.

The same sin of pride (or indifference) shaped China's response to European armament. Here we have anything but a toy. Cannon and muskets were instruments of death, hence of power. The Chinese had every reason to desire these artifacts, for the seventeenth century saw the Ming dynasty fighting to survive and losing to Tartars from the north. In these decades of war, European inventions might have tilted the balance of power.

And yet the Chinese never learned to make modern guns. Worse yet, having known and used cannon as early as the thirteenth century, they had let knowledge and skill slip away. Their city walls and gates had emplacements for cannon, but no cannon. Who needed them? No enemy of China had them.* But China did have enemies, without and within. No European nation would have been deterred from armament by enemy weakness; when it came to death, Europeans maximized. European technology was also incremental: each gain led to further gain. The Chinese record of step-forward, step-back, signaled an entirely different process.†

---

* The Jurchen Tartars (Manchus) who overthrew the Ming dynasty, replacing it with their own Qing line, opposed Chinese musketry with bows and arrows. Yet so ineffective were these muskets, presumably because they took so long to load and were hard to move about, that they were more handicap than advantage. See Wakeman, *The Great Enterprise,* I, 68.

† Students of Chinese technology and science, most notably Joseph Needham and his team, have made much of Chinese priority in discovery and invention, pushing the origins of important techniques and devices far back, well before their appearance in Europe. They see this quite properly as a sign of exceptional creativity and precocity, but they might better ask why the subsequent retreat and loss.

So it was that in 1621, when the Portuguese in Macao offered four cannon to the emperor by way of gaining favor, they had to send four cannoneers along with them. In 1630, the Chinese hired a detachment of Portuguese musketeers and artillerymen to fight for them, but gave up on the idea before they could put it into action. Probably a wise decision, because mercenaries have been the death or usurpation of more than one regime.* But the Mings did use some Portuguese as teachers, and later on they got their Jesuit theologian-mechanicians to build them a foundry and cast cannon.

These Jesuit cannon seem to have been among the best China had. Some still found use in the nineteenth century, two hundred fifty years later. Most Chinese guns saw short service, however, being notoriously unreliable, more dangerous to the men who fired them than to the enemy. (We even hear of Chinese cannonballs made of dried mud, but these at least allowed the force of the explosion to exit by the mouth of the tube.) In general, Chinese authorities frowned on the use of firearms, perhaps because they doubted the loyalty of their subjects. In view of the inefficacy of these weapons, one wonders what they had to fear. Presumably the improvement that comes with use.[7]

All of this may seem irrational to a means-ends oriented person, but it was not quite that; the ends were different. Europeans saw the purpose of war as to kill the enemy and win; the Chinese, strong in space and numbers, thought otherwise. Here is Mu Fu-sheng (a pseudonym) on the imperial viewpoint:

. . . military defeat was the technical reason why Western knowledge should be acquired, but it was also the psychological reason why it should not be. Instinctively the Chinese preferred admitting military defeat, which could be reversed, to entering a psychological crisis; people could stand humiliation but not self-debasement. . . . The mandarins sensed the threat to Chinese civilization irrespective of the economic and political issues and they tried to resist this threat without regard to the economic and political dangers. In the past the Chinese had never had to give up their cultural pride: the foreign rulers always adopted the Chinese civilization. Hence there was nothing in their history to guide them through their modern crisis.[8]

* The pressure actually came from Cantonese merchants, who feared losing the monopoly of foreign trade to such useful foreigners and bribed ministers at court to cancel the project—Wakeman, *The Great Enterprise,* I, 77, and n. 148.

Along with indifference to technology went resistance to European science. Christian clerics brought in not only clocks but knowledge (sometimes obsolete knowledge) and ideas. Some of this interested the court: in particular, astronomy and techniques of celestial observation were valuable to a ruler who claimed a monopoly of the calendar and used his mastery of time to control society as a whole. The Jesuits, moreover, trained gifted students who went on to do their own work: mathematicians who learned to use logarithms and trigonometry; astronomers who prepared new star tables.

Little of this got beyond Peking (Beijing), however, and soon the new learning ran into a nativist reaction that reached back to long-forgotten work of earlier periods. One leader of this return to the sources (Wen-Ting, 1635–1721) examined mathematical texts of the Song dynasty (tenth to thirteenth centuries) and proclaimed that the Jesuits had brought in little that was new. Later on, his manuscripts were published by his grandson under the title *Pearls Recovered from the Red River.*[9] The title was more eloquent than intended: by this time much Chinese scientific "inquiry" took the form of raking alluvial sediment.

Meanwhile European science marched ahead, and successive churchmen brought to China ever better knowledge (though still well behind the frontier). Here, however, constraints thwarted their mission. They had laid so much stress on the link between scientific knowledge and religious truth that any revision of the former implied a repudiation of the latter. How, then, deal with Europe's constantly changing science? In 1710, a Jesuit astronomer sought to use new planetary tables based on the Copernican system. His superior would not permit it, for fear of "giving the impression of a censure on what our predecessors had so much trouble to establish and occasioning new accusations against [the Christian] religion."[10]

This intellectual xenophobia did not apply to all Chinese. A few far-sighted officials and at least one emperor understood that the empire had much to gain by learning these new ways. Yet the curse of foreignness remained. In a letter of November 1640, the Jesuit von Bell wrote: "The word *hsi* [Western] is very unpopular, and the Emperor in his edicts never uses any word than *hsin* [new]; in fact the former word in used only by those who want to belittle us."[11]

The would-be modernizers were thwarted, moreover, not only by brittle insecurities but also by the intrigue of a palace milieu where innovations were judged by their consequences for the pecking order. No proposal that did not incite resistance; no novelty that did not frighten vested interests. At all levels, moreover, fear of reprimand (or worse) outweighed the prospect of reward. A good idea brought credit to one's superior; a mistake invariably meant blame for subordinates. It was easier to tell superiors what they wanted to hear.[12]

This prudent aversion to change struck generations of visitors. Listen to the Jesuit missionary Louis Le Comte (1655–1728): "They [the Chinese] are more fond of the most defective piece of antiquity than of the most perfect of the modern, differing much in that from us [Europeans], who are in love with nothing but what is new."[13] George Staunton, Lord Macartney's secretary, disheartened by Chinese indifference to suggestions for improvement of their canals, lamented that "In this country they think that everything is excellent and that proposals for improvement would be superfluous if not blameworthy." And a half century later a Christian friar, Evariste Huc, engaged in the sisyphean task of missionizing, despairingly observed: "Any man of genius is paralyzed immediately by the thought that his efforts will win him punishment rather than rewards."[14]

(Imperial China is not alone here. The smothering of incentive and the cultivation of mendacity are a characteristic weakness of large bureaucracies, whether public or private [business corporations]. Nominal colleagues, supposedly pulling together, are in fact adversarial players. They compete within the organization, not in a free market of ideas but in a closed world of guile and maneuver. The advantage lies with those in higher places.)

The rejection of foreign technology was the more serious because China itself had long slipped into technological and scientific torpor, coasting along on previous gains and losing speed as talent yielded to gentility. After all, China was its own world. Why did it not produce its own scientific and industrial revolutions? A thousand years ago, the Chinese were well ahead of anyone else—and certainly of Europe. Some would argue that this superiority held for centuries thereafter. Why, then, did China "fail"?

Some China scholars would mitigate the pain by euphemism: "Chinese society, though stable, was far from static and unchanging .... the pace was slower . . . the degree of change less."[15] (True, but the issue remains.) Others dismiss the question as unanswerable or illegitimate. Unanswerable because it is said to be impossible to explain a negative. (This is certainly not true in logic; the explanation of large-scale failure and success is inevitably complicated, but that is what history is all about.) Illegitimate because where is the failure? The very use of the word imposes non-Chinese standards and expectations on China. (But why not? Why should one not expect China to be curious about nature and to want to understand it? To cumulate knowledge and go from one discovery to another? To pursue economic growth and development? To want to do more work with less labor? The earlier successes of China in these respects make these questions the more pertinent.)[16]

What about the relations between science and technology? Did the one matter to the other? After all, science was not initially a major contributor to the European Industrial Revolution, which built largely on empirical advances by practitioners. What difference, then, to Chinese technology if science had slowed to a crawl by the seventeenth century?

The answer, I think, is that in both China and Europe, science and technology were (and are) two sides of the same coin. The response to new knowledge of either kind is of a piece, and the society that closes its eyes to novelty from the one source has already been closing it to novelty from the other.

In addition, China lacked institutions for finding and learning— schools, academies, learned societies, challenges and competitions. The sense of give-and-take, of standing on the shoulders of giants, of progress—all of these were weak or absent. Here was another paradox. On the one hand, the Chinese formally worshipped their intellectual ancestors; in 1734, an imperial decree required court physicians to make ritual sacrifices to their departed predecessors.[17] On the other, they let the findings of each new generation slip into oblivion, to be recovered later, perhaps, by antiquarian and archeological research.*

The history of Chinese advances, then, is one of points of light, separated in space and time, unlinked by replication and testing, obfuscated by metaphor and pseudo-profundity, limited in diffusion (nothing comparable to European printing)—in effect, a scattering of ephemera. Much of the vocabulary was invented for the occasion and fell as swiftly into disuse, so that scholars today spend a good deal of their effort deciphering these otherwise familiar ideograms. Much thought remained mired in metaphysical skepticism and speculation. Here Confucianism, with its easy disdain for scientific re-

---

* And this in spite of considerable effort to collect knowledge in encyclopedias. One such project, really an anthology, may well have been the biggest of its kind ever attempted: 800,000 pages—Spence, *Search for Modern China*, p. 86. But a plethora of encyclopedias is a bad sign: like still photographs, they aim to fix knowledge at a point of time. They are useful as reference works, especially for historians, but they can impede free inquiry.

search, which it disparaged as "interventionist" and superficial, contributed its discouraging word: "With the microscope you see the surface of things. . . . But do not suppose you are seeing the things in themselves."*

This want of exchange and challenge, this subjectivity, explains the uncertainty of gains and the easy loss of impetus. *Chinese savants had no way of knowing when they were right.* It is subsequent research, mostly Western, that has discovered and awarded palms of achievement to the more inspired. Small wonder that China reacted so unfavorably to European imports. European knowledge was not only strange and implicitly belittling. In its ebullience and excitement, its urgency and competitiveness, its brutal commitment to truth and efficacy (Jesuits excepted), it went against the Chinese genius.

So the years passed, and the decades, and the centuries. Europe left China far behind. At first unbelieving and contemptuous, China grew anxious and frustrated. From asking and begging, the Westerners became insistent and impatient. The British saw two embassies dismissed with contempt. The third time, in 1839, they came in gunboats and blew the door down. Other Western nations followed suit, and then the Japanese, with their own pretensions to dominion after the Meiji Restoration (1868), moved to secure their place alongside Great Britain, France, Germany, and Russia.

Even so, the outsiders barely scratched the surface of the porcelain kingdom: some trading cities along the coast; uncertain spheres of influence in the interior; the right to import opium, kerosene, and manufactures. These represented only a small fraction of the market, but the potential size of the market—so many people!—made China the legendary El Dorado of the nineteenth and twentieth centuries.

Inside the brittle skin, the empire was restless, the people unhappy, the mandarinate divided, the rulers insecure. The Qing (pronounced "Ching") dynasty (1644–1912), remember, was of Manchu origin. A small nomadic people of perhaps 1 million seized a nation of hundreds of millions and held them captive for two hundred fifty years. To be sure, the dynasty had adopted and been absorbed into Chinese culture,

---

* From a poem, early nineteenth century, by the son of the prime minister, himself a high state dignitary, quoted in Taton, ed., *General History*, II, 593. Of course, when the time came, one could find support in Confucianism for other positions. One can quote sacred writ to one's purpose. Which does not stop people from using it to bad purpose.

but the difference in manners, descent, and privilege remained. Markers (the obligation of Chinese males to wear the pigtail) distinguished rulers from ruled—a thorn in the flesh of the Chinese people. And while most of the administration was necessarily Chinese and these officials did not want for diligence and loyalty, they were inevitably diminished by their inherited inferiority and tainted by their collaboration.

The first years of the new dynasty saw improvement. Peace and order were restored; food supply kept up with demand. This was Europe's greatest gift to the people that thought it had everything: new crops (potatoes, sweet potatoes, peanuts) that could be grown on otherwise barren, upland soils. But now Chinese population grew sharply—the traditional Malthusian response—and when food supply leveled off, famine, hunger, and civil unrest returned. The Kangxi (K'ang Hsi) emperor (1662–1722) was barely in his grave when the trouble started, easily suppressed at first but a gathering storm.

Chinese thoughts turned easily to xenophobia. The foreigner became a focus of fear and hatred, the presumed source of difficulty, oppression, and humiliation. Much of this indictment was justified: superior power does not bring out the best in people. But insofar as it shifted responsibility for native ills, it was a self-defeating escapism. Most potent and costly of these internal explosions was the so-called Taiping rebellion (1850–64), a religiously inspired revolt that for all its nativism was part Christian-millenarian and took over a decade to suppress, at the cost of 20 million lives.

All this anger blocked economic modernization. Foreign ownership and management, for example, immensely complicated the introduction of railways. Steamboats were equated with gunboats—instruments of penetration and oppression. Mechanization, discouraged by an abundance of cheap labor and the reluctance of women to work outside the home, was tarred with the same brush.[18] As a result, factory industry barely had a foothold at the end of the nineteenth century, creeping into the foreign settlements of the treaty ports, extraterritorial carbuncles on the hide of the Chinese empire. Since the country could not defend itself against imports by tariffs—forbidden by the unequal treaties imposed from outside—these "plantation" enterprises had little exemplary influence on the domestic economy. China remained overwhelmingly agricultural with a scattered overlay of handicraft industry.

And poor. Evariste Huc, who traveled through China as a missionary from 1839 to 1851, bears witness to the misery:

. . . unquestionably there can be found in no other country such a depth of disastrous poverty as in the Celestial Empire. Not a year passes in which a terrific number of persons do not perish of famine in some part or other of China; and the multitude of those who live merely from day to day is incalculable. Let a drought, a flood, or any accident whatever occur to injure the harvest in a single province, and two thirds of the population are immediately reduced to starvation. You see them forming up into numerous bands—perfect armies of beggars—and proceeding together, men, women, and children, to seek some little nourishment in the towns and villages. . . . Many faint by the wayside and die before they can reach the place where they had hoped to find help. You see their bodies lying in the fields and by the roadside, and you pass without taking notice—so familiar is the horrible spectacle.[19]

⇝ ⇜

## "Modern Universal Science, Yes; Western Science, No!"

Nothing troubles a historian's spirit more than the wounds of the past. This seems to be especially true when studying those countries and peoples whom time has mistreated. Once rich, they have become poor. Once mighty, they have fallen. Such losers and victims carry with them the memory of better days and resentments that feed on bitter experience. And the historian, who seeks to understand them and to translate them for others, who wants to know and love them, finds himself caught up in the campaign to justify their past, to assert their dignity, to salve their wounds.

This is a worthy mission. It can, however, get in the way of science. Nowhere is this more evident than in the historiography of China, navel of the universe, the earth's richest and most populous empire a thousand years ago, still an object of admiration some three hundred years ago, only to be brought down to derision and pity thereafter. The desire of sinologists to defend China from outrageous outsiders has spawned a small industry of defensive scholarship, typically erudite and *ipso facto* intimidating, designed to enhance Chinese performance and correct Western criticisms.

Nowhere is this strain-to-maintain more prominent, indeed intrusive, than in discussions of the alleged failure of Chinese science and technology, especially in the context of Chinese contacts with Europe. Many China experts are not happy to be reminded of this failure, for two reasons primarily. First, Westerners have often seen it as a mark of weakness and as proof of their superiority. In the seventeenth and eighteenth centuries even those visitors who admired China in general, and its government, its philosophy, its walled cities, its rectangular street patterns, its manufactures, and number of other aspects in particular, usually condemned and scorned Chinese science. Very awkward.

Secondly, nothing has been more distressing to the people and government of the new China than this condescension. In the past, the Chinese saw their land as "the one true center of civilization."[20] How should they see it now—a caboose at the end of a European train? How to reconcile the pursuit of Western science with a legacy of sublime self-esteem? The answer: to stress the worldwide character of scientific inquiry and technological advance—one common stream—and highlight Chinese contributions to that enterprise. "The achievements of China's ancient science and technology prove that the Chinese people have the ability needed to occupy their rightful place among the world's peoples."[21]

Western sinologues have taken up the cudgels. One tactic has been to minimize the import of the contrast. What's all the fuss about? Why this fascination with West-East contacts and conflicts? China, these scholars contend, had its own history to live, and to see this solely in terms of confrontation, as a puppet of Europe-driven challenge and response, is to diminish it and empty it of its essence. Look in more than out.

The old emperors would have approved. But that kind of argument adds little to our understanding, for it is simply irrelevant to the issue of Chinese regression. You do not solve a major historical problem by pretending it does not exist and telling people to look elsewhere.

A somewhat similar dismissal says that we simply do not know enough about Chinese science to ask the question. To pose it would be "an utter waste of time, and distracting as well . . . until the Chinese tradition has been adequately comprehended from the inside."[22] (Until when? It is always a good idea to learn more about one's subject, but not at the expense of shelving important and timely questions. In fact, Nathan Sivin, author of this caution and collaborator with Joseph Needham in the exploration of the history of Chinese science, ignores his own advice and turns to this issue in other contexts.)

More to the point has been an effort to accentuate the positive by

painting a happy picture of Chinese achievements in the context of
ecumenical science. This we might call the multicultural approach:
knowledge is a house of many mansions, and diverse civilizations
have each taken their own path to their own truth. And then, in
science at least, all these truths merged in a common product. Here
is Sivin again:

> The historical discoveries of the last generation have left no basis for the
> old myths that the ancestry of modern science is exclusively European and
> that before modern times no other civilization was able to do science except
> under European influence. We have gradually come to understand that sci-
> entific traditions differing from the European tradition in fundamental re-
> spects—from techniques, to institutional settings, to views of nature and
> man's relation to it—existed in the Islamic world, India, and China, and in
> smaller civilizations as well. It has become clear that these traditions and the
> tradition of the Occident, far from being separate streams, have interacted
> more or less continuously from their beginnings until they were replaced by
> local versions of the modern science that they have all helped to form.[23]

This is the new myth, put forward as a given. Like other myths, it
aims to shape the truth to higher ends, to form opinion in some
other cause. In this instance, the myth is true in pointing out that
modern science, in the course of its development, took up
knowledge discovered by other civilizations; and that it absorbed and
combined such knowledge and know-how with European findings.
The myth is wrong, however, in implying a continuing symmetrical
interaction among diverse civilizations.

In the beginning, when China and others were ahead, almost all
the transmission went one way, from the outside to Europe. That
was Europe's great virtue: unlike China, Europe was a learner, and
indeed owed much to earlier Chinese inventions and discoveries.
Later on, of course, the story was different: once Europe had
invented modern science, the current flowed back, though not
without resistance. Here, too, the myth misleads by implying a kind
of equal, undifferentiated contribution to the common treasure. The
vast bulk of modern science was of Europe's making, especially that
breakthrough of the seventeenth and eighteenth centuries that goes
by the name "scientific revolution." Not only did non-Western
science contribute just about nothing (though there was more there
than Europeans knew), but at that point it was incapable of
participating, so far had it fallen behind or taken the wrong turning.
This was no common stream.

All of this has not discouraged the propagation of the new gospel, because in matters of this kind scholars are often the servants of their ideals and their needs. The extraneous ideological and political motivation here may be inferred from the following text:

> Educated people all over the world are now prepared to respond to new revelations about Chinese scientific traditions. . . . The heightened interest has meant a small but perceptible rise in the world's esteem for China. More to the point, it has meant that scientists all over the world are increasingly involved in the give and take that help Chinese scientists to be fully involved in the international scientific community.[24]

As though even now they needed encouragement.[25]

# 22

# Japan: And the Last
# Shall Be First

Wealthy we do not at all think [Japan] will ever become: the advantages conferred by nature, with the exception of climate, and the love of indolence and
pleasure of the people themselves, forbid it. The Japanese are a happy race,
and being content with little, are not likely to achieve much.
—*Japan Herald*, 9 April 1881[1]

Once in China, the Europeans would inevitably go on to the legendary Cipangu (Japan). (Actually, the first Europeans to arrive
on Japanese soil, in 1543, were thrown up on shore by a storm.) They
had heard wonderful things about these islands: "inexhaustible" gold
in the greatest abundance, palace roofed and ceilinged with gold, tables of pure gold "of considerable thickness" . . . gold, gold, gold.* To
say nothing of souls for saving.

The Japan they encountered was very different from the hearsay.
Gold there was, but not enough to arouse passions. As in China, the
people were ruled by an emperor, but more in principle than in fact,
for the land was divided into smaller kingdoms or domains (what the
Japanese called *han*), whose rulers seemed to enjoy absolute power
over their subjects. These kingdoms were then engaged in intermittent
wars with one another. Indeed, in that second half of the sixteenth century, Japan seemed awash in blood.

This favorably impressed European visitors, whose own behavior
gave them a well-founded respect for force and violence. As a Por-

---

* The picture is as given in Marco Polo's *Travels*, Book III, ch. 2. Polo himself never
visited Japan.

tuguese Jesuit put it, those who knew Japan "set it before all the countries of the East, and compared it with those of the West in its size, the number of its cities, and its warlike and cultured people."[2] This image persisted, even after the Japanese stopped fighting:

> The national character is strikingly marked, and strongly contrasted with that which generally prevails throughout Asia. The Japanese differ most especially from the Chinese, their nearest neighbors. . . . Instead of that tame, quiet, orderly, servile disposition which makes [the Chinese] the prepared and ready subjects of despotism, the Japanese have a character marked by energy, independence and a lofty sense of honour.[3]

The Europeans were used to strange peoples; the Japanese, not:

> The Japanese were first surprised to see the red-bearded, blue-eyed men, and then astonished by the natural power of their guns and powder. They were made to realize how great was the world . . . by the strange birds, curious beasts, precious silk, and beautiful damask brought from islands in the tropical zone and China. They wondered at the ideas and learning . . . the Japanese people, putting all this together, believed that there was a new heaven and earth far over the sea, and were thirsty to know this civilization. For this civilization was not like the quiet study of Confucianism, but a practical achievement before their eyes. Those who came from this new heaven and earth raised the price of merchandise, which had been almost a drug, to the great surprise of the Japanese, and demanded an unlimited supply, so that even a blade of grass or a tree had some value in the market. . . . The Japanese could not understand why this foreign trade was profitable to them. That they should become intimate with the Portuguese thus rich and thus strong, and learn their civilization, was the general idea of that time. . . .[4]

In these circumstances, European visitors got a much warmer greeting than they had received in China. The Chinese had wanted to quarantine them, like an infection. The Japanese, as soon as they realized the mighty powers of these strangers—their ability, for example, to shoot down birds in flight—took them in with open arms and vied with one another to learn their secrets. They also sought to trade with them, because the gains were substantial. And the Europeans, on their side, seeing an opportunity to plant themselves in this welcoming society and get rich, scurried to make themselves useful. These wonderfully exotic Japanese had good tradables and placed an inordinately high value on European things and a foolishly low value on their own. Two

JAPAN AND KOREA, C. 1850 — THE END OF
TOKUGAWA AND BEGINNING OF MEIJI
The Japanese islands constituted a little world of trading and competing urban
centers, semi-autonomous provincial units (the *han*), and offshore islands that
nevertheless lay inside the wall of isolation.

worlds embraced, and each thought itself fortunate and the other generous.

The Japanese were learners because they had unlimited aspirations. Their mythology told of a ruler descended from the sun goddess and a land at the center of creation. They thought of themselves as a people specially chosen, as warrior-dominators with all of East Asia as legitimate domain.* They had long been culturally subordinate to China, takers rather than givers, students rather than teachers. Their ideographic writing and writing implements came from China; much of their language as well.† Their knowledge of silk, ceramics, and printing, their furnishings and the style of their paintings, their Buddhist beliefs, their knowledge of Confucianism—all from China. Yet learning never made them feel smaller; on the contrary, they thought themselves inherently superior to the Chinese.[5]

So, when the Japanese encountered the Europeans, they went about learning their ways. They copied their arms; they imitated their timekeepers; they converted in large numbers to Christianity. And still felt superior.

The vogue for Christianity seemed destined to sweep all. The new faith had much success among local rulers, and even more among the marginal members of a hard, edge-of-subsistence population. These were classical conversion strategies: get the leaders to come along and let them compel their subjects; or give love and nourishment to those in need of moral and material support. Some *daimyō* (rulers of *han*) and *samurai* (members of the warrior aristocracy) became Christian out of conviction. Christianity offered a comfort and spirituality missing in traditional rites and gestures. Others converted for practical reasons: Christianity provided a channel to European trade and tech-

---

* Toyotomi Hideyoshi, "chancellor" *(dajo daijin)* and effective ruler of Japan from 1586 to 1598, thought it reasonable to envisage the conquest not only of Korea and China but also India. The Japanese clearly had no accurate idea of the size and population of these places. But who knows? Centuries later, some Japanese still saw all of this as a legitimate field of conquest. Writing of the Philippines in the sixteenth century, Yosoburo Takekoshi, author of *Economic Aspects of the History of the Civilization of Japan* (1930), expressed disappointment (I, 482): "Originally the Japanese occupied the Islands before Spain, and as they had thus the right of previous residence the sovereignty should have been theirs, whereas Spain acquired them." No wonder the Europeans liked the Japanese: they thought alike.

† Many of the Japanese ideographs have dual readings, one in the native Japanese, the other in a Chinese derivative; thus *hara-kiri* and *seppuku*. Others have only the "Chinese" reading. The adoption of these signs and meanings added enormously to Japanese vocabulary, particularly in abstract concepts.

nological assistance in a tough political arena. For a time, even the topmost leaders, Oda Nobunaga (dominated 1568–82) and then Toyotomi Hideyoshi (1586–98), went along.

It couldn't last. Older religious interests gnawed at this tolerance and planted seeds of suspicion about the motives of these foreign intruders. Their charges were reinforced by the innuendoes of non-Catholic rivals of Spain and Portugal—the Dutch of course—who painted Roman missionary activity as preparation for Iberian political and commercial ambitions. And truth to tell, Portuguese and, even more, Spanish captains and merchants gave color to these fears by their boastful and minatory behavior. They had picked up bad habits and sharp tongues to match in the Americas, the Philippines, and the Indonesian archipelago.

Example: In 1597 a rich Spanish galleon fetched up on Japanese shores. The Japanese wanted to keep the cargo. The pilot appealed to the *taiko* Hideyoshi, chiefest of warlords, and sought to intimidate him with the might of his master King Philip. Taking out his globe, he showed the worldwide extent of Spanish dominions, from the Americas to the Philippines. How come so small a nation has such extensive dominions? asked the *taiko*. Oh, said the incautious seaman, His Very Catholic Majesty would first send out priests to christianize the population, and these converts would then help the Spanish forces in their conquest. With that kind of encouragement, Hideyoshi refused to return the cargo and ordered the crucifixion of twenty-six Christians, seventeen of them Japanese, the others Jesuits and Franciscans from Europe.*

Besides, in this snakepit of conflict and intrigue, the one test that the Christians could not pass was that of earthly loyalty. For the rulers of Japan, no obligation stood higher than the personal allegiance a man owed his lord; no command more absolute than that of lord to man—even to the point of taking his own life. Even a hint that suicide was advisable amounted to a death sentence. How else prove one's loyalty than to take the hint? (The ability of Japanese superiors to compel subordinates to commit *hara-kiri* and their readiness to exercise this power are fairly stupefying. When warlords Tokugawa Ieyasu and Oda

---

* As reported by Father Martinez, then bishop of Japan. In a letter of 1602, Martinez lamented the bellicose penchant and intentions of the Spanish: their "religious preaching is merely an instrument of conquest. . . . All the calamities that the Church is now exposed to have their beginning in the arrival of these clerics from Luzon"—Elisseeff, *Hideyoshi*, p. 229.

Nobunaga were allies, Nobunaga conceived the notion that Ieyasu's wife and his son, who was married to Nobunaga's daughter (ergo his son-in-law), were plotting against him. Kill them both, he demanded of Ieyasu. So Ieyasu had his wife executed and ordered his son to kill himself. Which he did. It is hard to say which act was crueler: Nobunaga's demand or Ieyasu's obedience. But to ask is to not think like a *samurai*.)

Now for Japanese Christians, the highest loyalty and duty was to God. They had stopped thinking like good Japanese. So, when suspicious chieftains put their Christians to the test, the Christians failed. The Buddhists, Confucianists, and xenophobes were right. Here was a threat to Japanese values and political stability. In 1612, then, after backing and filling, Tokugawa Ieyasu banned the Christian religion. How many Japanese were Christian at that point is hard to say. Perhaps 300,000. Some estimates run as high as 700,000, in a population of 18 million.

The Japanese went about *eradicating* Christianity with characteristic ferocity. Nero would have been ashamed for his softness. Christians were compelled publicly to abjure. Those who refused or backslid were tortured and burned or beheaded. Those who helped missionaries, the same. The third Tokugawa shogun (army chief), Iemitsu, continuing the policy of his grandfather and father, often attended the torture sessions himself. Those who resisted were killed to the last babe in arms. One hundred thousand warriors invested some 37,000 Christian men, women, and children at Shimabara in 1637–38. Thirteen thousand of these *samurai* died in the bitter fighting—no quarter given or asked. Later, in 1671, the *Bakufu* (the Tokugawa government) made sure that no more of these Catholics would be born. All births had to be registered, from Kyushu in the south to Hokkaido in the far north, with evidence of Shinto or Buddhist religious affiliation.[6] This procedure lasted over a hundred years. It was the Spanish Inquisition all over again, this time against Christians.

Root-and-branch religious persecution stood apart at first from trade relations, which proved extremely profitable, but in the long run the two came together, leading to Japan's commercial and cultural isolation. No other way to keep Christian missionaries and propaganda out. In 1616, all foreign merchant vessels—except Chinese—were barred from ports other than Nagasaki and Hirado. Foreign residence was limited to Edo (later named Tokyo), Kyoto, and Sakai. In 1624, the Spanish were barred; in 1639, the Portuguese. The English just stopped coming. That left the Dutch.

From 1633, Japanese vessels needed official authorization to leave the country; three years later, all Japanese ships were confined to home waters. From 1637, no Japanese was allowed to leave the country by whatever means—no exit. What's more, no return, on penalty of death. Those Japanese who had moved abroad for trade, some tens of thousands to the Philippines and Southeast Asia, were now shipwrecked in exile. Then, in 1639, after suppression of the Christians at Shimabara (what the Japanese call the Shimabara rebellion), no foreigners were permitted to come and trade, except for Koreans at a small island off Honshu (the main island), and Dutch and Chinese on the artificial island of Deshima in Nagasaki Bay. Except when summoned, the Dutch were held under house arrest. They had two streets of warehouses and offices to promenade in. Their food, drink, servants, and sex came in to them from the mainland. They drank, smoked, played cards, and languished in boredom and stupefaction. Not a good assignment. The Japanese wanted it that way.

All of this was part of a larger process of self-petrification. Japan had had enough of discovery and innovation, enough fire and blood. The aim now: freeze the social order, fix relations of social and political hierarchy, prevent disagreement and conflict. Lines were drawn between statuses, and status was fixed from birth. As in medieval European schemas, each group had its social function. *Samurai* no longer owned land and ruled over its inhabitants. Once seigneurs, they now became stipendiaries, a service aristocracy charged to serve their lord; but no more to fight, because there would be no fighting. This stripped them of their raison d'être and promoted bluster. Strutting about with two swords, long and short (no one else was permitted to wear a sword), the *samurai* grunted their superiority to commoners. Many did nothing but live on their stipends and cherish vainglory and a military code *(bushido)* that entailed strenuous self-discipline and could be turned to better ends. A few devoted themselves to domanial *(han)* administration and cultivated an ethic of function that would one day turn personal loyalty into national duty. The poorer ones even took up the hoe; a *samurai* had to eat, and like his European counterpart (the French *hobereau*), he felt little shame in tilling the soil.

Peasants meanwhile were to stay put and grow food; merchants would trade and make money; artisans would create objects of use and value. Unions across status lines were forbidden, and even among *samurai*, high were not to marry low. Order and appropriateness above all, and this meant no change: "Generally speaking in all things the ancient laws must be followed. New practices must be prohibited." This immobilism was typically justified in Confucian terms: "It seems that in state affairs, if the laws and practices of those who founded the state are followed exactly and are not changed, the state will endure forever. If the descendants turn against the laws of their ancestors and devise new ones, the state will fall into chaos and will surely perish."[7]

It was one thing to enunciate principles; another to make them work. After decades of civil war, Japan's new dynasty was determined to stifle the merest whiff of rebellion. When Nobunaga ordered Ieyasu to kill his wife and son, he complied; and once Ieyasu triumphed in the Battle of Sekigahara (1600) and was appointed shogun (1603), he purged his enemies with equal ruthlessness. The Toyotomi family were killed to the last of kin, saving only two small children. Thousands of their allies were hunted down and executed, and their heads capped on pikes as a lesson to others.

This was get-even time. Enemy clans lost domain and income. The lucky ones were deported to distant places and given petty fiefs too meager to support their retainers. As a result, the land swarmed with masterless *samurai (ronin),* angry men of thirsty swords, trained only to fight and looking for trouble. Many of them did vex the Tokugawa, but so doing, declared themselves and died in the purge.* Others came into being when a *daimyō* died without heir. For a time the shogunate, seeking to consolidate its power, happily profited from such opportunities by escheating these estates and awarding them to allies and favorites. But the *ronin* problem so worsened that in 1651 the *Bakufu* decided to recognize the legitimacy of deathbed adoptions and leave these domains in the family.†

In order to ensure order in the empire, the Tokugawa conceived an extraordinary hostage arrangement. Under a system of alternate attendance *(sankin kotai)* instituted in 1634–35, all *daimyō* were required to set up residence in Edo as well as on their domain *(han),* and to leave wife and children there under the eye and hand of the shogu-

---

* The more prudent ones became teachers of swordsmanship and martial arts or of Confucianism. Others became warrior-farmers *(goshi).* Still others joined their masters in death—so many that the practice was forbidden in 1663.

† Oishi, "The Bakuhan System," p. 23. These *ronin,* always ready to avenge wrongs done their masters, were like a time bomb, threatening revenge from beyond the grave. The most famous such case is that of the "Forty-seven Ronin," whose cunning and bloody revenge (1702) is still remembered. They were ordered by the government to commit mass *hara-kiri* for having disturbed the peace and broken the law; but they remain heroes. Their grave in Tokyo is a much-visited shrine, and the Japanese have made literally hundreds of films singing their deeds.

nate. And although the lord himself obviously had to live and attend
to business in his domain, he was required to divide his residence between there and Edo—a year alternately in each. The lord in turn
brought many retainers along with him: better to have them in view
than making mischief far away. In emergencies, the lord could ask for
temporary leave to return to the *han* for a specified period. The *Bakufu*
posted troops at key points of passage to check on all comers and make
sure the trip was authorized. Dual residence plus travel cost a small fortune. *Sankin kotai* aimed not only at keeping an eye on these potential troublemakers but at draining their resources.*

Along with these personal controls went a deliberate exclusion of
foreign things and knowledge. European books, of course, were
banned, and Chinese books, a traditional source of morality and science, were now subject to careful scrutiny. Christian doctrines might
lurk between their covers.

Even potentially useful things were proscribed. Of the European artifacts that had so startled and impressed the Japanese, the most potent
and tempting was the gun; but this too was banned. The gun had
helped settle the battles of the civil wars. So well had the Japanese
taken to it that they learned to make their own and improved on European models. Indeed, at one point in the late sixteenth century the
Japanese may well have been manufacturing more muskets than any
single European nation.[8] Once these wars were settled, however, and
the nation united under a single government, guns no longer served a
useful purpose. On the contrary, they could only make trouble. Worse
yet, the gun was an equalizer. With it, the merest commoner could slay
the finest *samurai* swordsman. One couldn't have that. So, no guns.†
(But the skills that went into making guns were pertinent to a whole
range of machinery production and work with metals: screw fasteners,
mechanical clocks, eventually rickshaws and bicycles. One Japanese
scholar has argued that these guns were "the roots of Meiji technology.")[9]

---

* In some instances, these expenses consumed over half the revenues of the *han*. An
additional expense was the cost of rebuilding after fires—a perennial threat in a city of
wood and paper houses. One domain had to rebuild its compound sixteen times. In
the absence of insurance, it should have learned from experience and built differently.
Cf. Nakamura and Shimbo, "Why Was Economic Achievement . . . ?", p. 8.

† A few were kept in public arsenals, under seal, just as a few cannon were mounted
in seaports to fend off unwanted arrivals. On this story, see Perrin, *Giving Up the
Gun.*

The other two major European imports were eyeglasses and the clock. We know little about the former, except that the Japanese learned to make them. We know more about the clocks, because many of them have survived. Here again, the Japanese proved an ability to make a foreign object their own. Unlike the Chinese, they made clocks on a large scale, and not only for princes, but for a wider clientele and in forms distinctively Japanese. Nothing like them can be found anywhere else, and no other non-European country succeeded in so indigenizing this European innovation.[10] The Japanese, moreover, took to personal timekeeping as the Chinese did not. After a while, they bought no more European watches; nor did they buy watches in pairs as the Chinese did in hope that one would work; or wear them in pairs in hope that one would be right (but which one?). Rather, they miniaturized their own clocks so as to make them portable and wearable (the definition of a watch). These worked adequately.

I say "adequately" because these Japanese clocks could not be really accurate. That was because Japanese time measurement gainsaid the mechanical clock, and they were not about to change their system. The Japanese kept unequal hours—unequal as between day and night, unequal across seasons. They divided daytime and nighttime separately into equal parts, so daytime hours equaled night hours only at the equinoxes; and of course day hours were longer in summer, shorter in winter, and vice versa for night hours.

The mechanical clock, for its part, kept an equal rhythm—equal hours at all times; at least that was its intended nature. The Japanese tried to solve this dilemma by devising clocks that beat at different rhythms night and day, or by varying the display to show different hours; but these were at best makeshifts. Every setting was wrong from the start. In theory the clocks should have been adjusted daily, but this was a pain; so one corrected every two weeks—when one remembered. No matter, the time indicated was inevitably approximate.

To be sure, these approximations sufficed for social purposes. Even today, with quartz timekeepers that are accurate to seconds, we run our lives to a margin of tolerance—whether as a courtesy to other people or comfort to ourselves. Meanwhile want of precision timekeeping kept the Japanese from exploiting the clock for its scientific and technical potential. When the Japanese decided on modernization in the late nineteenth century, they early on gave up their own time and went over to equal hours. (The Europeans had done this from the start—had exchanged church hours for civil time.)

Japan's decision to isolate itself from the outside world, to return to tradition and live in a bubble, appears no different from China's refusal of the West. If anything, it was more adamant in its principled rigor. But how different the outcome! It was the Chinese who, though changing in detail and passing from one political challenge to another, remained the same in substance; and the Japanese who, clinging to old ways, so changed that they had every prospect of industrializing, even without the Western challenge, on the eve of the Meiji Restoration.

One may distinguish two aspects of the paradox: (1) the forces making for change within Japan; and (2) the effect of contacts with the outside world.

To understand the first, consider Tokugawa Japan as an approximate, rough miniature of medieval Europe. It had one overall government, the *Bakufu* or shogunate—something like the empire or the Roman Church, but stronger—and a host of provinces *(han)*. These were rather like separate nations—not sovereign, to be sure, but endowed with all manner of autonomies and capable of initiatives in law and in the regulation of the society and economy. Society in turn was ordered hierarchically: at the top, a landless nobility of warrior-retainers whose stipends were defined and paid in quantities of rice; toward the bottom, a new, "rising" mercantile class. In between, the peasants, respected for the food they grew, and craftsmen, for the quality of their work. At the very bottom were the marginal, hereditary "untouchables," in particular the *eta* or *burakumin,* contaminated by their work with dead animals or humans. (Ironically, the *samurai,* who did their fair share of butchery, were honored for it.)

In medieval Europe, feudal lords owned land and took most of their revenue in kind or in labor (which produced income in the form of crops). Over time, however, with the rise of a new world of cities and towns and exposure to strange things and people, the *seigneurs* and their ladies conceived new needs and wants. To satisfy these, landlords converted more and more of their traditional income into money, which could be spent as one pleased; hence a long-run tendency in western Europe to commute manorial dues into money rents (the key to peasant emancipation).

In Japan, the same. The fiscal system ran on rice, in other words, on the principal food staple, and this arrangement *(kokudaka-sei)* was designed to take care of the ruling elite. The lord *(daimyō)* took roughly 30 percent of the harvest, kept much of it for himself and his household, and distributed the rest to his stipendiary *samurai* retainers. Unlike European vassals, these *samurai* had no property in the land.

The system fed people according to rank. In principle, nothing more was needed. But since there is more to life than eating and the appetite for noncomestibles grows with status, the lord and his retainers needed to convert much of their rice income into money, the better to enjoy life's finer things. For this they turned to the despised merchants, who played an ever more active role in what was supposed to be a quiet economy but instead bubbled with desire. Here human nature married the political arrangements, for the system of alternate residence and the social ambiance of Edo incited to profligacy.[11]

This in turn pushed the sword-wearers to extract more from the peasants. As one superintendent of finance put it, "Peasants are like sesame seeds: the more you squeeze them, the more you get." Very witty; but squeeze too hard and you get peasant uprisings or flight, to towns or to other *han*. (As in Europe, the best protection against oppression was the possibility of exit.) Historians have counted almost three thousand peasant disturbances between 1590 and 1867, occurring more often and violently in the second half of the period and in the richer areas. Favored targets: the houses and warehouses of rich farmers, merchants, and moneylenders. Clearly economic change was shaking the social order and breaching the social contract.

It was easier to borrow than to wrest. *Daimyō* and *samurai* knew their merchants, many of them already active in the grain trade and tied into politics. The merchants in turn knew their customers personally and felt unable to refuse their requests for loans.* To be sure, nothing was riskier for the lender: his debtors were stronger than he and could refuse to pay. Only too often, moreover, these deadbeats had the support of higher authorities, who had their own reasons to resent the power of money and decreed general reductions and cancellations of debt.†

But this kind of thing cuts both ways: habitual borrowers and bad

---

* These loans often began as advances on anticipated rice revenues, converted into long-term loans at 10 to 20 percent per year—Miyamoto, "Emergence of National Market," pp. 300–01.

† In the second quarter of the eighteenth century, the shogun Yoshimune issued a number of decrees freeing *samurai* of their debts secured by their rice stipends if the price of rice fell and barring lawsuits over debt. Merchants began dunning their debtors personally, picketing their residences and stopping their litters and horses in the street. Some posted a paper protest flag in front of the house or on the gate—a practice that the decree of 1729 found "most outrageous" and inadmissible—Takekoshi, *Economic Aspects*, II, 362–66.

payers always need more. (Which is why debtor nations today prefer to negotiate deals; they still need money.) Just because they can repudiate debt does not mean than they can afford to. The news of default gets around, and soon no one wants to lend. So *daimyō* and *samurai* heaped scorn on merchants in their absence but wooed them in person. In Japan, where every detail of etiquette and language signaled superiority and inferiority, spendthrift warriors learned to bend their head, to speak softly, to give seasonal gifts, to grant merchants the right to wear a sword (but only one), and to confer commercial privileges (better than bows and smiles and gifts).

So merchants lent, and many grew rich. But others, hundreds of them, foundered on the rock of bad faith. The *samurai* were ready to die for their lord and master, yet their word was notoriously worthless, and not just to merchants. Often the merchant was caught in a no-win situation; he was damned if he did and damned if he didn't. The case of Yodoya Tatsugoro became legendary. The family had made an enormous fortune by being useful, among other things by undertaking public works in Osaka; no house did more to make that city the commercial center of Japan. But Tatsugoro, fifth-generation head of the house, was too rich for the public good. So many *daimyō* owed him money that state interest and Confucian morality required he be cut down to size. In 1705, the *Bakufu* confiscated his fortune and canceled his claims on the pretext that he was living beyond his social status.[12] So much for gratitude.

(That is not so bad as what happened to Nicolas Fouquet, from 1653 superintendent of finance in the government of Louis XIV of France. Grown too big and rich too fast, Fouquet was already marked for doom when he invited Louis to visit him in his new chateau and put on a welcome so lavish, indeed royal, that the king became implacably jealous. No functionary could afford such display except by cheating his master. So after the pretense of a trial, accompanied by the usual painful questions, Fouquet was condemned in 1661 and sentenced to prison for life.)

In the long run, in spite of all manner of constraints and betrayals, Japan's merchant class prospered, courted by the powerful and progressively exempted from restrictions. These businessmen developed their own ideology and sense of function and importance; also rules of prudence and tactic designed to shelter them from the men of the two swords. The key lay in single-mindedness, an ingrained suspicion of outsiders, fanatical thrift, and nerve. Above all, thrift and its reward, accumulation. "The samurai seeks fame and sacrifices profit, but the townsman dismisses fame and makes profit. He amasses gold and silver. That is what he calls his Way."[13]

That was the Way, and nothing must be allowed to get in the way. Here is Mitsui Takafusa (1684–1748), third generation of the great house of that name, still, after three hundred years, a major mercantile power:

> Never waste your attention on matters that have nothing to do with your work. Merchants who ape samurai or think that Shinto, Confucianism or Buddhism will preserve their inner heart will find that they will only ruin their houses if they become too deeply engrossed in them. How much more true is this of other arts and entertainments! Remember that it is the family business that must not be neglected for a moment.[14]

Again the parallel with Europe is striking. Japan did not have Calvinism, but its businessmen adopted a similar work ethic. The key lay in the commitment to work rather than to wealth. The Zen monk Suzuki Shosan (1579–1655) saw greed as a spiritual poison; but work was something else: "All occupations are Buddhist practice; through work we are able to attain Buddhahood [salvation]."[15] One does not have to be a Weberian Protestant to behave like one.

(Japanese scholars have noted that this work ethic was not universal in time or space, but that the latter half of the Edo period was marked by intensified labor and the propagation of work habits that stood the economy in good stead once it moved on to modern industry. In their words, an "industrious revolution" prepared the way for the industrial revolution.)*

Meanwhile, in Japan as in western Europe, rulers had learned that mercantile prosperity meant revenue and that revenue was convertible into pleasure and power. Here the multinational model is relevant: Japan was in effect a competitive economic world of over two hundred fifty nations, all of them wanting more and many of them sorely wanting.

Nothing so concentrates the mind as lack of money. In the effort to generate income over and above the rice stipends, *daimyō* began to make improvements (roads, canals, land reclamation, irrigation, new crops, and better strains of seed), or to promote specialization in trad-

---

* The inventor of the term, now commonly found in Japanese academic discourse, is Professor Akira Hayami.

ables, including the products of rural industry.[16] Support from above combined with private initiative to increase both area of cultivation and crops. Area cultivated doubled from 1598 to 1716–36; while crops increased some 65 percent from 1598 to 1834.[17] Another estimate has land and labor productivity in agriculture rising 30–50 percent from 1600 to 1867.[18] Such calculations focus on rice, but an important further source of gain lay in the development of side crops and specialties: sericulture, other cereal grains, new species such as sugar and sweet potatoes. Urbanization increased demand for specialties. Villages near cities turned to truck farming and gardening, just as happened around London in the sixteenth and seventeenth centuries.[19] Some *han* also dug out minerals not claimed by the *Bakufu*—copper and later coal.*

The Achilles heel of this development was the temptation for authorities to create monopolies and distort prices in their favor. Normally, competition from other *han* restored market order. Unlike Europe, where the market was fragmented by politics, custom, and high costs of transport, Japan's compactness and commercial unity tended to vitiate protection. Sometimes, however, as with Satsuma sugar, climatic advantages protected the *han* from most outside competition.[20] Some fifty-three "domain monopolies" were still in effect at the end of the Edo (Tokugawa) period. These monopolies no doubt offered advantages to the participants: the *han*, the merchants, the producers (farmers or manufacturers). The consumer paid.

An important innovation was the rise of a cottage cotton manufacture. As in Europe, cotton came late, not really spreading in Japan until the late sixteenth and early seventeenth centuries, but then quickly replacing hemp and winning a wide market for its cheapness, convenience, and comfort. Its manufacture in Japan took several forms: urban production by craft guilds; rural shops run by independent masters (peasants turned industrial entrepreneurs) and employing inside and outside spinners and weavers; rural putting-out, where merchants supplied the raw materials and even the tools and bought back the finished and semifinished product. In the long run, as in England, urban manufacture gave way to rural. Wages were lower in the countryside, and guild regulations in the towns were stifling. Numbers of agricultural villages turned into collective cotton *fabriques*. Farming was done in spare time or simply abandoned, sometimes to the distress of local rulers and notables.[21]

---

* The Tokugawa had confiscated gold and silver mines previously controlled by the domains.

This precocious development of pre-factory industry (what some economic historians would call proto-industry) paid off in the mid-nineteenth century, when the opening of the country to foreign goods exposed Japanese manufacture to the machine-made products of the West. The spinning branch crumpled, but weaving, using imported yarn, held up against foreign cloth. And then, as in Britain, cotton spinning became the leading sector of Japan's industrial revolution, building on a preexisting network of machine shops and skilled labor.[22]

Regional specialization, again as in England, depended on a unified national market—unified spatially and between town and country. Commercial agents scoured the villages for labor and commodities; successful rural entrepreneurs found their way to urban centers; businessmen took up residence in villages. Here we see the unintended effects of *sankin kotai* (alternate residence). The movement of several hundred *daimyō*, plus retainers and their families, from provincial *han* to Edo and back made for constant stir, an exposure to strange places and new commodities, a rapid proliferation of travel accommodations, a large demand for liquid funds and remittance facilities, a multiplication of crafts and shops and services.

Edo, a fishing village at the end of the sixteenth century, was the largest city in the world in the eighteenth, with over 1 million people out of perhaps 26 million for the nation as a whole. Like London in England, Edo became the heart and lungs of the country, pumping and renewing the economic life blood, drawing people in and out, promoting division of labor and the diffusion of wants, knowledge, and know-how.[23] Edo was the great marketplace, where *samurai* competed in conspicuous consumption and enriched a swarm of craftsmen and tradesmen. This was a shopkeeper's heaven that boasted the world's first department stores. But to say this is not to overlook the older business center: alongside Edo and much larger at first stood the Osaka-Kyoto duo, seat of the emperor and his court, hub of industry, banking, and trade.[24]

These two primary centers and their network of provincial connections fueled new techniques of buying (including futures trading), of distribution (much of it by coastal shipping in specialized vessels), and of remittance (bills of exchange, transferable warehouse receipts, clearing), much as in Europe's commercial revolution of the Middle Ages and early modern period, only more so.[25] And faster. This island economy was changing swiftly along Smithian lines of specialization, division of labor, and growing demand. But then it had some real advantages over Europe: (1) two hundred fifty years without war or revolution; (2) cheaper and more accessible water transport; (3) a single language and culture; (4) the abolition of old trade barriers and the prohibition of new; and (5) the development of a common merchant ethic.[26]

Division of labor and specialization fostered closer ties between country and town, a precocious "urbanization" of the countryside that was found in Europe only in England and, to a lesser degree, Holland. The remotest rural areas were crisscrossed by a network of peddlers, ready to sell for cash or on credit. The so-called Toyama drug sellers, for example, would leave a stock of their goods with farmers and return later on to be paid for whatever had been used. That says something about Japanese neatness (no small matter) and honesty (even more important).[27] More densely settled areas warranted the establishment of fixed outlets. We have the inventory of a village "general store" in 1813. The variety of goods is astonishing, some of them distinctive markers of an economy in an advanced preindustrial stage: thus a large range of manufactures, including hardware and garments that farm households had once made for themselves; and writing implements and paper in a country where literacy was not easy to come by.[28] One could not at that date have found such a store in the Continental European countryside, except perhaps in the watchmaking districts of Switzerland.

So busy, moving, and changing a society would not be caged intellectually. In spite of strenuous restrictions and controls, European knowledge seeped in, mostly by personal contact with the Dutch at Deshima. By the mid-eighteenth century the Japanese called this foreign knowledge *rangaku;* the *ran* is the *lan* of Holland (Japanese *Oranda;* Japanese has no letter "l"). This in itself signaled a new attitude: they had been calling it *bangaku,* "barbarian learning."[29]

One consequence of this awakening was the beginning of discrimination between helpful and harmful, acceptable and unacceptable. Christianity and its writings were still seen as undesirable and taboo. But some Japanese caught on that Japan had much to gain from Western secular knowledge.

So, in 1720, the first breach was made: the *Bakufu* agreed that non-Christian books could be imported; and while this relaxation had its periods of constriction and reaction, the way was open now for some few Japanese to study the new learning and to publish on the subject. This development led to a clash between the new learning and the dominant

Confucian school; that is the way of such challenges to orthodoxy. The *rangakusha* (experts in Dutch learning) tried at first not to provoke and diffidently defended their contributions; thus Ōtsuki Gentaku, author of a *Ladder to Dutch Studies* (1783): "Dutch learning is not perfect, but if we choose the good points and follow them, what harm could come of that? What is more ridiculous than to refuse to discuss its merits and to cling to what one knows best without hope of changing?"[30]

Such soft words could not turn away Confucianist wrath. The new learning challenged the very premises of Japanese culture, which had always learned from China. (The Chinese were the only foreigners not called barbarians.)* Much depended on the accidents of politics. Toward the end of the eighteenth century, for example, the government decreed that only Confucian philosophy should be taught—and a particular variety at that. In subsequent decades restrictions on Western learning grew more severe, to the point of outright persecution. The appointment of a Chinese scholar as governor of Edo in the 1830s was the signal for a tenacious hunt and chase of leading Dutch scholars, to the point of imprisonment and forced suicide. For a while, Japan was consuming its best and brightest.[31]

Much of *rangaku,* moreover, by contradicting traditional knowledge, shamed the old believers; and shame, in Japanese culture, is unbearable. European medicine, for example, as verified by dissections—seeing is believing—made a mockery of Chinese doctrine.[32] By the same token, in a world of East Asian isolation and complacency, geographical reality was intrinsically subversive. Here is Ōtsuki again: "Hidebound Confucianists and run-of-the-mill doctors have no conception of the immensity of the world. They allow themselves to be dazzled by Chinese ideas, and in imitation of Chinese practice, laud the Middle Kingdom, or speak of the way of the Middle Flowery Land. This is an erroneous view; the world is a great sphere. . . . "[33] Unfortunately for the Chinese, they persisted in this nonsense. The Japanese, on the other hand, were facing up to a new truth: "The sun and moon shine on every place alike."

A word of caution: to say that the Japanese had started to learn something of European science and technology does not mean they

---

* They had apparently been so called at one time, and some adherents of *rangaku* were now happy to recall this by way of discrediting Confucian learning. The aim now was not simply to say that the Chinese were not better than others; they were worse. That is the way of debate.

were near to catching up. They came into contact with European knowledge at a number of points, but these points were scattered and all of them lay well behind the frontier. Under the circumstances, although the extraordinary commercial and industrial development of the Tokugawa era prepared the Japanese, as no other non-Western people, to receive the lessons and techniques of the European scientific and industrial revolutions, they were still far from conceiving and making such advances.

How far is impossible to say, because the Europeans came and broke open the carapace of isolation, preempting chance and history. The newer historiography rejects a Eurocentric view of world history. It stresses the autonomy and initiative of non-Western peoples and deprecates the older focus on reactions to the imperialist challenge. In the matter of Japan, I sympathize with that point of view, because I believe—no way of proving this—that even without a European industrial revolution, the Japanese would sooner or later have made their own.

꙳ ꙴ

## *Han*, Inc.

The image of Japan as a collection of semi-independent units is confirmed by the enterprising *han* called Satsuma, southwesternmost province, far from Edo and *Bakufu* control. In 1825, Satsuma's government was bankrupt. Salaries of retainers were over a year in arrears; grass and weeds grew rank in the *han*'s compounds in Edo; the big bankers in Osaka refused to lend another cent. In 1831, the *han* leaders summarily repudiated all debt to local businessmen and effectively nullified obligations to merchants in Osaka and Edo by rescheduling payments over a period of two hundred fifty years.[34] Yet twenty years later, the *han* treasury was overflowing, and merchants were lining up to offer credit.

What happened in between? Sugar. Satsuma, blessed by a warm, maritime climate, was made for cane. Once the *han* realized the value of sugar, it mandated increased planting and forbade all other crops on its offshore islands. Cultivation was stringently controlled, and those peasants who failed the quality test were severely punished. It was the *han* that set the price and then sold the sugar in Osaka at two to five times that amount. No one, on pain of death, might market sugar privately. No more need to borrow. Satsuma was soon producing one half the national sugar crop.[35]

Meanwhile Satsuma had a privileged position in international trade. In theory, only Chinese and Dutch vessels could come to Japan, and then only to Nagasaki. But Satsuma was the effective ruler of the nominally Chinese Ryukyu Islands, and this made possible a lucrative smuggling operation bypassing the shogunate's controls. Again, no need for credit: the merchants were glad to pay cash for cheaper imports.

Unfortunately, these same imports hurt home industry, including manufacture of cotton goods in Satsuma itself. "Of all things Western, what do you dread most?" asked the Satsuma *daimyō* Shimazu Nariakira of his councilors. European guns and ships, came the answer. "No," said the *daimyō*. "It is cotton cloth. Unless we begin preparing now, we shall soon be dependent on Westerners for our clothing."[36] In an effort to prepare, the *han* began to distribute better cotton seeds, purchased better spindles and looms (not yet powered), built a manufactory near Kagoshima, and set unemployed *samurai* to work there. The result: cotton goods costing half as much as before.

At the same time, Satsuma began to invest in war and modernity. This was a *han* with a disproportionate number of *samurai*, one in three people as against a national average of one in seventeen. Idle warriors were the makings of power; also of management; also of trouble. Nariakira chose to focus on the first two. He built up the army, bought foreign arms and vessels, and undertook a program of economic development: a research center (the *Shuseikan*), an iron foundry using a reverberatory furnace (the first in Japan), an arsenal, a shipyard. In 1855, Satsuma was able to put a steam vessel into the water. In 1867, it opened a mechanized cotton mill. Way to go!

A terrible irony lurked here. Satsuma, by its enterprise, contributed not only to its own development but to that of Japan as a whole. But then it turned against the new Japan. It was technicians from Satsuma, often drawn from the lowest levels of *samurai* (thus talent before birth), who staffed key positions in the national government of the Meiji Restoration. But it was also Satsuma that became a stronghold of reaction after 1870 and led a revolt of the old order. All those *samurai* could not bear their eclipse by commoners, the abandonment of old dress and ways, the usurpation of their monopoly of war by general military conscription (1872). So in 1878 the Satsuma warriors, in their gorgeous robes and terrifying armor, brandishing steel swords that could cleave a body at a blow or slice a floating, gossamer piece of silk, pranced and bragged before the impassive, stolid ranks of a disciplined, uniformed peasant army equipped with muskets. And when the smoke cleared, the flower of Japanese chivalry lay dead.

# 23

# The Meiji Restoration

Japan had a revolution in 1867–68. The shogunate was over-thrown—really it collapsed—and control of the state returned to the emperor in Kyoto. So ended a quarter millennium of Tokugawa rule. But the Japanese do not call this overturn a revolution; a restoration rather, because they prefer to see it as a return to normalcy. Also, revolutions are for China. The Chinese have dynasties. Japan has one royal family, going back to the beginning.

It was in the 1180s that Japan was first ruled, not by the emperor but by a warrior chief called a shogun (literally, leader of the army). With some interruptions and interregnums, this rule by the strongest be-came the normal pattern. Such is the weakness of heredity kingship: even with the help of divine ancestry, a dynasty is hard-put to maintain competence indefinitely. Weak genes, bad marriages, whatever: strong men, mayors of the palace, will rise to power and sooner or later oust the legitimate monarch.

So it was in medieval France, where the Carolingians displaced the Merovingians and were pushed aside in turn by the usurper Capetians. In Japan, however, the solution was not to dethrone and expunge the dynasty, but to immure it. The emperor, his family, and his court were confined to their palaces and temples—under the Tokugawa shogunate, in Kyoto. There the Mikado wrote poetry, performed symbolic religious acts (like planting the first rice), let himself be entertained and ministered to. That was the Japanese version of virtual divinity: ceremonial isolation and sacred haplessness.

The existence of an emperor, however—of a legitimate ruler, then, above the real ruler—made it possible for enemies of the Tokugawa shogunate to look to an honorable alternative. In a society that valued nothing higher than personal loyalty, disaffected elites could set higher authority—the emperor *(Tenno)* and the nation—above their lord and the shogun above him, without being disloyal. They could make a revolution without being revolutionaries.

Meanwhile the symbols of national unity were already there; the ideals and passions of national pride, already defined. This saved a lot of turmoil. Revolutions, like civil wars, can be devastating to order and national efficacy. The Meiji Restoration had its dissensions and dissents, often violent. The final years of the old, the first of the new, were stained with the blood of assassinations, of peasant uprisings, of reactionary rebellion. Even so, the transition in Japan was far smoother than the French and Russian varieties of political overturn, for two reasons: the new regime held the high moral ground; and even the disaffected and affronted feared to give arms and opportunity to the enemy outside. Foreign imperialists were lurking to pounce, and internal divisions would invite intervention. Consider the story of imperialism elsewhere: local quarrels and intrigue had fairly invited the European powers into India.

The Tokugawa shogunate was already breaking down before the middle of the nineteenth century. The old rules of place and rank were openly flouted. Needy *samurai* married merchant heiresses. Wealthy peasants became local notables, the equivalent of country gentry. Obedience dissolved. The wealthier *han* (those of western Honshu and southern Kyushu) undertook their own foreign policy, thinking to deal with these outrageous, insolent barbarians better than the shogunate could. Hiring foreign technicians and advisers, they bought arms from abroad, built arsenals and shipyards. Some of them even conscripted peasants for military service, and the *Bakufu* began to do the same. In a country where peasants were forbidden to bear arms and *samurai* lorded it over commoners by the sword, here was a gross breach of public order and social propriety, of immeasurable consequences. But how else to arm for war? The *samurai* hated to fight with guns, which they saw as demeaning and dishonoring.

At this point, one short-reigned, ineffectual shogun followed another, fomenting intrigues over the succession, spawning cabals, inviting subversive appeals to Kyoto. And again and again, pressure from outside embarrassed the regime. In a society that had never admitted the stranger, the very presence of Westerners invited trouble. More than once Japanese bully-boys challenged and assaulted these impudent foreigners, the better to show them who was boss. Who was boss? Certainly not the shogunate. In the face of Western demands for retribution and for indemnities, the Japanese authorities could only temporize and, by waffling, discredit themselves in the eyes of foreigner and patriot alike.

But what was one to do? The outside powers *knew* they were stronger and would not yield to violence. In September 1862 a team of Satsuma warriors deliberately attacked some English merchants and a European woman; and when the *Bakufu* proved unwilling and unable to compel Satsuma to make reparation, the British sent a fleet in August 1863 to shell the castle town of Kagoshima. The lesson worked. Satsuma, confronted with reality, offered to establish direct trade and diplomatic relations with Great Britain—directly flouting the shogunate's traditional monopoly of foreign affairs. The same with Chōshū. On 25 June 1863, the date fixed by the imperial court in Kyoto for expulsion of the barbarians, impatient Chōshū patriots fired on an American ship passing through the Shimonoseki Straits. It took a year of palaver to come to a dead end; and then, in September 1864, a fleet of 17 British, American, French, and Dutch naval vessels with 305 cannon sailed into Shimonoseki Harbor and demolished all the forts. Chōshū capitulated and like Satsuma asked for direct and friendly relations with the Westerners. And Chōshū and Satsuma, traditionally antagonistic, now joined forces to get rid of the *Bakufu*.[1]

The *Bakufu* found itself fatally discredited by its weakness and ineptitude. Once it signed treaties with Townsend Harris (for the United States, in 1854) and then with the great European powers (1858), it lost honor and legitimacy. Meanwhile Japanese honor was not Western honor. The codes were different. One man's word was the other's prevarication. Twist and turn, the *Bakufu* might. It could send subordinates to negotiate, who would then plead the need of higher confirmation. It could sign but then argue that the agreement had not received the emperor's sanction. In short, it gave its word while withholding it; said yes while meaning no. Nothing could more envenom the conflict. The shogunate had better have succumbed to *force majeure* and said as much: You Westerners have the guns. All right, one day we'll have them too.

(Compare here the misunderstanding over Japan's attack on Pearl Harbor: for the Americans, a day that would "live in infamy"; for the Japanese, an unfortunate error in timing. The Americans were apparently supposed to receive notice that the Japanese were "breaking off negotiations" a half hour before the attack took place; they got it afterward. To this day, the Japanese think this the heart of the matter: previous warning, however short and oblique [but diplomats are supposed to be able to read between the lines], would justify a long-prepared surprise attack. For the Americans, such notice would in no way have diminished the infamy.)

The pretensions of the outsiders were the heart of the matter. *Sonnō jōi*, went the pithy slogan: Honor the emperor; expel the barbarians. The leaders of the move for change were the great fiefs of the far south and west, Satsuma and Chōshū, once enemies, now united against the shogunate. They won; and they lost. That was another paradox of this revolution-restoration. The leaders thought they were going back to days of yore. Instead, they found themselves caught up in tomorrow, in a wave of modernization, because that was the only way to defeat the barbarians.

Now the true revolutionaries took over: the *rangakusha*, the technicians, the forward-looking bureaucrats. The year 1868 began with the opening of more major ports to foreign trade. On April 6 the new emperor swore a "Charter Oath" promising representative institutions and the creation of a new democratic civil society. (It proved easier to promise than to do, and this gesture may have been directed more to outside observers than to the Japanese people.) What mattered more was the transformation of the central government: the abolition of feudal institutions, the conversion of the fiefs *(han)* into prefectures *(ken)* administered by government appointees, the appropriation by the center of revenues that had gone to the old warrior elite. Here again Satsuma and Chōshū set an example: in March 1869 their *daimyō* offered their lands to the emperor, that is, to the nation. The other *daimyō* then fell into line, because that was the right and loyal thing to do. (This gesture recalls the voluntary surrender of feudal dues by the French nobility on the fateful night of August 4, 1789.) Meanwhile Japanese peasants no longer paid dues to their *daimyō;* they paid taxes to the imperial government.

The Japanese went about modernization with characteristic intensity and system. They were ready for it—by virtue of a tradition (recollection) of effective government, by their high levels of literacy, by their tight family structure, by their work ethic and self-discipline, by their sense of national identity and inherent superiority.

That was the heart of it: the Japanese knew they were superior, and because they knew it, they were able to recognize the superiorities of others. Building on earlier moves under Tokugawa, they hired foreign experts and technicians while sending Japanese agents abroad to bring back eyewitness accounts of European and American ways. This body of intelligence laid the basis for choices, reflecting careful and supple consideration of comparative merit. Thus the first military model was the French army; but after the defeat of France by Prussia in 1870–71, the Japanese decided that Germany had more to offer. A similar shift took place from French to German legal codes and practice.

No opportunity for learning was lost. In October 1871, a delegation headed by Prince Iwakura Tomomi and including such innovators as Ōkubo Toshimichi and Prince Itō Hirobumi traveled to the United States and Europe to ask for rescission of the unequal treaties imposed in the 1850s. The Japanese wanted above all to (re)gain control over their tariff, the better to protect their "infant" industries. They ran into a stone wall: the Western nations had no intention of giving up their hard-won right of entry to the Japanese market. No matter. The delegation swallowed their pride and went about their calls, visiting factories and forges, shipyards and armories, railways and canals, not returning until September 1873, almost two years later, laden with the spoils of learning and "on fire with enthusiasm" for reform.

This direct experience by the Japanese leadership made all the difference. Riding on an English train and meditating on the industrial landscape, Okubo confided ruefully that, before leaving Japan, he had thought his work done: the imperial authority restored, feudalism replaced by central government. Now he understood that the big tasks lay ahead. Japan did not compare with "the more progressive powers of the world." England especially offered a lesson in self-development. Once a small insular nation—like Japan—England had systematically pursued a policy of self-aggrandizement. The navigation acts were crucial in raising the national merchant marine to a position of international dominance. Not until Britain had achieved industrial leadership did it abandon protection for laissez-faire. (Not a bad analysis. Adam Smith would not have disagreed.)

To be sure, Japan would not have the tariff and commercial autonomy that seventeenth-century England had enjoyed. All the more vexing was European refusal to renegotiate the unequal treaties. Here, however, the German example made sense. Germany, like Japan, had only recently come through a difficult unification. Also Germany, like Japan, had started from a position of economic inferiority, and look how far it had come. Okubo was much impressed by the German people he met. He found them thrifty, hardworking, "unpretentious"—like Japanese commoners, one imagines. And he found their leaders to be realists and pragmatists: focus, they said, on building national power. They were the mercantilists of the nineteenth century. Okubo came back and gave a German orientation to the Japanese bureaucracy.[2]

First came those tasks ordinary to government: a postal service, a new time standard,* public education (for boys and then for girls as well),† universal military service.** The last two in particular defined the new society. General schooling diffused knowledge; that is what schools are for. But it also instilled discipline, obedience, punctuality, and a worshipful respect for (adoration of) the emperor.[3] This was the key to the development of a we/they national identity transcending parochial loyalties and status lines. The nation's calendar was homogenized around the *Tenno* cult. Every school had its picture of the emperor, and on every national holiday, the same ritual was performed in front of this icon throughout the country *at the same time.*

The army (and navy) completed the job. Beneath the sameness of the uniform and the discipline, universal military service wiped out distinctions of class and place. It nurtured nationalist pride and democratized the violent virtues of manhood. In Japan, this meant generalization of the right to fight—an end to the *samurai* monopoly of arms. (Not every former commoner applauded the change. War and violence had always been the business of the elite, who were duly rewarded with stipends. Many of those too old to have been formed by the new common schools asked why they were now expected to engage in such foolishness. But they would not do the fighting.)

Higher authority saw a citizen army as a prerequisite of power, and power was the primary objective—power to be free, power to talk back to the Europeans, power to push others around the way Europeans

---

* Bringing equal hours and the Gregorian calendar. Even so, it remained customary to number years by the dates of the emperor's reign, a practice that has not been entirely abandoned over a century later. For foreigners, it makes for a crash course in Japanese political history.

† Minimum four years at first, six years from 1907. Given the difficulties of Japanese script, three or four years were needed to impart literacy.

** Exceptions were made initially for married men and only sons. One effect was to encourage early marriage.

did. In September 1871, the new Japan negotiated a treaty with China. The treaty did not accord Japan extraterritorial and commercial privileges like those already granted to the Western powers; but it was signed as between equals. A momentous "first"; inequality would come after. This was followed in 1874 by an expedition to Formosa (Taiwan), which in effect affirmed Japanese sovereignty over the Ryukyu Islands and laid the basis for a later claim to Formosa itself. Then, in 1876, a naval expedition to Korea extracted Chinese recognition of Korean independence. This poisoned gift removed Korea's cover against eventual Japanese aggression, while securing for Japan extraterritorial and commercial privileges that would whet the Japanese appetite and lead to further gains. New Nippon, bursting with energy and force, knew a victim when it saw one. Great China lay wounded, and the very largeness of its earlier pretensions invited attack.

Earlier, in November 1873, the imperial cabinet had already divided between a peace party, which wanted to concentrate on modernization and reconstruction at home, and a group of hawks calling for war against Korea. Five of the new oligarchs resigned, chief among them Saigō Takamori of Satsuma, one of the leaders in overthrowing the shogunate. That was not the end of the story. Now these ex-warriors, projecting their personal discontents onto the national stage, cried out against the Japan-China-Korea treaty of 1876, however advantageous. They had preferred to stay on in Korea, thereby realizing an old dream of mainland conquest.

Their disappointment was compounded by two acts of aggression against the *samurai* class. First, the traditional stipends, now converted to pensions, were commuted to a single payment of the capitalized equivalent. The *samurai* got state bonds instead of an annual revenue, and the value of the paper was hostage to monetary policy and the value of the yen. It was not long before inflation compelled the *samurai* to work for a living. Some did, and well indeed. Others sank into poverty and nursed their grievances. Still others tried to convert pride and sometime status into good jobs and marriages. That is what declassed aristocracies everywhere try to do: turn blue blood, patrician profiles, and grand manners into coin.

The second measure was even more painful in its symbolism: the ex-*samurai* were prohibited from walking about with their two swords. These weapons had made commoners tremble for their lives. Most commoners still trembled out of habit, but now even peasants might own a gun. Meanwhile statesmen and politicians vied in salutes to westernization. They went about in formal European dress more suitable to a Paris wedding than to everyday business in Tokyo; wore absurd top hats on cropped polls; brandished umbrellas in rain and shine; rode about in carriages; sat in chairs around tables; met in newly built stone structures that rebuked the paper-and-wood buildings of Japanese tradition.*

*Samurai* resentment boiled over into political assassinations. The most spectacular was the killing in May 1878 of Okubo Toshimichi, home minister and a principal builder of the new Japan, on his way in foreign horse carriage and Western regalia to a meeting of the Council of State at the Akasaka Palace in Tokyo.† The six assassins, five of them ex-*samurai*, defended their action by denouncing the waste of precious funds on economic trivia while warriors suffered want. But the symbolism also mattered. Many years later, the wife of the Belgian minister, then resident in Okubo's old house, wrote in her diary: "I am told that one of the reasons [for Okubo's] unpopularity, and incidentally the cause of [his] political murder was . . . the construction of this very European house."4

These murders changed little. Nor did the rebellions. Old met new—and old lost.

Meanwhile state and society went about the business of business: how to make things by machine; how to do more without machines; how to move goods; how to compete with foreign producers. Not easy. European industrial nations had taken a century. Japan was in a hurry.

To begin with, the country built on those branches of industry already familiar and changing even before Meiji—silk and cotton manufacture in particular, but also the processing of food staples immune from foreign imitation: sake, miso, soy sauce. From 1877 to 1900— the first generation of industrialization—food accounted for 40 percent of growth, textiles 35 percent.5 In short, the Japanese pursued comparative advantage rather than the will-o'-the-wisp of heavy industry. Much of this was small scale: cotton mills of two thousand spindles (as against ten thousand and up in western Europe); wooden water wheels

---

* These symbols held immense importance to a society that had systematically cultivated its particularities as virtues. Cf. the petition to the emperor in 1875 of Shimazu Hisamitsu, member of a powerful Satsuma clan, asking him to ban the wearing of Western clothes, among other things. The memorial was rejected, and Hisamitsu left Tokyo to sulk and plot. Cf. Brown, "Okubo Toshimichi," p. 189, n. 21.

† The Home Ministry was concerned not only with police and public order but also with economic development, working through its Bureau for the Promotion of Industry.

that were generations behind European technology;* coal mines whose tortuous seams and hand-drawn baskets made the infamous British pits of an earlier time look like a promenade.[6]

The economist's usual explanation for this inversion of the late-follower model (late is great and up-to-date) is want of capital: meager personal resources, no investment banks. In fact, some Japanese merchants had accumulated big fortunes, and the state was ready to build and subsidize industrial plant. As it did. But the long haul to parity needed, not so much money as people—people of imagination and initiative, people who understood economies of scale, who knew not only production methods and machinery but also organization and what we now call software. The capital would follow and grow.

These early decades of groping experiment saw many failures. In the early 1880s, the government sold off its factories to private enterprises. This decision did it much credit: bureaucrats rarely admit mistakes or give up power. The state mills were ceded on easy terms, usually to friends and connections—not the best arrangement, but one that in effect subsidized businessmen and permitted a fresh start. Around the same time, cotton merchants turned from hand-spun yarn to machine spinning.† Between 1886 and 1894, thirty-three new mills were founded, over half of them in the Osaka area; and from 1886 to 1897, total value of yarn output increased fourteen times, from 12 million to 176 million yen. By 1899, Japanese mills were producing some 355 million pounds of yarn; by 1913, 672 million pounds. The effect was to close out imports and move over to exports. In 1886,

---

* And yet exquisitely ingenious. The Japanese had to cope with special constraints on water use, in particular the inviolable rights of riparian cultivators to water for irrigation. The answer was found in anchoring boats in midstream, with water wheels that turned spinning machinery aboard—in effect, small floating factories—Minami, *Power Revolution*.

† And yet hand spinning survived in Japan far longer than elsewhere. One reason was the industriousness and patience of Japanese women (more on this later). Another was the invention of tube (*gara*) spinning in 1876 by a Shinto priest, Tatsuchi Gaun. This technique consisted of packing raw cotton into tinplate tubes, one inch in diameter and about six inches long, then rotating the tube while winding the cotton on to a spindle and thereby imparting twist. It was in effect a poor man's throstle or flyer and testified to Japanese ingenuity under capital scarcity. The *gara* technique increased the daily output of a woman spinner from 40–50 to 650 *monme*—some fifteen times. Even so, hand spinning could not compete once water wheels were installed, many of them on spinning boats. Output of this primitive branch continued to grow into the 1930s, partly owing to low capital costs and low wages, partly by making coarse yarns for use in carpets, blankets, flannel, soles for *tabi* (Japanese socks, for use with *geta* sandals), and the like.

some 62 percent of yarn consumed in Japan came from abroad; by 1902, just about nothing. In 1913, one fourth of the world's cotton yarn exports came from Japan, and Japan—along with India but more so—had become a major threat to Britain in third markets.[7]

It was one thing to spin and weave cotton; quite another to make the machines that did the work. Cotton spinning was a relatively easy gateway into modern industry, as shown by precocious performances in Catalonia, Egypt, and Brazil. One had only to buy the machines, normally from some British manufacturer, who would then send out the technicians to get them started and if necessary keep them running. Such mills could then supply domestic handloom weavers, and hocuspocus, the deed was done: one had the simulacrum of an industrial revolution.

Early on, the Japanese determined to go beyond consumer goods. If they were to have a modern economy, they had to master the heavy work: to build machines and engines, ships and locomotives, railroads and ports and shipyards. The government played a critical role here, financing reconnaissance abroad, bringing in foreign experts, building installations, and subsidizing commercial ventures. But more important were the talent and determination of Japanese patriots, ready to change careers in the national cause; and the quality of Japanese workers, especially artisans, with skills honed and attitudes shaped by close teamwork and supervision in craftshops.

This legacy paid off in quick learning. Waterpower for industrial use did not come in until the last years of Tokugawa, when the Japanese adapted it to textiles particularly. Yet waterpower was never so important as in European or American industry, because the Japanese were already moving on. Steam technology was available, with electricity close behind. Electric power especially suited light industry and small, dispersed workshops; no other form of energy delivered such small amounts as needed. To be sure, electricity called for large-scale generation and distribution. This did not pose a problem in urban areas. In remoter country districts, beyond the grids, internal combustion engines did the job.

Japan, then, moved into the second industrial revolution with an alacrity that belied its inexperience, generating and using electricity almost before it had gotten used to steam.* Arc lamps in Japan first lit up in 1878. Participating in this experiment was one Ichisuke Fujioka,

---

* One exception: chemical manufacture, not yet perceived as crucial to national power. But one should not expect Japanese economic policy to be complete and con-

a teacher at Kobu University, an engineering school founded in 1877 and later merged into Tokyo University. From his mix of study and practice, Fujioka saw the need for a central power station and sought private backing. When the first businessmen he approached declined, he went to a high government official from his home province. The official brought him together with a venture capitalist, and the two put together a syndicate of some sixty-four investors—former aristocrats, businessmen with official connections, and wealthy provincial merchants. So was born the Tokyo Electric Light Company (TELC). At first TELC built small private generating and lighting facilities for factories, business firms, and shipyards. It went on, beginning in 1887, to supply electricity to the general public. That same year similar companies started up in Kobe, Kyoto, and Osaka; two years later in Nagoya and Yokohama—thirty-three companies in all by 1896. By 1920, primary electric motors accounted for 52.3 percent of the power capacity in Japanese manufacturing. The comparable American figure was 31.6 percent in 1919, reaching 53 percent only in 1929. Great Britain was even slower, with 28.3 percent in 1924.[8] In respect of energy and power, then, Japan confirms the catch-up model: It pays to be late.

The traditional account of Japan's successful and rapid industrialization rings with praise, somewhat mitigated by distaste for the somber and intense nationalist accompaniment—the ruthless drive that gave the development process meaning and urgency. This was the first non-Western country to industrialize, and it remains to this day an example to other late bloomers. Other countries sent young people abroad to learn the new ways and lost them; Japanese expats came back home. Other countries imported foreign technicians to teach their own people; the Japanese largely taught themselves. Other countries imported foreign equipment and did their best to use it. The Japanese modified it, made it better, made it themselves. Other countries may, for their own historical reasons, dislike the Japanese (how many Latin Americans like *gringos?*); but they do envy and admire them.

It is a good, even edifying story. Yet one aspect of the Japanese achievement has not caught the attention of celebratory historians: the pain and labor that made it possible. The record of early industrialization is invariably one of hard work for low pay, to say nothing of

---

sistent. On the typically overoptimistic judgment of Japanese policy, see Okimoto, *Between MITI and the Market.*

exploitation. I use this last word, not in the Marxist sense of paying labor less than its product (how else would capital receive its reward?), but in the meaningful sense of compelling labor from people who cannot say no; so, from women and children, slaves and quasi-slaves (involuntary indentured labor).* The literature of the British Industrial Revolution, for example, is full of tales of abuse, especially of those so-called parish apprentices who were assigned to textile mills to relieve the taxpayers of welfare burdens. But not only the mills; the coal mines were a place of notorious travail; likewise many small metallurgical shops and even cottage workplaces. "When I was five, my mother took me to lace school [everything can be called a school] and gave the mistress a shilling. She learned me for half an hour, smacked my head six times, and rubbed my nose against the pins." Taskmasters and parents connived at this precocious enslavement: "Six is the best age, you can beat it into them better then. If they come later, after they have been in the streets, they have the streets in their minds all the while." And the more frightened the better, in the words of a lacemakers' ditty:

> There's three pins I done today,
> What do you think my mother will say?
> When she knows I done no more,
> She'll take and turn me out of door,
> Never let me come in any more.[9]

The most common ailment of these wretchedly unhappy children was a nervous stomach. Small wonder that many fell victim to sexual predators and went on to prostitution. It seemed a promotion.

The high social costs of British industrialization reflect the shock of unpreparedness and the strange notion that wages and conditions of labor came from a voluntary agreement between free agents. Not until the British got over these illusions, in regard first to children, then to women, did they intervene in the workplace and introduce protective labor legislation. When they did, they wrote it all down, so that social

* The Marxist term is one of the most misleading and abused words in the vocabulary of social science. It refers to a universal and inescapable condition of wage labor, whether in capitalist or socialist economies, hence has no meaning as a distinctive phenomenon; and in its attempt (pretension) to quantify a rate of exploitation by dividing wages by product (wage hours by total hours), it anomalously makes progressive, innovative capitalists—those who enhance labor productivity by investment in equipment and plant—the more exploitative for their enterprise.

historians have a library of reports and testimony to work with. Was England as bad as these records say? Or do we just have fuller records?

The European countries that followed England on the path of modern industry had their own labor problems and scandals, though less serious, largely because they had had warning and were able to introduce protections by anticipation. By comparison, Japan rushed into a raw, unbridled capitalism. As in England, but more so, cottage industry was already the scene of shameful exploitation. Why do I say "more so"? Because the Japanese home worker was able and willing to put up with hours of grinding, monotonous labor that would have sent the most docile English spinner or pinmaker into spasms of rebellion. The Japanese, for example, had no day of rest, no sabbath. Why did they need one? Animals did not get a day of rest. Nor was the backward-bending labor supply curve—the preference for leisure over income—a serious problem in Japan.

Why not? The answer lay partly in a more intense sense of group responsibility: the indolent, self-indulgent worker would be hurting not only himself but the rest of the family. And the nation—don't forget the nation. Most Japanese peasants and workers did not feel this way to begin with; under Tokugawa, they had scarcely a notion of nation. That was a primary task of the new imperial state: to imbue its subjects with a sense of higher duty to emperor and country and link this patriotism to work. A large share of school time was devoted to the study of ethics; in a country without regular religious instruction and ceremonial, school was the temple of virtue and morality. As a 1930 textbook put it: "The easiest way to practice one's patriotism [is to] discipline oneself in daily life, help keep good order in one's family, and fully discharge one's responsibility on the job."[10] Also to save and not waste.

Here was a Japanese version of Weber's Protestant ethic, the more effective because it jibed so well with atavistic peasant values. The classical peasant is a miser who saves everything, and plans and schemes and works accordingly. He lives for work and by work adds to his holding; that is his reason for being. (The precocious separation of British cottage workers from the soil and agriculture was an advantage to industry, but in some ways the attitudinal effects were negative. The landless industrial worker works to live. When he has enough, he stops to enjoy.)

The Japanese pushed this peasant mentality to the limit. This was, in the old days, a very poor society, squeezing out a mean subsistence. One lived on rice or, in colder climes, on millet and buckwheat. The

Keian edict of 1649 forbade peasants to eat the rice they grew, ordering them to make do with "millet, vegetables, and other coarse foods."
Little animal protein—some chicken maybe and seafood. Not so much
fish (including head, skin, bones, and tail) as the scavengings of the
ocean: seaweed, plankton, little tidal creatures. Even now, the Japanese show a catholicity of taste that testifies to the privation and improvisation of yesteryear.

Everything counted. You had to relieve yourself? Rush home and
empty your bowels on your own land. Division of labor? Mother's
time and work were too precious to waste on babies and self-
indulgence—up after childbirth! Older children could care for
younger; small children would learn early to perform light industrial
tasks. The smallest threads, even lint, could be saved and sold to rag-
pickers for a few sen (100 sen = 1 yen). Old folks, too old to labor, represented mouths to feed; better to turn them into ancestors. Such
households were miniature textile factories, a mine of profit to the energetic merchant putter-out.

We have the personal story of one such workhorse, an orphan married to a clever peasant who wanted to avoid military service and
needed a wife.* She brought nothing into the marriage except that military exemption, the strength to fetch water from a well eighty-six feet
deep, uncommon manual dexterity, and the humility and patience of
a saint before a mother-in-law from hell. Her father-in-law lived for
nothing but work: "I have no wish to see anything. I have no hobby.
Making the soil produce better crops is the only pleasure I have in
life."†

The mother-in-law told her right off that she would have to earn her
keep. "I don't intend to work hard by myself and let you, the young
wife, have an easy time of it. Now that you've joined our family, I want
you to work hard and skimp and save with me." They put her to work
at the loom, making cloth for the merchant, and she and her three

---

* The story comes to us in semifictional form: the prose poem *Fuki no tō (Bog
Rhubarb Shoots)* by Yamashiro Tomoe, a left-wing militant for agrarian reform, married to a Marxist labor organizer and imprisoned from 1940 to 1945 for "harboring
dangerous thoughts." It was in prison that she apparently learned the story of the
woman recounted above, which I take from the version of Hane, in *Peasants, Rebels,
and Outcasts*, pp. 85 ff. This last is a very important book, which deserves more attention from students of Japanese economic history.

† Again, the Keian edict: "Peasants must rise early and cut grass before cultivating the
fields. In the evening they are to make straw rope or straw bags. . . . The husband must
work in the fields, the wife must work at the loom. Both must do night work"—
Leupp, *Servants, Shophands*, p. 7.

sisters-in-law would send the shuttles flying from early morning, before light, to midnight, day in, day out, in cold weather and hot. No sabbath; no day of rest. No time even for cleaning: "This isn't the temple or a doctor's house," the harridan would scold. "If you have time to clean house, go out and work." And they worked. Three bolts of plain striped cloth per day. No English weaver could have come close. Sometimes, when they did some weaving for another peasant family, they were able to stretch the cloth and eke out an ell for themselves—no doubt everybody did it. Mother-in-law made sure that such "perks" also ended up with the merchant: no indulgences for the young women. The neighbors called the young weavers the moneybags of the family. Mother-in-law took all the credit.

The daughter-in-law was the best weaver of the household, the best in the village. Even her mother-in-law had to admit this, although she found reason to complain nevertheless. When the daughter-in-law gave birth, no one coddled her. No three days in bed. A piece of pickle to keep her going. And no one told her she'd done a fine job; that's what mothers are for. So the young mother got one meal a day, and when she nursed her babe, the mother-in-law would mutter about time lost: "I sure hate to see a young wife wasting her time feeding the baby. She could be working the loom and making some money."

The harder and better she worked, the harder they squeezed and the more they begrudged her time. Naturally; her marginal value was rising. "Our young mother takes a lot of time in the toilet"; or, "She sure takes a long time feeding the baby"; or, "She's so stupid, she's doing the washing again." She had better use for her time, and what matter if she could not wash herself or her clothes. The Japanese are renowned for their passion for cleanliness, but greed brings money closer to godliness.* And what if her underwear was soiled? Her husband was now away, serving as a border guard in northern Korea to earn one of those niggardly pensions that were the dream of poor peasant families. No need to be fastidious. (He never told her when he left how long that might take. It took twenty-four years.)

So the family saved the sen and the merchant-manufacturer made his yen and the Japanese textile industry flourished; and the day came when the family had put enough money aside to rebuild the house,

---

* On the importance of cleanliness for the Japanese and the urgent need for European visitors to learn these habits ("one will accept no failing in this regard"), see the strictures of the Jesuit Alessandro Valignano in his advice of 1583 to his brother missionaries—Valignano, *Les Jésuites au Japon,* p. 200.

with a tile roof this time. After all, what is more important than a house? "In this world what counts is the house. The house fixes the family's standing in society. It fixes a person's worth." When you call a doctor, he looks over the house while he takes your pulse. When you hire a priest for a funeral, he looks over the house and fixes accordingly the place of the deceased in the netherworld. The in-laws could talk of nothing else. They'd always been looked down on; people were not even polite. Well, they'd show them. And the daughter-in-law wove away—alone now, because her sisters-in-law had been married off; and she got thinner and thinner because she had to work for four and eating took time. And her son grew up and was sweet consolation, because her husband off in Korea in his dark uniform with gold stripes had forgotten her.

But then the boy went to school, and the mother never had time to see him take part in sports or in school plays because that would have kept her from the loom; and when teachers visited the house, Mother-in-law would tell her to sit away in the back room, because all she knew was how to weave and she would disgrace the boy if she spoke to the teacher. And then the boy graduated and sang with the other children: "Nothing can match the happiness we feel!" This was the first and only time the mother went to the school, in the spring, the yard full of peach blossoms; and ever after the mother would weep when she saw the peach blossoms in flower and remembered the children's graduation song.

So the mother wove and the merchant bought and the mother-in-law saved and the textile industry prospered; and the son went off to middle school because that was what his father the police captain in Korea wanted for him. And the mother saw him off and climbed through the gate and put her head on the rail to hear the diminishing hum of the train after it disappeared from sight.

And still the husband did not return. He would not have the privilege of building the new house. So they went ahead and had it built anyway, and relatives brought gifts, and Mother-in-law smiled and fawned on those who brought many gifts, and the others, even her own children returning her generosity, got nary a word. Her brother-in-law, a rich ox dealer, brought her many things, and while he was at it took the opportunity to tell the old grandmother off: "Old woman, aren't you dead yet?" You never did much, he told her; it was your daughter-in-law who made the money, bought rice paddies, paid for the house. The old woman laughed and nodded, and the ox dealer exclaimed, "Good thing she's deaf!" And then the old woman told the whole

thing to her granddaughter-in-law the weaver (whom else to talk to?):
"Did you hear what he said? It makes me feel bad." And the
granddaughter-in-law consoled her: "Grandma, don't let it bother
you. No one has worked so hard as you. I was able to keep weaving
without having to get off the loom only because you wound the thread
on the spindles for me. The money from weaving has gone into building the house. You must know that. Don't feel bad about it." And she
took her grandmother-in-law's hands in hers and wept. And the old
woman said, "What you say makes me feel better." Soon after, the
grandmother died. She looked like a withered tree.

And then the husband Uichi came back, in gold-striped uniform,
with gold-rimmed eyeglasses and upturned mustachios. And he built
an annex to the house. And then he began staying away in town—with
a woman, rumor had it—and stayed away longer and longer. And the
rumor was true. Uichi's wife was afraid to ask—he was so quick to
anger—but in a village community such things cannot be kept secret.

Nor did Uichi try to hide anything. He had known the woman in
Korea. She was Japanese and had been sent to Korea to work as a
"hostess." There a prominent government official had taken her for a
mistress, and she had become rich and had made her family rich on his
gains. And now she was Uichi's lady friend, like no one else in the peasant village, with her silk kimonos, a different one for every day, and her
silk bed sheets. And Uichi had no patience for his wife and beat her,
and his parents made no move to intervene, and his father even took
pleasure in his son's brutality: "Unless a person has that kind of
willpower, he cannot go out in the world and get ahead." And his
mother agreed: "That's how he scared the Koreans. No wonder they
were afraid of him. He really can be rough."

And then one day Uichi brought his mistress home, with her fancy
chests and dressers filled with costly silks. His mother knew of his plans
and told her daughter-in-law to clean the new annex. But when she
started wiping the new tatami mats, Uichi rushed up to her and kicked
her out: "You animal! How dare you step on the tatami with your
frostbitten feet!" And when the dazed woman staggered off, calling to
her long-gone son, away in China with the army: "Mii! Mii! On what
battlefield . . . ?" her mother-in-law drove her off: "Go away, you crazy
woman. We have no use for you." No use: they no longer needed the
income from the loom.

The women of the neighborhood understood: "He won his gold
stripes by doing brutal things to the Koreans. He did shady things to
get wealthy." No good would come of this, they said. But when they

saw Uichi's wife, moaning and whimpering in distress, they offered neither company nor sympathy. Toward evening, Uichi's mistress and her
maid arrived from town in a rickshaw. She was wearing pure white silk
socks, another product of Japanese looms. All Uichi's wife could remember after that was the closed door of the annex and the laughter
that came from within.

So she set the house on fire—and Japanese houses burn fast and
brightly. None of the woman's chests and dressers and silk kimonos
could be saved. And how much paper money gone with them? Then
Uichi's wife slid down into the deep well to disappear from the world,
but they found and revived her. She was tried for arson, aggravated by
the fact that the fire violated the blackout; one had to be prepared for
nonexistent Chinese bombers. She was sentenced to ten years' imprisonment, reduced to eight by extenuating circumstances.

No one came to see her in prison. She sat there huddled against the
cold and the wind and comforted herself with songs about rhubarb
shoots pushing through the snow—the same shoots she once picked
for her own mother when she was a little child and her mother in her
illness got comfort from them. Her son Mii wrote her only once: a
family that brutalizes its women does not make men of virtue and gratitude. It was a prison mate, Yamashiro, who heard her out and preserved her story. The orphan mother and wife was then fifty years old.

Of course, cottage outwork was the old; the mill and factory were the
new. The leading sector of Japan's industrial revolution was textiles, silk
and cotton above all, and there one had to create a new workforce. As
in Britain, these early mill hands were often women. One difference divided the two experiences: whereas in Britain early factory labor included many children, beginning with the ill-famed parish apprentices,
this was less true of Japan, which instituted compulsory education soon
after the Restoration. Children were in principle not available for factory work. I say "in principle" because reality often differed. As in
Britain, we have in Japan much evidence of deliberate lying about age;
also less than perfect school attendance.[11] The parents needed the
money, and schooling was not free.

In fairness, one should note that so poor was farm life, so hard the
work, that life in the mills could be attractive by comparison. The water
was cold on the farm and came from the bottom of a well; it was both
hot and cold in the mill dormitory and came out of a faucet. The food
was plain, coarse, and spare on the farm, fit for pigs more than humans;
the mill provided rice three times a day—foreign rice no doubt, not the

traditional sticky rice that Japanese are said to prefer. But just as other nations seem to like these other species, poor Japanese factory girls also found them tasty, nourishing, and habit-forming—as the Japanese would no doubt find today if they opened their home market to rice from abroad.

The wages in these mills were a pittance: it took years for a girl to save enough after deductions for food and lodging to pay the debt incurred by her father when he accepted the advance. (Lodging was often a pallet between the machines or a cot in a crowded dormitory that gave each sleeper the space of a tatami, that is, three by six feet—casket room.) A survey of sixty-two cotton plants in 1898 showed average monthly pay for women as 4.05 yen, as against 6.83 for men—4.67 yen for both sexes taken together. Even Indian workers made more, indeed almost double: wages equivalent to 8.07 to 9.18 yen a month in a sample of seven major textile plants.[12]

The heart of the story lay not so much in the low wages, however, as in the marginal product: Japanese labor worked well. It has been argued that low wages in newly industrializing and preindustrial countries reflect low productivity, but this does not seem to have been true for Japan. As long as the farm sector released hands to industry, factory enterprise had the best of both worlds: labor cheap and yet industrious, committed to task, to group, to family. One woman recalled:

> From morning, while it was still dark, we worked in the lamplit factory till ten at night. After work we hardly had the strength to stand on our feet. When we worked late into the night, they occasionally gave us a yam [to eat]. We then had to do our washing, fix our hair, and so on. By then it would be 11 o'clock. There was no heat even in the winter, and so we had to sleep huddled together. Several of the girls ran back to Hida. I was told that girls who went to work before my time had a harder time. We were not paid the first year. In the second year I got 35 yen, and the following year, 50 yen. . . . The life of a woman is really awful.[13]

The quotation tells much of the story: low pay, poor living conditions, the commitment to personal cleanliness, the gradual improvement. To which should be added unhealthful working conditions: humidification (to prevent static electricity), air filled with lint (hence a high rate of tuberculosis), a deafening din. Balzac, writing of business morals and the character of enterprise, put it well: no child comes into the world without dirty diapers. No industrial nation, either. Some young women ran away; chasers and catchers brought them back to punishment and humiliation before resuming work. Others made good their escape but came back anyway—because their family made them go back, or because they missed the poor creature comforts of the factory.

The point was, farm life and work were harder, at least physically. And then family loyalties ruled: the poor young women who worked in the silk filatures and cotton mills around Lake Suwa (today a center of electronics manufacture) saved desperately to give something to their parents and walked home through deep snow along treacherous mountain tracks, roped together against falling into bottomless gorges. Years later, when interviewed about these terrible years, many of them remembered only the good aspects. This is a natural survival reaction—we want to forget the pain; we want to "accentuate the positive." *"Haec olim meminisse iuvabit,"* said Aeneas to his desperate, discouraged comrades: some day you'll be happy to remember these things.

The men did better. Their wages were higher; their bargaining power greater. Japan was no different in this respect from European industrializers—a little worse perhaps, at least in the beginning. Factory workers, indeed industrial workers in general, were seen as a lower breed, like the *burakumin* outcasts, and indeed many of them were probably *burakumin* themselves.* They stood apart: "low class," "inferior," "base," "the defeated," "the stragglers." Mothers scared their children with the factory worker as bogeyman and exhorted them to do well in school for fear of falling into this slough of lowliness.

The workers fought back for status and dignity—not rights so much as dignity. "Don't despise a miner," went their slogan; "coal is not grown in a grain field."[14] (And when one could not get Japanese to work in the mines, especially when fighting wars, one could always conscript Koreans and Chinese. It is no accident that, so often in history, miners are slaves. With Japan's defeat in 1945, these slaves just walked off the job, and coal production, Japan's primary source of energy, fell from 3–4 million tons a month to 1 million. Needless to say, one could no longer get Japanese to do the work. They were used to

---

* Since the *burakumin* are indistinguishable from other Japanese, they have tended over time to pass into the larger society, although many continue to live in slum and crime neighborhoods. To this day, Japanese will employ detective agencies and genealogists to check on the possible *burakumin* ancestry of a prospective spouse. To counter this, authorities have closed certain official records. See N. D. Kristof, "Japan's Invisible Minority," *N.Y. Times,* 30 November 1995, p. A-18.

better and they were free. Japan, like other advanced industrial countries, eventually solved the problem by turning to oil.)*

Along with government initiatives and a collective commitment to
modernization, this work ethic and these personal values made possible the so-called Japanese economic miracle. It was as though an entire population subscribed to bygone *samurai* values—the banalization
of *bushido*. It would be a mistake of course to see this belief system as
universal, but any serious understanding of Japanese performance must
build on this phenomenon of culturally determined human capital. It
was the national *persona* that generated a harvest of ingenious adaptations of Western technologies, that made much of little, that drew extraordinary output from people who, in other societies, would have
resorted to massive sabotage and exit. Those who wonder at the resistance opposed by Japanese armed forces in the closing months of
World War II and ascribe it to fanaticism or suicidal impulse are missing the point. This is a society whose sense of duty and collective obligation, in all realms, sets it apart from the individualism cultivated in the
West. Individualism was an enormous advantage in the pursuit of economic wealth in the centuries preceding the Industrial Revolution, not
only in Europe but, as we have seen, in Tokugawa Japan. But once the
Japanese saw the path they wanted to follow, their collective values
proved a fabulous asset. (And a gross temptation.)

A common mistake of would-be scientific history is to assume that
today's virtues must also be tomorrow's and that a given factor, if positive once, must always pay. History doesn't work that way. The requirements of start-up and breakthrough economies are not the same
as those of front-runners and cruisers. Japanese success lay in the successful fight against petrification and nostalgia under Tokugawa and the
pursuit of a national effort under Meiji and successors. Different strategies in different circumstances.

---

* Reading, *Japan*, p. 51. Japan does not have the oil, but has the money to buy it.
Russia does have the oil, but it does not have the money to install oil burners; or to
pay the coal miners for that matter. As of December 1996, wages were seven months
in arrears.

# 24

# History Gone Wrong?

Arab male pride is very strong, and also very fragile.
—JAN GOODMAN, *Price of Honor*

No one can understand the economic performance of Muslim nations without attending to the experience of Islam as faith and culture. Islam, which means submission (to God), is one of the great world religions. Born in the desert like its two monotheistic predecessors, Judaism and Christianity, Islam proved uncommonly inspiring, carrying with it a small group of nomadic fighters to wide and rapid dominion. Within a century of the Prophet Muhammad's flight (Hegira) from Mecca to Medina (622, year 1 of the Muslim era), the mostly Arab warriors of the new faith crumpled the nations and empires of the Middle East and swept westward past Gibraltar to the Atlantic and through Spain into central France. Then, after a digestive respite, new armies pushed eastward into India and beyond. By the time Europeans entered the Indian Ocean by sea (1498), Islam had planted itself in parts of China and the Philippines, down the east coast of Africa, in southeastern Europe into the Danube basin, and along the trade routes of central Asia. Only in Spain and Portugal had a *reconquista* regained lands once Muslim and reversed a seemingly predestined course of conquest.

This explosion of passion and commitment was the most important feature of Eurasian history in what we may call the middle centuries—

the thousand years from the fall of the western Roman empire (traditionally dated 476) to the overseas expansion of Christian Europe. In this sense, it anticipates the potency of the later European imperial sweep, which would go even wider and deeper, imposing its calendar on the world and turning *"anno Domini"* into "Common Era."

The critical difference between the two rushes of power is the place of technology. The first—the Muslim—rested on old ways but new men, on the fighting zeal of fast-moving, horse-mounted warriors who were convinced that God and history were on their side. These men simply overpowered the salaried minions and indifferent subjects of despotic empires, pausing only for an occasional digestion of conquest and booty. The second—the European push—was based on superior firepower and moved by profit: loot yes, but above all, continuing, sustainable profit. (When I was a student, we learned about the three G's: God, Gold, and Glory. They all mattered, but the greatest of all was Gold, because gold paid the bills, armed the fleets, lured and consoled the flesh.)

The European rush was potentially stronger, because of its material basis. The Europeans at their peak could defeat anybody. Their only serious adversaries were other Europeans. But the Muslim rush was at once more uncompromising and more insatiable. The combination of prowess and faith held apocalyptic implications in both directions—in its triumphs and in its disappointments.

European expansion (imperialism) was not apocalyptic. It was at bottom an expression of power. As a response to a calculus of disparity and opportunity, it was cost-conscious, hence opportunistic in both directions. Oh yes, souls mattered to the Europeans, more to some countries than to others—so to Catholics more than to Protestants. (We saw this with the Dutch in Asia.) But rarely did souls count enough to get in the way of profit and loss. Prestige also mattered, but again prestige, like everything, had its price. That's why European empires dissolved as and when they did. When the European powers met colonial resistance and the cost of staying rose, they packed up and got out (India is the prime example), often at heavy cost to newly free native peoples.*

Not so for Islam. The Muslim warrior was doing God's work, and

---

* Some readers will recall as counterevidence the French reluctance to leave Vietnam and then Algeria. True enough, but the French had (and have) a higher pride quotient than other Europeans. And once the issue was settled, the French and other European *colons* cleared out of Algeria as fast as they could.

his defeat was a setback for humanity. So when, beginning in the eleventh century in Spain and the Levant, Christian knights came to push the faithful back and to occupy lands once part of the House of Islam, Muslims saw this as the triumph of evil. And when, in the eastern Mediterranean, Muslim armies drove the crusaders into the sea, this was not simply victory, but God's victory, the restoration of order and a redress of history. The expulsion of the Christian crusader kingdoms of the Levant became a kind of paradigm, a metaphor for all time. When, almost a millennium later, Saddam Hussein of Iraq seized Kuwait and took on the coalition of Western powers and their Muslim toadies, he did so in the name and memory of Saladin, the Kurdish chief who took Jerusalem back from the infidel.*

From that peak moment (1187), the course of Islam was mostly downhill. Not that the religion languished. It continued to make gains, especially among populations of animistic belief. The message of Islam is simple; the act of conversion also. Of the great monotheistic faiths, it makes the least demands on the new adherent, at least in the beginning.† But insofar as Islam links faith to power and dominion, as it does, the loss of might relative to infidel societies became a source of profound despair or active anguish. For a long time, the problem of decline was concealed by the sustained autonomy of Muslim states, the diversion of European power to other parts of the world, the instances of local triumph (in particular the territorial gains of the Ottoman Turks), the apparent imperviousness of Islam. But from the seventeenth century on, no one who looked around could be blind to the shifting balance of world power. Islam had become an economic and intellectual backwater. History had gone awry.

In two places this clash of faiths and empires was critical for the larger course of history: Moghul India, where the British began gobbling territory, revenues, and sovereignty; and the Ottoman empire, where the sultan's writ was flouted and his lands gnawed by the pretensions of Christian neighbors and the derived nationalism of Christian subjects. Both these entities were aristocratic (despotic) empires in the classical mold: societies divided between a small elite and a large mass of fleeceable subjects. Above the prime divider that separated the few and the many, nobles and officials held limitless power. They had

---

* Cf. Charnay, *Traumatismes musulmans,* p. 314. The Christian campaign in the Gulf was seen as a reprise of the crusader hatred for the Islamic spiritual heritage.
† I exclude from this comparison the phenomenon of forced conversion, which obviously makes no demands on faith or preparation.

a monopoly of violence, restrained only by the occasional, random, even whimsical wisdom of the ruler. These societies were not without a sense of justice: one historian even speaks of "the vitality of a constant moral code made self-aware by a compassionate society."[1] (Reading the laments of contemporaries, including visitors from Europe, I find such a view curiously optimistic.)

Below the divider, people had no rights, no security; only duties and submission. Resistance was next to impossible. The only escape from abuse was to fly or hide—the invisibility of nobodyhood. As one of the caliphs in Baghdad is said to have said: "The best life has he who has an ample house, a beautiful wife, and sufficient means, who does not know us and whom we do not know."[2] He knew. In such a society, to know and be known by power was to ask for trouble. A Sufi saint put it well when asked to receive the ruler: "My house has two doors; if the Sultan entered it through one, I would leave it by the other." Of course only a saint could afford to talk that way, and only a saint would be asked. How, then, could the masses identify with king or kingdom? Recruitment into the armed forces could only be a form of servitude. Fighters tended to be either slaves or mercenaries, wanting in zeal and loyalty.

In India, the Moghul empire was already fragmenting when the Europeans arrived; the death process was under way and nothing could have reversed it. This subcontinent, apparently destined to oneness by shape and religion, had in fact never been able to cohere. One invader after another had come in across the northwest passes and imposed its rule on the Indus and Ganges basins; but the south had always held out, tenacious in its linguistic and cultural nativism, like a spring in compression. So, no unity: "The country seemed to fall asunder at the touch."[3]

But then why not a system of independent nation-states as in Europe? Why, "given the makings of a similar set of competing polities, did no states system emerge?"[4] Because, I think, these aristocratic tyrannies, large and small, could not create the popular identities needed to bond a people and make it feel different from, even superior to, its neighbors. Religion might have done—Muslims vs. Hindus—but that would not serve as a national definer (discriminant) until the twentieth century. Had the Europeans not come in the seventeenth century, India would simply have reverted to the internecine divisions and troubles that had been its lot for millennia.

The British changed everything. They brought the administrative experience and superior technology that permitted a tiny force to govern a docile people thousands of times more numerous. Except for the Sepoy rebellion (1857–58), ruthlessly suppressed, and occasional religious riots, neither Muslims nor Hindus would resist. The British also came with decisive trade advantages. Like the Portuguese and Dutch before them, they were the active partner in this union of West and East. It was their ships that went and returned, their merchants who sailed forth into Asian waters. (Contrast here the symmetrical pattern of exchange and competition in the North Atlantic.) Old Asian commercial networks, for all their wealth and experience, yielded the juiciest transactions to foreign agency houses, and India's economic development from the late eighteenth century came to be shaped more by British imperial policy than by indigenous initiative.

British rule proved a school for scorn. The white sahibs and memsahibs felt themselves infinitely more civilized—cleaner, smarter, handsomer, better educated. The Indians returned the contempt in spades. The English, the Bengali folk myth had it, were descended from the union of a demon with a she-monkey. The more sophisticated Indians eschewed such fanciful genealogies but noted that their ancestors wrote poetry and knew about the zero when the British were still skulking through the woods. Sir Henry Maine, British social anthropologist of the late nineteenth century, deplored this self-indulgent nostalgia, on either side: "The Natives of India have caught from us Europeans our modern trick of constructing, by means of works of fiction, an imaginary Past out of the Present. . . . " And again: "On the educated Native of India, the Past presses with too awful and terrible a power for it to be safe for him to play or palter with it."*

Today, of course, we all do that. We think it good, and we call it multiculturalism.

The empire of the Ottoman Turks proved more durable. That in itself is a mystery, because after some two hundred fifty years of expansion (1300–1550), its downhill course should have brought about fragmentation and liquidation in a matter of decades. By the nineteenth century, Turkey was recognized as the "sick man of Europe," but the dying process had actually started three hundred years earlier.

---

* Quoted in N. Chaudhuri, *Thy Hand,* pp. 674–76, who notes that much of this counterpride was encouraged by romantic orientalists. But no such encouragement was necessary: this was a not uncommon response where European arrogance encountered older civilizations brought low by history. Cf. the lessons of Prince Tewfik, son of the Egyptian Khedive Ismail, which taught him in the 1860s that everything in Western science and technology—steam engine, railroad, etc.—came in the first place from Islam and the Arabs—Landes, *Bankers and Pashas,* p. 325.

How could a living corpse, rotting in all its parts, take so long to expire?

The Ottoman empire began in the late thirteenth century when the Osmanlis, a Turkish clan or tribe, somehow penetrated into northwest Anatolia, far from the plains and pastures of their ancestral home, very close to the center of Byzantine (Greek) power. This warrior people was swift to move and keen for loot—very dangerous. The Greeks should have known it and seen them as potential, inevitable enemies. Instead, these pseudo-Hellenes, too clever by half, thought they could turn the Ottomans into tools and allies.

So when, in the mid-fourteenth century, the Byzantine empire was riven by civil war, both sides began calling in Turks and Serbs (also invaders) for aid. This pattern went back centuries: co-opt the barbarians and get them to fight for rather than against you. Yet it's a high-risk strategy to let the enemy into the house. He may like it too well. When the Serbs got ambitious and decided to replace the Greek dynasty by one of their own, the Greeks called once more on the Turks for help, which they gave. But why stop there? Having beaten the Serbs, the Turks planted themselves in Gallipoli in 1354, then overran Thrace, and then in 1365 took Adrianople (the city of the Roman emperor Hadrian) as their new capital, a day's march from Constantinople. Now the Ottomans had one foot firmly established in Europe and one in Asia Minor. The Byzantine "empire" was reduced to shrunken nodules, Christian islets in a Muslim sea; and the Ottomans, like other Asian invaders before them, began to imitate the pomp and ceremony of the Greek court, though in their own way.

In 1453, when the Ottomans captured Constantinople and put an end to the Roman empire, bells tolled and worshippers mourned in courts and churches a thousand miles away. At that point, the Turks held as much territory in Europe as in Asia, and were seen and feared as the bearers of the Islamic sword against Christendom. The Turk became a new bogeyman, his name synonymous with "brute" or "cruel savage." Carnival targets, *"têtes de Turc,"* wore turbans and large mustaches.* Schoolboys did arithmetic problems that sought the most efficient way to dispose of Turkish passengers on a sinking ship.

These hostile (fearful) perceptions and intermittent aggressions marked off a restless, moving frontier of conflict. The fall of the great city, The City (which gives us the name Istanbul), constituted one of

---

* The expression has since been reduced to metaphor; a *tête de Turc* is now a butt of mockery and jest.

the fateful events of all time, one that changed history in ways that are still being worked out five hundred years later. Witness the fighting and the outrages of so-called ethnic cleansing in today's Bosnia.

The Ottoman empire was a typical despotism, only more warlike. The rulers took the surplus, though at first they apparently squeezed the masses less, or less effectively, than in Moghul India.* Perhaps this was because the Ottomans were too busy fighting. Every year brought its campaign, its forays into neighboring areas. So long as these incursions paid off, one could keep the *rayas,* the human cattle, on a loose leash. Besides, the Turks were eager to encourage commercial and industrial enterprise by minority communities—Christians (Greeks and Armenians, but also an increasing number of Levantines) and Jews. In effect they built their society on an ethnic division of labor, a sign of their own distaste for and superiority to trade and crafts. This segmentation opened enterprise to a few, but impeded its extension. In despotisms, it is dangerous to be rich without power. So in Turkey: capital accumulation proved an attractive nuisance. It aroused cupidity and invited seizure.

Over time, the size of the Ottoman empire grew to cover all the Muslim Middle East (including Syria and Iraq), all of North Africa (including Egypt, Tunis, and Algiers), and a large chunk of southeast Europe plus lands around the Black Sea. This congeries of opportunistic acquisitions could not be administered uniformly. Some closely governed pieces paid taxes; others were bound by ties of fealty and paid tribute. Others went in and out of Ottoman control with the fortunes of war and diplomacy. Sovereignty was often suzerainty, and power was as much virtual as real; that is, the Ottoman court ruled as much by what it could and might do if challenged, as by what it did.

In the beginning, such bonds could be strong; the Ottoman empire had a number of able leaders. In the long run, however, autocracies, like all hereditary monarchies only more so, suffer from two intrinsic weaknesses: the accidents of heredity and the problem of succession; and the two are connected. The first shortcoming is unavoidable: even a brilliant family will regress to the mean, and ordinary families will os-

---

* Not everyone would agree with this comparison. Eric Jones, *European Miracle,* for example, thinks Moghul India was easier, largely on the basis of population (survival) records. But these are incomplete, and it may well be that Ottoman subjects were less docile and squeezable. In any event, it is not easy to distinguish between oppressions. I think the Moghuls were worse; it may well have been the Ottomans.

cillate around it. The succession, meanwhile, is defined by social and political convention. In Muslim lands, succession often went to the oldest male member of the clan, conceivably an uncle, cousin, or the oldest son. The Turkish variant was succession by the ablest, later by the oldest, son.

In both systems the multiplication of spouses and concubines and the proliferation of descendants (what else could an idle ruler do— what better proof of vigor?) posed the question of legitimacy. The Ottoman way of dealing with this was to strangle all potential competitors, delicately to be sure, by a silken cord. Such definitive stakes incited to precautionary murder not only of rivals but of the rivals' mothers (stuffed into a bag and drowned in the Bosphorus); also to the prudent immurement of the heir-apparent in the harem, safe from intrusion and harm. This stultifying isolation led to intellectual and political impotence. From the seventeenth century on, the future sultan was typically an uneducated nonentity—an instrument for others to play.

Around this void at the center, courtiers maneuvered for influence and intrigued. As the Ottoman bureaucracy grew, as the paper piled up and regulations multiplied, the state came to rely on non-Turkish personnel, even at the highest levels. Many of these were recruited by a head tax in the literal sense (the *devshirme*): Christian subjects of the empire were required to supply sons to the state, to be reared as Muslims and used in peace and war in occupations high and low.[5] The system stirred jealousy among the older elites—"how come that those who enjoy rank and power are all Albanians and Bosnians?"—but this meant the Ottomans were open to talent, including renegades.* They were no longer a Turkish empire—indeed the very word "Turk" came to have negative connotations of ignorance and boorishness—but rather a pluralistic assemblage. Not a melting pot, though: the Turks never could create an Ottoman identity that commanded the loyalty of their diverse subjects.†

Meanwhile the Turkish warriors of old lost their fighting spirit, and

---

* The word is Jones's, *European Miracle,* p. 180. That was the Christian perspective. For the Muslims, conversion to Islam was a sign of sincerity.

† Very different, then, from open recruitment of talent from different German states into the Prussian bureaucracy. At the origin of German national identity was a common culture and the pride that went with it. The political frontiers were accidental. The Ottoman empire brought together a diversity of cultures, and the divisions were anything but superficial or accidental.

patriotic volunteers were not to be found. More and more, the state depended on slave soldiers, the janissaries in particular.* The janissaries began as the servants of the sultan, his right arm, his elite corps; but the power to kill is a key to power. In Constantinople (Istanbul to the Muslims),† the janissaries became a state within the state, a pretorian guard that made and unmade rulers, until in 1826 the sultan got the consent of religious leaders to rid the place of these troublemakers. First the sultan set up a new corps and told the janissaries they would be welcome to join—elimination by fusion. They refused and dug in. The sultan's loyal troops then brought up their artillery, cannonaded the barracks, and the mob did the rest. Balance sheet: six to ten thousand dead, and the janissaries had become history.

In Egypt, a similar corps, called Mamelukes, had actually taken over the kingdom and ruled it for some 260 years (1254–1517) as an aristocracy whose very name (Arabic *memalik,* slave) had changed its meaning. Even after the Ottoman conquest, they ran Egypt, up until the intrusion of the French under Bonaparte (1798) and the counter-invasion by British forces. In the train of these Europeans came an Albanian adventurer who made himself the sultan's viceroy and the new pasha of Egypt. This soldier of fortune, Mehemet Ali by name, decided he had had enough of the Mameluke parasites and needed to clarify his authority. So in 1811 he invited their chiefs to a banquet. They showed up at the palace all gay and hearty and dressed in their best and sat themselves down to the feast. Most of them never got up. The gates were closed, and shooters killed them from above like ducks on a pond. Finis to over 550 years.**

But here we get ahead of our story. After the defeat of the first Ottoman siege of Vienna (1529), the empire suffered repeated setbacks in Europe as inchoate Christian polities got organized. Among other changes that made a difference, European military technology kept improving. The Ottomans tried to keep up, but they were imitators

---

* The janissaries were originally conscripted by the *devshirme* and raised as Muslims; they also included young war captives. Later on, Turks were admitted to the corps; in between campaigns they were allowed to work at trades or serve as police.

† The Turkish version of Stamboul. The Turkish language does not like to begin a word with two successive consonants; so Stamboul becomes Istanbul and Smyrna becomes Izmir.

** The Bey of Algiers used a similar trap to eliminate his rivals. Ditto for Saddam Hussein of Iraq. It is precisely the force of obligations of hospitality that render such tactics effective.

rather than inventors. They understood the value of cannon and especially of siege artillery, but they depended on Christian technicians to do the founding. As the gap between Christian and Muslim guns grew, the Turks could not even make use of pieces captured in battle.[6]

Ditto at sea: the Ottomans replaced their battle vessels with more of the same, while Christian naval armament improved. Listen to the Ottoman historian Selaniki Mustafa Efendi reporting on the arrival in 1593 of the vessel that brought the second English ambassador to the Sublime Porte: "A ship as strange as this had never entered the port of Istanbul. It crossed 3700 miles of sea and carried 83 guns, besides other weapons. The outward form of the firearms was in the shape of a swine."[7] This image unconsciously testified to ignorance: these pigs (significant symbol: Christian fare, taboo to Muslims) were iron naval cannon, made in England in quantity as nowhere else. That ship and a few others like it could have blown the Ottoman fleet (and the Venetian to the bargain) out of the water before it got close enough to ram or grapple. Meanwhile the Ottomans tried to keep up by importing large quantities of war materiel: muskets, gunpowder, saltpeter, iron, blades. In spite of papal interdictions on arms sales to Muslims, in defiance of clerical anathemas and excommunications, much of this armament came from England, which also sold to Spain. But then, what to expect from conscienceless heretics?

And not only armament. Over time, trade relations between Europe and the Levant reversed. Eastern craftsmen had once supplied Europeans with fine cloth, carpets, tapestries, faience, and the like in exchange for metal (copper and tin), slaves, and money. From the sixteenth century on, Europe made and sold the manufactures in exchange for dried fruit, spices, cotton, cereal. The same for silk: in the Middle Ages Europe had bought Byzantine silk fabrics; now it imported raw silk, and local producers in Turkey found it hard to compete with European buyers for the raw material. And paper: this writing material was eagerly adopted in the Middle East (eighth century) from Chinese example; forage was short, hides were scarce, and so was parchment. The new technology took root slower in Europe, where parchment was relatively abundant; but once European makers learned to produce paper, they far surpassed their Levantine predecessors and were soon selling large quantities in the East.[8] Even such substances as coffee and sugar that had originally come to Europe from the East now went the other way—in the case of sugar, after refining and processing.[9]

Islam's greatest mistake, however, was the refusal of the printing press, which was seen as a potential instrument of sacrilege and heresy. Nothing did more to cut Muslims off from the mainstream of knowledge.

As a result of this intellectual segregation, technical lag, and industrial dependency, the balance of economic forces tilted steadily against the Ottomans, while a series of military defeats undermined their assumptions of superiority and paralyzed their ability to respond. A few farsighted observers tried to warn the ruling elite and pushed for reform, but to little effect. The evil was constitutional, founded in religious dogma and inculcated by habit. A byzantine bureaucracy made everything harder with thorny regulations in incomprehensible officialese. Corruption—the only way to get something done—just fed on itself.

This self-imposed archaism dissolved the loins of empire. "The Ottoman state was a plunder machine which needed booty or land to fuel itself, to pay its way, to reward its officer class."[10] The Ottomans had originally filled a power vacuum—had taken over a region once strong, now enfeebled—looting as they went. Now they could no longer take from outside. They had to generate wealth from within, to promote productive investment. Instead, they resorted to habit and tried to pillage the interior, to squeeze their own subjects. Nothing, not even the wealth of high officials, was secure. Nothing could be more self-destructive. The only thing that saved the empire from disintegration was its inefficiency, the venality of its officials, and the protective interests of stronger powers.

In these circumstances, the continued advance of European technology, in particular the Industrial Revolution, nailed shut the coffin of Ottoman industry. Except for some local specialties, nothing could stand up to cheap factory-made cottons and silks. The nineteenth century saw Britain protect the Ottoman empire from the territorial ambitions of its adversaries, while blithely killing off its manufactures. But from the British point of view, that was as it should be: British goods were cheaper, and the Ottomans could not possibly compete. They did not know enough; they did not have the capital; they could not count on political stability.

Across the Mediterranean, however, a piece of the Ottoman empire had other ideas. This was Egypt, long dozing under Mameluke misrule, to the point of forgetting the wheel—this, in the land of the Pharaohs, where archers in chariots had once driven black Nubians and fleeing Hebrews before them.* Turkish government had changed the country little, but the invasion in 1798 by a French expeditionary force under General Bonaparte shook Egypt to the core. A Mameluke army was simply brushed aside, while Bonaparte proclaimed French revolutionary slogans to a population that had no idea what he was talking about. The French were followed by the British—more technological humiliation—and with them came a new Turkish intrusion designed to remind the Egyptians of their fealty to Istanbul. One of the detachments so dispatched was under the command of Mehemet Ali— we met him earlier—who used the Mamelukes to unseat the Ottoman governor and made himself master of Cairo. Faced with reality, the sultan in Istanbul named Ali his viceroy in Egypt. In return, Mehemet Ali made war on Turkey, in the best Turkish tradition.

Mehemet Ali (now Muhammad Ali in Arabic as against Turkish style) was clearly a man of force and ambition. But he differed from conventional warlords in having a larger vision and the imagination to go with it. No isolation in the palace for him. Ali knew from personal experience how far the Ottoman empire had fallen behind, how much there was to learn. So no one of interest visited Egypt without talking with him. Ali also saw Egypt not as a term appointment, but as a personal estate and field for development. Normally the Ottomans moved officials about from post to post to prevent them from taking root. Ali converted Egypt into a hereditary fiefdom.

What is more, Muhammad Ali envisioned this development as a total process, encompassing advances in agriculture and industry, new technologies, innovations in schooling (what the economist would call improvements in human capital); also, and unfortunately, an arms program and the inculcation of martial virtues. To accomplish all this, he brought in foreign technicians, some of whom left Christianity for Islam. Although Britain clearly led the world in manufacturing, most of these experts were French, perhaps because the collapse of the Napoleonic empire had freed up talent, perhaps because France's defeat made it less redoubtable, perhaps because Muhammad Ali correctly saw Britain as an opponent of Egyptian industry.

Among the expats, the most important was probably Louis-Alexis Jumel, a French mechanic-cotton manufacturer turned agronomist.

---

* In the earlier discussion of China, I expressed surprise and skepticism that the Chinese had managed to forget earlier superior technologies. But such retrogression is clearly possible. The question is, how and why.

In 1822, Jumel transplanted a bush he had found on the Ile Bourbon (later renamed Réunion) and developed for Egypt the cotton we know by his name.[11] This species has a very long fiber, thin and yet tough, spinnable in combed form and suitable to the finest yarn and cloth.* In the new world of mechanized cotton manufacture, jumel cotton was a winner from the start. Muhammad Ali had it grown on his own estates, which occupied an increasing share of Egypt's best soil, and his officials quickly followed his example. By 1824, over 11 million kilograms were exported; by 1845, the figure was 15.5 million kilograms.[12] It was the earnings from jumel cotton, bought (expropriated) at artificially low prices and marketed through state monopolies (roughly half of total Egyptian exports in 1835), that paid for Ali's economic and military ambitions and for much of the Suez Canal. The rest came from other crops, also sold by official agencies. This was a quiet way to generate revenue without levying uncollectable taxes. The system drove European merchants wild.

Beginning in the 1820s, a good part of these earnings flowed into a massive educational and industrial effort—into technical and military schools, and a wide variety of mills and shops for the manufacture of textiles, metals and metal products, chemicals, rope, arms, ships, and the like—all the things necessary to replace imports and feed a growing war machine. The viceroy even sought a deeper independence by buying European machines and copying them in Egypt. In the face of British export prohibitions, the Egyptians got permission in 1826 to import five hundred power looms from Galloway's in Manchester. No harm would follow, assured a scornful William Huskisson, president of the Board of Trade; in six months "they would have been knocked to pieces."[13]

Some say that Muhammad Ali was trying to build a war machine; others, that he was aiming at an industrial revolution in a land far behind the European follower countries.† It was a quixotically bold vision, one that was bound to vex European industrial and trading interests: the first attempt by a backward, non-Western society to build a mod-

---

* At the time, the only finer cotton came from a few islands off the coast of Georgia and the Carolinas, the so-called sea island cotton. Little enough of this was ever grown (by 1835 the Egyptian crop was three times as large), and the crop has shrunk over time almost to nothing, as hotels, summer homes, and tourism have taken over these sandbars. Egyptian cotton today is to all intents and purposes the best in the world. On the early history of Jumel, see Lévy-Leboyer, *Les banques européennes,* p. 199.

† Issawi, "Economic Development," p. 362 f., says both, though he describes the economic objective as perhaps unwitting and possibly deliberate.

ern industrial economy—by command from above.[14]

The extent of Muhammad Ali's success and the reasons for his ultimate failure have been sharply debated. On the one hand, Egypt's cotton manufacture apparently grew smartly. An estimate of 400,000 machine spindles in 1834 would put it ninth in the world, ahead of Belgium, and fifth or sixth in spindlage per head of population.[15] At the end of the 1830s, Egypt was producing 1.2 million pieces of calico a year. On the other hand, visitors were struck by the crudeness of the machinery, the want of maintenance, the poor quality of the finished product. Jumel cotton was made for high counts, but Egyptian yarn was notoriously coarse and yet fragile. Some foreign observers, though, gave a favorable opinion, and we even have reports of shipment of these products to India, ancestral home of cotton manufacture.*

Whom to believe? The optimistic view leans toward a conspiratorial theory of Egyptian failure. Muhammad Ali's project threatened European industrial supremacy. Egypt should stick to cotton-picking and let the big boys make yarn and cloth (comparative advantage again). So the Europeans, Britain in the lead, took the first opportunity (1838) to deprive Egypt of those tariff barriers and market constraints necessary to its infant industries. Capitalism, the argument runs, coolly and cannily stifled a potentially dangerous competitor.

The pessimists retort that Egypt was never a serious competitor. The whole project was a loser and survived only so long as the state poured money into it. Nothing could be done without foreign technicians and machinists, and even then. Also, the prices of materials and products were set, not by the market, but by the authorities. The meager evidence of sales abroad proves nothing.

The primary problem, say the skeptics (realists), lay in Egypt's social and cultural incapability. Native entrepreneurs were rare. Most of them were drawn from the Coptic, Jewish, and Greek minorities—outsiders who had good reason to be discreet. Local manufacturing was done in shops and cottages, by owners lacking knowledge, money, and desire to shift to machine technologies. Foreign investors had better and quicker ways to make money, by lending, for example. The viceroy alone could imagine factories in Egypt, and he established them by fiat. But where would he find the motor energy? Egypt had neither wood nor coal fuel, and water had to be raised before it could be used to

---

* But Lévy-Leboyer, *Les banques européennes,* p. 189 and n. 31, based on reports to the British Foreign Office, says that Egyptian cottons could sell only in Egypt, and in Syria after the Egyptian conquest.

drive wheels. So he began with animal power—1,000 oxen to drive 250,000 cotton spindles. The English had done that at the start of their Industrial Revolution, but it is a costly and inefficient technique, especially in hot climates. It is one thing to use beasts for the intermittent tasks of agriculture and transport; quite another to make them drive insatiable machines.

And where would Muhammad Ali find managers? He hired numerous Europeans at good salaries, but what he wanted from them was know-how rather than direction. For this latter, he chose Muslims, Turkish and Egyptian, for reasons that may have had to do with workers' sensibilities and the building of a vested interest in the new industry. These *nazirs* received honors, medals, and generous salaries, but corruption was rife. "Being entrusted with the regulation of the expenses, and the paying of the workmen, they accept bribes to favour an indifferent artisan at the expense of the government, and commit innumerable other frauds difficult of detection."[16] All this entailed the appointment of inspectors to examine accounts and niggling regulations to prevent waste and theft. In this way, time, quality, and maintenance were sacrificed to form and order.

And where would Muhammad Ali find the workers? In the best Egyptian tradition, he started by using slaves (in England, remember, they began with women and children, the people who could not say no). But these slaves died in large numbers, which says something about working conditions.* He then had recourse to forced labor torn from family and household, scantily fed and housed, much abused by tyrannical superiors. (The one generosity was in blows of the *kurbash*.) Some recruits mutilated themselves to avoid conscription. Most, however, found that repugnant as well as painful and life-threatening; so they mutilated the machines instead.† Arson was an abiding threat,** and maintenance was systematically neglected, the more so as bureau-

---

* "At first no persons were employed in the factories but black slaves from Darfour and Kordofan, who displayed great intelligence, and quickly acquired a competent knowledge of the business; but so great a change of life, co-operating with the peculiar unhealthiness of the occupation, gradually thinned their ranks, so that the Pasha was shortly compelled to have recourse to the Fellahs"—Saint-John, *Egypt of Mohammed Ali*, pp. 410–11.

† Others fled the country, in spite of efforts to close the frontiers. Issawi, "Economic Development," p. 362, attributes the flight to hard times and military conscription. But labor conscription may well have been worse.

** "Of the twenty-three or twenty-four cotton-mills existing in Egypt, there is not one which has not, at various periods, been accidentally or designedly set on fire"—Saint-John, *Egypt,* p. 413.

cratic complications within the mills (antipilferage measures) made even lubrication a monumental task. In a sandy, dusty climate, bad maintenance spelled disaster.* More and more of the machines fell idle. Standard repair took the form of cannibalization. "For the small number of machines [the mills] contain, they are much more spacious than necessary."[17] Thus output fell, as it should have.

The British, in other words, had no reason to fear the competition of Egyptian manufactures. In spite (or because) of absurdly low wages, Egyptian costs were higher; and for all the fineness of the raw material, the quality of the final product was lower. But the British were immensely vexed by Ali's monopoly of the export cotton crop and by the barriers to import of foreign cotton goods into Egypt. So, with the help of the viceroy's own miscalculations and extravagant political ambitions, they forced free trade upon him.

Scholars of "progressive" bent see this as the assassination of Egypt's industrial revolution, or at the least a measure that stalled Egyptian industrialization for another century. The assumption here is that industrialization cannot succeed without "tariff protection, tax exemptions, rebates on transport rates, cheap power, special credit facilities to certain sectors, educational policies, etc., which only a government enjoying a large measure of political and fiscal independence can provide."[18]

My own sense is that all of this is wishful thinking. Muhammad Ali's Egypt ready for an industrial revolution? No. His grand project already lay moribund when the new commercial treaty went into effect. To be sure, the old pasha went on investing in industrial plant right up to his death in 1848; but the military incentive was gone, and he was just throwing good money after bad. Nor did tariffs hold the key. The Japanese had no protective tariffs from the 1850s to the new century. They were not happy about this. But they prospered. (Note that the anti-imperialist historians want to have it both ways: now they complain that Egypt could not shelter its infant industries; now they boast that these industries were doing so well that they could sell their products abroad and that their European competitors were quaking before them.)

All of this is fantasy history. Some of it reproduces an earlier time's enthusiasms: Muhammad Ali seemed to many of his contemporaries an

---

* Saint-John, *ibid.*, p.415, speaks of "the peculiar nature of dust, consisting of fine silicious atoms, which the most compact building, and the best glazed windows could never prevent from collecting in great quantities."

enlightened ruler (despot), a wise man, a savior sent to waken Egypt land from its long sleep. Some of it expresses anticapitalist, anti-imperialist, anti-European ideology. Yet for all the misdeeds of capitalism and imperialism, for all the hypocrisy of European exploiters, Egypt's problems went much deeper. Too deep for even an inspired Albanian outsider like Ali to solve.

Even now, Egyptian industrial efforts stutter, for reasons not unlike those of Ali's day. Technologies have been transformed, and economic lateness models tell us that newcomers should have opportunity and incentive to learn and catch up. But Egyptian society and culture have not changed much in those fundamentals that determine vocation and performance. Egypt was not ready then. Is it ready now?

Nor have other Middle Eastern societies done better. The highest incomes in the Muslim Arab world are of course to be found among the oil producers and exporters. The others are "going nowhere." Even among OPEC members, the torrent of wealth has not grown an economic transformation. A World Bank study of these economies with the hopeful title "Claiming the Future" notes that as recently as 1960, the seven leading Arab economies had an average income of $1,521, higher than the $1,456 of the seven East Asian comers—Taiwan, South Korea, Hong Kong, Singapore, Thailand, Malaysia, and Indonesia. By 1991, the Arab countries had fallen well behind: $3,342 as against $8,000. Today, the Arab Middle East attracts 3 percent of global direct foreign investment; East Asia, 58 percent.[19]

But do these Middle Eastern states need foreign investment? The best comparison is with sixteenth- and seventeenth-century Spain, cursed by easy riches and led down the path of self-indulgence and laziness. So with the oil-rich. They have traded black gold for money and sent the money back to the countries that paid it. They have purchased shares large and small in the enterprises of advanced industrial nations. They have also built handsome homes, hotels, and palaces, bought large, gas-guzzling automobiles (but fuel is cheap, like coal at the mine), acquired properties abroad where they can shelter their fortunes and permit themselves dress and behavior unacceptable at home. Saudi Arabia, for all its deserts, has paid handsomely to import beach sand from Australia. Most wasteful and counterproductive has been a huge investment in arms, including weapons condemned by international law and treaties. Much of this, presumably, buys the friendship of the manufacturers of these nasty toys.

These countries simply haven't developed an advanced economy.

Like the Spain of yesteryear, they've purchased the skills and services of others rather than learned to do things for themselves. "What is rich?" asks a merchant banker of the Persian Gulf:

> *Rich* is education . . . expertise . . . technology. *Rich* is knowing. We have money, yes. But we are not *rich*. We are like the child who inherits money from the father he never knew. He has not been brought up to spend it. He has it in his hands; he doesn't know how to use it. If you do not know how to spend money, you are not *rich*. We are not rich.
>
> Without this knowledge, this understanding, we are nothing. We import *everything*. The bricks to make houses, we import. The men who build them, we import. You go to the market, what is there that is made by Arabs? Nothing. It is Chinese, French, American . . . it is not Arab. Is a country rich that cannot make a brick, or a motorcar, or a book? It is not rich, I think.[20]

True, but why? Data on income or product per head show a high standard of living for some Arab countries—in some years higher even than that of advanced industrial nations. But this oily gain is precarious and in the long run evanescent. For one thing, petroleum is a wasting asset (it will not last forever); for another, wealth-cum-fragility invites opportunists and predators, private and public. So we have breaches of cartel agreements, and oil prices tumble;[21] or the vultures gather, especially relatives of the ruling family, to soak up the black gravy and waste it on high living;* or we have naked land grabs, as Iraq in Kuwait.† (Kuwait, of course, was just the stepping stone to the Gulf sheikhdoms and, beyond, to the huge Saudi reserves.)

Besides, not everyone has petroleum. The Muslim countries of the

---

* European and American university towns are a chosen mecca for student high flyers from the Middle East. In theory, they are going to school; what better? In fact, they support the local clubs, dens, dives, casinos. See Michele McPhee, "The Euro-Brats of Boston," *Boston Globe,* 20 September 1995, p. 77. To judge from the contents, the title is a misnomer; but it is "politically correct."

† Not everyone would agree that Iraq was the predator in invading Kuwait. Some scholars, both Arab and Western apologists for the Iraqi position, have argued that Saddam Hussein was lured in (Samir Amin), or "almost invited in" (Edward Said); or that the attack was justified in the higher cause of Arab unity, or of the mobilization against Zionism (Saddam as Bismarck or Saladin); or, implicitly, that this was a not unreasonable way to raise issues of international disagreement (Noam Chomsky). Such arguments tell volumes about the appeal and immanence of violence in the Arab world (even if Israel did not exist, they would be at one another's throats)—more on this below; and about the debasement and corruption of truth and intellectual argument in the higher cause of nationalism and anti-Westernism (anti-Americanism). The best source is Makiya, *Cruelty and Silence,* ch. 8: "New Nationalist Myths."

Middle East are either rich or poor depending on whether they have oil and have few or many people. The richest have lots of oil and few people (Saudia Arabia, Kuwait); the poorest have little oil and lots of people (Egypt); and in between are those that have oil but too many people (Iraq, Iran). The poor call for solidarity, but the rich have more immediate worries. They feel insecure, for wealth sleeps badly in a bed of poverty. So they try to buy their safety by paying off potential rebels or enemies; or they order costly arms from advanced industrial nations in the hope of getting their protection.[22] (One wants to take care of the customers.) Meanwhile the poor ones (such as Pakistan) make children and, when possible, export them; or sell them to richer co-religionists as servants, menial labor, or sources of pleasure.

No solution there; just first aid and crisis managment. Rich or poor, these countries are without exception despotisms, where leaders are not responsible, actions are unpredictable, loyalty is a ruse or a mirage of propaganda, and everything, including the economy, is subordinated to politics and can be turned around by an event. Instead of courting legitimacy by appeals to material improvement—have I made you better off?—Arab leaders have boasted of victories over colonialism or Zionism and waved the bloody shirt of jihad, promising to put history right.[23] I recall a conversation in Amman back in 1968. A leading American (Jewish) scientist was trying to persuade a group of local notables of the advantages of peace: knowledge and collaboration, he urged, could make the desert bloom. (This had long been a theme of liberal Zionist discourse.) In vain; his Arab interlocutors told him they had more pressing things to do—first of all, to defeat Israel. Prosperity could follow.

It is still following. Nor will it come, other than locally, even if the "peace process" succeeds. For the ill is far more general than the Israeli-Arab conflict.

It lies, I would argue, with the culture, which (1) does not generate an informed and capable workforce; (2) continues to mistrust or reject new techniques and ideas that come from the enemy West (Christendom);* and (3) does not respect such knowledge as members do manage to achieve, whether by study abroad or by good fortune at home. At the most elementary level, the rates of illiteracy are scandalously

---

* Thus Islam has long exercised a retardative influence on Arab intellectual and scientific activity. New knowledge and ideas have fallen under suspicion as *bid'a* or heresy. The subtext is that they represent an unacceptable insult to timeless truth. Cf. Tibi, *Islam*, p. 145.

high, and much higher for women than for men. That alone speaks of
a society that accords women an inferior place, and this is clearly related
to attitudes cultivated in Islam and especially in the Islam of the Arab
world.

A word of caution. Many Middle Eastern specialists, keen to defend
Islam against (Western) denigration or condescension, insist that Muslim gender relations, though shaped by religious doctrine, are in great
part independent of it. Among their arguments: these rules and practices
go back to pre-Islamic times, or were learned from non-Arab peoples,
or were linked to income and status (rich men's wives did not have to
work or shop), or were a response to the threats of urban life, shielding
women against insults to personal and family honor. They have a point:
*If Islam were to disappear tomorrow, Arab men would still see women as*
*they do today.* Other scholars, sometimes the same, stress the allegedly
hostile motivations of Western scholars: "orientalist" scorn and malev-
olence, "essentialist" ignorance and foolishness. The use of such pejorative code words is to dismiss rather than refute. Very convenient.

So these customs go way back; and once they were sanctified by
holy writ, they took on authority and rigor. Yet even sacred texts are
not immutable: "There has been much breaking and bending of
Quranic admonitions throughout Muslim history."[24] And indeed,
women's status in Arab lands does show changes backward and forward over time—now more liberal, now reactionary. One reads of exceptional figures: queens and princesses who have reigned, even
governed (also political leaders such as Benazir Bhutto in Pakistan,
Khaleda Zia in Bangladesh, and Tansu Çiller in Turkey); or of "liberated" women who have lived in the West and brought new attitudes
home with them, often to the shock of their more conventional compatriots. One even hears of lords and masters mocked in the privacy of
the harem (what is privacy good for?); and one buys a new kind of intimate, best-selling autobiography recounting the abuses of male domination (a call for help and a school for scandal).[25]

The historian Bernard Lewis, among others, tells us that "the steady
march of [Muslim] women into the public arena, as important players
in the economy and increasingly important players in politics, is . . . ir-
reversible and of enormous significance."[26] Women have the vote now
in Turkey, Egypt, and Iran, and even the Ayatollah Khomeini, fundamentalist though he was, never suggested that women should lose that
right.[27]

I am skeptical. I don't know what constitutes "important players."
Nor would I anticipate an early transformation of structures that rest

on the male-female divider. Halim Barakat, Arab sociologist and novelist, while acknowledging the subordinate status of women, tells us that "change toward the emancipation of women must [will] begin by transforming the prevailing socioeconomic structures to eliminate all forms of exploitation and domination."[28] (If that's what it takes, we're talking about the millennium.) Nor would I rest too much hope on the right to vote: for Arab politicians, especially the more conservative, the women's vote is a useful electoral card. The vote, yes; power, no.

Arab Muslim men, it seems to me, have been largely unmoved by these small innovations and pockets of resistance. For one thing, the lessons are blurred by the readiness of many (most?) women to accept and defend the old ways.* For another, gender privileges will not be taken; they must be surrendered. It is male opinion and behavior that matter (the men run the show), and their quasi-unanimous sense of superiority is little affected by occasional feminist challenges. The men will not be converted or intimidated by miniskirts in Beirut, only scandalized and confirmed in their sense of women's dire, demonic corporality.[†]

The economic implications of gender discrimination are most serious. To deny women is to deprive a country of labor and talent,** but—even worse—*to undermine the drive to achievement of boys and men*.[‡] One

---

* Cf. a mini-review (*TLS*, 1 Oct. 1993, p. 28) of a book by Arlene E. MacLeod, *Working Women, the New Veiling, and Change in Cairo* (New York: Columbia, 1993), which argues that veiling is both symbolism and the resolution of a double dilemma: it protests loss of identity and status and "signals women's acceptance and acquiescence to a view of women as sexually suspect and naturally suited only to the home." So we have resistance *cum* acquiescence—an "accommodating protest." If such double-think and double-talk are true—and they may be—abandon all hope, ye women of Cairo.

† Nor will they be cowed by feminist political agitation in other, more liberal Muslim lands. On the effort to redefine Islam in this regard, see Barbara Crossette, "Muslim Women's Movement Is Gaining Strength," *N.Y. Times*, 12 May 1996, p. A-3. On contrasts within Islam, see Ash Devare, "For Indonesian Families, Smaller Is Now Better," *Boston Globe*, 23 June 1996, p. 69.

** Not everyone would agree. In a letter to *The New York Times* of 26 July 1995, William J. Parente, who signs as professor of political science in the University of Scranton, argues against the "liberation of women" in Arab countries because they "would flood Arab labor markets and further depress wages."

‡ The demographic consequences are also serious. The ability of women to earn money in the workplace is critical to their status within the household and their say in family planning. It is negatively correlated, for example, with reproduction. Cf. Dasgupta, "Population Problem." It is no accident that a decision by a Muslim wife (often a woman of non-Muslim origin) to go to work outside the home (or even to leave the home without the husband's consent) is perceived as a threat to marital harmony and to the dignity and honor of the husband, and is treated accordingly. Cf. Goodwin, *Price of Honor, passim*; Barakat, *Arab World*, p. 101.

cannot rear young people in such wise that half of them think themselves superior by biology, without dulling ambition and devaluing accomplishment. One cannot call male children "Pasha," or, as in Iran, tell them that they have a golden penis, without reducing their need to learn and do.[29] To be sure, any society will have its achievers no matter what, if only because it has its own division of tasks and spoils. But it cannot compete with other societies that ask performance from the full pool of talent.

In general, the best clue to a nation's growth and development potential is the status and role of women. This is the greatest handicap of Muslim Middle Eastern societies today, the flaw that most bars them from modernity. To be sure, other societies depreciate women and adulate men. No one is pure. Think of Latin America with its *machismo,* or Japan with its male bonding and fatherless homes.[30] Even the so-called advanced societies of the West can do better in this regard. But if we view gender relations as a continuum running from nothing to full equality, the Muslim countries, and especially the Arab Muslim countries, would bottom out the scale. The women are humiliated from birth. The message: their very existence is a disaster, their body a sin.[31] The boys learn that they can hit their sisters, older and younger, with impunity—as I have seen one do, in public, before the eyes of his unprotesting mother. The sister did not even defend herself. Bad for the girls, but just as bad for the boys.

Is such a failing somehow inherent in Islam? No. Islam is multifarious. Global in its reach, it embraces a diversity of societies (and parts of societies) and cultures. It also contains within its sacred writings many lessons, some of them contradictory, which can be used to almost any purpose. The political scientist Fouad Ajami reminds us how, when the Muslim Brotherhood condemned Egypt's peace treaty with Israel, the Egyptian government promptly got the University of al-Azhar in Cairo to declare the treaty in harmony with Islamic law.[32] Interpretation varies, then, with time, place, and constituency.

Even so, one must not niggle or rule out generalization. This is a favorite line of defense by Muslim apologists, embarrassed by laws and institutions that are not thought "progressive," and quick to cite exceptions and variants. But Muslim societies do have common characteristics that rest on a shared faith. That both the Middle Eastern state and its opposition appeal to Islam for justification and support tells volumes about the authority of religious discourse. Islam is the argument that carries, and it carries backward as easily as forward.

One defence would dismiss the regressive influence of Islam by pointing to Muslim economic, spiritual, and intellectual openness in an earlier golden age. If they could do it then, the reasoning goes, they can do it now.* One would like to say yes, but for two reasons. First, the scope of competition and level of performance required is far greater now than it once was. The meaning of "modern" has changed drastically, far more than Islam. (Such an argument is like saying that because the British used to produce tennis champions, they should be able to turn them out today.)†

Secondly, failure to keep up generates its own immune reactions. In this regard, the huge oil windfall has been a monumental misfortune.[33] It has intoxicated rulers, henchmen, and purveyors, who have slept on piles of money, wasted it on largely worthless projects, and managed to exceed their figuratively (but not literally) limitless resources. Even Saudi Arabia cannot balance its books. In the process these spoilers have infuriated the Muslim poor, who in turn have sought an outlet for rage and outrage in fundamentalist doctrine.

This is the saddest part of the story. Islam, like all religions, has its pure and hard core, and in a society of extreme *machismo,* the combination can be explosive. Hence the quick recourse to violence, for *violence is the quintessential, testosteronic expression of male entitlement.* Hence massacre of religious opponents in Syria; revolution and suppression in Iran; autocratic despotism in Iraq and the Sudan; poison gas attacks against Kurds in Iraq; genocide in the black south of the Sudan; both random and targeted murder in Pakistan, Egypt, and Algeria.** The Algerian violence tells it all: there we have, not a civil war, but a war against civilians. A favorite murder mode: slit the throat. That saves bullets and brings the killer closer to God.[34] Gunmen have killed young women who refuse to 'marry' the heroes of the revolution.

---

* They *will* do it now, says Mohammed Talbi, historian and former dean at the University of Tunis. Talbi reminds us that for all the episodes of Muslim intolerance, the Muslim world has not been guilty of "systematic forcible conversion, nor arbitrary ghettoization, nor total and massive expulsion, nor genocide, nor, need it be said, a Holocaust." *Le Figaro,* 27 March 1997, p. B-27. His account is somewhat overkind, but the favorable comparison of Islamic with Christian persecution of minorities (implicitly Jews) is correct.

† The last of them, Fred Perry, champion in the 1930s, is memorialized by a statue at the entrance to Wimbledon: a memento of and salute to a happier era.

** An article by Jean-Paul Mari, "Enquête sur le massacre d'un peuple: Algérie: au delà de l'horreur," *Le nouvel observateur,* 23–29 March 1995, p. 58, remarks: "Algeria has always believed that only violence can found [establish] something." For more on this, see Miller, *God Has Ninety-nine Names,* pp. 168 ff. See also Fisk, "Sept journées."

These thugs see themselves as entitled, *first as men,* then as soldiers in the cause.

The most striking aspect of the Algerian fundamentalist campaign is its rapidity—how little time it took to turn the clock back centuries.

> "My name is Ozymandias, king of kings:
> Look on my works, ye Mighty, and despair!"
> Nothing beside remains . . . boundless and bare
> The lone and level sands stretch far away.

## Orientalists and Essentialists

Scholarly emotions run high on Middle Eastern matters. Readers and audiences know the answers in advance. Debates, often angry or sullen, are anything but debates. No one is ready to check his gun at the door; it may be needed. Among the *casus belli:* the Arab-Israeli conflict; European economic imperialism, formal and informal; and Western criticisms (hence slanders) of Arab or Islamic culture, especially the treatment of women.

In these circumstances, much of the debate has taken the form of name-calling. The purpose (or effect) of these labels is to marginalize or exclude the adversary. He is a . . . (fill in the classifier). Nothing more need be said.

The most influential of these dismissive strikes has been the invention of "orientalism." This is the sin of writing about Asia, but especially the Middle East, from the outside, that is, from the standpoint of the condescending, hostile, exploitative West. Attacks on the once respectable fascination with things Eastern go back at least to the 1960s; but it was the publication in 1978 of Edward Said's book of this name *(Orientalism)* that gave the charges currency and called into question most Western writing on the Middle East.[35] The bill of indictment ran as follows:

1. Studies by outsiders distort the subject of inquiry by turning persons into objects. These objects are by definition ripe for manipulation and domination. For Said, such systems as orientalism are "discourses of power, ideological fictions—mind-forg'd manacles."

2. Such pseudo-scholarship tends to stereotype in time and space. "Orientals"—the very designation is a Eurocentric imposition—are the same through the ages, and this essential sameness results from a perdurable Islam that "never changes." Hence the intellectual fellow-disease of "essentialism." Orientalists have no room for details, nuances, or texture.

3. Stereotyping lends itself to racism and prejudice. It separates one group from another, promotes arrogance on one side, resentment on the other. If we could get rid of "the Orient," we would have "scholars, critics, intellectuals, human beings, for whom the racial, ethnic, and national distinctions [are] less important than the common enterprise of promoting human community."[36]

One can hardly quarrel with lofty sentiments, but sentiments are not enough. The effort to purge the field of these factitious diseases has become an assault on knowledge. In the first place, the anti-"orientalist" method would exclude indispensable tools of inquiry. As any good comparativist knows, distinctions are the stuff of understanding. The anti-"orientalist" cannot have it both ways— denounce, that is, the pursuit of distinctive characteristics as "essentialist," while calling for an understanding of intergroup differences. It is this understanding that turns diversity into a sense of common humanity.

Ironically, those very "orientalists" so roundly condemned here— those philologists, archeologists, and travelers, sand-smitten Westerners in Middle Eastern garb—were desperately in love with the Arab Muslim world. Some of them were searching for paradise lost. To quote from an epigraph to a recent book: "The attraction, the spell of Arabia, as it is so frequently called, is a sickness of the imagination."[37] Today these orientalists are reproved as pretentious, racist imperialists. So much for their romance: no kindly sentiment goes unpunished. They were sincere? So what? Sincerity is the cheapest of virtues.

Secondly, the reality of nuance does not rule out the light that comes from generalization. Everything, to be sure, is more complex than appears. Every person, every event is unique. Even so, some effort must be made to simplify, to find patterns. Otherwise we have nothing but a grab bag of unrelated data.

Thirdly, bad news is not necessarily wrong. Substantive observations may cast an unfavorable light, but such evidence must be judged on its merits, not dismissed as *a priori* falsehood. That way lies self-censorship and dereliction of duty. Much of the anti-orientalist critique boils down to a lawyer's brief for the defense. Lawyers are paid to do that kind of thing. Scholars have a higher obligation.

In that regard, one must reject the implication that outsideness disqualifies: that only Muslims can understand Islam, only blacks understand black history, only a woman understand women's studies, and so on. That way lies separateness and a dialogue of the deaf. It also excludes the valuable insights of outsiders and lends itself to racism. I knew a Boston Brahmin once who could not understand why a student of Italian background would want to work on Christopher Columbus ("I thought Columbus was Italian," was the student's reply); and another who was surprised to find an African-American doing Roman history—as though he were any more Roman than the other.*

Discrimination in such exclusionary fields, moreover, invites a loyalty test: is a given scholar on the right side? This applies both to outsiders, who can "earn" acceptance by right-think, and to insiders, where it overrides even color. Thus an Afro-American historian or politician who does not meet the standards of political correctness is an "oreo"—which is the name of a well-known cookie consisting of a chocolate, cream-filled sandwich.

In the Middle Eastern anti-"orientalist" camp, the shibboleth is anti-Zionism. Any indulgence for Israel is proof of error and irrelevance, if not worse. Thus Edward Said and followers have worked to exclude and denigrate Bernard Lewis, a leading authority in the field, as "orientalist" and "essentialist," but also "too close to the Israeli cause to be regarded as capable of impartial judgment." To be sure, "Lewis has given as good as he has got. Nevertheless, Said's critique has found a body of support among Western scholars, while it has been echoed with relish by Islamists and others in the Middle East."[38]

On the other hand, some outside scholars qualify because they agree politically with the gatekeepers. So Edward Said makes an

---

* I consider the outside-inside dichotomy to be the most unfortunate, anti-intellectual aspect of the "orientalist" thesis. Interestingly, in an essay at self-definition destined to appear as afterword to a new edition of the Said book, he says nothing about this. Instead, he focuses on criticisms of the book's alleged anti-Westernism, which he says take the form of one or both of two erroneous inferences: that orientalism is symbolic of the entire West; and that, in distorting Islam and the Arabs, it is by implication an assault on a "perfect" system. A vigorous defense against strawmen. Said, "East Isn't East."

exception in *Orientalism* for a handful of Western scholars—pro-Palestinian, pro-Arab, pro-Muslim—who may or may not be right, but are on what he sees as the right side. Motive trumps truth and fact.[39]

That way lies censorship by exclusion and indifference. Scholarship and research are the losers.

⁌    ⁌

## Japanese Women Are Talking Tenor[40]

The Japanese case would seem to be the exception that proves the rule (everyone knows how *macho* Japanese men are), and apologists for the treatment of women in Muslim countries, or more accurately, for Arab Muslim culture, never fail to cite it by way of extenuation. If the Japanese could do so well while putting down their women, the argument runs, why label this a handicap in Muslim societies? And indeed, Japanese women have traditionally accepted inferior status, with direct economic consequences. They quit jobs after marriage and rarely reach posts that would put them in charge of men. Their very dress was traditionally designed to hobble them on the pretext of protecting their modesty and accenting their femininity. Their speech was differentiated and encumbered by a polysyllabic burden of deference; their voices were trained and tuned to a panting soprano squeak; their gestures drilled to a caricature of coy, tremulous humility. (Small wonder that Japanese men found consolation in bath- and other houses where they could meet more "natural" partners.)

Yet this artful female subordination, memorialized in Japanese prints, theater, and *samurai* films, was far more class than national practice. These were the ways of the nobility and landed gentry, those who could afford to be idle and pay for servants to minister to them. For almost all others, including wealthy commercial families, women had a duty to help manage the household (the *ie*). This meant not only keeping house and rearing children but also enforcing frugality, engaging in farming and industry, and building prosperity. Indeed, this primary task involved everyone, from husband (and maybe husband's mother) to little children. Of course the content of the task varied with social status and family income, but this common cause, which blended with the goal of national prosperity and greatness, gave women much more influence than a simplistic view of etiquette would lead one to think.

In the face, then, of conventional constraints on female behavior and rules for male precedence, the larger interest came first. Whatever the traditional discriminations, the educational authorities under Meiji (1870s on) mandated universal elementary schooling: four, later six, years for girls—enough to ensure literacy and more. Why the girls? Because the aim was modernization and equality with the West. This entailed a generalized ability to read, write, and reckon, and to help children with their lessons. Industrial development would see fathers working outside the home and farm; government and military service would also draw men away. Mothers had to fill the gap. At first, many poor families rebelled against this loss of children's earnings; school and school supplies did not come free. Some rebels went so far as to burn schools down. But the sacralization of the home as enterprise, as building block of national wealth and achievement, converted even the laggards. In 1890, only 30 percent of eligible girls attended school; twenty years later, the figure was 97.4 percent.[41]

At the same time, women's actiivities changed to fit the needs of a new economy. More and more of them found jobs outside the home, primarily in light industry (textiles, etc.), where the workforce was 60–90 percent female. These branches produced 40 percent of the GNP and 60 percent of foreign exchange at the end of the nineteenth century.[42] How were women wageearners going to rear and teach children? Answer: By leaving work upon marriage and focusing on household and family—unless of course they needed the earnings (a big "unless"). Priorities were the key: country and household first; gender next. As a result, the role of a woman was never simply reproductive. She was more than a vessel. She was a toiler, a consumer, a saver, a manager. And she always, both by right and by necessity, had access to public space. (The contrast here with Arab Muslim societies is striking and crucial.)

What Japanese women did not have was political rights. They neither voted nor governed, and Japanese men made a point of the justice of exclusion. Politics, to say nothing of military matters, were male by right and calling. (On the other hand, the Japanese military cheerfully accepted women nurses, because they released men for destructive activities.) Not until after World War II did Japanese women get the vote—no different in that respect from French women and quicker than the Swiss. Even so, they play little part in the executive branch. Again, Japan is not very different from other countries.

What has this pragmatic, partial discrimination done to men? The answer is mixed: Japanese men have enjoyed a sense of sexual privilege and superiority, which sometimes emerges on jam-packed subway trains, where anonymity protects.[43] On the other hand, Japanese men help out in domains conventionally linked to women. Here, at the very beginning of Tokugawa (1610), is a merchant instructing his son on his duties:

> With your own hands kindle the fire under the stove, for breakfast and dinner, damping the embers afterwards. . . . Going out behind the house, collect all the bits and pieces of rubbish: small lengths of rope should be cut up for mixing in cement . . . fragments of wood or broken bamboo, even as small as half an inch, should be stored, cleaned, and used as fuel for watchfires . . . when buying things for the first time . . . go out and buy for yourself. Buy at the cheapest rates, and make careful note of the prices. Afterwards . . . you will know whether the articles [the servant] brings are too expensive or not. . . . Housekeeping may be said to be a matter of firewood, charcoal, and oil. . . . No matter what his calling, if a man does not take these troubles upon himself, he can never run a household successfully.[44]

"No matter what his calling . . . " This was a merchant talking, giving expression to antique, primary virtues. Japanese male children, in other words, were spoiled and yet not spoiled.

Economic development and political transformation have changed the details, but the values remain. Schooling today is highly competitive; examinations are scenes of combat. As cities have grown, commuting to work is a long travail. Fathers see much less of home and children, but that has only enhanced the role and responsibilities of women. Also soured many of them on the alleged joys of marriage. Women now attend universities with the men, get advanced degrees, seek executive careers. They still bump against the glass ceiling, and they remain shy, even tongue-tied, in the presence of men. But many are ready to give up on family to concentrate on career. In a society where male commuters have little time for wife and children, single women do not want for attention. Muslims would say, I told you so.

When I visited Japan in 1991 and was received to dinner, the hostess, if grandmotherly, would decline to dine with the men, but she served. If younger, she ate with us, and the children too. In an

Arab house some years earlier, the women prepared the meal, but did not serve or even appear; the host received and served his guests. Two worlds.

There remains a common thread: Japanese society also has its testosteronic bravado and taste for violence. Japan has a long history of wars of aggression and oppression, all of them justified by national necessity. Nothing has done more to propel Japan. Nothing has done so much to set it back.

# ~ 25 ~

# Empire and After

Furopean overseas empire began in the fifteenth century with the Atlantic islands (Canaries, Madeiras) and pieces of North Africa, and more or less ended in the second half of the twentieth. Five hundred years of dominion, a long time. And yet, for all of colonialism's enormous effects, it was a passing phenomenon in the larger sweep of world history. Pomp and pride on the one side, humiliations on the other—all are gone. Not forgotten; the memories remain. Yet the losses are reparable; the gains are savable; the tasks and opportunities lie ahead.

*Empire, imperialism; colony, colonialism;* the terms need definition.* *Imperialism* is the system ("principle or spirit") and pursuit of empire—the dominion of one country over others. Empires arose as states arose, one stronger than another. Given this long pedigree and the link of empire to military conquest and diplomatic enterprise, to sta-

---

* For an excellent discussion of these terms and distinctions over time, space, and ideologies, see Klor de Alva, "Postcolonization." He is more discriminating than I, especially in his use of *imperialism* and *colonialism* and in his distinction between *postcolonialism* and *postcoloniality*. His approach has its advantages, but I shall trade nuance for brevity.

tus, power, and wealth, *"empire"* and *"imperialism"* have been (once were) proud words. Thus the last gasp of King George V in January 1936: "How is the Empire?"

To note that empires go back to the dawn of history may seem a truism, but in fact it is no trivial assertion. Some insist, for example, that imperialism, which peaked around the end of the nineteenth century, is somehow an invention or by-product of modern capitalism—in Lenin's words, "the highest stage of capitalism." Building on this, they argue that empire was necessary (indispensable) to the prosperity and survival of modern capitalism. The tenacity of this belief can be measured by a copious literature averring that imperialism aimed above all at material gain, even where it manifestly cost and lost.[1]

History belies such intrinsic links to capitalism. Consider the ancient empires of Egypt, China, Assyria, Persia, Rome, etc.; or, in modern times, the late, unlamented Communist-Socialist empire of the Soviet Union. That so much ink has been spilled on this issue reflects the need to discredit the imperialists and capitalists by way of encouraging resistance and revolution. They're in it for the money—what can be worse? Meanwhile bad definitions and explanations lead to bad conclusions.

*Colonialism* is *imperialism* writ dark: "For many it implies unjust social asymmetries, human abuses, and moral imperatives, which call for acts of resistance, demands for justice, and struggles for liberation."[2] The word *"colony"* started innocently enough: in the ancient world it meant a place of distant settlement—the Phoenician colony of Carthage or the Greek colonies in Italy. But settlement, we now know, implies some kind of displacement (nothing is so scarce as empty land), hence cannot be good or virtuous, at least not for the victims; so that settlement as system (colonialism) is clearly bad. In recent discourse, *colonialism* has broadened to denote "any economically or politically dependent condition," whether or not it leads to displacement of the native population.[3] This pejorative quality has led modern critics of foreign (Western) dominion to prefer *colonialism* to the older term of *imperialism*. *Colonialism* sounds worse.

European imperialism (colonialism)—I shall use the two terms interchangeably—goes back to the Middle Ages, to the *Drang nach Osten* (push to the east) of Teutons conquering Slavic lands, to the invasions by Norsemen of England and Normandy and by the English of Ireland, to the *reconquista* in Spain.[4] Much of this expansion took the form of absorption. The conquerors melted into the indigenous population, to the point of effacing their own identity, or swallowed the conquered. (The tests are intermarriage, language, and personal names.)* Thus the Normans defeated the Anglo-Saxons (1066 and after), who had earlier chased out the Romans and subdued the native Britons (a Celtic people who had themselves conquered the native inhabitants), driving many of the Celtic speakers before them into Wales and across the Channel into what came to be known as Brittany. To this day speakers of Breton can listen to radio broadcasts in Welsh and understand much of what is said.†

The whole island of Britain, in other words, is a palimpsest of successive invasions and seizures, most of which have blurred into a unitary society; although some members of the conquered Welsh and Scots populations still dream of earlier independence and distinctive identity. One can find similar foci of grievance in the Basque country of Spain (but less in that of France), in Catalonia and Corsica, in the debris of the old Habsburg and Romanov empires; and the current tragedy of Bosnia reminds us that memories of defeat and conquest do last, or can be reawakened and manipulated, and that life is short but revenge long. The Turks defeated the Serbs at Kossovo in 1389; the Turks have long forgotten, but the Serbs have made reversal of this defeat the lodestone of their national aspirations.

One can continue around the world. Over long centuries, the Chinese drove to the south, subjugating and absorbing non-Han peoples. The Japanese conquered their "home" islands from the Ainu, reducing them to a relic in the far north. The Burmese migrated from their original home in Mongolia and gave their name to a land far to the south, absorbing most of the natives but leaving a number of peoples to fight with to the present day. The Arabs burst out of the desert into the Fertile Crescent, then swept across North Africa, converting most of their subjects to Islam. They carved out Muslim states, and their language became the common definer of these diverse populations. (As of 1998, the only official language in once-French Algeria will be Arabic.) As a result, our Eurocentric term *Middle East* extends to the African shores of the Atlantic.

Clearly, the common view of imperialism as a Western invention and

---

* Cf. the *Polyptique* of Irminon, a census of the population of the estates of the abbey of Saint-Germain (just outside of Paris) in the early ninth century. Who bears a Frankish name and who a Gallo-Roman one?

† Later incursions and invasions by Danes led in the ninth century to cession of a substantial area in eastern England that was known as the Danelaw (Danelagh). The Danish invaders intermarried with the residents, and a half-century later the area was reabsorbed into the English kingdom.

monopoly visited on non-European peoples is wrong.* Yet that is what most people think of as imperialism. To be sure, something different happened when Europeans sailed or rode around the world and subdued strange tribes and nations by means of superior weapons and knowledge. These far places and peoples were culturally, geographically, and physically distant. Whereas earlier conquests were next door and implied absorption or assimilation, these strange lands were viewed as prizes, as fields of opportunity—not as components, but as annexes. The native population? A lesser breed—usable, improvable, but not potentially European. The mother country did not envisage a fusion of old and new, though this could and did happen, as in Spanish America and in Portuguese colonies in both the New and Old worlds.† Sport tells the story. In 1898, a British governor in West Africa had two cricket pitches built, one for Europeans, the other for natives. When the two teams sportingly played each other, these games became racial contests; and when the African side began to win, the competition had to be discontinued.[5] We have come a long way since then: less colonial pride and more colonial losses.

The annexation and exploitation of these distant lands took many forms. For the Spaniards, the heart of the matter was treasure. Their empire consisted of veins of ore linked to local and regional supply lines of labor, food, and manufactures, and to sea lines stretching back to Europe. The Portuguese in Asia, on the other hand, worked in lands inhabited by much larger and, for them, unconquerable populations. They had to build on small, defensible holdings such as Goa—points of presence—and radiate from there, buying, selling, and extorting protection money from local merchants.**

---

* Exception is sometimes made for modern Japan; but what of precolonial Africa? The same "progressive" thinkers who denounce European colonialism are quick enough to take pride in the expansion of the Zulu or Ashante. On this manichean view of world history, setting the demonic white man against victimized people of color, see Bruckner's emphatic *Tears of the White Man.*

† Thus the Spanish government originally envisaged keeping Spaniards and Indians apart, but the inevitable unions of invaders and natives *(castas)* led to a large mixed population that, owing to the ravages of disease, almost came to equal in numbers the Indians of pure race. It was this *mestizo* and *criollo* group that deliberately separated itself from the *castas* and eventually led the rebellion against Spanish rule and took over the new nations—Klor de Alva, "Postcolonization."

** Contrast in this regard Portuguese empire in Asia with that in South America (Brazil) and Africa (Angola and Mozambique). On these other continents, they encountered sparse populations lacking the political organization to oppose a serious resistance. So they took territory, with boundaries long undefined.

The Dutch and English sought trade, although commerce often led to intervention in local quarrels and land takings. Government and security cost money, for men of war and men at arms. But territory could be turned into privilege and monopoly, and the costs of governance could be shifted to both the home country and the subject population. Besides, the proconsuls in the field had their own agenda; the Spanish were not the only conquistadores.

Once installed, Dutch and British aimed at managed cultivation, going well beyond what nature provided. Empire is a story of botanical enterprise, moving crops to soils and climes of opportunity: sugar starting in the Indian Ocean and working round the globe to the Caribbean islands; tea transplanted from China to India and Ceylon (India tea vs. China tea); rubber seeds smuggled from Brazil and planted in Malaya; cinchona (source of quinine) from South America to St. Helena to Java; oleaginous plants from the New World to West Africa; coffee here, cocoa there. Here the Royal Botanic Gardens at Kew on the banks of the Thames, a princess's hobby to start with, played a leading role—a model of science and commerce conjoined. All of this was more profitable and durable than pillage or extraction, though obviously no one objected to treasure trove—over the centuries, diamonds in India and South Africa, gold in Australia and Africa, oil in Burma and the East Indies.

Private and special interests got in the way of rational, prudent intentions. The merchants themselves sought trade, not territory as such. They would have done business with the devil if it meant profits. But they did not want to be robbed or bullied by native dealers or officials, who saw all traders as potential prey. So when Europeans ran into trouble, they called on their home governments for help.

Governments typically pitched in. To be sure, their starchy, largely incompetent representatives, selected more for family and political connections than for merit, adored form and protocol.* (The biographies of these stuffed shirts make one wonder how the British ever built and held an empire. But a few exceptional individuals could make up for a horde of placemen, the more so as genteel favorites were only too happy to leave the work to their subordinates.) These wellborn officials

---

* Here is Sir George Robinson, Superintendant of British traders at Canton, groveling before Lord Palmerston in London: "I trust it is not necessary for me to add anything like an assurance of the most profound deference and respect with which I shall implicitly obey and execute the very spirit of such instructions as I may have the honour to receive, on this or any other point. Strict undeviating obedience to the orders and directions of which I may be in possession . . . is the foundation on which I

often resented the traders as crass and rude, greedy and importunate. Too bad. Businessmen were only too ready to go "outside channels" and appeal directly to London or Paris, where money counted.

Besides, officials had their own care for promotions and enrichment. Empire drew such types, men who did not want to spend their lives as magistrate in some bucolic home county, men of pride and power and, if we are to believe the reports, men sometimes drawn by the sexual ambiguities and freedoms of an interracial, anomic world. These were not healthful climes, and many an official died early; they drank like fish, and alcohol is a poison. But vigorous, mettlesome men think themselves immortal. Meanwhile they spoke of "duty" and "improvement"—a "call" to higher things.[6]

Higher things included conquest, "dominion over palm and pine." The sages in the Colonial Office might try to leash agents abroad, but it took months for instructions to arrive, plenty of time for the fait accompli. *"Peccavi* [I have sinned]," wrote Sir Charles Napier to his superiors in London—a one-word pun to soften his disobedience in taking Sindh in 1842 in the face of explicit orders to the contrary. So over the centuries, bit by bit and bite by bite, the British, for example, found themselves picking up large and small pieces of territory: the whole of India, much of Burma, Canada all the way to the Pacific, Australia and New Zealand, plus watering holes and refueling stations, strategic power points, refuges along the major trade routes and on the periphery of great markets (thus Gibraltar, Malta, St. Helena, Capetown, Bombay, Singapore, Hong Kong, Aden). Such places paid their cost and made a string of pearls around the globe. Some of them were prizes of imperial ambition; others, of mercantile interest. But at bottom, all of them were the reward of superior power.*

In the old days, students of world (or European) history learned of "Old" and "New" empires. The old were the territories taken from

---

build. . . . " At the end of two years of this, this toady was peremptorily fired. In mitigation, Sir George was acting in the best English courtly tradition. Cf. William Pitt's effusive gushings to King George III—Cook, *The Long Fuse,* p. 111.

* Frontiers were the lines of encounter of stronger and weaker, hence loci of testing and conflict. The Earl of Carnarvon spoke in 1878 of "the difficulties of frontier": "The same provocations, real or supposed . . . the same temptation of those on the spot to acquire territory" were a universal characteristic of empire—Hyam, *Britain's Imperial Century,* p. 283. On imperialism as an expression of disparity of power, see Landes, "Some Thoughts on the Nature of Economic Imperialism" and "An Equilibrium Model of Imperialism."

about 1500 to 1800: the American dominions of Spain, the English and French holdings in North America, the Portuguese, Dutch, and British grabs in the Indian Ocean. Then, around the turn to the nineteenth century, almost all of the American portions of these "old empires" broke away from the mother country. For many in Europe, these losses proved the folly of the whole enterprise: was ever so much wasted by so many on so few? As a result, we were taught, the appetite for colonies abated. For a century after 1763 (Treaty of Paris between Britain and France), imperialism was said to be marking time.

British domestic politics gave substance to this chronology. The Whigs, ever practical, called the whole business a mistake, money thrown away on uncivilized, ungrateful, disloyal subjects (George Washington and company)—"shrewd, artful, and cunning people."[7] Some even advocated freeing colonies that had not asked for independence.

But of course not. Something so clearly the expression of power was not going to stop just as the Industrial Revolution was empowering Europeans and enhancing their ability to survive in once fatal environments. To the contrary, imperialism was very busy during these decades, as the French Algerian venture (1830), the British occupation of India and advances in Burma, the Russian conquests in Siberia and the Caucasus, and the American expansion westward—among others—all showed. It was the historians who had a blind spot; that, and a doctrinaire notion that empire had to wait for the call of a mature (fading?) capitalism.

This call, we were taught, explained the "New Imperialism." Beginning in the late 1860s, the growing indocility of the proletariat at home turned covetous eyes toward exploitable workers abroad. Africa in particular, but also pieces of Asia and Pacific islands, became targets of opportunity for all the major European nations. Among them, Germany, which belatedly decided that it could not be a world power without overseas possessions. When the dust had settled, all of Africa lay under one or another European government. The only exceptions: Liberia, an American project for returning blacks to their home; and Ethiopia, which the Italians tried to grab and failed.

This "New Imperialism" differed from the Old. It too was supposedly based on rational, material interest, but in fact these late acquisitions promised little. To be sure, some of the lands did contain potentially valuable resources, but these treasures were generally unknown at the time of annexation. Much of the land-grabbing was strategic (cf. Cape to Cairo) or preemptive (better mine than yours).

Subsequent discoveries were happy surprises and sometimes so changed the incentives as to provoke new fighting for control. Thus southern African gold mines drew a flood of rough-and-ready prospectors to the Transvaal, spawned disputes with the Afrikaner authorities, brought Britain into the quarrel, and led to the Boer War.

Radical and skeptical observers denounced this late land grab as, first, the product of capitalist greed, and then of need—a prior condition of European prosperity. The first was partly true. Greed now had free play—not necessarily capitalist greed, but simple human greed. Thanks to repeating rifles and machine guns, grabbing and killing were now easy—so easy that European brutes rejoiced at massacring natives like game birds and called them "brutes." (For so-called gentlemen, hunting was a school for brutality and cowardice. It still is.) Here is the young Winston Churchill, anticipating the imminent battle of Omdurman, revenge for Gordon at Khartum: " . . . a good moment to live," he wrote, and: "Of course we should win. Of course we should mow them down." And: "Nothing like the battle of Omdurman will ever be seen again. It was the last link in the long chain of those spectacular conflicts whose vivid and majestic splendour has done so much to invest war with glamour." Native peoples soon learned to disappoint their conquerors by giving up too quickly. No killing; no medals and promotions.[8]

The second assertion, that Europe needed these acquisitions for capitalism's sake, is simply nonsense. Some businessmen made money in these strange and distant places; many more did not. But European economies as economies gained little if anything from these exotic connections. Good businessmen knew it. When Belgium's King Leopold, venality wearing a crown, invited the German banker Gerson Bleichröder to help with his huge domain in the Congo, Bleichröder politely declined. He was as interested as any good banker in the opportunities of such a partnership, but he could spot a clinker a long way off. A few years later (early 1880s), Bismarck thought to pick up some pieces in far-off Africa and among the Pacific islands. Would Bleichröder help? Here the banker had to be more forthcoming, because Bismarck was his private client and patron; even so, he asked for a guaranteed minimum return.

The public was a different matter. You can fool some businessmen some of the time; politicians much of the time; and voters almost all the time. Listen to Paul Leroy-Beaulieu explain to the French electorate why imperialism was a good thing: "The most useful function that colonies perform . . . is to supply the mother country's trade with a ready-made market to get its industry going and maintain it, and to supply the inhabitants of the mother country—whether industrialists, workers, or consumers—with increased profits, wages, or commodities." So colonial expansion became a *leitmotif* of electoral blather. No coy political correctness in those innocent times, but little accuracy either. Today's historians and political economists should know better than to take these campaign promises seriously.

Must one take a country to make a market? Here, too, scholarship has offered a reinterpretation. Where once historians wrote of (formal) empire, now they began to look more closely at informal dominion.[9] Take the history of European presence and influence in the Middle East. The region included the Ottoman empire, independent in name but increasingly subject to European demands; and Egypt, under Ottoman suzerainty but really in the European sphere of influence. No history of nineteenth-century Egyptian economic and political development would make sense that did not attend to the impact of informal, virtual controls.[10] The same for Persia, never a colony, but like the Ottoman empire more independent in memory than in reality.

One could say the same of European dominion in Latin America. Here an entire continent, once largely divided between Spain and Portugal, became formally independent by the 1820s except for a few minor gores and islands in the Caribbean. What's more, the very possibility of new territorial grabs in the western hemisphere was largely excluded by the Monroe doctrine.* Not that European powers were absolutely cowed by this unilateral declaration of the president of the American republic. One could perhaps get around it by using strawmen, as the French tried with Maximilian in Mexico.† But the threat of American intervention now entered the calculus, a deterrent to imperialist ambitions. No matter. More money could be made by trade:

* The formal declaration was made by President James Monroe in 1823, but was in fact written by John Quincy Adams and was foreshadowed by earlier statements of George Washington and Thomas Jefferson. The immediate impetus came from the successful revolt of the former Spanish colonies and the threats of European intervention to restore the *status quo ante;* also from hints of possible Russian expansion along the Pacific coast of North America. The declaration was never formalized by an act of Congress but it was accepted thereafter as an expression of American policy.

† The only reason that worked even for a short time was that the United States was busy with its own Civil War. But once the Americans turned their attention to this interloper and gave aid to the native resistance, Maximilian was doomed. His own European sponsors wrung their hands but abandoned him to the firing squad—*raison d'état.*

public works concessions, loan contracts, favorable market arrangements. It is no accident that much of the literature on dependency has been the work of Latin American economists and political scientists. They feel, with some justice, that their part of the world, though nominally free, has been put down and looted by stronger partners.

Formal empire is now a great rarity. Much here depends on definition (is Puerto Rico a colony of the United States?), but one still finds odd pieces (Guam, Samoa, Bermuda, the French DOM-TOM [*départements and territoires d'outre-mer*]) that come under someone else's rule. Sometimes, as with Bermuda, or New Caledonia, or Puerto Rico, the dependents prefer it that way because dependency pays.* Panama, after years of "working for the Yankee dollaaaah," as the old song has it, is also thinking twice about American departure from the Canal Zone. But most lands that were once colonies, dependencies, protectorates, dominions, metropolitan departments, or overseas departments are now free. Given the sensibility of once subject populations and accumulated resentments of subjugation and humiliation, material advantages have rarely stood up to separatism.

A wave of liberations more than tripled the world's nations after World War II. Each of these newcomers, however small and artificial, was sovereign and enjoyed a vote in the United Nations. Freedom promised growth and prosperity to countries once exploited, and—the important reverse of the coin—portended shrinkage to the capitalist nations that had thrived on oppression of others and would now have to make it on their own. Justice would be done.

Things have not worked out that way. Once-imperialist economies have prospered as never before. And most of the former colonial nations have found it hard to get on track. Their colonial masters, afraid of their incipient nationalism and contemptuous of their abilities, had not taught them much—barely enough to do the subaltern tasks of government. White rulers dreaded educated natives: detribalized, filled with "inappropriate" aspirations, they were, in the words of one British official (1886), "the curse of the [African] west coast."[11] The British, for all their reliance on local elites, systematically excluded these *déracinés* (uprooted ones) from posts of responsibility in government and trade.

---

* France is a holdout for global dominion, primarily for reasons of prestige and self-esteem. Such vanity costs, and the French, pressed by European constraints to reduce their budget deficit, are supposedly reconsidering—*Wall Street Journal*, 25 January 1996, p. 1. Don't count on it.

So, although the colonialists often left behind an infrastructure of roads, ports, railroads, and buildings, maintenance was another matter. The ability of the ex-colonies to neglect and run down their material legacy was stunning, as visitors could attest. (The same thing happened in central and East European countries drawn into the inept bureaucratic world of socialism.)[12] Much of what these subject populations learned in the schools and universities of the colonial master was political and social discourse rather than applied science and technical know-how—the makings of revolution rather than production. And maybe that was the first priority: freedom first, economy later; because freedom is a necessary if not sufficient condition of development.

The first post-freedom numbers for product and income per head were encouraging, but probably misleading. They reflected more appearance than reality. As more transactions became commercialized, for example, as more product went to market rather than to home consumption, the results showed up in the data where they had not before. Economic pundits predicted bright futures for such ex-colonies as Nigeria (oil), Ivory Coast/Côte d'Ivoire (cocoa), Algeria (oil and gas).

Then disappointment. Few of these ex-colonies maintained consistent growth per head,* and their dependence on highly variable terms of trade (agricultural commodities vs. manufactures) inflicted painful swings in income. As President Julius Nyerere of Tanzania complained in 1976, why should his country have to give twice as many bales of sisal this year as last to buy the same farm tractor? Of course, he had not complained earlier (1970–74), when the price of sisal rose more than four times in four years.[13] (Mercurial commodity prices were an old story. Between 1925 and 1928, the world price of rubber fell from 73 cents to 22 cents a pound, and then with the Great Depression, to less than 3 cents a pound in 1932.[14] The plantations of Southeast Asia [Malaya, East Indies, Indochina] took a beating. But from there the price could only go up, as it did up to and into the war. War is hell on tires and great for the rubber business.)

In the face of freedom's disappointments, the law of undiminishing conviction took over. Those accustomed to blame material failure on foreign wrongs now decided that exploitation had merely assumed

* Thus, after good years in the 1960s and 1970s, the Côte d'Ivoire showed negative growth over the next decade, –4.7 percent per year per head from 1980 to 1992— World Bank, *World Development Report 1994*, Table 1. Algeria and Nigeria show a similar pattern, although their rates of decline are lower, –0.5 and –0.4 percent from 1980 to 1992. In the latter two, civil war has had a disastrous effect on the economy, in Nigeria from 1967 to 1970, in Algeria today.

new guises. The old colonial areas were only nominally free, they said, still bound to exploiters by invisible ties of unequal trade and dependency; also by subventions and bribes in return for political allegiance and loyalty. Hence failure.

Some critics of this new colonialism (neocolonialism) even argued that all exchanges between the advanced industrial nations and the backward "Third World" are intrinsically unfair. Logically, the poor should cut all commerce with the rich.[15] No better recipe for poverty maintenance could have been found, and fortunately most Third World governments knew better than to shut themselves off from trade in goods and knowledge; also from loans, gifts, and subsidies. One exception was Burma (Myanmar), where a self-imposed embargo made it necessary to cannibalize vehicles to keep them running, and to use gasoline so crude that black gouts of poison spout into the streets. Only the light traffic saves the lungs of passersby.

Since independence, the heterogeneous nations that we know collectively as the South, or as the Third World (and sometimes the Third and Fourth worlds, to distinguish between poor and very poor), have achieved widely diverse results. These have ranged from the spectacular successes of East Asia to mixed results in Latin America to outright regression in such places as Burma and much of Africa.

This diversity of outcomes shows that colonization in itself, even enslavement, does not dictate failure.* In the long sweep of history, this is the heart of the matter: down is not out. Some countries have made something of the colonial legacy; of the heritage of social overhead capital, education, ideas; even of their own anger, resistance, and pride.† Others have run down what the colonial power left behind and have not learned to replace it. Still others were left little, usually be-

---

* Two examples from pre-modern history: the ancient Israelites after the exodus from Egypt; and the Aztecs who fled slavery into the marshes and emerged to conquer all the peoples around.

† The significance of resistance and pride is the principal theme of much of the new work on the history of imperialism—what Michael Adas conveys as "The End of the White Hero in the Tropics"—" 'High' Imperialism and the 'New' History," p. 318. Whereas older studies focused on European conquistadors, governors, and entrepreneurs, on European modernity vs. native backwardness, on improvement vs. stagnation, the recent stress has been on the forms and consequences of resistance, not only the rebellions, riots, and "mutinies," but also the quotidian sabotage and withholding of cooperation. On this last, cf. Scott, *Weapons of the Weak*. The point is to restore "agency," that is, to show passive victims as purposeful actors and indigenous cultures as sources of energy and inspiration.

cause the colonial power did not see the payoff to improvement. Still others were too poor even to attract the cupidity of stronger nations.

The example of a few thriving ex-colonies has little consoled the failures. For them, the whole experience has been humiliating, enraging; and subsequent disappointments have only aggravated their resentments. They have a point. But having sucked on it, they would do well to spit it out. None of this had to do with intentions, good or bad. It was built into the logic of the situation, and all would have argued, from the heart, that they were doing the best for everyone else.

Take the French. They thought of themselves as bearers of universal reason and virtue, to say nothing of the highest literary culture; and while they did little to educate their subject peoples, that little was inspired by a sense of mission and infinite perfectibility—you too can be French. Classroom instruction was typically in French, which produced a class of literates estranged from parents and native culture—one of the teachers called it an "alienation machine." Substance consisted in French historical clichés—*"Nos ancêtres les Gaulois* [our ancestors the Gauls] . . . " and such literary classics as Racine's *Andromaque* and Corneille's *Le Cid*.[16] The best students, those who did well enough to win fellowships to French universities, learned the treasures of French republican virtue, just the kind of thing that would lead them to hate their status if not themselves and turn them into leaders of rebellion. Witness the careers of Ho Chi Minh in Vietnam or Pol Pot in Cambodia.

What's the balance sheet? Has imperialism been good or bad for subject peoples? Let me attempt a series of propositions:

(1) A principal aim of imperialism has been to extract wealth and labor, more than was available at a free market price. The results have not always matched expectations. On the other hand, in (almost) every instance, a few people have done well—tough traders, concessionaires, functionaries, intermediaries (compradores), local elites—on both sides of the divide between rulers and ruled, stronger and weaker.

(2) Almost all imperialisms have brought material and psychological suffering for the subject people; but also material gains, direct and indirect, intended and not. Some of these gains flowed from opening and trade. To cite John Stuart Mill, writing from a British/Smithian perspective in the middle of the nineteenth century, " . . . the tendency of every extension of the market [is] to improve the processes of production."[17]

All of these trade effects depended on the nature of colonial rule. Some masters were richer and more ambitious. The colonials typically built useful things—roads, railroads, port facilities, buildings, water supply, waste disposal units, and the like. They made the natives pay for these improvements in labor and taxes, but they could have just kept the money. Meanwhile the gain to natives was incidental, for such improvements were made primarily for the ruling power and its commercial interests; after all, one had to make these distant places livable and profitable, defend the frontiers, maintain order. It was nonetheless gain. The same holds for health facilities, which initially served the masters (note, however, that roads and clearances could help spread disease). Yet motive matters less than consequences. No one can segregate the benefits of such efforts. Also, builders and doctors had their own sense of duty to the larger society.

Would more of these facilities have been built if these countries had been free? Under the precolonial regimes, unlikely. Even now, when development has become a universal religion and business enterprise stands ready to respond, public works in former colonies too often disappoint. Worse, successor regimes have allowed the colonial legacy to deteriorate. The great exceptions have been the postcolonial societies of East and Southeast Asia: South Korea, Taiwan, Singapore. And, of course, new technologies have made for inexorable improvement— airports and air transport, for example.

In ex-colonies, however, such projects are often the conspicuous consumption of rulers who prefer to spend (other people's money) for new, rather than care for old. We are left with a succession of layers on the middens and ruins of an earlier generation. The usual archeological pattern of successive civilizations is now revived in the ill-prepared societies of the twentieth century and will presumably be the delight of future diggers. Among the future ruins: lavish hotels, already displacing caravanseries and the kind of inn that sets the stage for adventure novels and cinema. Today's business travelers and bureaucrats expect one-class service around the globe; also CNN broadcasts and Sky-News.

(3) The map of the colonial world was drawn by Europeans. The boundaries did not reflect the realities of place and people. This was particularly true of Africa (but India and Burma too), where tribes were split and others joined (including the young tribe of white settlers and immigrants), laying the basis for irredentism and strife. Freedom, when it came, came to peoples ill-prepared to live together. And yet the

new nations saw these artificial boundaries as sacred, for fear of what might replace them. Quite right: the record of territorial disputes in ex-colonial areas shows much ado about little and heavy penalties for both winners and losers.[18]

(4) The energy, resources, and potential goodwill of these successor states have been depleted in the process of defining themselves. A very few (the best example is Korea) already had something of a national or ethnic identity at the time the colonial power took over, and could build their resistance on it or pick it up again after the outsiders left.* The others have suffered the instability and violence that accompany uncertain identity and legitimacy, careening from coup to coup, from one explosion to another.[19] Meanwhile the advanced industrial nations have mouthed pieties, succored victims, propped up tyrannies, created new victims, wrung their hands, generally botched every intervention—done good as well as bad and both at the same time, consoling themselves the while with virtuous intentions, larger causes, and the satisfaction that comes with moral superiority. (That is the point of the exercise.) Pictures of starving and fly-specked children fill the public prints and the TV screen. The supply of charitable causes exceeds the supply of funds. Little goes beyond first aid.

(5) Let us try the counterfactual: the economically backward nations would have grown and progressed (in the sense of technique and productivity) faster had they never known colonialism. The argument *pro* rests on hypothesis: on the assumption that these subject peoples would otherwise have been free of domestic as well as of foreign exploitation; also able to learn and change. The argument *con* rests on history: imperialism has not prevented a few colonies from developing as autonomous centers and from learning and inventing the techniques of an industrial economy.[20] Hence the British colonies in North America, Finland as part of the Russian empire, Norway under Sweden, Hong Kong under Britain. The first example of a non-Western nation to do so, Japan, though remaining independent (no small matter), did it under the tariff limits of an informal imperialism. But then again, as everyone knows, Japan is special.

---

* In some instances, these subjugated peoples had built their own empires before the white man came: the Aztecs and Incas of course; but also the Annamites in Indochina, the Burmese in Burma; the Zulus in Africa; and so on. Freedom did not necessarily entail the restoration of equality. Equality had never existed, and new state structures rested on old hierarchies.

History suggests that tutelage can be a school. Of course, a lot depends on the teacher. Some imperial nations were better rulers than others and their colonies did better after independence. This criterion would have the Spanish and Portuguese bad, the Dutch and French less bad, and the British least bad because of their willingness and ability to invest in social overhead (railways in India, for example) and their reliance on local elites to administer in their name. In 1900, India had thirty-five times the railway mileage of nominally independent China—a salute to Britain's sense of imperium and duty.[21] (A cynic might argue that these railways were intended primarily to get raw cotton and other primary products to port and soldiers to points of unrest. Still, the linking of Indian markets eased food distribution in a country vulnerable to local famines. And sometimes it might take a famine to get a line built.)*

By this standard, however, the best colonial master of all time has been Japan, for no ex-colonies have done so well as (South) Korea and Taiwan, where annual growth rates per head from 1950 to 1973 exceeded those of the advanced industrial nations (Japan itself excepted). This achievement reflects in my opinion the culture of these societies: the family structure, work values, sense of purpose. (I say this even though many economists do not accord importance to culture, which cannot be measured and, for these experts, just gets in the way of good ideas.) These values were already there under Japanese rule, partly in reaction to it, and showed in the response to profit opportunities whenever the alien master gave the natives some working room.[22] But the postcolonial success also testifies to the colonial legacy: the economic rationality of the Japanese administration, which undertook in the colonies "the superbly successful modernization effort which Japan itself had undertaken."[23]

To be sure, the inhabitants of Korea and Taiwan would not agree with this. They remember tyranny, torture, and abuse—memories embittered by an "in-your-face" Japanese refusal of regret or remorse.[24] Remorse for what? The system worked.[25] Besides,

---

* Note that the technical quality of the Indian railways was low; also that it was the Indian taxpayer who involuntarily paid much of the cost in the form of guaranteed returns to the British investors. (For all their occasional wealth, the Indians were not interested in investing in these projects.) On this checkered story, see Headrick, *Tentacles of Progress,* ch. 3.

> [Japan] was as responsible in its policies toward its colonial populations
> . . . as was Belgium in the Congo, France in Indo-China, Holland in the East
> Indies, or Germany, Italy, Spain, or Portugal in Africa. And in all fairness, it
> can be argued, it is against these other colonial situations, rather than against
> some theoretical utopia, that Japan's colonial efforts should be judged.[26]

The world belongs to those with a clear conscience, something Japan
has had in near-unanimous abundance.

Korea and Taiwan would say they succeeded in spite of Japan, which
steered them into agriculture and away from industry. Japan subjected
them to repeated reminders of their political and social subordination;
made them, in the Korean case, change their names and assume a
second-class, imitation Japanese identity; assigned them to jobs that
Japanese found too dangerous and disagreeable (for example, mining
in the home islands). When freedom came, Koreans remembered. But
they did not let memory get in the way of material development.
"Don't get angry; get even."

Korea and Taiwan are the exception. Most of the new postwar nations remembered too well and took the wrong path. The economic
system of their former rulers was anathema: capitalism was seen as inefficiency laced with corruption and injustice. In the light of the Soviet
victory in World War II, socialism *cum* dictatorship was the assurance
of production and promise. They couldn't have been more wrong.

Looking back, then, on the imperialism experience, one sees a persistent
conflict between theory and reality. For most of the past century, the ruling orthodoxy has been not simply anticolonialist. It has incorporated
anticolonialism into a larger vision (explanation) of economic history:
colonies as pillars of a dying capitalism. In this model, colonies paid,
whether by nourishing the growth of imperialist economies or by transferring wealth from poor to rich—empire as vampire. Without colonies,
bourgeois domination would come tumbling down. Or to put it differently, Europe could not afford to give up its colonies. Conversely,
once the subject peoples free, they would rise swiftly to prosperity.

Could not afford . . . Not at all. Over the course of the twentieth
century, resistance to imperial masters grew. European ideals of freedom and the rights of man proved contagious, and subject peoples
learned from their masters how to resist their masters. Meanwhile public opinion, once blithely supportive of empire, now deplored it. Major
scandals—the revelations of torture and mutilation in King Leopold's
Congo and of atrocities (including concentration camps) in the war

against the Afrikaners (1899–1902)—gave arguments to anti-imperialist liberal and radical writers and politicians. Empire, pride of the powerful and consolation of the little people, the thing that made small countries big and big countries huge, lost legitimacy.*

World War II dealt the *coup de grâce*. Not only did Western nations lose their reputation of invincibility, but their war aims deprecated dominion. Now the burden of mastery grew unbearably heavy. Some countries, prouder than others, held on (France in Indochina and, even more, Algeria). Others (Britain in India and Palestine, Holland in Indonesia) could not wait to let go. They were right. To the disappointment of the anticolonialist doctrinaires, the ex-imperial nations suffered not a whit by the loss of these territories; on the contrary.

The second thesis also proved to be wrong. In 1961, an Indian economist named Surendra Patel published an essay that demonstrated by irrefutable arithmetic that India, now free of the British Raj, would in some thirty years pass France in income per head, and in another few years, the United States.[27] He was not alone; one could find other romantic predictions. They reflected fair hope and tenacious doctrine; also national pride and a kind of virtual revenge.

∽ ∾

# It's Easy to Remember, and
# So Hard to Forget

One of the worst legacies of colonialism has been the explosion of ill-will against the former masters and their representatives—not so much on the level of governments, where deals and money are to be made, as of relations between people. A number of colonies, among them some of the most important, became outlets for overseas

---

* Among the powerful anti-imperialist statements: Joseph Conrad's short novel *Heart of Darkness* (1902). This eloquent testimony to the abuses of imperialism and the hypocrisy of the West was based on personal experience in the heart of Africa: "Going up that river was like travelling back to the earliest beginnings of the world. . . . " The novella has since been denounced as a racist, "orientalist" document and hence to be excluded from the literary canon. Conrad, we are told, presented the native Africans as primitive and helpless (Africa as the heart of darkness), and we can't have that. Such are the anachronistic imperatives of political correctness. This assault on what has always been considered a masterpiece of empathy and humanity has produced what the current jargon awkwardly calls a "site of contestation." See the fascinating article by David Denby, "Jungle Fever."

settlement, lands of opportunity for Westerners seeking to start over or get away. Some of these settlers developed a great love for their new homelands, for the earth, the streams, the landscapes, the towns and markets and soukhs; and yes, for the people, whom they loved for their dependency, or their mystery, or their strangeness, or their innocence. Many of them thought that they had found a new paradise, were founding a new race—not by mixture but by coexistence in newness. Read Albert Camus on his boyhood in Algeria.* He was not the only European to feel this way; he just wrote better.

It came, then, as a terrible shock to learn that many natives did not return this love and resented the intrusion of these strangers— their appropriation of the best soil, their political and social privileges, their unavoidable, irresistible condescension.

Not all natives felt this way. But as independence movements simmered and boiled, as consciousness awoke, it was hard to remain neutral ("Which side are you on?"). And so, when independence came, the colonials withdrew. Most could not abide the loss of their privileges and withdrawal of deference, and even those who would have stayed, who wanted to stay, were sped on their way by insults, threats, violence, seizures back of property seized in the first place.

Algeria was paradigmatic: over a million Europeans among ten times as many natives. These *colons* did not want independence. They wanted France to stay; indeed, many were ready to fight to keep Algeria French. (The French themselves almost had a civil war over the issue.) The new government of Charles de Gaulle was ready at first to make concessions to persuade the Algerian independence movement to remain united with France; to no avail. And once the French government decided the game was not worth the candle, that was it. The *colons* were told they were on their own, that France would recognize Algerian independence. Some die-hards would have fought on, but who was going to help them in a world pledged to the demise of colonialism? Within a couple of years, all the *pieds-noirs* pulled out.† Not all these Europeans were rich; they had come there poor and often stayed poor. But the successful ones owned the best land, grew the wine and wheat that were the great exports, handled the shipping, managed the banks, made the economy go.

---

* *The First Man* (New York: Alfred Knopf, 1995), an autobiographical novel.
† *Pieds-noirs:* literally "blackfeet." The term given to European settlers in Algeria, by analogy with barefoot natives.

Their departure did not leave the Algerians bereft. They had their land back; the Christians (and Jews) were gone. (They also kept the oil in the Sahara.) Yet the loss of these human resources was a crushing blow. Over the years, the Algerian economy slowed, and even oil and gas could not stem the tide. Algeria started exporting people to France, where economic growth increased the demand for labor. So much for the alleged capitalist need for empire.

# 26

# Loss of Leadership

The market is supposed to be a level place of combat, often (usually) peaceful. Not that the players would have it so: if they had their way, they would be given every advantage and keep what they have from those who come after. The same for groups and industries and national economies: all want to get and keep. Fortunately, the presence of competitors imposes a duty to strive; in the long run, nothing for nothing.

So with international economic rivalries. Cities and nations have come to the fore, have yielded to newcomers, been passed in turn by other newcomers. The process is not a pleasant one for the losers, although the pain is much eased by willful myopia; also by the fact that these losses of place do not usually entail absolute decline.* On the contrary, earlier advances will have been converted into a stock of wealth that comforts those who have it; and into human and material capital that continues to yield income and growth. Still, leadership is habit- and pride-forming. No one likes to lose place.

Jealousy signals ambition. When English "political arithmeticians" of

---

* Much of the literature on this subject tacitly uses the term *decline* to denote relative rather than absolute loss of place. It were better to specify that explicitly.

the latter seventeenth century pointed to Holland as exemplar and adversary; when French writers of the eighteenth century noticed and deplored English commercial and financial achievements—they were venting their envy, hopes, and dissatisfaction in an age of state building and intense national rivalry. That was the nature of Europe, very different here from ecumenical China or anarchical India and Islam. Europe consisted of states big and small, each steered by the pride and interest of the ruler, but increasingly by self-aware nationalism. All vied. All knew the significance of money for standing and power.

The primacy of money in the service of power found expression in economic thought. Mercantilism was not a doctrine, nor a set of rules. It was a general recipe for political-economic management: whatever enhanced the state was right. Even Adam Smith had his mercantilist moments: the navigation acts, he noted, may have cost the British consumer, but they worked wonderfully to put down Dutch seapower.

By Smith's day, the era of Dutch primacy was over. It had been a hundred-year wonder: this small country dominating the oceans; moving goods, bulky and rare, in thousands of vessels; standing up to and defeating more populous nations; setting an example to all of rationality and purpose. Nothing shows this better than the conquest of England by William of Orange, Stadholder of the United Provinces, in 1688. This was the last successful invasion of England, and the first since another William, him of Normandy, in 1066. To be sure, the British do not remember it that way. The Whig interpretation of the overthrow of James II as the "Glorious Revolution" has obscured the character of the event. Yet invasion it was, and it was intended to take over the English crown to prevent it from joining with France against the Netherlands. The Dutch fleet assembled that September was four times the size of the Spanish Armada and carried the best troops in the Dutch army, plus foreign volunteers, animals, equipment, and a huge artillery train. "When all dimensions are considered—military, naval, financial, logistical, diplomatic, domestic . . . it was arguably one of the most impressive feats of organization any early modern regime ever achieved."[1]

As late as 1776, Adam Smith still thought of Holland as richer than England. How did he know? He compared interest rates in the two countries and found that the Dutch government could borrow at 2 percent, private parties at 3. English rates, he wrote, ran about a point higher; Scottish rates, maybe two points. This implied, he said, that capital was more abundant in Holland and profits lower. To be sure, Dutch entrepreneurs complained that business was poor; but for

Smith, low profits were "the natural effect of prosperity," and Dutch merchants were suffering in effect from what Marxists would later call false consciousness.[2]

Smith also noted that "the wages of labour are said to be higher in Holland than in England," and this too showed that Holland was richer. Well, it might mean that, but it might also imply that Holland was growing faster than England, and that was simply not true.* Recall that Smith had already made such a link between high wages and growth in comparing the American colonies with the mother country. "[T]hough North America," he wrote, "is not yet so rich as England, it is much more thriving, and advancing with much greater rapidity to the further acquisition of riches."[3]

Smith should have applied the standards of his Britain–North America comparison to that between Britain and Holland; that is, distinguished between wealth and growth, between being rich and thriving. They would have prepared him for signs of Dutch slowdown.† Instead, he focused on a Holland overflowing with capital and seeking outlets for investment abroad, which was true enough. Already in the early eighteenth century, the Dutch were placing large sums in the British and French funds, as well as in Bank of England, East India, and South Sea stock. They were doing this, of course, because British and French placements paid more; but the point is, they paid more because domestic demand was greater and supply shorter, and all this because, in England at least, economic growth was more rapid.**

Meanwhile Dutch industry had fallen on hard times. (This is one instance when Smith would have gained by visiting.) Output of Leiden fine cloth had fallen from 25,000 rolls a year in 1700 to 8,000 by the late 1730s; of Leiden camlets from 37,000 pieces in 1700 to 12,600 in 1750, 3,600 by 1770. Haarlem linen bleaching shriveled in the 1730s and '40s. The famous windmill-driven complex on the Zaan (timber, sail-canvas, ropemaking, shipbuilding) went into free fall by the 1750s, many of the mills still and silent. Cotton printing and to-

---

* His laconism in this instance may lead us to believe that his comparison, whatever its accuracy, was of nominal rather than real wages—in other words, not based on purchasing power.
† "The trade of Holland, it has been pretended by some people, is decaying, and it may perhaps be true that some particular branches of it are so."
** They might also have paid more because English business was bad, risks greater, and they were looking for outside gulls to save the day—like Mexico in 1994. (Not true, of course.) Prices are determined by demand as well as supply. In this instance Smith looks only at the Dutch side—supply—and ignores demand.

bacco processing in Amsterdam were declining even before midcentury. An index of industrial production setting 1584 at 100 shows a peak of 545 in 1664, dropping to 108 in 1795.[4] Among the toughest competitors: the rapidly growing cottage industries of Flanders, Rhenish Germany, Saxony, and Silesia.[5] Nor was commerce spared: the "rich trades" to the Levant and Spanish America dwindled, along with bulk carrying of herring, salt, and wine in European waters. A few sectors held up, notably the import, processing, and re-export of such colonial wares as sugar, coffee, tobacco, tea, and cocoa. Yet even there, Holland lost relatively, to Britain and France in particular.[6]

Economic contraction pulled at the social fabric. The major cities shrank as skilled craftsmen and small entrepreneurs sought better opportunities in other lands. The decline, though moderate, contrasted significantly with steady and even rapid urbanization elsewhere.[7] That Dutch towns did not shrink more was because rents and food prices fell and some poor relief was available; this was a matter of public order if not of charity. Besides, Dutch wages still topped those in surrounding lands, in large part owing to the resistance of craft guilds, and this gap drew cheap labor from abroad to compete with the newly unemployed. Increasing hostility and conflict found an outlet in strikes, until nothing was left to strike about.

Some of this may remind readers of conditions in the United States in the last quarter of the twentieth century. As branches of manufacture have shrunk before foreign competition, enterprises have discharged redundant labor or moved to lower-wage areas. New workers cost less than old, as the airlines know only too well. Poor immigrants have kept coming. Unions have struck, sometimes only hastening plant closings or transfer of orders to cheaper suppliers. (*Mutatis mutandis,* one finds similar developments today in western Europe.)

So in Holland two centuries ago. The United Provinces pared and trimmed to meet the competition, but the best they could do was run in place. Many businessmen gave up the fight and retired to the country and to a life of passive investment. Incomes polarized between the rich few and the poor many, with a diminishing middle in between. Tax returns show that by the late 1700s, most wealthy Dutch were big landowners, high state officials, or *rentiers.* Gone the prosperous enterprisers of the "golden age": employers were now confined to the middle and lower ranks.

In the process, the United Provinces abdicated as world leader in trade and manufacture and went into a postindustrial mode. Italy had gone that way before. In Venice, for example, the wool craft had sunk under the burden of taxes, key industries had migrated to cheaper lands, and businessmen had reinvested their fortunes in agriculture on the mainland.[8] In Genoa, active merchants had become bankers to Habsburg Spain. Both Venice and Florence were already taking on the new role of tourist magnets, living on the wealth of erstwhile competitors. In the aggregate, Holland was still wealthy, as Adam Smith's impressions show, but estimates of income or product per head 1750–1870 have it going nowhere. Other, more active nations were passing it by.[9] *No absolute decline, then, but a long pause and a mutation.*

Why this should have been so is a difficult but important historical question. Some scholars cite mistakes of strategy: the Dutch stayed with Indonesia and spices while the British and then the French bet on India and textiles; or the Dutch mishandled their commercial ties with China and thus lost out on the lucrative tea trade; or the Dutch, for this and other reasons, lost ground in inter-Asian commerce. More persuasive is the argument from catch-up and convergence: other centers, advantaged by lower wages, learned to make the textiles and other manufactures that had been a mainstay of Dutch exports and shipping, and having learned, shut their doors against imports. In a world of mercantilist rivalry, navigation acts and protectionism were killing the old workshop and chief middleman. No wonder the Dutch exported capital: they could get more for it abroad than at home.

In the nineteenth century, the example of more successful industrializers, Britain above all, but also the southern Netherlands (from 1815 actually part of the Kingdom of the Netherlands, then from 1831 on, independent Belgium), did not lead at first to a redefinition of Dutch vocation. Perhaps the persistently higher price of labor discouraged manufacturing, at least in the coastal provinces,[10] or the Dutch may have had trouble abandoning ingrained habits and refiguring the opportunities.[11]

On this point, scholars have pointed to a Dutch distaste for modernity and high aversion to risk. One historian wrote:

> In nearly all the industrial towns in our land one saw the owners of factories and *trafieken* rather give up the unequal struggle with a more dynamic neighbour than adapt the new machine power to the increasingly old-fashioned inherited means of production. Yes, many regarded the smoke of the fuming steam engine as the hideous smoke from the pit of the abyss.[12]

And another:

> The Dutch merchant seemed to be dozing off on the soft cushions of formerly gathered riches and the leaders of industrial business from this period strike us as belonging to the respectable class of slow fat-bellied trade bosses whose brains, suffering from spiritual flabbiness, prevented them from hazarding the leap from the traditional way of doing business.[13]

A harsh judgment, but one could cite others like it. How important were such attitudes? Economists and "new economic historians" are skeptical of entrepreneurship as explanation, because it is hard to pin down and does not lend itself to measurement or prediction. Some business people may be indifferent or lazy, but others will take their place. After all, if peasants act quickly on differences in crop returns, how much quicker should merchants and manufacturers respond to new technologies! (On the other hand, the stakes in industry are typically bigger, the payoff slower, the penalties for error heavier.)

That is the point of innovation and initiative: they are not there until they are there. In the meantime, one has to ask why they took so long, and longer in some places than others. "Postindustrial" Holland did not want for capital or cheap labor or experience of industry. What it lacked, it could import. Transport might have been better, but that too could be had for the enterprise. We even find a few sports, unexpected entrepreneurs, people whose assets were, not business know-how, but rather technical knowledge and government connections. Thus the ex-naval officer Gerard Moritz Roentgen, back from a failed expedition to Indonesia, commissioned by the Dutch navy to look into new techniques of ship construction and iron manufacture. In so doing, he helped found Holland's first steamship yard, in Rotterdam in 1825.[14]

But mavericks did not add up to a self-sustaining, general movement. Some adventurers found an outlet in Indonesia. Meanwhile Holland itself marked time and found the long pause congenial. That is where culture came in: it defined patterns of recruitment, avenues of opportunity, and sources of satisfaction.

To be sure, culture changes. In the latter nineteenth century, Holland got back into modern industry on an internationally competitive basis. A protected market in Indonesia helped. The first gains came in textile manufacture, not coincidentally in the inland, off-the-beaten-track Twente district; but the real takeoff had to await the "second industrial revolution" of electricity, internal combustion (diesel motors), chemicals and artificial fibers; also scientific agriculture and horticulture. Soon Dutch income, never far behind, converged with that of the European leaders.[15]

Britain succeeded Holland. In the seventeenth century, England harassed and fought the United Provinces at every opportunity: hence a tax on the export of unfinished woolens and Alderman Cockayne's Project (1614–17) to take back from the Dutch the valuable dyeing and finishing (unsuccessful);* two navigation acts, designed to hurt the Dutch in their role as chief carriers and middlemen (they did); and a pair of naval wars that displaced the Dutch as masters of the seas, extruded them from North America, and led indirectly to their containment in India. Then the Dutch placed William of Orange on the English throne (1688), and from then on, the two countries partnered in war and peace; but the Dutch were the junior partners. In particular, the Dutch were Britain's barrier to French territorial ambitions on the Continent. So useful were they in this role that, once the takeover by Revolutionary-Napoleonic France liquidated, the British gave back (1815) to the newly created Kingdom of the Netherlands its lost colonies, including Indonesia (one major exception: Cape Colony in South Africa). In the bargain came what is now Belgium, then a mosaic of the Austrian Netherlands and sundry bishoprics and principalities.

The point was, Britain no longer had to fear Dutch economic rivalry. Whatever the Dutch had done, the British now did bigger and better. Josiah Child, London merchant, M.P., later governor of the East India Company, and political arithmetician, saw the issue clearly in his *New Discourse of Trade* (1668 and 1690):

> The prodigious increase of the Netherlanders in their domestick and foreign trade, riches, and multitude of shipping, is the envy of the present, and may be the wonder of all future generations. And yet the means whereby they have thus advanced themselves are . . . imitable by most other nations but more easily by us of this kingdom of England.[16]

Exactly. By Child's time, Holland was exporting capital to Britain, while Britain led the way to modern industry and took over as the world's premier mercantile and financial center.

---

\* An estimate of 1614 figured that dyeing and dressing would add 50 to 100 percent to the value of exports—see Supple, *Crisis and Change,* pp. 33–51. The scheme failed because exporters of unfinished cloth (the company of Merchant Adventurers) had their own clout and more money. And of course the Dutch fought the import of finished cloth.

After 1815 the British, sure of their hegemony, began abolishing the restrictions introduced in an earlier mercantilist spirit: thus prohibitions on export of machinery and emigration of artisans and some major tariff barriers and navigation acts. At the same time, using unimpeachable arguments about division of labor and gains from trade, they sought to persuade other countries to reciprocate. They did make some progress, but unfortunately for comparative advantage and classical doctrine, most other countries saw this as a device to keep them in their agricultural place. Free trade became British dogma and practice; most other countries flirted with it and found the water cold. Or perceived it as a British trap: if perfidious Albion wanted it, it couldn't be good.[17]

Meanwhile British industry throve in a world that wanted cheap manufactures. If European nations would not take these goods, buyers could be found on other continents, the more so as improved transport steadily lowered the cost of delivery. When in 1851 the British held the first worldwide exposition of technical and industrial achievement, they thought to celebrate their own mastery. They gave room and prizes to other, lesser nations, to be sure, but the principal theme was Britain as workshop to the world. And to the future: the very architecture of the Crystal Palace, hall to the exhibits, marked farewell to stone and brick and welcomed in a new age of iron and glass, of light and open space, of modular components and mechanized washings. It was the equivalent of the medieval shift from heavy Romanesque to vaulting Gothic. (Such boldness entailed a few surprises. The palace was big enough to plant trees; the trees received birds; the birds left souvenirs on the throngs below. What to do? Shoot them? But how to do that without breaking the glass walls and roof? "Sparrow hawks, Ma'am," suggested the duke of Wellington to Her Majesty the Queen.)

Even then, small clouds appeared. Some potential competitors displayed quality and taste that made their products unbeatable: French silks, Saxon porcelains, or vintage wines, for example. But that was an old story, perfectly comprehensible in a regime of inherited skills, natural favors, and comparative advantage. More vexing were signs of non-British technological superiority in a branch that Britain tended to see as its own—the production of machines and machine-made objects. The first hints of trouble came in American clocks and firearms, mass-produced with quasi-interchangeable parts.[18] In 1854, the British government sent a mission to the United States to look further into this "American system." Back came the message that, yes, the British had to start learning again.[19]

Serious unease set in toward the end of the century. It was linked to political changes signaling a shift in the balance of power: Germany's sudden rise to primacy on the Continent; its defeat of France in 1870 and establishment of a Deutsches Reich; its colonial ambitions in Africa and the Pacific; its projects of railway construction and trade in the Ottoman empire, which the British saw as threats to the India lifeline; the departure of the prudent, sagacious Bismarck and his replacement by a chauvinistic emperor who bullied his political advisers and resented his British cousins (so much for family ties); finally, Germany's decision to build a big navy, that is, to challenge Britannia's God-given right to rule the waves. All of this, moreover, rested on substantial economic gains: rapid growth of heavy industry (iron, steel, chemicals); special strength in the newer technologies (electricity, organic chemicals, internal combustion, and gas and oil motors); a banking sector exceptionally supportive of manufacturing and commercial enterprise; an educational system that was turning out large numbers of technicians, engineers, and applied scientists. Britain had cause to worry.

For the student of economic performance, this growing concern raises interesting questions. Was Britain failing? Was Britain declining? If so, whose fault? What remedies? The debate, believe it or not, has been going on for more than a century, indeed, is still going on. In April 1993, Professor Barry Supple of the University of Cambridge devoted his presidential address to the British Economic History Society to the question of Britain's alleged "failure" and suggested that the fear was greater than the reality.[20] In September 1995, an international colloquium met at Montpellier, France, to deal with the same issue and came to similar conclusions. And in May 1997, still another group convened in the shadow of Windsor Castle to treat of national "hegemonies"—the very word pronounced in as many different ways as there were countries present. Subjects of special attention: Britain in the nineteenth century; the United States in the twentieth. How long must we worry this old bone?

Forever. For all kinds of reasons:

1. The terms of the quarrel betray a confusion or misunderstanding of the issues—matter for endless disagreement. People speak or write of "decline."* Yet Britain clearly has not declined in a material sense. It is richer today than a hundred years ago. To be sure, entire branches

---

* The word recurs repeatedly. A small sample: Eatwell, *Whatever Happened . . . The Economics of Decline;* Gamble, *Britain in Decline;* Pollard, *Britain's Prime and*

have shriveled. Also it has suffered *relative* decline: other countries, once poorer, have passed it by and become richer. Yet a term like *relative decline* is technical, needs explanation, lacks punch. So people talk of decline and worse. The believers have used the term to attack the government or the business classes or both, sometimes with a view to political gain. The critics have denounced its use as "declinism"— clearly a *bad thing*. So doing, they demolish a strawman and falsify the debate.[21]

2. The economic merges with the political. A decline of relative economic strength (loss of market share, of industrial branches) means less political power, if only because armed forces cost money. The Britain of today is a far cry from the "Rule Britannia" of 1914–18 or even 1939–45. Such power as it has stems from possession of nuclear arms and its special tie, for what that is worth, with the United States. Now, hard as loss of relative wealth may be, it is not the pain of powerlessness.[22] Nationalism is an expression of identity, and via identity, of dignity and self-esteem. When one's country becomes smaller, one's self becomes smaller. When one has known and enjoyed the greatness of Great Britain, ebb tide is hard to take.

Perceptions rule here. Some scholars have wanted to treat this sense of loss as an illusion—like the one experienced by passengers in a stationary train who see another train going by and imagine they are moving in the opposite direction.[23] Besides, does not this kind of loss flow inevitably from the growth of other powers? The world does not stand still, and the diffusion of technology and industry was bound to raise up new, and often bigger rivals.[24] Britain could not but lose standing. But that does not make the loss easier to bear. Perception is subjective, and the dispassion of the scholar is like caviar to the general: it doesn't taste good.

Appeals to national vanity, we are cautioned, are the work of politicians. "But they mislead us." After all, there can be only one top dog, only one number one. So, "if not being top is failure then Britain has been in good and abundant company . . . " But is that the same as *losing* first place? The pain, w are told, is sharpest for those who remember better days, especially when one recalls long-standing superiorities. It is one thing to see the United States richer and stronger. But France, Italy! Ask English football fans who go from Merseyside and the Mid-

---

*Britain's Decline;* Rubinstein, *Capitalism, Culture, and Decline;* Elbaum and Lazonick, eds., *The Decline of the British Economy;* Coates and Hillard, eds., *The Economic Decline.* Lorenz, *Economic Decline in Britain,* deals with a particular branch.

lands to watch matches in Milan and find Italians living better and more modern than they. Still, that kind of pain eases with time. Soon no one will be left to remember. Besides, the world is filled with much poorer people. In the club of advanced industrial nations, Britain may have sunk to the lower ranks, but think how much better off it is than Mexico or India.[25]

3. The issue has its religious aspects, and nothing rouses more contention than issues of faith. In this matter, we are talking about economic religion, the religion of free trade. Where did free trade come in? Well, no sooner did Britain feel the heat of competition than home producers called for a return to protection. Free trade, they said, may have been fine when Britain was the workshop of the world, but now other nations could make things cheaper if not so well. These nations, moreover, did not play fair. They had tariffs and other barriers to foreign imports, while Britain opened its doors to everyone. They subsidized their industries, sold (dumped) their goods at less than home market prices, engaged in "unfair" business practices in order to gain market share. As a result, one after another branch of British manufacture found itself pressed into a corner, compelled to cut back on investment, to close down plant.

But free trade was become a matter a matter of faith—faith not only in the gains from trade but also in the power of material progress and international exchange to create peace and love. The logic was economic, the rationality of comparative advantage. But the passion was moral. Listen to John Bowring, our peripatetic agent of British commercial interests, recalling a visit to the Holy Land (what better place?) and gushing about trade, peace, and love:

> What a satisfaction it is to every man going from the West to the East, when he finds one of the ancient Druses clothed in garments with which our industrious countrymen provided him. What a delight it is in going to the Holy City to stop within the caravan at Nazareth—to see four thousand individuals and scarcely be able to fix upon one to whom your country has not presented some comfort or decoration! Peace and industry have been doing this and much more; for be assured that while this country is diffusing blessings, she is creating an interest, she is erecting in the minds of those she serves an affection towards her, and that commerce is a communication of good and a dispensing of blessings which were never enjoyed before.[26]

Does it make a doctrine less a matter of belief because it claims to be scientific? Here is W. S. Jevons, one of the icons of British political economy, smiting the heretics during the business crisis of the mid-1880s:

> Freedom of trade may be regarded as a fundamental axiom of political economy. . . . We may welcome *bona fide* investigation into the state of trade, and the causes of our present depression, but we can no more expect to have our opinions on free trade altered by such an investigation, than the Mathematical Society would expect to have axioms of Euclid disproved during the investigation of a complex problem.[27]

As a result, concerns about Britain's loss of industrial leadership were rejected by many—including many economists—because they could be and were used to challenge the sacred.

4. An economy built on exports was losing its export markets. In response to labor unions and political pressure, the British government subsidized and socialized the old standbys—iron and steel, cotton textiles, coal. But no growth there. Just underemployed labor, encrusted practices, and torturous decline.

As for new technologies and manufactures, well, jobs were opening up in lesser lines. The Cambridge economic historian J. H. Clapham pointed out that such a shift was normal: as branches close down, people have to leave them and move "to some expanding occupation, say, chocolate-making or chorus singing." He said this in 1942; had he been able to see the future, he would have spoken of the Beatles. The problem with such specialties is that some of them are culture-specific and do not travel well, at least not everywhere. Some people, for example, do not care for British chocolate—too milky, too sweet. But it suits British taste, and children like it, and it sells in U.S. supermarkets. *De gustibus* . . .

More important, these new lines may not have the same social and economic value as older employments. That was the gravamen of the Chamberlain argument. Not clear, says Barry Supple. "Is the production of cigarettes or tanks inherently more useful than the supply of nurses or violinists?" he asks, loading the choices and inviting a "no" answer. Other comparisons—say autos or computers vs. movies or saxophonists—might yield a "yes," though not to all.[28] Many of these new products do not have the same payoff in skills, knowledge, and high-wage jobs that high-tech items do. All of this raises a fundamental question: are some activities more fruitful than others? Economists are sharply divided on this, but the neoclassicists would insist that a dollar of hamburger is the same as a dollar of computer chip; or in Ricardian terms, a pound's worth of port wine equaled a pound's worth of machine-spun cotton. The dissenters, strangely cowed, caught between logic and intuition, object *sotto voce*.

5. "Did Victorian Britain Fail?"—a loaded question. It was the title of an article that defined failure as doing less well than rational behavior would have permitted.[29] Did British entrepreneurs miss opportunities to make more money because of want of character, knowledge, or rationality? The answer of the historical economist (the "new economic historian") was no: if Britain did less well than some other countries in, say, coal or steel or cotton manufacture, it was because it could not have done better. Coal deposits were not thick enough; better iron ores could wait while older, poorer ores were used up; faster spinning machines did not suit fine British yarn. Given competition, all had to be for the best in the best of all possible worlds.

True, foreign rivals now ran faster and better machines and more of them. But new is not always cheaper, at least not for the early comer. Never underestimate the tenacity and ingenuity of older devices where touch and hand skills play a role lost with automation. Even where British equipment aged, it did not always pay to replace it. These older machines had already been paid for, and their net return might be higher than a new device's. New might be more productive, but it still had to be amortized.

And then some things were beyond the entrepreneur's control. External costs (related costs), for example, were greater in Britain, which was stuck with relatively narrow-gauge track, small freight cars, low bridges, narrow, winding roads. These installations had been built economically when volume was smaller. Now they reduced economies of scale and hurt mass production. Similarly, Britain had developed a system of commission brokers and multimark distributors between manufacturer and potential customers.[30] These arrangements had once promoted division of labor. Now they got in the way of big deals. Some British enterprises did find ways to bypass the bottlenecks; but too few.

Ironically, many of the production changes deemed unnecessary and unprofitable before 1914 were made after the war—everything in its time. They came then too late.* And when one sees evidence of de-

---

* Thus Clapham, speaking of improvements in iron and steel technology: "Yet it is hard to believe that a process employed so extensively in 1925 and 1913 might not have been employed to advantage rather more than it was in 1901 and earlier"— *Economic History*, III, 148.

layed remedies in the decades since the World War II, one is inclined to define the British disease as a case of hard tardiness; entrepreneurial constipation.

For the defenders of British performance—let's call them the optimists because they see things in the best light—evidence of "declining market shares, [reduced] scale of operation, [lower] capital intensity, [old] capital vintage and average labour productivity" does not demonstrate "entrepreneurial backwardness."[31] Nor does evidence of belatedness. Why, they say, accord so much importance to the old standby industries: cotton, iron and steel, chemicals? These branches make intermediate goods. What about consumer industries? Don't they count? The business of an economy is to make people happy, not to perform "statistical feats."[32]

So the optimists dismiss the figures on cotton consumption, make of iron, output of sulfuric acid. Too embarrassing. Instead, they put forward statistical constructs of total product and productivity—"undoubtedly a major advance" over "ad hoc" data for "a few select industries."[33] These number figments have made a deep impression on economic historians, first, and then on those general historians who feel obliged to accept them at face value. The figures seem so precise (one or two decimal places) and, as asserted by some of the cliometricians, so peremptory.

Yet when all is said and done, the older data on individual branches, based as they were on direct measures, were far more accurate and reliable than aggregate constructs, as these same cliometricians conceded when their figments went against them. This happened as soon as the focus on British loss of leadership widened from the Victorian and Edwardian eras to include the period after World War I. Now, for the twentieth century, the comparative estimates of productivity, like the industry data, told a story of Britain's further loss of place. And now, suddenly, the optimists warned readers of the unreliability of macroestimates—of the "frailty of the calculations," of "errors and imprecision in measurement" and "very large margins of error"; and cautioned that national aggregates were a "fragile foundation" on which to build theories of British performance.[34] One leading yea-sayer, more faithful to theory, did not even bother: he simply dismissed calculations of higher productivity in other countries (say, the United States) as trivial or incredible: why should such large gaps exist and persist?[35]

But, of course, they do exist. They just don't persist. The annals of competition show entire national branches dragging and withering—

not this and that enterprise, but the whole industry.* Sometimes, having learned their lesson, the last members of the branch move away, generally to cheaper labor; that is smart, but also easy, and is evidence of rationality more than enterprise. And sometimes, as in Britain and in Holland earlier, entrepreneurs retire to a life of interest, dividends, rents, and ease. That is also evidence of rationality more than enterprise. One can understand the choice: enterprise is strenuous and risky; who needs it?

6. Does entrepreneurship matter? Some would argue that it does, but that it is dependent on growth. By this reasoning, Britain's spirit of enterprise suffered for want of opportunity and expansion. "Because [Britain] already had a large industrial plant which in many branches was adequate to the demands made upon it in the '80's and '90's, the incentive to install new capacity and the opportunity of trying out new methods were circumscribed."[36] So we have change in slow motion: why rush to put in electrical lines if one already has an excellent supply of gas lighting? (Answer: Electricity is better and safer, if less romantic; also much more versatile.) Especially if municipal authorities have sunk large sums into gas production and distribution.[37] (More related costs and vested interests.)

But Britain was not the only market for British industry. It sent much of its output abroad, as we have seen, and foreign demand with concomitant growth was there for the swifter and smarter, in sum for all. As one student of the British retreat in Asia put it: "There was nothing inevitable, for example, in the fact that Britain's share of imports into Hong Kong and Singapore fell between 1960 and 1980 from 11.3% to 4.9% and from 8.9% to 3.0%, while Japan's share of imports into those two economies rose from 16.1% to 23% and from 7.3% to 18.8%. Japanese business provided what those two fast-growing economies required; British business did not."[38]

"Nothing inevitable," then; and yet one could think of enterprises,

---

* In the aftermath of World War II, British shipyards made over half the gross tonnage produced in the world—1.3 million tons in 1950. These were admittedly exceptional circumstances, for almost all potential competitors had been knocked out by war. Over the following quarter century, a period that saw the introduction of radically new ship types (giant tankers, for example) and rapid growth of the industry, British output stood still, and then in a dozen years (1975–87) plunged 96 percent. Wipe-out. E. Lorenz, *Economic Decline in Britain*, ch. 4, while pointing to protectionist policies and subsidies abroad, notes "the failure of British builders to benefit from . . . high throughput technology" and better methods of work organization, the latter due to "lack of trust between labour and management" (pp. 90–91). See also D. Thomas, "Shipbuilding," in Williams, *et al.*, *Why Are the British Bad?*, pp. 179–216.

like people, as suffering from hardening of the arteries. This is partly because people create them, people who age. Succession of control is a difficult and invidious process, pitting insiders against outsiders, some insiders against others, blood against talent, blood against blood, talent against talent. At stake, decisions regarding choice of product and methods of production. Here the British were late in exploiting newer fields and ways, stressing instead learning by doing, in the shop and at the bench. Such job apprenticeship has its virtues and successes, but nothing is better calculated to preserve the old in aspic and miss the possibilities of innovation.

Both historians and contemporaries have pinpointed such technological and scientific shortcomings as a major cause of British loss of leadership. The "cliometric" optimists have retorted by defending British performance in such older industries as cotton and steel—the staples that had made Britain the workshop of the world. But what about the new branches of manufacture, the industries of the second industrial revolution? Back in 1965, a Cambridge economic historian urged scholars to go beyond "pig iron and cotton stockings" and pay more attention to soap, patent medicines, mass-produced foodstuffs, and light engineering, "the production of vigorous and ingenious entrepreneurs as dynamic as any of their predecessors."[39]

In vain; the defenders of British enterprise have done little with these success stories because they were in fact few and small. The second industrial revolution misfired. The most egregious failure was the abortion of the protean industry of organic chemicals (dyestuffs, plastics, pharmaceuticals). Here Britain was actually the pioneer and leader, with strong advantage in the key raw material (coal tar) and in demand (the textile industry), but lost out for want of knowledge, imagination, and enterprise to Germany, Switzerland, even France.[40] Management made no commitment to systematic research. R. J. Friswell, a working industrial chemist at the turn of the century, regretted (1905) that the men in charge of the chemical industry "looked upon all these [scientific] discoveries as isolated and not connected in any way . . . that they were discovered by lucky flukes." Small wonder that a key role was played by foreign immigrants—enterprise moving to opportunity. Thus Ivan Levinstein, immigrant Jew and hence outsider, deplored in 1886 the neglect of the newer, nonstaple industries, the "insufficient appreciation of the importance of the chemical industries . . . the absence of any intimate connection or intercourse between our scientific men and our manufacturers."[41]

Here one recognizes the extent of British abdication. In these new branches, the industrial countries began together, and the high science content of these innovations ensured that knowledge and technique would spread rapidly. Britain's chances were as good as or better than the next country's. Nor was Britain backward in science—no more than France in the eighteenth century. But like France earlier, the Britain of the late nineteenth and twentieth centuries cared more for pure science than its applications.[42] Part of the difficulty lay in British schooling: the Continental countries had created technical and scientific institutions as a matter of policy, whereas Britain had let this kind of education grow like a weed and had treated it, once grown, like a poor relation of "proper" schools and universities.*

Some have explained the shortcoming by exogenous factors, notably culture. They have sought to explain Britain's retreat from hegemony by the triumph of an antibusiness, antimaterialist outlook and its negative consequences for recruitment.[43] The teachers, poets, men and women of letters, and intellectuals—the people who set the tone and orchestrated the values—nurtured a sense of scorn for the shop and the office. The point was to rise above the material to higher things. Such pretensions found particular resonance among those older elites who found themselves jostled by grubby newcomers, and of course among the grubby newcomers who wanted to degrub themselves.[44] Snobbery is the revenge of the haughty and the humbug of the ambitious.

Others have countered by pointing to similar attitudes in other countries. Surely Germany nursed antibourgeois prejudices. All of Europe did. If anything, Britain was freer from these outworn biases than countries round. One could argue, however, that as industry lagged, Britain proved more vulnerable and succumbed more easily, its resistance sapped by its disappointments.

For twentieth-century Britain to stay with the rest, nothing less than a new industrial revolution would do: innovation and enterprise in electronics, pharmaceuticals, optics and glass, engines and motors. Some few firms did make a start and gains along these lines. One thinks of

---

* One aspect of this semispontaneous, pluralistic approach was the appearance of evening classes, many of them for workers desirous of improving knowledge and skills. These courses harked back to the itinerant lecturers of the eighteenth century and were intended as a response to the shortcomings of the regular school system. Some have argued that they were substantial, even adequate compensation. I do not agree: voluntary evening classes for tired laborers are no substitute for full-time, professional, lab-centered, exam-monitored, sequential curricula.

ICI, Pilkington, Glaxo, Courtauld, Dunlop, all of which bear witness to the commercial power of innovation. But these examples were not contagious. In the decades after World War II, Britain (along with the United States) lagged the club of advanced industrial nations (see Table 26.1).

What would such differences mean for the long run? A growth rate of 2.8 percent yields a sixteen-fold increase over the course of a century, as against 2,200 times for an annual rate of 8 percent. Such is the power of compound interest. Of course, no country can maintain a gain of 8 percent per year over a century, what with linked constraints, accidental reverses, cyclical downers, changes in government, competition, and the soothing corruption of success. Even Japan has had its setbacks in real estate and banking; while the increase in the exchange value of the yen chilled demand for Japanese manufactures. In contrast British industry, buoyed by North Sea oil, hospitality to foreign enterprise, and Margaret Thatcher's showdown with tool-dragging labor chiefs, has done better since the 1980s.*

A final word about the United States of America. At the end of World War II, with just about all industrial rivals in ruins, America accounted for the greater part of world industrial product. Its labor pro-

Table 26.1. Annual Percentile Rates of Growth by Country,
1950–87

|  | GDP | Labor Productivity in Manufacturing |
|---|---|---|
| Japan | 7.9 | 8.0 |
| Germany | 4.6 | 4.3 |
| United Kingdom | 2.5 | 2.8 |
| USA | 3.2 | 2.6 |

SOURCE: Porter, *Comparative Advantage,* pp. 279–80.

---

* And even earlier by some calculations. Estimates of annual growth in value added per hour in manufacturing, 1950–90, show Japan at 7.4 percent, France at 4.9, Germany at 4.5, Britain at 4.1, the USA at 2.6—Eaton and Kortum, "Engines of Growth," p. 6. Even allowing for error, we clearly are not in the presence of decline; rather, of apparent convergence.

ductivity in 1950, after a few years of cleanup and a new start in Germany and Japan, was more than twice that of the world's most advanced economies, and it was still twice as high in 1960.[45]

No country could expect to hold such an overwhelming lead indefinitely. Follower countries were gaining disproportionately by jumping to state-of-the-art technologies. (That's what catch-up is all about.) From 1950 on, mean labor productivity of these emulators gained consistently on that of the United States: 1.82 percent per year from 1950 to 1973; 1.31 percent from 1973 to 1987.[46]

What do these figures add up to? International comparisons are arbitrary and often contradictory, so that it was not clear whether, around 1990, the United States was in first or third place in income per head, whether its lower rate of productivity increase would persist, whether these other, faster-growing economies, plus several newcomers, were converging with it or on the way to passing it.* These issues were further embroiled by the conjuncture of the early 1990s: the Japanese found themselves in the throes of a slowdown, while the American economy continued to grow. Perhaps the Japanese had come to the end of their "miracle."†

Not to worry. The American data recall the earlier retreats of the Netherlands and Great Britain: loss of market share in manufactures; wastage of entire branches; new hires in service jobs, usually poorer-paid; polarization of incomes.[47] On the other hand, U.S. unemployment remains low (lower than European, but not Japanese), and continued American dominance in new lines, among them the high-tech, computer-linked manufactures (software and hard), gives reason for confidence (hope?). A new report argues that, while Americans save less (15 percent of income as against 33 percent in Japan), they put their savings to better use; capital productivity in Germany and Japan is reckoned to be only two thirds the American level. So "we can spend more of our current income on investment without jeopardizing future living standards."[48] Similarly, although manufacturing performance in

---

* From 1960 to 1973, U.S. total factor productivity (that is, gains in productivity after increases in capital and labor have been deducted) grew by 1.5 percent per year, against 6.3 percent for Japan. The oil shock of 1973 hit Japan hard, reducing TFP growth to 1.5 percent 1973–79, 2 percent 1979–88. But U.S. TFP actually turned negative 1973–79, rising to less than 0.5 percent in 1979–88—Hart, "Comparative Analysis," p. 207.

† Nothing is riskier than building prognoses on the last year's (or last quarter's) performance. Japan seems to be doing better in 1996; but see the *Wall St. J.*, 20 June 1996, p. A-13: "Despite a Spurt of Growth, Japan Isn't in Fast Lane Yet."

Japan is excellent, overall productivity is substantially lower (55 percent of the American), because agriculture is cosseted and the service sector is overmanned, highly fragmented, and uncompetitive. The whole system is designed to create and preserve vested interests, and so much the worse for the consumer. Meanwhile the yen is overvalued, and international comparisons based on exchange rates tilt grotesquely in Japan's favor. The reality is very different. Japanese housing is so fragile and space so scarce that it is often easier to tear down a house and rebuild than to look for better accommodation. Unless, of course, one is ready to go out into the endless suburbs and do a daily calvary to and from work.

A mixed picture, then. From the economists, to say nothing of self-appointed pundits, journalists, and politicians, we have cacophony. This division of opinion in itself gives one pause; for it recalls the century-long debate about Britain's performance. Does this kind of ebb tide invite denial? Is the evidence so abundant that each temperament can find what it wants? Or is the whole issue of leadership now irrelevant? Have we now entered a new era of global enterprise, such that nationality no longer matters?

Hardly.

⋙ ⋘

# The Rise and Fall of
# the British Auto Industry

The invention of the automobile should have boosted British industry. No country had a longer tradition of machine manufacture and engineering; none so large a pool of skilled metal workers. The potential demand was good. British income levels topped all of Europe, and imperial dominions and possessions offered sheltered markets overseas. Yet Britain was slow on the pickup and saw first France and then the United States take the lead. In 1913, only one British car stood amongst the top ten of American and British producers—the Maxwell, in sixth place with 17,000 units, against 202,667 by Ford.[49]

Given the winding, narrow roads, British car makers might have concentrated on small vehicles. Some of them did; but early on, the industry moved to large, pricey models that appealed to richer buyers (many with drivers) and brought larger unit profits. As a result, the industry was characterized by models galore (198 in 1913), short runs, and costly techniques, with much adjustment and fitting. Some observers thought auto makers underestimated demand. Said *The Times* in 1912: "no firm . . . has been sufficiently enterprising to lay down a large enough plant to make small cars in sufficient numbers to make their production really cheap."[50]

World War I and the introduction of assembly-line technology by Ford in the United States pushed the British industry to change. British firms bought heavy-duty machines and began to standardize models, though tentatively, like dipping their feet in cold water. That was the easy part. They found it hard to follow the Americans in buying labor cooperation with general wage increases. Nothing like money to ease the pain of faster work and labor-saving techniques. When Herbert Austin (of Austin Motors) visited the Ford plants after World War I, he was most impressed by the "energetic" work performance, the hustle and bustle, which he attributed to the "diversity of the Races employed" (interracial competition?) and the compulsion of the line flow. "I saw the famous Ford shops . . . the point that interested me and made me marvel was the way in which everybody in the establishment seemed to be trying to do their best."[51]

British management did not want higher wages across the board. It preferred to target and reward the more productive workers. So, following established custom, employers offered piecework wages. These helped some, but they had a serious disadvantage: they gave the work rhythm over to the workers. The good, rational assumption was that piece wages would lead workers to maximize productivity, as some no doubt did. But it allowed others to set such pace as the group or team found comfortable as well as rewarding. The group was only as fast as its slowest member.

What an irony! In the eighteenth century the British had developed the factory system with its supervised labor to counter the independence of cottage workers. Now they had permitted a comparable system of worker independence to take root in their factories.

So the British sacrificed productivity to custom and individuality and felt virtuous for it. American methods, one Briton snorted, were "herd methods." To be sure, wage arrangements, like production methods, varied from one car maker to another, but in general, British management saw bonus systems as a way of economizing on management. (Never underestimate the leisure preference of bosses, any more than of workers.) In the long run it was a false economy. When, after World War II, foreign cars invaded the British market, employers blamed labor for want of diligence and attention, and labor blamed the bosses for want of competence and attention. Both were right.[52]

On a scale of labor efficiency, the British system was at the low end, the American and German considerably better, the Japanese just about the best. Piecework wages and bonuses in a world of rapid innovation and sharp competition invited conflict. Every change in work and pace was pretext for disagreement; every settlement a source of disappointment; every gain a sacred and vested right; every loss something to be made up; and no one forgot anything. The strike statistics are not dismaying, but they omit the run-of-the-mill, wildcat interruptions, the explosions of anger, the fury between supervisors and labor stewards.

All of this sent the British auto industry into terminal decline. Car registrations went from 2.5 million in 1951 to over 9.5 in 1966 to over 15 million in 1980, but the big winners were the foreign makers, once they got their postwar act together: 5 percent of the British market in 1965, 14 in 1970, 49 in 1978, 58 percent in 1982.[53] The multinationals with branches in Britain—General Motors, Ford, and Chrysler—did little to exploit the export possibilities of their British subsidiaries; they had easier platforms to work with.[54] On the contrary, thanks to the Common Market, they were able to import parts into Britain. From 1973 to 1983—ten years—local content in GM cars made in Britain fell from 98 to 22 percent; in Fords, from 88 to 22. Expressed in car equivalents, this represented an import of 150,000 vehicles. When added to full auto imports, these together constituted two thirds of the British market in 1984.

The native British firms, without affiliates abroad, outsourced less. (The indifference of Morris [later Lord Nuffield] to the opportunity to acquire Volkswagen in 1945, thus a major bridgehead on the Continent, tells volumes.)[55] Instead, the British resorted to mergers at home. These were intended to promote a rational division of labor, but in vain. Plants were closed and workers laid off, especially after British banks stopped spending in a lost cause. How to design new models without fresh cash, and how to sell cars without new models? The state stepped in with subsidies, £2,400 million from 1975 to 1984—this, in the heyday of Tory laissez-faire, *laissez-crever* (leave 'em on their own and let 'em croak).[56] To no avail.

By 1989, British Leyland (renamed Rover Group), the residual conglomerate of a generation of mergers (1936–68) that had just about swallowed the entire home industry, accounted for only 13.6 percent of domestic car sales. Had it not been for foreign transplants, including some Japanese factories using Britain as a springboard to the European Common Market, the British auto manufacture was headed for extinction. As it was, it now depended "on the financial resources, design and production technology, managerial methods, working practices and approaches to industrial relations" of American, French, and especially Japanese multinationals.[57]

The explanation for this sad calvary is, as always, multiple. Here is Sidney Pollard: "[In addition to government policy], other factors in the decline have been poor management, complacency, poor industrial relations, an over-fragmented industrial structure, unhelpful financial institutions and a relatively stagnant home market."[58] And the first of all was poor management—another way of saying poor entrepreneurship.

# 27

# Winners and . . .

The twentieth century divides neatly at two points: 1914 and 1945. The first date marked the start of the so-called Great War—one of the most absurd conflicts in human history. These four years of combat left 10 million dead and many more maimed and stunted. They also took a prosperous and improving Europe and left it prostrate. The tragedy lay in the stupidity of kings, politicians, and generals who sought and misfought the conflict, and in the gullible vanity of people who thought war was a party—a kaleidoscope of handsome uniforms, masculine courage, feminine admiration, dress parades, and the lightheartedness of immortal youth.*

Colonial wars should have provided a warning, but the use of repeating and automatic weapons against "savages" left the confidence of the white man intact. Still, the Boer War in South Africa, where the British took terrible casualties, should have instilled a prudent fear. Not at all: a decade later, the havoc wrought by machine guns in Flan-

---

* On the arrogant stupidity of the generals, see the comments *passim* in Len Deighton, *Blood, Tears, and Folly*. Deighton is primarily a writer of adventure and spy novels, but he also does nonfiction, and when he does, he has the story right.

ders fields seems to have come as a great surprise. Obtuse commanders reckoned with impeccable logic that the army with the last troops standing and shooting would win. The generals got promotions, honors, and statues, usually on horseback. Their men died in the mud.

The losses of war were compounded by the blunders of peace. Perhaps that is unfair, and statesmen and diplomats were stuck with a legacy of hatred and revenge that left little room for reason. Could France be generous to Germany? In 1870, Germany invaded France, and after few casualties and no damage to its own territory, had used its victory to compel an extortionate indemnity. Now Germany had invaded France again, killing well over a million Frenchmen and wasting the richest industrial regions, pulling out as soon as the Allied armies threatened to move on to German land. Could France let them get away with that? How to calculate such losses? How much for vicious intentions? What if the Germans had won?

And what about the home fronts? The Germans did not surrender in 1918; they concluded an armistice. They had lost, but had not admitted defeat. German (and Austrian) malcontents and chauvinists cried betrayal: we were stabbed in the back. Villains were there for the marking—Jews to begin with, also socialists, and even better, the two together. Meanwhile tsarist Russia had collapsed, first into civil war and then into a Bolshevist regime that fomented in every country a festering conflict between revolution and status quo. The Soviet rulers may have settled momentarily for "revolution in one country," but agents abroad, working with local socialist parties, posed everywhere an implicit threat to property, hierarchy, and order.

The response, at the extreme, was fascism—a label of diverse content for a corporatist, status-conscious society under dictatorial rule. The political rhetoric of the day stressed the differences between socialism-communism on the far left, fascism on the far right. In fact, the extremes met and resembled each other: in their contempt for democracy, their pretense to virtue, their abhorrence of bourgeois values, their emphasis on state rather than market direction of the economy. Both sides would have rejected any thought of similarity; but the number of people who managed to slither from the one to the other testified to their compatibility.

To contemporaries, the year 1945 was one of triumph and defeat, of revelation and ruin, of relief and despair, of joy and sorrow. The war years had witnessed atrocities and cruelties beyond experience: 55 million dead, 35 million wounded, 3 million lost; some 30 million civilian deaths, including 6 million European Jews. Some survivors consoled themselves with the hope that war had become unthinkable. Others nursed incurable wounds and insatiable grievances. Still others set about to make a better world.

These responses, often fused in the same person, sparked a diversity of objectives and means. The larger goals were the same: restoration and repair, material improvement, peace and happiness. Like motherhood—everyone was in favor. For all the idealistic consensus, however, the world after 1945 was riven by the rivalry between bourgeois, capitalist countries on the one hand, Socialist and Communist societies on the other. This conflict had slept during the war, permitting all to collaborate against a Germany gone berserk in the pursuit of racial "purity" and world dominion.

The reaction to the German threat had been slow and reluctant. How could the land of Goethe and Beethoven become a cesspool of savagery and a threat to all?* Also, after the folly of the Great War, what could possibly justify another conflict? Fatigue and fear engendered an unconditional tolerance for evil, so long as the victims were strangers and far away. Only when it became clear that Germany's appetite was growing with the eating, and when the Nazi-Soviet pact freed German's rear for aggression against the West, did the democratic governments face up to reality and declare war.

They did not do well; and once Germany had taken just about all of Continental western Europe, it turned eastward against the Soviet Union, which had slept with the devil and now felt his fangs. So democratic (capitalist) and socialist countries joined against the common enemy. The West poured in supplies, played Russian songs, romanticized "Uncle Joe" Stalin and the Red Army, fought a two-front war in the Atlantic and Pacific. Colonial troops helped their masters out. The Soviets did most of the dying: of a population of almost 200 million, more than one out of four was killed or wounded. (The Germans also lost heavily, but that's the price of trying to take over the world.) Meanwhile the Western Allies unwittingly provided shelter for Soviet spies, both insiders and outsiders. Military collaboration had not removed the underlying differences, and the Communist regime was determined to use the alliance to lay groundwork for postwar success.

---

* In fact, the German record of racism and group hate in the decades preceding the Nazi regime gave ample warning that this was a very sick society. See Weiss, *Ideology of Death*.

Even before World War II was over, the cold war between the two systems had begun, or, more accurately, had resumed.

In the decades that followed, Western market economies put the Great Depression and wartime losses behind them and entered a period of unprecedented growth. Much of this was due to pent-up technological innovation. France-1948, for example, after decades of economic standstill followed by war and occupation, was a tired version of France-1900. Paris, empty of vehicles, needed neither traffic lights nor one-way streets; all cars had to be garaged at night; gas stations hand-cranked the pumps. Many small flats and houses had electrical services as low as 3 ampères—enough for a light bulb, a radio, perhaps an electric iron; anything more would blow the fuse wire. (No ready-made, screw-in fuses. One bought wire of given resistance and wound it around the terminals.) Some Paris dwellings had no electricity, and it was common in apartment buildings to share the privies, inside for the lucky (rich) ones, in the courtyard for the others. (Try walking down and up again five or six flights every time you have serious business. As the French say, it's good for the legs—*ça fait les jambes*.) Rich people might have an indoor toilet for their own use, an outdoor privy for the servants; or running hot water for their own use but none for the kitchen. One whole department, the Lozère, admittedly a poor region, had three bathtubs in all—presumably one in the prefecture, another in the "Hôtel Moderne," and who knows where the third. Many places that had tubs used them to store firewood or debris. Refrigerators were little known; people used iceboxes and screened *garde-manger* (foodboxes). No point to a refrigerator unless one bought for several days at a time; no point to such shopping unless one could find all food needs in one place, and then only if one had a car to carry the comestibles home and an elevator in the apartment building to haul up the bags and bottles. The knee bone was connected to the shin bone, the shin bone to the ankle bone, the ankle bone to the foot bone, and France had not really entered the twentieth century.

In the next three decades—what came to be known as the *trente glorieuses* (the thirty wonderful years from 1945 to 1975)—France moved in with alacrity. New construction, new industrial installations, a new road network—new, new, new—all of this was an opportunity to install up-to-date facilities, to electrify and mechanize and motorize. The automobile and telephone told the story. Once seen as luxuries for the rich, they now became necessities. Whereas in 1953, only 8 percent of French workers owned a car, fourteen years later half of them did. From 1954 to 1970, households-with-auto rose from 22.5 to 56.8

percent. Streets filled with cars day and night; vehicles could be seen parked outside farms that, even after the war, had still relied on horses. Rush-hour traffic became a pain and worse, and cities like Paris began to measure air pollution and warn the citizens of unavoidable poisons. No one really cared; the freedom that came with mobility trumped all the rest. Besides, a society that could smoke *gauloises* could breathe anything.

Meanwhile the same people who had once sat for hours in a cafe waiting for a long-distance call to go through (and maybe drinking a little and playing cards; the *cafetier* had to make a living too), now began to have home telephones. They might have to wait a year or two to get their connection. Central switchboards were swamped, particularly in Paris, and the post office, which ran the telephone service, had little sympathy for this rival mode of communication. People renting apartments to foreign vistors made much of the fact that they already had a phone. But not only foreigners; telephones are addictive, and the French can talk with the best. In the end, P.T.T. (Postes, Telegraphs, Telephones) hived off the phone system and the government created France Telecom to deal with these matters—an indispensable first step to autonomy, initiative, and market responsiveness.

In all this, the French economy grew and changed under government direction and planning *(dirigisme, étatisme)*—much more than in other European countries. This accorded with national tradition, going back to the Colbertism of the Old Regime and relying heavily on the competitive recruitment of the best and brightest into the *grandes écoles*—Polytechnique, Mines, Normale; and now a new one: the Ecole Nationale d'Administration, ENA, with its graduating classes of fledgling bureaucrats and rulers-to-be—the *énarques,* as they quickly came to be called.

Government engineers and functionaries, with and without the cooperation of private enterprise, modernized the infrastructure: roads, railroads, communications, public housing, equipment. The results exceeded expectations, and France in some areas, such as high-speed rail service, set the pace for the rest of the world. Whether such developments were always profitable is not clear; state subsidies, manifest and discreet, obscure the realities of the market. But what a pleasure for the privileged railway passenger, especially one favored by discount ticket prices (state employees, for example), to ride some of the smoothest and fastest lines in the world! France never became a giant maker of standardized industrial products. The French typically bought household machines in Germany and Italy, and as income rose, the richer among them tended to buy their cars from Germany. But France remained the master of quality, making articles set above and apart by taste (in both senses) and beauty. And France, the country, remained one of the world's most beautiful places to visit, a work of natural and man-made art, a tourist paradise. By the 1990s France had one of the highest standards of living in the world, with income a quarter again as high as that of old rival Great Britain. The old staples had slumped; France did not learn to mass-produce the high-tech devices of the computer age. But wine and cheese and fabrics and fashions remained.

One sticking point, source of weakness as well as strength: the French are proud. They have their way of doing things and, unlike the British, do not take easily to loss of power. This makes them poor learners of foreign ways. They have their own way. Today, French workers enjoy a generous social safety net and excellent medical and child care, along with strong vested privileges (long paid vacations, early retirement). This, plus cultural advantages, makes France a marvelous country to grow old in. But it also makes employers slow to hire, because every hire is laden with associated costs and potential liabilities. The effect: a high unemployment rate that hits especially hard at the young. The state, concerned for social peace (how does one argue peaceably and reasonably with truckers who block major roads?), would preserve these social arrangements, fears to adulterate them, yet wants more jobs. Such countries as the United States, persuaded of the value of free markets and committed to survival of the fittest, shower the French with advice. The French reply: Get lost; we don't need any lessons from you. Especially not from you, with your crime, racial antagonisms, imperfect assimilation.

The German comeback was even more astonishing. The country had suffered heavy war damage, and much of what was left was seized by the Russians, who had good reason to make the losers pay for what they had destroyed and taken—but did not always know what to do with the machines and materials. Heaps were left to rust at roadside. Better junk than German. In 1945, Germans had stopped taking baths for lack of hot water or soap. Young women gave themselves to occupation troops for a pack of cigarettes. Bourgeois in coat and tie could be seen scavenging horse droppings to use as fuel.

These German hardships and humiliations elicited little sympathy. Some Allied experts called for the pastoralization of the country: no more industry. Others argued that if the country was to pay reparations, some industry was unavoidable—say, half the output of 1938. All such retributive projects fell before the imperatives of cold war: the

Western powers needed and wanted Germany. So, unlike the hard, if often futile, enforcement of reparations after World War I, this time the victors offered substantial aid to their defeated enemies. The prospect of Soviet aggression defined everything.

But one should credit above all the energy and work habits of the defeated Germans. In 1945 their currency was worthless. The only money that mattered was dollars or cigarettes, and American GI's, smokers or not, were entitled to a carton a week.* (I myself bought a Harley motorcycle, minus generator, for five cartons—strictly against the rules.) The years that followed were marked by hard winters, food and fuel shortages, endless cleanup of rubble, and political repair, if not retribution. And then in 1948 the new Germany issued a new currency, exchanging 1 deutsche Mark for 10 Reichsmark. Price controls came off, and hoarded stocks came out of hiding. The economy took off.[1] In twenty years, the deutsche Mark, along with the Swiss franc, became the strongest currency in Europe. New plants sprang up and German goods sold everywhere, enjoying a nonpareil reputation for solidity and design.

As spectacular as was the German "economic miracle," the Japanese one was even more so. Destruction and casualties from American bombing were horrific, in large part owing to flammable housing and the tenacious refusal of a proud country, never defeated in war, to acknowledge its situation. Toward the end, the Americans "owned" the skies and could attack at will. Even so, it took the atom bomb to persuade the emperor and many (but even then not all) of his advisers and military to surrender.[2]

The Japanese, like the Germans, built their recovery on work, education, determination. They too were helped by American financial assistance; here, as in Europe, the aim was to parry the perceived Russian threat. The rapidity of Japanese development was the more astonishing in that it took place without the advantages of empire. Prewar Japan had been convinced that control of raw materials was a *sine qua non* of power and wealth, indeed had gone to war to secure this control. Now they had lost everything and found to their surprise what the economists could have told them all along, namely, that raw materials can be delivered on competitive terms anywhere in the world. All it takes is money to buy them. If the Western powers were so difficult before the war, it was because Japan's militaristic policy invited precau-

---

* Other currency commodities were coffee and silk or nylon stockings, but these were clearly less convenient. Cf. Kindleberger, *Financial History*, p. 403.

tions and reprisals. Now the Japanese learned that they had more to gain by buying than by grabbing.

Their quickness stunned Japan's competitors. Some know-how came to them because producers in other countries hired Japanese firms to make objects (watches, auto parts) that the more advanced country could label and sell as its own. Much they copied by reverse engineering, taking Western models apart and learning to make them better. They also sent missions to visit Western lands and humbly learn by watching and asking, photographing and tape-recording. "Humbly" was the word: the Japanese are the proudest of people, but that very sense of pride raises humility to an art and a virtue. These bowing and hissing embassies were repeatedly astonished by the openness of their hosts, especially in the United States. But why not? The Americans thought they had little to fear from these defeated little people.[3]

Even more impressive was the Japanese ability to go beyond imitation and invent. A visit to a Japanese showroom is a look into the future: the objects look familiar, but they do new things. Their greatest success came in automobiles, an industry so voracious and varied in its appetite for materials and parts that it could act as locomotive to most of the manufacturing sector. Beyond that they set their eyes on the most advanced and demanding high-tech products: optical devices, precision machinery and instruments, robotics and electronics. Before the war, the Germans held a quasi-monopoly on high-quality cameras; names like Leica and Zeiss were legendary. At the end of the century, Leica is still there, but a good Leica camera costs three times as much as the Japanese equivalent. For rich aficionados, price does not matter. But for most users, including professional photographers, that kind of difference is prohibitive. Japan dominates the market, leaving niches to others.

All of this has been supported by the world's most effective quality controls. Before the war, Japanese goods were scorned as rubbish— shoddy, meretricious, unreliable—made for five-and-dime stores. That was partly a rational response to deep depression and sharply restricted demand. But now, in the growing affluence of postwar growth, the last had become first, and Japanese cars, cameras, TVs, and minicomputers set the industrial standard. How did they do it? Partly they were inspired by American example, in particular, the doctrine of W. Edwards Deming, who became an honored prophet far from his own land. But the idea alone would not have been enough. It was the Japanese ethic of collective responsibility—one simply does not let the side down— that made for effective teamwork, sharing of ideas between labor and management, attention to detail so as to eliminate error (zero defects).

Competitors in older industrial nations woke up late and looked around for someone to blame—anyone but themselves. Their first excuse was that the Japanese were not playing fair, that they enjoyed access to foreign markets but refused to open their own. The complaint had merit, although the Japanese were only following earlier European and American examples: protect until you're so strong you don't have to worry about competition. In the late Tokugawa and Meiji periods (1850s to 1900), when Japan was prevented by treaty from imposing customs duties, much of the resistance to foreign goods came from deep-rooted, culturally determined consumer preferences. Also from bureaucratic regulations that tormented importers; the open-door period was a school in nontariff barriers to trade. Once Japan was free to set tariffs, it set them high enough to shelter home industry.

After World War II, world trade policy changed direction. The disastrous experience of the thirties, when industrial nations closed doors and windows and beggared neighbors, had led most economists and politicians to recognize the advantages of free trade, not only for economic prosperity but international harmony. Sentiment along these lines was, to be sure, far from unanimous, but with the United States leading the way, diplomacy and expertise urged everyone to open up. America here was following the British precedent of a century earlier: now that it was the richest, most powerful economy in the world, it renounced old protectionist habits; though in a nation of frequent elections and political deals, it was not always easy to find and erase the heresies. (Some of these vested interests bordered on the ludicrous. During the war, Americans had learned to make a sort of vermouth to replace the French and Italian versions. With peace, this infant industry found it could not compete with the genuine article. So it called for protection on national security grounds and almost got it.)

Japan went along with this move to freer trade, but no country was so effective in enforcing nontariff barriers.* The ingenuity of Japanese contumacy became legendary. Baseball bats were drilled on arrival to make sure they were all-wood. High-tech new medical equipment was generously allowed in, but the procedures using these machines were excluded from health coverage (the ban was lifted once the Japanese

---

* On these (mal)practices, which many American economists are inclined to discount or trivialize and others dismiss as "Japan-bashing" (an expression invented to dispose of awkward charges without having to answer them), see Lincoln, *Japan's Unequal Trade*. The word "bashing" is a favorite resort of the intellectual scoundrel.

had built their own devices). Automobiles were taken apart and checked inside and out before they might be sold to consumers. Once, vexed by increasing imports of French skis, the Japanese tried to exclude them on the pretext that Japanese snow was different. The French responded by threatening to exclude Japanese motorcycles on the ground that French roads were different. Understood; the Japanese dropped their plans.

All of these vexations testify to a sly cunning, of a sort to permit indefinite delays, evasions, and flip-flops, and always with politely straight face. More serious in the long run are business ties and social expectations that exclude shopping for cheaper imports. The Japanese do not think of the market as an open space. It consists of enclosures, and business people who violate the boundaries will be warned that when and if such imports should be unavailable, the maverick bargain hunter will not find Japanese suppliers ready to help out.

What kinds of imported manufactures do get in? Primarily prestige brands, typically linked to national specializations: Scotch whisky, French cognac, Belgian and Swiss chocolates, Vuitton luggage, Patek and Rolex watches, Italian designer clothing—the sort of thing that makes a statement, whether as gift or conspicuous marker of success. All of Japan's big department stores have separate boutiques for these items: a country ready to spend a hundred dollars for a supermelon with ribbon attached can afford to spoil itself. No room, though, for Kodak film; the Japanese have their own Fuji brand—and Japanese light is different.

This mercantilist policy has aroused indignation among trading "partners" and puzzlement among economists. Don't the Japanese understand that such a policy is a deliberate impoverishment of their own population, who pay that much more for what they buy? No one would call the Japanese fools, even if they do occasionally make mistakes. Don't they understand comparative advantage? Don't they know that free trade promotes growth and wealth?

To these rhetorical questions, the Japanese reply that the end of economic policy is not low prices and discount distribution. The goal is market share, increased capacity, industrial and military strength.* Pro-

* On the technological links in Japan between industrial development and military strength, see especially Samuels, *"Rich Nation, Strong Army."* The one thing I would add to his analysis is the role of export-oriented manufacture in expanding industrial capacity. The Japanese have not forgotten the strategic consequences of their relative industrial weakness in World War II.

ducers are more important than consumers. Anyone can buy, but not everyone can make. If people spend less now, they save more (about one third of income). Their children will have more and Japan will be the stronger.

Behind the Japanese, who by some measures may now be the richest people in the world, come the "little tigers" (or "dragons" if you prefer), the ambitious Asian newcomers who have shown the way to other aspirants. Two of these are the former Japanese colonies of Taiwan and Korea; two, Singapore and Hong-Kong, are global city-states that hark back to the commercial-industrial centers of late medieval Italy.[4] No group has grown "more rapidly and more consistently" over the last thirty-five years.* In all four the primary assets have been a work ethic that yields high product for low wages; and, as in Japan, an exceptional manual dexterity that comes from eating with chopsticks and is especially useful in micro-assembly. (This last argument brings smiles from my colleagues, but I stand by it. Much of modern assembly is fine tweezer work, and nothing prepares for it better than eating with chopsticks from early childhood.)†

The availability of fine-skilled, low-wage labor has made all of these countries—plus regional followers such as Malaysia, Thailand, and Indonesia—attractive to advanced enterprises elsewhere, especially from places with overvalued currencies.** Nothing has so persuaded the Japanese to manufacture abroad as the costly yen. Never has capital

---

* World Bank, *East-Asian Miracle*, p. 28. We are talking of growth rates averaging 6 or more percent per year. Taiwan, it should be noted, for all its economic power, is the invisible man. The World Bank's *Annual Development Report* does not include data on Taiwan or even list it among the world's nations—this, apparently to avoid offending the People's Republic, which resents any hint of recognition of Taiwan as a separate entity. In the *East Asian Miracle,* Taiwan appears as "Taiwan, China." Give the World Bank a tin medal for pusillanimity.

† Almost everyone who writes about the economic performance of these East Asian units comments on the quality of the workforce, but equally takes it somehow for granted. Manuel Castells, "Four Asian Tigers," p. 55 and *passim,* finds the most important common characteristic to be the role of the state, even in Hong Kong. My only problem with that is that one finds state intervention all over the place, sometimes wise, sometimes foolish. States may helpeconomic developement, but it takes a world of good work and enterprise to make the state look good.

** The World Bank calls these the "high-performing Asian economies," which seems appropriate, but then vitiates its nomenclature by offering dubious growth data for other countries. What is one to make of a list of countries in order of growth per head per year 1960–85 that has Egypt, Greece, Syria, and Portugal up in the top twenty, and Botswana (diamonds) leading all the rest?—*East Asian Miracle,* p. 3, based on Summers and Heston, "A New Set."

been so mobile. In the 1980s, foreign direct investment (FDI) by industrial nations was growing five times faster than world trade, ten times faster than world output; and even when these flows slowed in the 'nineties, FDI to the developing countries kept growing.[5]

In this way, investment and technique have cascaded from country to country, with wages rising accordingly. The Koreans moved into automobile manufacture with orders and technical assistance from American firms hard-pressed to meet Japanese competition. The Swiss and Japanese contracted for watches and parts made in Hong Kong, then in Malaysia. Japanese (NEC, Sony), European (Philips, Rollei), and American (G.E., Seagate Technologies) multinationals have made Singapore a world center of electronics and photographics, while Hong Kong, where refugee labor could once be had for a low wage and a pallet to sleep on among the machines, is busily setting up plants and leasing work in mainland China. Singapore has outsourced for telephones in Malaysia and the Philippines.

No economy is too advanced to be penetrated, no wall too high. By late 1996, more than thirty Korean companies had manufacturing units in Britain. Wales was congratulating itself on "revitalisation" by foreign, largely Asian, investors, and five thousand people applied for three hundred jobs with the first Korean company to come in. Other European countries are less hospitable. In France, the Korean conglomerate Daewoo Electronics agreed to take over the consumer electronics branch of the French firm Thomson Multimedia. This would have put it ahead of Sony as the world's biggest maker of TV sets, which Thomson had been selling under the RCA label. The deal aborted. The Koreans were furious.*

In choosing investment targets, wage levels are clearly decisive, but

---

* On Wales, see *The Times* (London), 6 January, 1997, p. 40. On Daewoo: *Int. Herald-Tribune*, 18 October 1996, p. 20; 19–20 October 1996, p. 15. Daewoo got its slice of Thomson for a symbolic one-franc piece, but the gift came with a load of debt. (The French government is trying to reduce its deficit to pave the way for entry into the new currency union.) As of December 1996, however, the deal was off. French opponents of foreign invasion made much fuss about the symbolic franc, but said little or nothing about the debt. In pulling out, the French government tried to hide behind the European Community, but fooled nobody. In Korea, people speak of French racism—if it had been an American buyer, no trouble—and the Korean government calls French bad faith (xenophobia) "a national concern." "France cannot be trusted." *Int. Herald-Tribune*, 6 December 1996, p. 1; 9 December 1996, p. 13; 15 January 1997, p. 11. Note, however, that Korea itself is notoriously hostile to foreign ownership. A tale of Eastern pot calling Western kettle black. Even so, Daewoo may still be interested.

market barriers and feelings, immaterial and personal, also matter. Thus American outsourcers found Korean partners far less expensive than Japanese; also a lot easier to work with. But when the Japanese set up affiliates in Korea, they soon found wages going up and pulled out for cheaper climes. And maybe the Koreans were glad to see them go.

(Why Malaysia? It has a population of only 19 million, so labor, at least unskilled labor, is hard to come by. But it has entrepreneurs, and they draw workers like a magnet. Illegal immigrants, mainly from Indonesia [population 190 million] and Bangladesh [115 million], pour in despite strenuous efforts to guard the gates. As everywhere, a thriving business smuggles people for outlandish fees. The outsiders don't look that different, but they are; so that it's not the competition for jobs that bothers the natives, it's mixed sex. The prime minister of Malaysia cites complaints by village leaders: girls running off with foreign boyfriends, unwed mothers ditched by partners, wives abandoning their families to elope with foreigners, who may well treat them better.[6] Can't have that.)

Ethnic connections also count, particularly among expatriate (overseas) Chinese. The Chinese, middleman minority par excellence, are the leaven and lubricant of Southeast Asian trade, and from there around the world. They cherish a work ethic that would make a Weberian Calvinist envious, and they somehow pass it on through richer and poorer from one generation to the next.

(I recall my first visit to Hong Kong a generation ago. It was evening, and outside my hotel I passed a tiny camera shop tucked into a staircase landing. I glanced in, and that was enough. The merchant immediately asked me what I was looking for. Well, I had begun with nothing in mind, but then I remembered that I could use a special lens; so I asked for it. His face fell; he did not have it in stock. Then he brightened up. If I came back later, he would have it for me. I told him I was off to dinner, would not come back until midnight at least. "Don't worry," he said. "You come back. I be here with lens." A little after midnight I returned and started up to my room. Then I remembered, but told my sleepy self it was a waste of time. But then I felt guilty, went back to the shop, and of course found the store open and my man there, with lens. Find me an American or a European to do that.)

The Chinese played a crucial role from the start in the success of European rule—in Dutch Indonesia and the Spanish Philippines, and then in the late nineteenth century in French Indochina. They continue to thrive in the successor states.[7] International partnerships have developed along ethnic lines. Thus Hong Kong, Taiwan, and Singapore are launching platforms to Thailand, where many Chinese have taken Thai names, the better to fit in;* and to Malaysia, where the Chinese run the business show, although affirmative action and smart politics urge them to adopt Malay partners.† Thailand prides itself on transcending differences, in part by strongly discouraging separate Chinese schooling. The Chinese smile politely, publicly approve, but often supplement the Thai curriculum with school abroad. The community balances "on an invisible see-saw between two or more identities."[8] In economic matters, that means that the Chinese know who they are and can work with one another.

In Malaysia ethnic differences are sharper, *ressentiment* keener. Malaysia has known violence, race riots—nowhere near so bad as in Indonesia, but bad enough to make a point. So everyone plays down the ethnic factor. In the meantime, on the island of Penang (northwest coast), disk-drive capital of the world (over 40 percent of output), the Chinese hold most of the executive and engineering positions. "They're more like Americans," says one exec, "they live to work."[9] Members, then, of a rare aristocracy: most people work to live.

Riding the wave of economic growth, the worldwide network of Chinese traders and entrepreneurs grows daily stronger. The success of this diaspora would justify calling the so-called East and Southeast Asian miracle an ethnic, that is, cultural triumph. In Indonesia, where the Chinese form 4 percent of the population, they controlled in the early 1900s seventeen of the twenty-five largest business groups. In Thailand (10 percent Chinese), they number more than 90 percent of the richest families and own the same proportion of commercial and manufacturing assets. That they do not own just about everything is due less to indigenous competition than to the claims made by political insiders, who have founded their own privileged enterprises or expect a piece of whatever looks good.

Guesses about the overall output of Chinese-controlled businesses, including China itself, but excluding Indonesia, Thailand, Malaysia, and the Philippines, speak of $2.5 trillion $(10^{12})$ in 1990, ahead of Japan ($2.1 trillion), half as big as the United States, and growing faster than both.[10] Some feel that Japan's moment of leadership is al-

---

* I am told, however, that the list of Thai names they draw on is such that informed Thais can recognize the Chinese origin.

† The Thais feel that they have been more welcoming than the Malaysians of their Chinese middleman minority—Kaplan, *Ends of the Earth*, p. 377.

ready past.[11] Japan's strength and weakness—both—are its sense of national distinctiveness and superiority. This stimulates the Japanese to high levels of performance, but it also makes it hard for them to work with others as equal partners.* My own sense, however, is that the Japanese will learn—as always.

Two caveats to this East Asian success story. The first concerns promotion from plantation industry to autonomous enterprise. Using modern technology is much easier than inventing it. A handful of countries are responsible for the vast bulk of industrial patents. These rampageous comers, with their lusty infant industries, have yet to stand on their own feet. Some of the hardest work still lies ahead.

Secondly, the faster the growth, the greater the negative side effects, material and psychological (haste makes waste). Remedies require social and political institutions capable of mastering the problems and undertaking solutions. These institutions may not be in place. Time marches on; the remedies never catch up. Often it is simply a question of priorities: money matters; people are expendable; related costs can wait.

Take Thailand. The metropolitan area of Bangkok has both exploded and imploded. Industry and trade have rushed in, drawing throngs of job hunters after, and *nominal* household income has increased tenfold in twenty years.[12] Happy builders have filled every open and underused space. Even canals, once lifeblood arteries, have been cemented over to gain ground for construction. Rising income has made cars proliferate, both for commerce and private use, and the traffic jams are monumental. When I visited Bangkok in 1979, the American Embassy put a car and driver at my disposal. The car had a mobile phone (in my innocence, I'd never seen one) to notify the embassy if we were stuck in a jam; and I was told to make only two appointments a day, one for A.M., one for P.M. Today, Bangkok has 10 million people (twenty times its population in 1900) and many of them prefer big cars. Vehicles pour in every day from the suburbs and surrounding countryside. Drivers need not only a mobile phone but a potty. Powerful people order motorcades, even for wife and children, but the effect on the hundreds of vehicles blocked off and piled up may well be imagined. In 1979, I quickly learned not to walk in the streets during

---

* On the other hand, Chinese clannishness makes them in some places a designated target for crime, the more so as they are richer than the majority population. This in turn discourages them from investing locally: who knows when they may have to run? Cf. Seth Mydans, "Kidnapping of Ethnic Chinese Rises in Philippines," *N.Y. Times,* 17 March 1996, p. 3.

the day; the air was unbreathable. Today, half the traffic cops in the city are suffering from respiratory illness, and a 1990 study reports that bad air (lead levels three times those in Europe or the United States) costs six points in IQ by age seven.[13]

In short, urban Thais are richer, but also poorer. Not in income, but in quality of life.* Only 2 percent of Bangkok's population is tied to proper sewage disposal. The water table is falling; the city is sinking into a treeless river delta that lies open to ocean flooding. Bad living conditions impede further development. Thailand has gone about as far as it can on the basis of cheap labor; cheaper labor lies just across the border. It now needs high-tech, knowledge-intensive industry, which calls for foreign investors and expatriate technicians, and they won't come to breathe poison. Meanwhile the macroeconomic figures show spectacular growth and are swelled by the very effort to correct these maladies. Antipollution devices and measures, waste disposal, medical care, and similar expenditures show up on the plus side of income and product accounts.

## "They Can Have Any Color They Want": The American and Japanese Automobile Industries

Henry Ford, in one of his wry brags, said that the buyers of his cars could have them in any color they wanted, so long as it was black. This was in the heyday of the Model T, which in fact was made at various times in a number of colors, though only one color at a time. That was the essence of Ford's philosophy of mass production: make all the cars alike, and make a lot of them. Sell them cheap and everyone will buy them. People who wanted styling and individuality could look elsewhere. Or buy a Model T chassis and have the coachwork done to order.[14]

The Ford principles became the basis of the American automobile manufacture, and of other branches as well. The American car industry became the world bellwether: biggest maker and exporter,

* Annual income per household in 1995 for the Bangkok metropolitan area was estimated at 2.5 times the average for the entire kingdom. Achavanuntakul, "Effects of Government Policies," p. 9.

tastemaker and style leader, mass producer of vessels of freedom and love.*

The number of registered motor vehicles in Japan in 1917 was 3,856; in 1923, the number had risen only to 13,000, all imported. The big movers were still rickshaws and horse-drawn carriages and wagons, plus trams, and trains for long-distance travel.† But the war, as everywhere, sharpened the sense of need and opportunity. The military had learned to value trucks and now moved to develop a home manufacture. They spoke to the leading *zaibatsu* (conglomerates)—Mitsui, Mitsubishi, Sumitomo—and found them singularly uninterested. So they recruited lesser players, and the Japanese automobile industry came largely into the hands of "new men."

Entering a fallow but fertile field, Ford and General Motors built auto assembly plants in Yokohama (1925) and Osaka (1927). The Japanese came to see these not as an advantage to their consumers but as a deterrent to the development of their own industry, still unfamiliar with mass-production technology. Low as were wages, a Japanese-made vehicle cost 50 percent more than an American-assembled car or import. Between 1926 and 1935, these last accounted for more than 95 percent of new vehicle registrations.[15]

Meanwhile the state, with aggression aforethought, had focused on manufacture for military use: hence the Military Automobiles Assistance Law of 1918, which offered large subsidies for utilitarian vehicles that met specified standards.** Passenger cars could wait.

---

* The assembly-line principle was adaptable to various methods of manufacture. Henry Ford stressed long runs and stuck to technologies long after they were obsolete. When he was right, he was very, very right. And when he was wrong, other producers took market share. Flink, "Unplanned Obsolescence," states that the Model T was in some respects obsolete from the start. But it was cheap, the price of the standard model going from $825 in 1908 to $260 in 1927. That was the end: in May 1927, the last of over 15 million Model T's rolled off the line.

† It is easy to underestimate the contribution of the rickshaw, but it was the key vehicle of urban Japan: some 38,000 in Tokyo alone in 1888. Morris-Suzuki, *Technological Transformation*, p. 97, argues that "the rikisha was just as important to Japan's modern economic development as the railway." She goes on to stress two aspects: it was the first Japanese vehicle to be exported, opening markets that would later take bicycles and motor vehicles; and it was made by networks of small suppliers of components, thereby anticipating the structures of the automobile and other assembly industries.

** Since Japan at this point had no enemies in prospect, one must see these measures as an anticipation of imperial expansion. On the law of 1918, see Morris-Suzuki, *Technological Transformation*, p. 124.

But could they? A decade later, when private enterprise had not yet shown interest, some officials began to worry. In 1929, the Ministry of Commerce and Industry (predecessor of the Ministry of International Trade and Industry [MITI]) published a study, "Policy for Establishing the Motor Vehicle Industry," and this was followed by renewed overtures to the biggest business groups.

By way of example and encouragement, the government designed and started making in 1931 a small 45-hp car that would do 40 kilometers an hour. This slowpoke did not catch on, however, and in 1936 the two American giants still accounted for some three quarters of national output. Now the Japanese army proposed that these foreign firms be purely and simply expelled. After all, war is war, and trade is war.* The pusillanimous politicians found this a little indelicate, though, so the Diet passed a law, drafted by the army, offering big subsidies to Japanese makers and requiring that auto companies be owned and directed in their majority by Japanese citizens. At the same time, the government laid heavy duties on import of complete vehicles and knockdown sets for assembly. These tariffs did the job: by 1938 the production share of Nissan, Toyota, and Isuzu was up to 57 percent. The Americans tried to stick it out, seeking to merge with Japanese makers. No way: all plans to merge, dissolve, or get around these discriminations were subject to government approval. In 1939, the American firms gave up and cleared out. For the Japanese, this turned out to be a good exercise in mercantilism and a preparation for the trade wars of the future.

Where all this would have led, we can guess. But war changes everything, including the best-laid plans. In 1945, plants and equipment lay in ruins, and the American occupation authorities saw no reason why Japan should bother itself with an auto industry. Some officials at the Bank of Japan and the Ministry of Transport agreed. But MITI saw automobiles as the focus of a whole range of related branches and worked out a stimulus package: low-cost loans, tax privileges, protection against foreign competition. For tax purposes, export sales were deductible from income; imports of tools

---

* This is an old theme in the Japanese nationalist refrain. Haruhiro Fukui, "The Japanese State," p. 206, offers an eloquent exposition in a prefectural governor's speech of 1904: " . . . war in peace time goes on constantly. In this kind of war, that is, struggle for survival, those who exploit scientific instruments to expand industry, produce goods at low costs, and thus absorb financial resources will nurture the strength of their own nation, enrich its resources, and thus emerge as winners. . . . "

and equipment were exempted from duty.[16] (Later on [1960s], the
General Agreement on Tariffs and Trade would forbid some of these
discriminatory practices. No use; the Japanese stayed ahead of all
efforts to level the playing field. Every economist knows that there's
more than one way to skin an international bureaucrat.)

This time, the home industry, led by Toyota and Nissan, did catch
fire. In 1950, Japan made 32,000 vehicles—about one and a half
days of American manufacture. At that point the Korean War
brought a rush of orders and gave the automobile industry an
impulse that it never lost, the more so as the American occupation
ended in 1952, leaving Japan free to pursue its own industrial
destiny. This was that of a major exporter, not only because bigger
sales meant lower unit costs and higher profits, but because *greater
productive capacity enhanced the power of the nation*. Defeat—the first
ever suffered by Japan—had left a bitter taste. The Japanese *knew*
they had lost the war not because the Americans were better or
braver fighters, but because of America's industrial output.

By 1960, car output stood at 482,000 units, 39,000 of them
exported, about 8 percent. A decade later, Japan made an
astounding 5.3 million cars, of which 1.1 million sold abroad. By
1974, Japan had replaced West Germany as the world's largest
exporter of automobiles. By 1980, it was shipping some 6 million
vehicles, 54 percent of total output, and had passed the United
States as the biggest carmaker in the world.[17] What's more, other
things equal, these Japanese cars were not winning market share by
lower prices. Japanese cars actually cost more, often more than
sticker price, while American cars typically sold for less than list. Why
so? Because Japanese cars had fewer defects and stood up better to
wear, hence sold higher on the used-car market.

These growth rates of 30 and 40 percent a year in the face of
immensely rich and firmly entrenched competitors will be studied in
the future as a lesson in energy, ingenuity, and enterprise. Henry
Ford must have been spinning in his grave.

Americans, looking for explanations (excuses), pointed to Japanese
state subventions and protectionism. They helped; but they did not
make the industry. That was the work of the people who made the
cars—the labor force, the engineers, the entrepreneurs. Also of the
ineptness of American car makers, who had been going from
triumph to triumph, who equated their enterprises with their
country, who thought the American consumer owed them a living,
and who paid themselves salaries and bonuses that bore little relation

to profits.[18] For them, this Japanese ascent was *lèse-majesté* on a global scale.

How did the Japanese do it? First, they made a virtue of handicaps. Since their home market was too small for the long runs that justified the mass-production methods of the American industry, the Japanese diversified their product, catering to special needs and tastes and switching models as demand dictated. To this end, they learned to design and test faster: 46 months in Japan vs. 60 in the United States (1.7 million man-hours vs. 3.1 million) to craft a new model; 1.4 months vs. 11 to return to normal quality after introduction of the new model.[19] The latter comparison is crucial. Haste makes waste, quality is decisive, and the annals of American car production are dotted with instances of quick savings swallowed by long repairs.*

These quick-change techniques made it possible for Japan to gain first-mover advantage;† to copy quickly the successes of other makers; to drop mistakes in a hurry. Here was the flexible production that some have put forward as the technology of the future.[20] It was not a shift to small scale ("small is beautiful") as some have thought; on the contrary, big firms had the resources to do it better and pay the costs of variation. But it was a major change from "any color, so long as it's black."[21]

Variety required a suitably versatile technology. After the war, the Japanese needed new equipment, and this gave them the opportunity to imagine and combine ingenious tools and machines—most of them, ironically, made to order in the United States. It also opened the way to the latest devices—automation, robotics, computerization. The key change took the Japanese from single-purpose to multipurpose machines, which required a workforce trained to deal with a range of jobs, shifting quickly from one to the other. The Japanese did this by adapting the equipment and learning the drill, so that by the 1970s, for example, they could change dies in stamping presses in five minutes, compared with eight

---

* Cf. Lee Iacocca, then chairman of Chrysler, on the $7-per-car economy on rust-proofing the *Aspen,* followed by $100 million in repairs and an even costlier loss of consumer confidence—Holusha, "Detroit's Push," p. D-8.

† March 1983: "Japanese auto makers introduced three cars this spring that make Detroit's newest models seem dated already." Nag and Simison, "With Three New Cars," on the prospective impact of the Toyota *Camry,* the Honda *Prelude,* and the Mazda 626.

to twenty-four hours in an American plant.[22] This strategy had profound implications for labor-management relations. American emphasis on single-purpose machines and hard assignments had the effect of deskilling; it also led unions to insist on job segmentation and management to accept it.

Multiple models, of course, multiplied inventories, and inventory idles capital, increases storage costs, invites delays. Where American car makers, with their long runs and rare changeovers, dreaded interruption (from strikes, for example) and accumulated a buffer of ready components, Japanese makers strove to minimize stocks by using the system we know as "just in time."* The idea, we are told, came from visits to the United States—not to the automobile plants but to the supermarkets, with their extraordinary diversity of products. They watched American housewives, who kept track and bought as needed; and the markets also kept track and did the same. The goods were pulled through rather than pushed. Why couldn't cars be made that way? (They were, in American auto plants, but the Japanese refined a procedure that had room for improvement.) All of these ideas testify to the value of curiosity, observation, and lateral thinking; in short, to the importance of the human actor.[23]

The Japanese also worked to exclude error, aiming at the unreachable goal of zero defects. Instead of pulling cars off the line, they tried to catch the mistake when it happened, stopping the line if necessary. That might have been expensive, but the point was to prevent rather than repair. "Where are the inspectors?" asked an American visitor. "We have no inspectors," came the answer. "The workers do it."

These innovations completely turned around Japan's reputation as manufacturer; whereas before the war, the Japanese had been associated with five-and-dime ticky-tacky and tin-can vehicles, now their products were quality leaders. American car manufacturers found it hard to accept the new reality, clinging to their cherished stereotypes past the point of no return. They also ridiculed the idea of small cars; the very name "Toyota" made them smile. Americans,

---

* The role of labor conflict and its interruptions is crucial. Ford, in the heyday of the $5 dollar wage and patriarchal management (1910s and early '20s), could afford to squeeze inventories from the 204 days of 1903 to 17 days in 1922. In general, write Abernathy and Clark, "Notes on a Trip," p. 36, "Japanese practice has not extended process rationalization too far beyond the state of the art . . . in Ford's Rouge River facility during the 1920s."

they knew, wanted big cars you could love and make love in. When someone at Chrysler designed a low-slung model, the top exec sneered: "Chrysler builds cars to sit in, not to piss over."[24]

Meanwhile Japanese compacts took a growing share of the American market, and when trade measures set bounds on the number of cars the Japanese could ship, they just moved upscale, first to midrange vehicles, and then to the best. So, the foilers foiled. This was also a way to build customer loyalty, bringing them up as their income and social status rose.[25] When the Japanese announced that they planned to compete with German luxury cars, it seemed a joke. A year or two later and Mercedes and BMW were no longer laughing. The Japanese had just about swept aside their higher-priced success symbols.

It would be wrong to see these gains as simply a matter of technique, there for the taking or copying. People made all the difference. For anyone who has ever visited Japan and suffered in the traffic that is one of the vexatious, even nightmarish features of overcrowded urban and industrial agglomerations, the ability to run a just-in-time system comes across as miraculous. How can anyone deliver parts on call and on time? The answer: by sleeping on the job. The driver takes his lorry close by the factory gate and parks there overnight, curling up in the cab. On the morrow he's there.

But that makes another point: what's sauce for the goose is not for the gander. The just-in-time mother plant is saving its time. Very smart. But the supplier is spending his time. The whole Japanese system of outsourcing rests on pressing down, on squeezing the purveyors while they in turn squeeze their workforce. All is not immaculate, then, in the Japanese industrial heaven. On the other hand, the mother firm is not unreasonable: it squeezes, but it also helps with equipment, technique, and funding. These are tough, resilient people, as always very hierarchical, but with a strong sense of reciprocal obligation up and down the scale.

In the automobile manufacture, all of this depends on a team approach that unites management and labor, in a commitment not only to efficient performance but to continuing improvement. Labor is not expected to oppose innovation, even of the labor-saving variety,[26] and in the big firms every worker feels obliged, indeed is pushed, to make suggestions, mounting to the tens of thousands, for saving effort here and money, even a few yen, there. (One can only wonder how management vets this flood of ideas.) Everyone on the line, moreover, is trained to do a range of tasks, and an interruption is not an opportunity to rest but rather to do something else. (None of this segmentation—"that's not my job"—which can be "murder" in work that brings together different trades.)* In Japan, the worker has and feels a duty to be useful at all times.†

All of this may sound good, but it is not easy, nor is it kind to the organism or the ego. It entails a rigorous subordination of the person to superiors and to the group. The company has a thousand ways to reward the cooperative worker, to punish the nonconformist. Groups that make trouble can see their tasks turned over to an outside supplier. Firms like Toyota swallow their employees; they have their own calendar, independent of national holidays and weekends (but most Japanese have no religious sabbath). What with overtime and commuting, workers are often away from home eleven and twelve hours a day; but that goes for cadres and bosses too. That's where wives come in: they rear the children and put them to bed before Father comes home. Off can mean on: 40 percent of the manufacturing employees work more than one of their days off each month; 30 percent more than five extra days a month. Most of them engage in company-sponsored activities on at least one holiday a month; a third do more than that. The company makes this easy, what with private recreational facilities, organized activities, and assiduous monitors. Ask a Japanese worker what he does, and he'll tell you the name of his company.[27]

Observers have justly contrasted this teamwork, this sacrifice of the individual to the group, and yes, this hyperintensification of labor, to the adversarial relationship that embodies and sanctions the self-respect of Western labor. In effect, the American firm is pluralistic:

---

* Note that things might have gone differently. In the postwar years, Japanese labor, often led by militant Communists, adopted an combative mode that was rejected and abandoned only after some fierce battles with company unions. The American occupation played its role: initially, it opened the door by legalizing trade unions; subsequently, its primary concern was to tame the unions by way of reducing Soviet influence.

† The economist Harvey Leibenstein states the contrast in general terms: " . . . the ideal in the West is a short-run *contractual* view or contractual *ideal* of firm association rather than a long-run *belonging* ideal. There is a sense in which the Western approach represents a series of contracts . . . involves devotion to a particular skill or job (even a 'property right' in the job) rather than loyalty to the firm in general"—"Japanese Management System," p. 9. See p. 11 for contrasting results of attitude surveys: in 1976 49 percent of Japanese workers said they should help others when their own tasks were completed; only 16 percent of American workers felt that way.

the bosses have their aims; the workers, theirs; the shareholders, theirs. And while all are theoretically united by loyalty to the enterprise, the meaning of that loyalty is subject to competing interests. Hence a constant, latent tension, punctuated by conflicts and showdowns.

Japan does not work that way. Japanese company unions almost always obtain their wage demands because they have been negotiated with management in advance.* Such strikes as occur are often symbolic, one-day affairs, just to show that the workers are serious.† Contrast the United States: there the talks are often *pro forma,* and issues are resolved by test of force. Sometimes, by miscalculation, the battle ends in closure of company or plant—who needs all this trouble? Too often the combat leaves a residue of hard feeling that embitters relations and invites another round. Both sides proclaim victory, but just wait until next time.[28]

Is this Japanese mode of "lean production," quality control, and labor-management partnership exportable? Can Americans learn new ways? We have the beginning of an answer in the performance—in the United States but also in Britain—of Japanese affiliates: Honda, Toyota, Mitsubishi, *et al.* These plants owe their origin to trade barriers; they were built to get behind the walls. They pay about the same wages as American firms, but they have been able to keep out the unions with their task segmentation and divided sovereignty. They also have relied extensively on imported components, to the point of raising questions about the nationality of the product. But that is the nature of global industry: one buys cheapest. In the meantime, these transplants seem to show higher labor productivity and quality than all-American firms, though Japanese factories in Japan do somewhat better.[29]

These results tell us what American workers can do starting from scratch. These non-unionized transplants are free of suspicions and

---

* The same in Japanese criminal trials: by the time the matter comes to court, the accused has largely conceded, so that the conviction rate is almost 100 percent.

† The nature of Japanese labor relations has been a puzzle to specialists. Is this absence of conflict a stage that labor will outgrow? Or does it reflect deep-rooted social values and traditions? Many Japanese incline to the latter explanation, but Galenson and Odaka, "The Japanese Labor Market," p. 627, do not think it necessary "to fall back on well-worn generalizations about family structure and the hierarchical, traditionalist nature of Japanese society." Is an explanation less persuasive or valid because it is "well-worn"?

negatives left by generations of combat by the United Auto Workers. On the other hand, some of the contrasts between Americans and Japanese workers go back to child rearing. Union or no union, people are different. Douglas Fraser, president of the UAW and a reasonable man, when asked if American workers had to adopt Japanese values and attitudes to compete, said he thought not, and argued from temperament: " . . . the American worker has an individuality and a willingness to dissent that does not respond to dictatorial instruction."[30] "Dictatorial"? The word proclaims the gap.

Plenty of blame to go around. Much of the initial failure of the American auto industry to hold its own against this bull of a competitor was its own fault—of labor partly, because of its hormonal reluctance to change ways or give way; but of management even more. The list of sins is long: (1) complacency (we're the best, have always been the best); (2) want of empathy (did they really expect the Japanese, with their often narrow roads and left-side driving, to buy big cars with steering on the left?); (3) residual, two-faced reliance on government support (we're all for free enterprise, but how else counter official favors to the Japanese auto industry?);* and (4) a short and selfish time horizon that led American management to use respites from Japanese competition to raise prices and dividends rather than invest and improve techniques.

But the Americans have been learning and are doing better. Here and there, increasingly, car makers have adopted Japanese methods— to much oohing and ahing and self-congratulation, as though they had discovered America. Example: Ford's decision to stop the assembly line at its Louisville truck assembly plant long enough to allow workers to lower the body onto the chassis. Simple enough, and it meant more accurate work and less damage: "You just line up two pins and drop it." The idea came from workers on the line. In the old days, management would have paid no heed. Now they were listening.[31]

So the American industry is poised today between old ways and new. The big auto makers are relying more than before on parts suppliers, within and without the enterprise, to do much of the component assembly, in effect pushing the burden back *à la*

---

* Cf. the Chrysler bailout, where the government took stock as security. The stock appreciated enormously when Chrysler got back on track, at which point Chrysler tried to argue that the government should not get the capital gain. One can well imagine what Chrysler would have said had things gone the other way. Where fair play?

*japonaise* and holding their wage bill down. To keep inventories lean, they are demanding just-in-time deliveries, some of them at twenty-minute intervals. Some affiliated partsmakers are now working for outside car makers as well as for the mother assembly plant, thereby maximizing the rate of utilization. Come a strike against the parent company, should the workers in the plant continue to produce for competitors? That's a hard one. Old-timers say no; others point to painful reality. If labor gets too difficult, they warn, the auto makers will turn to more cooperative suppliers, say in Mexico. *(Viva la NAFTA!)* The big boys cannot afford to let a parts supplier hang up the whole process. The pragmatists have been winning the argument. (In effect, the possibility of such diversion has sapped labor's bargaining power.) Labor ideologues are not happy: "You're seeing a taste of business unionism," they scold. Labor in bed with management.[32] Can this be love?

Meanwhile Japanese car makers are beginning to feel such Asian rivals as Korea nipping at their heels. No rest or end in this kind of war.

# 28

# Losers

S trung out behind the leaders and followers—in the sense of those who are keeping pace or catching up—are most of the world's peoples.

By comparison with East Asia, the rest of the world looks like a study in slow motion, or even one step forward, two steps back. The Middle East has much going for it, in particular, huge oil revenues (some \$2 trillion [$10^{12}$] in the twenty years after 1973), but its political, social, and cultural institutions do not ensure security of enterprise or promote autonomous technological development. Also, cultural attitudes, and above all, gender biases, inhibit industrial undertakings. One result is high rates of unemployment and underemployment, made worse and angrier by education: people who have been to school expect more.[1]

To be sure, well-meaning governments in the region have tried to substitute for private initiative. Thus Egypt, recalling the industrial projects of Muhammad Ali one hundred years earlier, decided after World War II to invest in cotton-spinning mills. The idea seemed foolproof. Egypt grew the finest long-fiber cotton in the world; why not work it up and gain the value added? The trouble was, the yarn turned out by these callow mills was not of international quality, while foreign growers sought to upgrade their raw cotton and weavers looked for ways to make high-quality cloth with poorer varieties. Never underestimate the ingenuity of good technicians: before the Egyptians could turn around, they were stuck with poor cloth for the home market and had lost part of their export market for raw cotton. Egypt, unfortunately, was not the only example of industry aborted. The African continent abounds in projects and disappointments.

Failure hardens the heart and dims the eye. Up to now, Middle Eastern losers have sought compensation in religious fundamentalism and military aggression. On the popular level, prayer and faith console the impotent and promise retribution. Hence the apocalyptic tone of much Muslim preaching and discourse: the End will bring redress. Meanwhile, the strong resort to force. They find it easier to seize and screw than to make and do. So for Iraq, which thought to get rich quicker by grabbing oil and looting houses in Kuwait than by manufacturing salable commodities. Why buy arms if not to use them?

Will these counterproductive tendencies pass? Impossible to say. They are not accidental but visceral. The international experts keep their chin up (that's what they're paid for) and offer modest recipes for improvement. Thus the World Bank, with its talk of "adjustment," reminds us that good policies pay. What are good policies? Realistic, competitive exchange rates, low or no budget deficits, low or no barriers to trade, markets, markets, markets.

Such "improvements in the macroeconomic framework" do help. They clear major distortions and obstacles. But they do not come easy. How does one eliminate budget deficits when half the workforce is employed by the state unproductively and political stability is tied to inefficiency? (This kind of problem afflicts even rich nations. Look at Europe and the Maastricht criteria for the euro curency.)

And that's only the beginning. The real work of building structures and institutions remains. Besides, what happens when the oil is gone?*

Latin America has had almost two hundred years of political independence to graduate to economic independence. It remains, however, a mixed area, wanting in local initiatives, technologically patchy, entre-

---

* Field, *Inside the Arab World*, p. 21, points out that at rates of extraction in the early 1990s, oil in the Gulf has 130 years to go. (The assumption, of course, is that we know what's there. People are still looking.) But that's the Gulf; for other oil producers in the Middle East and North Africa, the end is nearer. Meanwhile progressive exhaustion is an incentive to a search for new energy technologies. In the end, for oil as now for coal, a fair amount may be left in the ground.

preneurially needy. This pattern of arrested development reflects the tenacious resistance of old ways and vested interests. In particular, the apparently rational focus on land and pastoralism (long live comparative advantage!), reinforced by social and political privilege, bred powerful, reactionary elites ill-suited and hostile to an industrial world. This disjuncture, when combined with social discontents—so many poor—invited antidemocratic, though populist, solutions *(caudillismo)*, terrible when durable, destructive when fragile.

So industry came late. This need not be a handicap; lateness has its advantages. But everything depends on the quality of enterprise and the technological capability of the society. In most of Latin America, industry came in under the shelter of import substitution: high tariffs, discriminatory legislation and regulations, nontariff barriers to imports. As we know from American experience in the nineteenth century and Japanese in the twentieth, such measures may work in a context of energetic emulation, of exigent, world-level (export-capable) standards, of domestic competition. In Latin America, this impulse was largely wanting. Not everywhere. Some industry is on the cutting edge. But most is well behind the frontier, panting behind protective walls.

This protection has been justified by national interest or by anticolonialist ideologies that, if pushed to their logical conclusion, would suggest an end to all exchange with the more advanced industrial nations abroad. (Latin America has been a field of dichotomous perspective: center vs. periphery, neocolonialists vs. victims, bad guys against good.) Fortunately, that has not happened. Such exercises in pure reason (or unreason) are more suited to scholars' studies than to the halls of government, as President Cardoso of Brazil, once a flag-bearer of the dependency school, has now discovered.

We should not underestimate the importance of that discovery: just because something is obvious does not mean that people will see it, or that they will sacrifice belief to reality. In the effort to have things both ways, or every way, to appease old interests, to encourage new, to keep the foreigner away while bringing him in, most Latin nations have resorted to the manipulation of trade and money: import barriers and quotas, differential rates of exchange, a carapace of restrictions that some have called the "inward-looking model"—and, of course, to borrowing.[2]

Such measures can provide temporary relief, but at a heavy price: constant adjustments, currency black markets, runaway inflations, high transaction costs, a chilling of foreign investment. Even so, some Latin American countries were able to borrow ridiculously large sums from official international lenders (World Bank, IMF) and from private commercial banks, acting with the encouragement of their governments and, no doubt, tacit assurances of a rescue safety net. Much of this money found its way back to secret private accounts in the United States, Switzerland, and other cozy shelters.

The combination of mismanagement, profligacy, corruption, and open-ended borrowing—development without efficiency constraints—cannot long endure. Such structures are intrinsically brittle, because everyone is straining to the limit and everything is interconnected. Sooner or later, someone gets worried; the balance sheets do not balance; the lenders get cold feet; it becomes impossible to pay old debts with new. Panic!

This happened in the Mexican peso crisis of 1994–95. It couldn't have come at a worse (some would say, a better) time, just after the American administration managed to squeeze through the North American Free Trade Agreement (NAFTA) by calling in every political chip and committing to a mountain of anti-economic favors. Now it had to find tens of billions to reassure the market and give investors and monetary allies the time to pull their chestnuts out. But this time it could not get fast action from a recalcitrant, narrow-minded Congress. Not to worry: the technicians, led by economist Lawrence Summers, found some $20 billion lying quietly in an account established over half a century earlier with the profits realized in the 1930s by repudiating obligations in gold. These ill-gotten gains had been set aside at the time to protect the American dollar . . . Well, one could say that a collapse of the peso and the liquidation of American holdings in Mexico would have done terrible damage to NAFTA and the American dollar . . . Those $20 billion plus another $30 billion cobbled together from international lending organizations saved the day. The American government subsequently made much of quick repayment by Mexico, and the press played down, or never noticed, the fact that the Mexicans had to borrow the money. New debt for old.

The heart of the matter is Latin America's need to go on borrowing, if only to pay interest on older loans. A research student from Latin America once complained to me about this burden of old debt and the vexatious, small-minded foreign insistence on repayment. "You don't have to repay," I pointed out; "a sovereign nation can always repudiate." "Yes," he replied, "but then where shall we go to borrow more?" Exactly. Now, however, the banks are wary, and international lending organizations are tying their support to fiscal and trade reform in the direction of openness. The code word is "adjustment"—surely a good thing. A more open market is a force for rationality and efficiency, a re-ordering of economic activity in the direction of comparative advantage, a constraint on corruption and favoritism. And the prospect of aid may be an incentive to cooperation in the struggle against the drug trade—an industry whose growth can only be guessed at.[3] No guarantees. But better a push in the right direction than a return to the *status quo ante*.

Among the heaviest losers in this period of record-breaking economic growth and technological advance were the countries of the Communist-Socialist bloc: the Soviet Union at the bottom of the barrel, Romania and North Korea almost as bad, and a range of satellite victims and emulators struggling to rise above the mess. Best off were probably Czechoslovakia and Hungary, with East Germany (the DDR) and Poland trailing behind. The striking feature of these command economies was the contradiction between system and pretensions on the one hand, performance on the other. The logic was impeccable: experts would plan, zealots would compete in zeal, technology would tame nature, labor would make free, the benefits would accrue to all. From each according to his ability; to each according to his deserts; and eventually, to each according to his needs.*

The dream appealed to the critics and victims of capitalism, admittedly a most imperfect system—but as it turned out, far better than the alternatives. Hence the Marxist economies long enjoyed a willfully credulous favor among radicals, liberals, and progressives in the advanced industrial nations; and a passionate, almost religious endorsement by the militant "anti-imperialist" leaders of the world's poor countries. Many colonies, now independent, turned to the socialist paradigm with a hunger and passion that defied reality.[4]

These favorable predilections long concealed the weaknesses of such command economies. In fact, although the Russian state was capable

---

* The Soviets anticipated and perhaps taught the Germans. The "tens of thousands" of slave labor deaths incurred building the White Sea–Baltic canal (early 1930s)—picks, shovels, and wheelbarrows against snow, ice, and hunger—were justified by the allegedly redemptive character of the work, which would turn enemies of the people into good socialists. The slogan: "We will instruct nature and we will receive freedom." Compare the motto at the entrance to the Nazi death camps: *Arbeit macht frei*—Work makes free. On the Soviet dream (nightmare) of ruthless gigantism (gods do not weep), see Josephson, " 'Projects of the Century.' "

of mobilizing resources for specific projects, technique was generally backward and overall performance shoddy. The impressive production data were intrinsically and deliberately exaggerated. They should have been heavily discounted for propaganda; also for deterioration and unsold (unsalable) commodities. (Except for caviar, vodka, and folkloric mementoes, nothing Russia made could compete on the world market.) Apartment buildings hung nets around the perimeter to protect pedestrians from falling tiles or stones. Thrifty consumers paid a small fortune for tiny, primitive motor vehicles and then waited years for delivery. Even after they got a car, they found replacement parts unobtainable, and motorists routinely took their windshield wipers with them when they parked their automobiles. Electrical appliances were at the mercy of fluctuating house current. National income data excluded services, for reasons of economic doctrine—only real product counted. But in fact, the less said about services the better: inconveniences balanced advantages. No friend like a good plumber. Or someone in the *nomenklatura,* the privileged elite, with their special stores and clubs, their access to foreign imports, their quasi-exemption from dregs and dross.

Some see this endemic mess as a dirty secret of the system: rulers nourished privation by way of rewarding favorites, building desire in the ambitious, and dulling the rest in the tedium of endless queues. The capitalist economies stimulated labor by the prospect of reward: "ya pays yer money an ya takes yer choice." Communism offered "singing tomorrows." But waiting had to be paid for, and tomorrow never came. When did the people in the queues work? The joke had it, they made believe they worked, and the state made believe it paid them.

The worst aspect of the system, however, was its indifference to, nay, its contempt for, good housekeeping and human decency. Prosperity forgone was bad enough. In a world that had once created and still preserved some beautiful things, the new system mass-produced ugliness: buildings and windows out of true; stained and pocked exteriors, raw cement block; equipment out of order, rusting machinery, abandoned metal corpses—in short, raging squalor.

Necessarily, what the system did to things, it did to people. How to survive in a wasteland dotted with junkheaps? In a world of systematic contempt for humanity? "White coal," they called the people shipped in jammed, fetid freight cars to useless labor and oblivion in frigid wastes. (The USSR anticipated here the death trains and marches of Nazi Germany.) Some, spared or overlooked, heroically maintained oases of warmth and culture in tiny flats and rooms. Many more drowned disappointment and despair in vodka.

Still, nature's gifts remained. The greatest asset of the revolutionary regime was the unspoiled natural treasures it inherited from a late-developing economy. It ran these down with the recklessness that comes with self-proclaimed virtue.

One *place* and one *event* stand for the whole. The place is the Aral Sea, once the fourth largest body of fresh water on the face of the earth, today a dying hole—half the original surface, a third of its volume, reeking with chemicals, fish gone, air hot and poisoned. Children in the region die young, one in ten in the first year. Decades of insolent plans, haste and waste, tons of pesticide, herbicide, and fertilizer, false economies such as unlined irrigation trenches enabled the Soviet Union to grow lots of cotton ("white gold"), while reversing gains in life expectancy and leading the way backward.[5]

Aral, moreover, was not unique, though it was a worst case. In general, Soviet projects for diversion and reversal of water and for construction of industrial plants in previously clean settings took no account of environment. Priority went to virtual jobs and economic growth, and the bigger and more costly the task, the more ennobling. Siberia especially was seen as a *tabula rasa,* empty tundra, space and more space, to do with as one pleased: rivers to be turned backwards, the snows of the north to water the deserts of the south. Creation corrected: communism saw itself as antireligious and scientific, but it aimed at making gods of men. The biggest of these megalomaniacal schemes, which would have altered global climate, had to be abandoned. Prometheus fortunately re-bound.

Aral was the *place.* The *event* was the meltdown of the atomic power reactors at Chernobyl in the Ukraine in 1986. The fire burned out of control for five days and spread more than 50 tons of radioactive poison across White Russia (Belarus), the Baltic states, and parts of Scandinavia—far more than the bombs at Hiroshima and Nagasaki combined. The prevailing winds blew north-northwestward, but no one will convince those Turks who later came down with blood diseases or the thousands of pregnant women from Finland to the Adriatic who had precautionary abortions that they were not victims too. Among the unquestioned casualties were the brave men sent in to fight the fire and clean up afterwards. They were promised special compensation and did not always get it. Relief funds disappeared down the local party maw. The workers' exposure was systematically understated, so that they did their job at the price of a lingering death. (Could they have said no?) Withal, the task was apparently botched: the core was not completely smothered; "the situation" not stabilized.*

The area around the plant has become a place of fear. Is the fear justified? The definitive answer may not come for decades: low levels of radiation work slowly. Some scientists speak of fifty years. By then all the victims will be dead. The residents of the area have chosen caution and terror. Most have left and not returned; but some never left and some have come back to take advantage of empty land. One such diehard, a woman of sixty-five, reassures herself that she is still feeling fine. She has rules of thumb: plant apple seeds deep in the ground; eat no more than ten kilos of mushrooms; "if you feel too much radiation, you have to drink some vodka." Her neighbor believes what she sees: "Look at this place. Where do you see any radiation? If anything, this place is better now that there are less people." And some try to laugh about their plight. They tell the joke about the farmer who is selling apples under a big sign, APPLES FROM CHERNOBYL. "You must be mad," says a passerby. "No one wants to buy apples from Chernobyl." "Sure they do," says the vendor. "Some people buy them for their mother-in-law, others for their wife."[6] (And maybe others for their husband.)

As a result, although other accidents and natural catastrophes may have cost more lives—the chemical leak at Bhopal, India, in 1984, perhaps—none has been more damaging to reputation and prestige.[†] Repugnance and repudiation were in direct proportion to the technological arrogance and gigantism that inspired and sanctified Soviet programs and projects.[7] The socialist command economy was tarred with incompetence, credulity, stupidity, and indifference to the public weal—among other sins—the more so because of clumsy attempts at concealment and mitigation. "It is now clear that the political repercussions from Chornobyl accelerated the collapse of the Soviet empire."[8]

A dozen nuclear plants on the Chernobyl model are still in operation.

---

* This was not what the Soviet authorities told the public; or, for that matter, what the International Atomic Energy Agency was ready to admit. Cf. Alexander R. Rich, "10 Years Later, Chernobyl's True Story Is Hard to Nail Down," *Boston Globe,* 26 April 1996, p. 21.

† The human cost of Chernobyl may never be known. Officials, including medical personnel, were under great pressure to minimize casualties. (Contrast Bhopal, where the injured had a financial incentive to make claims.) Feshback and Friendly, *Ecocide in the USSR,* p. 152, think doctors cleared out because they feared public anger. They may have feared radiation more.

Pretense and promises are vulnerable to truth and experience. When the dream vanished, when people came to know the difference between the systems, communism lost its legitimacy. The walls came down and the Soviet Union collapsed, not by revolution, but of abandonment.

> . . . the ecological inheritance [of Africa] could never have been less than difficult. Africa was "tamed" by its historical peoples, over many centuries, against great handicaps not generally present in other continents, whether in terms of thin soils, difficult rainfall incidence, a multitude of pests and fevers, and much else that made survival difficult.[9]

All the ills that have hurt Latin America and the Middle East are exponentially compounded in sub-Saharan Africa: bad government, unexpected sovereignty, backward technology, inadequate education, bad climate, incompetent if not dishonest advice, poverty, hunger, disease, overpopulation—a plague of plagues. Of all the so-called developing regions, Africa has done worst: gross domestic product per head increasing, maybe, by less that 1 percent a year; statistical tables sprinkled with minus signs; many countries with lower income today than before independence. The failure is the more poignant when one makes the comparison with other parts: in 1965, Nigeria (oil exporter) had higher GDP per capita than Indonesia (another oil exporter); twenty-five years later, Indonesia had three times the Nigerian level.[10]

The pain of reality hurts more for the initial exhilaration. With independence, the burden of exploitation would be lifted. Time now for rewards. Some early growth figures seemed to confirm this: "Some areas—like the Rhodesias, the Belgian Congo, Morocco, Gabon, Kenya—were given as growing at 6 to 11 per cent per year, rates among the highest in the world."[11] Few people deflated these estimates to take account of upward bias in countries moving toward urbanization and a growing share of monetized, hence countable, transactions. And no one paused to ask why the colonial powers were so quick to leave. People wanted Africa to do well. Here is a Western observer, writing in 1962:

> Africans in general are the most present-minded people on earth. . . .
> Without significant exception, all African leaders . . . share the passionate desire to acquire all the good things which western civilization has produced in the two millennia of its history. They want especially to get the technological blessings of American civilization, and to do so as quickly as

possible. The lack of historical consciousness of their people gives the African leaders a great advantage in moving rapidly toward this goal of modernization.[12]

And yet . . . Basil Davidson, Africanist of unquestioned sympathy and bona fides, writes sadly of the moment of disillusion—that point when the Africans of one or another place realized that freedom was not an automatic gateway to happiness and prosperity.[13]

Specialists in these matters distinguish between food security and food self-sufficiency; Africa is wanting on both scores. A large and increasing number of people—and that means women and children especially—are hungry and malnourished, whether for want of purchasing power or for bad distribution. Recalling the anarchy of the late Roman empire, city and country are at war with each other. The new bureaucrats try to squeeze the land and pay less than market value. The farmers hold back or give up. The rootless urbanites have learned tastes that cannot be satisfied locally. So, even in the best of circumstances, the land produces too little food or the wrong kind of food, and must bring it in from outside, at a growing cost to earnings and balance of payments. No other part of the globe is so much prisoner to survival.[14]

Unlike other poor regions, moreover, Africa's shortfalls in food supply afflict, not the food buyers in the cities, but the small farmers who scratch the soil and raise the livestock.* Here nature—material impediments and climatic variations—plays a nasty role, not only swinging widely from fat years to lean, but cumulating trends over longer periods. In the quarter century from 1960 to 1984, food output did not keep up with population, and only a rapid increase in imports kept nourishment up to inadequate (as against catastrophic) levels. Market forces encouraged the trend: food grains from the United States, for example, could be had in Lagos in 1983 at a quarter of the locally grown price.[15] Import dependency (6 percent of caloric intake in 1969–71, 13 percent in 1979–81) switched tastes from old, boring sta-

---

* Typically the farmers will get enough to eat (will feed themselves first) if the government does not expropriate food supplies for distribution in cities or for sale abroad. So in Europe during World War II. But in the Soviet Union, seizure of farm crops in the 1930s in the Ukraine led to a ghastly famine that killed millions. But then, this was the intent. These were nationalists and kulaks, marked as enemies of the Revolution. For a brief, vivid description of this atrocious crime, see Moynahan, *The Russian Century*, pp. 114–22. To know this is to understand the eventual collapse of a rotten regime.

ples to new cereals, while new urban eating habits led to an increased
demand for meat by those who could not afford it. In this way, more
and more of Africa's food crops went to animal feed. All along, the
highest natural rates of population growth in the world (3+ percent per
year) were pushing farmers on to marginal soils that quickly wore out.
Or driving them from country to slums in the city.[16] In countries where
political agencies are fragile and ineffective, the scars of mismanagement do not easily heal, and the good and bad do not balance.

One should not blame these outcomes on smallholder ignorance or
incapacity, for in Africa, as much as anywhere, farming methods and reproductive behavior mix old values and rituals with a rational response
to material circumstances. African farmers are not fools, and children
start paying their way early in a land where firewood and water are
scarce and much time is spent foraging and carrying. The result is a reasonable preference for large families. Large families are also proof of
virility and a source of pride.[17] In general, the women do as they are
told, especially in those cultures where polygamy prevails; and when
the men come home, for they often work far off, they have their way,
often at great risk to health. AIDS? Forget condoms; the men don't
like them. And the women? "They have so many other problems to
think of, why should they think about something that kills you in 10
years?"[18]

In the latter days of empire, some governments and foreign advisers
tried to remedy these ills, although their calculations were often distorted by extraneous motives and personal interest. Take agriculture.
Even before independence, some colonial rulers tried to correct for
past mistakes and indifference and to introduce "modern" methods.

The "mother" of all such projects was the British groundnut (in
American English, peanut) scheme, launched and sunk in Tanganyika
over the period 1946–54 and "intended to demonstrate what the state
was capable of . . . when it harnessed modern Western technology and
expertise."[19] The idea came originally from the managing director of
the United Africa Company, a subsidiary of Unilever, a company reputed to know its oil. The plan was vetted and approved at British
cabinet level. The immediate objective: to alleviate British postwar oil
and fat shortages without spending dollars (buy colonial). In the words
of Food Minister John Strachey, "On your success depends, more than
on any other single factor, whether the harassed housewives of Britain
get more margarine, cooking fat and soap, in the reasonably near future."[20]

The ultimate aim was to "raise the standard of living of the African peasant" by demonstrating the possibilities of modern technology. To be sure, these peanuts were not destined for consumption by Africans, hungry as they might be; but the peasants would see (would be given an "ocular demonstration," in bureaucratese) and copy the superiority of large-scale, mechanized agriculture. No hands; everything would be done by machine: bulldozers, tractors, rooters, sowers, combines.

At the same time, as though to prove the virtues of British-style socialism (the project was intended, among other things, to demonstrate a superior alternative to Soviet ideology), the British Labour government sent officials to teach the African employees how to strike for higher pay. This altruism succeeded beyond expectations. The natives took up spears, idled the tractors, blocked the roads, stopped the railway. Police had to be brought in; the union leaders, put in prison. The strike failed, but the natives had learned a thing or two.[21]

The planners went in without a plan. They chose a central site because it was empty. It was empty because it had no water. Members of the mission acknowledged "a total lack of any experience of mechanised agriculture." No one had ever tried this kind of thing. Information on rainfall patterns and their effect on yields was wanting; ditto regarding the soil; and estimates on cost of clearing bush drew on experience with airstrips during the war. Supplies took the form of left-over army stores from the Philippines, some useful, some worthless, all the worse for neglect. The mission had no engineering expert. As one member, an accountant, put it: "It was all guesswork, and our guess was as good as anybody else's."

Both British housewives and African peasants had a long wait in prospect. African farmers raised peanuts in some areas, but they (usually the women) did so at enormous pain and effort, scratching and clawing every step of the way. Even so, they did better than these machines, which for all their steel, rubber, and internal combustion engines, sickened in the African climate. Breakdowns were common, repair shops lacking, and what would they have done anyway without replacement parts? Clearance of the gnarled brush and roots was a nightmare. It cost ten times original estimates, and the ground, once cleared, dried to brick hardness.* Very soon the projectors had to scale back expectations and substitute sunflowers for some of the peanut bushes. The changes did not help. Nature refused to cooperate, and yields were far below expectations.

The effects on the local economy and society were deplorable. The

---

* On lateritic soil, see Chapter I.

British employes had enough money to buy the natives out of food, and the natives in turn got jobs with the project and gave up traditional cultivation. So food production went down and large amounts had to be imported to feed those who were supposed to be producing a surplus for export. Liquor came in too; and prostitutes, charging "stupendous fees of five shillings and more";[22] and thieves—all the afflictions and corruptions of unexpected wealth. Meanwhile the British tried to teach the natives the virtues of working-class solidarity and equality. The natives saw this as a subversion of order and morality.

By 1950, failure was inescapable; time now for remorse and liquidation. The groundnut does not lend itself to mass cultivation. Economic yields require intensive farming. The plan to grow in huge 30,000 acre units proved utterly impractical. It took four years to dispose of the equipment and installations. The British turned as much as possible over to the government of newly independent Tanganyika, which saw these ill-favored leftovers as nuisance more than assets. It wasn't hard for observers to note that the money could have been put to better use.

Needless to say, the fiasco hurt British prestige and discouraged other "imaginative schemes of economic development." Would these have done better? The record is not encouraging, except to ever renewable planners and technicians, who seem to use these projects as children might a dollhouse, and who learn with every failure. I would not depreciate the motives and deeds of these experts. They remain our hope for large-scale, long-range amelioration. Yet nothing is more inebriating and seductive than making a world and feeling virtuous for it. In the end, the British shrugged the failure off. The nation was tired and had better things to worry about than peanuts in Africa.

The British groundnut scheme was not the exception. Colonial governments were liable to these temptations, which held out the irresistible promise of doing well while doing good. The French tried for cotton on the Niger River, upstream from Timbuktu (today Mali), from the 1910s to the 1940s. Again Africa was to supply European needs—this time the potential demand by French spinners, pressed to find precious dollars for American cotton. The colonial administrators involved were concerned to protect their African constituents, even against themselves, while ensuring a supply of raw cotton that could compete on the world market. The French also wanted to preserve freedom of enterprise where possible. So, with consummate Gallic logic, they came up with a compromise formula: the peasants had a "strict obligation" to grow cotton from dawn to dusk, but complete freedom to sell it.[23] Then the French uprooted and replanted peasants and made them plant cotton bushes, and if the peasants made trouble or brought in unsatisfactory cotton, they were marched off to jail. It was, some like to think, a loose, easygoing jail—enough though to make the point.

One would like to think that liberation changed all that, but in fact the new governments had their own schemes of economic development and social engineering, inspired by a new world of peripatetically eager experts and technicians—eager to spend money, to do good, to wield power. These doers, be it said, had no trouble imagining schemes, the bigger the better. And when the schemes failed?

> That is the fault of the West. The West told us to build power stations, bridges, factories, steel mills, phosphate mines. We built them because you said so, and the way you told us. But now they don't work, you tell us we must pay for them with our money. That is not fair. You told us to build them, you should pay for them. We didn't want them.[24]

Much of the gap between expectation and realization came from unpreparedness. The postcolonial Africans had no experience of self-government, and their rulers enjoyed a legitimacy bounded by kinship networks and clientelist loyalties. Abruptly, these new nations were pressed into the corset of representative government, a form alien to their own traditions and unprepared by colonial paternalism. In some instances, this transition had been preceded by a war of liberation, which mobilized passion and identity. But the legacy was rule by a strongman, autocratic embodiment of the popular will, hence slayer of democracy. Stability depended on one man's vigor, and when he weakened or died (or was helped to die), the anarchy of the short-lived military coup followed.

The governments produced by this strong-man rule have proved uniformly inept, with a partial exception for pillage. In Africa, the richest people are heads of state and their ministers.[25] Bureaucracy has been inflated to provide jobs for henchmen; the economy, squeezed for its surplus. Much (most?) foreign aid ends in numbered accounts abroad.[26] These kleptocrats have much to gain by living in Switzerland, near their banks. But maybe money alone is not enough.

Basil Davidson gives us two case studies in incoherence. The first, Zaire (ex-Belgian Congo), was a skeleton of a state. The tyrant Mobutu Sese Seko ruled in the capital Kinshasa and a few other cities, and in those localities where foreign companies were extracting mineral wealth. All of these paid him tribute, and his accounts in Switzerland were said to total billions of dollars. Between these few points of effective control, the only transport was by air, for the roads below are neither passable nor safe. Under Belgian rule in 1960, the Congo had 88,000 miles of usable road; by 1985 this was down to 12,000 miles, only 1,400 of them paved. But then dirt roads are better than holed and cracked hard surfaces. Paving is only as good as its maintenance.

Almost the whole of the country and the society was in but not of the pseudo-nation. In the east, foreign invaders were driving foreign refugees to their death while supporting rebellion against Kinshasa. In the capital, the parliamentary opposition denounced rebel plans and warned against a new despotism: "We are not getting rid of one strongman to replace him with another." The rebel reply: "If the opposition leader "wants to pilot a ship that is going down," he'd better learn to swim.[27] Meanwhile Western agents worked to persuade Mobutu into retirement (or keep him in office) while jockeying for influence with what might follow. The primary Western concern was to keep getting those minerals out. The French also wanted to keep Zaire in the francophone orbit, as though the dignity of France depended on it. (The Belgians had thrown up their hands long ago.) The Americans . . . well, it wasn't clear what might be the American interest, except maybe to "stick it" to the French.

In the midst of this anarchy, international relief agencies tried to keep refugees alive but had to break off every time marauders drew near. Some emergency supplies got in, but for whom? Some mineral resources were still getting out, but for whom? The capture by rebels in April 1997 of the country's diamond capital portended a change in regime. Without revenues, Mobutu could not pay his troops, now given to pillage (a soldier's got to live); nor could he hold the hearts of the great powers, even if he spoke French. Footnote: Zaire had vanished by then from the tables of the World Bank. This was prescient: the victorious rebels, after forcing Mobutu out in June, changed the name of the country back to (the Republic of) Congo.

The second case is Benin, formerly Dahomey. This country's biggest products from 1960 to 1989 were Marxist-Leninist propaganda and political coups. The official statistics showed product and trade as almost nonexistent. Yet Benin was planting and harvesting palm oil and peanuts. It simply did not yield up its product to the authorities or to official markets. Just about everything moved in parallel channels. These yielded the farmer more than he would ever get from an official marketing board, and the farmer bought off the swollen bureaucracy. On the record, then, Benin is an empty husk with big negative trade balance and negative growth; but it's really a smuggling machine.

The lesson one draws from these and similar instances is that Africa is not so badly off as it appears, just worse. Look at a photo or TV screen, at these prostrate fly-specked children, all bones, saggy skin, bulging eyes and belly, and you are overwhelmed by the misery. You *know* that the children you are looking at are dead by the time you see them. Look at another scene, especially in the picturesque pages of the *National Geographic,* and you marvel at the smiles and vigor of the dancers or traders in an exotic landscape. The continent bears witness to hope and hopelessness, courage and despair. Circumstances are appalling, but somehow people find ways to cope, survive, die, yet multiply.

Meanwhile the international placemen and experts sing their little songs of innocence and inexperience. "Adjustment" is the current refrain: a touch of freedom here, of market and exchange rate realism there, and things will be better, may even get well. One of the games economists play may be called "statistical misinference." Compare more or less comparable numbers from different countries and draw conclusions, past and future. So with Africa: as we saw earlier, comparing Nigeria and Indonesia, Africa has done less well than East Asian countries that started at a lower level. (One can make a similar invidious comparison between Turkey and South Korea.) But why not turn that around? If Indonesia could do so well, why not Nigeria? The same World Bank report that deplores African performance in 1965–90 cites Asian figures for 1965 ("conditions similar to those in Africa in 1990") to envisage African growth over the next quarter century. Equal levels at different times constitute for these experts similar conditions. Oh yes, the proportion of children in school was higher in Asia, but that is easily remedied. Otherwise, no problem. Of cultural and institutional differences, nothing.

News item: The United Nations, in collaboration with the World Bank and the International Monetary Fund, has announced a plan to raise $25 billion over the next decade, over and beyond what these international agencies can find (much to come from private sources), and invest it in African improvement.[28] At present twenty-two of the twenty-five poorest countries in the world are in Africa, and 54 percent of Africans live below the UN poverty line; what's more, Africa is the only region where poverty is expected to increase over the next ten years. How much can $25 billion do? Well, as of 1994, the debts of

African nations totaled $313 billion (almost 2.5 times total export income), so the $25 billion could pay the interest for one year. In the meantime, of $231 billion in direct foreign investment in the Third World in 1995, some $2 billion, less than 1 percent, went to Africa. Businessmen know to go elsewhere.

No matter: accentuate the positive. The worse the situation, the greater the potential for improvement. Better policies (structural adjustment) can/will put Africa back on the growth track. But there would still be lots to do. The continent's problems go much deeper than bad policies, and bad policies are not an accident. Good government is not to be had for the asking. It took Europe centuries to get it, so why should Africa do so in mere decades, especially after the distortions of colonialism? And how about no government? At the moment, for example, Somalia is a political vacuum: even if one wants to send help, what address to send it to? "We don't even know how to send them a message."[29]

In a fragile world, good policies are hostages to fortune. In Africa, as in much of the world only more so, the clocks go backward as well as forward.

⁀ ⁀

## Country Interrupted: Algeria

One of the most chastening exercises in economic history is to recall the expert prognoses of yesterday and appreciate their vacuity.

In the euphoria of the 1970s, when Algeria was raking in abruptly inflated oil revenues and, after South Africa, had the largest industrial base on the continent, a happy minister of industry predicted that Algeria would be "Africa's first, and the world's second, Japan." From his mouth to God's ear. Plant and equipment may not mean output, and output may not mean utility and salability. Like other developing nations before it, including those in nineteenth-century Europe, Algeria set about creating a modern industrial infrastructure. Like some of them, it aimed especially to promote heavy industry, the more so as good socialist doctrine saw that as the only way to go. Comparative advantage (a bourgeois-capitalist doctrine) be damned.

All of this costly, state-owned apparatus featured overemployment, inefficiency, nonmarket prices, and cooked books. Just about none of the industrial product was exportable, and even in the captive domestic market, much was unusable or liable to rapid deterioration. The factories went rapidly downhill. Many stood idle or lay underused for want of maintenance and spare parts. Cannibalization, always the accomplice of poor repair, consumed equipment before its time. Manufacturing output fell by 1.9 percent per year from 1980 to 1992; and sank from 15 to 10 percent of GDP in the quarter century from 1970 to 1992.[30]

Meanwhile population tripled in the thirty years after independence (10 million in 1960, 27 million in 1993), in spite of substantial emigration to Europe. The ambitious revolutionary government encouraged big families in order to enhance military power and international influence, and reproduction turned out to be the one efficient branch of production. Unfortunately, children have to grow up to produce, and this rapid increase (almost half the population is now under fifteen years of age) has imposed a heavy if temporary burden. Birth promotion, for example, implied a big investment in education, yet 43 percent of the population were illiterate in 1990, and 55 percent of the women.* It also presupposed an abundant food supply, but the country has not added to its arable land (the same 2.9 percent of the area as in 1910), has made a mess of collective farming, and can no longer feed itself. Algeria imports increasing quantities of basic and not-so-basic foods (cereals, milk, sugar, bananas, cooking oil) and subsidizes them for consumers.

While at it, the government has also imported consumer durables and sold them to favored insiders at concessionary prices. Highly coveted contracts to furnish such goods have become the object of keen competition among foreign suppliers. One might have expected the bids and counterbids to yield lower prices; on the contrary, they have yielded bigger bribes. And big as these are, they are but a small part of a much larger pool of privatized state funds. Algerians speak of $26 billion ($10^9$) in secret bank accounts abroad.[31]

Cover of imports by exports was running in the early 1990s between 3 and 10 percent, coming almost entirely from oil and gas

---

* Algerian nationalists would now lay the blame for illiteracy on the French. Half the population, they say, was literate when the French came in 1830, but the French shut indigenous schools and admitted almost no Muslims to their new state schools. It takes willful credulity to believe that 50 percent figure (presumably none of the women and all of the men).

shipments. That may seem like little, but remember, two thirds of these oil revenues, as well as other export income, go to pay interest on the debt. (The oil, in other words, is mortgaged, and reserves are dwindling fast.)[32] Again, Algeria could, like any other sovereign country, tell its creditors to get lost. But it needs to borrow more, if only to feed itself. The IMF has offered the usual "structural adjustment" financing: We will pay you to change your ways. The Algerian government has accepted with alacrity: We will change our ways. Besides, we owe so much, a little more can't hurt.

French-educated Algerian observers have compared the country to the grasshopper of La Fontaine's fable:

> Que faisiez-vous au temps chaud? . . .
> Je chantais, ne vous déplaise.
>
> *What were you doing when it was warm? . . .*
> *I sang, I hope you don't mind.*[33]

Fortunately for Algeria, the IMF is not so hard and exigent as La Fontaine's ant: *"You sang, eh? I like that. Well, now dance."*

It won't be easy for Algeria to change. State socialism is not only a mode of production; it is a symbol and legacy of the revolution, an "irrevocable commitment" (to cite the original constitution), an egalitarian ideal, the banner under which Algeria has played a major role in Third World political movements.

In the last few years, the country has faltered and festered. Almost three quarters of the young men from seventeen to twenty-three years of age are unemployed. These are the "wall people," so called because they have nothing to do but lean against a wall and watch the street go by. They are a pool of resentment, brooders of dark fantasy, bomb and gun fodder. Civil war has killed more than sixty thousand people. Untimely death is never pleasant, but rebels in Algeria have gone out of their way to be cruel, dispatching victims whenever possible by cutting their throat. This saves bullets and supposedly brings the killer nearer to God.[34]

Much of the death has been random, the victims innocent passersby, many of them women and children. But Islamist terrorists have particularly targeted "shameless women" and key personnel: trained jurists and bureaucrats, foreign technicians, intellectual leaders. In this way, they roll back any progress toward freedom of thought and gender equality. Outsiders are particularly vulnerable: a few exemplary murders can discourage the rest and persuade them to leave. (Compare the effect of attacks on foreign tourists in Egypt.) The state responds with its own violence: torture, rape, murder. Presumably an end will come—on which side of the line, no one can say. Meanwhile the secular, francophone elements flee to France. The French do not want them, in part because Algerians bring the struggle with them. France has already had its premonitory explosions of Algerian terror.

෴ ෴

# From Leftist Scholar to President of Brazil:
## The Advantages of Realism

For years Fernando Henrique Cardoso was a leading figure of the Latin American dependency school, ideological flagship of anticapitalist anticolonialism. The doctrine had first been defined by the Argentine Raoul Prebisch, who drew his inspiration from center-and-periphery theories of European and American exploitation of weaker economies overseas; and it found powerful resonance in countries aggrieved by the growing gap between rich and poor. In the 1960s and 1970s, the sociologist Cardoso wrote or edited some twenty books on the subject. Some of them became the standard texts that shaped a generation of students. Perhaps the best known was *Dependency and Development in Latin America*. In its English version, this ended with a turgid, less-than-stirring credo:

> The effective battle . . . is between technocratic elitism and a vision of the formative process of a mass industrial society which can offer what is popular as specifically national and which succeeds in transforming the demand for a more developed economy and for a democratic society into a state that expresses the vitality of truly popular forces, capable of seeking socialist forms for the social organization of the future.[35]

Then, in 1993, Cardoso became Brazil's minister of finance. He found a country wallowing in an annual inflation rate of 7,000 percent. The government had become so inured to this monetary narcotic and Brazilians so ingenious in their personal countermeasures (taxis used meters that could be adjusted to the price index, and perhaps to the client) that serious economists were

ready to make light of this volatility on the pretext that the certainty
of inflation was a form of stability.

This may have been true for those Brazilians able to take
precautions; but inflation played havoc with Brazil's international
credit, and this country needed to borrow. It also needed to trade
and work with other countries, especially those rich, capitalist nations
that were marked as the enemy. So Cardoso began to see things
differently, to the point where observers praised him as a pragmatist,
"without a strong ideological core."[36] Gone now were the
anticolonialist passions; gone the hostility to foreign links, with their
implicit dependency. Brazil has no choice, says Cardoso. If it is not
prepared to be part of the global economy, it has "no way of
competing. . . . It is not an imposition from the outside. It's a
necessity for us."[37]

To each time its virtues. Two years later Cardoso was elected
president, in large part because he had given Brazil its first strong
currency in many years: the *real,* rated at slightly more than a dollar.
The *real* is still there, and what a boost to national pride: more than
a dollar!

Epilogue: A stable currency does not cure all. As of mid-1996,
public finances showed a larger deficit; export growth had slowed;
real product fell in the first quarter; real interest rates, though lower,
were still prohibitive; and productivity gains in manufacturing had
fallen sharply, indeed, to negative rates in such key sectors as
metallurgy, machinery, and textiles in 1995.[38]

# 29

# How Did We Get Here?
# Where Are We Going?

The millennial record seems simple enough. From a world of great and little empires and kingdoms, more or less equal in wealth and power, we have become a world of nation-states, some far richer and stronger than others. From hundreds of millions of people, we have become 6 billion and counting. From working with modest if ingenious tools and techniques, we have become masters of great machines and invisible forces. Putting aside magic and superstition, we have passed from tinkering and intelligent observation to a huge and growing corpus of scientific knowledge that generates a continuing flow of useful applications.*

Most of this is to the good, although intellectual and material power has often been abused to evil and destructive ends. Or just simply used, with unintended but nefarious consequences.[1] We suffer from the asymmetry between our knowledge of nature and our knowledge of

---

* I am reminded that superstition and magic are not dead; and some would argue that religious faith is part of this package. No doubt, because weak mortals that we are, we look for comfort where it is to be found. Even scientists and technicians are vulnerable, for science and reason are tough companions. Nonetheless, illusions, delusions, and faith are excluded in principle and practice from inquiry and discovery.

man, between outside awareness and self-ignorance. Still, few people would prefer a return to earlier times. Those who secede from the rich material world to find spiritual renewal in nature may leave their watches behind. But they take books, eyeglasses, and manufactured clothing; also sometimes CD players; and they usually know enough to get medical help when they need it.

Note that my assumption of the ultimate advantage and beneficence of scientific knowledge and technological capability is today under sharp attack, even in the Academy. The reasons for this reaction, often couched in preferences for *feeling* over *knowing*, range from disappointment at Paradise Unfound to fear and resentment by laymen of unknowable knowledge.[2] Some of the anti's are millenarians: they look to an apocalyptic revolution to right wrongs and generalize happiness. Marxian Socialists and Communists, for all their lip service to science, fall in this category. Others are nostalgics, harking back to the mythic blessings of stateless, communal, primitive societies. The first group well illustrates the human limits of good intentions. The second is pissing into the wind. That is not where the world is going.*

Until very recently, over the thousand and more years of this process that most people look upon as progress, the key factor—the driving force—has been Western civilization and its dissemination: the knowledge, the techniques, the political and social ideologies, for better or worse. This dissemination flows partly from Western dominion, for knowledge and know-how equal power; partly from Western teaching; and partly from emulation. Diffusion has been uneven, and much Western example has been rejected by people who see it as an aggression.

Today, the very account of this story is seen by some as an aggression. In a world of relativistic values and moral equality, the very idea of a West-centered (Eurocentric) global history is denounced as arrogant and oppressive. It is intended, we are told, "to justify Western domination over the East by pointing to European superiority."[3] What we should have instead is a multicultural, globalist, egalitarian history that tells something (preferably something good) about everybody. The European contribution—no more or less than the invention and

---

* This approach has found adepts in anthropology, which is confronted by the dilemma of its traditional subject matter: to cherish and preserve as in a gel; or to study and, so doing, promote the alteration and disappearance of the subject. On the virtues of the primitive, see Diamond, *In Search of the Primitive;* also Jordan, "Flight from Modernity."

definition of modernity—should be seen as accidental or, to use the modish word, contingent.

We have seen examples of this Europhobia in recent discussions of the age of voyages and discovery. The Chinese, we are told, might have (should have) found the Americas. Or the Japanese, or Africans. Maybe they did. Europe was just lucky. Or, in an angry variant, the Europeans were not lucky. They were nasty and vicious. They stole the silver of the New World, used it to pay for empire and trade in Asia, beat up more cultivated peoples, and then praised themselves for their wealth, technical achievements, civilizing mission, and spirituality.

Above all, say the globalists, we must not account for European priority by "essentializing" it, that is, by tying it to European institutions and civilization—explaining it by European "presences" as against non-European "absences." Thus the manifest asymmetry between Europe's systematic curiosity about foreign civilizations and cultures and the relative indifference of these "others" is denied a priori by apologists who unknowingly reaffirm the contrast.[4] The point, say some globalists, is that *there is nothing to explain*. Or, if one prefers, one can "problematize" both European and non-European history by including what did not happen: "failed struggles as well as successful ones are all part of history."[5] To be sure, attention to failure is open to the charge of biased negativism: who says non-Europeans had to pursue goals similar to those of the West?

This line of anti-Eurocentric thought is simply anti-intellectual; also contrary to fact. But how popular, especially among those allegedly chauvinist Westerners. The new globalists, not liking the message, want to kill the messenger—as though history hadn't happened. The fact of Western technological precedence is there.* We should want to know why, all of us, because the *why* may help us understand today and anticipate tomorrow.[6]

Historians like to look back, not ahead. They try to understand and explain the record. Economists also want to know the past, but believe what they know about it only insofar as it accords with theory and logic; and since they have the assurance of basic principles, they are less averse to telling a future shaped by rationality. To be sure, economists

---

* Some would argue (thus A. G. Frank) that Europe's knowledge and know-how did not surpass those of other civilizations until the Industrial Revolution, say, around 1800—as though European dominion were an accident and the Industrial Revolution an illumination. Bad history.

recognize the possibility of accident and unreason, but these can in the long run only delay the logically inevitable. Reason will triumph because reason pays. More is better, and in choosing goals, material achievement is the best argument.

So, whereas historians are agnostics about the future, hence virtual pessimists, economists and business people tend to be optimists.[7] Optimism has to do, above all, with increase of wealth, what Adam Smith called "the natural progress of opulence." Even for the poor: "In almost any way you care to measure, life is getting better for people in developing nations."[8] Also longer; and these data on life expectancy should settle the issue. In the same way, poor people are *on average* better off. Not fewer; but better off. Economists now opine that the world will continue to get richer, that the poor will catch up with the rich, that islands of growth will become continents, that knowledge can solve problems and overcome material and social difficulties along the way.* So it was, and so shall be.

Economists have not always felt this way.† Adam Smith's successors anticipated stagnation: Malthus, with his inexorable press of people on food supply; Ricardo, with his "stationary state" as land and rent soaked up the surplus; Jevons, with his bogey of fuel exhaustion. In those times, economics wore the sobriquet of "the dismal science." Subsequent progress has allayed these fears, although some see the Malthusian doom as only postponed.**

Meanwhile a new rider joins the horsemen of the apocalypse: eco-

* Islands of growth: not everyone is enthralled. Paul Kennedy asks in *Preparing for the Twenty-first Century:* "How comfortable would it be to have islands of prosperity in a sea of poverty?" Rifkin, *End of Work,* is comparably scandalized by the contrasts of rich and poor. If that's the way it's going to be, we should move on to a "post-market society," whatever that is. Cf. Mount, "No End in Sight." What with the proliferating succession of post-this and post-that, we may soon see post-post and post-post-post.

† Smith does give some credence to limits, for he speaks of a country "which had acquired that full complement of riches which the nature of its soil and climate, and its situation with respect to other countries, allowed it to acquire; which could, therefore, advance no further"—*Wealth of Nations,* Book I, ch. 9: "Of the Profits of Stock." But he treats this as a distant prospect, "perhaps" not as yet experienced, and adverts to the opportunities for transcending these limits with better "laws and institutions."

** Thanks to botanical research and the invention of "miracle rice," the world rice harvest nearly doubled from 1967 to 1992. India had its "Green Revolution." Now population is once again pressing on supply, and the International Rice Research Institute promises a "super rice" that will yield 20 to 25 percent more—Seth Mydans, "Scientists Developing 'Super Rice' to Feed Asia," *N.Y. Times,* 6 April 1997, p. A-9. Will that be enough? And what about Africa?

logical disaster. We no longer have to worry about the exhaustion of this or that resource; technology will find substitutes.[9] But we do have to attend to the serious, progressive, and possibly irremediable damage we are inflicting on the environment. This threat to well-being ties directly to economic development, for waste, pollution, and environmental damage grow with wealth and output. *Other things equal, it is the rich who poison the earth.*

To be sure, the rich see the peril—at least some do—and their wealth permits them to spend on clean-up and dump their waste elsewhere.* They also abound in good ecological advice to the new industrializers. These in turn are quick to point to the pollution perpetrated by today's rich countries in their growth period. Why should today's latecomers have to be careful? Besides, most developing countries are ready to pay the environmental price: wages and riches now; disease and death down the road. To be sure, no one has taken a poll, but this preference seems plausible. Young people—and developing countries are full of young people—think they'll live forever. Meanwhile who can confine pollution and disease? The rich are frightened, even if the poor are not. The rich have much more to lose.

If we learn anything from the history of economic development, it is that culture makes all the difference. (Here Max Weber was right on.) Witness the enterprise of expatriate minorities—the Chinese in East and Southeast Asia, Indians in East Africa, Lebanese in West Africa, Jews and Calvinists throughout much of Europe, and on and on. Yet culture, in the sense of the inner values and attitudes that guide a population, frightens scholars. It has a sulfuric odor of race and inheritance, an air of immutability. In thoughtful moments, economists and social scientists recognize that this is not true, and indeed salute examples of cultural change for the better while deploring changes for the worse. But applauding or deploring implies the passivity of the viewer—an inability to use knowledge to shape people and things. The technicians would rather do: change interest and exchange rates, free up trade, alter political institutions, manage. Besides, criticisms of culture cut

* But not always, because nobody wants that stuff. On 7 May 1996 rioters in Germany protested the return of radioactive wastes, German in origin, sent to France for processing and then brought back to Germany for presumably safe storage. The Germans spent millions of dollars to contain the angry crowds. That is why one economist recently proposed that rich nations dump unwanted wastes in such poor places as Africa—all that sand, and the Africans need the money. The very idea is symbolically unacceptable.

close to the ego, injure identity and self-esteem. Coming from outsiders, such animadversions, however tactful and indirect, stink of condescension. Benevolent improvers have learned to steer clear.

Besides, if culture does so much, why does it not work consistently?
Economists are not alone in asking why some people—the Chinese,
say—have long been so unproductive at home and yet so enterprising
away. If culture matters, why didn't it change China? (It is doing so,
now.) An economist friend, master of political-economic therapies,
solves this paradox by denying any connection. Culture, he says, does
not enable him to predict outcomes. I disagree. One could have foreseen the postwar economic success of Japan and Germany by taking account of culture. The same with South Korea vs. Turkey, Indonesia vs.
Nigeria.

On the other hand, culture does not stand alone. Economic analysis cherishes the illusion that one good reason should be enough, but
the determinants of complex processes are invariably plural and inter-
related. Monocausal explanations will not work. The same values
thwarted by "bad government" at home can find opportunity elsewhere. Hence the special success of emigrant enterprise. The ancient
Greeks, as usual, had a word for it: these *metics*, alien residents, were
the leaven of societies that sneered at crafts (hence the pejorative sense
of "banausic") and at money. So strangers found and sold the goods
and made the money.

Meanwhile, because culture and economic performance are linked,
changes in one will work back on the other. In Thailand, all good
young men used to spend years undergoing a religious apprenticeship
in Buddhist monasteries. This period of ripening was good for the
spirit and soul; it also suited the somnolent pace of traditional economic activity and employment. That was then. Today, Thailand moves
faster; commerce thrives; business calls. As a result, young men spiri-
tualize for a few weeks—time enough to learn some prayers and rituals and get back to the real, material world. Time, which everyone
knows is money, has changed in relative value. One could not have imposed this change, short of revolution. The Thais have voluntarily adjusted their priorities.

The Thai story illustrates culture's response to economic growth
and opportunity. The reverse is also possible—culture may shift against
enterprise. We have the Russian case, where seventy-five years of anti-
market, antiprofit schooling and insider privilege have planted and
frozen anti-entrepreneurial attitudes. Even after the regime has fallen—
people fear the uncertainties of the market and yearn for the safe te-

dium of state employment. Or for equality in poverty. As the Russian joke has it, peasant Ivan is jealous of neighbor Boris, because Boris has a goat. A fairy comes along and offers Ivan a single wish. What does he wish for? That Boris's goat should drop dead.

Fortunately, not all Russians think that way. The collapse of Marxist prohibitions and inhibitions has led to a rush of business activity, the best of it linked to inside deals, some of it criminal, much of it the work of non-Russian minorities (Armenians, Georgians, *et al.*). The leaven is there, and often that suffices: the initiative of an enterprising, different few. In the meantime, old habits remain, corruption and crime are rampant, culture war rages, elections hang on these issues, and the outcome is not certain.*

*Convergence* is the watchword of the day, the promise of eventual equality, of the generalization of prosperity, health, and happiness. That, at any rate, is what economic theory tells us, assuming mobility of the factors of production.

Experience is another matter. The numbers for the small set of advanced industrial countries seem to confirm convergence, but individual countries do not always stay with the pack. Will Japan continue to pull ahead? Will the United Kingdom continue to fall behind, or is this decade's good news the promise of tomorrow? Will this be the East Asian century? And what about the United States? Americans should remember the refusal of the British to face up to their troubles before they too let themselves be soothed by optimistic prognoses. That's the weakness of futurism: the soothsayers do not hang around to take responsibility for their errors. Even if they do, no one notices them any more; and they themselves remember only the good guesses. (Besides, remember the basic law: I was right when I said it.)

Meanwhile advanced and backward, rich and poor do not seem to be growing closer. Optimistic number-crunchers point to overall mini-convergence, but they put Asia with the poor, and only the special success of East Asia yields this optical illusion. Africa and the Middle East are still going nowhere. Latin America is doing a mixed job, mixed over time and space. The former Socialist bloc is in transition: some countries are doing well; others, particularly the former Soviet Union, swing in high uncertainty.

---

* Russia is not a safe place to do business. Cf. Remnick, *Lenin's Tomb* and *Resurrection*. Ukraine may well be worse. Cf. R. Bonner, "Ukraine Staggers on Path to the Free Market," *N.Y. Times,* 9 April 1997, p. A-3.

And what about contingency and mess? So many things to go wrong—war, revolution, natural disaster, bad government, crime, antiproductive ideology. Many success stories seem brittle, dependent on the political status quo. Every day's newspaper brings messages of hope: India is changing and beginning to encourage foreign investment; peace and order "take root" in Sierra Leone; after years of internecine strife, Argentina is coming back; Russia bubbles with new enterprise as Pepsi-Cola plans new investments. Can one take these happy turns as definite? Every other day, the same newspaper brings its warnings of trouble and reversal.

The British colony of Hong Kong is perhaps the best example of wobbling uncertainty. It went back to China on 1 July 1997. The returns are not yet in. China may choose to cherish it; or it may decide to force it into line with the mainland economy. To be sure, it seems improbable that China would kill the goose that lays so many golden eggs. But how important are Hong Kong's eggs in the larger Chinese picture? Besides, history has known similar irrationalities, and China has a history of sacrificing trade to imperial principle. Meanwhile Hong Kong business families have taken their precautions, both ways—to stay or to go. They have taken up citizenship in safer havens (some 600,000 of them hold foreign passports).[10] They are also learning to speak Mandarin as well as their native Cantonese and replacing Western executives with Chinese.[11] A rational "minimax" strategy: minimize maximum potential loss.

Do globalization and convergence signal the end of national striving? Does the very idea of international economic competitiveness no longer make sense? The economist Paul Krugman would say so: the "views [of those who call for a national economics] are based on a failure to understand even the simplest economic facts and concepts."[12]

Peremptory and dismissive, and yet the proponents of state intervention have not surrendered. We are talking here of two goals, power and wealth; and two ideals, distributive justice and impersonal efficiency. All of these hang together. Each has its own appeal, constituency, and justification.

Even within the economics profession, opinions differ. The neoclassicists say no: for them, no signals more reliable than market signals. They follow here in the steps of the great master: "Great nations are never impoverished by private, though they sometimes are by public prodigality and misconduct. The whole, or almost the whole public revenue, is in most countries employed in maintaining unproductive hands."[13] Adam Smith worried that these place servers might consume the produce needed to sustain the productive members of the society. (There are countries like that.)

Yet Adam Smith also understood that the state can (will) do some things—defense, police—better than private enterprise. In Ottoman Turkey, firefighting was in the hand of private companies, who came running when the alarm sounded. They competed with one another and negotiated price with house owners on the spot. As the negotiation proceeded, the fire burned higher and the stakes diminished. Or spread. Neighbors had an interest in contributing to the pot. 'Twixt meanness and greed, many a house fire turned into mass conflagration.

The issue presses in those countries where enterprise is wanting. In a world of rapid change and international competition, can society afford to wait for private initiative? Look at the role of the state in such exemplary countries as Korea, Taiwan, and even Japan: triggering, sheltering, and guiding nominally free market enterprise. To which the free marketeers make reply by recalling Pearl Harbor.

The record, then, is clearly mixed. State intervention is like the little girl who had a little curl right in the middle of her forehead: when she was good, she was very, very good; and when she was bad, she was horrid.

Besides, the state can be very useful as the servant of business. Officials have always been liable to temptation (bribes); that's human nature. But the growth of private salaries and bonuses in expanding economies has inflated and accelerated this venalization of government and administration. Men of money can buy men of power. Presidents and prime ministers act as traveling salesmen and judge their success by deals closed and contracts signed. The British are talking of replacing the royal yacht with an even bigger vessel, the equivalent of a cruise ship for two, plus guests. This liner would cost hundreds of millions of pounds, and if experience be a guide, would eventually take more to run than to build—the more so as the very existence of such an expensive toy compels its use. (Royalty has no notion of the doctrine of sunk costs.) No matter. The ship's proponents assure the British taxpayer that it will bring in trade. Meanwhile ideals yield to interest. China is behaving badly? The best way to straighten it out is to say nothing and do business. That may seem cynical; but it may be as good a cure as any for despotic irrationality.

The selection process goes on. Today's search for cheap labor has moved jobs from rich countries to poor, or more precisely, to some poor countries.[14] Happiness to some, deprivation to others. This mix of good news and bad is what economic change is all about. Economists and moralists applaud such transfers as rational, reflecting comparative advantage, hence reasonable and desirable. Why should employment for Malaysians and Mexicans be any less desirable than for Americans and Germans? Krugman again: "One might have expected everyone to welcome this change in the global landscape, to see the rapid improvement in the living standards of hundreds of millions of people, many of whom had previously been desperately poor, as progress—and as an unprecedented business opportunity."[15]

No reason, except that job losers are unhappy and angry, and in advanced industrial nations, job losers vote. They also demonstrate and riot. The same observers who worry about the mistakes of "strategic" trade policy might focus instead on the risks and costs of conflict. A cool economist may argue that nations do not compete as corporations do; or that loss of export markets and jobs does not make that much difference to a rich country like the United States;[16] or that bars to imports will not promote productivity or raise the standard of living at home; or that loss of jobs in branches that are no longer "advantageous" will be compensated by the creation of other jobs in other areas. These reasonings and clevernesses will not help workers and unions intimidated by the threat of job emigration. Nor will they console someone who loses a place and must take something less satisfying and less well paid, or who is of that twilight age that makes the very idea of starting over impractical.[17]

How much more vexing are the sassy dismissals that tell the public to rejoice at the prospect of cheaper cars and TV sets, which they can no longer afford, and advise them to seek jobs growing soy beans or servicing bank accounts. This, remember, is a replay of the advice John Bowring gave the member states of the German Zollverein in 1840: grow wheat, and sell it to buy British manufactures. This was a sublime example of economic good sense; but Germany would have been the poorer for it. Today's comparative advantage, we have seen, may not be tomorrow's. Is protection legitimate only for infant industries? Are rich countries morally obliged to eschew the devices routinely adopted by developing countries? Proponents of dependency theory have long stressed the injustice of allegedly unequal trade between strong and weak, rich and poor. But asymmetry goes both ways.

These questions do not have simple, unambiguous answers. It is one thing to advocate an active government policy; quite another to take the right measures and carry them out. One thing seems clear to me, however. The present tendency to global industrial diffusion will entail, for the richer countries, a leveling down of wages, increased inequality of incomes, and/or high levels of (transitional?) unemployment. No one has abrogated the law of supply and demand. Many, if not most, economists will disagree. They rely here on the sacred certainty of gains from trade for all. International competition, they tell us, is a positive-sum game: everyone benefits.

In the long run. This is not the place to attempt, in a few pages, a survey of the differences of opinion on this issue, which continues to generate a library of material.[18] I would simply argue here, from the historical record, that

—The gains from trade are unequal. As history has shown, some countries will do much better than others. The primary reason is that comparative advantage is not the same for all, and that some activities are more lucrative and productive than others. (A dollar is not a dollar is not a dollar.) They require and yield greater gains in knowledge and know-how, within and without.

—The export and import of jobs is not the same as trade in commodities. The two may be fungible in theory, but the human impact is very different.

—Comparative advantage is not fixed, and it can move for or against.

—It always helps to attend and respond to the market. But just because markets give signals does not mean that people will respond timely or well. Some people do this better than others, and culture can make all the difference.

—Some people find it easier and more agreeable to take than to make. This temptation marks all societies, and only moral training and vigilance can hold it in check.

Withal, I do not want to advocate any particular national policy, the less so as activist intervention can as easily make things worse as better. Each case must be judged on the merits, and governments are capable of as many mistakes, and bigger, than the businessmen who try to shape and play the market. (And vice versa. Much depends on what one is trying to maximize—wealth, equality, security, salvation, or what have you.)[19] I just want to say that the current pattern of technological diffusion and catch-up development will press hard on the haves, especially the individual victims of economic regrouping, while bringing "goodies" and hope to some of the have-nots, and despair, disappointment, and anger to many of the others.

To be sure, the rich, industrial countries can defend themselves (ease but not eliminate the pain) by remaining on the cutting edge of research, by moving into new and growing branches (creating new jobs), by learning from others, by finding the right niches, by cultivating and using ability and knowledge. They can go a long way on cruise control and safety nets, helping the losers to learn new skills, get new jobs, or just retire. Much will depend on their spirit of enterprise, their sense of identity and commitment to the common weal, their self-esteem, their ability to transmit these assets across the generations.

Meanwhile what about the poor, the backward, and the disadvantaged? After all, the rich industrial countries, however much pressed by the new competition, are so much better off that it is hard to work up concern and sympathy. With all their troubles, they have a continuing obligation, moral even more than prudential, to those less fortunate. Should they give for the sake of giving? Give only when it makes sense (pays) to give? Give, as bankers do, preferably to those who do not need help? Hard love, soft? Both? I ask these questions not because I know the answers (only true believers claim to know), but because one must be aware of the inextricable tangle of conflicting motives and contradictory effects. Navigation through these rapids demands constant adjustment and correction, the more difficult because policy is constrained by domestic politics.

And what of the poor themselves? History tells us that the most successful cures for poverty come from within. Foreign aid can help, but like windfall wealth, can also hurt. It can discourage effort and plant a crippling sense of incapacity. As the African saying has it, "The hand that receives is always under the one that gives."[20] No, what counts is work, thrift, honesty, patience, tenacity. To people haunted by misery and hunger, that may add up to selfish indifference. But at bottom, no empowerment is so effective as self-empowerment.

Some of this may sound like a collection of clichés—the sort of lessons one used to learn at home and in school when parents and teachers thought they had a mission to rear and elevate their children. Today, we condescend to such verities, dismiss them as platitudes. But why should wisdom be obsolete? To be sure, we are living in a dessert age. We want things to be sweet; too many of us work to live and live to be happy. Nothing wrong with that; it just does not promote high productivity. You want high productivity? Then you should live to work and get happiness as a by-product.

Not easy. The people who live to work are a small and fortunate elite. But it is an elite open to newcomers, self-selected, the kind of people who accentuate the positive. In this world, the optimists have it, not because they are always right, but because they are positive. Even when wrong, they are positive, and that is the way of achievement, correction, improvement, and success. Educated, eyes-open optimism pays; pessimism can only offer the empty consolation of being right.

The one lesson that emerges is the need to keep trying. No miracles. No perfection. No millennium. No apocalypse. We must cultivate a skeptical faith, avoid dogma, listen and watch well, try to clarify and define ends, the better to choose means.

> *. . . I have set before thee life and death, the blessing and the curse; therefore choose life.*
>
> —Deuteronomy 30:19

# Epilogue 1999

In theory, everything up to *now* is history. But as every historian knows, the closer one gets to the present, the more uncertain and precarious the story.

No sooner had I sent in the final text for this volume when the countries of East Asia, featured as big winners in the contest for growth and development, fell into crisis and contraction. The baby tigers—Thailand, Indonesia, Malaysia—went into contagious convulsions. Their better established regional competitors—South Korea, Taiwan, Singapore, and Hong Kong—resisted awhile but then succumbed to investors' doubts and fears. China—enormous and mysterious—seemed impervious in its relative isolation to market movements; but China's turn would come. Even Japan—bellwether and second largest economy in the world but strongly linked by export and investment to the region's emerging economies—saw major sectors such as banking and real estate shudder and stall. For the first time since the oil embargo of the 1970s, this paragon of success saw national product shrink.

The problem, in a way, was *too* much success. These economies had grown too fast, had become the focus of a gold rush yielding inebriating rates of profit and spectacular capital gains—the kind of returns that gild a balance sheet in London or New York and promise fast advancement for investment prodigies. But high returns imply/entail high risk, and good businessmen should be as suspicious of spectacular profits as they are alarmed by big losses.[1] The basic rule of business, as of physics, is the law of conservation of mass and energy: nothing for nothing. And another law: every action gives rise to reaction, in other words, no bulls without bears. Failure lurks in the shadow of success, in the inevitable, all-too-human excess of greed.

So with the great East Asian leap forward. In 1993, the World Bank, in a report ebulliently entitled *The East Asian Miracle,*[2] fairly rhapsodized:

> Since the 1960s, the high performing Asian economies have grown more than twice as fast as the rest of East Asia, roughly three times as fast as Latin America and five times faster than sub-Saharan Africa. They also significantly outperformed the industrial economies and the oil-rich Middle East–North Africa region. Between 1960 and 1985, real income per capita increased more than four times in Japan and the Four Tigers [South Korea, Taiwan, Singapore, Hong Kong] and more than doubled in the Southeast Asian NIEs.[3]

And to this list should be added China, which finally, in the 1980s, freed itself from some of the toils and servitudes of Marxist ideology and began encouraging enterprise, to the point of inviting in the agents of predatory capitalism. One might have expected these capitalists to be wary of so unsympathetic a regime, but the prospect of over a billion customers ("oil for the lamps of China") trumped caution, and they accepted conditions more onerous than in other Third World countries. The result: average growth in Chinese GDP 1981–96 of slightly more than 10 percent per annum—*if the official figures are to be believed.*[4]

In 1996, however, came signs of trouble. Anti-Chinese riots in Indonesia told of frictions between the business community and the native Muslim majority. One might have expected the authorities to keep the peace, but no, these were pogroms waged with tacit approval from above and intended to put Chinese merchants and money lenders in their place. It is easier to borrow money than to repay, easier to lend than collect. As the months went by, the IMF not only told Malaysia to cool the overheated economy but also put both Thailand and Indonesia on notice. Caution lights were blinking.

Then, in 1997, after initial expressions of confidence, came further

warnings. The central bank of Thailand labeled some ten finance companies insolvent, and this implied a small throng of pinched debtors.
The *baht* (Thai currency unit) immediately came under attack—hold-
ers understandably wanted out—and hit an eleven-year low against the
dollar by mid-May. The stock market fell in sympathy, to 17 percent
below the year's start level.

The weakness of the baht, which had been pegged to the dollar,
was an invitation to dump the currencies of the two other would-be
tigers, the Malaysian *ringgit* and the Indonesian *rupiah*. In many ways
both countries, in spite of shiny statistics, were seriously ill, crawling
with corruption and caught on a treadmill of easy, insider credit. Once
the business community awoke to the risks, and the endless stream of
funds abated, foreign speculators jumped ship; indigenous entrepreneurs and investors not only moved funds to safer havens but also deferred commitments, inevitably creating job loss, popular discontent,
and political instability.

Matters were not helped in Malaysia by the ethnocentric reaction of
the prime minister, Mahathir bin Mohammad, a militant Islamist who
spit at foreign speculators for bringing low the ringgit. He was particularly incensed by alleged Jewish enemies of Islam such as George
Soros. It was as if Mahathir had been reading and believing the anti-
Zionist twaddle that was one of the Arab Middle East's most successful products, or perhaps listening to too many Friday sermons, or just
expressing irritation at the refusal of foreigners to heel and obey in the
same manner that Malays did.[5] In any event, such antisemitic foolishness, however plausible in the frontier Islam of a racist society, could
only alienate and frighten foreign money men. It did not help the ringgit. In addition, the Malaysian authorities tried to ease the strain of industrial contraction by ordering the Indonesian *Gastarbeiter* out. Go
home! Any jobs, they said, should be reserved to natives. This was the
same tactic European countries had used in the 1930s but could no
longer get away with. Malaysia, however, had fewer compunctions.

In Indonesia, more than elsewhere, the link between power and
favor was particularly blatant. Normally the state would have bailed out
the fat cats, but this time the debts far exceeded the reserves, and much
of the debt was denominated in dollars. The best one could do was to
slow the decline in the exchange value of the rupiah, keep it high long
enough to pay off dollar obligations and enable insider favorites to
convert rupiahs into strong currency, and give foreign investors and
speculators more time to pull out. Meanwhile the rising price of basic
commodities and the stench of corruption inflamed the population

against the regime. This time violent repression could not still the populace, and, in the end, Suharto had to resign.

At first the older tigers felt superior and pitied the parvenus, but finally they too felt the squeeze. Korea especially suffered the same easy-credit syndrome. A number of major manufacturing enterprises had been rolling over debt, borrowing the while, but now the finance companies found their own money sources drying up. Panic turned into recession; major industries contracted and closed, leaving the usual jobless debris. "Businesses are almost paralyzed," said the chief representative of an American investment bank in December 1997. "They're not out there producing and marketing. They're just trying to get liquidity."[6] Even Singapore and Hong Kong, long seen as paragons, saw their currencies lose value, their stock markets tumble, their guest money men turn or even move away.

The IMF sought to stem the tide by putting together emergency aid packages: $17.2 billion for Thailand, of which 4 from the IMF; $35 billion for Indonesia, of which 10 from the IMF, 4.5 from the World Bank, and 3.5 from the Asian Development Bank; $57 billion for South Korea, of which 21 from the IMF, 10 from the World Bank, and 4 from the Asian Development Bank. (All these packages included further contributions by creditor nations.) All well and good, but IMF aid came with unpleasant constraints. Beneficiary countries were expected to clean up their finances, tighten credit, stop helping insider favorites, and in all of this, let the IMF see the books. No part of IMF loans could be used to bail out industrial enterprises, long considered sinkholes of favoritism. No part could be used to revive an insolvent financial institution. No part could go to compensate shareholders in these enterprises. Given the suspicions of Malaysia's Mahathir, one can well understand why no IMF package proved acceptable. As any child can tell you, medicine never tastes good, and some children would rather be sick than swallow.

Meanwhile, alongside the Asian crisis, the advanced industrial nations were having trouble in Russia, where foolish speculators and banks that should have known better found that even state bonds were not immune to repudiation. (They should have studied history and learned something about tsarist certificates turned into wallpaper.) And as ever, Latin America looked shaky. But so what? Latin America always looked shaky. American financial statesmen congratulated themselves on saving Mexico in 1994 and then again in 1997 and, whistling in the dark, told themselves that the market was sound; all it needed was an occasional transfusion. The IMF to the rescue. The U.S. treasury to the rescue. Who was rescued? First and foremost, American and other foreign lenders and speculators. That made sense: if one didn't save the lenders, how could they lend again? And who better to save than one's own people? In January 1999, it was Brazil's turn. Again, the United States to the rescue. And after Brazil? Why not Mexico again? Or Argentina?

Japan, however, was more important than all these tremblers combined, and Japan was in trouble. For one thing, the country was closely linked to the others as both supplier and investor. When East Asia swooned, Japan languished. More serious, however, Japan found itself sinking into a structural morass: bad commercial habits, an inefficient banking sector, too easy credit, credulous inflation of property values, bad collection, and much corruption and connection—the kind of thing one can hide or live with during a period of rapid growth and innovation, but not in time of slowdown. Some enterprises responded vigorously, but most firms were stuck with the obligations of consensus, which was easier to achieve in good times than in bad. And all that guidance from above—MITI, the Ministry of Finance: it's good when it works, but it is not responsive to crisis.

Some see the recent Japanese recession as a warning of long-run decline, a parallel to Britain's loss of place toward the end of the nineteenth century. The old ways that had brought success had now turned into impediments. Others reject the analogy, noting that the British economy, even in hard times, had never turned negative (but then again, neither had the British economy ever grown so fast as the Japanese). Still, Britain had not adapted to the new technologies (automobiles, electricity and electronics, numerical controls) so well as the Japanese had. Manufacturing was stronger in Japan. And there was another difference, this time one that should have favored Britain: whereas the British had more or less welcomed immigrants, the Japanese did their best to keep all of them out except for Koreans, who were brought in for dirty tasks and, until recently, fingerprinted and politically segregated. The country didn't want them marrying or melting into the Japanese bloodstream.

Comparisons are never perfect. The above analogy intended a link between two nations that had been riding high and then found themselves ill-prepared to deal with new circumstances. The British had adapted poorly to the new technologies of the second industrial revolution. The Japanese were responding ineptly to the follies of prosperity: tiny houses in Tokyo going for millions of dollars, the Imperial Palace and grounds having an imputed value greater than all of California, golf club memberships selling for a million dollars. And against this, central bank discount rates falling close to zero percent and yet people saving. Even if they could afford a large, up-to-date television, where would they put it?

When the Asian crisis broke in 1997, I thought it very inconsiderate of these countries to make of me an optimistic fool. What unfortunate timing! Some readers rejoiced at my imagined discomfiture: if culture was so important, why were these culturally advantaged societies, these allegedly successful societies, having so much trouble?

My answer would be that economic prowess has never exempted anyone from the ups and downs of the business cycle, indeed, that success is its own worst enemy and a temptation to greed and folly. Rectifying mistakes has to be painful. Take Thailand: in December 1997, the government finally agreed to close fifty-six of fifty-eight finance companies, but selling the assets of these companies was another matter. Other countries are still trying to put off the most painful liquidations, in part because the losers include very influential people. But this too shall pass, and I would expect that the east Asian and southeast Asian economies will soon resume the path of growth, because they have the skills and are capable of learning. But they will achieve this only *on condition that* they overcome the racist friction that invites fear, risk avoidance, and even flight. How long will this take? Impossible to say.

On the other hand, and on reflection, this Asian *contretemps* implicitly supports the emphasis I would place on the role of the West as the driving force of economic development and modernity. Of all the critical responses to this book, the noisiest and most passionate has been the rejection of what is seen as Western triumphalism, decried and derided as politically incorrect and morally repugnant. This rejection has pursued two principal lines of argument, one based on the alleged past, the other on present prospects. On the alleged past: Europe was a poor latecomer and did not catch up with Asia until about 1800. (To say this, one has to trivialize or ignore European advances made in science and technology since the twelfth and thirteenth centuries, as well as the obvious European advantage in mobility and power since the end of the fifteenth century.)[7] This European dominance was short-lived, as shown by the rapid economic growth of East Asia over the last century and culminating in the last third (1960–95).[8] That's where the current Asian debacle comes in. It casts doubt on this fairy-tale reconstruction of the past and should help people avoid the seductions of ideology.

On present prospects: the Asians, it is said, had developed an ethic of economic enterprise drastically different from the market orientation and criteria followed by the West. Where the West pursues only "self-ish" motives of profit and loss, Asia prefers a "sponsored capitalism," in which government does the larger planning and takes the initiative in sponsoring meritorious branches and enterprises. The East also prefers to work, help, and lend (borrow) through a network of personal and political friends and allies. Credit worthiness is not the point. It is connections that count.

In all fairness, one should note that such personal ties are not absent from Western enterprise. People everywhere prefer to work with people they know and like. The records of European as well as Asian banking are full of network patterns: Jewish, Calvinist, Greek, Lebanese, Pakistani, Chinese.[9] The so-called Asian way of business is not that different from the Western; and insofar as it is different, the current debacle would seem to indicate that it is neither foolproof nor intrinsically superior. Again, a lesson in the dangers of overconfidence.

Much of this eagerness to cut the West down to size comes from Asian chauvinists. The Japanese in particular requite resentment of military defeat with affirmations of spiritual superiority. But much of the disparagement comes from Western dissenters. Our civilization more than any other generates skepticism and discontent. Some of this reaction is justified by misbehavior; some reflects natural and personal disappointment translated to the larger scene. Such negativism may actually reflect success, for anger thrives on ease.

What does this mean for the longer future? Some "experts" see the Asian crisis as part of a larger pattern of poisoned globalization, the effect of capitalism gone wild.[10] They warn of depression, poverty, war, disease, ecological disaster—the horsemen of the apocalypse. As for me, I haven't changed my mind and continue to expect the best, however difficult and interrupted. As I confessed above, I'd rather be an optimist than a pessimist.

# Notes

## INTRODUCTION

1. In "Illogic of Neo-Marxian Doctrine," p. 107.
2. Thus Wilson, *Rothschild*, p. 102.
3. I am relying here, with some modifications, on bold estimates by Paul Bairoch, "Ecarts internationaux des niveaux de vie avant la Révolution industrielle," *Annales: économies, sociétés, civilisations,* 34, 1 (Jan.–Feb. 1979), 145–71. If one calculates in real terms (PPP), the range in GDP (gross domestic product) is given in *Human Development Report 1996* as 80:1. Ram, "Tropics and Human Development," p. 1.

## CHAPTER 1

1. One thing for the French school: they were very sure of themselves. Thus Edmond Demolins, back around the turn of the century: "If the history of mankind were to begin over, without any change in the world's surface, it would broadly repeat itself"—*Comment la route crée le type social* (Paris, n.d.), I, ix. For a skeptical view of this European interest in geography—decried as training for colonialism—see Blaut, *The Colonizer's Model*, p. 45, n. 3.
2. See Andrew Kamarck, *The Tropics and Economic Development.*
3. Cf. Arnold Guyot, *The Earth and Man* (1849; reprinted 1897), p. 251. Also Livingstone, "The Moral Discourse of Climate," p. 414.
4. On this story, see Smith, "Academic War," pp. 155, 162; also S. B. Cohen, "Reflections on the Elimination of Geography," p. 148.
5. So it is easier, and no doubt more practical (though not for what I am trying to do), to confine discussions of African agriculture to what can and cannot be done in circumstances such as they are. Cf. R. P. Moss, "Environmental Constraints." For a more

or less unconditionally egalitarian view of geography (no one is better off than anyone else, because no one should be), see Blaut, *The Colonizer's Model.*

6. David Smith, "Climate, Agriculture, History: An Introduction," pp. 1–2. Further to the point, Smith tells us that scholarship in this field demands "a willingness to accept much badinage or even rejection from colleagues."

7. "Conditions for Economic Change in Underdeveloped Countries," *Journal of Farm Economics,* 33 (November 1951), 693. Cited in Andrew Kamarack's valuable and undeservedly neglected book, *The Tropics and Economic Development,* p. 4.

8. "How Poor Are the Poor Countries?" in Seers and Joy, eds., *Development in a Divided World,* p. 78. Cf. Rati Ram's regressions of income, life expectancy, etc., on distance from the equator, "highly significant and quantitatively substantial"—"Tropics and Economic Development," p. 10.

9. L. Don Lambert, "The Role of Climate," p. 339 and n. 1, compares the economist's one-sided approach to that of a doctor who focused only on well people and treated the ill by prescribing the "good life" of the well. " . . . the relevant questions," he writes, "are not only: What causes development? but also: What causes stagnation?"

10. "The Deadly Hitch-hikers," *The Economist,* 31 October 1992, p. 87.

11. Elvin, *The Pattern of the Chinese Past,* p. 186, notes a Chinese text of 1264 describing schistosomiasis and other worm infestations. Cited in Jones, *The European Miracle,* p. 6.

12. *The Economist,* 27 July 1991, pp. 74–75. Cf. Giblin, "Trypanosomiasis Control."

13. Morbidity data from the military hospital in Bône—Curtin, *Death by Migration,* pp. 65–66.

14. These data from World Bank, *World Development Report 1994,* Table 1, pp. 162–63.

15. World Bank, *World Development Report 1991,* Table 28, pp. 258–59, and *1994,* Table 27, pp. 214–15. Richard Easterlin calls these gains a "mortality revolution"—one that is still under way.

16. The price remains high in spite of modern laboratory techniques and security precautions. On the battle against deadly, newly discovered viruses, most of them of tropical origin, see Altman, "Researcher's Infection."

17. Sattaur, "WHO to Speed Up Work on Drugs for Tropical Diseases," p. 17. Once again, some would disagree. Blaut, *The Colonizer's Model,* pp. 77–78, contends that until very recently, "midlatitude" climes (he prefers to avoid the word "temperate") have been just as disease-ridden as tropical; and that inhabitants of the tropics develop appropriate immunities to pathogens and parasites. Other things equal, "is there, then, a remainder that can be called 'the innate [intrinsic?] unhealthiness of the tropics'? Probably the answer is no."

18. *N.Y. Times,* 16 February 1997, p. 1.

19. On the conflict between the Western, scientific school and indigenous medicine, see Verma, "Western Medicine," who feels that the Europeans have kept their own secrets. The Westerners came with methods and printed books; the native practitioners had no books, only practice and secrets. The Westerners wanted help, especially for such mass procedures as vaccination. But they taught the natives less than they taught their own countrymen, for equal education would have undermined authority (p. 134).

20. Cf. Gwyn Prins, who tells us, "Hygæa was for many Africans seen as the colonialist's whore"—"But What Was the Disease?", p. 164. This is an unhappy article, alert to the failings and wrongs of colonial medicine, sympathetic to traditional therapies without being credulous, almost angry. The author is torn between science and a different kind of "knowledge": "why should those explanations which are found to be widely applicable be assumed to be universally pre-eminent" (p. 178)? But are Africans biologically different?

21. See Paul Harrison, "The Curse of the Tropics," p. 602. These variations make a difference. Cf. Sah, "Priorities," pp. 339–40, on the great British peanut (groundnut) fiasco of the late 1940s, killed, among other things, by the failure to reckon with fluctuations in rainfall (discussed below, chapter xxviii).

22. Wade, "Sahelian Drought," 234–37.

23. Kamarck, *Tropics and Economic Development*, p. 16.

24. This passage draws on Raaj Sah, "Priorities of Developing Countries," p. 337.

25. Bandyopadhyaya, *Climate and World Order*, p. vi.

CHAPTER 2

1. Tortella, "Patterns of Economic Retardation and Recovery in South-western Europe."

2. "Speech on Mr. Fox's East India Bill," 1 December 1783.

3. Charlene L. Fu, "China Paper Details Risk of Hepatitis in Transfusions," *Boston Globe*, 30 June 1993, p. 2.

4. On the implications of disease and malnutrition for economic performance, see Alan Berg, "Malnutrition and National Development," pp. 126–29.

5. Oshima, *Economic Growth*, p. 21.

6. Lattimore, *Inner Asian Frontiers*, p. 23.

7. Leeming, *Changing Geography*, pp. 11–12. Some 65 percent of China is mountain, hill, and plateau.

8. Cited in Elvin, *The Pattern of the Chinese Past*, p. 37.

9. From the *Chin History*, cited by Elvin, *ibid.*, p. 39.

10. The *Wei History* (compiled in the sixth century by Wei Shou), cited by Elvin, *op. cit.*, p. 45.

11. Jones, *European Miracle*.

12. Chang, "Agricultural Potential," p. 338. On the other hand, Debeir, *et al., In the Servitude of Power*, p. 47, give paddy (unhusked rice) as superior to wheat and corn "because of the quality of its proteins and its richness in essential amino acids."

13. Karl A. Wittfogel, *Oriental Despotism: A Comparative Study of Total Power.*

14. Thus Chi Ch'ao-ting, *Key Economic Areas in Chinese History*, who tells a story of food and politics: he who controlled the big granaries held the key to the kingdom.

15. March, *The Idea of China*, pp. 94–95.

16. Cf. Stevens, "The High Risks of Denying Rivers Their Flood Plains."

17. Debeir, *et al., In the Servitude of Power*, p. 50.

CHAPTER 3

1. Cf. Kautsky, *Politics of Aristocratic Empires;* Richard Landes, "While God Tarried" (forthcoming).

2. *Tract on the Popery Laws.*

3. Michael Cook, "Islam: A Comment," in Baechler *et al.*, eds., *Europe and the Rise of Capitalism*, p. 134.

4. Cf. Crone, *Pre-Industrial Societies*, pp. 161–62, who stresses the plurality of the barbarian strike forces that brought down the Western empire and the consequent plurality of political and, I would add, cultural and linguistic units. The one unified entity was the Church, with its more or less common language, and the pope, Crone points out, had no interest in promoting a secular rival.

5. As cited in Lévi, *Le grand empereur*, p. 187. This is a novel, but it draws heavily and often verbatim from contemporary documents.

6. Balazs, *La bureaucratie céleste*, pp. 22–23. Cf. John Fairbank, who speaks of "Oriental" societies, "organized under centralized monolithic governments in which the

bureaucracy was dominant in almost all aspects of large-scale activity—administrative, military, religious, and economic—so that no sanction for private enterprise ever became established . . ." *The United States and China,* p. 47. Note the use of the word "Oriental," not then frowned upon.

7. On the significance of law and justice for medieval political rule, see Crone, *Pre-Industrial Societies,* pp. 157–58, who stresses the contribution of this function to royal revenues. But perverse consequence: he who gets his living by the law must live by the law.

8. Cited in Edmonds, *Northern Frontiers,* p. 55.

9. Some have argued that this is not so; thus Rowe, *Hankow: Commerce and Society in a Chinese City,* and Perdue, *Exhausting the Earth,* p. 263, n. 6. Such arguments miss the explicit political autonomies and status privileges of European communes.

10. Robert Lopez, cited by Pounds, *Economic History,* p. 104.

11. On rural privileges and their link to projects of land reclamation and extension of cultivation, going back to the eleventh century, see the important article of Bryce Lyon, "Medieval Real Estate Developments and Freedom," *Amer. Hist. Rev.,* 63 (1957), 47–61.

12. Cf. Bartlett, *The Making of Europe: Conquest, Colonization and Cultural Change.*

13. "Far from being stultified by imperial government, Europe was to be propelled forward by constant competition between its component parts." And, stressing the paradox of redemption in the loss of imperial paradise: "Europe failed: had it succeeded, it would have *remained* a pre-industrial society"—Crone, *Pre-Industrial Societies,* pp. 161, 172.

14. Hippocrates, *Air Waters Places,* cited in March, *Idea of China,* p. 29. For March, the very idea of Asia is a myth—an opposing "they" that defines Europe in terms of what it is not or does not want to be. This, he feels, reflects ideological and class interests: "Our modern 'Asia' is perpetuated not for science but on behalf of those strata whose care is to maintain the ideal of western civilisation and who benefit from its sacred myths of individualism, private property, and aggressive defence of liberty" (p. 35). None of which necessarily invalidates these contrasts.

15. On the "Peace of God" movement of the late tenth, early eleventh century, which took the form of mass public encounters of clergy, nobility, and populace and produced a series of social compacts, cf. Head and Landes, eds., *The Peace of God: Social Violence and Religious Response.* These compacts were not always honored, but principle matters, and again, such evidences of popular initiative and expression were distinctively European.

CHAPTER 4

1. The key piece is the seminal article of Lynn White, Jr., "Technology and Invention in the Middle Ages," *Speculum,* 15 (1940): 141–59.

2. Jean Gimpel, *The Medieval Machine,* p. 14. Cf. White, *Medieval Religion and Technology,* pp. 226–27. White also points out that whereas paper from Muslim lands (not mechanically produced) never shows watermarks, such trademarks appear in Italian paper by the 1280s, a sign of commercial enterprise.

3. On these glasses before eyeglasses, see the work of Zecchin, *Vetro e vetrai di Murano* (Venice, 1989), cited by Ilardi, "Renaissance Florence," p. 510.

4. The speaker is the Dominican Fra Giordano of Pisa, in a sermon at Santa Maria Novella in Florence in 1306. Quoted in White, "Cultural Climates," p. 174; also in reprint, 1978, p. 221. White cites the Italian original. I have made small stylistic changes in the translation. See also Rosen, "Invention of Eyeglasses"; and Ilardi, *Occhiali* and "Renaissance Florence."

5. Moses Abramovitz argues that a longer life span encourages investment in human capital and makes people readier to move to new places and occupations. How much more when the extra years can be the best—"Manpower, Capital, and Technology," p. 55.

6. "The clock is not merely a means of keeping track of the hours, but of synchronizing the actions of men. The clock, not the steam-engine, is the key-machine of the modern industrial age . . . at the very beginning of modern technics appeared prophetically the accurate automatic machine. . . . In its relationship to determinable quantities of energy, to standardization, to automatic action, and finally to its own special product, accurate timing, the clock has been the foremost machine in modern technics; and at each period it has remained in the lead; it marks a perfection toward which other machines aspire"—Mumford, *Technics and Civilization*, pp. 14–15.

7. Cited in Lewis, *The Muslim Discovery of Europe*, p. 233.

8. Sivin, "Science and Medicine," p. 165, says that printing with movable type did not replace the older method until the twentieth century.

9. Cf. Hall, *Powers and Liberties*, p. 49.

10. Elvin, *Pattern of the Chinese Past*, p. 180.

11. Needham, "The Guns of Khaifeng-fu," p. 40.

12. Levathes, *When China Ruled the Seas*, p. 102.

13. On this point, note the development, as early as the sixteenth century, of a formal claim by victorious armies to all bells, or to the best bell, in and around a conquered place: "the right to the bells." Cipolla, *Guns, Sails, and Empires*, p. 30, n. 1.

14. In 885, all professional copyists in Baghdad were required to swear an oath not to copy books of philosophy. On the conflicts of Muslim science and Islamic doctrine, see Hoodbhoy, *Islam and Science,* especially chs. 9 and 10.

15. Ibn Khaldūn, *The Muqaddima: An Introduction to History* (London: Routledge and Kegan Paul, 1978), p. 373, cited in Hoodbhoy, *Islam and Science,* pp. 103–04. We have an analogous example of arrant cynicism and zealotry in Christian annals: when the French "crusader" army sent to repress the Cathar heresy broke into Béziers and was permitted (ordered) to put its inhabitants to the sword, the commander was asked how they might distinguish the good Christians from the heretics; to which he replied: "God will know his own."

16. White, *Medieval Religion and Technology*, p. 227.

17. Elvin, *Pattern of the Chinese Past*, p. 184.

18. *Ibid.*, p. 85. Elvin gives the figure as "between 35,000 to 40,000 tons and 125,000 tons," but says he prefers the higher estimate. He relies here on Yoshida Mitsukuni, a Japanese specialist writing in 1967. Subsequent work by Robert Hartwell, "Markets, Technology, and the Structure of Enterprise," p. 34, also advances the higher figure. In Hall, *Powers and Liberties*, p. 46, this becomes "at least 125,000 tons." That's the way of historical numbers—they grow.

19. Elvin, *Pattern of the Chinese Part*, pp. 297–98.

20. Cf. Goldstone, "Gender, Work, and Culture."

21. Balazs, *La bureaucratie céleste*, pp. 22–23.

22. Cited in White, *Medieval Religion and Technology*, pp. 245–46.

## CHAPTER 5

1. Schama, "They All Laughed," p. 30, says that even in 1892, protestors objected to the celebration and delayed it by a year.

2. Cf. "The Invasion of the Nina, the Pinta, and the Santa Maria," *New York Times,* 2 June 1991; and the indignant rebuttal of Teresa de Balmaseda Milam, *ibid.,* 4, July 1991.

3. James Barron, "He's the Explorer/Exploiter You Just Have to Love/Hate," *New York Times,* 12 October 1992, p. B7. See also Sam Dillon, "Schools Grow Harsher in Scrutiny of Columbus," *ibid.,* p. A1. Although "Native American" is now the accepted and acceptable name for people descended from the original (first) inhabitants of the western hemisphere, some have objected that "American" is a European, and hence inappropriate, designation. One should speak of "natives" instead. But what of all the other people born in the hemisphere? Are they not natives? Apparently some natives are more native than others.

4. See Joel Sable, "Mexico Hails Aztecs with Multiple Issues," *Boston Globe,* 3 April 1994, p. B34.

5. Cf. Schama, "They All Laughed." The superbly illustrated catalogue: Levenson, ed., *Circa 1492: Art in the Age of Exploration.*

6. Vitorino Magalhaes Godinho rightly speaks of the absurdity of this no-discovery thesis, which he describes as an "infantile trap." "Rôle du Portugal," p. 58.

7. On these issues, see King, *Art of Mathematics,* pp. 41–46.

8. Ibn Khaldūn, *The Muqaddimah,* cited in Fernandez-Armesto, *Before Columbus,* p. 50.

9. Fernandez-Armesto, *Before Columbus,* p. 49.

10. See the discussion *ibid.,* pp. 84–85.

11. *Ibid.,* p. 12.

12. For the Portuguese, the first encounter with the Madeiras seems to date from 1419. Huygue, *Coureurs d'épices,* p. 119, gives it as accidental.

13. Bennassar and Bennassar, *1492,* p. 252.

14. Axtell, *After Columbus,* p. 168.

15. Bartolomé de Las Casas, *Brief Relation of the Destruction of the Indies,* cited in Josephy, *Indian Heritage,* p. 287.

16. These reports are from a letter of 1516 from a group of Dominican friars to the minister of Charles I (later Charles V) in Spain, cited in Todorov, *La conquête de l'Amérique,* p. 146. The letter cites among other atrocities the case of a poor mother with nursing child who had the misfortune to pass before a group of Spaniards whose dog was hungry. Exaggerated? We have corroborative evidence from other witnesses.

17. Most of what follows is drawn from the vivid presentation of Fernandez-Armesto, *Before Columbus,* pp. 143–47.

18. Bruckner, *The Tears of the White Man,* p. 10, suggests that Columbus was prepared to believe by reading in Pierre d'Ailly's *Imago mundi* (written 1410, published 1480) that the Garden of Eden had to be in a warm land somewhere on the other side of the equator. To be sure, this new land, though warm, was not on the other side of the equator. But what really mattered to Columbus in my opinion was the nakedness and innocence of these beautiful people. How could Ailly know which side of the equator the Garden was on?

19. The above quotations come from Bruckner, *ibid.,* who has them from a French translation of Columbus's journals: Christophe Colomb, *La découverte de l'Amérique,* 2 vols. (Paris: Maspero, 1979).

20. See the article by Henley, "Spanish Stew," p. 5, reviewing Boucher, *Cannibal Encounters:* "Boucher reviews the current state of the argument among the specialists, concluding that the evidence for cannibalism is very weak. If it was practised at all, it was probably only a highly ritualized procedure which may have involved the eating of the fat of slain enemies on certain restricted occasions. Certainly, they would never simply have boiled somebody up in a stew-pot."

See also Wright, "The Two Cultures," p. 3, who argues that European accounts of this practice should be treated with suspicion. "The case against the Mexicans is far from proven, and the Spaniards, by their own reports, were not above an occasional lapse in this regard." Wright notes that during the siege of Mexico, there were plenty of dead

bodies lying about and yet the defenders starved. But that might simply mean that cannibalism had ritual aspects that did not allow the eating of otherwise dead people. Cf.
the Hebrew food ban of dead animals (that is, not ritually slaughtered), even though
kosher.

21. Maybury-Lewis, "Societies on the Brink," p. 56.

22. Todorov, *La conquête de l'Amérique*, p. 150.

23. On the "Black Legend," it is instructive to read Stern, *Peru's Indian Peoples*, pp.
xli–xlii. Stern, who has a pressing urge to be politically correct, recognizes the misdeeds
of the Spanish but concedes to the apologist position by alluding to "simplification"
and "anti-Hispanic prejudice." He also points to "an equally brutal history of racial violence and exploitation by other European colonizers." Then a word of criticism: he
laments that the anti-Legend thesis "reduces the Conquest to a story of European villains and heroes." What about the Amerindians and their responses? he asks. It is no
longer acceptable among ethnologists to portray native populations as helpless victims;
as Stern says, they were not "mere objects upon which evil is enacted." Fair enough,
but what about the Amerindians? As we shall see below, they perpetrated their own
cruelties; they imposed their own imperialisms. Imperialism is not the monopoly of Europeans or Westerners. The orthodoxy of Latin American history prefers to pass over
that part of the story. The whole business is a minefield of traps for moral judgment.
Latin American historians face the further dilemma that they often descend from both
victims and victimizers. Where, then, should their sympathies go?

CHAPTER 6

1. On the psychological and physical significance of Bojador, see Randles, "La signification."

2. Quoted in Huyghe, *Coureurs d'épices*, p. 121.

3. On the special navigational problems of the South Atlantic, see Landes, "Finding
the Point at Sea," in Andrewes, ed., *The Quest for Longitude;* and Seed, *Ceremonies of
Possession*, ch. 4: "A New Sky and New Stars." This latter is a superb treatment of the
scientific basis for Portuguese oceanic navigation and discovery.

4. Zacut was the author of the *Almanach Perpetuum* (1478), which worked out the
position of the sun for each day at each latitude. This work, intended for astronomers,
was simplified and converted into a table for use at sea by his co-religionist John Viz-
inho—Jones, *Sail the Indian Sea*, pp. 37–38.

6. The above is taken from the valuable article of Godinho, "Rôle du Portugal," pp.
81–83.

7. Introduction to his *Tratado im defensam da carta de marear,* cited in Seed, *Ceremonies of Possession*, p. 126.

8. Cf. the splendid discussion in Needham, "China, Europe, and the Seas Between,"
paper originally presented to the International Congress of Maritime History, Beirut,
1966, and republished in Needham, *Clerks and Craftsmen*, pp. 40–70. But the largest
treatment of these voyages, rich and fascinating in its detail and broad in its coverage,
is the recent book of Louise Levathes, *When China Ruled the Seas.*

9. "By Sung times, Chinese junks had become very much more sophisticated. They
were built with iron nails, and waterproofed with the oil of the t'ung tree, a superb natural preservative. Their equipment included watertight bulkheads, buoyancy chambers,
bamboo fenders at the waterline, floating anchors to hold them steady during storms,
axial rudders in place of steering oars, outrigger and leeboard devices, oars for use in
calm weather, scoops for taking samples off the sea floor, sounding lines for deter-
mining the depth, compasses for navigation, and small rockets propelled by gunpowder for self-defence"—Elvin, *Pattern of the Chinese Past*, p. 137. This tradition
continued under the Mongol dynasty: Khubilai Khan (Marco Polo's emperor) had

ships of more than ten sails, big enough to carry a thousand men. The biggest, running to about 450 feet, were lake vessels, which "moved through the water with great stability and made the passengers feel as if they were on dry land"—Levathes, *When China Ruled the Seas,* p. 81. Of course, lake water is not the ocean sea.

10. Needham gives the number of vessels as seventy-three.

11. The above relies especially on Levathes, *When China Ruled the Seas,* pp. 73 ff.

12. Huang, *China,* pp. 155–57.

13. Levathes, *When China Ruled the Seas,* pp. 174–75.

14. Levathes emphasizes the link of indifference to trade to Confucian doctrine on the one hand, imperial legitimacy on the other. To seek trade was to admit that China needed something from elsewhere, and "the mere expression of need was unworthy of the dragon throne"—*When China Ruled the Seas,* p. 180.

## Chapter 7

1. *Wealth of Nations,* Book IV, ch. 7, Part I: "Such in reality is the absurd confidence which almost all men have in their own good fortune, that wherever there is the least probability of success, too great a share of it is apt to go to them [projects of mining] of its own accord."

2. Cf. Fernandez-Armesto, *Millennium,* pp. 211–20, on Aztec pride in their military success.

3. Stuart, *The Mighty Aztecs,* p. 73. Bartolomé de Las Casas, that great defender of Indian rights, came eventually to praise, not their rites, but the devotion that infused them. "One could argue convincingly," he wrote in his *Apologia,* "on the basis that God ordered Abraham to sacrifice his only son Isaac, that God does not entirely hate human sacrifice." And further: " . . . in religiosity, [the Aztecs] surpassed all other nations, because the most religious nations are those that offer their own children in sacrifice for the good of their people." Cited in Todorov, *La conquête de l'Amérique,* pp. 194, 196.

4. On the intellectual pains of anthropology (ethnology) as a discipline torn between "universal values" and "cultural relativism"—should we criticize another culture from some higher ground?—see Fluehr-Lobban, "Cultural Relativism and Human Rights."

5. This kind of *tu quoque* exculpation goes back to Las Casas at least—Todorov, *La conquête de l'Amérique,* p. 194.

6. Sahlins, "Cosmologies of Capitalism," p. 19, n. 24, citing George Macartney's journal of his embassy to China in 1793. Poor Macartney: he sought by his own dignified conduct to convince the Chinese that the British were civilized. But all his efforts to preserve his dignity, that is, to establish his parity with his hosts, only convinced them that he had much to learn before he could be accounted civilized.

7. From the chronicler Pedro Aguado, as cited in Gomez, *L'invention,* p. 171. Cf. Smith, *Wealth of Nations,* Book IV, ch. 7, Part 2.

8. Kirkpatrick, *Les conquistadors espagnols,* p. 147.

9. Fernandez-Armesto, *Millennium,* p. 224.

10. Bernand, *The Incas,* p. 28.

11. Diamond, *Guns, Germs, and Steel,* p. 80.

12. The demographic history of the Amerindians has been a subject of controversy and imagination. Estimates of the pre-Columbian population of the Americas vary from 13 million according to A. Rosenblatt, *La poblacion de America* (1971) to 100 million by the Berkeley school. Cf. Woodrow Borah, Sherburne Cook, L. B. Simpson, *Essays in Population History* (1971). The latter would strike most scholars as wildly hyperbolic, and a figure between 50 and 70 million, the great majority in the corn-eating areas of Mexico and Peru, now seems more reasonable. Part of this is ideological: to magnify

the demographic catastrophe by way of aggravating European guilt—as though it were not great enough already. Can it be that the Indian population of the west coast of South America was composed of a different gene pool, one that had had some exposure to these pathogens? See the speculations of Dickinson and Mahn-Lot, *1492–1992*, pp. 93–94.

13. On more than one occasion, plans for rebellion were betrayed via the confessional and reported to the authorities—Rowe, "The Incas" (1957), p. 158. Cf. Chklovski, *Voyage of Marco Polo*, p. 162, on the comparable role of astrologers (interpreters of dreams) in the Mongol Chinese empire of Kublai Khan. To be sure, these astrologers had never obligated themselves to keep these confidences secret.

14. The idiom is one of dismissal. But history has its own obligations, and Fernandez-Armesto, *Millennium*, p. 225, argues that we must not forget: " . . . it is important to restore the imperial careers of these African and American states to their place in the commonly received record of the past . . . without a broad picture of the expanding and convergent movements which met in the 'age of expansion,' the nature of the world moulded by European initiatives in the second half of our millennium cannot be fully grasped, nor the scale of the achievement realistically envisaged."

15. Among the most important are (1) the account by Father Bernabe Cobo, *History of the Inca Empire: An Account of the Indians Customs and Their Origin Together with a Treatise on Inca Legends, History, and Social Institutions* (finished 1653). Rowe, "Inca Culture," p. 195, describes Father Cobo's *History* as "still the best and most complete description of *Inca* culture in existence." And (2) Garcilaso de la Vega El Inca, *Royal Commentary of the Incas and General History of Peru* (finished 1616). De la Vega, related to the Inca royal family on his mother's side, was the son of a Spanish conquistador. On de la Vega's somewhat edulcorated account of Inca conquests, see Bernand, *The Incas*, p. 28.

16. I say "humiliating" deliberately. In confrontations with the Spanish, the Araucanians would parade captured and visibly pregnant Spanish women before their former spouses, skirts tucked above the waist—Padden, "Cultural Change and Military Resistance."

17. Cobo, *History*, pp. 228–30. Much has been made of the excellence of the Inca roads, and the Spanish themselves were impressed by the broader, straighter sections; although truth to say, the Spanish did not have good examples at home to go by. Two major routes ran north-south, one along the coast, the other along the highland ridge; these were fed by east-west transversals and local paths. From an economist's point of view, the excellence of these roads lay in their practicality: they were no better than they had to be. In the more difficult terrain, they were often nothing more than a track, perhaps a yard wide, paved with stone as required and stepped to save distance. They were protected where necessary from rockfalls, but the users were expected to keep themselves from falling. At intervals, in towns or along the road, the Incas built shelters and storehouses for travelers. Almost all travelers were on official business. The Inca state discouraged private trade and had an effective monopoly of long-distance commerce. Cf. Rowe, "Inca Culture," pp. 229–33.

## CHAPTER 8

1. Around 1600, Spain's Caribbean island empire had a population of maybe 75,000–80,000, of whom one in ten Spanish, the rest black and mixed. Few traces of natives. Thus one person for 5 sq. km., one Spanish "settler" for 50 sq. km.—Chaunu, *L'Amérique*, p. 112.

2. Twenty-five sugar refineries in Amsterdam alone in 1622—Rich, "Colonial Settlement," p. 334.

3. Wood, *Spanish Main*, p. 125, gives a total of something under 5,000.

4. On bugs in the Caribbean, see Starkey, *Economic Geography,* p. 60; on animal pests, Watts, *The West Indies,* p. 195. Needless to say, the combination of climate, pests, and pathogens made for high death rates, of work animals even more than of humans. (I owe these references to Stanley Engerman.)

5. Parry, *Age of Reconnaissance,* p. 276. Dunn, *Sugar and Slaves,* p. 55, says this figure is "impossible." On the basis of poll tax returns, he suggests a population of about 10,000 in 1640, equal to that of Massachusetts or Virginia.

6. Parry, *Age of Reconnaissance,* p. 276.

7. Chaunu, *L'Amérique,* p. 113.

8. *Wealth of Nations,* Book IV, ch. 7, Part 2.

9. Littleton, *Groans of the Plantations,* p. 20, cited in Dunn, *Sugar and Slaves,* p. 194.

10. Rich, "Colonial Settlement," p. 322.

11. Joseph Miller, in his book on the Angolan slave trade, *Way of Death.*

12. Sheridan, "Eric Williams," p. 326, citing Williams, *Capitalism and Slavery,* pp. vii, 52, 105. Sheridan writes (p. 327) that Williams's book "inaugurated the modern period of West Indian historiography."

13. Inikori, "Slavery and the Development of Industrial Capitalism," p. 101.

14. Sheridan, "Eric Williams," p. 327.

15. Thus Oxaal: "Williams attacked the moral complacency associated with Britain's understanding of its slave-holding past." He describes Williams (along with James) as a "marginal, black intellectual whose personal experiences had made him aware of the hypocrisy behind the metropolitan country's pious self-congratulation over its dealings with the colonies"—*Black Intellectuals,* pp. 75–76.

16. In a review in the *American Sociological Review,* Wilson Gee criticized Williams for exaggerating the role of slavery "by claiming that it was almost the indispensable foundation stone in the establishment of modern capitalism." Cited by Sheridan, "Eric Williams," p. 320.

17. Anstey, "Capitalism and Slavery"; also his *Atlantic Slave Trade.* Anstey goes on to estimate the part of slave profits in British capital formation at 0.11 percent—"derisory." Stanley Engerman, "The Slave Trade and British Capital Formation," plays with the numbers "under some implausible assumptions" and comes up with hypothetical figures, strongly and knowingly biased upward, ranging from 2.4 percent to 10.8 percent over the period 1688–1770, which he says "should give some pause to those attributing to the slave trade a major contribution to industrial capital formation in the period of the Industrial Revolution." He also compares the "gross value of slave trade output" to British national income and comes up with an average of about 1 percent, climbing to 1.7 percent in 1770, too small by itself to explain much. He goes on to suggest that the contribution of the slave trade itself has to be joined to that of the plantation system; and that these together were better seen in a dynamic context of linkages.

18. Inikori, "Market Structure," p. 761, n. 52. Inikori estimates profits at 50 percent, intermittently but over a number of years. This is based on an investment that does not include debts incurred in the purchase of trade goods: "What the individual slave trader actually put into the ventures as his investment (the actual cash outlay) was often less than half of the total outward cost. . . ." (p. 775).

19. On gains to planters, see Sheridan, "The Wealth of Jamaica," and Ward, "The Profitability of Sugar Planting." There is a rebuttal to Sheridan from a macroeconomic point of view: R. P. Thomas, in "The Sugar Colonies," points in good Smithian fashion to the overhead costs of empire and the cost to consumers of a protected, monopolistic market in Britain for sugar from British plantations. This, of course, is an old story: privatize the gains and socialize the costs. Net out, and one finds that the macroeffects differ from partial results.

20. Along these lines, cf. Zahedieh, "London and the Colonial Consumer."

21. Solow and Engerman, eds., *British Capitalism*, pp. 10–11.

22. Most of the following material on Mexican sugar is drawn from Cardoso, *Negro Slavery in the Sugar Plantations*.

## CHAPTER 9

1. William Hunter, *History of British India*, I, 109, cited by Masselman, *Cradle of Colonialism*, p. 218. Masselman writes: "There were many more examples of this kind, all part of a deliberate policy of intimidation to gain control over India." On this practice of cutting off nose and hands—because it was a deliberate practice—see chapter v (above) on Spanish policy.

2. Cited by Boxer, *The Portuguese Seaborne Empire*, p. 297.

3. Lang, *Portuguese Brazil*, p. 34.

4. Cf. Boxer, *Portuguese Seaborne Empire*, p. 59.

5. The words are from *The Letter-Book of William Clarke, Merchant in Aleppo*, cited in Domenico Sella, "Crisis and Transformation in Venetian Trade," in Pullan, ed., *Crisis and Change in the Venetian Economy*, p. 97.

6. On all of this, see especially the works of K. N. Chaudhuri: *The Trading World of Asia and the English East India Company 1660–1760; Trade and Civilisation in the Indian Ocean;* and *Asia Before Europe.*

7. I take these verses from Boxer, *The Dutch Seaborne Empire*, p. 115. On the weakness of Portugal vs. the Dutch and English, see Meilink-Roelofsz, *Asian Trade*, pp. 116–35.

8. Boxer, *Portuguese Seaborne Empire*, p. 57.

9. From Luis da Camoëns, *The Lusiads* (*Os Lusiadas*, "The Lusitanians"). The great epic poem was written over a period of many years and finally published in 1572.

10. Cited by Boxer, *Portuguese Seaborne Empire*, p. 147.

11. The expression is from Father Antonio Vieira, S.J. (1608–1697), cited in Boxer, *Portuguese Seaborne Empire*, p. 340.

12. Seed, *Ceremonies of Possession*, pp. 135–37 and n. 133.

13. Boxer, *Portuguese Seaborne Empire*, p. 350.

14. From Dom Luis da Cunha, cited in Boxer, *Portuguese Seaborne Empire*, p. 356. The allusion is surely to the Methuen treaty of 1703, by which Portugal agreed to admit British wool and woolens duty-free, while Britain would take Portuguese wines (porto and madeira) at sharply reduced rates.

15. *Ibid.*, pp. 340–42.

16. *Ibid.*, p. 350.

17. *Ibid.*, p. 344.

## CHAPTER 10

1. From his *Werken*, III, 628–29, translated by Keene, *The Japanese Discovery of Europe*, p. 3. Keene's book, little known outside the field of Japanese studies, is a gem.

2. As given in Braudel, *Civilisation matérielle*, III: *Le temps du monde*, p. 149. This quotation, from a report by a certain abbé Scaglia, has passed through several avatars on its way to my page.

3. Israel, *Dutch Primacy*, p. 24.

4. Cf. Peyrefitte, *Du "miracle,"* pp. 146–47.

5. Cf. Israel, *The Dutch Republic*, pp. 183–84.

6. Directors to Admiral Pieter Verhoef, 29 March 1608, cited in Masselman, *Cradle of Colonialism*, pp. 257–58. The anticipated deadline for a territorial freeze was 1 September 1609. On profit from rare spices, see Prakash, "Dutch East India Company," p. 189 and n. 6.

7. J. P. Coen to the Heeren XVII (the board of directors of the VOC), 27 December 1614, cited by Boxer, *Dutch Seaborne Empire*, p. 107. On the career of Coen, see Masselman, *Cradle of Colonialism*.
8. J. P. Coen to the Heeren XVII, in Boxer, *Dutch Seaborne Empire*, p. 107.
9. Cf. C. P. Thunberg, *Travels in Europe, Africa and Asia, 1770–1779*, I, 277, cited in Boxer, *Dutch Seaborne Empire*, pp. 238–39.
10. Hannay, *The Great Chartered Companies*, cited in Boxer, *Dutch Seaborne Empire*, pp. 225–26.
11. Furnivall, *Netherlands Indies*, p. 49.
12. Early on, in the 1620s, the VOC apparently accepted to share with the English its monopoly in the Spice Islands, on condition that the English share the cost of garrisoning the area. The English found it cheaper to withdraw—Prakash, "Dutch East India Company," p. 188.
13. Furnivall, *Netherlands India*, p. 39.
14. In regard to English (British) trade with the North American colonies, Adam Smith reasons that monopoly due to the navigation acts raised the rate of profit above what it would have been in a free market—*Wealth of Nations*, Book IV, ch. 7, Part 3. But he does not factor in the effect on revenue in the colonies and hence on tax revenues to the mother country. Had he done so, he would have found one more reason to disapprove of such interference with the market.
15. Furnivall, *Netherlands India*, p. 39; Vlekke, *Nusantara*, pp. 203–04.
16. *Wealth of Nations*, Book III, ch. 7, Part 3.
17. Braudel, *Civilisation matérielle*, III: *Le temps du monde*, p. 191.
18. Braudel notes *(ibid.)* that Johannes Hudde, chairman of the board at the end of the seventeenth century, was well aware of the difficulty and tried to revise (transform) the system of accounts. He never succeeded. "For a thousand reasons and real difficulties. But perhaps also because the directors of the Company were not keen on publishing clear accounts." Opacity has its advantages. This too is not unknown in modern business management, the more so when there are conflicts of interest among owners, directors, and managers.

CHAPTER 11

1. Sainsbury, ed., *Calendar of State Papers, East Indies*, para. 321, cited in Masselman, *Cradle of Colonialism*, p. 281.
2. The English, building on an imperial firman exempting them from custom duties, took all manner of merchants under their protection and sold them passes, while levying upon agents and representatives of the Nawab and taxing land transfers and marriages in the area under their control. The result: a constant outcry at the court of Bengal that made war inevitable—Edwardes, *Battle of Plassey*, pp. 23–24, citing Captain Rennie, in 1756.
3. Cited in Bhattacharya, *East India Company*, p. 19 f.
4. Both *ibid.*, p. 22.
5. Edwardes, *Battle of Plassey*, p. 24.
6. Chaudhuri, *Trading World of Asia*, p. 195.
7. On all this, see Steensgaard, "Trade of England," pp. 123–26. His Table 3.8 shows summary estimates of imports of Indian (plus some Chinese) textiles into Europe, 1651–1760, by VOC and EIC. These data show that the EIC was in a stronger position than its rivals even before the Battle of Plassey. Steensgaard attributes this among other things to the greater decentralization of the English company and the initiative allowed its agents in the field.
8. *Journal of the House of Commons*, 14 February 1704, XIV, 336, cited in Chaudhuri, *Trading World of Asia*, p. 277.

9. Moreland, *India at the Death of Akbar,* pp. 9–22; cited in Habib, "Potentialities," p. 54, n. 6.

10. Habib, "Population," p. 167, gives a probable figure of "a little under 150 million in 1600." Habib, "Potentialities," pp. 34–35. Comparing 1600 and 1900, Habib argues that, balancing abundant land in the earlier period (hence higher average fertility) against increased social overhead capital in the later (British investments in irrigation canals, railroads, etc.), and allowing for stagnant techniques of cultivation over the interval, one may infer that productivity per head in Indian agriculture was at least as high at the earlier date as at the later. He also thinks that per capita productivity in Moghul India was "not in any way backward when compared with other contemporary societies, including those of western Europe." I think this unlikely. For similar arguments, cf. Parthasarathi, "Rethinking Wages."

11. Kautsky, *Politics,* p. 188, citing Lybyer, *The Government of the Ottoman Empire,* p. 295. And Kautsky points out that since these estimates were based on pre–World War I dollars, one would have to multiply them by 10 to convert to 1981 values. My own multiple would be 20 or 25 to match 1994 values.

12. Lybyer, *Government,* p. 293, quotes Alexander Dow, *The History of Hindostan,* 3 vols. (London, 1770–72), that "to be born a prince" of the Moghul empire was "a misfortune of the worst and most embarrassing kind. He must die by clemency, or wade through the blood of his family to safety and empire." Cited in Kautsky, *Politics,* p. 240; he also quotes Herbert A. Gibbons, *The Foundation of the Ottoman Empire,* p. 180, who refers to the theological sanction for these bloody intrafamilial conflicts: "The new emir justified this crime by a verse conveniently found for him by his theologians in the Koran: 'So often as they return to sedition, they shall be subverted therein; and if they depart not from you, and offer you peace and restrain their hands from warring against you, take them and kill them wheresoever ye find them' (Sura IV, verse 94). They declared that the temptation to treason and revolt was always present in the brothers of the ruler, and that murder was better than sedition."

13. On the huge personal fortunes of the Moghul ruling class and the consequences of their systematic hoarding, see Raychaudhuri, "The Mughal Empire," p. 183. The ultimate beneficiaries were the British, who pensioned off the local potentates and still had plenty to spare for the Raj (the British government in India) and themselves.

14. Cf., among many others, Chaudhury, "Trade, Bullion and Conquest." At stake here are larger issues about the role of the Europeans in a world already prosperous: Why so much fuss about them? Who needed them?

15. Cf. Root, "Le marché des droits de propriété," p. 299.

16. J. Ovington, *A Voyage to Surat in the Year 1689,* ed. H. G. Rawlinson (London, 1929), cited by Raychaudhuri, "The Mughal Empire," p. 185, who calls this description of "fear and servitude" "typical of a hundred others."

17. Macaulay, "Lord Clive," p. 222.

18. On the business interests of the company and its agents, many of them engaged in all manner of private enterprises, and the British desire to help the local government into friendly hands, see Chaudhury, "Trade, Bullion and Conquest," pp. 27–30.

19. The quote is from a letter of 9 April 1757 from Luke Scrafton to "Clive's confidant" John Walsh—Chaudhury, "Trade, Bullion and Conquest," p. 28.

20. Cf. Adas, " 'High Imperialism' and the 'New History,' " pp. 9–10; also Edwards, *Battle of Plassey.*

21. Keay, *Honourable Company,* pp. 318–19.

22. Macaulay, "Clive," p. 253.

23. *Ibid.,* p. 250.

24. Marshall, *Problems of Empire,* p. 60.

25. Cf. Pearson, "India and the Indian Ocean," p. 72: "For the sixteenth century, we are distressingly dependent on European sources."

26. Habib, *Agrarian System,* pp. 90, 350, 390. The latter story is from John Fryer, *A New Account of East India and Persia being Nine Years' Travels, 1672–81.* The whole is cited from Kautsky, *Politics of Aristocratic Empires,* p. 103, n. 14.

27. Thus Andre Wink affirms that "at the dawn of the Industrial Revolution income per capita was possibly higher in many parts of Asia than in Europe."—Wink, " 'Al-Hind,' " p. 65. Cf. Bairoch, "Ecarts internationaux," and "The Main Trends in National Economic Disparities," p. 7. Also Parthasarathi, "Rethinking Wages."

28. Cf. Alam, "How Rich Were the Advanced Countries in 1760 After All?"

29. Macaualay, "Clive," p. 228.

<h2 style="text-align:center">CHAPTER 12</h2>

1. Thus Salaman, *History and Social Influence;* and Langer, "Europe's Initial Population Explosion."

2. And not only the early centuries. Cf. S. K. Coll, "Anti-Malaria Drugs Post Hard Choice for Parents," *Int. Herald-Tribune,* 18 October 1996, p. 11.

3. Curtin, "Epidemiology and the Slave Trade," Table 1, p. 203, cited in Sheridan, *Doctors and Slaves,* p. 12. These figures are based on the mortality of British military personnel, white and black, posted to different parts of the world, 1817–36. On the assumption of some learning, death rates were presumably lower then than they had been in the seventeenth and eighteenth centuries.

4. Cited by Edwy Plénel, "Le conquérant oublié," *Le Monde,* 1–2 September 1991, p. 2. One can find similar orgies of destructive self-indulgence among the oil-rich countries of the late twentieth century.

5. Spanish industry was not equal to that of Italy or the countries of northwestern Europe; but neither was it negligible in the sixteenth century. Cf. Peyrefitte, *Société,* p. 134. On shrinkage in the seventeenth, see Lynch, *Hispanic World,* pp. 210 ff.

6. Alfonso Nuñez de Castro, quoted in Cipolla, *Before the Industrial Revolution,* p. 251.

7. Cited in Lewis, *Muslim Discovery,* p. 197. The Italian historian and statesman Francesco Guicciardini said much the same thing, though he put it in terms of who got the value added. Guicciardini, *Relazione di Spagna,* p. 131, quoted in Cipolla, *Before the Industrial Revolution,* p. 250.

8. Bernaldez, ch. cxii, p. 257, cited in Bernand and Gruzinski, *Histoire du nouveau monde,* I, 78–79, 643. Note that in some cultures, tanning and leather trades have been traditionally despised as intrinsically foul and degrading; thus Japan, which included such workers among the *eta,* a group of social untouchables that also included undertakers and gravediggers. In Ottoman Turkey, a society that like Spain cultivated the arts and habits of war, industrial crafts were primarily in the hands of religious minorities, notably the Armenians.

9. Cf. Peyrefitte, *Société,* pp. 141–42.

10. On the riches and trade of the North Atlantic, see Axtell, "At the Water's Edge: Trading in the Sixteenth Century," in his *After Columbus,* pp. 144–81. Of whale oil, he writes (p. 146), it was "as profitable as liquid gold" (but much less tempting to freebooters). "For whale oil lit the lamps of Europe, made soap and soup, lubricated everything from frying pans to clocks, and, since the whale was classified as a fish, served as *lard de carême*—Lenten fat—during holy days when meat products were prohibited."

11. On the decline of the Italian textile manufacture (far and away the principal branch of industrial production), see Cipolla, *Before the Industrial Revolution,* pp. 253–63. We have much to learn about new industries taking hold in smaller towns and even in the countryside. Cf. Ciriacono, "The Venetian Economy" and "Venise et la Vénétie." But the older urban centers seem to have used economic and political power to keep

these in their modest place. See Sella, *Crisis and Continuity*, and Moioli, "De-Industrialization in Lombardy."

12. [Anthony Walker], *The Holy Life of Mrs Elizabeth Walker* (1690), cited in Thomas, "Cleanliness and Godliness," p. 56. Thanks to Keith Thomas for making this available in advance of publication.

13. Baxter, "Of Redeeming Time," *Practical Works*, p. 228. Again, thanks to Keith Thomas.

14. Cf. H. M. Robertson, *Aspects of the Rise of Economic Individualism.*

15. On this older, defensive ethic of gentility, see the important article of Arthur Livingston, "Gentleman, Theory of the," in the *Encyclopedia of the Social Sciences.* Also Kautsky, *Politics of Aristocratic Empires,* pp. 177–97.

16. Candolle, *Histoire des sciences et des savants.* Some have dismissed these figures on the ground that Candolle's counting starts in the 1660s, when the scientific revolution was already well under way. Cf. Smith, *Science and Society,* p. 48. Such an objection does not, of course, rule out the possibility that a similar survey of the earlier period might yield similar results; but the implication is that it would not. The point is that Candolle had countable data to work with after the founding of the scientific academies. It would seem unreasonable to dismiss them for the period they deal with, where Protestant leadership in science would seem to be a fact. Whether the explanation lies in Protestantism or Catholic hostility to the new science, or both, is another matter.

17. Cited by Mason, "Scientific Revolution."

18. This is the Swedish historian Kurt Samuelsson, in a slim monograph translated into English as *Religion and Economic Action.*

19. Samuelsson's statistical critique of Weber's data on Baden, for example, is unpersuasive, although he makes the point that Protestants were likelier to live in urban areas where technical schools were invariably located. But that was no accident either.

20. Landes, *Revolution in Time,* pp. 92–93. Cf. de Vries, *Dutch Rural Economy,* p. 219: on the basis of household inventories, possession of clocks in the Leewarderadeel district rose from 2 percent in 1677–86 to 70.5 percent in 1711–50. Of course these were households sufficiently well off to make an inventory after death.

21. Cf. Michaud, "Orléans au XVIIIᵉ siècle," p. 11. Even so, certain orders of chivalry were closed to such new men, and such exclusions worked against these efforts to honor business success, to the point where some argued for the creation of a new kind of order by way of raising the status of these underappreciated achievers. These protestations of esteem do not ring hollow; but they tell us that other people did not agree.

22. Bennassar, *L'Inquisition espagnole,* ch. viii: "Refus de la Réforme," especially pp. 289–90. Once again Spain's reaction was shaped, to its own cost, by its long history of uncompromising religious conformity and the passions it engendered. Cf. Goodman, "Scientific Revolution," pp. 163–64, who suggests that the dearth of Old Catholic physicians in sixteenth-century Spain may have reflected the racial (congenital) link that some Spaniards made between Jewishness and medicine. "It could well be that, in a society which gave esteem to those who could establish freedom from Jewish or Moorish descent, the Old Christians avoided the medical profession in case success there might arouse suspicions of Jewish blood." Poisoned bread upon the waters.

23. Goodman, "Scientific Revolution in Spain and Portugal," in Porter and Teich, eds., *Scientific Revolution,* p. 172. Some Spanish historians, seeking to defend the indefensible, have argued that outside universities were so poor and hidebound that Spanish students were not missing much. Perhaps; although Protestant universities, in England and Holland for example, were substantially better. But drinking at the fountain of heresy was simply out of the question. Cf. Smith, *Wealth of Nations,* Book V, ch. i, Part 3, Article 3d, on the drain of talent from university teaching to the Church in Catholic countries.

24. Crow, *Spain: The Root and the Flower,* p. 149.

25. In his *Carta filosofica, medico-chymica* (Madrid, 1687), cited by Goodman, "Scientific Revolution," p. 173.

26. Trevor-Roper, "Religion, the Reformation and Social Change," in the collection of essays of the same title. The paper was originally delivered in 1961 to the Fifth Irish Conference of Historians in Galway. It must have upset many listeners.

27. On Bruno and the Church campaign to domesticate science, see Minois, *L'Eglise et la science,* I, ch. ix: "Contre-Réforme et reprise en main des sciences." On the provenance of Bruno's "science," see Yates, *Giordano Bruno,* and the discussion in Copenhaver, "Natural Magic."

28. Grenet, *Passion des astres,* p. 87.

29. *Ibid.,* p. 79.

30. See especially La Lumia, *Histoire de l'expulsion des Juifs de Sicile.*

CHAPTER 13

1. *OED, s.v.* Revolution, III, 6, b.

2. On the breast wheel: Mokyr, *Lever of Riches,* pp. 90–92. On waterpower vs. steam: Tunzelmann, *Steam Power;* and Greenberg, "Reassessing the Power Patterns."

3. This is the traditional explanation—see Ashton, *Iron and Steel.* Hyde, *Technological Change,* p. 40, argues that this was not the reason; rather that Darby succeeded because he knew how to cast thin-walled iron vessels using sand instead of loam, thereby saving one half the metal, and these could be more easily made from coke-blast pig.

4. John U. Nef, *Rise of the British Coal Industry.* The scholar who has argued most cogently for the importance of fossil fuel and steampower is E. A. Wrigley. See his *Continuity, Chance and Change* and his essay on "The Classical Economists, the Stationary State, and the Industrial Revolution," p. 31. Adam Smith, *Wealth of Nations,* Book V, ch. 2, Art. 4, notes the tendency of British industry to concentrate near coal deposits. He attributes it to the effect of cheap fuel on wages (they could be lower) and on the costs of such fuel-intensive (heat-using) industries as glass and iron. He does not speak of coal as fuel for engines and machines; for that matter, he does not speak of steam engines and says little about machines. Smith had his blind spots.

5. This is the estimate of A. P. Usher, *History of Mechanical Inventions.*

6. A. Rees, *The Cyclopaedia,* Vol. 38 (London, 1819), cited in Randall, *Before the Luddites,* p. 13.

7. Cited in Kindleberger, *World Economic Primacy,* viii, 6.

8. This sequence led A. P. Usher, the pioneer student of the links between technology and industry, to track the progress and timing of the Industrial Revolution by just these data—*Industrial History,* pp. 304–13.

9. *Ibid.,* p. 306.

10. Thus T. S. Ashton, whose classic and "classy" little handbook, *The Industrial Revolution,* takes as its terminal dates 1760 and 1830.

11. Compare the similar analysis by Christopher Freeman of the slowdown in productivity gains in advanced industrial countries in the 1970s and 1980s—*The Economics of Hope,* pp. 86–89.

12. Cf. Landes, "What Room for Accident in History?"

13. McCloskey, "Statics, Dynamics, and Persuasion."

14. Aldcroft, "Europe's Third World?", p. 2. The pioneer work on these historical comparisons comes from Paul Bairoch; see his "Main Trends in National Economic Disparities."

15. Yet even in these apparently straightforward matters, one can make egregious mistakes. See the discussion in J. Cuenca Esteban, "British Textile Prices," of N. F. R.

Crafts' and Knick Harley's cotton cloth prices, used in the calculation of British industrial growth. These latter purport to show increases (*sic*) or stability of cotton prices over the course of the Industrial Revolution. They were, unfortunately, badly chosen for the purpose (among other things, the indexes rest on contract rather than market prices), in part no doubt because of convenience and availability. Still, all kinds of alarm bells should have gone off. Numbers should make sense, and anyone who is ready to believe that yarn or cloth prices stood still or went up after the invention of the water frame, mule, and power loom is ready to believe anything. On the dangers and banality of numerical credulity, see Landes, "What Room for Accident in History?"

16. Theodore W. Schultz, "On Investing in Specialized Human Capital," p. 343.

17. Jeffrey Williamson figures 0.3 percent—"New Views on the Impact," p. 1.

18. Crafts, "British Industrialization in an International Context," p. 425. For a more reliable, empirical analysis of growth and gains across the industrial board, see Temin, "Two Views."

19. See the article, "The Price of Light," *The Economist*, 22 October 1994, p. 84.

20. For an early example of such avoidance, see Youngson, *Possibilities of Economic Progress*, ch. viii: "The Acceleration of Economic Progress in Great Britain, 1750–1800," especially p. 117: " . . . nothing can be proved or disproved about the economy as a whole." Youngson avers there that "progress was never constant" and that the respective contributions of different sectors were always changing. Result: many trees, no forest.

21. Ward, "Industrial Revolution and Imperialism," p. 58, commenting on Cain and Hopkins, "Gentlemanly Capitalism," pp. 510–12. It does not seem to me that Cain and Hopkins quite say that.

22. Eric Jones in *Growth Recurring*, p. 19. See Landes, "The Fable of the Dead Horse," which deals with the larger debate.

23. Cited in Massie, *Dreadnought*, p. 475.

## CHAPTER 14

1. As cited in McCloskey, "1780–1860: A Survey," p. 243.

2. As cited by White, "Cultural Climates and Technological Advance," in *Medieval Religion and Technology*, p. 221, n. 16. The sermon, it should be noted, was delivered in the vernacular. I have slightly modified the White translation of the original.

3. In his *Coloquios dos simples e drogas he cousas medicinais da India* [*Dialogues on the Simples, Drugs, and Materia medica of India*] (Goa, 1563), cited in Goodman, "Scientific Revolution," pp. 168–69.

4. Quoted in Smith, *Science and Society*, p. 51. Cf. today's version of this dependence on mathematics, this time in the field of cosmology: " . . . supergravity theory, Kaluza-Klein theory, and the Standard Model [work], but we are at a total loss to explain why. . . . String field theory exists, but it taunts us because we are not smart enough to solve it. The problem is that while 21st-century physics fell accidentally into the 20th century, 21st century mathematics hasn't been invented yet." Michio Kaku, *Hyperspace* (New York: Oxford, 1993), cited *New York Times*, 20 March 1994, "Book Review," p. 21.

5. The reference here is to the work of Frances Yates: *Giordano Bruno* and "The Hermetic Tradition." Yates suggests that the scientific revolution may well be seen as a two-step process: "the first phase consisting of an animistic universe operated by magic, the second phase of a mathematical universe operated by mechanics"—"The Hermetic Tradition," p. 273.

6. Hansen, "Science and Magic," p. 495.

7. Cf. Edward Rosen, "Was Copernicus a Hermetist?" in Roger H. Stuewer, ed., *Historical and Philosophical Perspectives of Science*, pp. 163–71: " . . . out of Renaissance

magic and astrology came, not modern science, but modern magic and astrology," cited in Hansen "Science and Magic," p. 505 n. 35. Of course, if one sees science as derivative rather than autonomous, one can lament "the ungrateful way science 'repaid' its debt: by bankrupting magic's metaphysics" (*ibid.*, p. 497).

8. *Ibid.*

9. I owe this reference to Mr. Noah Efron, doctoral candidate at the Hebrew University, currently preparing a thesis on the response of Jewish scholars to the new science of the seventeenth century.

10. Cf. Sarton, "Arabic Science," p. 321: "While the Western people had discovered the secret of experimental science and were using the new methods with increasing confidence and frequency, Muslim doctors were rereading the selfsame books and turning in hopeless circles. Stagnation in the vicinity of progressing people means regression; the distance between Eastern and Western thought was steadily increasing, the Western men went further and further ahead and the Muslims—remaining where they were—were left further and further behind."

11. Dumas, *Scientific Instruments*, pp. 49–55.

12. Sarton cites an Algerian-Turkish claimant to the invention of logarithms: Ibn Hamza al-Maghribi—"Arabic Science," p. 305, n. 2. The operative question is, to what end?

13. Cited in R. Lenoble, "The Seventeenth-Century Scientific Revolution," in Taton, ed., *A General History of the Sciences*, II: *The Beginnings of Modern Science*, p. 183.

14. Dooley, "Processo a Galileo," English translation, pp. 8–9.

15. Landes, *Revolution in Time*, pp. 125–27. Part of the problem was that Hooke was hoping to profit from this and related horological ideas and was afraid he would lose a fortune if he revealed his secret. So he ended up with nothing.

16. "Although Dr. Black's theory of latent heat did not *suggest* my improvements on the steam-engine, yet the knowledge upon various subjects which he was pleased to communicate to me, and the correct modes of reasoning, and of making experiments of which he set me the example, certainly conduced very much to facilitate the progress of my inventions...." Fleming, "Latent Heat," citing John Robinson, *A System of Mechanical Philosophy* (Edinburgh, 1822), II, ix.

17. On all this, see Musson and Robinson, *Science and Technology*, pp. 80–81.

18. On efforts of industrial spies to learn about a silk-throwing mill established in 1681 at Utrecht in Holland, see Davids, "Openness or Secrecy?" p. 338.

19. On Lombe and mechanized silk throwing: Wadsworth and Mann, *Cotton Trade*, pp. 106–108; Usher, *History of Mechanical Inventions*, pp. 275–76.

CHAPTER 15

1. Compare the analysis of the contribution of agriculture to Japanese economic development in Ohkawa and Rosovsky, "A Century of Japanese Economic Growth," and Hayami and Ruttan, "Korean Rice, Taiwan Rice."

2. On market gardening, see F. J. Fisher, "Development of the London Food Market."

3. Some historians would emphasize the material constraints. Thus Wrigley on coal as the key factor—*People, Cities and Wealth*, pp. 90–91: " . . . in this world [of Adam Smith] there was a ceiling to the possible size of industrial production set by the difficulty of expanding raw material supply at constant or declining prices as long as most industrial raw materials were organic. When this was no longer true, the ceiling disappeared." For transport as the key, see Szostak, *Role of Transportation*.

4. On the question of accident and chance in economic history, see Landes, "What Room for Accident in History? Explaining Big Changes by Small Events." This is in part a response to a well-known and perhaps intentionally provocative essay by Nick

Crafts on the question of *ex ante* probabilities: "Industrial Revolution in Britain and France: Some Thoughts on the Question 'Why Was England First?' "

5. This point begs a lot of questions. Some would argue—more in the past than now—that the most productive economy would be one directed from above. Such a command economy implies government appropriation of the surplus, the better to reinvest it with planning aforethought. Or would argue that government does some things better than the market does. But that's another book, and other people have written it. Cf. Kuttner, *Everything for Sale*.

6. One of the best discussions here is in Liah Greenfeld, "The Worth of Nations," p. 580 and *passim*. Recall again Adam Smith's justification of the navigation acts in terms of national power—*Wealth of Nations*, Book IV, ch. 2.

7. Cf. Berend and Ránki, *European Periphery*, p. 66, on limits to state action in the poor, underdeveloped societies of eastern and southeastern Europe. Also Batou and David, "Nationalisme économique," p. 6, concerning the lack of a sufficiently broad "social consensus" in nineteenth-century Poland.

8. *Wealth of Nations*, Book IV, ch. 5: "Digression on the Corn Trade."

9. Macfarlane, "On Individualism." Industry in the countryside: we have already noted the importance of rural putting-out in bringing previously unused or underused labor into production. For the merchant-manufacturer, such labor was cheap and profitable; for the rural cottager, the new work opportunities meant a substantial increase in income. Cf. Faujas de Saint Fond, *Journey Through England*, Vol. I. In 1778 a French inspector of manufactures opposed the introduction of spinning machinery into France because it would prevent the spread of cottage industry; he was less interested in economic development than in the income of the rural population. Wadsworth and Mann, *Cotton Trade*, p. 504, n. 2.

10. Fortescue, *Governance*, pp. 114–15. Cf. similar sentiments a century later by Bishop John Aylmer, cited in Fisher, ed., *Essays in the Economic and Social History*, pp. 12–13.

11. On the significance of such sentiment, cf. Greenfeld, "The Worth of Nations."

12. Cf. Crouzet, "Les sources de la richesse de l'Angleterre, vues par les Français du XVIIIᵉ siècle," in his *De la supériorité*, ch. 5, and the sources given there, pp. 488–93. Also Lacoste, *Voyage philosophique*, I, 93; Chantreau, *Voyage*, I, 7; Moritz, *Travels*, p. 31. *Et al.*

13. Defoe, *A Plan of the English Commerce*, pp. 76–77.

14. Crouzet, *De la supériorité*, p. 115, citing J. Meyer, *L'armement nantais dans la deuxième moitié du XVIIIᵉ siècle* (Paris, 1968), p. 252; and Crouzet, "Les Français," p. 28. The statement dates from 1792. On the link between high consumption and industrialization (demand and supply), see the important article by de Vries, "The Industrial Revolution."

15. On Biencourt, see Crouzet, *De la supériorité*, p. 115.

16. See among others McKendrick, Brewer, and Plumb, *The Birth of a Consumer Society;* Hopkins, *Birmingham;* Shammas, *The Pre-industrial Consumer;* Weatherill, *Consumer Behaviour;* Berg, ed., *Markets and Manufacture;* and Berg, *Age of Manufactures* (2d ed.).

17. Cf. Muller, "Justus Möser," pp. 170–71.

18. On the effort of the Habsburg emperor to remedy these wrongs through a controversial ordinance of 1731, *ibid.* pp. 162–63.

19. Thus Warren Scoville, *The Persecution of Huguenots*.

20. On these tenacious, yet highly diluted Jews, ready for quick assimilation, see Endelman, *Radical Assimilation*, pp. 9–33.

21. Cf. Crouzet, "The Huguenots and the English Financial Revolution," in Higonnet *et al.*, eds., *Favorites of Fortune*, pp. 221–66.

22. Studeny, *L'invention de la vitesse*, p. 184.

23. Fukazawa, "Non-Agricultural Production," pp. 314–15.
24. Raychaudhuri, "Non-Agricultural Production," p. 286.
25. Thus Raychaudhuri, *ibid.*, p. 295: "If necessity is the mother of invention, its pressure in the Indian case was not insistent."
26. *Ibid.*, pp. 286–87.
27. F. Buchanan, *A Journey from Madras . . .* (1807), cited *ibid.*, p. 291. Raychaudhuri agrees.
28. Brennig, "Textile Producers," p. 86. The words in quotes are his.
29. On these Banjara (a nomadic caste) caravans, see Habib, *Agrarian System*, p. 62, and Brennig, "Textile Producers," pp. 68–69. As Brennig puts it, "time was of little importance."
30. Chaudhuri, *Trading World*, Appendix 5, Table C.20, pp. 540–41.
31. Wadsworth and Mann, *The Cotton Trade*, p. 117.
32. Spear, *The Nabobs*, p. 75. Indian shipbuilders, be it noted, were highly reputed and built vessels not only for locals but for customers in other parts of Asia. The Europeans relied on them almost exclusively, not only because their work was good (teak was better than oak) and cost less, but also because European-made vessels were already in well-used condition by the time they reached the Indian Ocean.
33. Habib, "Potentialities," p. 63.
34. Raychaudhuri, "Non-Agricultural Production," p. 292, speaks of Indian shipwrights riveting planks and says this was superior to European caulking. Is this a misreading for "rabbeting"? On Indian techniques, see Barendse, "Shipbuilding" and Bhattacharya, "A Note on Shipbuilding." This ferruginous temper was an old story in Europe. Gimpel, *Medieval Machine*, pp. 65–66, cites the number and variety of nails kept in store: half a million in Calais in 1390; tens of thousands in a dozen different sizes (listed with their prices) at York Castle in 1327. The specialization of nails by use is indicative of the sophistication of this technology.
35. Kuppuram, "A Survey of Some Select Industries," p. 46.
36. Habib, "Potentialities," p. 62 and n. 4, citing J. Ovington, *A Voyage to Surat in the Year 1689* (London, 1929), pp. 166–67. Ovington says that Indian craftsmen found it hard to make clocks because dust clogged the wheels. Implausible. That may have been a problem, but not insoluble with Indian technology. As for Chinese clocks, they were poor imitations of European work. On Claude Martin, who left a large estate that still finances schools called La Martinière in Lucknow, Calcutta, and Lyons, see Landes, *Revolution in Time* and *L'heure qu'il est*.
37. Chaudhuri, *Trading World*, pp. 273–74. Cf. Bernier, *Voyage dans les états*, p. 168.
38. Kerr, "Colonialism and Technological Choice," pp. 95–97. Kerr sees the Indian choice as quite rational, but rationality is a function of ends as well as means.

CHAPTER 16

1. Cf. the references to McCloskey in Landes, "Fable," p. 163, n. 27. Pollard, *Peaceful Conquest,* does not see the story of European industrialization as one of strenuous response to the British challenge, but rather as a harmonious diffusion of technology along lines defined by the market. It was that . . . too. Cf. Davis, "Industrialization in Britain and Europe," pp. 54–55.
2. Cited by Crouzet, *De la supériorité*, p. 105.
3. *Ibid.*, p. 107.
4. Voltaire, *Essai sur les moeurs et l'esprit des nations* (Paris: Garnier, 1963), II, 695–97; cited in Crouzet, "Les Français," p. 24. The date of the first Navigation Act was actually 1651, followed by another in 1660, just after the restoration of the monarchy.

5. Crouzet, *De la supériorité*, p. 110. Crouzet notes (p. 489, n. 28) that this resentment of English trade practices is already found in Jacques Savary's commercial manual, *Le parfait négociant* (1st ed. 1675). On the other hand, a memorandum of 1711 states that England went over to heavy protection only after France had set the example and that the English actually traded more fairly [*noblement*] than other nations. One should not take these opinions as more than perceptions.

6. So Crouzet, tongue-in-cheek, citing a variety of sources, p. 490, n. 31.

7. Riem, IV, 17.

8. Mirabeau, p. 47.

9. Karl Marx, preface to *Capital*, p. 13. One consequence of this faith in laws was the definition of a properly socialist path to development, with strong emphasis on the priority of heavy industry—a kind of metallurgical fetishism. (It was no accident that Josef Dzhugashvili took Stalin [steel] as his *nom de parti*.)

10. Although empirical research has long demonstrated the particularities of national patterns of development (see, for example, Clapham, *Economic Development* [1923]), the myth of "a single and multilinear model of industrialization based on the English experience" remains an irresistible strawman, to be knocked down by successive revisions of an allegedly conventional wisdom. Thus the wonderful (in more ways than one) findings of O'Brien and Keyder, *Economic Growth in Britain and France,* which announced with flourishes that France had found its own "path to the twentieth century." For a critical if indulgent view of these exercises in iconoclasm, see Davis, "Industrialization in Britain and Europe," pp. 48–54.

11. This is the sense of Jordi Nadal in his *Fracaso de la Revolución industrial en España*, which he describes as an "analysis of the causes that limit the attempt to apply in Spain the classic model—English style—of economic development."

12. Good, *Economic Rise,* pp. 11–12; Kemp, *Industrialization,* pp. 26–27. For what we would call today a politically correct attack on the bias of such We-centered temporalities, see Fabian, *Time and the Other.* Cf. Landes, "Time of Our Lives," p. 719, n. 7.

13. Cf. Domar, "Causes of Slavery or Serfdom."

14. Cited in Bradley, *Guns for the Tsar,* p. 132.

15. Crisp, "Labour and Industrialization in Russia," in Mathias and Postan, eds., *The Cambridge Economic History of Europe,* Vol. VII, Pt. 2, p. 330. This figure (4 m.) represented some 6.5 percent of total population. Small, then, relatively, but large absolutely.

16. Some scholars would stress the incompleteness of the emancipation, in particular the maintenance of collective village obligations, as the reason for its inefficacy—cf. Gerschenkron, "Die Vorbedingungen," p. 25. As the above text indicates, I would put more stress on the effect of freedom on the workforce in industry—those already there and those to be recruited.

17. Report of spring 1859, cited in Hamerow, *Social Foundations,* p. 120. The phrase "prohibitive system" is an allusion to prohibitions on the import of certain manufactures, particularly cottons, by way of protecting and promoting the local infant industry.

18. By the middle of the 1860s, sixteen states of the German Confederation with 34 million inhabitants had come under the new dispensation; seven states with 7 million people were in the process of transition; and twelve states with only 3.5 million people, most of them agricultural in character, held out for the old order—Hamerow, *Social Foundations,* p. 121.

19. Heckscher, *Mercantilism,* I, 64.

20. Heckscher, *ibid.,* I, 72, states that the highest officials connived at this secrecy tactic; thus the toll director of East Prussia was given the tariff of 1644 with the strict in-

junction not to reveal it to anyone. It is hard to understand such a strategy, unless the ill-gotten gains were being shared right up the hierarchy.

21. For an example with economic implications, see Koerner, "Linnaeus' Floral Transplants," on the project of cultivating foreign flora in the Swedish climate in the eighteenth century. Linnaeus' ambition to grow tea in the north did not succeed, but he was following on and anticipating here one of the major gains to knowledge of geographical discovery.

22. I take this analysis from Tortella, "Patterns of Economic Retardation," pp. 8–9.

23. Tortella puts it differently: the comparative disadvantage of Switzerland in agriculture, he says, was much greater. Citing Bergier, *Histoire économique,* pp. 106, 179, he points out that from the Middle Ages on, Switzerland has imported nearly 50 percent of its food. But comparative advantage is implicitly relative, and this is just another way of saying that Swiss industry paid better—in spite of government subsidies to agriculture.

24. Tortella, "Patterns of Economic Retardation," p. 11.

25. On this, see Tortella, "La pénurie d'entrepreneurs," pp. 63–64.

26. Bradley, *Guns for the Tsar,* p. 45.

CHAPTER 17

1. Freudenberger, "The Schwarzenberg Bank," p. 51 and *passim.*

2. On this banking world, see Landes, "Vieille banque et banque nouvelle," and *Bankers and Pashas.*

3. For Rothschild interests in industry and transport, see the forthcoming history of the bank and family by Niall Ferguson.

4. Cf. Barbier, *Finance et politique,* ch. 14: "Fould après Fould," tracing ties of the Fould banking family to the bank Heine and others in Germany, the Gunzburgs (business successors of Stieglitz; now related by marriage to the Bronfmans) in St. Petersburg, the Lazards and Furtados in France, plus noble clans (feudal and Napoleonic) with vineyards, horses, and pocket boroughs.

5. Aside from the Société Générale of Brussels, one has the A. Schaffhausen'sche Bankverein in Cologne, a private bank driven to failure in the crisis of 1848 and then converted to the corporate form. The general impression that the brothers Pereire invented a new form comes from such studies as Plenge, *Gründung und Geschichte des Credit Mobilier,* as picked up by Gerschenkron in his *Economic Backwardness in Historical Perspective.* (The title essay goes back to 1951.)

6. The Germans too, by law of 11 June 1870. The point was whether businessmen could establish a joint-stock company with limited liability without obtaining prior government permission, whether by charter from the crown or a bill of the legislature. Tsarist Russia never got around to instituting such routine registration: by a decree of 1836, in effect until the revolution of 1917 (after which nothing mattered), any such company had to be authorized by law—F. Crouzet, in Moss and Jobert, eds., *Naissance et mort,* p. 201. In the United States, the rules varied from state to state, but despite routine incorporation in some states well before the Civil War, partnerships continued to dominate until the 1870s. One reason was that banks preferred to lend on the security of unlimited liability.

7. On "assistance for the strong," see R. Tilly, "German Banking, 1850–1914."

8. *Ibid.,* p. 113. All industrial capital? Or just that held in public joint-stock companies?

9. On the triumph of trade liberalization, see Levasseur, *Histoire des classes ouvrières . . . de 1789 à 1870,* Vol. II, Book VI, ch. 5. It should be noted that this move to freer trade was short-lived. In the wake of a severe financial and commercial crisis (1873–), the major industrial nations moved back toward protection (Germany, Austria, Italy,

1878–79; France, Méline tariff, 1892). The United States, meanwhile, was imposing a much higher level of protection than prevailed in Europe (outside Russia). Only Great Britain remained faithful to free trade, although there, too, agitation for protection grew. On all this, see Bairoch, *Economics and World History,* pp. 16–55, who, unlike mainstream economists, argues that protection has its rewards.
10. On all this, see André Thuillier, *Economie et société nivernaises,* chs. ix and x.
11. On this not infrequent shift from trade to banking, generally via a buildup of transactions in commercial paper, see Landes, *Bankers and Pashas,* ch. i.
12. On the Seillière and the "ascent" of Lorrain businessmen to Paris during the revolution and under the Empire, see Bergeron, *Banquiers,* pp. 54–55. On the Seillière role in the career of Ignace de Wendel and the later repurchase of the family ironworks, plus the later purchase of the forge of Moyeuvre, see Woronoff, *L'industrie sidérurgique,* p. 485.
13. For further and sometimes discordant views on this point, see Sylla and Toniolo, eds., *Patterns of European Industrialization.*

CHAPTER 18

1. Harris, "The First British Measures" and "Law, Espionage, and the Transfer of Technology"; Cellard, *John Law,* pp. 180–81.
2. Landes, *Revolution in Time,* p. 161.
3. Young, *A Six Months Tour through the North of England* (2d ed., 1771), cited in Musson and Robinson, *Science and Technology,* p. 216, n. 3.
4. We do have instances of patriotic sensibilities triumphing over material advantage. See Landes, *Revolution in Time,* ch. 10: "The French Connection," on the international competition for the invention of the marine chronometer.
5. On Boulton's tireless search for skilled workmen (he "was always alert to French inventions in the luxury trades"), see Musson and Robinson, *Science and Technology,* pp. 218–21.
6. *Ibid.,* pp. 225–27.
7. Harris, "Industrial Espionage in the Eighteenth Century," in his *Essays in Industry,* pp. 164–65. Harris has given us a detailed account of one of these snoopers in "A French Industrial Spy."
8. Harris, *Essays in Industry,* p. 170.
9. *Ibid.,* p. 171. Harris points out, quite correctly, that the convergence of these spies on Britain "emphasises the centrality of technology to the industrial revolution, and confirms overwhelmingly British technological leadership." Also that "British technological advance was cumulative and attracted attention before the major take-off into economic growth"—*ibid.,* p. 164.
10. On Alcock, see Harris, "Attempts to Transfer English Steel" and "Michael Alcock and the Transfer of Birmingham Technology." The second of these articles notes that Alcock's girlfriend's father denied that she was Alcock's mistress once Mrs. Alcock got to La Charité. But he would say that, wouldn't he, especially since Alcock's French competitors were using rumors of the liaison to discredit him with the authorities. (The French have since outgrown such compunctions and wonder at the puritanical zeal of the American armed forces.)
11. On the Cockerills, see Mokyr, *Industrialization in the Low Countries,* ch. ii; also Demoulin, *Guillaume I^{er},* and Henderson, *Britain and Industrial Europe.* The above quote is cited by Mokyr from an article by Nisard, "Souvenirs de voyage, le pays de Liège," *Revue de Paris,* 24 (1835): 130–46. John had two older brothers, William Jr. and James. Both settled in Prussia, where William founded a wool-spinning mill at Guben and James built machines in Aachen—Henderson, *State and the Industrial Revolution,* p. 113.

12. Héron de Villefosse in 1803, cited in Woronoff, *L'industrie sidérurgique,* p. 318. The reference may be to the brief Peace of Amiens, which gave the French a chance to bring in British entrepreneurs and technicians.

13. MacLeod, "Strategies for Innovation," p. 302.

14. Kuznets saw this era as beginning in the seventeenth century. He was too hasty in his dating. But the link is correct: it is the combination of science and technology that made the difference.

15. See a devastating critique of Réaumur's judgment and influence by Frédéric Le Play in the *Annales des Mines,* 9 (1846), cited in Harris, "Attempts to Transfer English Steel Techniques," in *Essays in Industry,* p. 109, n. 18. On Réaumur, see *ibid.,* p. 84.

16. Woronoff, *L'industrie sidérurgique,* p. 351.

17. *Ibid.,* pp. 352–53.

18. On Fischer, see Henderson, *J. C. Fischer.* Fischer kept invaluable diaries, which have been edited and published by Karl Schib.

19. On this story, see Haber, *Chemical Industry,* pp. 128–36, 169–98; and Travis, *The Rainbow Makers,* pp. 237–39, who stresses the open-mindedness of young German chemists on a technological roll.

20. Haber, *Chemical Industry,* p. 84.

21. Milward and Saul, *Economic Development,* p. 230.

CHAPTER 19

1. I take these figures from Engerman and Sokoloff, "Factor Endowments," Table 4; see the sources cited there. It should be remembered that such estimates, especially those for earlier years, are figments, the product of heroic manipulations and guesswork, to say nothing of errors and distortions in the original data—cf. Randall, "Lies, Damn Lies, and Argentine GDP." The matter is further complicated by the fragility of international comparisons that do not rest on purchasing power parity. If one were to incorporate the collapse of the Mexican peso in December 1994–January 1995, for example, the Mexican results would look even weaker. Whatever; the general picture of more rapid American growth is reliable. For another set of estimates, based on estate data converted to income (grossly approximate), see Garcia, "Economic Growth," pp. 53–54.

2. See, among other discussions: Caves, " 'Vent for Surplus' Models of Trade" and "Export-Led Growth"; Baldwin, "Patterns of Development"; Watkins, "A Staple Theory of Economic Growth"; and Garcia, "Economic Growth and Stagnation."

3. This is the thesis of Stanley Engerman and Kenneth Sokoloff in their essay on "Factor Endowments." An important and ingenious analysis. For parallel arguments concerning the "endogenous" exploitation and production of raw materials (the U.S. was more than lucky), see David and Wright, "Increasing Returns."

4. Fischer, *Albion's Seed,* p. 174.

5. Smith, *Wealth of Nations,* Bk. IV, ch. 7, Part 2: "Causes of the Prosperity of New Colonies."

6. Smith, *Wealth of Nations,* Bk. I, ch. 8: "Of the Wages of Labour."

7. Both quotations come from Fischer, *Albion's Seed,* p. 560.

8. See Hartley, *Ironworks on the Saugus.*

9. Cited in Oliver, *History of American Technology,* p. 89.

10. Fischer, *Albion's Seed,* p. 860.

11. A newer generation of economic historians is not happy with what are dismissed as "intellectually unproductive cultural essentialist explanations," "notoriously slippery and difficult to assess," and argues for regression analysis using "clearly, specified,

broadly applicable measures"—Carlton and Coclanis, "The Uninventive South?" pp. 304, 326. Aside from the question why culture should be deemed "intellectually un-productive" or "essentialist" (it may be hard to quantify, but the real question is, does it matter?), the problem with regression analysis is that it excludes what it omits and can be specified so as to leave little "unexplained" residual. It works well to measure the relative importance of the factors specified, presumably quantifiable economic variables, but is dumb on the rest.

12. Jeremy, *Transatlantic Industrial Revolution*, p. 254.
13. Gibb, *Saco-Lowell Shops*, p. 10, cited in Oliver, *History of American Technology*, p. 158. See also Rosenberg, "Anglo-American Wage Differences," who suggests that al-though American wages for unskilled labor were higher than British, Americans could hire "best" machine makers for less.
14. On this reverse flow, see Musson and Robinson, *Science and Technology*, pp. 62–64. They cite Matthew Curtis, machine maker in Manchester, to a parliamentary committee in 1841: ". . . I apprehend that the chief part . . . of the really new inven-tions, that is, of new ideas altogether, in the carrying out of a certain process by new machinery, or in a new mode, have originated abroad, especially in America."
15. Jeremy, *Transatlantic Industrial Revolution*, p. 253.
16. *Ibid.*, p. 252.
17. See Broadberry, "Comparative Productivity in British and American Manufactur-ing."
18. See Eisler, ed., *The Lowell Offering*.
19. On the negative aspects of factory labor, see Dublin, *Women at Work*, and Zon-derman, *Aspirations and Anxieties*.
20. Quoted in Jeremy, *Transatlantic Industrial Revolution*, p. 253.
21. Rosenberg, *Perspectives on Technology*, pp. 39–40.
22. On the significance of the balloon house, see Giedion, *Space, Time, and Architec-ture;* and Rosenberg, *Perspectives on Technology*, p. 38. It has been argued that the va-riety of goods, including houses, available to British consumers, constituted an amenity that does not show up in standard income or production figures but substantially en-hanced the standard of living—cf. Prais, "Economic Performance and Education," p. 155. But a few stays in British stone and brick houses—cold even in August—would suggest that American construction, however dull and utilitarian, provided more space and comfort for the money. What is more, the nature of the balloon house is such that plumbing and electrical wiring can easily be installed in the walls, and this con-tributed to the early adoption of such amenities as hot and cold running water and cen-tral heating. On the other hand, the European masonry and plaster construction is significantly more resistant to fire, and this can make the difference between life and death.
23. Rosenberg, *Perspectives on Technology*, p. 42.
24. On the difference and on standards of interchangeability, see Landes, *Revolution in Time*, pp. 283–85, and ch. xix: "Not One in Fifty Thousand."
25. Nathan Rosenberg, *Perspectives on Technology*, p. 17, calls this phenomenon *tech-nological convergence*, because he sees different branches converging on the same tech-niques. But I would prefer something like *technological proliferation* or *interrelatedness*, the better to emphasize the spread of the techniques into multiple applications.
26. George Talcott, in S. V. Benet, ed., *A Collection of Annual Reports . . . Relating to the Ordnance Department*, I, 395, cited in Gordon, "Who Turned the Mechanical Ideal," p. 746.
27. Cf. Rosenberg, *American System of Manufactures*.
28. Erickson, *American Industry*, p. 132.
29. Cited in Oliver, *History of American Technology*, p. 375.

30. Abramovitz and David, "Convergence and Deferred Catch-up," p. 21. The data are taken from Angus Maddison, "Explaining the Economic Performance of Nations," Tables 2-1 (p. 22) and 2-4 (p. 28), and are measured in PPE (purchasing power equivalent) dollars.

31. This and the quotations that follow are from *Wealth of Nations,* Book IV, ch. 7, Part 2: "Causes of the Prosperity of New Colonies."

32. *Wealth of Nations,* Book II, ch. 5: "Of the Different Employment of Capitals."

33. Cook, *The Long Fuse,* pp. 58–59.

34. Modern quantitative economic historians have tried to measure the burden of these acts on the American colonists and have argued that it was insignificant. The implication is that economic "justifications" were a pretext and that the colonists had other motives for war, or worse yet, were simple ingrates. Aside from errors in the calculation of the burden and problems with fanciful counterfactuals of what might have been if no navigation acts, the very notion that one can quantify a perceived grievance and thereby judge whether a war is justified strikes me as naive. On this abundant debate, see Thomas, "A Quantitative Approach," and in rejoinder, Sawers, "The Navigation Acts Revisited," and the articles cited there.

35. Cited in Cook, *The Long Fuse,* p. 59.

## CHAPTER 20

1. Cf. Humboldt, *Relation historique,* ed. Tulard, p. 252.

2. Fischer, *Albion's Seed,* p. 26 and n. 5. In Virginia, a land of plantations and indenture, the ratio was 4 to 1; in Brazil a land of sugar and slaves, 100 to 1.

3. An article in the *Quarterly Review,* 35, speaks (p. 537) of the segmentation of Latin American society by color: "the different classes, who in process of time, more by the rules of society than by the influence of the laws, assumed a variety of ranks according to the greater or less affinity to the white race." Quoted in Rodney and Graham, *Reports of the Present State,* p. 12.

4. Cf. Fischer, *Albion's Seed,* pp. 240–46, on the hierarchical values and institutions of southern England.

5. "Independence was not so much sought after by the people of Buenos Ayres, as thrown in their way"—Rodney and Graham, *Reports of the Present State,* pp. 28–29.

6. The contrast is Furtado's, *Economic Growth of Brazil,* p. 109.

7. Cf. Faith, *The World the Railways Made,* p. 156, citing Ferns, *Britain and Argentina:* "Argentine interests were not concerned either to invest in or gain control of such undertakings, no matter how freely they might criticise their activities in their newspapers and in the halls of the Congress . . . it was . . . more profitable to speculate in land, sell cattle and wool, and institute share-cropping, all of which railways greatly stimulated by opening a way to the markets first of Buenos Aires and then the world. . . ."

8. Mullet des Essards, *Voyage en Cochinchine,* p. 95.

9. The above is drawn from Rock, *Argentina,* p. 25. On nails, see E. A. J. Clemens, *The La Plata Countries of Latin America* (1886), cited in Rock, "Features of Industrial Development," p. 8; also Mullet des Essards, *Voyage en Cochinchine,* p. 89.

10. Rock, "Features of Industrial Development," p. 7.

11. The words are Sarmiento's, writing in the 1840s, cited in Rock, *ibid.*

12. Juan Bautista Alberdi, *Bases e puntos de partida para la organización politica de la República Argentina* (1852), cited by Shumway, *Invention of Argentina,* p. 149.

13. "Even today, Argentine church leaders are arguably the most conservative, if not reactionary, in Latin America"—Shumway, *Invention of Argentina,* p. 150.

14. Adelman, *Frontier Development,* p. 105.

15. Krout and Fox, *The Completion of Independence,* pp. 53–57.

16. Fish, *Rise of the Common Man,* p. 130. It should be noted that not everyone agreed with this general encouragement to westward settlement. The older states were opposed on the ground that such generous terms would encourage their inhabitants to emigrate, which they did in fact. And the slave states were upset by a policy that gave no special consideration to slaveowners: their allotments would be no larger than those of nonslaveowners. The aim was to promote homesteads, not plantations.

17. Fish, *Rise of the Common Man,* p. 118.

18. R. Cortés Conde, "The Growth of the Argentine Economy," in Bethell, ed., *Argentina Since Independence,* p. 75.

19. Bethell, ed., *Argentina,* p. 55. One indicator of the difference between the American sense of identity and purpose as against the Argentine is that the United States conducted national censuses every decade from the founding of the republic, whereas Argentina did not do its first national census until 1869, the second in 1895—*ibid.,* p. 54.

20. The primary source for these figures is Rock, *Argentina 1516–1987,* pp. 141–45, 164–67.

21. The figures come from *Historical Statistics of the United States,* Series A and C.

22. *Ibid.,* series C 115–32.

23. Rock, *Argentina, 1516–1987,* p. 89.

24. Juan B. Justo, *Internacionalismo y patria* (Buenos Aires, 1933), cited in Cornblit, "European Immigrants," p. 233.

25. Even the most efficient farmers working the most fertile soil found (find) their profits vanishing in the form of lower prices. The gains went (go) largely to the customers. Erik Reinert, "Symptoms and Causes of Poverty," stresses the contrast between this "classical" pattern of distribution of gains from technological change, which he sees as especially typical of agriculture and distribution, and the "collusive" pattern of industries that are marked by barriers to entry and increasing returns to knowledge. He uses the term *collusive* because "the forces of the producing country (capital, labour, and government) in practice—although not as a conspiracy—'collude' to appropriate these gains" (p. 84).

26. Landes, *Revolution in Time,* p. 326.

27. Shumway, *Invention of Argentina,* p. 156, n. 3.

28. Rock, *Argentina, 1516–1987,* p. 233.

29. Cortés Conde, *Corrientes immigratorias;* Cornblit, "European Immigrants," p. 230. In the early censuses, about a tenth of the so-called industrial establishments were what we would call services: shoe repair shops, photography studios, seamstresses' shops, barber shops, and hairdressing parlors—all the necessary paraphernalia of urban life. The 1935 census dropped them from the industrial sector—Lewis, *Crisis of Argentine Capitalism,* p. 35.

30. Lewis, *Crisis,* ch. 6: "Labor." The quotation that follows is from p. 103.

31. See *ibid.,* p. 492.

32. Pedro de Azevedo, cited in Freyre, *The Masters and the Slaves,* p. 41.

33. Batou, *Cent ans,* ch. 8: *"L'essor économique du Paraguay."*

34. On this so-called revisionist school, see Pastore, "State-led Industrialisation," who cites, among others, Whigham, "The Iron Works of Ybycui"; a manuscript by Vera Blinn Reber, "Modernization from Within: Trade and Development in Paraguay, 1810–1870" (Shippensburg Univ., Carlisle, PA, 1990); and Batou, *Cent ans,* who sees this as one more example of a much wider pattern of European hostility to "Third World" (anachronism) initiatives. For a similar revisionist approach to Argentine history, Pastore cites Tulio Halperin Donghi, *El revisionismo historico argentino* (Buenos Aires, 1970).

35. Cf. Batou, *Cent ans,* p. 223, n. 13, who attributes this concept to Gramsci.

36. Batou, *Cent ans,* p. 232, citing A. Garcia Mellid, *Proceso a los falsificadores de la historia del Paraguay* (Buenos Aires, 1963).

37. Batou, *Cent ans,* p. 260. By comparison, Batou cites 8–10 percent for Argentina in 1865, 10–15 percent for Colombia before 1870, 18–20 percent for Mexico in 1873.

38. As part of this campaign, the rulers and merchant interests in Buenos Aires repeatedly closed the mouth of the Parana river and cut the "Guarani republic" off from the sea. See a table of these blockades in Batou, *Cent ans,* p. 241. By international law, which defines a blockade as an act of war, Argentina was at war with Paraguay from 1827 to 1852.

39. On these industries, most of them created in the 1850s under the rule of Carlos Antonio Lopez, see Batou, *Cent ans,* ch. 8; Pastore, "State-led Industrialisation"; Whigham, "Iron Works of Ybycui."

40. For a pro-Paraguayan point of view, see Batou, *Cent ans,* pp. 263–66.

41. See the table assembled by Batou, *Cent ans,* p. 249, which gives population as 750,000 in 1865, 230,000 in 1872. Not all scholars agree with these losses, which have long been accepted as gospel. Thus Reber, "The Demographics of Paraguay," suggests that the dead in the Great War, rather than more than half the population and the great majority of males, may have been as few as 8.7 to 18.5 percent of the prewar population. Others find these revisionist estimates, which are "based on a nonlinear regression with very few degrees of freedom" (Pastore, "State-led industrialisation," p. 296, n. 3), implausible.

42. Batou, *Cent ans,* p. 267.

CHAPTER 21

1. From Welsh, *A Borrowed Place,* p. 16, who quotes without reference.

2. On the morning ceremonial, see Landes, *Revolution in Time,* pp. 51–52; also Huang, *1587, a Year of No Significance.*

3. Nathan Sivin speaks of "a large measure of social stability and cultural homogeneity that left traditional values and forms practically unchallenged as the creativity behind them was sapped by intellectual orthodoxies"—"Science and Medicine," in Ropp, ed., *Heritage of China,* p. 166.

4. Letter to the French minister Colbert, undated but of 1675—Landes, *Revolution in Time,* p. 45.

5. On this story, see Cipolla, *Clocks and Culture;* also Landes, *Revolution in Time,* ch. 2.

6. Spence, *Emperor of China,* p. 74.

7. On all of this, the best source is still Cipolla, *Guns, Sails, and Empires,* especially pp. 116–19. Cipolla is not a sinologist and had to rely exclusively on European sources, including the testimony of Christian missionaries and travelers; but his "global vision" gives him crucial insights that are missing in the specialist literature.

8. Mu, *The Wilting of the Hundred Flowers* (New York, 1963), pp. 76–77, cited in Cipolla, *Guns, Sails, and Empires,* p. 120.

9. Taton, ed., *General History,* II, 592.

10. *Ibid.,* 590.

11. *Ibid.,* 589, n. 1.

12. This is one of the major contribution's of Alain Peyrefitte's book, *L'empire immobile.* Because he gained access to the Chinese archives, including papers read and annotated by the emperor, Peyrefitte can show the inner workings of bureaucratic equivocation.

13. Cipolla, *Guns, Sails, and Empires,* p. 120 f.

14. Peyrefitte, *L'empire immobile,* p. 286. The Staunton quote is from the French edition of his travels: *Voyage en Chine et en Tartarie* (6 vols.; Paris, 1804), VI, 6. The Huc is from his *Souvenirs d'un voyage,* IV, 81. Eric Jones, "The Real Question," pp. 12–13, dismisses such personal recollections of stasis as "snapshot impressions." I think he is wrong. These witnesses do concur; they report a state of mind; and their testimonies do fit what we know about technological change in China. Jones recalls "similar" conservatism in England after the war (worker rejection of American technology), and England, he says, "soon adopted many American practices." Bad example.

15. Fairbank and Reischauer, *East Asia,* p. 291, citing Oshima, *Economic Growth,* p. 34. Fairbank and Reischauer suggest that the reason for Chinese "stability" was "the very perfection that Chinese culture and social organization had achieved by the thirteenth century." The contrast with Europe, roiling with imperfection, could not be sharper. Cf. Crone, *Pre-Industrial Societies,* pp. 172–73: "China is a star example of a successful civilization. . . . China reached the pinnacle of economic development possible under pre-industrial conditions and stopped: no forces pushing it in a different direction are in evidence. . . ."

16. Cf. Jones, "The Real Question," pp. 8–9, who is equally nonplussed by these *a priori* objections to this line of inquiry: "I cannot see why; [the sinologists] are not being blamed and the question does not seem tendentious with respect to a society that had achieved so much and then passed so many centuries without achieving it again."

17. Taton, ed., *General History,* II, 590.

18. Cf. Goldstone, "Gender, Work, and Culture," who argues that support for such constraints came from the imperial government, which saw its primary function as "enforcing *positional roles*" (p. 25). China was very different in this regard from Europe or Japan.

19. Cited in Lippit, "Development of Underdevelopment," pp. 266–67. I have amended the translation slightly, for purely stylistic reasons.

20. Sivin, "Science and Medicine," p. 195.

21. From a publication of the Chinese Academy of Sciences addressed to teenage readers—*ibid*. Interestingly enough, this exhortation was omitted from the English translation, perhaps because the translators did not think the ideological agenda was or should be of concern to non-Chinese.

22. Nathan Sivin, as cited in Spence, *Chinese Roundabout,* p. 148. Spence is skeptical of the defensive arguments of the Needham school. On the other hand, he welcomes the prospect of further study of the lines of inquiry that they have opened up.

23. Sivin, "Science and Medicine," p. 164. Cf. Needham, "Poverties and Triumphs," in Crombie, ed., *Scientific Change,* p. 149: "Modern universal science, yes; Western science, no!"

24. *Ibid.,* p. 196.

25. This policy of the helping hand is analogous to the efforts of some scholars—many fewer, to be sure—and so-called educators to promote or defend the new Afrocentric view of the rise of Western civilization. Cf. Bernal, *Black Athena,* and numerous reviews.

## CHAPTER 22

1. Cited in Wilkinson, *Japan versus the West,* p. 121. We have a similar disparagement of Japanese productivity by an Australian expert in 1915: ". . . to see your men at work made me feel that you are a very satisfied easy-going race who reckon time is no object. When I spoke to some managers they informed me that it was impossible to change the habits of national heritage,"—Jagdish Bhagwati, cited in Meier and Seers, eds., *Pioneers in Development,* p. 53.

2. Gaspare Gonsalves in 1585, cited in Fisher, "The Britain of the East?", pp. 345–46, from Lach, *Asia in the Making of Europe,* I, 696.

3. Hugh Murray, *An Encyclopaedia of Geography* (London, 1834), p. 1102, cited in Fisher, "The Britain of the East?", p. 346.

4. Takekoshi, *Economic Aspects,* I, 291.

5. Cf. Wilkinson, *Japan versus the West,* p. 108, citing a report of 1812 by Sir Stamford Raffles, then governor of Java.

6. Oishi, "The Bakuhan System," p. 28. These records are still carefully shelved in Japanese provincial archives and present an unrivaled and still largely unexplored source for demographic analysis, including family reconstitution.

7. Hane, *Premodern Japan,* pp. 142–43.

8. Sakaiya, *What Is Japan?,* pp. 128–29, says Japan had 100,000 guns in 1600, compared to some 10,000 in the French army, and that national output exceeded that of all of Europe. See also Samuels, *"Rich Nation, Strong Army,"* pp. 79–80.

9. Sawada Taira, cited Samuels, *"Rich Nation, Strong Army,"* p. 80 and p. 358, n. 6.

10. On Japanese timekeepers, see Robertson, *Evolution of Clockwork,* pp. 190–287; Mody, *Japanese Clocks;* Fernandez, "Precision Timekeepers of Tokugawa Japan."

11. On the rice revenue system and some of its unanticipated consequences, see Keisuke, "The VOC and Japanese Rice."

12. Sakudo, "Management Practices," pp. 150–51, 154.

13. From a play of 1718 by Monzaemon Chikamatsu (1653–1724), cited in Yamamoto, "Capitalist Logic of the Samurai," p. 2.

14. Hane, *Premodern Japan,* p. 150.

15. Cited in Yamamoto, "A Protestant Ethic," p. 2.

16. On canals and reclamation, see Takekoshi, *Economic Aspects,* III, 409–16.

17. Hane, *Premodern Japan,* p. 194. See also Miyamoto, "Emergence of National Market," p. 297, whose dating does not correspond to Hane's. These figures imply that the Japanese were reclaiming and taking into cultivation less fertile soils, partly no doubt to cope with population growth, but also because the tax burden on these new lands was lower than on the old. On tax incentives and recruitment of cultivators— Takekoshi, *Economic Aspects,* III, 413–14.

18. Cited in Nakamura and Shimbo, "Why Was Economic Achievement . . . ?", p. 9.

19. Cf. Fisher, "Development of the London Food Market."

20. Cf. Nakamura and Shimbo, "Why Was Economic Achievement . . . ?", p. 18.

21. See the valuable discussion by Satoru Nakamura, "The Development of Rural Industry," in Nakane and Oishi, eds., *Tokugawa Japan,* pp. 81–90.

22. *Ibid.,* p. 96. Cho, "The Evolution of Entrepreneurs," p. 15, links the success of new, imported forms of industrial production to the prior existence of an indigenous support network. Without this, "the foreign companies must bring their subcontractors with them as suppliers of necessary parts."

23. See Rozman, "Edo's Importance." On London's comparable contribution to British development, see E. A. Wrigley, "A Simple Model." One big difference, however. London, almost as large as Tokyo by the end of the eighteenth century, was the capital of a nation of around 9 million, about one third the population of Japan.

24. Nakamura and Shimbo, "Why Was Economic Achievement . . . ?", p. 7.

25. "The Japanese institutions may have had a comparable, if not a higher, degree of functional sophistication"—*ibid.,* p. 14. Cf. Hauser, *Economic Institutional Change.*

26. I take much of this list from Nakamura and Shimbo, pp. 14–15.

27. *Ibid.,* p. 19. Compare the readiness of British itinerant traders in the eighteenth century, and later on, of United States peddlers, to sell clocks and watches in rural areas on installment credit.

28. For the complete list of goods, see Crawcour, "Tokugawa Heritage," p. 41.

29. Keene, *Japanese Discovery of Europe*, p. 25.
30. Cited *ibid.*, p. 25.
31. On this persecution, see Takekoshi, *Economic Aspects*, III, 233–35.
32. See Keene, *Japanese Discovery*, pp. 21–22, on the dissection of "Old Mother Green Tea."
33. Cited *ibid.*, pp. 26–27.
34. Totman, *Early Modern Japan*, p. 519.
35. Craig, *Chōshū in the Meiji Restoration*, p. 71.
36. Tsuru Shigeto, "Development of Capitalism and Business Cycles in Japan" (MS, Harvard University), cited in Brown, "Okubo Toshimichi," p. 186.

## CHAPTER 23

1. On these and other episodes of these years of reciprocal trial and measure, see Miyoshi, *As We Saw Them*, ch. 4: "Lives."
2. Brown, "Okubo Toshimichi," p. 190.
3. On all this, see Shimada, "Social Time and Modernity in Japan."
4. Brown, "Okubo Toshimichi," p. 191, n. 27. Okubo's enemies used his house to hurt him. They even sent photographs of a new public building to Satsuma and said that this was Okubo's accursed mansion; and it is said that this photo convinced Saigo to break with Okubo and his circle.
5. Minami, *Economic Development*, p. 99.
6. Cf. Samuels, *Business of the Japanese State*, ch. 3, especially the illustrations, pp. 76–79.
7. Hirschmeier, *Origins of Entrepreneurship*, p. 99; Hane, *Peasants, Rebels, and Outcasts*, p. 173; Ohkawa and Kohama, *Lectures on Developing Economies*, p. 35.
8. Minami, *Power Revolution*, ch. vi.
9. Landes, "What Do Bosses Really Do?", p. 593.
10. Fukui, "Japanese State," p. 205.
11. *Ibid.*, p. 204: by the opening of the new century, almost all children were enrolled, but no more than three quarters attended class regularly.
12. Hane, *Peasants, Rebels, and Outcasts*, pp. 177–78.
13. *Ibid.*, p. 182.
14. The above is based on Thomas Smith, "The Right to Benevolence: Dignity and Japanese Workers, 1890–1920," in Smith, *Native Sources*, pp. 236–70.

## CHAPTER 24

1. Chaudhuri, *Asia before Europe*, p. 71.
2. Cited *ibid.*, p. 73.
3. This vivid formulation is by Eric Jones, *European Miracle*, p. 194. Jones's ch. 9, "Islam and the Ottoman Empire," is probably the best and most compact discussion of these matters.
4. *Ibid.*, p. 194.
5. Cf. Lewis, *Muslim Discovery of Europe*, pp. 190–91.
6. Cf. Jones, *European Miracle*, p. 185, citing Braudel, *La Méditerranée*.
7. Lewis, *Muslim Discovery*, p. 161.
8. Jones, *European Miracle*, p. 177; Lewis, *Muslim Discovery*, p. 199.
9. Lewis, *Muslim Discovery*, pp. 195–96.
10. Jones, *European Miracle*, p. 185.
11. On Jumel, see Batou, *Cent ans de résistance*, p. 96. Like many of his kind, he was drawn to Egypt by financial incentives; and sent on his way by matters of the heart (*"une déception sentimentale"*).

12. Issawi, "Economic Development," p. 362, gives the figures as "over 200,000 qantars" and 345,000 qantars respectively. But he says, p. 518, that the definition of the qantar changed in 1835, and I have converted to kilograms accordingly.

13. Lévy-Leboyer, *Les banques européennes,* p. 189.

14. The most convenient discussion in English is to be found in Batou, "Muhammad-'Ali's Egypt." Batou feels that the Egyptian industrial project has been underestimated and unrecognized. Also that its demise was the work of European adversaries, particularly the British.

15. Batou, "Muhammad-'Ali's Egypt," p. 185, Table 1.

16. Saint-John, *Egypt,* p. 412.

17. *Ibid.,* p. 417.

18. Issawi, "Economic Development," p. 363.

19. Friedman, "Egypt Runs for the Train."

20. Mohammed Mannei, merchant banker in the Persian Gulf, as cited by Jonathan Raban, *Arabia: A Journey Through the Labyrinth,* p. 63.

21. On the distinction between resource exhaustion and cartel market constraints, see Dasgupta, "Natural Resources," p. 112.

22. On ransom money to extremists, see Goodwin, *Price of Honor,* pp. 15–17.

23. Cf. Friedman, "Egypt Runs for the Train."

24. Keddie, in Keddie and Baron, eds., *Women in Middle Eastern History,* p. 5.

25. On this new, scandalous literature, available in Muslim countries only as *samizdat,* see Amy Dockser Morris, "These Potboilers Stir Widespread Interest in 'Islamic Affairs,' " *Wall St. J.,* 22 December 1995, p. 1.

26. The words cited are those of Professor Francis Hamilton, reviewing Lewis, *The Middle East,* in the *TLS* of 8 December 1995, p. 4. Roy Mottahedeh, "The Islamic Movement," p. 123, is also hopeful. He notes the role of women political leaders in a number of Islamic (but not Arab) countries, and states that "the enfranchisement of women offers a compelling proof of the ability of Islamic political cultures to evolve." Yes and no: what is "compelling"? The status of women in these countries, even secular Turkey, remains constrained by Islamic prescriptions and custom, to the point where we must temper our assumptions about the liberating power of political rights. We must also keep in mind the spatial segmentation of societies where cities evolve differently from countryside. Turkey, with Istanbul in one world and time, Anatolia in another, and Anatolia crowding into Istanbul, is a fascinating case study of this cultural and temporal schizophrenia. Hence the election returns of late 1995, which gave a plurality to the Islamist party.

27. Mottahedeh, "Clash of Civilizations," p. 11.

28. Barakat, *Arab World,* p. 105.

29. Mosteshar, *Unveiled,* p. 353. This book, a tumbleweed basket of experience and observation, is a fascinating insight into an Iran that thought it was modernizing; that made a revolution in the name of greater freedom and saw it hijacked by religious fundamentalists; and then saw the clock turned back centuries. And a terrifying insight into the nature of a sloppy, capricious tyranny: eyes and tongues everywhere, vengeful snitches, undefined rules, random violence.

30. On Latin America, see among other things, Calvin Sims, "Justice in Peru: Rape Victim Is Pressed to Marry Attacker," *N.Y. Times,* 3 December 1997, p. A1.

31. Makiya, *Cruelty and Silence,* p. 298, citing a Palestinian nurse from Acre. Cf. Goodwin, *Price of Honor,* p. 4.

32. Ajami, *Arab Predicament,* p. 233.

33. On oil as a misfortune, see Ajami, *Arab Predicament.*

34. Fisk, "Sept journées," p. 7—an important article.

35. See Landes, "Passionate Pilgrims."

36. Said, *Orientalism,* p. 327.

37. In Tidrick, *Heart Beguiling Araby*, which is not tender toward the British victims of romantic illusion. See the foreword by Albert Hourani.
38. The quotations are from Francis Robinson, "Through the Minefield," pp. 3–4. Robinson, a professor at the University of London, is generally sympathetic to Lewis and respectful of his scholarship. His observations of the intellectual climate are all the more telling.
39. This stress on motive shows again in Said's denunciation of Western work on Islam and Arab societies. Rather than confront data and theses, he dismisses the whole business as inspired by "antagonisms and hostility," by "cultural antipathy." See his lecture at the Collège de France, "Comment l'Occident voit les Arabes," *Le Monde,* 3 December 1996, p. 16.
40. See Nicholas D. Kristof, "Japan's Feminine Falsetto Falls Right Out of Favor," *N.Y. Times,* 13 December 1995, p. A-1.
41. Nolte and Hastings, "Meiji State's Policy," p. 157.
42. *Ibid.*
43. See Sheryl WuDunn, "On Tokyo's Packed Trains, Molesters Are Brazen," *N.Y. Times,* 17 December 1995, p. A-3.
44. Shimai Soshitsu, cited in Uno, "Women and Changes," p. 33.

CHAPTER 25

1. In recent years, an effort has been expended to test by the numbers what was once a little contested orthodoxy: among others, Davis and Huttenback, *Mammon and the Pursuit of Empire;* or on an individual case, Kimura, "The Economics of Japanese Imperialism in Korea," especially pp. 568–70. Michael Adas, " 'High' Imperialism," pp. 327–28, terms these "grand attempts to draw up balance sheets" an exercise in "oversimplification and ultimately futility." Translation: they don't come out as the materialist interpreters of imperialism would like; not enough profit.
2. Klor de Alva, "Postcolonization," p. 242.
3. *Ibid.,* p. 267. Cf. Prakash, in Prakash, ed., *After Colonialism,* p. 3.
4. On this, see especially Bartlett, *Making of Europe.*
5. Hopkins, *Economic History,* p. 256.
6. Hyam, *Britain's Imperial Century,* p. 290, cites the consolation of the "bottle, the bullet, and the bible" (source not given) and offers figures on alcohol consumption, not only by officials and officers, but also of course by the troops and subalterns. On sex, he cites (p. 291) Alfred Milner (1854–1925), activist proconsul in South Africa: "Sex enters into these Great Matters of State. It always has, it always will. It is never recorded, therefore history will never be intelligible." The historian may safely assume that in such private matters, the scattered relationships we know about are only the tip. Cf. Hyam, *Empire and Sexuality.*
7. Cook, *The Long Fuse,* p. 227, citing Charles Stuart in a letter of 1775 to his father the earl of Bute, after fighting the American rebels at the Battle of Bunker Hill.
8. On empire as blood lust, see Lindqvist, *"Exterminate All the Brutes,"* pp. 52 ff. I do not think he exaggerates.
9. Hence the seminal article of Gallagher and Robinson, "The Imperialism of Free Trade."
10. Cf. Landes, *Bankers and Pashas,* ch. 3, on the practices and profits of informal imperialism.
11. Hyam, *Britain's Imperial Century,* p. 164.
12. Cf. S. Erlanger, "Retired People Are Struggling in the New Russia," *N.Y. Times,* 8 August 1995, p. A-3: "This House of Veterans, opened in 1986 and already crumbling in typical Soviet fashion. . . ."
13. Harrison, *Inside the Third World,* p. 336.

14. Murray, *The Development of Capitalism in Colonial Indochina.*

15. On the use of the term *neocolonialism,* see Stavrianos, *Global Rift,* pp. 177–78.

16. Harrison, *Inside the Third World,* ch. 17: "The Alienation Machine: The Uneducated and the Miseducated." See p. 325: "It is bad enough that French children must addle their brains with these stilted and constipated works, but to teach them to African children is positively criminal." (I don't know. I am moved by *Andromaque.*)

17. Mill, *Principles of Political Economy,* cited in Meier, "Theoretical Issues," pp. 42–43.

18. On the "costly and futile wars" of Latin America, see Harrison, *Inside the Third World,* p. 384 f. But add to his list the conflicts between Mexico and the United States and abortive incursions from the United States into British Canada. Some Mexican maps still show Texas and the southwestern United States as Mexican territory, waiting to be reclaimed.

19. Harrison, *Inside the Third World,* p. 388, cites S. E. Finer to the effect that of 104 *coups d'état* between 1962 and 1975, all but a handful took place in Third World countries. In 1975, one quarter of all member states in the UN were ruled by regimes that had come to power via a coup.

20. Alam, "Colonialism, Decolonisation and Growth Rates," p. 235 and n. 2, would not agree. He notes that in the nineteenth century those countries that developed modern manufacturing sectors were "either sovereign or self-governing states" and infers that "domestic control over economic policies was a necessary condition for industrialisation."

21. India 23,627 miles; China 665 miles—Kerr, "Colonialism and Technological Choice," pp. 93–94. On belated British support for Indian iron and steel manufacture, see Bahl, "Emergence," and her *Making of the Indian Working Class.*

22. See the response to a fall-off of Japanese manufactured imports during World War I. Ho, "Colonialism and Development," in Myers and Peattie, eds., *Japanese Colonial Empire,* p. 365.

23. Mark Peattie in Myers and Peattie, eds., *Japanese Colonial Empire,* p. 23. On these data and the special reasons for development in Korea and Taiwan, where Japanese policy was further shaped by strategic military considerations and the need for cheap food, see Alam, "Colonialism," pp. 250–53; and Hayami and Ruttan, "Korean Rice, Taiwan Rice."

24. On Japanese complacency in the matter of Korea, see the *N.Y. Times,* 12 October 1995, p. A-5; 14 November 1995, p. A-14. On Korean memory and outrage, Yoichi Serikawa, "Deux peuples empêtrés dans leur passé [two peoples mired in their past]," *Courrier international,* 211 (17–25 Nov. 1994), p. 32, with illustration of a wax figure exhibit in the Korean independence memorial showing Japanese army torture of a Korean patriot. On the larger matter of aggression before and during World War II, see Buruma, *The Wages of Guilt.* The latest "flap" has come over the statement of a Japanese official that "Japan did some good things. Japan built schools in every town in Korea to raise the standard of education and also constructed railroads and ports."

25. The pro-Japanese point of view, as expressed by a Westerner, speaks of "modern and superbly efficient police forces, supplemented by the clever exploitation of indigenous systems of community control." Peattie in Myers and Peattie, eds., *The Japanese Colonial Empire,* p. 27.

26. *Ibid.,* p. 47.

27. Patel, "Rates of Industrial Growth."

CHAPTER 26

1. Israel, *The Dutch Republic,* p. 850. Like the Japanese, who also prefer to see the history of their country in terms of divine intervention through favorable winds *(kamikaze),* the Dutch and English have attributed the success of the invasion to a "Protestant wind"—strong easterlies that sped the Armada across the North Sea and locked the English fleet in the Thames, where all it could do was watch the enemy go by—*ibid.,* p. 851.

2. *Wealth of Nations,* Book I, ch. ix: "Of the Profits of Stock."

3. *Ibid.,* Book I, ch. viii: "Of the Wages of Labour."

4. Cited in Wallerstein, "Dutch Hegemony," p. 98. Such apparent precision must be taken with a grain of salt, but the overall trend is unmistakable.

5. Vandenbroeke, "Regional Economy," p. 170, argues that these low-wage industries posed a terrible challenge to Britain, which found a riposte in mechanization; but the same argument can be used to account for Dutch failure: they did not mechanize.

6. Most of the above is from Israel, *The Dutch Republic,* pp. 998–1003. See also Wallerstein, "Dutch Hegemony."

7. Israel, *Dutch Republic,* p. 1011.

8. On the decline of Venetian wool output, see Rapp, *Industry and Economic Decline,* pp. 140–41, 148, and n. 24; and Sella, "Rise and Fall." Trade policy seems to have been appallingly counterproductive. On migration of capital to the mainland, see Woolf, "Venice and the Terraferma." Also Ciriacono, "Venetian Economy" and "Venise et la Vénétie."

9. Cf. van Zanden, "The Dutch Economy in the Very Long Run."

10. Cf. Mokyr, *Industrialization in the Low Countries,* who makes the wage comparison with Belgium. But Dutch wages, if higher than Belgian along the coast, were just as low in the interior and lower overall than those in England, for example. Griffiths, *Industrial Retardation,* pp. 3, 62–65, argues that the causes of Dutch lateness have to be sought elsewhere; that Belgium then had a strong industrial base and could modernize more easily. It had good coal resources, a precociously mechanized cotton and wool manufacture, an old yet vigorous tradition of metallurgy, and the beginnings of machine building in the Liégeois. The Netherlands had once been strong in industry, but after a century of decline, it had trouble starting up.

11. Mokyr, *Lever of Riches,* p. 260, notes the persistence of Luddite opposition to cotton-spinning machinery in the Netherlands.

12. H. J. Koenen, *Voorlezingen over de geschiedenis der nijverheid in Nederland* (Haarlem, 1956), p. 140, cited in Griffiths, *Industrial Retardation,* p. 41.

13. Peter W. Klein, *Traditionele ondernemers en economische groei in Nederland, 1850–1914* (Haarlem, 1966), p. 3, cited in Griffiths, *Industrial Retardation,* p. 42.

14. Griffiths, *Industrial Retardation,* p. 121.

15. On this later period, cf. Pollard, *Peaceful Conquest,* pp. 237–38. The quiet entry of the Netherlands into the world of modern industry is reflected in the general indifference of economic histories. The country barely gets on stage.

16. Cited from a 1693 edition in Chaudhuri, *Trading World of Asia,* p. 5.

17. On French sensibilities, cf. Ratcliffe, "Great Britain and Tariff Reform," p. 102.

18. On clocks and American manufacture, see Landes, *Revolution in Time,* pp. 310–13. On firearms, Smith, *Harpers Ferry Armory and the New Technology;* Uselding, "Technical Progress at the Springfield Armory."

19. On this wake-up call, see Rosenberg, *American System of Manufactures.*

20. Supple, "Fear of Failing." The address is in large part a reprise of Clapham's thoughts and tone on the subject, as expressed in his *Economic History of Modern Britain,* III (1938), ch. 3: "The Course of Industrial Change."

21. Cf. Tomlinson, "Inventing 'Decline' "; also Supple, "Fear of Failing," pp. 442–43.

22. Supple, p. 444, speaks of "disturbing psychological and political repercussions."

23. Supple, p. 444, n. 9, citing W. A. P. Manser, *Britain in the Balance* (1971), p. 179.

24. Cf. Clapham, *Economic History*, II, 113, writing in gloomy 1932 of the trade crisis of 1885: "The mechanical and industrial movement has become once for all international, and there is very little echelon in the advance. . . . Engines are toiling indifferently for all. Mechanical or scientific industrial monopolies are short lived." Clapham did not know the word "convergence," but he understood the phenomenon. Also *ibid.*, III, 122: "Half a continent is likely in course of time to raise more coal and make more steel than a small island. . . ." How are the mighty fallen!

25. On the good fortune of being among the rich, Clapham, *ibid.*, III, 554; Mc-Closkey, *If You're So Smart*, p. 48; Supple, "Fear of Failing," p. 443: ". . . the differences between Britain and other advanced societies are much less (and much less important) than the differences between the advanced and less developed countries." McCloskey actually waxes indignant that people so fortunate should complain that they are losing ground to other rich people: "at best tasteless in a world of real tragedies . . . ; at worst . . . immoral self-involvement, nationalist guff. . . ." That's the trouble with people: they think first of Number One. They also think that being first is better than being second or fourteenth.

26. Cited in Burn, *Age of Equipoise*, p. 64.

27. W. S. Jevons, *Methods of Social Reform* (London: Macmillan, 1883), pp. 181–82, cited in Supple, "Official Economic Inquiry," p. 325.

28. Here is McCloskey, offering compatriots cold comfort: "Americans are better off when Japan 'defeats' them at car-making, because then they will do something they are comparatively good at—banking, say, or growing soybeans—and let the Japanese do the car making or the consumer electronics." McCloskey, "1066 and a Wave of Gadgets," in McCloskey and Dormois, eds., "British Industrial 'Decline,' " p. 21.

29. McCloskey, *Econ. Hist. Rev.*, 2d ser., 3 (1970).

30. Cf. Wilson, *British Business History*, pp. 90–93. One would have expected these ambivalent distributors to sort things out and focus on the more profitable brands. Or the manufacturers to set up their own sales and service networks, as occurred in the United States and later on in Japan.

31. Peter H. Lindert and Keith Trace in McCloskey, ed., *Essays on a Mature Economy*, p. 242.

32. Wilson, "Economy and Society," pp. 185, 190, cited in Dintenfass, "Converging Accounts," p. 19.

33. The quotes are from Dintenfass, "Converging Accounts," p. 22. The optimists have been equally dismissive of entrepreneurial testimony to poor performance. See Edgerton, "Science and Technology in British Business History" and *Science, Technology*, p. 11. For a pessimistic view based on business histories, Coleman and MacLeod, "Attitudes to New Techniques."

34. Floud, "Britain," in Floud and McCloskey, eds., "Economic History," 1st ed., II, 23.

35. McCloskey, "International Differences in Productivity?" in McCloskey, ed., *Essays on a Mature Economy*, pp. 286–87.

36. Habakkuk, *American and British Technology*, p. 212.

37. Cf. Clapham, *Economic History*, III, 131.

38. Davenport-Hines and Jones, eds., *British Business in Asia*, p. 21. One could make similar observations about the British steel manufacture. British makers had every preference and advantage in the Indian market and yet saw themselves increasingly displaced: £8,000 for Belgian steel in 1885/86 as against £98,000 for the U.K.; £280,000 for Belgium in 1895/96 as against £274,000 for the U.K.—and this, in spite of British steel's reputation as superior. Saul, *Studies in British Overseas Trade*, p. 199.

39. Charles Wilson, "Economy and Society," in Payne, "Industrial Entrepreneurship," p. 208.
40. James Foreman-Peck, "The Balance of Technological Transfers 1870–1914," in McCloskey and Dormois, eds., "British Industrial 'Decline,' " p. 11, dismisses the loss as "merely a different pattern of international specialisation." Pollard, *Britain's Prime*, ch. 3, sees dyestuffs as small stuff.
41. Friswell and Levinstein cited in Haber, *Chemical Industry*, p. 168. (This is just the kind of witness that the optimists find awkward; so they dismiss it as self-interested.) The best-known Jews in British chemicals were the managing partners in Brunner, Mond & Co., the leading firm in alkali manufacture. They brought in the Solvay process, without effect on the outworn technology of the rest of the industry—except, that is, to encourage them to shelter themselves behind agreements in restraint of trade. Brunner, Mond went along and garnered monopoly rents.
42. Rubinstein, *Capitalism, Culture and Decline*, pp. 94–96, makes much of British contributions in pure science, recognized by a disproportionate share of Nobel prizes. But he says little about applications, except to agree that most of these "often, now regularly" found use in other countries. On the electrical industry, where engineering clearly mattered, see Byatt, *British Electrical Industry*, pp. 188–90: "British business men were not very good at using their engineers." For a favorable view of British scientific and technical education, see Edgerton, *Science, Technology*, especially ch. 5.
43. See, among others, Landes, *The Unbound Prometheus*, ch. 5; and Wiener, *English Culture and the Decline of the Industrial Spirit*. Also a passing remark by Habakkuk, *American and British*, p. 212: "An Englishman's choice of career was, it is true, very much influenced by tradition, convention and inertia, and no doubt in England these tended to channel talent away from business towards the professions." On the other hand, see Dintenfass, *Decline*, pp. 61–64.
44. Cf. Livingston, "Gentleman, Theory of the." This cultivation of superiority to the material also found expression in the memoirs of British travelers to the United States. Whereas in the eighteenth century it was England that was the object of criticism or admiration because of its social mobility and material success, in the nineteenth century the United States incarnated these virtues and vices and became the object of scorn and condescension by snobs and fortune hunters alike.
45. Abramovitz and David, "Convergence and Deferred Catch-up," pp. 26–27. The sixteen advanced countries grouped for comparison are twelve European leaders: Austria, Belgium, Denmark, Finland, France, Finland, Germany, Italy, the Netherlands, Norway, Sweden, Switzerland, plus the U.K.; plus Australia, Canada, and Japan.
46. *Ibid.*, p. 27, Table 1.
47. See Steven A. Holmes, "Income Disparity between Poorest and Richest Rises," *N.Y. Times*, 20 June 1996, p. A-1. Also Keith Bradsher, "More Evidence: Rich Get Richer," *ibid.*, 22 June 1996, p. A-31. Paul Krugman, *Pop Internationalism*, is cutting in his rejection of those who would argue that the retreat of the United States is linked to the advance of international competitors. Yet I find a similarity to the earlier instances of loss of leadership.
48. Robert Samuelson, "Is There a Savings Gap?" *Newsweek*, 17 June 1996, p. 56, citing a study by the McKinsey Global Institute.
49. Lewchuk, *American Technology*, p. 117.
50. Quoted *ibid.*, p. 117. Of the three leading producers in the prewar years, only Great Britain fell substantially short of home demand. France shipped more than half its output abroad and was the leading exporter in the world.
51. *Ibid.*, pp. 171–72.
52. For a case study in dysfunctional management, going back to the interwar years, see Church, "Deconstructing Nuffield." On leisure preference, Church notes (p. 572)

Nuffield's annual months-long voyages to Australia, on a slow boat well equipped for deck quoits.

53. Pollard, *Development of the British Economy*, pp. 242–43.

54. Cf. Channon, *Strategy and Structure*, p. 109: " . . . their strategy did not appear promising for the long-run development of the British automobile industry."

55. Church, "Deconstructing Nuffield," p. 578, n. 127.

56. Pollard, *Development of the British Economy*, p. 400.

57. Church, *Rise and Decline*, pp. 77, 104, 115, and *passim;* and his "Effects of American Multinationals."

58. Pollard, *Development of the British Economy*, p. 401.

CHAPTER 27

1. Kindleberger, *Financial History*, p. 407: "I regard the German monetary reform of 1948 as one of the great feats of social engineering of all time."

2. On those last days, see Toland, *The Rising Sun*.

3. On these ritualistic encounters, cf. Halberstam, *The Reckoning*, p. 310.

4. I take the phrase "global city-state" from Murray and Perera, *Singapore*.

5. "A Survey of Multinationals," *The Economist*, 24 June 1995, p. 4.

6. M. Richardson, "Malaysia Readies a Crackdown on Illegal Workers," *Int. Herald-Tribune*, 7 October 1996, p. 4.

7. On Indochina, cf. Murray, *Development of Capitalism*, p. 619, n. 345. He cites René Dubreuil, *De la condition des Chinois et de leur rôle économique en Indochine* (Bar-sur Seine, 1910), p. 71: "When the French administration was installed in Cochin China, it discovered that the Chinese . . . were a priceless help in carrying out its colonialization. . . . In order to get . . . [the Vietnamese] to change their habits and ill-will, to educate them in the field of commerce and to make them take out of their earthen jars the piasters needed to sustain our administrative machine, we needed an intermediary living side-by-side with them, speaking their language and marrying women of their race. That intermediary was the Chinese. The Chinese is flexible, skillful, without prejudice, and loves gain."

8. Pan, *Sons of the Yellow Emperor*, p. 247; see, on much of this, ch. 13: "Cultural and National Identities."

9. Ohmae, *End of the Nation State*, 179. On renewed trouble in Indonesia, see: *Int. Herald Tribune*, 11–12 January 1997, p. 1.

10. These and the preceding figures from Rohwer, *Asia Rising*, pp. 228–29.

11. Thus Naisbitt, *Megatrends Asia*, p. 17: "The Chinese are coming. Asia and much of the world today is shifting from Japanese-dominated to Chinese-driven." If Naisbitt is right, the period of Japanese leadership will be one of the shortest in history. But what will follow? Where is leadership in a world of global enterprises?

12. Achavanuntakul, "Effects of Government Policies," p. 9. According to the World Bank, inflation ran at 9.2 percent from 1970 to 1980, 4.2 percent from 1980 to 1992.

13. On all this, see Thomas L. Friedman, "Bangkok Bogs Down," *N.Y. Times*, 20 March 1996, p. A-19; and Kaplan, *Ends of the Earth*, pp. 380–82. The problem is aggravated by extensive and growing use of coal fuel, much of it lignite—the worst kind. On motorcades: *Int. Herald-Tribune*, 9 January 1997, p. 2.

14. On Model T diversity, see Flink, "Unplanned Obsolescence."

15. Cusumano, *Japanese Automobile Industry*, p. 7.

16. I take this from Cusumano, pp. 18–19. He notes that whatever reservations may have been felt in some quarters, the Bank of Japan, the Japan Development Bank, and the Industrial Bank of Japan lent large sums to keep Nissan, Toyota, and Isuzu out of bankruptcy in the late 1940s. Had MITI not won the argument, he writes, "postwar Japanese (and world) history would have been considerably different" (p. 19).

17. These figures from Cusumano, pp. 4–5.

18. The best and most readable source here is Halberstam's *The Reckoning*. Forget the economists and economic historians. Halberstam understands the industry, but even more he understands the people in it. See also, along similar lines, Lacey, *Ford*.

19. From Womack *et al., The Machine That Changed the World,* p. 118.

20. Friedman, "Beyond the Age of Ford." Cf. Piore and Sabel, *The Second Industrial Divide.*

21. On the difference between size and flexibility, see Landes, "Piccolo e bello. Ma e bello davvéro?"

22. Dertouzos *et al., Made in America,* p. 180. Not that Japanese technical strategies were homogeneous from one company to another. Nissan and Toyota, for example, show significant differences—the former closer to the American pattern; the latter given to more flexible methods. Cf. Cusumano, *Japanese Automobile Industry.*

23. Abernathy and Clark, p. 36, speak of "fascinating parallels but ultimately sharp contrasts." Cf. Cusumano, *Japanese Automobile Industry,* ch. 5, on the Toyota production system and the extraordinary career of Taiichi Ohno, who came to autos from the mother firm (Toyoda automatic looms), saw everything anew, and transformed the character of mass production.

24. Halberstam, *The Reckoning,* pp. 43, 50.

25. Cf. Womack *et al., The Machine That Changed the World,* p. 109, on the Honda *Accord.*

26. See Johnson, *Japan,* p. 31.

27. On much of this, see Tabb, *The Postwar Japanese System,* p. 160.

28. Cf. Keith Bradsher, "Cost-Cutting Strategy," *N.Y. Times,* 17 March 1996, p. A-1, on the pros and cons of the strike at the Dayton, Ohio, brake plant of General Motors.

29. Cf. Stopford and Strange, *Rival States,* pp. 84–85.

30. *N.Y. Times,* 13 May 1983, p. D-3.

31. Holusha, "Detroit's New Labor Strategy."

32. See Keith Bradsher, "New Union Tactics," *N.Y. Times,* 10 March 1996, p. A-16.

CHAPTER 28

1. Cf. Ishac Diwan, "Hard Time for More Labor Economics," *Forum* (Newsletter of the Economic Research Forum for the Arab Countries, Iran & Turkey), 2, 2 (July–August 1995), 1–3; and N. Fergany, "Unemployment in Arab Countries: The Menace Swept Under the Rug," *ibid.,* pp. 4–5.

2. Bulmer-Thomas, *Economic History of Latin America,* p. 278.

3. The U.N. International Drug Control Programme, in its first World Drug Report, estimates the trade in illicit drugs at $400 billion—about 8 percent of total world trade. Between 28 and 53 percent of Bolivia's export revenues are estimated to come from narcotics; some 6 percent of Colombia's GDP—*Financial Times,* 26 June 1997, p. 4. Guesses all.

4. For a fascinating insight into the fairy-tale economics of the Socialist countries, in this case, the German Democratic Republic, see Merkel and Mühlberg, eds., *Wunderwirtschaft.*

5. Feshbach and Friendly, *Ecocide in the USSR,* ch. 4; Kaplan, *Ends of the Earth,* p. 277; David Filipov, "A Sea Dies, Mile by Mile," *Boston Globe,* 23 March 1997, p. A-1.

6. Filipov, "In Chernobyl Soil, Fatalism Thrives," *Boston Globe,* 21 April 1996, p. 17.

7. Cf. Josephson, " 'Projects of the Century' " p. 546 and *passim.*

8. Shcherbak, "Ten Years of the Chornobyl Era," p. 44. See also Marples, *Social Impact;* Medvedev, *Truth About Chernobyl;* Michael Specter, "10 Years Later, Through Fear, Chernobyl Still Kills in Belarus," *N.Y. Times,* 31 March 1996, p. A-1.

9. Davidson, *Black Man's Burden*, p. 216.
10. World Bank, *Adjustment in Africa*, p. 17. See also the Bank's *World Development Report 1997: The State in a Changing World.* One difficulty with these numbers is that the margin of error is huge. On the one hand, African authorities make up figures as needed. On the other, all manner of parallel economic activities escape measurement. Do these biases even out?
11. Kamarck, *Economics of African Development*, p. 17.
12. H. J. Spiro, *Politics in Africa*, cited in Kamarck, *Economics*, p. 48.
13. Davidson, *The Black Man's Burden*, p. 197.
14. On all this, see Platteau, "Food Crisis in Africa."
15. *Ibid.*, p. 451.
16. Some welcome this premature urbanization as the seedbed of modernity, democracy, and business enterprise. Cf. A. Frachon, "L'Afrique n'est plus rurale," *Le monde*, 10–11 November 1996.
17. Cf. Dasgupta, "Population, Poverty, and the Local Environment."
18. J. C. McKinley, Jr., "Anguish of Rwanda Echoed in a Baby's Cry," *N.Y. Times*, 21 February 1996, p. A-8. See also Howard W. French, "Migrant Workers Take AIDS Risk Home to Niger," *N.Y. Times*, 8 February 1996, p. A-3.
19. Havinden and Meredith, eds., *Colonialism and Development*, p. 276.
20. *Ibid.*, p. 278.
21. I take this from Evelyn Waugh's account, *Tourist in Africa*, p. 98.
22. *Ibid.*, p. 99.
23. Roberts, "The Coercion of Free Markets," p. 224; also Davidson, *Black Man's Burden*, p. 217.
24. An educated and traveled police captain in Mali, quoted in Biddlecombe, *French Lessons*, p. 247.
25. George B. N. Ayittey, "The U.N.'s Shameful Record in Africa," *Wall St. J.*, 26 July 1996, p. A-12.
26. According to Ayittey, the United Nations estimated that some $200 billion was shipped from Africa to foreign banks in 1991 alone—equal to 90 percent of sub-Saharan Africa's GDP. *Ibid.*
27. H. W. French, "Personal Rivals Fight to Finish in War in Zaire," *N.Y. Times*, 6 April 1997.
28. Barbara Crossette, "U.N., World Bank and IMF Join $25 Billion Drive for Africa," *N.Y. Times*, 17 March 1996, p. A-6. The New York–based *African Observer* denounced the scheme as a charade, cooked up by Boutros Boutros-Ghali by way of promoting his campaign for renewal as secretary-general of the UN (if so, it didn't help)—Ayittey, "U.N.'s Shameful Record."
29. *N.Y. Times*, 17 March 1996, p. A-6.
30. These data from the World Bank, *World Development Report 1994.*
31. As of 1993. Field, *Inside the Arab World*, p. 135, notes that the sum matched the country's foreign debt as of that date, so that people were able to dream of owing nothing. If they could put their hands on that money.
32. On this, see Abdelaziz, "Une économie paralysée."
33. Field, *Inside the Arab World*, p. 134.
34. Fisk, "Sept journées ordinaires," p. 7.
35. Cardoso and Faletto, *Dependency and Development*, p. 216. In all fairness, the text may read better in Spanish.
36. Matt Moffett, "Foreign Investors Help Brazil's Leader Tame Its Raging Inflation," *Wall St. J.*, 15 December 1995, p. A-1.
37. *Ibid.* On the assumption that the quotes are translations, I have taken the liberty of changing the language ever so slightly without changing the meaning.

38. Sebastian Edwars, "Why Brazil Is Not Mexico—Yet," *Wall St. J.,* 26 July 1996, p. A-13.

## CHAPTER 29

1. On the negatives and "excesses" of technology, see Salomon, *Le destin technologique.*

2. See Holton, *Einstein, History.*

3. Islamoğlu-Inan, "Introduction," p. 222. In a witty, understated excursion on the subject, Khoo Khay Jin suggests that among the sources of this preeminently Western *crise de conscience* is "the collapse of the socialist project in thought and reality." H-World @ h-net.msu.edu, 31 October 1996.

4. Thus Tavakoli-Targhi, "Orientalism's Genesis Amnesia."

5. Islamoğlu-Inan, "Introduction," p. 229.

6. Cf. Hall, "A Theory of the Rise of the West," p. 231.

7. On the proliferation of what Ferdinand Mount calls "Endist" books, see his review "No End in Sight," *TLS,* 3 May 1996, p. 30. He writes: "One thing is common to this grand cacophony of prophecy and prescription: the refusal to pause and consider, with even the appearance of care, any arguments of their opponents or any weaknesses in their own."

8. B. Biggs, chairman, Morgan Stanley Asset Management, cited in Kaplan, *Ends of the Earth,* p. 297.

9. Cf. Dasgupta, "Natural Resources." This speaks of a third stage, the "Age of Substitutability": "In this final Age, economic activities will be based almost exclusively on materials that are virtually inexhaustible, with relatively little loss in living standards" (p. 1128).

10. Cf. Edward A. Gargan, "A Year from Chinese Rule, Dread Grows in Hong Kong," *N.Y. Times,* 1 July 1996, p. A-1; and Peter Stein, "China Is Slow to Handle Issues on Hong Kong," *Wall St. J.,* p. B7D.

11. Compare the precautions of Russian firms, setting up headquarters in Cyprus to get away from the crime and potential chaos at home. Mark M. Nelson, "Economic Fugitives," *Wall St. J.,* 9 May 1996, p. 1.

12. Krugman, *Pop Internationalism,* p. 70.

13. *Wealth of Nations,* Book II, ch. 3.

14. *N.Y. Times,* 19 June 1996, p. D-5: "Moulinex [French maker of household appliances] Is Shifting Production to Mexico." Not all: four of eleven plants, 2,600 of 11,300 jobs. The firm had suffered a loss of 702 m. francs for the year ended 3/31, after a loss of 213 m. a year earlier.

15. *Pop Internationalism,* p. 50.

16. Cf. *ibid.,* pp. 112–13, which says that even a successful "strategic trade policy" would add no more than 1/15 of 1 percent to American national income. This puts such policy "as an issue in the same league as pricing policies for ranchers and miners operating on federal land." I disagree. Insofar as government can promote competitiveness, it should, on the principle that more knowledge and better performance are contagious. And insofar as government is leasing federal land for less than market value, it should stop, on the principle that successful rent seeking is a bad habit and also contagious. The only real argument against government intervention is that it often botches the job. And that's also contagious.

17. Cf. Uchitelle, "Like Oil and Water." This article is a comparison of the economics—content and tone—of Lester Thurow and Paul Krugman.

18. Among the more recent contributions are the essays in Krugman, *Pop Internationalism,* which denounce protectionism and other efforts to manage trade. Krugman

is especially severe toward his intellectual adversaries, defining "pop internationalism" as "glib rhetoric that appeals to those who want to sound sophisticated without engaging in hard thinking." Cited in review by Charles Wolf, Jr., in the *Wall St. J.*, 1 June 1996, p. A-12.
19. For a skeptical view of market efficiency and a defense of the advantage of government intervention, see Kuttner, *Everything for Sale*.
20. See le Masson, *Faut-il encore aider?*, p. 145.

## EPILOGUE 1999

1. Cf. Fay, *The Collapse of Barings*, p. 123.
2. It is a good rule to avoid the word "miracle" in speaking of economic achievement, though in all fairness, critics are less inclined to condemn such use in the Asian than in the European context. European "miracles" are decidedly out of fashion.
3. Cited in Henderson, *Asia Falling*, p. 7.
4. Henderson, *Asia Falling*, p. 7, Table 1. It is not clear whether this is growth in real (deflated) terms.
5. "The question is whether we have to bow to their pressure. These are not pressures from governments but [from] individuals who are not elected by anyone, whilst we are a sovereign country, having a government elected by the people." Gill, *Asia under Siege*, p. 160.
6. Gough, *Asia Meltdown*, p. 68.
7. For a statement of this position, see Frank, *ReOrient*.
8. The eighteenth century poses a special problem to this school. Western economic and political pre-eminence would seem clear-cut, but a number of scholars would now argue that the real mover in world growth at that time was China, whose huge population made it the focus of international trade. Among the proponents of this thesis: Kenneth Pomeranz, Gunder Frank, William McNeill. I do not question the size of the Chinese market, nor the volume and value of its industrial output. But that was not where the innovations were taking place that changed the world. We have a real disagreement here about the nature and causes of historical change.
9. See Landes, *Bankers and Pashas*, ch. i.
10. On the negative aspects of fast and furious enterprise, see Luttwak, *Turbo-Capitalism*. Economists point out that he is not an economist, hence unauthoritative. But I think he makes many good points.

# Bibliography

Abdelaziz, Malika. 1993. "Une économie paralysée," *Courrier international*, 156 (28 Oct.): 12.

Abe, Etsuo, and Robert Fitzgerald, eds. 1995. *The Origins of Japanese Industrial Power: Strategy, Institutions and the Development of Organisational Capability.* London: Cass.

Abel, Christopher, and Colin M. Lewis, eds. 1985. *Latin America, Economic Imperialism and the State: The Political Economy of the External Connection from Independence to the Present.* London: Athlone Press.

Abernathy, William J., and Kim B. Clark. 1982. "Notes on a Trip to Japan: Concepts and Interpretations." Graduate School of Business Administration, Harvard Univ. Working Paper HBS 82–58.

———, and Alan M. Kantrow. 1983. *Industrial Renaissance: Producing a Competitive Future for America.* New York: Basic Books.

Ablin, Eduardo, and Jorge M. Katz, "From Infant Industry to Technology Exports: The Argentinian Experience in the International Sale of Industrial Plants and Engineering Work," in Katz, ed., *Technology Generation,* pp. 446–77.

Abramovitz, Moses. 1972. "Manpower, Capital, and Technology," in Ivar Berg, ed., *Human Resources and Economic Welfare: Essays in Honor of Eli Ginzburg.* New York: Columbia Univ. Press.

———. 1986. "Catching-up, Forging Ahead and Falling Behind," *J. Econ. Hist.,* 46, 2 (June), 385–406.

———. 1989. *Thinking About Growth; and Other Essays on Economic Growth and Welfare.* Cambridge: Univ. Press.

———. 1993. "The Search for the Sources of Growth: Areas of Ignorance, Old and New," *J. Econ. Hist.,* 53, 2 (June): 217–43.

———, and Paul A. David. 1973. "Reinterpreting Economic Growth: Parables and Realities," *Amer. Econ. Rev.,* 63, 2 (May), 428–39.

———. 1994. "Convergence and Deferred Catch-up: Productivity Leadership and the Waning of American Exceptionalism," in Landau, Taylor, and Wright, eds., *Mosaic of Economic Growth,* pp. 21–62.

Achavanuntakul, Sarinee. 1996. "Effects of Government Policies on Poverty Incidence and Income Distribution in Thailand." Harvard College, Senior Honors Essay in Economics.

Adams, Robert McC. 1996. *Paths of Fire: An Anthropologist's Inquiry into Western Technology.* Princeton: Princeton Univ. Press.

Adas, Michael. 1989. *Machines as the Measure of Men: Science, Technology, and Ideologies of Western Dominance.* Ithaca: Cornell Univ. Press.

———, ed. 1993. *Islamic and European Expansion: The Forging of a Global Order.* Philadelphia: Temple Univ. for the American Historical Assn.

———. 1993. " 'High' Imperialism and the 'New' History," in Adas, ed., *Islamic and European Expansion,* pp. 311–44. Also issued in "Essays on Global and Comparative History," American Historical Assn., Washington, DC, n.d.

Adelman, Jeremy. 1994. *Frontier Development: Land, Labour, and Capital on the Wheatlands of Argentina and Canada 1890–1914.* Oxford: Clarendon Press.

Adler, Emanuel. 1986. "Ideological Guerillas and the Quest for Technological Autonomy: Brazil's Domestic Computer Industry," *International Organization,* 40 (Summer), 673–705.

Aerts, Erik, and John H. Munro, eds. 1990. *Textiles of the Low Countries in European Economic History.* Session B-15. Proceedings of the 10th International Economic History Congress. Leuven, August 1990. Leuven: Leuven Univ. Press.

Ahmad, Jalal Al-i. 1984. *Occidentosis: A Plague from the West.* Berkeley: Mizan Press. The Persian original dates from 1947.

Ainval, Henri d'. 1994. *Deux siècles de sidérurgie française: De 1003 entreprises à la dernière.* Grenoble: Presses Universitaires.

Ajami, Fouad. 1992. *The Arab Predicament: Arab Political Thought and Practice Since 1967.* Cambridge: Univ. Press; Canto ed.

Alam, M. S. 1994. "Colonialism, Decolonisation and Growth Rates: Theory and Empirical Evidence," *Cambridge J. of Econ.,* 18: 235–57.

———. 1996. "Sovereignty and Human Capital Formation: An Empirical Study of Historical Links." Dept. of Economics, Northeastern Univ., Boston. Typescript.

———. 1996. "How Rich Were the Advanced Countries in 1760 After All?" Dept. of Economics, Northeastern Univ., Boston. Typescript.

Alapuro, Risto. 1988. *State and Revolution in Finland.* Berkeley: Univ. of California Press.

Albuquerque, Luis de. 1987. *As Navegações e Sua Projecção na Ciência e na Cultura.* Lisbon: Gradiva.

Aldcroft, Derek H. 1996. "Europe's Third World? The Peripheral Companies in the Interwar Period." Typescript; to be presented at conference in Lausanne, October 1997.

———, and Michael Freeman, eds. 1983. *Transport in the Industrial Revolution.* Manchester: Univ. Press.

Alden, Dauril. 1968. *Royal Government in Colonial Brazil.* Berkeley: Univ. of California Press.

Alder, Ken. 1997a. *Engineering the Revolution: Areas and Enlightenment in France, 1763–1815.* Princeton: Princeton Univ. Press.

————. 1997b. "Innovation and Amnesia: Engineering Rationality and the Fate of Interchangeable Parts Manufacture in France," *Technology and Culture*, 38, 2 (April): 273–311.

Alexander, David. 1970. *Retailing in England During the Industrial Revolution*. London: Athlone Press.

Algazi, Gadi. 1993. "The Social Uses of Private War: Some Late Medieval Views Reviewed," *Tel Aviver Jahrbuch fur deutsche Geschichte*, 22: 253–73.

al-Hassan, Ahmad Y., and Donald R. Hill. 1986. *Islamic Technology: An Illustrated History*. Cambridge: Univ. Press.

Al-i Ahmad, Jalal. 1984. *Occidentosis: A Plague from the West*. Berkeley: Mizan Press.

al-Khalil, Samir. 1989. *Republic of Fear*. Berkeley: Univ. of California Press.

Altman, Lawrence K., M.D. 1994. "Researcher's Infection Raises Concerns for Laboratory Safety," *New York Times*, 23 Aug. p. C-3.

Amalric, J.-P., and B. Bennassar, eds. 1984. *Aux origines du retard économique de l'Espagne XVI<sup>e</sup>–XIX<sup>e</sup> siècle. Paris: CNRS.*

"American Business: Back on Top?" 1995. *The Economist*, 16 Sept., Survey, pp. 2–18.

Anderson, B. L. 1969. "The Attorney and the Early Capital Market in Lancashire," in Harris, ed., *Liverpool and Merseyside*, 50–77.

————. 1970. "Money and the Structure of Credit in the Eighteenth Century," *Business History*, XII.

Anderson, P., Paul Bairoch, Carlo Ginzburg, and E. J. Hobsbawm, eds. 1997. *Storia d'Europa*. Vol. IV. Turin: Einaudi.

Andrewes, William J. H., ed. 1996. *The Quest for Longitude*. Cambridge, MA: Collection of Historical Scientific Instruments, Harvard Univ.

Andrews, Kenneth R. 1984. *Trade, Plunder and Settlement: Maritime Enterprise and the Genesis of the British Empire 1480–1630*. Cambridge: Univ. Press.

Annino, Antonio. 1995. "Some Reflections on Spanish American Constitutional and Political History," *Itinerario*, 19, 2: 26–47.

Anstey, Roger T. 1968. "Capitalism and Slavery: A Critique," *Econ. Hist. Rev.*, 2d ser., 21 (August): 307–20.

Antony, Robert J. 1993. "Aspects of the Socio-Political Culture of South China's Water World, 1740–1840," *The Great Circle*, 15, 2 (October): 75–90.

Appelbaum, Richard P., and Jeffrey Henderson, eds. 1992. *States and Development in the Asian Pacific Rim*. Newbury Park, CA: Sage.

Appleby, Joyce Oldham. 1978. *Economic Thought and Ideology in Seventeenth-Century England*. Princeton: Princeton Univ. Press.

Arasaratnam, S. 1980. "Weavers, Merchants and Company: The Handloom Industry in Southeastern India 1750–1790," *Indian Econ. and Soc. Hist. Rev.*, 17: 257–81.

Aridjis, Homero. 1991. *1492: The Life and Times of Juan Cabezon of Castile*. Trans. Betty Ferber. New York: Summit Books.

Armus, D. 1986. "Diez años de historiografia sobre la inmigracion masiva," *Estudios migratorios latinoamericanos* (December): 431–660.

Arrow, Kenneth J. 1969. "Classificatory Notes on the Production and Transmission of Technological Knowledge." *Amer. Econ. Rev.*, Papers and Proceedings, 59 (May): 29–35.

————. 1962. "The Economic Implications of Learning by Doing," *Rev. Econ. Studies*, 29 (June): 155–73.

Artz, Frederick B. 1966. *The Development of Technical Education in France, 1500–1850*. Cambridge, MA, and London: Soc. for the Hist. of Technology and MIT Press.

Ashton, T. S. 1924/1951. *Iron and Steel in the Industrial Revolution*. Manchester: Univ. Press.

————. 1948. *The Industrial Revolution, 1760–1830*. Oxford: Oxford Univ. Press.

————. 1945. "The Bill of Exchange and Private Banks in Lancashire, 1790–1830," *Econ. Hist. Rev.,* 15, 1/2: 25–35.

Ashworth, W. 1977. "Typologies and Evidence: Has 19th-Century Europe a Guide to Economic Growth?" *Econ. Hist. Rev.,* n.s., 30 (February): 140–58.

Atkins, Keletso E. 1988. " 'Kafir Time': Preindustrial Temporal Concepts and Labour Discipline in Nineteenth-Century Colonial Natal," *J. African Hist.,* 29: 229–44.

Axtell, James. 1988. *After Columbus: Essays in the Ethnohistory of Colonial North America*. New York: Oxford Univ. Press.

Aymard, Maurice, ed. 1982. *Dutch Capitalism and World Capitalism*. Cambridge: Univ. Press; Paris: Maison des Sciences de l'Homme.

Aziz, Philippe. 1996. *Le paradoxe de Roubaix*. Paris: Plon.

Baark, Erik, and Andrew Jamison, eds. 1986. *Technological Development in China, India and Japan: Cross-Cultural Perspectives*. New York: St. Martin's Press.

Baber, Zaheer. 1996. *The Science of Empire: Scientific Knowledge, Civilization, and Colonial Rule in India*. Albany: SUNY Press.

Baechler, Jean, John A. Hall, and Michael Mann, eds. 1988. *Europe and the Rise of Capitalism*. Oxford: Basil Blackwell.

Bagchi, Amiya Kumar. 1976. "De-industrialization in India in the Nineteenth Century: Some Theoretical Implications," *J. Devel. Studies,* 12, 2 (January), 135–64.

Bahl, Vinay. 1994. "The Emergence of Large-scale Steel Industry in India under British Colonial Rule, 1880–1907," *Indian Econ. and Soc. Hist. Rev.,* 31, 4 (October–December), 413–60.

————. 1995. *The Making of the Indian Working Class: The Case of the Tata Iron and Steel Company, 1880–1946*. New Delhi: Sage.

Bailyn, Bernard. 1955. *New England Merchants in the Seventeenth Century*. Cambridge, MA: Harvard Univ. Press.

————. 1996. "The Idea of Atlantic History," *Itinerario,* 20, 1: 19–44.

Bairoch, Paul. 1969/1973. "Agriculture and the Industrial Revolution 1700–1914," in Carlo M. Cipolla, ed., *The Fontana Economic History of Europe: The Industrial Revolution*. London: Collins/Fontana, pp. 452–506.

————. 1975. *The Economic Development of the Third World Since 1900*. Transl. Cynthia Postan. Berkeley: Univ. of Calif. Press.

————. 1979. "Ecarts internationaux des niveaux de vie avant la Révolution industrielle," *Annales: économies, sociétés, civilisations,* 34, 1 (January–February), 145–71.

————. 1981. "The Main Trends in National Economic Disparities Since the Industrial Revolution," in Bairoch and Lévy-Leboyer, eds., *Disparities in Economic Development,* pp. 3–17.

————. 1993. *Economics and World History: Myths and Paradoxes*. Chicago: Univ. of Chicago Press; New York: Harvester Wheatsheaf.

———— and Maurice Lévy-Leboyer, eds. 1981. *Disparities in Economic Development Since the Industrial Revolution*. London: Macmillan.

————. 1997. *Victoires et déboires: Histoire économique et sociale du monde du XVI$^e$ siècle à nos jours*. 3 vols. Paris: Gallimard; "Folio histoire."

Baladouni, Vahe. 1986. "Armenian Trade with the English East India Company: An Aperçu," *J. Europ. Econ. Hist.,* 15, 1 (Spring): 153–62.

Balazs, Etienne. 1964. *Chinese Civilization and Bureaucracy: Variations on a Theme*. New Haven: Yale Univ. Press.

————. 1968. *La bureaucratie céleste: Recherches sur l'économie et la société de la Chine traditionnelle*. Paris: Gallimard.

Baldwin, K. D. S. 1957. *The Niger Agricultural Project: An Experiment in African Development.* Oxford: Basil Blackwell.

Baldwin, R. 1956. "Patterns of Development in Newly Settled Regions," *Manchester School of Econ. and Soc. Studies,* 24.

Bandt, Jacques de, and Philippe Hugon, eds. 1988. *Les tiers nations en mal d'industrie.* Paris: Economica; Nanterre: CERNEA.

Bandyopadhyaya, Jayantanuja. 1978. "Climate as an Obstacle to Development in the Tropics," *Int. Soc. Science J.,* 30, 2: 339–52.

———. 1983. *Climate and World Order: An Inquiry into the Natural Cause of Underdevelopment.* Atlantic Highlands, NJ: Humanities Press.

Bankes, George. 1977. *Peru Before Pizarro.* Oxford: Phaidon Press.

Barakat, Halim. 1993. *The Arab World: Society, Culture, and the State.* Berkeley: Univ. of Calif. Press.

Barbour, Violet. 1963. *Capitalism in Amsterdam in the 17th Century.* Ann Arbor: Univ. of Michigan Press.

Barbey-Say, Helene. 1994. *Le voyage de France en Allemagne de 1871 à 1914: Voyages et voyageurs français dans l'Empire germanique.* Nancy: Presses Universitaires.

Barbier, Frédéric. 1991. *Finance et politique: La dynastie des Fould XVIIIᵉ–XXᵉ siècle.* Paris: Armand Colin.

Barendse, R. J. 1995. "Shipbuilding in Seventeenth-Century Western India," *Itinerario,* 19, 3: 175–95.

Barnett, Correlli. 1986. *The Pride and the Fall: The Dream and Illusion of Britain as a Great Nation.* New York: The Free Press. British ed., 1986: *The Audit of War.*

Barrett, Ward. 1990. "World Bullion Flows, 1450–1800," in Tracy, ed., *Rise of Merchant Empires,* pp. 224–54.

Barro, Robert J. 1991. "Economic Growth in a Cross Section of Countries," *QJE,* 106, 2: 407–43.

———. 1996. "Determinants of Economic Growth: A Cross-Country Empirical Study." Nat. Bureau Econ. Research (NBER) Working Paper Series 5698.

———, and Xavier Sala-i-Martin. 1991. "Convergence Across States and Regions," *Brookings Papers on Economic Activity* 1, pp. 107–82.

———. 1995. *Economic Growth.* New York: McGraw-Hill.

Bartlett, Robert. 1993. *The Making of Europe: Conquest, Colonization and Cultural Change 950–1350.* London: Penguin.

Bartlett, Roger P. 1979. *Human Capital: The Settlement of Foreigners in Russia 1762–1804.* Cambridge: Univ. Press.

Bataillon, Marcel, and André Saint-Lu, eds. 1971. *Las Casas et la défense des Indiens.* Paris: Julliard ("Collection Archives").

Bates, Marston. 1952/1963. *Where Winter Never Comes: A Study of Man and Nature in the Tropics.* New York: Charles Scribner's Sons.

Batou, Jean. 1990. *Cent ans de résistance au sous-développement: L'industrialisation de l'Amérique latine et du Moyen-Orient face au défi européen, 1770–1870.* Geneva: Droz, for the Centre of International Economic History.

———, ed. 1991. *Between Development and Underdevelopment 1800–1870.* Geneva: Droz, for the Centre of International Economic History.

———. 1991. "Muhammad-'Ali's Egypt, 1805–1848. A Command Economy in the 19th Century?" in Batou, ed., *Between Development and Underdevelopment,* pp. 181–217.

———. 1993. "Nineteenth-Century Attempted Escapes from the Periphery: The Cases of Egypt and Paraguay," *Review* (Centre d'Efudes Industrialles, Gereva), 16, 3: 279–318.

———, and Thomas David. 1996. "Nationalisme économique et industrialisation de la périphérie européenne: de la Révolution industrielle à la Deuxième guerre mondiale." To be published in Italian in Anderson, Bairoch, *et al.*, eds., *Storia d'Europa*. Vol. IV.

Bauer, P. T. 1981. *Equality, the Third World and Economic Delusion*. Cambridge, MA: Harvard Univ. Press.

Baumol, William J. 1994. "Multivariate Growth Patterns: Contagion and Common Forces as Possible Sources of Convergence," in Baumol *et al.*, eds., *Convergence of Productivity*, pp. 62–85.

———, Sue Anne Batey Blackman, and Edward N. Wolff. 1989. *Productivity and American Leadership: The Long View*. Cambridge, MA: MIT Press.

———, Richard R. Nelson, and Edward N. Wolff, eds. 1994. *Convergence of Productivity: Cross-National Studies and Historical Evidence*. New York: Oxford Univ. Press.

Bayly, C. A. 1986. "The Middle East and Asia During the Age of Revolutions, 1760–1830," *Itinerario*, 10, 2: 69–84.

Beaujouan, Guy. 1967. *La science en Espagne aux XIVe et XVe siècles*. Paris: Univ. de Paris, Palais de la Découverte.

Beck, Lois, and Nikki Keddie, eds. 1978. *Women in the Muslim World*. Cambridge, MA: Harvard Univ. Press.

Becker, Gary S., and Kevin M. Murphy. 1992. "The Division of Labor, Coordination Costs, and Knowledge," *QJE*, 107, 4 (November), 1137–60.

Bellah, Robert N. 1957/1985. *Tokugawa Religion: The Cultural Roots of Modern Japan*. New York: The Free Press.

Bennassar, Bartolomé. 1975. *L'homme espagnol: attitudes et mentalités du XVIe au XIXe siècle*. Paris: Hachette. English translation, 1979: *The Spanish Character: Attitudes and Mentalities from the Sixteenth to the Nineteenth Century*. Berkeley: Univ. of Calif. Press.

———, ed. 1979/1994. *L'Inquisition espagnole XVe–XIXe siècles*. Paris: Hachette.

———, *et al.* 1992. *Histoire des Espagnols: VIe–XXe siècle*. *Paris: Robert Laffont*.

Bennassar, Bartolomé, and Lucile Bennassar. 1991. *1492: Un monde nouveau?* Paris: Perrin.

Berend, Ivan T., and Gyorgy Ránki. 1982. *The European Periphery and Industrialization 1780–1914*. Cambridge: Univ. Press.

Berg, Alan D. 1967. "Malnutrition and National Development," *Foreign Affairs*, 46, 1 (October), 126–36.

Berg, Maxine, ed. 1991. *Markets and Manufacture in Early Industrial Europe*. London: Routledge.

———. 1994. *The Age of Manufactures 1700–1820: Industry, Innovation and Work in Britain*. 2d ed., London: Routledge.

———. 1994. "Growth and Change: A Comment on the Crafts-Harley View of the Industrial Revolution," *Econ. Hist. Rev.*, 47: 147–49.

———, and Pat Hudson. 1992. "Rehabilitating the Industrial Revolution," *Econ. Hist. Rev.*, 45, 1: 24–50.

Bergeron, Louis. 1978. *Banquiers, négociants et manufacturiers parisiens du Directoire à l'Empire*. Paris and The Hague: Mouton.

Bernal, Martin. 1987. *Black Athena: The Afroasiatic Roots of Classical Civilization*. London: Free Association Books.

Bernaldez, Andres. 1962 [end 15th century]. *Memorias del reinado de los reyes catolicos*. Ed. Manuel Gomez Moreno and Juan de Mata Carriazo. Madrid: Real Academia de la Historia.

Bernand, Carmen. 1988/1994. *The Incas, People of the Sun*. New York: Harry N. Abrams.

———, and Serge Gruzinski. 1991/1993. *Histoire du nouveau monde*, I: *De la découverte à la conquête, une expérience européenne 1492–1550*; II: *Les métissages (1550–1640)*. Paris: Fayard.

Bernecker, Walther L., and Hans Werner Tobler, eds. 1993. *Development and Under-development in America: Contrasts of Economic Growth in North and Latin America in Historical Perspective.* Berlin and New York: Walter de Gruyter.

Bernier, François. 1670–72/1981. *Voyage dans les états du Grand Mogol.* Paris: Fayard.

Bernstein, Gail Lee, ed. 1991. *Recreating Japanese Women, 1600–1945.* Berkeley: Univ. of Calif. Press.

Bernstein, Michael A., and David E. Adler, eds. 1994. *Understanding American Economic Decline.* Cambridge: Univ. Press.

Berque, Augustin. 1976. *Le Japon: Gestion de l'espace et changement social.* Paris: Flammarion.

Bethell, Leslie, ed. 1993. *Argentina Since Independence.* Cambridge: Univ. Press.

Bhattacharya, Bhaswati. 1995. "A Note on the Shipbuilding in Bengal in the Late Eighteenth Century," *Itinerario,* 19, 3: 167–74.

Bhattacharya, Sukumar. 1954. *The East India Company and the Economy of Bengal from 1704 to 1740.* London: Luzac.

Biagioli, Mario. 1993. *Galileo Courtier: The Practice of Science in the Culture of Absolutism.* Chicago: Univ. of Chicago Press.

Biddlecombe, Peter. 1993. *French Lessons in Africa: Travels with My Briefcase Through French Africa.* Boston: Little, Brown.

Bigelow, Bill. 1994. "Good Intentions Are Not Enough: Children's Literature in the Aftermath of the Quincentenary," *The New Advocate,* 16, 7, 4 (Fall), 265–79.

Birch, Alan. 1967. *The Economic History of the British Iron and Steel Industry, 1784–1879.* London: Frank Cass.

Biswas, Margaret R., and Asit K. Biswas, eds. 1979. *Food, Climate, and Man.* New York: John Wiley.

Bix, Herbert P. 1986. *Peasant Protest in Japan, 1590–1884.* New Haven: Yale Univ. Press.

Blackwell, William L. 1968. *The Beginnings of Russian Industrialization 1800–1860.* Princeton: Princeton Univ. Press.

Blaut, James M. 1993. *The Colonizer's Model of the World: Geographical Diffusionism and Eurocentric History.* New York: Guilford.

Blomström, Magnus, Robert E. Lipsey, and Mario Zejan. 1994. "What Explains the Growth of Developing Countries?", in Baumol *et al.,* eds., *Convergence of Productivity,* pp. 243–59.

———. 1996. "Is Fixed Investment the Key to Economic Growth?" *QJE,* 111, 1 (February), 269–76.

Bluestone, Barry, and Bennett Harris. 1982. *The Deindustrialization of America: Plant Closings, Community Abandonment, and the Dismantling of Basic Industry.* New York: Basic Books.

Blum, Jerome. 1956. "Prices in Russia in the Sixteenth Century," *J. Econ. Hist.,* 16, 2: 182–99.

Bodmer, Beatriz Pastor, ed. 1992. *The Armature of Conquest: Spanish Accounts of the Discovery of America, 1492–1589.* Stanford: Univ. Press.

Bonheur, Gaston. 1963. *Qui a cassé le vase de Soissons? L'album de famille de tous les Français.* Paris: Laffont.

Bonin, Hubert. 1994a. *La Société Générale en Russie.* [Paris]: Société Générale.

———. 1994b. "L'activité des banques françaises dans l'Asie du Pacifique des années 1860 aux années 1940," *Rev. française d'hist. d'outre-mer,* 81, 305: 401–25.

Bonwick, James. 1884. *The Lost Tasmanian Race.* London: Sampson Low.

Borah, Woodrow, Charles Gibson, and Robert Potash. 1963. "Colonial Institutions and Contemporary Latin America," *Hisp. Amer. Hist. Rev.,* 43: 371–94.

Borgstrom, Georg. 1972. *The Hungry Planet: The Modern World at the Edge of Famine.* 2d rev. ed., New York: Macmillan.

Boskin, Michael J., and Lawrence J. Lau. 1992. "Capital, Technology, and Economic Growth," in Rosenberg, Landau, and Mowery, eds., *Technology and the Wealth of Nations,* pp. 17–55.

Bottineau, Yves. 1977. *Le Portugal et sa vocation maritime: Histoire et civilisation d'une nation.* Paris: Boccard.

Boucher, Philip P. 1992 *Cannibal Encounters: Europeans and Island Caribs, 1492–1763.* Baltimore: Johns Hopkins Univ. Press.

Boulnois, Luce. 1963/1986. *La route de la soie.* Genève: Olizane.

Bowden, Witt. 1925. *Industrial Society in England Towards the End of the Eighteenth Century.* New York: Macmillan.

Boxer, Charles R. 1962. *The Golden Age of Brazil, 1695–1750: Growing Pains of a Colonial Society.* Berkeley and Los Angeles: Univ. of Calif. Press in cooperation with the Sociedade de Estudos Historicos Dom Pedro Segundo, Rio de Janeiro.

———. 1965/1990. *The Dutch Seaborne Empire 1600–1800.* London: Penguin.

———. 1969. *The Portuguese Seaborne Empire 1415–1825.* London: Hutchinson. Reprinted Lisbon: Carcanet, 1991.

Boyd-Bowman, Peter. 1973. *Patterns of Spanish Emigration to the New World (1493–1580).* Buffalo: State Univ. of New York; Council on International Studies.

Bradley, Joseph. 1990. *Guns for the Tsar: American Technology and the Small Arms Industry in Nineteenth-Century Russia.* De Kalb, IL: Northern Illinois Univ. Press.

Braudel, Fernand. 1979. *Civilisation matérielle, économie et capitalisme, XV³–XVIII$^e$ siècle. 3 vols. Paris: Armand Colin. Vol. III.* Le temps du monde.

Braun, Hans-Joachim. 1974. *Technologische Beziehungen zwischen Deutschland und England von der Mitte des 17. bis zum Ausgang des 18. Jahrhunderts.* Düsseldorf: Schwann.

Bray, Francesca. 1978. "Swords into Plowshares: A Study of Agricultural Technology and Society in Early China," *Technology and Culture,* 19, 1 (January), 1–31.

———. 1986. *The Rice Economies: Technology and Development in Asian Societies.* Oxford: Basil Blackwell; 1994 ed., Berkeley: Univ. of Calif. Press.

Brennig, Joseph J. 1990. "Textile Producers and Production in Late Seventeenth Century Coromandel," in Subrahmanyam, ed., *Merchants, Markets and the State,* pp. 66–87.

Brewer, John. 1988. *The Sinews of Power: War, Money and the English State, 1688–1783.* New York: Knopf; 1990 ed., Cambridge, MA: Harvard Univ. Press.

Brewer, John, and Roy Porter, eds. 1993. *Consumption and the World of Goods.* London: Routledge.

Brezis, Elise. 1995. "Foreign Capital Flows in the Century of Britain's Industrial Revolution," *Econ. Hist. Rev.,* 48, 1 (February): 46–67.

———, Paul R. Krugman, and Daniel Tsiddon. 1993. "Leapfrogging in International Competition: A Theory of Cycles in National Technological Leadership," *Amer. Econ. Rev.,* 83, 5 (December): 1211–19.

*Britannia Languens, or a Discourse of Trade* (London, 1680), in McCulloch, ed., *Early English Tracts,* pp. 275–506.

Broad, William J. 1995. "Watery Grave of the Azores to Yield Shipwrecked Riches," *New York Times,* 6 June, p. C-1.

Broadberry, S. N. 1994. "Comparative Productivity in British and American Manufacturing During the Nineteenth Century," *Explor. Econ. Hist.,* 31: 521–48.

Brockway, George P. 1995. *The End of Economic Man: Principles of Any Future Economics.* New York: W. W. Norton.

Brosse, Jacques. 1981. *La découverte de la Chine.* Paris: Bordas.

Brown, Sidney D. 1961–62. "Okubo Toshimichi: His Political and Economic Policies in Early Meiji Japan," *J. Asian Studies*, 21: 183–97.

Bruckner, Pascal. 1983/1986. *The Tears of the White Man: Compassion as Contempt.* New York: Free Press.

Brunel, Sylvie, ed. 1987. *Tiers mondes: Controverses et réalités.* Paris: Economica.

———. 1995. *Le Sud dans la nouvelle économie mondiale.* Paris: P.U.F.

Bruno, Michael, and Boris Pleskovic, eds. 1997. *Annual World Bank Conference on Development Economics.* Washington, DC: World Bank.

Buc, Philippe. 1994. *L'ambiguité du livre: prince, pouvoir et peuple dans les commentaires de la bible au Moyen-Age.* Paris: Beauchesne.

Buchanan, J., R. Tollison, and G. Tullock, eds. 1980. *Toward a Theory of the Rent-seeking Society.* College Station, TX: Texas A. & M. Press.

Bulliet, Richard W. 1994. *Islam: The View from the Edge.* New York: Columbia Univ. Press.

Bulmer-Thomas, Victor. 1994. *The Economic History of Latin America Since Independence.* Cambridge: Univ. Press.

Burawoy, Michael. 1985. *The Politics of Production: Factory Regimes Under Capitalism and Socialism.* London: Verso.

Burke, Peter. 1974. *Venice and Amsterdam: A Study of Seventeenth Century Elites.* London: Temple Smith.

Burn, D. L. 1931/1970. "The Genesis of American Engineering Competition, 1850–1870," in Saul, ed., *Technological Change,* pp. 77–98.

Burn, W. L. 1964. *The Age of Equipoise: A Study of the Mid-Victorian Generation.* London: Allen & Unwin.

Burrage, Michael. 1969. "Culture and British Economic Growth," *Brit. J. of Sociology,* 20, 2 (June), 117–33.

Burrish, Onslow. 1728. *Batavia illustrata.* 2 vols. London: William Innys.

Buruma, Ian. 1994. *The Wages of Guilt: Memories of War in Germany and Japan.* New York: Farrar, Straus & Giroux; Penguin/Meridian.

Butel, Paul. 1990. "France, the Antilles, and Europe in the Seventeenth and Eighteenth Centuries: Renewals of Foreign Trade," in Tracy, ed., *Rise of Merchant Empires,* pp. 153–73.

Byatt, I. C. R. 1979. *The British Electrical Industry 1875–1914: The Economic Returns to a New Technology.* Oxford: Clarendon Press.

Cadieux, Francois. 1986. "Western Technology and Early Russian Pipelines, 1877–1917," *J. Europ. Econ. Hist.,* 15, 2 (Fall): 335–44.

Cain, P. J., and A. G. Hopkins. 1980. "The Political Economy of British Expansion Overseas, 1750–1914," *Econ. Hist. Rev.,* 2d ser., 33, 4: 463–90.

———. 1986. "Gentlemanly Capitalism and British Expansion Overseas, I. The Old Colonial System, 1688–1850," *Econ. Hist. Rev.,* 39: 501–25.

Cairncross, A. K. 1962. *Factors in Economic Development.* New York: Praeger.

Calvert, Monte, A. 1967. *The Mechanical Engineer in America, 1830–1910: Professional Cultures in Conflict.* Baltimore: Johns Hopkins Univ. Press.

Cameron, Rondo E. 1961. *France and the Economic Development of Europe.* Princeton: Princeton Univ. Press.

———, ed. 1967. *Banking in the Early Stages of Industrialisation: A Study in Comparative History.* New York: Oxford Univ. Press.

———, ed. 1972. *Banking and Economic Development: Some Lessons of History.* New York: Oxford Univ. Press.

———, and Charles E. Freedeman. 1983. "French Economic Growth: A Radical Revision," *Soc. Science Hist.,* 7, 1 (Winter), 3–30.

Campbell, R. H. 1980. *The Rise and Fall of Scottish Industry 1707–1939.* Edinburgh: John Donald.

Candolle, Alphonse de. 1885. *Histoire des sciences et des savants depuis deux siècles.* 2d enl. ed., Geneva: H. Georg.

Cantrell, J. A. 1981. "James Nasmyth and the Bridgewater Foundry: Partners and Partnerships," *Business History,* 23, 3 (November): 346–58.

———. 1984. *James Nasmyth and the Bridgewater Foundry: A Study of Entrepreneurship in the Early Engineering Industry.* Manchester: Manchester Univ. Press for the Chetham Society.

Cardoso, Eliana, and Ann Helwege. 1995. *Latin America's Economy: Diversity, Trends, and Conflicts.* Cambridge, MA: MIT Press.

Cardoso, Fernando Henrique, and Enzo Faletto. 1979. *Dependency and Development in Latin America.* Berkeley: Univ. of Calif. Press.

Cardoso, Gerald. 1983. *Negro Slavery in the Sugar Plantations of Veracruz and Pernambuco 1550–1680: A Comparative Study.* Washington, DC: Univ. Press of America.

Cardwell, D. S. L. 1972. *Turning Points in Western Technology: A Study of Technology, Science, and History.* New York: Neale Watson.

Carlton, David L., and Peter A. Coclanis. 1995. "The Uninventive South? A Quantitative Look at Region and American Inventiveness," *Technology & Culture,* 36, 2 (April): 302–26.

Caro Baroja, Julio. 1961. *Los judíos en la España moderna y contemporanea.* 3 vols. Madrid: Arion (reprint Madrid, 1978).

Caron, François, Paul Erker, and Wolfram Fischer, eds. 1995. *Innovations in the European Economy Between the Wars.* Berlin: Walter de Gruyter.

Carpenter, Kenneth J. 1986. *The History of Scurvy and Vitamin C.* Cambridge: Univ. Press.

Carpentier, Elisabeth, and Michael Le Mené. 1996. *La France du XI^e au XV^e siècle: Population, société, économie.* Paris: P.U.F.

Carrasco, Raphael, Claudette Derozier, and Annie Molinie-Bertrand. 1991. *Histoire et civilisation de l'Espagne classique 1492–1808.* Paris: Nathan.

Carus-Wilson, Eleanora M. 1952. "The Woollen Industry," in Postan and Rich, eds., *The Cambridge Economic History of Europe.* II: *Trade and Industry in the Middle Ages,* pp. 355–428.

Cassidy, Vincent H. 1978. "New Worlds and Everyman: Some Thoughts on the Logic and Logistics of Pre-Columbian Discovery," *Terrae incognitae* (Annals of the Society for the History of Discoveries), 10: 7–13.

Cassis, Youssef, ed. 1992. *Finance and Financiers in European History 1880–1960.* Cambridge: Univ. Press.

Castells, Manuel. 1992. "Four Asian Tigers with a Dragon Head: A Comparative Analysis of the State, Economy, and Society in the Asian Pacific Rim," in Appelbaum and Henderson, eds., *States and Development,* pp. 33–70.

Castro, Americo. 1949/87. *Aspectos de vivir hispanico.* Santiago de Chile: Cauz del Sur.

Caves, Richard. 1965. " 'Vent for Surplus' Models of Trade and Growth," in Robert E. Baldwin *et al.,* eds., *Trade, Growth, and the Balance of Payments.* Chicago: Rand McNally.

———. 1971. "Export-led Growth and the New Economic History," in J. N. Bhagwati *et al.,* eds., *Trade, Balance of Payments and Growth.* Amsterdam: North Holland.

Cellard, Jacques. 1996. *John Law et la Régence 1715–1729.* Paris: Plon.

Chaloner, W. H., and Barrie M. Ratcliffe, eds. 1977. *Trade and Transport: Essays in Economic History in Honour of T. S. Willan.* Manchester: Manchester Univ. Press; Totowa, NJ: Rowman & Littlefield.

Chandeigne, Michel, ed. 1990. *Lisbonne hors les murs, 1415–1580: L'invention du monde par les navigateurs portugais.* Paris.

Chandler, Alfred D., Jr. 1990. *Scale and Scope: The Dynamics of Industrial Capitalism.* Cambridge, MA: Harvard/Belknap Press.

Chang, Han-yu, and R. H. Myers. 1963. "Japanese Colonial Development Policy: A Case of Bureaucratic Entrepreneurship," *J. Asian Studies,* 22 (August): 433–49.

Chang, Jen-hu. 1968. "The Agricultural Potential of the Humid Tropics," *Geographical Rev.,* 58, 3 (July), 333–61.

Chang, Pin-tsun. 1989. "The Evolution of Chinese Thought on Maritime Foreign Trade from the Sixteenth to the Eighteenth Century," *Int. J. Maritime Hist.,* 1, 1 (June): 51–64.

———. 1992. "Maritime China in Historical Perspective," *Int. J. Maritime Hist.,* 4, 2 (December): 239–55.

Channon, Derek F. 1973. *The Strategy and Structure of British Enterprise.* Boston: Harvard GSBA.

Charnay, Jean-Paul. 1993. *Traumatismes musulmans: Entre chari'a et géopolitique.* Paris: Editions AFKAR.

Chassagne, Serge. 1993. "Industrie et proto-industrie en France au XVIIIᵉ siècle," *Bull. de la Soc. d'hist. moderne et contemp.,* 1–2: 12–20.

Chauchadis, Claude. 1984a. *Honneur, morale et société daus l'Espagne de Philippe II.* Paris: CNRS.

———. 1984b. "Honneur, morale et société dans l'Espagne de Philippe II," in Amalric and Bennassar, eds., *Aux origines du retard économique de l'Espagne.*

Chaudhuri, K. N. 1974. "The Structure of the Indian Textile Industry in the Seventeenth and Eighteenth Centuries," *Indian Econ. and Soc. Hist. Rev.,* 11 (June–September), 127–82.

———. 1978. *The Trading World of Asia and the English East India Company 1660–1760.* Cambridge: Univ. Press.

———. 1985. *Trade and Civilisation in the Indian Ocean: An Economic History from the Rise of Islam to 1750.* Cambridge: Univ. Press.

———. 1990. *Asia Before Europe: Economy and Civilisation of the Indian Ocean from the Rise of Islam to 1750.* Cambridge: Univ. Press.

Chaudhuri, Nirad C. 1987. *Thy Hand, Great Anarch! India 1921–1952.* Reading, MA: Addison-Wesley.

Chaudhury, Sushil. 1991. "Trade, Bullion and Conquest: Bengal in the Mid-Eighteenth Century," *Itinerario,* 15, 2: 21–32.

Chaunu, Pierre. 1964. *L'Amérique et les Amériques.* Paris: Armand Colin.

Chenery, Hollis, T. N. Srinivasan, and Paul Streeten, eds. 1988. *Handbook of Development Economics.* Vol. I. North-Holland: Elsevier.

Chesnais, Jean-Claude. 1987. *La revanche du tiers-monde.* Paris: Robert Laffont.

Chevalier, François. 1963. *Land and Society in Colonial Mexico: The Great Hacienda.* Berkeley: Univ. of Calif. Press.

Chevalier, Michel, ed. 1989. *La géographie de la créativité et de l'innovation.* Actes du Colloque du 9–10 juin 1987 à l'Univ. de Paris-Sorbonne. Paris: Dept. de Géographie de l'Univ. de Paris-Sorbonne et du Labo. CNRS, "Espace et Culture," 18.

Chevedden, Paul E., Les Eigenbrod, Vernard Foley, and Werner Soedel. 1995. "The Trebuchet," *Scientific American,* 273, 1 (July): 66–71.

Chi, Ch'ao-ting. 1936. *Key Economic Areas in Chinese History, as Revealed in the Development of Public Works for Water-Control.* London: Allen & Unwin.

Chiappelli, Fredi, ed. 1976. *First Images of America: The Impact of the New World on the Old.* Berkeley, CA: Univ. Calif. Press.

Chirot, Daniel, ed. 1989. *The Origins of Backwardness in Eastern Europe: Economics and Politics from the Middle Ages until the Early Twentieth Century.* Berkeley: Univ. of California Press.

Chklovski, Victor. 1938/1993. *Le voyage de Marco Polo*. Paris: Payot.

Chomsky, Noam. 1993. *Year 501: The Conquest Continues*. Boston: South End Press.

Christelow, Allan. 1947. "Great Britain and the Trades from Cadiz and Lisbon to Spanish America and Brazil, 1759–1783," *Hisp. Amer. Hist. Rev.*, 27: 2–29.

Christensen, Thomas and Carol, eds. 1992. *The Discovery of America & Other Myths: A New World Reader*. San Francisco: Chronicle.

Church, Roy. 1986. "The Effects of American Multinationals on the British Motor Industry: 1911–83," in Teichova *et al.*, eds., *Multinational Enterprise*, pp. 116–30.

————. 1994. *The Rise and Decline of the British Motor Industry*. London: Macmillan; Economic History Society.

————. 1996. "Deconstructing Nuffield: The Evolution of Managerial Culture in the British Motor Industry." *Econ. Hist. Rev.*, 49, 3 (August): 561–83.

Cipolla, Carlo M. 1965. *Guns, Sails, and Empires: Technological Innovation and the Early Phases of European Expansion 1400–1700*. New York: Pantheon.

————. 1967. *Clocks and Culture, 1300–1700*. New York: Walker.

————, ed. 1970. *The Economic Decline of Empires*. London: Methuen.

————. 1980. *Before the Industrial Revolution: European Society and Economy, 1000–1700*. 2d ed., New York: W. W. Norton.

————. 1988/1991/1992. *Between Two Cultures: An Introduction to Economic History*. New York: W. W. Norton.

Ciriacono, Salvatore. 1993. "The Venetian Economy and Its Place in the World Economy of the 17th and 18th Centuries. A Comparison with the Low Countries," in H.-J. Nitz, ed., *The Early-Modern World-System in Geographical Perspective*. Stuttgart: Franz Steiner, pp. 120–35.

Clapham, John H. 1923. *The Economic Development of France and Germany, 1815–1914*. Cambridge: Univ. Press.

————. 1926/1932/1938 (rev. and reprinted 1950/1952/1951). *An Economic History of Modern Britain*. 3 vols. Cambridge: Univ. Press.

Clark, Christopher. 1990. *The Roots of Rural Capitalism: Western Massachusetts, 1780–1860*. Ithaca: Cornell Univ. Press.

Clark, Rodney. 1979. *The Japanese Company*. New Haven: Yale Univ. Press.

Clendinnen, Inga. 1991. *Aztecs: An Interpretation*. Cambridge: Univ. Press.

————. 1993. "Fierce and Unnatural Cruelty: Cortés and the Conquest of Mexico," in Greenblatt, ed., *New World Encounters*.

Coase, R. H. 1994. *Essays on Economics and Economists*. Chicago: Univ. of Chicago Press.

Coates, David, and John Hillard, eds. 1986. *The Economic Decline of Modern Britain: The Debate Between Left and Right*. London: Harvester Wheatsheaf.

Cobb, James C. 1984. *Industrialization and Southern Society 1877–1984*. Lexington, KY: Univ. of Kentucky Press.

————. 1988. "Beyond Planters and Industrialists: A New Perspective on the New South," *J. Southern Hist.*, 54 (February): 45–68.

Cobo, Father Bernabe. 1653/1979. *History of the Inca Empire*. Trans. and ed. by Roland Hamilton. Austin: Univ. of Texas Press.

Cochet, François, and Gérard Marie Henry. 1995. *Les révolutions industrielles: Processus historiques, développements économiques*. Paris: Armand Colin.

Coe, David T., and Elhanan Helpman. 1995. "International R&D Spillovers," *Europ. Econ. Rev.*, 39: 859–87. Cambridge, MA: NBER Reprint No. 2018.

———— and Alexander W. Hoffmaister. 1997. "North-South R&D Spillovers," *Econ. J.*, 107 (January): 134–49.

Cohen, Elie. 1996. *La tentation hexagonale: La souveraineté à l'épreuve de la mondialisation*. Paris: Fayard.

Cohen, Roger. 1997. "France vs. U.S.: Warring Views of Capitalism," *New York Times,* Oct. 20, p. 1.

Cohen, Saul B. 1988. "Reflections on the Elimination of Geography at Harvard, 1947–51," *Annals Amer. Assn. Geographers* 78, 1 (March): 148–51.

Cohen, Yves. 1994. "Inventivité organisationnelle et compétitivité: L'interchangeabilité des pièces face à la crise de la machine-outil en France autour de 1900," *Entreprises et histoire,* 5 (June), 53–72.

Coleman, Donald C., and Christine MacLeod. 1986. "Attitudes to New Techniques: British Businessmen 1800–1950," *Econ. Hist. Rev.,* 39.

Collins, K. J., and D. F. Roberts, eds. 1988. *Capacity for Work in the Tropics.* Society for the Study of Human Biology, Symposium 26. Cambridge: Univ. Press.

Confino, Michael. 1960. "Maîtres de forges et ouvriers dans les usines métallurgiques de l'Oural aux XVIIIᵉ–XIXᵉ siècles," *Cahiers du monde russe et soviétique,* I (Janvier–Mars): 239–84.

Conrad, Robert Edgar. 1984/1994. *Children of God's Fire: A Documentary History of Black Slavery in Brazil.* Princeton: Princeton Univ. Press; rev. paperback, University Park, PA: Pennsylvania State Press.

Conze, Werner. 1976. "Sozialgeschichte 1800–1850," in Wolfgang Zorn, ed., *Handbuch der deut. Wirtschafts- u. Sozialgeschichte,* II. *Das 19. und 20. Jahrhundert.* Stuttgart: E. Klett, pp. 426–94.

Cook, Don. 1995. *The Long Fuse: How England Lost the American Colonies, 1760–1785.* New York: Atlantic Monthly Press.

Coppock, D. J. 1956. "The Climacteric of the 1870's: A Critical Note," *Manchester School Econ. and Soc. Studies,* 24, 1 (January): 1–31.

Cornblit, Oscar. 1967. "European Immigrants in Argentine Industry and Politics," in Veliz, ed., *Politics of Conformity,* pp. 221–48.

Cortés Conde, Roberto. 1964. *Corrientes immigratorias y surgimento de industrias en Argentina 1870–1914.* Buenos Aires: Galerna.

Cosandey, David. 1997. *Le secret de l'occident: du miracle passé au marasme présent.* Paris: Arléa.

Cottrell, P. L. 1980. *Industrial Finance 1830–1914: The Finance and Organization of English Manufacturing Industry.* London: Methuen.

———, and D. H. Aldcroft, eds. 1981. *Shipping, Trade and Commerce: Essays in Memory of Ralph Davis.* Leicester: Leicester Univ. Press.

Cottret, Bernard. 1986. "Le Roi, les Lords et les Communes: monarchie mixte et états du royaume en Angleterre (XVIᵉ–XVIIIᵉ siècles)," *Annales E.S.C.,* 1 (janvier–fevrier), 127–50.

Crafts, N. F. R. 1977. "Industrial Revolution in England and France: Some Thoughts on the Question 'Why Was England First?'" *Econ. Hist. Rev.,* 2d ser., 30: 429–41. Reprinted in Mokyr, *Economics of the Industrial Revolution,* pp. 119–31.

———. 1985. *British Economic Growth During the Industrial Revolution.* Oxford: Clarendon Press.

———. 1989. "British Industrialization in an International Context," *J. Interdisc. Hist.,* 19 (Winter): 415–28.

———. 1993. *Can De-industrialization Seriously Damage Your Wealth?* London: Inst. Econ. Affairs.

———. 1995. "The Golden Age of Economic Growth in Western Europe, 1950–1973," *Econ. Hist. Rev.,* 48, 3 (August), 429–47.

———. 1995. "Macroinventions, Economic Growth, and 'Industrial Revolution' in Britain and France," *Econ. Hist. Rev.,* 48, 3 (August), 591–98.

———, and Knick Harley. 1992. "Output Growth and the British Industrial Revolution: A Restatement of the Crafts-Harley View," *Econ. Hist. Rev.,* 45: 703–30.

————, and T. C. Mills. 1994. "The Industrial Revolution as a Macroeconomic Epoch: An Alternative View," *Econ. Hist. Rev.*, 47, 4 (November), 769–75.

Craig, Albert M. 1961. *Chōshū in the Meiji Restoration.* Cambridge, MA: Harvard Univ. Press.

Cranmer-Byng, J. L. 1957–58. "Lord Macartney's Embassy to Peking in 1793 (from Official Chinese Documents)," *J. Oriental Studies,* 1: 117–87.

————. 1962. *An Embassy to China: Being the Journal Kept by Lord Macartney During His Embassy to the Emperor Ch'ien-lung 1793–1794.* London: Longman.

Crawcour, E. Sydney. 1965. "The Tokugawa Heritage," in Lockwood, ed., *The State and Economic Enterprise in Japan,* pp. 17–44.

Crisp, Olga. 1972. "The Pattern of Russia's Industrialization up to 1914," in Léon *et al.,* eds., *L'industrialisation en Europe,* pp. 435–66.

Crombie, A. C. 1953. *Robert Grosseteste and the Origins of Experimental Science 1100–1700.* Oxford: Clarendon Press.

————, ed. 1963. *Scientific Change: Historical Studies in the Intellectual, Social and Technical Conditions for Scientific Discovery and Technical Invention, from Antiquity to the Present.* Symposium on the History of Science, Oxford University, 9–15 July 1961. London: Heinemann.

Crone, Patricia. 1989. *Pre-Industrial Societies.* Oxford: Basil Blackwell.

Crosby, Alfred W., Jr. 1972. *The Columbian Exchange: Biological and Cultural Consequences of 1492.* Westport, CT: Greenwood.

————. 1994. *Germs, Seeds & Animals: Studies in Ecological History.* Armonk, NY: M. E. Sharpe.

Crosland, Maurice. 1967. *The Society of Arcueil: A View of French Science at the Time of Napoleon I.* Cambridge, MA: Harvard Univ. Press.

Crouzet, François. 1980. "Les Français et le 'miracle' anglais," *L'Histoire,* 28: 21–30.

————. 1981. "The Sources of England's Wealth: Some French Views in the Eighteenth Century," in Cottrell and Aldcroft, eds., *Shipping, Trade and Commerce,* pp. 61–79.

————. 1985. *De la supériorité de l'Angleterre sur la France: L'économique et l'imaginaire XVIIᵉ–XXᵉ siècles.* Paris: Perrin.

Crow, John A. 1985. *Spain: The Root and the Flower: An Interpretation of Spain & the Spanish People.* 3rd ed., Berkeley: Univ. of Calif. Press.

Cuenca Esteban, Javier. 1994. "British Textile Prices, 1770–1831: Are British Growth Rates Worth Revising Once Again?" *Econ. Hist. Rev.,* 47, 1 (February), 66–105.

————. 1995. "Further Evidence of Falling Prices of Cotton Cloth, 1768–1816," *Econ. Hist. Rev.,* 48, 1 (February), 145–50.

Cullen, L. M. 1972. *An Economic History of Ireland Since 1660.* London: Batsford.

Cullen, L. M., and T. C. Smout, eds. 1978. *Comparative Aspects of Scottish and Irish Social and Economic History 1600–1900.* Edinburgh: John Donald.

Curtin, Philip D. 1964. *The Image of Africa: British Ideas and Action, 1780–1850.* Madison: Univ. of Wisconsin Press.

————. 1968. "Epidemiology and the Slave Trade, *Pol. Sci. Q.,* 83: 190–216.

————. 1989. *Death by Migration: Europe's Encounter with the Tropical World in the Nineteenth Century.* Cambridge: Univ. Press.

Cusumano, Michael A. 1985. *The Japanese Automobile Industry: Technology and Management at Nissan and Toyota.* Cambridge, MA: Harvard Univ. Press for the Council on East Asian Studies.

Daget, Serge, ed. 1988. *De la traite à l'esclavage: Actes du colloque sur la traite des noirs.* Nantes: Centre de Recherche sur l'Histoire du Monde Atlantique. Paris: Soc. française d'Histoire d'Outre-mer; L'Harmattan.

Danaher, Kevin. 1994. *50 Years Is Enough: The Case Against the World Bank and the International Monetary Fund*. Boston: South End.

Daniels, John, and Christian Daniels. 1988. "The Origin of the Sugarcane Roller Mill," *Technology and Culture*, 29, 3 (July), 493–535.

Darity, William, Jr. 1990. "British Industry and the West Indies Plantations," *Soc. Sci. Hist.*, 14 (Spring), 117–49.

———. 1992. "A Model of 'Original Sin': Rise of the West and Lag of the Rest," *Amer. Econ. Rev.*, 82, 2 (May), 166–71.

Das Gupta, Ashin, and M. N. Pearson, eds. 1987. *India and the Indian Ocean, 1500–1800*. Calcutta: Oxford Univ. Press.

Dasgupta, Partha S. 1993a. *An Inquiry into Well-Being and Destitution*. Oxford: Clarendon Press.

———. 1993b. "Natural Resources in an Age of Substitutability," in A. V. Kneese and J. L. Sweeney, eds., *Handbook of Natural Resource and Energy Economics*. Amsterdam: Elsevier, III, 111–30.

———. 1995a. "Population, Poverty, and the Local Environment," *Scientific American*, 272, 2 (February), 40–45.

———. 1995b. "The Population Problem: Theory and Evidence." *J. Econ. Lit.*, 33, 4 (December): 1879–1902.

———. 1995c. "Nutritional Status, the Capacity for Work and Poverty Traps." In press with *J. Econometrics*.

Daumas, Maurice. 1972. *Scientific Instruments of the Seventeenth and Eighteenth Centuries*. New York: Praeger (translation of French ed. of 1953).

———, and René Taton, eds. 1973. *L'acquisition des techniques par les pays non-initiateurs*. Colloques internationaux du Centre National de la Recherche Scientifique No. 538, Pont-à-Mousson, 28 juin–5 juillet 1970. Paris: Editions du CNRS.

Daunton, M. J. 1989. " 'Gentlemanly Capitalism' and British Industry 1820–1914," *Past & Present*, 122 (February): 119–58.

Davenport-Hines, R. P. T., and Geoffrey Jones, eds. 1989. *British Business in Asia Since 1860*. Cambridge: Univ. Press.

Davids, Karel. 1995. "Openness or Secrecy? Industrial Espionage in the Dutch Republic," *J. Europ. Econ. Hist.*, 24, 2 (Fall): 333–48.

Davidson, Basil. 1992. *The Black Man's Burden: Africa and the Curse of the Nation-State*. New York: Random House; Times Books.

Davis, John A. 1989. "Industrialization in Britain and Europe Before 1850: New Perspectives and Old Problems," in Mathias and Davis, eds., *The First Industrial Revolutions*, pp. 44–68.

Davis, Lance E., and R. A. Huttenback. 1986. *Mammon and the Pursuit of Empire: Political Economy of British Imperialism, 1860–1912*. Cambridge: Univ. Press.

Davis, Ralph. 1973. *The Rise of the Atlantic Economies*. Ithaca: Cornell Univ. Press.

Dawson, Raymond. 1978. *The Chinese Experience*. New York: Charles Scribner's Sons.

Debeir, Jean-Claude, Jean-Paul Deléage, and Daniel Hemery. 1991 [1986]. *In the Servitude of Power: Energy and Civilisation Through the Ages*. London and Atlantic Highlands, NJ: Zed Books.

Decraene, Philippe. 1995. *Lettres d'Afrique entre Cancer et Capricorne*. Paris: Denoel.

Dedieu, Jean-Pierre. 1984. "Responsabilité de l'Inquisition dans le retard économique de l'Espagne? Eléments de réponse," in Amalric and Bennassar, eds., *Aux origines du retard économique de l'Espagne*.

Defoe, Daniel. 1728/1928. *A Plan of the English Commerce, Being a Compleat Prospect of the Trade of This Nation, as well the Home Trade as the Foreign*. Oxford: Basil Blackwell.

De Gregori, Thomas R. 1969. *Technology and the Economic Development of the Tropical African Frontier.* Cleveland: Case Western Reserve.

Deighton, Len. 1993. *Blood, Tears and Folly: An Objective Look at World War II.* New York: HarperCollins.

Denby, David. 1995. "Jungle Fever." *The New Yorker,* 6 November, pp. 118–29.

Denevan, Wm. L., ed. 1976. *The Native Population in the Americas in 1492.* Madison: Univ. of Wisconsin Press.

Dertouzos, Michael L., Richard K. Lester, Robert M. Solow, and the MIT Commission on Industrial Productivity. 1989. *Made in America: Regaining the Productive Edge.* Cambridge, MA: MIT Press.

Desmond, Ray. 1995. *Kew: The History of the Royal Botanic Gardens.* Kew: Harvill with The Royal Botanic Gardens.

Devoto, L. F. J., and G. Rosoli, eds. 1988. *L'Italia nella società argentina.* Rome: Centro Studi Emigrazione.

De Vries—see Vries.

Dewey, Clive J., ed. 1988. *Arrested Development in India: The Historical Dimension.* New Delhi: Manohar.

Diamond, Jared M. 1992. *The Third Chimpanzee: The Evolution and Future of the Human Animal.* New York: HarperCollins.

———. 1994. "Ecological Collapses of Past Civilizations," *Proc. Amer. Philosoph. Soc.,* 138, 3 (September): 363–70.

———. 1997. *Guns, Germs, and Steel: The Fates of Human Societies.* New York: W. W. Norton.

Diamond, Stanley. 1974. *In Search of the Primitive: A Critique of Civilization.* New Brunswick, NJ: Transaction Books.

Dickinson, John A., and Marianne Mahn-Lot. 1991. *1492–1992: Les Européens découvrent l'Amérique.* Lyons: Presses Universitaires de Lyon.

Dickson, D. 1978. "Aspects of the Rise and Decline of the Irish Cotton Industry," in Cullen and Smout, eds., *Comparative Aspects,* pp. 100–15.

Dickson, P. G. M. 1967. *The Financial Revolution in England: A Study in the Development of Public Credit, 1688–1740.* London: Macmillan.

Diffie, Bailey W. 1960. *Prelude to Empire: Portugal Overseas Before Henry the Navigator.* Lincoln: Univ. of Nebraska Press.

———, and George D. Winius. 1977. *Europe and the World in the Age of Expansion.* Vol. I. *Foundations of the Portuguese Empire 1415–1580.* Minneapolis: Univ. of Minnesota Press.

Dintenfass, Michael. 1992. *The Decline of Industrial Britain 1870–1980.* London: Routledge.

———. 1996. "Converging Accounts, Misleading Metaphors, and Persistent Doubts: Reflections on the Historiography of Britain's 'Decline,' " in McCloskey and Dormois, eds., "British Industrial 'Decline' Reconsidered," pp. 1–37.

Disney, A. R. 1978. *Twilight of the Pepper Empire: Portuguese Trade in Southwest India in the Early Seventeenth Century.* Cambridge, MA: Harvard Univ. Press.

Dixon, Chris. 1991. *South East Asia in the World-Economy.* Cambridge: Univ. Press.

Dixon, William J., and Terry Boswell. 1996. "Dependency, Disarticulation, and Denominator Effects: Another Look at Foreign Capital Penetration," *Amer. J. Sociol.,* 102, 2 (September): 543–62.

———. 1996. "Differential Productivity, Negative Externalities, and Foreign Capital Dependency: Reply to Firebaugh," *Amer. J. Sociol.,* 102, 2 (September): 576–84.

Dobbin, Christine. 1996. *Asian Entrepreneurial Minorities: Conjoint Communities in the Making of the World Economy, 1570–1940.* Richmond, Surrey: Curzon Press.

Dohrn-van Rossum, Gerhard. 1996. *History of the Hour: Clocks and Modern Temporal Orders.* Chicago: Univ. of Chicago Press.

Domar, Evsey. 1970. "Causes of Slavery or Serfdom: A Hypothesis," *J. Econ. Hist.*, 30 (March): 18–32.

Dooley, Brendon. 1995. "Processo a Galileo" (English translation), forthcoming in *Belfagor.*

———. 1995. "The *Storia letteraria d'Italia* and the Rehabilitation of Jesuit Science." Forthcoming in the *Rivista storica italiana.*

Dore, Ronald. 1987. *Taking Japan Seriously: A Confucian Perspective on Leading Economic Issues.* Stanford: Stanford Univ. Press.

Dormois, Jean-Pierre. 1997. *L'économie française face à la concurrence britannique à la veille de 1914.* Paris: L'Harmattan.

Drèze, Jean. 1995. "Famine Prevention in Africa: Some Experiences and Lessons," in Drèze, Sen, and Hussain, eds., *Political Economy of Hunger*, pp. 554–93.

———, Amartya Sen, and Athar Hussain, eds. 1995. *The Political Economy of Hunger: Selected Essays.* Oxford: Clarendon Press.

Drouin de Bercy. 1818. *L'Europe et l'Amérique comparées.* 2 vols. Paris, chez Rosa. Reprinted 1968, Upper Saddle River, NJ: Gregg Press.

Dublin, Thomas. 1979. *Women at Work: The Transformation of Work and Community in Lowell, Massachusetts, 1826–1860.* New York: Columbia Univ. Press.

Dubreuil, René. 1910. *De la condition des Chinois et de leur role économique en Indochine.* Bar-sur-Seine: C. Caillard.

Dumas, Maurice. 1953/1972. *Scientific Instruments of the Seventeenth and Eighteenth Centuries.* New York: Praeger.

Dunn, Richard S. 1972. *Sugar and Slaves: The Rise of the Planter Class in the English West Indies, 1624–1713.* Chapel Hill: Univ. of North Carolina Press; New York: W. W. Norton.

Du Plessis, Robert, and Martha C. Howell. 1982. "Reconsidering the Early Modern Urban Economy: The Cases of Leiden and Lille," *Past and Present*, 94 (February).

Durand, Robert. 1992. *Histoire du Portugal.* Paris: Hatier.

Duus, Peter. 1984. "Economic Dimensions of Meiji Imperialism: The Case of Korea," in Myers and Peattie, eds., *Japanese Colonial Empire*, pp. 128–63.

———. 1989. "Zaikabo: Japanese Cotton Mills in China, 1895–1937," in Duus *et al.*, eds., *Japanese Informal Empire*, pp. 65–100.

———, Ramon H. Mayers, and Mark R. Peattie, eds. 1989. *The Japanese Informal Empire in China, 1895–1937.* Princeton: Princeton Univ. Press.

Eamon, William. 1990. "From the Secrets of Nature to Public Knowledge," in Lindberg and Westman, eds., *Reappraisals*, pp. 333–65.

Easterlin, Richard. 1995. "Industrial Revolution and Mortality Revolution: Two of a Kind?" *J. Evolution. Econ.*, 5: 393–408.

Easterly, William, Michael Kremer, Lant Pritchett, and Lawrence H. Summers. 1993. "Good Policy or Good Luck? Country Growth Performance and Temporary Shocks," *J. Monetary Econ.*, 32: 459–83.

Eaton, Jonathan, and Samuel Kortum. 1995. "Engines of Growth: Domestic and Foreign Sources of Innovation." Boston University, Inst. for Economic Development, Discussion Paper Series 63.

Eatwell, John. 1982. *Whatever Happened to Britain? The Economics of Decline.* Oxford: Univ. Press; New York: Oxford Univ. Press, 1984.

Eckstein, Otto, Christopher Caton, Roger Brinner, and Peter Duprey. 1984. *The DRI Report on U.S. Manufacturing Industries.* New York: McGraw-Hill.

Edgerton, David. 1987. "Science and Technology in British Business History," *Business Hist. Rev.*, 29.

———. 1996. *Science, Technology, and the British Industrial "Decline," 1870–1970.* Cambridge: Univ. Press.

Edgerton, Samuel Y., Jr. 1991. *The Heritage of Giotto's Geometry: Art and Science on the Eve of the Scientific Revolution*. Ithaca: Cornell Univ. Press.

Edmonds, Richard Louis. 1985. *Northern Frontiers of Qing China and Tokugawa Japan: A Comparative Study of Frontier Policy*. Chicago: Dept. of Geography, Univ. of Chicago.

Edwardes, Michael. 1963. *The Battle of Plassey and the Conquest of Bengal*. London: Batsford; New York: Macmillan.

Edwards, Sebastian. 1995. *Crisis and Reform in Latin America: From Despair to Hope*. New York: Oxford Univ. Press for the World Bank.

Eichengreen, Barry. 1988. "The Australian Recovery of the 1930s in International Comparative Perspective," in R. G. Gregory and N. G. Butlin, eds., *Recovery from the Depression: Australia and the World Economy in the 1930s*. Cambridge: Univ. Press.

Eisenstadt, Shmuel N. 1963. *The Political Systems of Empires*. New York: Free Press.

————, ed. 1968. *The Protestant Ethic and Modernization: A Comparative View*. New York: Basic Books.

Eisler, Benita, ed. 1977. *The Lowell Offering: Writings by New England Mill Women (1840–1845)*. Philadelphia: Lippincott.

Elbaum, Bernard, and William Lazonick, eds. 1989. *The Decline of the British Economy*. Oxford: Clarendon Press.

Elisseeff, Danielle. 1986. *Hideyoshi: Bâtisseur du Japon moderne*. Paris: Fayard.

Elliott, John H. 1970. *The Old World and the New 1492–1650*. Cambridge: Univ. Press; Canto ed., 1992.

————. 1989. *Spain and Its World 1500–1700*. New Haven: Yale Univ. Press.

Ellis, Henry. 1817. *Journal of the Proceedings of the Late Embassy to China; Comprising a Correct Narrative of the Public Transactions . . . etc*. London. Reviewed in the *Quarterly Review*, Vol. 17, No. 34 (July): 463–506. Ellis was Third Commissioner of the embassy.

Eltis, David. 1987. *Economic Growth and the Ending of the Transatlantic Slave Trade*. New York: Oxford Univ. Press.

Elvin, Mark. 1973. *The Pattern of the Chinese Past: A Social and Economic Interpretation*. Stanford: Stanford Univ. Press.

Emmanuel, Arghiri. 1972. "White Settler Colonialism and the Myth of Investment Imperialism," *New Left Rev.*, 73 (May–June), 35–57.

————. 1974. "Myths of Development versus Myths of Underdevelopment," *New Left Rev.*, 85 (May–June), 61–82.

Endelman, Todd M. 1990. *Radical Assimilation in English Jewish History, 1656–1945*. Bloomington: Indiana State Univ. Press.

Endrei, Walter. 1990. "Manufacturing a Piece of Woollen Cloth in Medieval Flanders: How Many Work Hours?" in Aerts and Munro, eds., *Textiles of the Low Countries*, pp. 14–23.

Engerman, Stanley L. 1972. "The Slave Trade and British Capital Formation in the Eighteenth Century: A Comment on the Williams Thesis," *Business Hist. Rev.*, 46, 4: 430–43.

————. 1982. "Economic Adjustments to Emancipation in the United States and the British West Indies," *J. Interdiscipl. Hist.*, 12 (Autumn), 191–220.

————. 1983. "Contract Labor, Sugar, and Technology in the Nineteenth Century," *J. Econ. Hist.*, 43 (September), 635–59.

Engerman, Stanley L., and Kenneth L. Sokoloff. 1994. "Factor Endowments, Institutions, and Differential Paths of Growth Among New World Economies: A View from Economic Historians of the United States." NBER Working Paper Series on Historical Factors in Long Run Growth, Historical Paper No. 66.

Erber, Fabio Stefano. 1985. "The Development of the 'Electronics Complex' and Government Policies in Brazil," *World Development*, 13 (March): 293–310.

Erickson, Charlotte. 1957. *American Industry and the European Immigrant 1860–1885*. Cambridge, MA: Harvard Univ. Press.

Erman, J. P., and F. Reclam. 1782–99. *Mémoires pour servir à l'histoire des réfugiés françois dans les états du roi*. Berlin: J. Jasperd.

Esposito, John L. 1995. *The Islamic Threat: Myth or Reality?* 2d ed., New York: Oxford Univ. Press.

Esquer, Gabriel, ed. 1951. *L'anticolonialisme au XVIIIᵉ: Histoire philosophique et politique des établissements et du commerce des Européens dans les Deux Indes par l'abbé Raynal*. Paris: P.U.F.

Etemad, Bouda, Jean Batou, and Thomas David, eds. 1995. *Pour une histoire économique sociale et internationale: Mélanges offerts à Paul Bairoch*. Geneva: Editions Passé Présent.

Evans, Peter B. 1986. "State, Capital, and the Transformation of Dependence: The Brazilian Computer Case," *World Development*, 14 (July), 791–808.

Evenson, Robert. 1988. "Technology, Productivity Growth, and Economic Development," in Ranis and Schultz, eds., *State of Development Economics*, pp. 486–536.

Fabian, J. 1983. *Time and the Other: How Anthropology Makes Its Object*. New York: Columbia Univ. Press.

Fager Jan. 1994. "Technology and International Differences in Growth Rates," *J. Econ. Literature*, 32 (September): 1147–75.

Fairbank, John K. 1962. *The United States and China*. 2d ed.; New York: Viking.

Fairbank, John K., and Edwin O. Reischauer. 1960. *East Asia: The Great Tradition*. Boston: Houghton Mifflin.

Fairnie, D. A. 1962. "Commercial Empire of the Atlantic, 1607–1783," *Econ. Hist. Rev.*, 15: 205–18.

Faith, Nicholas. 1990/1994. *The World the Railways Made*. London: Bodley Head; Pimlico.

Fallows, James. 1995. *Looking at the Sun: The Rise of the New East Asian Economic and Political System*. New York: Vintage.

Farley, John. 1991. *Bilharzia: A History of Imperial Tropical Medicine*. Cambridge: Univ. Press.

Faroqhi, Suraiya. 1986. "The Venetian Presence in the Ottoman Empire (1600–1630)," *J. Europ. Econ. Hist.*, 15, 2 (Fall): 345–84.

Favier, Jean. 1991. *Les grandes découvertes d'Alexandre à Magellan*. Paris: Fayard.

Fay, Stephen. 1996. *The Collapse of Barings*. London: Arrow Books; New York: Norton.

Fazal, Qazi M. 1994. "Let's Pretend Nature Exists: Measuring the Impact of Climate on Economic Growth." Harvard College, Senior Honors Essay in Economics.

Feachem, Richard G. A., Tord Kjellstrom, *et al.*, eds. 1992. *The Health of Adults in the Developing World*. Oxford: Oxford Univ. Press for the World Bank.

Felix, David. 1956. "Profit Inflation and Industrial Growth: The Historic Record and Contemporary Analogies," *QJE*, 70 (August), 441–63.

Feltham, Owen. 1660. *A Brief Character of the Low Countries Under the States, Being Three Weeks Observations of the Vices & Virtues of the Inhabitants*. London.

Fernandez, M. P. and P. C. 1996. "Precision Timekeepers of Tokugawa Japan and the Evolution of the Japanese Domestic Clock," *Technology & Culture*, 37, 2 (April): 221–48.

Fernandez-Armesto, Felipe. 1987. *Before Columbus: Exploration and Colonisation from the Mediterranean to the Atlantic, 1229–1492*. "New Studies in Medieval History," ed. Maurice Keen. London: Macmillan.

————. 1991. *Columbus.* Oxford: Oxford Univ. Press.

————. 1992. " 'Aztec' Auguries and Memories of the Conquest of Mexico," *Renaissance Studies,* 6: 287–305.

————. 1995. *Millennium: A History of the Last Thousand Years.* New York: Charles Scribner's Sons.

Ferns, H. S. 1960. *Britain and Argentina in the Nineteenth Century.* Oxford: Oxford Univ. Press.

Ferrie, Joseph P. 1996. "The Entry into the U.S. Labor Market of Antebellum European Immigrants, 1840–60." NBER Working Paper Series on Historical Factors in Long Run Growth, Historical Paper No. 88.

Feshbach, Murray, and Alfred Friendly, Jr. 1992. *Ecocide in the USSR: Health and Nature Under Siege.* New York: Basic Books.

Feuerwerker, Albert. 1978. "A White Horse May or May Not Be a Horse, But Megahistory Is Not Economic History," *Modern China,* 4, 3 (July), 331–50.

————. 1990. "Chinese Economic History in Comparative Perspective," in Ropp, ed., *Heritage of China,* pp. 224–41.

Field, Michael. 1994. *Inside the Arab World.* Cambridge, MA: Harvard Univ. Press.

Fieldhouse, D. K. 1973. *Economics and Empire 1830–1914.* Ithaca: Cornell Univ. Press.

————. 1994. *Merchant Capital and Economic Decolonization: The United Africa Company, 1929–1987.* Oxford: Clarendon Press.

Firebaugh, Glenn. 1992. "Growth Effects of Foreign and Domestic Investment," *Amer. J. Sociol.,* 98: 105–30.

————. 1996. "Does Foreign Capital Harm Poor Nations? New Estimates Based on Dixon and Boswell's Measures of Capital Penetration," *Amer. J. Sociology,* 102, 2 (September): 563–75.

Fischer, David Hackett. 1989. *Albion's Seed: Four British Folkways in America.* New York: Oxford Univ. Press.

Fischer, Wolfram, R. Marvin McInnis, and Jürgen Schneider, eds. 1986. *The Emergence of a World Economy 1500–1914.* Papers of the Ninth International Congress of Economic History. 2 vols. Wiesbaden: Franz Steiner.

Fish, Carl Russell. 1927. *The Rise of the Common Man 1830–1850.* "A History of American Life," Vol. VI. New York: Macmillan.

Fisher, Charles A. 1968. "The Britain of the East? A Study in the Geography of Imitation," *Modern Asian Studies,* 2, 4: 343–76.

Fisher, F. J. 1935. "The Development of the London Food Market, 1540–1640," *Econ. Hist. Rev.,* 5, 2 (April): 46–64.

————, ed. 1961. *Essays in the Economic and Social History of Tudor and Stuart England.* Cambridge: Univ. Press.

Fisher, H. E. S. 1963. "Anglo-Portuguese Trade, 1700–1750," *Econ. Hist. Rev.,* 16: 219–33.

Fisk, Robert. 1996. "Sept journées ordinaires dans la vie des Algériens," *Courrier international,* 319 (12–18 Dec.), 5–7.

Fitton, R. S. 1989. *The Arkwrights: Spinners of Fortune.* Manchester: Manchester Univ. Press.

Fleming, Donald. 1952. "Latent Heat and the Invention of the Watt Engine," *Isis,* 43: 3–5.

Fletcher, Anthony, and Peter Roberts, eds. 1994. *Religion, Culture, and Society in Early Modern Britain; Essays in Honour of Patrick Collinson.* Cambridge: Univ. Press.

Flink, James J. 1996. "Unplanned Obsolescence," *Invention and Technology,* 12, 1: 58–62.

Flinn, M. W. See Svedenstierna.

Floud, Roderick, and D. N. McCloskey, eds. 1994. *The Economic History of Britain, 1700 to the Present*. 2d ed., 3 vols. Cambridge: Univ. Press.

Fluehr-Lobban, Carolyn. 1995. "Cultural Relativism and Universal Rights," *Chronicle of Higher Education*, 9 June, pp. B1–B2.

Fogel, Robert W. 1989. *Without Consent or Contract: The Rise and Fall of American Slavery*. New York: W. W. Norton.

Fohlen, Claude. 1956. *L'industrie textile au temps du Second Empire*. Paris: Plon.

Foley, Vernard, Darlene Sedlock, Carole Widule, and David Ellis. 1988. "Besson, Da Vinci, and the Evolution of the Pendulum: Some Findings and Observations," *History and Technology*, 6, 1: 1–43.

Foreman-Peck, James. 1995. *A History of the World Economy: International Economic Relations Since 1850*. 2d ed., Hemel Hempstead: Harvester Wheatsheaf.

Fortescue, John. 1926. *The Governance of England,* ed. Charles Plummer. 2d ed., London Oxford Univ. Press; Humphrey Milford.

Foster, William, ed. 1940. *The Voyages of Sir James Lancaster to Brazil and the East Indies 1591–1603*. London: Hakluyt Society.

Fox, Robert, and George Weisz, eds. 1980. *The Organization of Science and Technology in France 1808–1914*. Cambridge: Univ. Press.

Fox, Robert, and Anna Guagnini, eds. 1993. *Education, Technology, and Industrial Performance in Europe, 1850–1939*. Cambridge: Univ. Press.

Francks, Penelope. 1992. *Japanese Economic Development: Theory and Practice*. London: Routledge.

Frank, Andre Gunder. 1998. *ReOrient: Global Economy in the Asian Age*. Berkeley: University of California Press.

Freedeman, Charles E. 1979. *Joint-stock Enterprise in France, 1807–1867: From Privileged Companies to Modern Corporations*. Chapel Hill: Univ. North Carolina Press.

———. 1993. *The Triumph of Corporate Capitalism in France 1867–1914*. Rochester: Univ. of Rochester Press.

Freeman, Christopher. 1982. *The Economics of Industrial Innovation*. 2d ed., Cambridge, MA: MIT Press.

———. 1992. *The Economics of Hope: Essays on Technical Change, Economic Growth and the Environment*. London and New York: Pinter.

Freudenberger, Herman. 1996. "The Schwarzenberg Bank: A Forgotten Contributor to Austrian Economic Development, 1788–1830," *Austrian History Yearbook*, 27: 41–64.

Freyre, Gilberto. 1971. *The Masters and the Slaves: A Study in the Development of Brazilian Civilization*. 2d English-lang. ed., New York: Knopf.

Fridenson, Patrick, and André Straus, eds. 1987. *Le capitalisme français 19ᵉ–20ᵉ siècles: blocages et dynamismes d'une croissance*. Paris: Fayard.

Fried, Aaron L. 1988. *The Weary Titan: Britain and the Experience of Relative Decline, 1895–1905*. Princeton: Princeton Univ. Press.

Friedman, David. 1983. "Beyond the Age of Ford: The Strategic Basis of the Japanese Success in Automobiles," in Zysman and Tyson, eds., *American Industry in International Competition*, pp. 350–90.

Friedman, Thomas L. 1995. "Egypt Runs for the Train," *New York Times*, 18 October, p. A-23.

Fuhrmann, Joseph T. 1972. *The Origins of Capitalism in Russia: Industry and Progress in the Sixteenth and Seventeenth Centuries*. Chicago: Quadrangle Books.

Fujimura-Fanselow, Kumiko, and Atsuko Kameda, eds. 1995. *Japanese Women: New Feminist Perspectives on the Past, Present, and Future*. New York: Feminist Press at the City University.

Fukazawa, Hiroshi. 1982. "Non-Agricultural Production: Maharashtra and the Deccan," in Raychaudhuri and Habib, eds., *Cambridge Economic History of India*, I, 308–15.

Fukui, Haruhiro. 1992. "The Japanese State and Economic Development: A Profile of a Nationalist-Paternalist Capitalist State," in Appelbaum and Henderson, eds., *States and Development in the Asian Pacific Rim*, pp. 199–225.

Furner, Mary O., and Barry Supple, eds. 1990. *The State and Economic Knowledge: The American and British Experiences*. New York: Cambridge Univ. Press for the Woodrow Wilson International Center for Scholars.

Furnivall, J. S. 1939. *Netherlands India: A Study of Plural Economy*. Cambridge: Univ. Press.

———. 1948. *Colonial Policy and Practice: A Comparative Study of Burma and Netherlands India*. Cambridge: Univ. Press.

Furtado, Celso. 1963. *The Economic Growth of Brazil: A Survey from Colonial to Modern Times*. Berkeley: Univ. of Calif. Press.

Gabor, Andrea. 1992. *The Man Who Discovered Quality. How W. Edwards Deming Brought the Quality Revolution to America—The Stories of Ford, Xerox, and GM*. New York: Penguin.

Galenson, Walter, and Konosuke Odaka. 1976. "The Japanese Labor Market," in Patrick and Rosovsky, eds., *Asia's New Giant*, pp. 587–671.

Gallagher, John, and Ronald Robinson. 1953. "The Imperialism of Free Trade," *Econ. Hist. Rev.*, 2d ser., 6, 1: 1–15.

Gallagher, Nancy Elizabeth, ed. 1995. *Approaches to the History of the Middle East: Interviews with Leading Middle East Historians*. Reading: Garnet.

Gamble, A. 1985. *Britain in Decline: Economic Policy, Political Strategy and the British State*. 2d ed., London: Macmillan.

Garcia S., Daniel D. 1993. "Economic Growth and Stagnation in the Colonial Americas: An Exploratory Essay," in Bernecker and Tobler, eds., *Development and Underdevelopment in America*, pp. 51–87.

Garrett, Laurie. 1994. *The Coming Plague: Newly Emerging Diseases in a World Out of Balance*. New York: Farrar, Strauss & Giroux.

Garrisson, Janine. 1985. *L'Edit de Nantes et sa révocation: Histoire d'une intolérance*. Paris: Seuil.

Gartman, David. 1986. *Auto Slavery: The Labor Process in the American Automobile Industry, 1897–1950*. New Brunswick: Rutgers Univ. Press.

Gates, David M. 1972. *Man and His Environment: Climate*. New York: Harper & Row.

Gay, Yves. 1994. "Matteo Ricci et l'introduction de la mesure du temps en Chine," *Bull. de l'Assn nat. des Collectionneurs et amateurs d'horlogerie ancienne*, 71 (automne–hiver), 5–34.

Geiger, Reed G. 1974. *The Anzin Coal Company, 1800–1833: Big Business in the Early Stages of the French Industrial Revolution*. Newark, DE: Univ. of Delaware Press.

Gellner, Ernest. 1988. *Plough, Sword and Book: The Structure of Human History*. London: Collins Harvill.

Gemery, Henry A., and Jan S. Hogendorn, eds. 1979. *The Uncommon Market: Essays in the Economic History of the Atlantic Slave Trade*. New York: Academic Press.

Gennaro, Giuseppe de. 1984. *Industrializzazione et Mezzogiorno: Le manufatture tessili nel Nord Barese, 1771–1816*. Naples: ESI.

———. 1990. "The Mechanical Spinner and Resistance to Change in the Mezzogiorno," *J. Regional Policy* (English ed., *Mezzogiorno d'Europa*), 10, 2 (April–June): 273–86.

Gereffi, Gary, and Donald L. Wyman, eds. 1990. *Manufacturing Miracles: Paths of Industrialization in Latin America and East Asia*. Princeton: Princeton Univ. Press.

Germani, Gino. 1962. *Politica y sociedad en una época de transición: De la sociedad tradicional a la sociedad de masas.* Buenos Aires: Paidos.

Gernet, Jacques. 1985. *China and the Christian Impact: A Conflict of Cultures.* Cambridge: Univ. Press.

Gerschenkron, Alexander. 1962. *Economic Backwardness in Historical Perspective: A Book of Essays.* Cambridge, MA: Harvard Univ. Press.

———. 1968. *Continuity in History and Other Essays.* Cambridge, MA: Harvard Univ. Press.

———. 1968. "Die Vorbedingungen der europäischen Industrialisierungen im 19. Jahrhundert," in Wolfram Fischer, ed., *Wirtschafts- und Sozialgeschichtliche Probleme der frühen Industrialisierung.* Berlin: Colloquium, pp. 21–28.

———. 1977. *An Economic Spurt That Failed: Four Lectures in Austrian History.* Princeton: Princeton Univ. Press.

Gibb, George Sweet. 1950. *The Saco-Lowell Shops: Textile Machinery Building in New England 1813–1949.* Cambridge, MA: Harvard Univ. Press.

Gibbons, Herbert Adams. 1916. *The Foundation of the Ottoman Empire.* Oxford: Clarendon Press.

Giblin, James. 1990. "Trypanosomiasis Control in African History: An Evaded Issue?" *J. African Hist.,* 31: 59–80.

Gibson, Charles. 1964. *The Aztecs Under Spanish Rule. A History of the Indians of the Valley of Mexico, 1519–1810.* Stanford: Stanford Univ. Press.

———. 1966. *Spain in America.* New York: Harper & Row.

Giedion, Siegfried. 1941. *Space, Time, and Architecture.* Cambridge, MA: Harvard Univ. Press.

———. 1948–1969. *Mechanization Takes Command: A Contribution to Anonymous History.* Oxford: Univ. Press; New York: W. W. Norton.

Gies, Frances and Joseph. 1994. *Cathedral, Forge, and Waterwheel: Technology and Invention in the Middle Ages.* New York: HarperCollins.

Gilder, George. 1981. *Wealth and Poverty.* New York: Basic Books.

Gill, Ranjit. 1998. *Asia under Siege: How the Asian Miracle Went Wrong.* Singapore: Epic Management Services.

Gille, Bertrand. 1959. *La banque et le crédit en France de 1815 à 1848.* Paris: P.U.F.

———. 1968. *La sidérurgie française au XIX^e siècle.* Geneva: Droz.

Gillet, Marcel. 1973. *Les charbonnages du nord de la France au XIX^e siècle.* Paris and The Hague: Mouton.

Gilmartin, Christina K., Gail Hershatter, Lisa Rofel, and Tyrene White, eds. 1994. *Engendering China: Women, Culture, and the State.* Cambridge, MA: Harvard Univ. Press.

Gimpel, Jean. 1976. *The Medieval Machine: The Industrial Revolution of the Middle Ages.* Harmondsworth: Penguin.

———. 1995. *The End of the Future: The Waning of the High-Tech World.* London: Adamantine Press.

Gingerich, Owen. 1993. *The Eye of Heaven: Ptolemy, Copernicus, Kepler.* New York: American Inst. of Physics.

Girard, Albert. 1932. *Le commerce français à Seville et a Cadix au temps des Habsbourg: Contribution à l'étude du commerce étranger en Espagne aux XVI^e et XVII^e siècles.* Paris: Boccard; Bordeaux: Féret et Fils.

Gleave, M. Barrie, ed. 1992. *Tropical African Development: Geographical Perspectives.* Burnt Hill, Harlow: Longman.

Glejser, Herbert. 1995. "National X-Efficiency," in Etemad, Batou, and David, eds., *Pour une histoire économique,* pp. 301–09.

Gluck, Carol. 1985. *Japan's Modern Myths: Ideology in the Late Meiji Period.* Princeton: Princeton Univ. Press.

Godinho, Vitorino Magalhaes. 1963–65. *Os descobrimentos e a economia mundial.* 2 vols. Lisbon: Arcadia.

———. 1993. "Rôle du Portugal aux XV$^e$–XVI$^e$ siècles—Qu'est-ce que découvrir veut dire? Les nouveaux mondes et un monde nouveau," in Thorens *et al.*, eds., *1492*, pp. 55–92.

Godley, Michael R. 1981. *The Mandarin-Capitalists from Nanyang: Overseas Chinese Enterprise in the Modernization of China 1893–1911.* Cambridge: Univ. Press.

Golay, F. H. 1976. "Southeast Asia: The 'Colonial Drain' Revisited," in C. D. Cowan and O. W. Wolters, eds., *Southeast Asian History and Historiography.* Ithaca: Cornell Univ. Press, pp. 368–87.

Goldman, Marshall. 1956. "The Relocation and Growth of the Pre-Revolutionary Russian Ferrous Metal Industry, *Explor. Entrepr. Hist.*, 9, 1 (October): 19–36.

Goldstone, Jack A. 1987. "Cultural Orthodoxy, Risk, and Innovation: The Divergence of East and West in the Early Modern World," *Sociological Theory*, 5 (Fall): 119–35.

———. 1991. "The Causes of Long Waves in Early Modern Economic History," *Research in Econ. Hist.*, Suppl. 6: 51–92.

———. 1996. "Gender, Work, and Culture: Why the Industrial Revolution Came Early to England But Late to China." *Sociological Perspectives*, 39, 1 (Spring): 1–20.

Gomez, Thomas. 1992. *L'invention de l'Amérique: Rêve et réalités de la conquête.* Paris: Aubier.

Gommans, Jos. 1995. "Trade and Civilization Around the Bay of Bengal, c. 1650–1800," *Itinerario*, 19, 3: 82–108.

Good, David F. 1984. *The Economic Rise of the Habsburg Empire 1750–1914.* Berkeley: Univ. of Calif. Press.

Goodman, David. 1988. *Power and Penury: Government, Technology and Science in Philip II's Spain.* Cambridge: Univ. Press.

———. 1992. "The Scientific Revolution in Spain and Portugal," in Porter and Teich, eds., *The Scientific Revolution.*

Goodman, Jordan. 1993. *Tobacco in History: The Cultures of Dependence.* London: Routledge.

Goodwin, Jan. 1994. *Price of Honor: Muslim Women Lift the Veil of Silence on the Islamic World.* Boston: Little, Brown.

Goody, Jack. 1996. *The East in the West.* Cambridge: Univ. Press.

Gordon, Andrew. 1985. *The Evolution of Labor Relations in Japan: Heavy Industry, 1853–1955.* Cambridge, MA: Harvard, Council on East Asian Studies.

Gordon, David M. 1996. *Fat and Mean: The Corporate Squeeze of Working Americans and the Myth of Managerial "Downsizing."* New York: Martin Kessler, The Free Press.

Gordon, Murray. 1989. *Slavery in the Arab World.* New York: New Amsterdam. French ed.: *L'esclavage dans le monde arabe.* Paris: Robert Laffont, 1987.

Gordon, Robert B. 1988. "Who Turned the Mechanical Ideal into Mechanical Reality?" *Technology and Culture*, 29, 4 (October), 744–78.

Goris, J. A. 1925. *Etude sur les colonies marchandes méridionales (Portugais, Espagnols, Italiens) à Anvers de 1488 à 1567: Contribution à l'histoire des débuts du capitalisme moderne.* Louvain: Librairie universitaire.

Gough, Leo. 1998. *Asia Meltdown: The End of the Miracle?* Oxford: Capstone.

Gourou, Pierre. 1983. *Terres de bonne espérance: Le monde tropical.* 2d ed., Paris: Plon.

Graham, A. C. 1973. "China, Europe, and the Origins of Modern Science: Needham's 'The Grand Titration,' " in Nakayama and Sivin, eds., *Chinese Science.*

Gray, H. L. 1924. "The Production and Exportation of English Woollens in the Fourteenth Century," *Engl. Hist. Rev.*, 39: 13–35.

Greasley, David, and Les Oxley. 1994. "Rehabilitation Sustained: The Industrial Revolution as a Macroeconomic Epoch," *Econ. Hist. Rev.*, 47, 4 (November): 760–68.

Green, William A. 1986. "The New World and the Rise of European Capitalist Hegemony: Some Historiographical Perspectives," *Itinerario*, 10, 2: 53–68.

Greenberg, Dolores. 1982. "Reassessing the Power Patterns of the Industrial Revolution: An Anglo-American Comparison," *Amer. Hist. Rev.*, 87: 1237–61.

Greenberg, Michael. 1951. *British Trade and the Opening of China 1800–42*. Cambridge: Univ. Press.

Greenblatt, Stephen, ed. 1993. *New World Encounters*. Berkeley: Univ. of California Press.

Greenfeld, Liah. 1992. *Nationalism: Five Roads to Modernity*. Cambridge, MA: Harvard Univ. Press.

———. 1995. "The Worth of Nations: Some Economic Implications of Nationalism," *Critical Review*, 9, 4 (Fall): 555–84.

Grenet, Micheline. 1994. *La passion des astres au XVII<sup>e</sup> siècle: De l'astrologie à l'astronomie*. Paris: Hachette.

Griffin, Charles C. 1949. "Economic and Social Aspects of the Era of Spanish-American Independence," *Hisp. Amer. Hist. Rev.*, 29: 170–87.

Griffin, Keith. 1978. "The Roots of Underdevelopment: Reflections on the Chinese Experience," *Modern China*, 4, 3: 351–57.

Griffin, Keith, and John Gurley. 1985. "Radical Analyses of Imperialism, the Third World, and the Transition to Socialism: A Survey Article," *J. Econ. Lit.*, 23 (September), 1089–1143.

Griffiths, Richard T. 1979. *Industrial Retardation in the Netherlands 1830–1850*. The Hague: Martinus Nijhoff.

Grigg, David. 1970. *The Harsh Lands: A Study in Agricultural Development*. London: Macmillan.

———. 1980. *Population Growth and Agrarian Change: An Historical Perspective*. Cambridge: Univ. Press.

———. 1982. *The Dynamics of Agricultural Change: The Historical Experience*. London: Hutchinson.

Griliches, Zvi. 1995. "The Discovery of the Residual: A Historical Note." Harvard Inst. Economic Research, Discussion Paper No. 1742.

Grossman, Gene M., and Elhanan Helpman. 1991. *Innovation and Growth in the Global Economy*. Cambridge, MA: MIT Press.

Grove, Richard H. 1995. *Green Imperialism: Colonial Expansion, Tropical Island Edens, and the Origins of Environmentalism, 1600–1860*. Cambridge: Univ. Press.

Gruzinski, Serge. 1987/1992. *The Aztecs: Rise and Fall of an Empire*. New York: Harry N. Abrams, "Discoveries."

Guerlac, Henry. 1979. "Some Areas for Further Newtonian Studies," *Hist. of Science*, 17: 75–101.

Guile, Bruce R., and Harvey Brooks, eds. 1987. *Technology and Global Industry: Companies and Nations in the World Economy*. Washington, DC: National Academy Press for the National Academy of Engineering.

Guy, Donna J. 1980. *Argentine Sugar Politics: Tucumán and the Generation of Eighty*. Tempe: Arizona State Univ. Press.

Habakkuk, H. J. 1962. *American and British Technology in the Nineteenth Century: The Search for Labour-Saving Inventions*. Cambridge: Univ. Press.

Haber, L. F. 1958. *The Chemical Industry During the Nineteenth Century: A Study of the Economic Aspect of Applied Chemistry in Europe and North America*. Oxford: Clarendon Press.

Habib, Irfan. 1963. *The Agrarian System of Mughal India (1556–1707)*. London: Asia Publishing House.

———. 1969. "Potentialities of Capitalistic Development in the Economy of Mughal India," *J. Econ. Hist.,* 29, 1 (March): 32–78.

———. 1980. "The Technology and Economy of Mughal India," *Indian Econ. and Soc. Hist. Rev.,* 17, 1 (January–March): 1–34.

———. 1982. "Population," in Raychaudhuri and Habib, eds., *Camb. Hist. of India,* I, 163–71.

Hahn, Roger. 1971. *The Anatomy of a Scientific Institution: The Paris Academy of Sciences, 1666–1803.* Berkeley: Univ. of Calif. Press.

Hakluyt, Richard. 1599/1903/5. *The Principal Navigations Voyages Traffiques and Discoveries of the English Nation . . .* 12 vols. Glasgow; reprinted London: J. M. Dent; New York: Dutton (Everyman's Library).

Halberstam, David. 1986. *The Reckoning.* New York: William Morrow.

Hale, Sondra. 1989. "The Politics of Gender in the Middle East," in Sandra Morgen, ed., *Gender and Anthropology: Critical Reviews for Research and Teaching.* Washington, DC: American Anthropology Association.

———. 1994. "Gender Politics and Islamization in the Sudan," *South Asia Bull.,* 14, 2: 51–66.

Hall, John A. 1990. "Will the United States Decline as Did Britain?" in J. Michael Mann, ed., *The Rise and Decline of the Nation State.* Cambridge, MA, and Oxford: Basil Blackwell.

———. 1995. "A Theory of the Rise of the West," *METU Studies in Development,* 22, 3: 231–41.

Hall, John W. 1988. "The Tokugawa Legislation," *Trans. Asiatic Soc. of Japan,* 41.

Halle, Francis. 1993. *Un monde sans hiver: Les tropiques, nature et sociétés.* Paris: Seuil.

Halliday, Fred. 1996. *Islam and the Myth of Confrontation: Religion and Politics in the Middle East.* London: I. B. Tauris.

Hamerow, Theodore S. 1969. *The Social Foundations of German Unification 1858–1871.* Princeton: Princeton Univ. Press.

Hamilton, Richard F. 1995. "Max Weber's *The Protestant Ethic:* A Commentary on the Thesis and Its Reception in the Academic Community." Madrid: Center for Advanced Study in the Social Sciences, Juan March Institute, Working Paper 1995/73.

Hammarstrom, I. 1957. "The 'Price Revolution' of the Sixteenth Century: Some Swedish Evidence," *Scand. Econ. Hist. Rev.,* 5: 118–54.

Hancock, Graham. 1991. *Lords of Poverty.* London: Mandarin paperback; originally London: Macmillan, 1989.

Hane, Mikiso. 1982. *Peasants, Rebels, and Outcasts: The Underside of Modern Japan.* New York: Pantheon.

———. 1991. *Premodern Japan: A Historical Survey.* Boulder: Westview.

Hanke, Lewis, ed. 1964. *Do the Americas Have a Common History? A Critique of the Bolton Theory.* New York: Knopf.

Hansen, Bent. 1989. "Capital and Lopsided Development in Egypt under British Occupation," in Sabagh, ed., *Modern Economic and Social History,* pp. 66–88.

Hansen, Bert. 1978. "Science and Magic," in Lindberg, ed., *Science in the Middle Ages,* pp. 483–506.

Harberger, Arnold C., ed. 1984. *World Economic Growth: Case Studies of Developed and Developing Nations.* San Francisco: ICS Press.

Hardach, Karl W. 1967. *Die Bedeutung wirtschaftlicher Faktoren bei der Wiedereinführung der Eisen- und Getreidezölle in Deutschland 1879.* Berlin: Duncker & Humblot.

Harding, Jeremy. 1994. *Small Wars, Small Mercies: Journeys in Africa's Disputed Nations.* London: Penguin.

Harley, C. K., and N. F. R. Crafts. 1995. "Cotton Textiles and Industrial Output Growth During the Industrial Revolution," *Econ. Hist. Rev.*, 48, 1 (February), 134–44.

Harner, Michael. 1977. "The Ecological Basis for Aztec Sacrifice," *American Ethnologist*, 4: 117–35.

Harries, Meirion and Susie. 1991. *Soldiers of the Sun: The Rise and Fall of the Imperial Japanese Army*. New York: Viking.

Harris, John R., ed. 1969. *Liverpool and Merseyside: Essays in the Economic and Social History of the Port and Its Hinterland*. London: Frank Cass.

———. 1972. *Industry and Technology in the Eighteenth Century: Britain and France. An Inaugural Lecture*. Birmingham: Birmingham Univ. Press.

———. 1978. "Attempts to Transfer English Steel Techniques to France in the Eighteenth Century," in *Business and Businessmen: Studies in Business, Economic and Accounting History*. Liverpool: Liverpool Univ. Press, pp. 199–233.

———. 1986. "Michael Alcock and the Transfer of Birmingham Technology to France Before the Revolution," *J. Europ. Econ. Hist.*, 15, 1 (Spring): 7–58.

———. 1988. *The British Iron Industry 1700–1850*. Houndmills and London: Macmillan.

———. 1989. "The Transfer of Technology Between Britain and France and the French Revolution," in Ceri Crossley and Ian Small, eds., *The French Revolution and British Culture*. Oxford: Univ. Press, pp. 156–86.

———. 1992a. "Movements of Technology Between Britain and Europe in the Eighteenth Century," in Jeremy, ed., *Transfer of International Technology*, pp. 9–30.

———. 1992b. "The First British Measures Against Industrial Espionage," in Ian Blanchard, A. Goodman, and J. Newman, eds., *Industry and Finance in Early Modern History*. Stuttgart: Franz Steiner, pp. 205–25.

———. 1992c. *Essays in Industry and Technology in the Eighteenth Century: England and France*. Hampshire, U.K.: Variorum.

———. 1996a. "A French Industrial Spy: The Engineer Le Turc in England in the 1780s," *Icon*, 1: 16–35.

———. 1996b. "Law, Espionage and the Transfer of Technology from Eighteenth Century Britain," in Robert Fox, ed., *Technological Change: Methods and Themes in the History of Technology*. Amsterdam: Harwood Academic Publishers, pp. 123–36.

Harris, Nigel. 1987. *The End of the Third World: Newly Industrializing Countries and the Decline of an Ideology*. London: Pelican (originally Tauris, 1986).

Harrison, Lawrence E. 1985. *Underdevelopment Is a State of Mind: The Latin-American Case*. Cambridge, MA: Center for International Affairs, Harvard Univ.; Lanham, MD: Madison Books.

Harrison, Paul. 1979a. *Inside the Third World: The Anatomy of Poverty*. Harmondsworth: Penguin.

———. 1979b. "The Curse of the Tropics: It's Hard to Make a Living in Hot Climates," *New Scientist*, 84 (22 Nov.), 602–04.

Hart, Jeffrey A. 1994. "A Comparative Analysis of the Sources of America's Relative Economic Decline," in Bernstein and Adler, eds., *Understanding American Economic Decline*, pp. 199–239.

Hartley, E. N. 1957. *Ironworks on the Saugus: The Lynn and Braintree Ventures of the Company of Undertakers of the Ironworks in New England*. Norman: Univ. of Oklahoma Press.

Haskins, Charles H. 1925. "Arabic Science in Western Europe," *Isis*, 7, 3: 478–85.

Hassig, Ross. 1993. *War and Society in Ancient Mesoamerica*. Berkeley: Univ. of Calif. Press.

Hatton, Timothy J., and Jeffrey G. Williamson, eds. 1994a. *Migration and the International Labor Market 1850–1939.* London: Routledge.
———. 1994b. "What Drove the Mass Migrations from Europe in the Late Nineteenth Century?" *Population and Devel. Rev.,* 20, 3 (September), 533–59.
Hau, Michel. 1987. *L'industrialisation de l'Alsace (1803–1939).* Strasbourg: Association des Publications près les Universités de Strasbourg.
Hauser, William. 1974. *Economic Institutional Change in Tokugawa Japan: Osaka and the Kinai Cotton Trade.* Cambridge: Univ. Press.
Havinden, Michael, and David Meredith, eds. 1993. *Colonialism and Development: Britain and Its Tropical Colonies, 1850–1960.* London: Routledge.
Hayami, Yujiro, and V. W. Ruttan. 1970. "Korean Rice, Taiwan Rice, and Japanese Agricultural Stagnation: An Economic Consequence of Colonialism," *QJE,* 84, 4 (November): 562–89.
Hazlitt, W. Carew. 1915. *The Venetian Republic: Its Rise, Its Growth, and Its Fall A.D. 409–1797.* 2 vols. London: Adam and Charles Black.
Head, Thomas, and Richard A. Landes, eds. 1992. *The Peace of God: Social Violence and Religious Response in France around the Year 1000.* Ithaca: Cornell Univ. Press.
Headrick, Donald R. 1981. *The Tools of Empire: Technology and European Imperialism in the Nineteenth Century.* New York: Oxford Univ. Press.
———. 1988. *The Tentacles of Progress: Technology Transfer in the Age of Imperialism, 1850–1940.* New York: Oxford Univ. Press.
Heckscher, Eli F. 1955. *Mercantilism.* 2d ed., rev., 2 vols. London: Allen & Unwin.
Heerding, A. 1988. *The History of N. V. Philips' Gloeilampenfabrieken.* Vol. II. *A Company of Many Parts.* Cambridge: Univ. Press.
Heikkinen, Sakari, and Riitta Hjerppe. 1987. "The Growth of Finnish Industry in 1860–1913: Causes and Linkages," *J. Europ. Econ. Hist.,* 16: 227–44.
Helliwell, John, and Alan Chung. 1992. "Convergence and Growth Linkages Between North and South." NBER, Working Paper No. 3948.
Henderson, Callum. 1998. *Asia Falling: Making Sense of the Asia Crisis and Its Aftermath.* New York: McGraw-Hill; BusinessWeek Books.
Henderson, W. O. 1958. *The State and the Industrial Revolution in Prussia 1740–1870.* Liverpool: Liverpool Univ. Press.
———. 1963. *Studies in the Economic Policy of Frederick the Great.* London: Frank Cass.
———. 1966. *J. C. Fischer and His Diary of Industrial England 1814–1851.* London: Frank Cass.
———. 1954/1965. *Britain and Industrial Europe 1750–1870: Studies in British Influence on the Industrial Revolution in Western Europe.* Liverpool: Liverpool Univ. Press; Leicester: Leicester Univ. Press.
———. 1975. *The Rise of German Industrial Power 1834–1914.* London: Temple Smith.
Henley, Paul. 1993. "Spanish Stew: Justifications of Conquest in the New World," *TLS,* 22 October, pp. 4–5.
Hershatter, Gail. 1986. *The Workers of Tianjin, 1900–1949.* Stanford: Stanford Univ. Press.
Hess, Andrew C. 1978. *The Forgotten Frontier: A History of the Sixteenth-Century Ibero-African Frontier.* Chicago: Univ. of Chicago Press.
Heston, Alan, and Robert Summers. 1980. "Comparative Indian Economic Growth: 1870 to 1970," *Amer. Econ. Rev.,* 70, 2 (May): 96–101.
Hibbert, Christopher. 1970. *The Dragon Wakes: China and the West, 1793–1911.* London: Longman.
Higonnet, Patrice, David S. Landes, and Henry Rosovsky, eds. 1991. *Favorites of Fortune: Technology, Growth, and Economic Development Since the Industrial Revolution.* Cambridge, MA: Harvard Univ. Press.

Hill, Christopher. 1965. *Intellectual Origins of the English Revolution*. Oxford, Clarendon Press.

Hills, Richard L. 1970. *Power in the Industrial Revolution*. Manchester: Manchester Univ. Press.

Himmelstrand, Ulf, Kabiru Kinyanjui, and Edward Mburugu, eds. 1994. *African Perspectives on Development: Controversies, Dilemmas and Openings*. London: James Currey; New York: St. Martin's Press.

Hirschman, Albert. 1981. *Essays in Trespassing*. New York: Cambridge Univ. Press.

———. 1995. *A Propensity to Self-Subversion*. Cambridge, MA: Harvard Univ. Press.

Hirschmeier, Johannes. 1964. *The Origins of Entrepreneurship in Meiji Japan*. Cambridge, MA: Harvard East Asian Series No. 17.

———. 1965. "Shibusawa Eiichi: Industrial Pioneer," in Lockwood, ed., *The State and Economic Enterprise*, pp. 209–47.

Hirst, Paul. 1975. "The Uniqueness of the West," *Economy and Society*, 4: 446–73.

Ho, Ping-ti. 1955. "The Introduction of American Food Crops into China," *Amer. Anthropol.*, 57: 191–201.

———. 1959. *Studies on the Population of China, 1368–1953*. Cambridge, MA: Harvard Univ. Press.

Ho, Samuel Pao-san. 1968. "Agricultural Transformation under Colonialism: The Case of Taiwan," *J. Econ. Hist.*, 28, 3 (September): 315–40.

———. 1984. "Colonialism and Development: Korea, Taiwan, and Kwantung," in Myers and Peattie, eds., *Japanese Colonial Empire*, pp. 347–98.

Hodder, B. W. 1968. *Economic Development in the Tropics*. London: Methuen.

Hodgson, Marshall G. S. 1974. *The Venture of Islam: Conscience and History in a World Civilization*. 3 vols. Chicago: Univ. of Chicago Press.

Hodne, Fritz. 1992. "New Perspectives in Economic History," *Scand. Econ. Hist. Rev*, 40, 1: 76–88.

Hoffmann, Walther G. 1955. *British Industry, 1700–1950*. Oxford: Basil Blackwell.

———. 1963. "The Take-off in Germany," in Rostow, ed., *The Economics of Take-off*, pp. 95–118.

Hohenberg, Paul M. 1991. "Urban Manufactures in the Proto-industrial Economy: Culture versus Commerce?" in Berg, ed., *Markets and Manufacture*, pp. 159–72.

———, and Lynn Hollen Lees. 1985. *The Making of Urban Europe 1000–1950*. Cambridge: Harvard.

Holtfrerich, Carl-Ludwig, ed. 1989. *Interactions in the World Economy: Perspectives from International Economic History*. New York: N.Y.U. Press.

Holton, Gerald J. 1996. *Einstein, History, and Other Passions: The Rebellion Against Science at the End of the Twentieth Century*. Reading, MA: Addison-Wesley.

Holusha, John. 1983a. "Detroit's New Push to Upgrade Quality." *New York Times*, 12 May, p. D-1.

———. 1983b. "Detroit's New Labor Strategy." *New York Times*, 13 May, p. D-1.

Honig, Emily. 1986. *Sisters and Strangers: Women in the Shanghai Cotton Mills, 1919–1949*. Stanford: Stanford Univ. Press.

Hoodbhoy, Pervez A. 1991. *Islam and Science: Religious Orthodoxy and the Battle for Rationality*. London and Atlantic Highlands, NJ: Zed Books.

Hooykaas, R. 1972. *Religion and the Rise of Modern Science*. Edinburgh: Scottish Academic Press.

———. 1987. "The Rise of Modern Science: When and Why?" *Brit. J. Hist. of Science*, 20, 4: 453–73.

Hopkins, A. G. 1973. *An Economic History of West Africa*. New York: Columbia Univ. Press.

Hopkins, Eric. 1989. *Birmingham, the First Manufacturing Town in the World, 1760–1840*. London: Weidenfeld & Nicolson.

Hoppit, Julian. 1990. "Counting the Industrial Revolution," *Econ. Hist. Rev.*, 2d ser., 43, 2 (May), 173–93.

Horwitz, Tony. 1992. *Baghdad Without a Map, and Other Misadventures in Arabia*. New York: Penguin (Plume).

Hossain, Ahmeeda. 1979. "The Alienation of Weavers: Impact of the Conflict between the Revenue and Commercial Interests of the East India Company, 1750–1800," *Indian Econ. and Soc. Hist. Rev.*, 16 (July): 323–45.

Hourani, George F. 1951/1995. *Arab Seafaring in the Indian Ocean in Ancient and Early Medieval Times*. Rev. and expanded by John Carswell. Princeton: Princeton Univ. Press.

Howe, Christopher. 1996. *The Origins of Japanese Trade Supremacy: Development and Technology in Asia from 1540 to the Pacific War*. London: Hurst.

Howells, Jeremy. 1995. "Tacit Knowledge and Technology Transfer." ESRC Centre for Business Research, Univ. of Cambridge, Paper No. 16.

Howells, William W. 1977. "Requiem for a Lost People [the Tasmanians]," *Harvard Magazine* (January–February): 48–55.

Howse, Derek. 1980. *Greenwich Time and the Discovery of the Longitude*. Oxford: Oxford Univ. Press.

Hsia, R. Po-Chia. 1989. *Social Discipline in the Reformation: Central Europe 1550–1750*. London: Routledge.

Huang, Ray. 1981. *1587, a Year of No Significance: The Ming Dynasty in Decline*. New Haven: Yale Univ. Press.

———. 1990. *China: A Macro History*. Armonk, NY: M. E. Sharpe.

Huc, Evariste. 1850/1925–28. *Souvenirs d'un voyage dans la Tartarie, le Thibet et la Chine*. 4 vols. Paris: Plon.

Hufton, Olwen H. 1974. *The Poor of Eighteenth-Century France 1750–1789*. Oxford: Clarendon.

Hughes, Thomas P. 1989. *American Genesis: A Century of Invention and Technological Enthusiasm*. New York: Penguin.

Hugill, Peter J. 1993. *World Trade Since 1431: Geography, Technology, and Capitalism*. Baltimore: Johns Hopkins Univ. Press.

Humble, Richard. 1979. *The Seafarers: The Explorers*. Alexandria, VA: Time-Life Books.

———. 1989. *Warfare in the Middle Ages*. Wigston, Leicester: Magna Books.

Humboldt, Alexander von. 1814–25/1965. *Relation historique du Voyage aux régions équinoxiales du Nouveau Continent*. Selections edited by Jean Tulard under the title, *L'Amérique espagnole en 1800, vue par un savant allemand Humboldt*. Paris: Calmann-Lévy.

Hunter, William W. 1912/1919. *History of British India*. 2 vols. London: Longmans Green.

Huyghe, Edith and François-Bernard. 1995. *Les coureurs d'épices [sur la route des Indes fabuleuses]*. [Paris]: J. C. Lattes.

Hyam, Ronald. 1990. *Empire and Sexuality: The British Experience*. Manchester: Manchester Univ. Press.

———. 1993. *Britain's Imperial Century, 1815–1914: A Study of Empire and Expansion*. 2d ed., London: Macmillan.

Hyde, Charles K. 1977. *Technological Change and the British Iron Industry, 1700–1870*. Princeton: Princeton Univ. Press.

Ignatieff, Michael. 1994. *Blood and Belonging: Journeys into the New Nationalism*. London: Vintage.

Ilardi, Vincent. 1976. "Eyeglasses and Concave Lenses in Fifteenth-century Florence and Milan: New Documents," *Renaissance Quarterly*, 29, 3: 341–66.

———. 1978. *Occhiali alla corte di Francesco e Galeazzo Maria Sforza con documenti inediti del 1462–1466.* Milan: Metal Lux.

———. 1993. "Renaissance Florence: The Optical Capital of the World," *J. Europ. Econ. Hist.,* 22, 3: 507–41.

Iliffe, John. 1983. *The Emergence of African Capitalism.* Minneapolis: Univ. of Minnesota Press.

Inikori, Joseph E. 1976. "Measuring the Atlantic Slave Trade: An Assessment of Curtin and Anstey," *J. African Hist.,* 17: 197–223.

———. 1977. "The Import of Firearms into West Africa (1750–1807): A Quantitative Analysis," *J. African Hist.,* 18: 339–68.

———. 1981. "Market Structure and the Profits of the British African Trade in the Late Eighteenth Century," *J. Econ. Hist.,* 41: 745–76.

———, ed. 1982. *Forced Migration: The Impact of the Export Slave Trade on African Societies.* New York: Africana.

———. 1987. "Slavery and the Development of Industrial Capitalism in England," in Solow and Engerman, eds., *British Capitalism,* pp. 79–101.

Inkster, Ian. 1991. "Mental Capital: Transfers of Knowledge and Technique in Eighteenth Century Europe," *J. Europ. Econ. Hist.,* 19, 2: 403–41.

———. 1991. *Science and Technology in History: An Approach to Industrial Development.* London: Macmillan Education.

Innes, Stephen. 1995. *Creating the Commonwealth: The Economic Culture of Puritan New England.* New York: W. W. Norton.

"The Invasion of the Nina, the Pinta, and the Santa Maria." 1991. *New York Times,* 2 June.

Irwin, Douglas A. 1996. *Against the Tide: An Intellectual History of Free Trade.* Princeton: Princeton Univ. Press.

Irwin, Robert. 1995. "Burying the Past: The Decline of Arab History and the Perils of Occidentosis," *TLS,* 3 Feb., pp. 9–10.

Isaacman, Allen, and Richard Roberts, eds. 1995. *Cotton, Colonialism, and Social History in Sub-Saharan Africa.* London: James Currey.

Ishizaka, Akio. 1982–83. "Die Industrialisierung und Modernisierung Japans vom Standpunkt der vergleichenden Wirschaftsgeschichte betrachtet," *Hokudai Economic Papers,* 12: 46–64.

Islam, Nazrul. 1995. "Growth Empirics: A Panel Data Approach," *QJE,* 110, 4 (November), 1127–70.

Islamoğlu-Inan, Huri., ed. 1987. *The Ottoman Empire and the World Economy.* Cambridge: Univ. Press.

———. 1995. "Introduction: Why European History?" *METU Studies in Development,* 22, 3: 222–30.

Israel, Jonathan I. 1989a. *European Jewry in the Age of Mercantilism 1550–1750.* 2d ed., Oxford: Clarendon Press.

———. 1989b. *Dutch Primacy in World Trade, 1585–1740.* Oxford: Clarendon Press.

———. 1995. *The Dutch Republic: Its Rise, Greatness, and Fall 1477–1806.* Oxford: Clarendon Press.

Issawi, Charles. 1961. "Egypt Since 1800: A Study in Lopsided Development," *J. Econ. Hist.,* 21: 1–25. Reprinted as "The Economic Development of Egypt, 1800–1960," in Issawi, ed., *Economic History of the Middle East,* pp. 359–74.

———, ed. 1966. *The Economic History of the Middle East 1800–1914: A Book of Readings.* Chicago: Univ. of Chicago Press.

———. 1970. "The Decline of Middle Eastern Trade, 1100–1850," in D. S. Ricards, ed., *Islam and the Trade of Asia: A Colloquium.* Oxford: Bruno Cassirer; Philadelphia: Univ. of Pennsylvania Press, pp. 245–66.

Itzkowitz, Norman. 1972. *Ottoman Empire and Islamic Tradition.* Chicago: Univ. of Chicago Press.

[Jackson, W. F.]. 1893. *James Jackson et ses fils*. Paris: Privately printed.

Jacob, Margaret C. 1997. *Scientific Culture and the Making of the Industrial West*. New York: Oxford Univ. Press.

Jalal al-ᶜAzm, Sadik. 1981. "Orientalism and Orientalism in Reverse," *Khamsin*, 8, 5–26.

James, C. L. R. 1938/1980. *The Black Jacobins: Toussaint Louverture and the San Domingo Revolution*. London: Allison & Busby.

Jansen, Marius. 1994. *Sakamoto Ryōma and the Meiji Restoration*. New York: Columbia Univ. Press (original ed. Princeton, 1961).

Jansen, Marius B., and Gilbert Rozman, eds. 1986. *Japan in Transition from Tokugawa to Meiji*. Princeton: Princeton Univ. Press.

Jenkins, D. T. 1975. *The West Riding Wool Textile Industry 1770–1835: A Study of Fixed Capital Formation*. Edington, Wilts.: Pasold Research Fund.

Jenkins, Stephen. 1991. "The Measurement of Income Inequality," in Osberg, ed., *Economic Inequality*, pp. 3–38.

Jeremy, David J. 1981. *Transatlantic Industrial Revolution: The Diffusion of Textile Technologies between Britain and America, 1790–1830s*. Cambridge, MA: MIT Press.

———, ed. 1992. *The Transfer of International Technology: Europe, Japan and the USA in the Twentieth Century*. Aldershot, Hants.: Edward Elgar.

Johnson, Chalmers. 1995. *Japan: Who Governs? The Rise of the Developmental State*. New York: W. W. Norton.

Johnson, Donald S. 1994. *Phantom Islands of the Atlantic: The Legends of Seven Lands That Never Were*. New York: Walker.

Jones, Eric L., ed. 1967. *Agriculture and Economic Growth in England 1650–1815*. London: Methuen.

———. 1981. *The European Miracle: Environments, Economies and Geopolitics in the History of Europe and Asia*. Cambridge: Univ. Press. 2d ed., 1987.

———. 1988. *Growth Recurring: Economic Change in World History*. Oxford: Clarendon Press.

———. 1990. "The Real Question About China: Why Was the Song Economic Achievement Not Repeated?" *Austral. Econ. Hist. Rev.*, 30, 2 (September): 5–22.

Jones, William O. 1965. "Environment, Technical Knowledge, and Economic Development in Tropical Africa," Stanford, *Food Research Institute Studies*, 5, 2, 101–16.

Jordan, Glenn. 1995. "Flight from Modernity: Time, the Other and the Discourse of Primitivism," *Time and Society*, 4, 3: 281–303.

Josephson, Paul R. 1995. " 'Projects of the Century' in Soviet History: Large-Scale Technologies from Lenin to Gorbachev," *Technology and Culture*, 36, 3 (July): 519–59.

Kadir, Djelal. 1993. *Columbus and the Ends of the Earth: Europe's Prophetic Rhetoric as Conquering Ideology*. Berkeley: Univ. of California Press.

Kafadar, Cemal. 1995. "When Coins Turned into Drops of Dew and Bankers Became Robbers of Shadows: Ottoman Economic Imagination and Decline Consciousness at the End of the Sixteenth Century." In press with Harvard Univ.

Kahan, Arcadius. 1962. "Entrepreneurship in the Early Development of Iron Manufacturing in Russia," *Econ. Devel. and Cult. Change*, 10, 395–422.

———. 1965. "Continuity in Economic Activity and Policy During the Post-Petrine Period in Russia, *J. Econ. Hist.*, 25, 61–85.

———. 1966. "The Costs of 'Westernization' in Russia: The Gentry and the Economy in the Eighteenth Century," *Slavic Rev.*, 25, 40–66.

Kamarck, Andrew M. 1967. *The Economics of African Development*. New York: Praeger.

———. 1976. *The Tropics and Economic Development: A Provocative Inquiry into the Poverty of Nations*. Baltimore and London: Johns Hopkins Univ. for the World Bank.

———. 1983. *Economics and the Real World*. Philadelphia: Univ. of Pennsylvania Press.

Kamen, Henry. 1978. "The Decline of Spain: A Historical Myth?", *Past & Present*, 81: 24–50.

Kaplan, Robert D. 1994. "The Coming Anarchy," *Atlantic Monthly* (February), pp. 44 ff.

———. 1996. *The Ends of the Earth: A Journey at the Dawn of the 21st Century*. New York: Random House.

Kaplan, Yosef. 1992. "The Jewish Profile of the Spanish-Portuguese Community of London During the Seventeenth Century," *Judaism*, 41, 3 (Summer): 229–40.

Katz, Jorge M., ed. 1987. *Technology Generation in Latin American Manufacturing Industries*. London: Macmillan.

Kautsky, John H. 1982. *The Politics of Aristocratic Empires*. Chapel Hill: Univ. of North Carolina Press.

Kearney, Hugh F. 1964. "Puritanism, Capitalism, and the Scientific Revolution," *Past & Present*, 28 (July).

Keay, John. 1991. *The Honourable Company: A History of the English East India Company*. New York: Macmillan.

Keddie, Nikki R., and Beth Baron, eds. 1991. *Women in Middle Eastern History: Shifting Boundaries in Sex and Gender*. New Haven: Yale Univ. Press.

Keene, Donald. 1952/1969. *The Japanese Discovery of Europe, 1720–1830*. Rev. ed., Stanford: Stanford Univ. Press.

Keisuke, Yao. 1995. "The VOC and Japanese Rice in the Early Seventeenth Century," *Itinerario*, 19, 1: 32–47.

Keith, Robert G. 1971. "Encomienda, Hacienda and Corregimiento in Spanish America: A Structural Analysis." *Hisp. Amer. Hist. Rev.*, 51, 3 (August), 431–46.

———. 1980. "The Encomienda and the Genesis of a Colonial Economy in Spanish America." *Res. in Econ. Anthropol.*, 3, 135–60.

Kemp, Tom. 1969. *Industrialization in Nineteenth-Century Europe*. London: Longman. 2d ed., 1985.

———. 1993. *Historical Patterns of Industrialization*. 2d. ed., London: Longman.

Kennedy, Paul. 1987. *The Rise and Fall of the Great Powers: Economic Change and Military Conflict from 1500 to 2000*. New York: Random House.

———. 1993. *Preparing for the Twenty-first Century*. New York: Random House.

Kerr, Ian J. 1995. "Colonialism and Technological Choice: The Case of the Railways of India," *Itinerario*, 19, 2: 91–111.

Kiesewetter, Hubert. 1994. "Europe's Industrialization—Coincidence or Necessity?" *German Yearbook of Business History 1994*, Munich, pp. 9–39.

———, and Rainer Fremdling, ed. 1985. *Staat, Region und Industrialisierung*. Ostfildern: Scripta Mercaturae.

Kimura, Mitsuhiko. 1995. "The Economics of Japanese Imperialism in Korea, 1910–1939," *Econ. Hist. Rev.*, 48, 3 (August), 555–74.

Kindleberger, Charles P. 1993. *A Financial History of Western Europe*. 2d ed., New York: Oxford Univ. Press.

———. 1996. *World Economic Primacy: 1500 to 1990*. New York: Oxford Univ. Press.

Kiple, Kenneth F. 1984. *The Caribbean Slave: A Biological History*. Cambridge: Univ. Press.

Kirby, Maurice W., and May B. Rose, eds. 1994. *Business Enterprise in Modern Britain from the Eighteenth to the Twentieth Century.* London: Routledge.

Kirchner, Walther. 1986. *Die deutsche Industrie und die Industrialisierung Russlands 1815–1914.* St. Katharinen: Scripta Mercaturae.

Kirkpatrick, F. A. 1934. *The Spanish Conquistadores.* London: A. & C. Black.

———. 1935/1992. *Les conquistadors espagnols.* Paris: Editions Payot.

Klein, Herbert S. 1990. "Economic Aspects of the Eighteenth-Century Atlantic Slave Trade," in Tracy, ed., *Rise of Merchant Empires,* pp. 287–310.

Klep, Paul, and Eddy van Cauwenberghe, eds. 1994. *Entrepreneurship and the Transformation of the Economy (10th–20th Centuries): Essays in Honour of Herman Van der Wee.* Leuven: Leuven Univ. Press.

Klitgard, Robert. 1990. *Tropical Gangsters: One Man's Experience with Development and Decadence in Deepest Africa.* New York: Basic Books.

Klor de Alva, J. Jorge. 1995. "The Postcolonization of the (Latin) American Experience: A Reconsideration of 'Colonialism,' 'Postcolonialism,' and 'Mestizaje,' " in Prakash, ed., *After Colonialism,* pp. 241–75.

Knight, Franklin W., and Peggy K. Liss, eds. 1991. *Atlantic Port Cities: Economy, Culture, and Society in the Atlantic World, 1650–1850.* Knoxville, TE: Univ. of Tennessee Press.

Koditschek, Theodore. 1990. *Class Formation and Urban Industrial Society: Bradford, 1750–1850.* Cambridge: Univ. Press.

Koerner, Lisbet. 1994. "Linnaeus' Floral Transplants," *Representations,* 47 (Summer), 144–69.

Komroff, Manuel, ed. 1926. *The Travels of Marco Polo [the Venetian]. Revised from Marsden's translation.* New York: Liveright.

Koning, Hans. 1976/1991. *Columbus: His Enterprise. Exploding the Myth.* New York: Monthly Review Press.

Krejci, Jaroslav. 1990. *The Civilizations of Asia and the Middle East: Before the European Challenge.* London: Macmillan.

Kriedte, Peter. 1986. "Demographic and Economic Rythms [sic]: The Rise of the Silk Industry in Krefeld in the Eighteenth Century," *J. Eur. Econ. Hist.,* 15, 2 (Fall): 259–89.

Kroker, Werner. 1971. *Wege zur Verbreitung technologischer Kenntnisse zwischen England und Deutschland in der zweiten Hälfte des 18. Jahrhunderts.* Berlin: Duncker & Humblot.

Krout, John Allen, and Dixon Ryan Fox. 1944. *The Completion of Independence 1790–1830.* "A History of American Life," Vol. V. New York: Macmillan.

Kriegel, Maurice. 1994. "Autour de Pablo de Santa Maria et d'Alfonso de Cartagena: alignement culturel et originalité 'converso,' " *Rev. d'hist. mod. et contemp.,* 41, 2 (April–June), 197–205.

Krueger, Anne O. 1974. "The Political Economy of the Rent-seeking Society," *Amer. Econ. Rev.,* 64: 291–303.

Krugman, Paul. 1994. "The Myth of Asia's Miracle," *Foreign Affairs,* 73, 6 (November–December), 62–78.

———, ed. 1995. *Trade with Japan: Has the Door Opened Wider?* Chicago: Univ. of Chicago Press.

———. 1996. *Pop Internationalism.* Cambridge, MA: MIT Press.

———, and Anthony J. Venables. 1995. "Globalization and the Inequality of Nations," *QJE,* 110, 4 (November): 857–80.

Krum, Horsta, ed. 1985. *Preussens Adoptivkinder: die Hugenotten, 300 Jahre Edikt von Potsdam.* Berlin: Arani.

Kuisel, Richard, 1993. *Seducing the French: The Dilemma of Americanization.* Berkeley: Univ. of California Press.

Kulischer, Josef. 1931. "Die kapitalistischen Unternehmer in Russland (insbesondere die Bauern als Unternehmer in den Anfangsstadien des Kapitalismus," *Archiv fur Sozialwissenschaft und Sozialpolitik,* 65: 309–55.

Kumar, Deepak. 199X. *Science and the Raj, 1857–1905.* Oxford: Oxford Univ. Press.

Kuppuram, G. and K. Kumudamani, eds. 1990. *History of Science and Technology in India.* 12 vols. Delhi: Sundeep Prakashan.

Kuttner, Robert. 1997. *Everything for Sale: The Virtues and Limits of Markets.* New York: Knopf.

Kuznets, Simon. 1929. "Retardation of Industrial Growth," *J. Econ. and Bus. Hist.,* I, 4 (August), 534–60.

———. 1959. *Six Lectures on Economic Growth.* Glencoe, IL: Free Press.

———. 1965. *Economic Growth and Structure: Selected Essays.* New York: W. W. Norton.

Lacey, Robert. 1974. *Sir Walter Ralegh.* New York: Atheneum.

———. 1986. *Ford: The Men and the Machine.* Boston: Little, Brown.

Lach, Donald F. 1965/1994. *Asia in the Making of Europe.* Vol. I. *The Century of Discovery.* Chicago: Univ. of Chicago Press.

Lafargue, Jean-André. 1909. *L'immigration chinoise en Indochine: Sa réglementation, ses conséquences économiques et politiques.* Paris: Henry Jouve.

Lai, Chi-kong. 1995. "The Historiography of Maritime China since c. 1975," *Research in Maritime History,* 9 (December): 1–27.

Lall, Sanjaya. 1987. *Learning to Industrialize: The Acquisition of Technological Capability by India.* London: Macmillan.

La Lumia, Isidoro. 1992. *Histoire de l'expulsion des Juifs de Sicile 1492.* Paris: Editions Allia.

Lambert, Jacques. 1967. *Latin America: Social Structure and Political Institutions.* Berkeley: Univ. of Calif. Press.

Lambert, L. Don. 1971. "The Role of Climate in the Economic Development of Nations," *Land Economics,* 47, 4, 339–44.

Lamoreaux, Naomi R. 1995. "Constructing Firms: Partnerships and Alternative Contractual Arrangements in Early-Nineteenth-Century American Business." Paper presented to Economic History Workshop, Harvard Univ. Typescript.

Lamoreaux, Naomi, and Kenneth Sokoloff. 1994. "Patents and the Market for Technology in the Late-Nineteenth and Early-Twentieth Century United States." Paper presented to the Economic History Workshop, Harvard Univ. Typescript.

Lampe, John R., and Marvin R. Jackson. 1982. *Balkan Economic History, 1550–1950: From Imperial Borderlands to Developing Nations.* Bloomington: Indiana University Press.

Landau, Ralph, and Nathan Rosenberg. 1992. "Successful Commercialization in the Chemical Process Industries," in Rosenberg, Landau, and Mowery, eds., *Technology and the Wealth of Nations,* pp. 73–119.

Landau, Ralph, Timothy Taylor, and Gavin Wright, eds. 1996. *The Mosaic of Economic Growth.* Stanford: Stanford Univ. Press.

Landes, David S. 1952. "Bankers and Pashas: International Finance in Egypt in the 1860's," in Miller, ed., *Men in Business,* pp. 23–70.

———. 1956. "Vieille banque et banque nouvelle: La révolution financière du dix-neuvième siècle," *Rev. d'hist. mod. et contemp.,* 3: 204–22.

———. 1958. *Bankers and Pashas: International Finance and Economic Imperialism in Egypt.* London: Heinemann; Cambridge, MA: Harvard Univ. Press.

———. 1961. "Some Thoughts on the Nature of Economic Imperialism," *J. Econ. Hist.,* 21 (December), 496–512.

———. 1965. "Factor Costs and Demand: Determinants of Economic Growth: A Critique of Professor Habakkuk's Thesis," *Business History,* 7, 1 (January): 15–33.

———. 1969. *The Unbound Prometheus: Technological Change and Industrial Development in Western Europe from 1750 to the Present*. Cambridge: Univ. Press.

———. 1980–81. "An Equilibrium Model of Imperialism," in S. Bertelli, ed., *Per Federico Chabod (1901–1960)*, II. *Equilibrio europeo ed espansione coloniale (1870–1914)*. Perugia: "Annali della Facoltà di Scienze Politiche," Vol. 17.

———. 1981. "The Foundations of European Expansion and Dominion: An Equilibrium Model," *Itinerario*, 5, 1:46–61.

———. 1983a. *Revolution in Time: Clocks and the Making of the Modern World*. Cambridge, MA: Harvard Univ. Press.

———. 1983b. "Passionate Pilgrims and Others: Visitors to the Holy Land in the 19th Century," in Moshe Davis, ed., *With Eyes Toward Zion. Vol. II. Themes and Sources in the Archives of the United States, Great Britain, Turkey and Israel*. New York: Praeger, pp. 3–21.

———. 1986. "What Do Bosses Really Do?" *J. Econ. Hist.*, 46, 3 (September): 585–623.

———. 1987a. *L'heure qu'il est: Les horloges, la mesure du temps et la formation du monde moderne*. Paris: Gallimard (rev. enl. transl. of American ed.).

———. 1987b. "Piccolo e bello. Ma e bello davvèro?" in Landes, ed., *A che servono i padroni: le alternative storiche dell'industrializzazione*. Torino: Bollati Boringhieri, pp. 162–78.

———. 1990a. "The Time of Our Lives," *Social Science Information*, 29, 4: 693–724.

———. 1990b. "Why Are We So Rich and They So Poor?", *Amer. Econ. Rev.*, 80, 2 (May): 1–13.

———. 1991. "Does It Pay to Be Late?" in Batou, ed., *Between Development and Underdevelopment*, pp. 43–66.

———. 1992. "Homo Faber, Homo Sapiens: Knowledge, Technology, Growth, and Development," *Contention*, I, 3 (Spring): 81–107, 133–35.

———. 1993. "The Fable of the Dead Horse; or, the Industrial Revolution Revisited," in Joel Mokyr, ed., *The British Industrial Revolution: An Economic Perspective*. Boulder: Westview, pp. 132–70.

———. 1994. "What Room for Accident in History? Explaining Big Changes by Small Events," *Econ. Hist. Rev.*, 47, 4: 637–56.

———. 1995. "Some Further Thoughts on Accident in History: A Reply to Professor Crafts," *Econ. Hist. Rev.*, 48, 3 (August), 599–601.

———. 1995. "Convergence and Divergence: What Do Numbers Tell?" in Etemad, Batou, and David, eds., *Pour une histoire économique*, pp. 111–19.

———. 1996. "Finding the Point at Sea," in Andrewes, ed., *The Quest for Longitude*, pp. 19–30.

Lane, Frederic C. 1965. *Navires et constructeurs à Venise pendant la Renaissance*. Paris: SEVPEN.

Lang, James. 1975. *Conquest and Commerce: Spain and England in the Americas*. New York: Academic Press.

———. 1979. *Portuguese Brazil: The King's Plantation*. New York: Academic Press.

Langer, William. 1963. "Europe's Initial Population Explosion, *Amer. Hist. Rev.*, 69: 1–17.

Laqueur, Walter. 1994. *The Dream That Failed: Reflections on the Soviet Union*. New York: Oxford Univ. Press.

Larner, John P. 1993. "North American Hero: Christopher Columbus 1702–2002," *Proc. Amer. Philosoph. Soc.*, 137, 1 (March): 46–63.

Larrain, J. 1991. "Classical Political Economists and Marx on Colonialism and 'Backward' Nations," *World Development*, 19, 2/3: 225–43.

Larraz, Jose. 1943. *La epoca del mercantilismo en Castilla (1500–1700)*. Madrid: Aguilar.

Latham, A. J. H., and Heita Kawakatsu, eds. 1994. *Japanese Industrialization and the Asian Economy.* London: Routledge.

Lattimore, Owen. 1940. *Inner Asian Frontiers of China.* American Geographical Society, New York, Research Series No. 21.

Lau, Lawrence, and Jong-Il Kim. 1994. "The Sources of Growth of the East Asian Newly Industrialized Countries," *J. Japanese and Int. Economies,* 8, 3 (September): 235–71.

Laurens, Henry. 1993. *L'Orient arabe: Arabisme et islamisme de 1798 à 1945.* Paris: Armand Colin.

Law, Robin. 1986. "Dahomey and the Slave Trade: Reflections on the Historiography of the Rise of Dahomey," *J. African Hist.,* 27: 237–67.

Lazonick, William. 1990. *Competitive Advantage on the Shop Floor.* Cambridge, MA: Harvard Univ. Press.

Lazonick, William, and Mary O'Sullivan. 1996. "Organization, Finance and International Competition," *Industrial and Corporate Change,* 5, 1: 1–47.

Lebergott, Stanley. 1980. "The Returns to U.S. Imperialism, 1890–1929," *J. Econ. Hist.,* 40: 229–52.

Lee, J. 1982. "Food Supply and Population Growth in South-west China, 1250–1850," *J. Asian Studies,* 41, 4: 711–46.

Lee, Keun. 1993. *New East Asian Economic Development: Interacting Capitalism and Socialism.* Armonk, NY: M. E. Sharpe.

Leeming, Frank. 1993. *The Changing Geography of China.* Oxford: Basil Blackwell.

Leff, Nathaniel H. 1982. *Underdevelopment and Development in Brazil.* Vol. I. *Economic Structure and Change 1822–1947.* London: Allen & Unwin.

———, and Kazuo Sato. 1993. "Homogeneous Preferences and Heterogeneous Growth Performance: International Differences in Saving and Investment Behaviour," *Kyklos,* 46, 2: 203–23.

Lefkowitz, Mary. 1996. *Not Out of Africa: How Afrocentrism Became an Excuse to Teach Myth as History.* New York: Basic Books.

Lehmann, Hartmut, and Guenther Roth, eds. 1995. *Weber's Protestant Ethic: Origins, Evidence, Contexts.* Cambridge: Univ. Press.

Leibenstein, Harvey. 1976. *Beyond Economic Man: A New Foundation for Microeconomics.* Cambridge, MA: Harvard Univ. Press.

———. 1982. "The Japanese Management System: An X-Efficiency-Game Theory Analysis." Harvard Inst. of Economic Research, Discussion Paper No. 938.

Leithäuser, Joachim G. 1955. *Worlds Beyond the Horizon.* New York: Knopf.

le Masson, Hugues. 1992. *Faut-il encore aider les pays en développement? Histoire d'un cas exemplaire.* Paris: Editions du Félin.

Léon, Antoine. 1968. *La Révolution française et l'éducation technique.* Paris: Société des Etudes Robespierristes.

Léon, Pierre, François Crouzet, and Richard Gascon, eds. 1972. *L'industrialisation en Europe au XIXᵉ siècle: cartographie et typologie. Colloques internationaux du Centre National de la Recherche Scientifique, Sciences humaines, Lyon, 7–10 October. Paris: CNRS.*

Leon-Portilla, Miguel. 1977. *L'envers de la conquête.* Lyons: Federop. Original edition, in Spanish: *El reverso de la conquista.* Mexico: J. Mortiz, 1963.

———. 1971/1982. *Aztec Thought and Culture: A Study of the Ancient Nahuatl Mind.* Norman: Univ. of Oklahoma Press.

Lequenne, Michel. 1991. *Christophe Colomb: Amiral de la Mer Océane.* Paris: Gallimard.

Leshi, Bao. 1995. "Ruling Out Change: Institutional Impediments to Transfer of Technology in Ship Building and Design in the Far East," *Itinerario,* 19, 3: 142–51.

Leupp, Gary P. 1992. *Servants, Shophands, and Laborers in the Cities of Tokugawa Japan*. Princeton: Princeton Univ. Press.

Leur, Jacob Cornelis van. 1955. *Indonesian Trade and Society: Essays in Asian Social and Economic History*. The Hague: W. van Hoeve.

Levasseur, Emile. 1900. *Histoire des classes ouvrières et de l'industrie en France avant 1789*. 2d ed., 2 vols. Paris: Rousseau.

———. 1903. *Histoire des classes ouvrières et de l'industrie en France de 1789 à 1870*. 2d ed., 2 vols. Paris: Rousseau.

———. 1907. *Questions ouvrières et industrielles en France sous la Troisième République*. Paris: Rousseau.

Levathes, Louise E. 1994. *When China Ruled the Seas: The Treasure Fleet of the Dragon Throne, 1405–33*. New York: Simon & Schuster.

Levenson, Jay, ed. 1991. *Circa 1492: Art in the Age of Exploration*. Exhibit at the National Gallery, Washington, DC, 12 October 1991 to 12 January 1992. Washington, DC: National Gallery of Art; New Haven: Yale Univ. Press.

Lévi, Jean. 1985. *Le grand empereur et ses automates*. Paris: Albin Michel. English ed.: *The Chinese Emperor*. San Diego: Harcourt Brace Jovanovich, 1987.

Levine, A. L. 1967. *Industrial Retardation in Britain 1880–1914*. London: Weidenfeld & Nicolson.

Levy, Frank. 1988. *Dollars and Dreams: The Changing American Income Distribution*. New York: W. W. Norton.

Lévy-Leboyer, Maurice. 1964. *Les banques européennes et l'industrialisation internationale dans la première moitié du XIX^e siècle*. Paris: Presses Universitaires de France.

Lewchuk, Wayne. 1987. *American Technology and the British Vehicle Industry*. Cambridge: Univ. Press.

Lewis, Bernard. 1982. *The Muslim Discovery of Europe*. New York: W. W. Norton.

———. 1984. *The Jews of Islam*. Princeton: Princeton Univ. Press.

———. 1995. *The Middle East: 2,000 Years of History from the Rise of Christianity to the Present Day*. London: Weidenfeld & Nicolson.

Lewis, Colin M. 1985. "Railways and Industrialization: Argentina and Brazil, 1870–1929," in Abel and Lewis, eds., *Latin America*, pp. 199–230.

Lewis, David Levering. 1987. *The Race to Fashoda: European Colonialism and African Resistance in the Scramble for Africa*. New York: Weidenfeld & Nicolson.

Lewis, Gwynne. 1994. "Proto-industrialization in France," *Econ. Hist. Rev.*, 47, 1: 150–64.

Lewis, Paul H. 1990. *The Crisis of Argentine Capitalism*. Chapel Hill: Univ. of North Carolina Press.

Lewis, W. Arthur. [1969]. *Aspects of Tropical Trade 1883–1965*. Wicksell Lectures 1969. Stockholm: Almqvist & Wiksell.

Lincoln, Edward J. 1990. *Japan's Unequal Trade*. Washington: Brookings Institute.

Lindauer, David L., and Michael Roemer, eds. 1994. *Asia and Africa: Legacies and Opportunities in Development*. San Francisco: ICS Press.

Lindberg, David C., ed. 1978. *Science in the Middle Ages*. Chicago: Univ. of Chicago Press.

———. 1992. *The Beginnings of Western Science*. Chicago: Univ. of Chicago Press.

———, and Robert S. Westman, eds. 1990. *Reappraisals of the Scientific Revolution*. Cambridge: Univ. Press.

Lindqvist, Sven. 1992/1996. *"Exterminate All the Brutes."* New York: New Press.

Link, Perry. 1993. "A Harvest of Empty Notes: The Hectic Pace of Modernization in China," TLS, 10 September, pp. 6–8.

Lippit, Victor D. 1978. "The Development of Underdevelopment in China," *Modern China*, 4, 3 (July), 251–327.

Lis, Catharina, and Hugo Soly. 1979. *Poverty and Capitalism in Pre-Industrial Europe.* Atlantic Highlands, NJ: Humanities Press.

Livingston, Arthur. 1931. "Gentleman, Theory of the," *Enc. Social Sciences,* VI, 616–20.

Livingstone, David N. 1991. "The Moral Discourse of Climate: Historical Considerations on Race, Place and Virtue," *J. Histor. Geog.,* 17, 4: 413–34.

———. 1992. *The Geographical Tradition: Episodes in the History of a Contested Enterprise.* Oxford: Basil Blackwell.

Lockhart, James. 1968. *Spanish Peru, 1532–1560: A Colonial Society.* Madison: Univ. of Wisconsin Press.

———, and Stuart B. Schwartz. 1983. *Early Latin America: A History of Colonial Spanish America and Brazil.* Cambridge: Univ. Press.

Lockwood, William W., ed. 1965. *The State and Economic Enterprise in Japan: Essays on the Political Economy of Growth.* Princeton: Princeton Univ. Press.

Lombroso, Gina. 1931. *La rançon du machinisme.* Paris: Payot.

Lone, Stewart, and Gavan McCormack. 1993. *Korea Since 1850.* Melbourne: Longman Cheshire.

Lopez, Robert S. 1971. *The Commercial Revolution of the Middle Ages, 950–1350.* Englewood Cliffs, NJ: Prentice Hall.

Lorenz, Edward H. 1991. *Economic Decline in Britain: The Shipbuilding Industry 1890–1970.* Oxford: Clarendon Press.

Lovejoy, Paul E. 1983. *Transformations in Slavery: A History of Slavery in Africa.* Cambridge: Univ. Press.

———. 1989. "The Impact of the Atlantic Slave Trade on Africa: A Review of the Literature," *J. African Hist.,* 30: 365–94.

Lovejoy, P. E., and Nicholas Rogers, eds. 1985. *Unfree Labour in the Development of the Atlantic World.* Ilford, Essex: Frank Cass.

"The Lunar Society of Birmingham." Special issue of the *Univ. of Birmingham Historical Journal,* 11, 1 (1967).

Lüthy, Herbert. 1959, 1961. *La banque protestante en France, de la révocation de l'édit de Nantes à la Révolution.* Paris: SEVPEN.

———. 1963. "Calvinisme et capitalisme: après soixante ans de débat," *Cahiers Vilfredo Pareto,* 2 (December).

Luttwak, Edward. 1998. *Turbo-Capitalism: Winners and Losers in the Global Economy.* London: Weidenfeld & Nicolson; New York: HarperCollins.

Lybyer, Albert Howe. 1913. *The Government of the Ottoman Empire in the Time of Suleiman the Magnificent.* Cambridge, MA: Harvard Univ. Press.

Lynch, John. 1991. *Spain 1516–1598: From Nation State to World Empire.* Oxford: Basil Blackwell.

———. 1992. *The Hispanic World in Crisis and Change 1598–1700.* Oxford: Basil Blackwell.

Lyon, Bryce. 1957. "Medieval Real Estate Developments and Freedom," *Amer. Hist. Rev.,* 63: 47–61.

Macaulay, William Babington. 1840/1898. "Lord Clive," in *The Works of Lord Macaulay, Essays and Biographies.* Vol. III. London: Longmans, Green. This is a review article in the *Edinburgh Review,* January 1840, on Sir John Malcolm, *The Life of Robert Lord Clive* (3 vols., London, 1836).

Macfarlane, Alan. 1993. "On Individualism," *Proc. Brit. Acad.,* 82: 177–99.

Mackenney, Richard. 1993. *History of Europe. Sixteenth Century Europe: Expansion and Conflict.* New York: St. Martin's Press.

MacLeod, Christine. 1988. *Inventing the Industrial Revolution: The English Patent System, 1660–1800.* Cambridge: Univ. Press.

———. 1992. "Strategies for Innovation: The Diffusion of New Technology in Nineteenth-Century British Industry," *Econ. Hist. Rev.,* 45, 2 (May): 285–307.

Maddison, Angus. 1994. "Explaining the Economic Performance of Nations, 1820–1989," in Baumol, Nelson, and Wolff, eds., *Convergence of Productivity*, pp. 20–61.

———. 1998. "Chinese Economic Performance in the Long Run." (forthcoming; Paris: OECD Development Center).

Mahn-Lot, Marianne. 1991. *Bartolomé de Las Casas: L'Evangile et la force*. Paris: Editions du Cerf.

Makiya, Kanan. 1993. *Cruelty and Silence: War, Tyranny, Uprising and the Arab World.* New York: W. W. Norton.

Malcomson, Scott L. 1994. *Empire's Edge: Travels in South-Eastern Europe, Turkey and Central Asia*. London: Verso.

Mamdani, Mahmood. 1996. *Citizen and Subject: Contemporary Africa and the Legacy of Late Colonialism*. Princeton: Princeton Univ. Press.

Mankiw, Gregory, David Romer, and David Weil. 1992. "A Contribution to the Empirics of Economic Growth," *QJE*, 107, 2 (May), 407–37.

Manning, Patrick. 1988. "The Impact of Slave Trade Exports on the Population of the Western Coast of Africa, 1700–1850," in Daget, ed., *De la traite à l'esclavage*.

Mannix, Daniel P., with Malcolm Cowley. 1962. *Black Cargoes: A History of the Atlantic Slave Trade, 1518–1865*. New York: Viking.

March, Andrew L. 1974. *The Idea of China: Myth and Theory in Geographic Thought.* New York: Praeger.

Marco Polo—see Komroff.

Marcus, G. J. 1981. *The Conquest of the North Atlantic*. New York: Oxford Univ. Press.

Marin, Manuela, et Joseph Perez, eds. 1992. *Minorités religieuses dans l'Espagne médiévale*. Special issue of *Revue du monde musulman et de la Méditerranée*, 63–64. Aix-en-Provence: Editions EDISUD.

Markham, Clements R., ed. 1877. *The Voyages of Sir James Lancaster, Kᵗ, to the East Indies*. London: Hakluyt Society.

Marples, David R. 1988. *The Social Impact of the Chernobyl Disaster.* Edmonton: Univ. of Alberta Press.

Marseille, Jacques. 1984. *Empire colonial et capitalisme français: Histoire d'un divorce.* Paris: Albin Michel.

———. 1997. *Puissance et faiblesses de la France industrielle XIXᵉ–XXᵉ siècle*. Paris: Seuil.

Marshall, Joseph. 1773. *Travels Through Holland, Flanders, Germany, Denmark . . . in the Years 1768, 1769 and 1770. 3 vols. London.*

Marshall, Peter James. 1968. *Problems of Empire: Britain and India, 1757–1813*. London: Allen & Unwin.

———. 1976. *East Indian Fortunes: The British in Bengal in the Eighteenth Century.* Oxford: Clarendon Press.

———, ed. 1981. *The Writings and Speeches of Edmund Burke*. Vol. 5. *India: Madras and Bengal 1774–1785*. General editor, Paul Langford. Oxford: Oxford Univ. Press.

———. 1988. "British Assessments of the Dutch in Asia in the Age of Raffles," *Itinerario*, 12, 1: 1–15.

Marshall, Ray, and Marc Tucker. 1992. *Thinking for a Living: Education and the Wealth of Nations*. New York: Basic Books.

Martin, John Frederick. 1991. *Profits in the Wilderness: Entrepreneurship and the Founding of New England Towns in the Seventeenth Century*. Chapel Hill: Univ. North Carolina Press.

Martin Acena, Pablo, and Leandro Prados de la Escosura, eds. 1985. *La nueva historia economica en España*. Madrid: Tecnos.

Martinez, Albert B., and Maurice Lewandowski. 1911. *The Argentine in the Twentieth Century*. London: T. Fisher Unwin.

Marx, Karl. 1906. *Capital: A Critique of Political Economy*. 2d American ed., from 4th German; ed. Frederick Engels. New York: Charles H. Kerr; reprint Modern Library.

Mason, S. F. 1953. "The Scientific Revolution and the Protestant Reformation," *Annals of Science*, 9, 1 (March), 64–87; 9, 2 (June), 154–75.

———. 1953. "Science and Religion in Seventeenth-century England," *Past & Present*, 3 (February).

Mass, William, and William Lazonick. 1991. "The British Cotton Industry and International Competitive Advantage: The State of the Debates," in Rose, ed., *International Competition*, pp. 9–65.

Masselman, George. 1963. *The Cradle of Colonialism*. New Haven: Yale Univ. Press.

Massie, Robert K. 1991. *Dreadnought: Britain, Germany, and the Coming of the Great War*. New York: Random House.

Masters, Bruce. 1988. *The Origins of Western Economic Dominance in the Middle East: Mercantilism and the Islamic Economy in Aleppo, 1600–1750*. New York: NYU Press.

Mathias, Peter, ed. 1972. *Science and Society, 1600–1900*. Cambridge: Univ. Press.

———. 1973. "Capital, Credit and Enterprise in the Industrial Revolution," *J. Europ. Econ. Hist.*, 2, 1 (Spring), 121–43.

———. 1975. "Skills and the Diffusion of Innovations from Britain in the Eighteenth Century," *Trans. Royal Hist. Soc.*, 5th series, 25: 93–113.

———, and John A. Davis, eds. 1989. *The First Industrial Revolutions*. Oxford: Basil Blackwell.

Mathias, Peter, and M. M. Postan, eds. 1978. *The Cambridge Economic History of Europe*. Vol. VII. *The Industrial Economies: Capital, Labour, and Enterprise*. Part 2. *The United States, Japan, and Russia*. Cambridge: Univ. Press.

Mathur, Gautam. 1965. *Planning for Steady Growth*. Oxford: Oxford Univ. Press.

Matossian, Mary. 1958. "Ideologies of Delayed Industrialization: Some Tensions and Ambiguities," *Econ. Devel. and Cult. Change*, 6.

Matthews, R. C. O., C. H. Feinstein, and J. C. Odling-Smee. 1982. *British Economic Growth 1856–1973*. Stanford: Stanford Univ. Press.

Mauny, Raymond. 1960. *Les navigations médiévales sur les côtes sahariennes antérieures à la découverte portugaies* [sic] *(1434)*. Lisbon: Centro de Estudios historicos ultramarinos.

Mauro, Frédéric. 1960. *Le Portugal et l'Atlantique au XVIIᵉ siècle (1570–1670): Étude économique*. Paris: SEVPEN.

———. 1990. "Merchant Communities, 1350–1750," in Tracy, ed., *Rise of Merchant Empires*, pp. 255–86.

Mauro, Paolo. 1995. "Corruption and Growth," *QJE*, 110, 3 (August), 681–712.

Maybury-Lewis, David. 1977. "Societies on the Brink," *Harvard Magazine* (January–February): 56–61.

McAlister, Lyle N. 1984. *Spain and Portugal in the New World, 1492–1700*. Minneapolis: Univ. of Minnesota Press.

McCloskey, Donald N. 1970. "Did Victorian Britain Fail?", *Econ. Hist. Rev.*, 2d ser., 23, 3 (December), 446–59.

———, ed. 1971. *Essays on a Mature Economy: Britain After 1840*. Princeton: Princeton Univ. Press.

———. 1990. *If You're So Smart: The Narrative of Economic Expertise*. Chicago: Univ. of Chicago Press.

———. 1994. "1780–1860: A Survey," in Floud and McCloskey, eds., *Economic History of Britain*, 2d, rev. ed., I, 242–70.

————, and Lars G. Sandberg. 1971. "From Damnation to Redemption: Judgments on the Late Victorian Entrepreneur," *Explor. Econ. Hist.,* 9, 1 (Fall), 89–108.

McCloskey, D. N., and Jean-Pierre Dormois, eds. 1996. "The British Industrial 'Decline' Reconsidered." Papers presented at a conference on "Roots of the British Industrial Decline . . . " Montpellier, 22–23 September 1995.

McConnell, Anita. 1994. "From Craft Workshop to Big Business: The London Scientific Instrument Trade's Response to Increasing Demand, 1750–1820," *London J.,* 19: 36–53.

McCulloch, J. R., ed. 1856/1952. *[A Select Collection of] Early English Tracts on Commerce.* London: Political Economy Club; reprint Cambridge: Econ. Hist. Society.

McCusker, John J., and Russell R. Menard. 1985. *The Economy of British America, 1607–1789.* Chapel Hill: Univ. of North Carolina Press.

McKendrick, Neil. 1960. "Josiah Wedgwood: An Eighteenth-Century Entrepreneur in Salesmanship and Marketing Techniques," *Econ. Hist. Rev.,* 2d ser., 13 (April), 408–33.

McKendrick, Neil, John Brewer, and J. H. Plumb. 1982. *The Birth of a Consumer Society: Commercialization of Eighteenth-Century England.* London: Europa Publications.

McNeill, William H. 1963. *The Rise of the West: A History of the Human Community.* Chicago: Univ. of Chicago Press. Eul. ed., 1991.

————. 1982. *The Pursuit of Power: Technology, Armed Force, and Society since A.D. 1000.* Chicago: Univ. of Chicago Press.

————. 1991. "American Food Crops in the Old World," in A. Viola and C. Margolis, eds., *Seeds of Change: A Quincentennial Celebration.* Washington, DC: Smithsonian Institution.

McRae, Hamish. 1995. *The World in 2020: Power, Culture and Prosperity.* Boston: Harvard Business School.

Medvedev, Grigori. 1991. *The Truth About Chernobyl.* New York: Basic Books.

Mehrens, Bernhard. 1911. *Die Entstehung und Entwicklung der grossen französischen Kreditinstitute mit Berücksichtigung ihres Einflusses auf die wirtschaftliche Entwicklung Frankreichs.* Stuttgart and Berlin: J. G. Cotta.

Mehta, Ved. 1970/1993. *Portrait of India.* New York: Farrar, Strauss & Giroux; New Haven: Yale Univ. Press.

Meier, Gerald M. 1989. "Theoretical Issues Concerning the History of International Trade and Economic Development," in Holtfrerich, ed., *Interactions in the World Economy,* pp. 33–58.

Meier, Gerald M., and Dudley Seers, eds. 1984. *Pioneers in Development.* New York: Oxford Univ. Press for the World Bank.

Meilink-Roelofsz, M.A.F. 1962. *Asian Trade and European Influence.* The Hague: W. Nijhoff.

Meinig, Donald William. 1986. *The Shaping of America: A Geographical Perspective on 500 Years of History.* Vol. I. *Atlantic America, 1492–1800.* New Haven: Yale.

Mendelssohn, Kurt. 1976. *The Secret of Western Domination.* New York: Praeger.

Merlin, Pierre. 1996. *Espoir pour l'Afrique noire.* 2d ed., Dakar: Présence Africaine.

Mernissi, Fatima. 1993. *Islam and Democracy: Fear of the Modern World.* London: Virago.

Meyer, Gordon. 1965. *The River and the People.* London: Methuen; Readers' Union ed., 1967.

Meyer, Jean. 1975. *Les Européens et les autres: De Cortés à Washington.* Paris: Armand Colin.

Michaud, Claude. 1995. "Orléans au XVIII$^e$ siècle: Quelques perspectives nouvelles," *Bull. de la Soc. d'hist. mod. et contemp.* (Supplement to the *Rev. d'hist. mod. et contemp.*, 42), 1–2, pp. 7–13.

Mill, John Stuart. 1869/1975. *The Subjection of Women.* Oxford: Oxford Univ. Press, paperback ed.: John Stuart Mill, *Three Essays.*

Miller, Joseph C. 1988. *Way of Death: Merchant Capitalism and the Angolan Slave Trade 1730–1830.* Madison: Univ. of Wisconsin Press.

Miller, Judith. 1996. *God Has Ninety-nine Names: Reporting from a Militant Middle East.* New York: Simon & Schuster.

Miller, Rory. 1995. "British Investment in Latin America, 1850–1950: A Reappraisal," *Itinerario,* 19, 3: 21–52.

Miller, Russell. 1980. *The Seafarers: The East Indiamen.* Alexandria, VA: Time-Life Books.

Miller, William, ed. 1952. *Men in Business: Essays in the History of Entrepreneurship.* Cambridge, MA: Harvard Univ. Press.

Milward, Alan S., and S. Berrick Saul. 1973. *The Economic Development of Continental Europe 1780–1870.* Totowa, NJ: Rowman & Littlefield.

Minami, Ryoshin. 1987. *Power Revolution in the Industrialization of Japan: 1885–1940.* Institute of Economic Research, Hitotsubashi University, Economic Research Series No. 24. Tokyo: Kinokuniya.

———. 1994. *The Economic Development of Japan: A Quantitative Study.* 2d ed., London: Macmillan.

Minois, Georges. 1990/91. *L'Eglise et la science: Histoire d'un malentendu.* 2 vols. Paris: Fayard.

Mintz, Sidney W. 1985. *Sweetness and Power: The Place of Sugar in Modern History.* New York: Viking, Elisabeth Sifton.

Miquel, Pierre. 1994. *Les Polytechniciens.* Paris: Plon.

Mirabeau, Honoré Gabriel Riquetti, Comte de. 1832. *Mirabeau's Letters, during His Residences in England.* 2 vols.; London: Effingham Wilson. These letters date from the 1780s.

Mitchell, Timothy. 1991. *Colonising Egypt.* Berkeley, CA: Univ. of Calif. Press.

Mitra, Debendra Bijoy. 1978. *The Cotton Weavers of Bengal 1757–1833.* Calcutta: Firma KLM.

Mitsui, Takafusa. 1961. "Some Observations on Merchants" (trans. and ed. E. S. Crawcour), *Trans. Asiatic Soc. Japan,* 3rd Ser.8: 1–139. The text dates from the 1720s.

Miyamoto, Matao. 1986. "Emergence of National Market and Commercial Activities in Tokugawa Japan, with Special Reference to the Development of the Rice Market," *Osaka Economic Papers,* 36, 1–2 (September), 291–310.

———. 1988. "The Products and Market Strategies of the Osaka Cotton Spinning Company," *Japanese Yearbook on Business History,* 5: 117–59.

Miyoshi, Masao. 1994. *As We Saw Them: The First Japanese Embassy to the United States.* New York: Kodansha International.

Mody, H. H. N. 1967. *Japanese Clocks.* Rutland, VT: Tuttle.

Moffett, Matt, and Jonathan Friedland. 1996. "A New Latin America Faces a Devil of Old: Rampant Corruption," *Wall Street Journal,* 1 July, p. 1.

Moine, Jean-Marie. 1989. *Les barons du fer: Les maîtres de forges en Lorraine du milieu du 19$^e$ siècle aux années trente; histoire sociale d'un patronat sidérurgique.* Nancy: Editions Serpenoise; Presses Universitaires de Nancy.

Mokyr, Joel. 1976. *Industrialization in the Low Countries, 1795–1850.* New Haven: Yale Univ. Press.

———, ed. 1985. *The Economics of the Industrial Revolution.* London: Allen & Unwin.

———. 1990. *Lever of Riches: Technological Creativity and Economic Progress*. New York: Oxford Univ. Press.

———, ed.. 1993a. *The British Industrial Revolution: An Economic Perspective*. Boulder: Westview.

———. 1993b. "Urbanization, Technological Progress and Economic History." Typescript.

———. 1994. "Technological Change, 1700–1830," in Floud and McCloskey, eds., *Economic History of Britain Since 1700*, 2d ed., I, 12–43.

Molinas, C., and L. Prados de la Escosura. 1989. "Was Spain Different? Spanish Historical Backwardness Revisited," *Explor. Econ. Hist.*, 26, 4 (October), 385–402.

Mollat, Michel, ed. 1965. *Les grandes voies maritimes dans le monde: XV^e–XIX^e siècles*. Paris: SEVPEN.

Monaghan, Peter. 1994. "A Writer 'to Be Reckoned With,' " *Chronicle of Higher Education*, 40, 45 (13 July): A-8, A-12.

Mondain, P. 1976. "Un conflit oublié: la guerre du Paraguay contre la Triple Alliance, 1864–1870," *Rev. historique*, 520: 385–418.

Montenay, Yves, and Le Club de l'Horloge, eds. 1983. *Le socialisme contre le tiers monde*. Paris: Albin Michel.

Montgomery, James. 1840. *A Practical Detail of the Cotton Manufacture of the United States of America*. Glasgow.

Moor, J. A. De, and H. L. Wesseling, eds. 1989. *Imperialism and War: Essays on Colonial Wars in Asia and Africa*. Leiden: Brill; Leiden University Press.

Moore, Sally Falk. 1958. *Power and Property in Inca Peru*. New York: Columbia Univ. Press.

Morawetz, David. 1977. *Twenty-five Years of Economic Development, 1950 to 1975*. Washington, DC: World Bank.

Morison, Elting E. 1966. *Men, Machines, and Modern Times*. Cambridge, Mass.: MIT Press.

Morita, Akio, with Edwin M. Reingold and Mitsuko Shimomura. 1986. *Made in Japan: Akio Morita and Sony*. New York: Dutton.

Morley, Samuel A. 1975. "What to Do about Foreign Direct Investment: A Host Country Perspective," *Studies in Comp. Internat. Develop.*, 10: 45–66.

Mörner, Magnus. 1976. "Spanish Migration to the New World Prior to 1810: A Report on the State of the Research," in Chiappelli, ed., *First Images of America*, II, 723–82.

Morris, Jan. 1985/1997. *Hong Kong: Epilogue to an Empire*. New York: Vintage Departures.

Morris-Suzuki, Tessa. 1994. *The Technological Transformation of Japan from the Seventeenth to the Twenty-first Century*. Cambridge: Univ. Press.

Morse, Richard M. 1964. "The Heritage of Latin America," in Louis Hartz *et al.*, *The Founding of New Societies*. New York: Harcourt, Brace and World, pp. 123–77.

Mosk, Sanford A. 1948. "Latin America and the World Economy, 1850–1914," *Inter-American Econ. Affairs*, 2: 53–82.

———. 1951. "Latin America versus the United States," *Amer. Econ. Rev.*, 41, 2 (May), 367–83.

Moss, R. P. 1992. "Environmental Constraints on Development in Tropical Africa," in M. B. Gleave, ed., *Tropical African Development: Geographical Perspectives*. Burnt Mill, Harlow: Longmans; New York: John Wiley, pp. 50–92.

Mossner, Ernest Campbell, and Ian Simpson Ross, eds. 1987. *The Correspondence of Adam Smith*. 2d ed., Oxford: Clarendon Press.

Mosteshar, Cherry. 1995. *Unveiled: One Woman's Nightmare in Iran*. New York: St. Martin's Press.

Mottahedeh, Roy P. 1995. "The Islamic Movement: The Case for Democratic Inclusion," *Contention*, 4, 3 (Spring), 107–27.

———. 1996. "The Clash of Civilizations: An Islamicist's Critique," *Harvard Middle Eastern & Islamic Rev.*, 2, 2: 1–26.

Mousnier, Roland. 1951. "L'évolution des finances publiques en France et en Angleterre pendant les guerres de la Ligue d'Augsbourg et de la Succession d'Espagne," *Rev. historique*, 205: 1–23.

Moussa, Pierre. 1962. *The Underprivileged Nations*. London: Sidgwick & Jackson. French ed., 1959, *Les nations prolétaires*. Paris: Presses Universitaires de France.

Mowery, David C., and Nathan Rosenberg. 1989. *Technology and the Pursuit of Economic Growth*. Cambridge: Univ. Press.

Moynahan, Brian. 1994. *The Russian Century: A History of the Last Hundred Years*. New York: Random House.

Muller, Jerry Z. 1990. "Justus Möser and the Conservative Critique of Early Modern Capitalism," *Central European History*, 232, 2/3 (June–September): 153–78.

Mullet des Essards, Louis-Gabriel. 1996. *Voyage en Cochinchine 1787–1789*. Paris: Editions de Paris. (Mullet, b. 1763, was supply officer [*commis aux revues*] on the voyage.)

Mumford, Lewis. 1939. *Technics and Civilization*. New York: Harcourt, Brace.

Munro, John H. 1990. "Urban Regulation and Monopolistic Competition in the Textile Industries of the Late-Medieval Low Countries," in Aerts and Munro, eds., *Textiles of the Low Countries*, pp. 41–52.

———. 1994. "Patterns of Trade, Money, and Credit," in Thomas A. Brady, Jr., *et al.*, eds., *Handbook of European History 1400–1600: Late Middle Ages, Renaissance and Reformation*, Vol. I. *Structures and Assertions*. Leiden: Brill, pp. 147–95.

———. 1995. "Anglo-Flemish Competition in the International Cloth Trade, 1340–1520," *Publication du Centre européen d'Etudes bourguignonnes (XIVe–XVIe s.)*, 35: Rencontres d'Oxford, 22–25 September 1994.

Murdoch, Tessa, *et al.* 1985. *The Quiet Conquest: The Huguenots 1685 to 1985*. Catalogue of an exhibition. London: Museum of London.

Murphey, Rhoads. 1974. "The Treaty Ports and China's Modernization," in Mark Elvin and G. William Skinner, eds., *The Chinese City Between Two Worlds*, Stanford Univ. Press, pp. 17–71.

———. 1977. *The Outsiders: The Western Experience in India and China*. Ann Arbor: Univ. of Michigan Press.

Murphy, K., Andre Shleifer, and R. Vishny. 1989. "Income Distribution, Market Size, and Industrialization," *QJE*, 104.

———. 1989. "Industrialization and the Big Push," *J. Pol. Econ.*, 97.

Murray, Geoffrey, and Audrey Perera. 1996. *Singapore: The Global City-State*. New York: St. Martin's Press.

Murray, Martin J. 1980. *The Development of Capitalism in Colonial Indochina (1870–1940)*. Berkeley: Univ. of California Press.

Musson, A. E., ed. 1972. *Science, Technology and Economic Growth in the Eighteenth Century*. London: Methuen.

Musson, A. E., and Eric Robinson. 1969. *Science and Technology in the Industrial Revolution*. Manchester: Manchester Univ. Press.

Myers, Ramon H. 1974. "Transformation and Continuity in Chinese Economic and Social History," *J. Asian Studies*, 33, 2: 265–77.

Myers, Ramon H., and M. R. Peattie, eds. 1984. *The Japanese Colonial Empire, 1895–1945*. Princeton: Princeton Univ. Press.

Nadal Oller, Jordi. 1959. "La revolución de los precios españoles en el siglo XVI," *Hispania*, 19: 503–29.

————. 1973. "The Failure of the Industrial Revolution in Spain, 1830–1914," in Cipolla, ed., *The Fontana Economic History*, IV, *The Emergence of Industrial Societies*, pp. 532–626.

————. 1975. *El fracaso de la Revolución industrial en España, 1814–1913*. Barcelona: Ariel.

Nag, Amal, and Robert L. Simison. 1983. "With Three New Cars, the Japanese Outdo U.S., Move into New Market," *Wall Street Journal*, 17 March, p. 37.

Naipaul, V. S. 1964. *An Area of Darkness*. Harmondsworth: Penguin.

————. 1981. *The Return of Eva Perón*. New York: Vintage.

Naisbitt, John. 1996. *Megatrends Asia: Eight Asian Megatrends That Are Reshaping Our World*. New York: Simon & Schuster.

Nakamura, James, and Hiroshi Shimbo. 1988. "Why Was Economic Achievement So Easy for Japan?" Typescript.

Nakamura, Satoru. 1990. "The Development of Rural Industry," in Nakane and Oishi, eds., *Tokugawa Japan*, pp. 81–96.

Nakane, Chie, and Shinzaburo Oishi, eds. 1990. *Tokugawa Japan: The Social and Economic Antecedents of Modern Japan*. Trans. and ed. by Conrad Totman. Tokyo: Univ. of Tokyo Press.

Nakayama, Shigeru, and Nathan Sivin, eds. 1973. *Chinese Science: Explorations of an Ancient Tradition*. Cambridge, MA: MIT Press.

Narain, Brij. 1929. *Indian Economic Life*. Lahore: Uttar Chand Kapur & Sons.

National Academy of Sciences (USA). 1967. *Applied Science and Technological Progress*. Washington, DC: GPO.

Neal, Larry. 1990. *The Rise of Financial Capitalism: International Capital Markets in the Age of Reason*. Cambridge: Univ. Press.

Needham, Joseph, *et al.* 1954–. *Science and Civilization in China*. Cambridge: Univ. Press.

Needham, Joseph. 1963. "Poverties and Triumphs of the Chinese Scientific Tradition," in Crombie, ed., *Scientific Change*, pp. 117–53.

————. 1964. *The Development of Iron and Steel Technology in China*. Dickinson Memorial Lecture to the Newcomen Society 1956. Cambridge: W. Heffer & Sons for the Newcomen Society.

————. 1969. *The Grand Titration: Science and Society in East and West*. London: Allen & Unwin.

————. 1970. *Clerks and Craftsmen in China and the West. Lectures and Addresses on the History of Science and Technology*. Cambridge: Univ. Press.

————. 1980. "The Guns of Khaifeng-fu," *TLS*, 11 January, pp. 39–42.

Needham, Joseph, Wang Ling, and Derek J. de Solla Price. 1960. *Heavenly Clockwork: The Great Astronomical Clocks of Medieval China*. Cambridge: Univ. Press.

Nef, John U. 1932. *Rise of the British Coal Industry*. 2 vols. London: Routledge.

Nelson, Richard R. 1993. *National Innovation Systems: A Comparative Analysis*. New York: Oxford Univ. Press.

Nelson, Richard R., and Gavin Wright. 1992. "The Rise and Fall of American Technological Leadership: The Postwar Era in Historical Perspective," *J. Econ. Lit.*, 30 (December), 1931–64.

Netanyahu, Benzion. 1995. *The Origins of the Inquisition in Fifteenth Century Spain*. New York: Random House.

New York Times. 1996. *The Downsizing of America*. New York: Times Books.

Newland, Carlos. 1991. "Spanish American Elementary Education before Independence: Continuity and Change in a Colonial Environment," *Itinerario*, 15, 2: 79–95.

Noiríel, Gérard. 1984. *Longwy: immigrés et prolétaires 1880–1980*. Paris: PUF.

Nolte, Sharon H., and Sally Ann Hastings. 1991. "The Meiji State's Policy Toward Women, 1890–1910," in Bernstein, ed., *Recreating Japanese Women*, pp. 151–74.

Nora, Dominique. 1991. *L'étreinte du samuraï: le Défi japonais*. Paris: Calmann-Lévy.

Nordhaus, William. 1994. "The Price of Light." Cowles Foundation Discussion Paper 1078.

Norgaard, Richard B. 1994. *Development Betrayed: The End of Progress and a Coevolutionary Revisioning of the Future*. London: Routledge.

Northrup, David. 1995. *Indentured Labor in the Age of Imperialism, 1834–1922*. Cambridge: Univ. Press.

Nossiter, Bernard D. 1987. *The Global Struggle for More: Third World Conflicts with Rich Nations*. New York: Twentieth Century Fund; Harper & Row.

O'Brien, Patrick K., ed. 1983. *Railways and the Economic Development of Western Europe, 1830–1914*. London: Macmillan.

———. 1986. "Do We Have a Typology for the Study of European Industrialization in the XIXth Century?" *J. Europ. Econ. Hist.*, 15, 2: 291–334.

———. 1988. "The Costs and Benefits of British Imperialism, 1846–1914," *Past & Present*, 120: 163–200.

O'Brien, Patrick K., and Stanley Engerman. 1991. "Exports and the Growth of the British Economy from the Glorious Revolution to the Peace of Amiens," in Solow, ed., *Slavery*, pp. 177–209.

O'Brien, Patrick K., T. Griffiths, and P. A. Hunt. 1996. "Theories of Technological Progress and the British Textile Industry from Kay to Cartwright," *Revista de historia económica*, 14, 3 (otoño-invierno): 533–35.

O'Brien, Patrick K., and Caglar Keyder. 1978. *Economic Growth in Britain and France, 1780–1914: Two Paths to the Twentieth Century*. London: Allen & Unwin.

O'Brien, Patrick K., and Roland Quinault, eds. 1993. *The Industrial Revolution and British Society*. Cambridge: Univ. Press.

O'Connor, Anthony M. 1991. *Poverty in Africa: A Geographical Approach*. London: Belhaven.

Ohkawa, Kazushi, and Henry Rosovsky. 1960. "The Role of Agriculture in Modern Japanese Economic Development," *Econ. Dev. and Cult. Change*, 9 (October): 43–68.

———. 1965. "A Century of Japanese Economic Growth," in Lockwood, ed., *The State and Economic Enterprise*, pp. 47–92.

———. 1973. *Japanese Economic Growth: Trend Acceleration in the Twentieth Century*. Stanford: Stanford Univ. Press.

———. 1978. "Capital Formation in Japan," in Mathias and Postan, eds., *Cambridge Economic History of Europe*, VII, 2, 134–65.

Ohkawa, Kazushi, and Gustav Ranis, eds. 1985. *Japan and the Developing Countries: A Comparative Analysis*. Oxford: Basil Blackwell.

Ohkawa, Kazushi, and Hirohisa Kohama. 1989. *Lectures on Developing Economics: Japan's Experience and Its Relevance*. Tokyo: Univ. of Tokyo Press.

Ohmae, Kenichi. 1995. *The End of the Nation State: The Rise of Regional Economies*. New York: HarperCollins.

Oishi, Shinzaburo. 1990. "The Bakuhan System," in Nakane and Oishi, eds., *Tokugawa Japan*, pp. 11–36.

Okimoto, Daniel I. 1989. *Between MITI and the Market: Japanese Industrial Policy for High Technology*. Stanford: Stanford Univ. Press.

Okyar, Osman. 1987. "A New Look at the Problem of Economic Growth in the Ottoman Empire (1800–1914)," *J. Europ. Econ. Hist.*, 16, 1 (Spring): 7–49.

Oliphant, Laurence. 1859/1970. *Elgin's Mission to China and Japan*. 2 vols. Hong Kong and Tokyo: Oxford Univ. Press. Reprint of original ed. by Oliphant,

*Narrative of the Earl of Elgin's Mission to China and Japan in the Years 1857, '58, '59.* 2 vols. Edinburgh and London: William Blackwood & Sons.

Oliver, John W. 1956. *History of American Technology.* New York: Ronald Press.

Olson, Mancur. 1982. *The Rise and Decline of Nations: Economic Growth, Stagflation, and Social Rigidities.* New Haven: Yale Univ. Press.

Omoto, Keiko, and Francis Macouin. 1990. *Quand le Japon s'ouvrit au monde.* Paris: Gallimard.

Orhant, Francis. 1991. *Bartolomé de Las Casas: Un colonisateur saisi par l'Evangile.* Paris: Editions Ouvrières. The cover page has the title *Bartolomé de Las Casas: De la colonisation à la défense des Indiens.*

O'Rourke, Kevin, and Jeffrey G. Williamson. 1995. "Open Economy Forces and Late 19th Century Scandinavian Catch-up." Harvard Inst. Econ. Research, Discussion Paper 1709. NBER Working Paper Series 5112.

———. 1995. "Around the European Periphery 1870–1913: Globalization, Schooling and Growth." NBER Working Paper Series 5392.

Ortiz de Montellano, Bernard R. 1978. "Aztec Cannibalism: An Ecological Necessity?" *Science,* 200, 4232 (12 May), 611–17.

Osborne, Milton. 1995. *Southeast Asia: An Introductory History.* 6th ed., St. Leonards, NSW, Australia: Allen & Unwin.

Oshima, Harry T. 1987. *Economic Growth in Monsoon Asia: A Comparative Survey.* Tokyo: Univ. of Tokyo Press.

Osberg, Lars, ed. 1991. *Economic Inequality and Poverty: International Perspectives.* Armonk, NY: M. E. Sharpe.

Oxaal, Ivar. 1968. *Black Intellectuals Come to Power: The Rise of Creole Nationalism in Trinidad and Tobago.* Cambridge, MA: Schenkman Publ.

Oxley, G. W. 1969. "The Permanent Poor in South-West Lancashire Under the Old Poor Law," in Harris, ed., *Liverpool and Merseyside,* pp. 16–49.

Pack, Howard. 1988. "Industrialization and Trade," in Hollis Chenery and T. N. Srinivasan, eds., *Handbook of Development Economics,* Vol. I (North-Holland: Elsevier), pp. 333–80.

Pack, Howard, and Larry E. Westphal. 1986. "Industrial Strategy and Technological Change: Theory versus Reality," *J. Develop. Econ.,* 22: 87–128.

Padden, R. Charles. 1957. "Cultural Change and Military Resistance in Araucanian Chile, 1550–1730," *Southwestern J. of Anthropology,* 13, 103–21.

———. 1967. *The Hummingbird and the Hawk.* Columbus: Ohio State Univ. Press.

Paepke, C. Owen. 1993. *The Evolution of Progress: The End of Economic Growth and the Beginning of Human Transformation.* New York: Random House.

Pagden, Anthony. 1982. *The Fall of Natural Man: The American Indian and the Origins of Comparative Ethnology.* New York: Cambridge Univ. Press.

———. 1995. *Lords of All the World: Ideologies of Empire in Spain, Britain and France, c1500–c1800.* New Haven: Yale Univ. Press.

Page, Thomas J. 1859. *La Plata, the Argentine Confederation, and Paraguay.* New York: Harper & Bros.

Pakenham, Thomas. 1979. *The Boer War.* New York: Avon Books.

Pan, Lynn. 1994. *Sons of the Yellow Emperor: A History of the Chinese Diaspora.* New York: Kodansha.

Paquette, Robert L. 1988. *Sugar Is Made with Blood: The Conspiracy of La Escalera and the Conflict Between Empires Over Slavery in Cuba.* Middletown, CT: Wesleyan Univ. Press.

Pares, Richard. 1936/1963. *War and Trade in the West Indies, 1739–63.* London: Frank Cass.

———. 1956. *Yankees and Creoles: The Trade between North America and the West Indies Before the American Revolution.* London: Longmans, Green.

————. 1960. *Merchants and Planters. Economic History Review,* Supplement 4. Cambridge: Univ. Press.

Park, Yung Chul, and Won-Am Park. 1995. "Changing Japanese Trade Patterns and the East Asian NICs," in Krugman, ed., *Trade with Japan,* pp. 85–115.

Parry, John H. 1964. *The Age of Reconnaissance.* London: Weidenfeld & Nicolson.

————. 1971a. *The Spanish Seaborne Empire.* New York: Knopf.

————. 1971b. *Trade and Dominion: The European Overseas Empires in the Eighteenth Century.* New York: Praeger.

————. 1974. *The Discovery of the Sea.* New York: Dial Press.

Parry, Vernon J., and M. E. Yapp, eds. 1975. *War, Technology and Society in the Middle East.* London: Oxford Univ. Press.

Parsons, Talcott. 1949. *The Structure of Social Action.* 2d ed., Glencoe, IL: Free Press.

Parthasarathi, Prasannan. 1998. "Rethinking Backwardness in the Eighteenth Century: Wages and Competitiveness in Britain and South India before the Industrial Revolution." To appear in *Past & Present.*

Pastor Bodmer, Beatriz. 1992. *The Armature of Conquest: Spanish Accounts of the Discovery of America, 1492–1589.* Stanford: Stanford Univ. Press.

Pastore, C. 1978. "Introduction a una historia economica del Paraguay en el siglo XIX," *Ateneo Paraguayo de historia/Historia Paraguaya* (Asuncion), 16: 103–26.

Pastore, Mario. 1994a. "State-led Industrialisation: The Evidence on Paraguay, 1852–1870," *J. Lat. Amer. Studies,* 26, 2 (May): 295–324.

————. 1994b. "Trade Contraction and Economic Decline: The Paraguayan Economy Under Francia, 1810–1840," *J. Lat. Amer. Studies,* 26, 3 (October): 539–95.

Patel, Surendra J. 1961. "Rates of Industrial Growth in the Last Century, 1860–1958," *Econ. Devel. and Cultural Change,* 9, 3 (April), 316–30.

Patrick, Hugh T., ed. 1976. *Japanese Industrialization and Its Social Consequences.* Berkeley: Univ. of Calif. Press.

————, and Henry Rosovsky, eds. 1976. *Asia's New Giant: How the Japanese Economy Works.* Washington, DC: Brookings Institute.

Pavitt, Keith, ed. 1980. *Technical Change and British Economic Performance.* London: Macmillan.

Payen, Jacques. 1969. *Capital et machine à vapeur au XVIII^e siècle: Les frères Perier et l'introduction en France de la machine à vapeur de Watt.* Paris and The Hague: Mouton.

Payne, Peter L. 1978. "Industrial Entrepreneurship and Management in Great Britain," in Mathias and Postan, eds., *Cambridge Economic History of Europe,* Vol. VII, ch. 4, pp. 180–230.

Pearson, M. N. 1976. *Merchants and Rulers in Gujarat: The Response to the Portuguese in the Sixteenth Century.* Berkeley: Univ. of California Press.

————. 1987. "India and the Indian Ocean in the Sixteenth Century," in Das Gupta and Pearson, eds., *India and the Indian Ocean,* pp. 71–93.

Peattie, Mark. R. 1984. "Japanese Attitudes Toward Colonialism, 1895–1945," in Myers and Peattie, eds., *Japanese Colonial Empire,* pp. 80–127.

Pedemonte Castillo, Javier. 1988. *El Problema judío en la España moderna: Sintesis del hecho diferencial judeoconverso.* Barcelona: PPU.

Perdue, Peter C. 1987. *Exhausting the Earth: State and Peasant in Hunan, 1500–1850.* Cambridge, MA: Harvard, Council on East Asian Studies.

Perez, Carlota. 1983. "Structural Change and the Assimilation of New Technologies in the Economic and Social Systems," *Futures,* 15, 5: 357–75.

————. 1985. "Microelectronics, Long Waves and World Structural Change: New Perspectives for Developing Countries," *World Development,* 13, 3 (March), 441–63.

Perlin, Frank. 1983. "Proto-Industrialization and Pre-Colonial South Asia," *Past & Present*, 98 (February): 30–95.

Perrin, Noel. 1979. *Giving Up the Gun. Japan's Reversion to the Sword 1543–1879.* Boston: Godine.

Persson, Karl Gunnar, ed. 1993. *The Economic Development of Denmark and Norway Since 1870.* Aldershot: Elgar.

Peterson, Barbara Bennett. 1994. "The Ming Voyages of Cheng Ho (Zheng He), 1371–1433," *The Great Circle*, 16, 1 (April), 43–51.

Pétré-Grenouilleau, Olivier. 1996. *L'argent de la traite: milieu négrier, capitalisme et développement: un modèle.* Paris: Aubier.

Peyrefitte, Alain. 1992. *The Immobile Empire.* New York: Knopf. French ed., 1989: *L'empire immobile ou le choc des mondes: Récit historique.* Paris: Fayard.

———. 1995a. *Du "Miracle" en économie: Leçons au Collège de France.* Paris: Odile Jacob.

———. 1995b. *La société de confiance: Essai sur les origines et la nature du développement.* Paris: Odile Jacob.

Phelps Brown, E. H., and S. J. Handfield-Jones. 1952. "The Climacteric of the 1890's," *Oxford Economic Papers*, n.s., 4, 3 (October): 266–307.

Philippe, Robert. 1984. "L'Eglise et l'énergie pendant le XIe siècle dans les pays entre Seine et Loire," *Cahiers de civilisation médiévale Xe–XIIe siècles*, 27: 107–17.

Phillips, Gregory D. 1979. *The Diehards: Aristocratic Society and Politics in Edwardian England.* Cambridge, MA: Harvard Univ. Press.

Picon, Antoine. 1992. *L'invention de l'ingénieur moderne: L'Ecole des Ponts et Chaussées 1747–1851.* Paris: Ponts et Chaussées.

Pike, Ruth. 1966. *Enterprise and Adventure: The Genoese in Seville and the Opening of the New World.* Ithaca: Cornell Univ. Press.

Piore, Michael J., and Charles F. Sabel. 1984. *The Second Industrial Divide: Possibilities for Prosperity.* New York: Basic Books.

Pirenne, Henri. 1936. *Histoire de l'Europe des invasions au XVIe siècle.* 3rd ed.; Paris: Félix Alcan; Brussels: Nouv. Soc. d'Editions.

Platt, D. C. M. 1985. "Dependency and the Historian: Further Objections," in Abel and Lewis, eds., *Latin America*, pp. 29–39.

Platteau, Jean-Philippe. 1995. "The Food Crisis in Africa: A Comparative Structural Analysis," in Drèze, Sen, and Hussain, eds., *Political Economy of Hunger*, pp. 445–553.

Plenge, Johann. 1903. *Gründung und Geschichte des Crédit Mobilier.* Tübingen.

Pluchon, Pierre. 1984. *Nègres et Juifs au XVIIIe siècle: Le racisme au siècle des Lumières.* Paris: Tallandier.

Polanyi, Micheal. 1967. *The Tacit Dimension.* London: Routledge & Kegan Paul.

Pollard, Sidney. 1981. *Peaceful Conquest: The Industrialization of Europe, 1760–1970.* Oxford: Oxford Univ. Press.

———. 1983. *The Development of the British Economy, 1914–1980.* 3rd ed. London: Edward Arnold.

———. 1989. *Britain's Prime and Britain's Decline.* London: Edward Arnold.

Pope-Hennessy, James. 1968. *Sins of the Fathers: A Study of the Atlantic Slave Traders, 1441–1807.* London: Weidenfeld & Nicolson.

Portal, Roger. 1950. *L'Oural au XVIIIe siècle Etude d'histoire économique et sociale.* Paris: Institut d'Etudes slaves.

———. 1961. "Origines d'une bourgeoisie industrielle en Russie," *Rev. d'hist. moderne et contemporaine*, VIII, 35–60.

Porter, Michael E. 1990. *The Competitive Advantage of Nations.* New York: Free Press.

Porter, Roy, and Mikulas Teich, eds. 1992. *The Scientific Revolution in National Context.* Cambridge: Univ. Press.

Postlethwayt, Malachy. 1757/1968. *Great-Britain's True System; Wherein Is Clearly Shown . . .* London. Reprint; Farnborough: Gregg International.

Pounds, Norman. 1974. *An Economic History of Medieval Europe.* London: Longmans, Green.

Pounds, N. J. G. 1952. *The Ruhr: A Study in Historical and Economic Geography.* Bloomington: Indiana Univ. Press.

———. 1958. *The Upper Silesian Industrial Region.* Bloomington: Indiana Univ. Press.

——— and William Parker. 1957. *Coal and Steel in Western Europe.* Bloomington: Indiana Univ. Press.

Powell, Raymond. 1968. "Economic Growth in the U.S.S.R.," *Scientific American,* 219, 6 (December), 17–23.

Powelson, John P. 1994. *Centuries of Economic Endeavor: Parallel Paths in Japan and Europe and Their Contrast with the Third World.* Ann Arbor: Univ. of Michigan Press.

Prado, Caio, Jr. 1967. *The Colonial Background of Modern Brazil.* Berkeley: Univ. of Calif. Press.

Prados de la Escosura, Leandro. 1988. *De imperio a nación: Crecimiento y atraso económico en España (1780–1930).* Madrid: Alianza Editorial.

——— and Vera Zamagni, eds. 1992. *El desarrollo económico en la Europa del sur: España e Italia en perspectiva histórica.* Madrid: Alianza Universidad.

Prais, S. J. 1994. "Economic Performance and Education: The Nature of Britain's Deficiencies," *Proc. Brit. Acad.,* 84: 151–207.

Prakash, Gyan, ed. 1995. *After Colonialism: Imperial Histories and Postcolonial Displacements.* Princeton: Princeton Univ. Press.

Prakash, Om. 1988. "Opium Monopoly in India and Indonesia in the Eighteenth Century," *Itinerario,* 12, 1: 73–90. Republished in Subrahmanyam, ed., *Merchants, Markets and the State,* pp. 121–38.

———. 1987. "The Dutch East India Company in the Trade of the Indian Ocean," in Das Gupta and Pearson, eds., *India and the Indian Ocean,* pp. 185–200.

Preston, Richard. 1991. *American Steel: Hot Metal Men and the Resurrection of the Rust Belt.* New York: Prentice-Hall.

———. 1994. *The Hot Zone.* New York: Random House.

Price, Barbara J. 1978. "Demystification, Enriddlement, and Aztec Cannibalism: A Materialist Rejoinder to Harner," *American Ethnologist,* 5: 98–115.

Prins, Gwyn. 1989. "But What Was the Disease? The Present State of Health and Healing in African Studies," *Past & Present,* 124 (August): 159–79.

Proust, Jacques. 1997. *L'Europe au prisme du Japon: XVIe–XVIIIe siècle: Entre humanisme, Contre-Réforme et Lumières.* Paris: Albin Michel.

Pryor, John H. 1988. *Geography, Technology, and War: Studies in the Maritime History of the Mediterranean 649–1571.* Cambridge: Univ. Press.

Pullan, Brian, ed. 1968. *Crisis and Change in the Venetian Economy in the Sixteenth and Seventeenth Centuries.* London: Methuen.

Qadir, C. A. 1988. *Philosophy and Science in the Islamic World.* London: Croom Helm.

Qian, W. Y. 1985. *The Great Inertia: Scientific Stagnation in Traditional China.* London: Croom Helm.

*Quarterly Review.* See Ellis, Henry.

Quinn, Arthur. 1994. *A New World: An Epic of Colonial America from the Founding of Jamestown to the Fall of Quebec.* Boston: Faber & Faber.

Quinn, David Beers, ed. 1979. *New American World: A Documentary History of North America to 1612.* 5 vols. New York: Arno Press and Hector Bye.

Raban, Jonathan. 1979. *Arabia: A Journey through the Labyrinth.* New York: Simon & Schuster.

Rahman, Abdur. 1973. "Sixteenth- and Seventeenth-Century Science in India and Some Problems of Comparative Studies," in Teich and Young, eds., *Changing Perspectives*, pp. 52–67.

Ralston, David B. 1990. *Importing the European Army: The Introduction of European Military Techniques and Institutions into the Extra-European World 1600–1914.* Chicago: Univ. of Chicago Press.

Ram, Rati. 1996. "Tropics and Economic Development: An Empirical Investigation." Economics Dept., Illinois State Univ. Typescript.

Ramaswamy, Vijaya. 1985. *Textiles and Weavers in Medieval South India.* Delhi: Oxford Univ. Press.

Ramsey, John Fraser. 1973. *Spain: The Rise of the First World Power.* Tuscaloosa, AL: Univ. of Alabama Press.

Randall, Adrian. 1991. *Before the Luddites: Custom, Community and Machinery in the English Woollen Industry, 1776–1809.* Cambridge: Univ. Press.

Randall, Laura. 1976. "Lies, Damn Lies, and Argentine GDP," *Latin Amer. Res. Rev.,* 11, 1: 137–58.

Randles, W. G. 1961/1986. "La signification cosmographique du passage du Cap Bojador," in N. Broc, ed., *La géographie de la Renaissance 1420–1620.* Paris: Editions du CTHS.

Ranis, Gustav. 1955. "The Community Centered Entrepreneur in Japanese Development," *Explor. Entrepr. Hist.,* 8, 2 (December), 80–98.

—— and T. Paul Schultz, eds. 1988. *The State of Development Economics: Progress and Perspectives.* New York: Basil Blackwell.

Ransford, Oliver. 1972. *The Slave Trade: The Story of Transatlantic Slavery.* Newton Abbot: Readers' Union.

Rapp, Richard Tilden. 1976. *Industry and Economic Decline in Seventeenth-Century Venice.* Cambridge, MA: Harvard Univ. Press.

Ratcliffe, Barrie. 1977. "Great Britain and Tariff Reform in France 1831–36," in Chaloner and Ratcliffe, eds., *Trade and Transport,* pp. 98–135.

—— and W. H. Chaloner, eds. 1977. *A French Sociologist Looks at Britain: Gustave d'Eichthal and British Society in 1828.* Manchester: Manchester Univ. Press.

Rau, Virginia. 1968. *Estudos de historia.* Porto: Editorial Verbo.

Rawski, Thomas G., and Lillian M. Li, eds. 1992. *Chinese History in Economic Perspective.* Berkeley: Univ. of Calif. Press.

Ray, G. F. 1969. "The Diffusion of New Technology: A Study of Ten Processes in Nine Industries," *Nat. Inst. Econ. Rev.,* 48, 1; 134–87.

Raychaudhuri, Tapan. 1982a. "The State and the Economy, I. The Mughal Empire," in Raychaudhuri and Habib, eds., *Cambridge Economic History of India,* I, 172–93.

——. 1982b. "Non-Agricultural Production: Mughal India," in Raychaudhuri and Habib, eds., *Cambridge Economic History of India,* I, 261–307.

——. 1985. "Historical Roots of Mass Poverty in South Asia: A Hypothesis," *Economic and Political Weekly* (Delhi), 20, 18 (May 4), 801–06.

—— and Irfan Habib, eds. 1982. *Cambridge Economic History of India.* Vol. I. c. 1200–c. 1750. Cambridge: Univ. Press.

Reader, W. J. 1970. *Imperial Chemical Industries: A History.* Vol. I. *The Forerunners 1870–1926.* London: Oxford Univ. Press.

Reading, Brian. 1993. *Japan: The Coming Collapse.* London: Orion.

Reber, Vera Blinn. 1988. "The Demographics of Paraguay: A Reinterpretation of the Great War, 1864–1870," *Hispanic Amer. Hist. Rev.,* 68, 2: 289–319.

Rediker, Marcus. 1987. *Between the Devil and the Deep Blue Sea: Merchant Seamen, Pirates, and the Anglo-American Maritime World, 1700–1750.* Cambridge: Univ. Press.

Redondo, Augustin, and Marc Vitse, eds. 1994. *Quelques aspects des peurs sociales dans l'Espagne du siècle d'or: L'individu face à la société.* Toulouse: Presses universitaires du Mirail.

Reid, Anthony. 1988/1993. *Southeast Asia in the Age of Commerce 1450–1680.* Vol. I. *The Lands Below the Winds.* Vol. II. *Expansion and Crisis.* New Haven: Yale Univ. Press.

Reinert, Erik S. 1994. "Symptoms and Causes of Poverty: Underdevelopment in a Schumpeterian System," *Forum for Devel. Studies,* 1–2: 73–109.

———, and Arno Mong Daastol. 1995. "Exploring the Genesis of Economic Innovations: The Religious Gestalt-switch and the *Duty to Invent* as Preconditions for Economic Growth." Forthcoming in Reinert, ed., *Christian Wolff.* London: Routledge.

Remnick, David. 1993. *Lenin's Tomb: The Last Days of the Soviet Empire.* New York: Random House.

———. 1997. *Resurrection: The Struggle for a New Russia.* New York: Random House.

Reynolds, Lloyd G. 1986. *Economic Growth in the Third World: An Introduction.* New Haven: Yale Univ. Press.

Reynolds, Robert L. 1961. *Europe Emerges: Transition Toward an Industrial Worldwide Society 600–1750.* Madison: Univ. of Wisconsin Press.

Reynolds, Terry S. 1983. *Stronger Than a Hundred Men: A History of the Vertical Water Wheel.* Baltimore: Johns Hopkins Univ. Press.

Rich, E. E. 1967. "Colonial Settlement and Its Labour Problems," in E. E. Rich and Charles H. Wilson, eds., *Cambridge Economic History of Europe.* Vol. IV. *The Economy of Expanding Europe in the 16th and 17th Centuries,* pp. 302–73.

Richardson, Bonham C. 1992. *The Caribbean in the Wider World, 1492–1992: A Regional Geography.* Cambridge: Univ. Press.

Riem, Andreas. 1795–97. *Europeans Politische Lage und Staats-interesse.* 6 parts. in 2 vols.

Riesser, Jacob. 1911. *The German Great Banks and Their Concentration in Connection with the Economic Development of Germany.* 3rd ed., Washington, DC: 61st Congress, 2d Sess., Senate Doc. 593. Washington, DC: GPO for the National Monetary Commission.

Rifkin, Jeremy. 1995. *The End of Work: The End of the Global Labor Force and the Dawn of the Post-Market Era.* New York: Putnam.

Ritter, Ulrich Peter. 1961. *Die Rolle des Staates in den Frühstadien der Industrialisierung.* Berlin: Duncker & Humblot.

Robbins, David. 1995. *Aspects of Africa.* New York: Viking Penguin.

Robequain, Charles. 1944. *The Economic Development of French Indo-China.* London: Oxford Univ. Press.

Roberti, Mark. 1994. *The Fall of Hong Kong: China's Triumph and Britain's Betrayal.* New York: John Wiley.

Roberts, Richard. 1995. "The Coercion of Free Markets: Cotton, Peasants, and the Colonial State in the French Soudan, 1924–1932," in Isaacman and Roberts, eds., *Cotton, Colonialism,* pp. 221–43.

Robertson, H. M. 1933. *Aspects of the Rise of Economic Individualism: A Criticism of Max Weber and His School.* London: Cambridge Univ. Press.

Robertson, John Drummond. 1931. *The Evolution of Clockwork.* London: Cassell.

Robinson, Francis. 1995. "Through the Minefield: Bernard Lewis and 'the Wonder of Arab Empire,' " *TLS,* 8 December 95, pp. 3–4.

Robison, Richard, and David S. G. Goodman, eds. 1996. *The New Rich in Asia: Mobile Phones, McDonalds and Middle-Class Revolution.* London: Routledge.

Rochebrune, Renaud de, and Jean-Claude Hazera. 1995/1997. *Les patrons sous l'occupation*, Vol. I: *Collaboration, résistance, marché noir;* Vol. II: *Pétainisme, intrigues, spoliations*. Paris: Odile Jacob; "Opus."

Rock, David. 1987. *Argentina 1516–1987: From Spanish Colonization to Alfonsin*. Rev. ed., Berkeley: Univ. of Calif. Press.

———. 1988. "Features of Industrial Development in Argentina: 1870, 1910, 1945." Typescript prepared for meeting on Latin America, Harvard Univ.

Rodney, C. A., and John Graham. 1818, reprinted 1969. *The Reports of the Present State of the United Provinces of South America . . . Laid Before the Congress of the United States*. New York: Praeger.

Rodney, Walter. 1972. *How Europe Underdeveloped Africa*. London: Bogle-L'Ouverture.

Rogers, Everett. 1995. *Diffusion of Innovation*. 4th ed., New York: Basic Books.

Rohwer, Jim. 1996. *Asia Rising: How History's Biggest Middle Class Will Change the World*. London: Nicholas Brealey.

Romer, Paul M. 1987. "Growth Based on Increasing Returns due to Specialization," *Amer. Econ. Rev.*, 77 (May), 56–62.

———. 1996. "Why, Indeed, in America? Theory, History and the Origins of Modern Economic Growth." NBER Working Paper Series 5443.

Root, Hilton. 1991. "The Redistributive Role of Government: Economic Regulation in Old Régime France and England," *Comp. Studies Society and Hist.*, 33, 2 (April): 338–69.

———. 1994. "Le marché des droits de propriété en France et en Angleterre à l'époque moderne," *J. des économistes et des études humaines*, 5, 2/3 (June–September), 295–318.

Ropp, Paul S., ed. 1990. *Heritage of China: Contemporary Perspectives on Chinese Civilization*. Berkeley: Univ. of Calif. Press.

Roques, Georges. 1996. *La manière de négocier aux Indes 1676–1691: La Compagnie des Indes et l'art du commerce*. Paris: Maisonneuve & Larose.

Rorabaugh, W. J. 1986. *The Craft Apprentice from Franklin to the Machine Age in America*. New York: Oxford Univ. Press.

Rose, Mary B., ed. 1991. *International Competition and Strategic Response in the Textile Industries since 1870*. London: Frank Cass.

Rosen, Edward. 1956. "The Invention of Eyeglasses," *J. Hist. Med. and Allied Sciences*, 11: 13–46, 183–218.

Rosen, Fred, and Deidre McFayden, eds. 1995. *Free Trade and Economic Restructuring in Latin America*. New York: Monthly Review Press.

Rosenberg, Nathan. 1967. "Anglo-American Wage Differences in the 1820's," *J. Econ. Hist.*, 27, 2 (June): 221–29.

———. 1969. *The American System of Manufactures: The Report of the Committee on the Machinery of the United States 1855 and the Special Reports of George Wallis and Joseph Whitworth 1854*. Edinburgh: Univ. Press.

———. 1976. *Perspectives on Technology*. Cambridge: Univ. Press.

———. 1982. *Inside the Black Box: Technology and Economics*. Cambridge: Univ. Press.

———. 1994. "How the Developed Countries Became Rich," *Daedalus*, 123, 4 (Fall), 127–40.

Rosenberg, Nathan, Ralph Landau, and David C. Mowery, eds. 1992. *Technology and the Wealth of Nations*. Stanford: Stanford Univ. Press.

Rosenthal, Franz. 1983. *"Sweeter Than Hope": Complaint and Hope in Medieval Islam*. Leiden: E. J. Brill.

Rosoli, G., ed. 1993. *Identità degli italiani in Argentina: Reti sociali, famiglia, lavoro*. Rome: Edizioni Studium.

Rostow, Walt W., ed. 1963. *The Economics of Take-off into Sustained Growth*. London: Macmillan.

Rothermund, Dietmar. 1988. *An Economic History of India from Pre-Colonial Times to 1991.* 2d ed., London: Routledge.

Rouse, Irving. 1992. *The Tainos: Rise and Decline of the People Who Greeted Columbus.* New Haven: Yale.

Rowe, John Howland. 1946. "Inca Culture at the Time of the Spanish Conquest," in Julian H. Steward, ed., *Handbook of South American Indians.* Vol. II. *The Andean Civilizations.* Smithsonian Institution, Bureau of American Ethnology, Bulletin 143. Washington, DC: GPO.

———. 1957. "The Incas under Spanish Colonial Institutions." *Hisp. Amer. Hist. Rev.,* 37, 2 (May), 155–99.

Rowe, William T. 1984. *Hankow: Commerce and Society in a Chinese City, 1796–1889.* Stanford: Stanford Univ. Press.

Roy, Joseph-Antoine. 1962. *Histoire de la famille Schneider et du Creusot.* Paris: M. Rivière.

Rozman, Gilbert. 1974. "Edo's Importance in the Changing Tokugawa Society," *J. Japanese Studies,* 1, 1 (Autumn), 91–112.

Rubinstein, Murray A., ed. 1994. *The Other Taiwan 1945 to the Present.* Armonk, NY: East Gate.

Rubinstein, W. D. 1993. *Capitalism, Culture and Decline in Britain 1750–1990.* London: Routledge.

Rucquoi, Adeline. 1993. *Histoire médiévale de la Péninsule ibérique.* Paris: Seuil.

Rudolph, Richard L. 1985. "Agricultural Structure and Proto-Industrialization in Russia: Economic Development with Unfree Labor," *J. Econ. Hist.,* 45, 1 (March), 47–70.

Runge, Joachim. 1966. *Justus Mösers Gewerbetheorie und Gewerbepolitik im Fürstbistum Osnabrück in der zweiten Hälfte des 18. Jahrhunderts.* Berlin: Duncker & Humblot.

Ruscio, Alain. 1995. *Le Credo de l'homme blanc: Regards coloniaux français XIXᵉ–XXᵉ siècles.* Paris: Editions Complexe.

Russell, Colin A. 1983. *Science and Social Change 1700–1900.* London: Macmillan.

Sabagh, Georges, ed. 1989. *The Modern Economic and Social History of the Middle East in Its World Context.* Cambridge: Univ. Press.

Sabben-Clare, E. E., D. J. Bradley, and K. Kirkwood, eds. 1980. *Health in Tropical Africa During the Colonial Period.* Oxford: Clarendon Press.

Sachs, Jeffrey D., and Andrew Warner. 1995. "Economic Reform and the Process of Global Integration," *Brookings Papers on Economic Activity,* 1: 1–118. Washington, DC.

Sah, Raaj. 1979. "Priorities of Developing Countries in Weather and Climate," *World Development,* 7: 337–47.

Sahlins, Marshall. 1988. "Cosmologies of Capitalism: The Trans-Pacific Sector of 'The World System,' " *Proc. Brit. Acad.,* 74: 1–51.

———. 1995. *How "Natives" Think: About Captain Cook, for Example.* Chicago: Univ. of Chicago Press.

Said, Edward W. 1978. *Orientalism.* New York: Vintage.

———. 1995. "East Isn't East: The Impending End of the Age of Orientalism," *TLS,* 3 February 1995, pp. 3–6.

———. 1995. "Orientalism, an *Afterword,*" *Raritan,* 14, 3 (Winter): 32–59.

Saint-John, J. A. 1834. *Egypt of Mohammed Ali; or, Travels in the Valley of the Nile.* 2 vols. London.

Sakaiya, Taichi. 1993. *What Is Japan? Contradictions and Transformations.* New York: Kodansha International.

Sakudo, Yotaro. 1990. "The Management Practices of Family Business," in Nakane and Oishi, eds., *Tokugawa Japan,* pp. 147–66.

Salama, Pierre, and Jacques Valier. 1994. *Pauvretés et inégalités dans le tiers monde.* Paris: Editions La Découverte.

Salaman, Redcliffe N. 1949. *The History and Social Influence of the Potato.* Cambridge: Univ. Press.

Salamé, Ghassan, ed. 1994. *Democracy Without Democrats? The Renewal of Politics in the Muslim World.* London and New York: Fond. Eni Enrico Mattei; I. B. Tauris.

Sale, Kirkpatrick. 1990. *The Conquest of Paradise: Christopher Columbus and the Columbian Legacy.* New York: Knopf.

Salomon, Jean-Jacques. 1992. *Le destin technologique.* Paris: Balland.

Salvucci, Richard J. 1987. *Textiles and Capitalism in Mexico: An Economic History of the Obrajes, 1539–1840.* Princeton: Princeton Univ. Press.

Samuels, Richard J. 1987. *The Business of the Japanese State: Energy Markets in Comparative and Historical Perspective.* Ithaca: Cornell Univ. Press.

———. 1994. *"Rich Nation, Strong Army": National Security and the Technological Transformation of Japan.* Ithaca: Cornell Univ. Press.

Samuelson, Paul A. 1976. "Illogic of Neo-Marxian Doctrine of Unequal Exchange," in David A. Belsley *et al.,* eds., *Inflation, Trade and Taxes: Essays in Honor of Alice Bourneuf,* Columbus: Ohio State Univ. Press, pp. 96–107.

Samuelsson, Kurt. 1961. *Religion and Economic Action.* New York: Basic Books. Translated from the Swedish: *Ekonomi och religion.* Stockholm: Kooperativa forfundets, 1957.

Sánchez-Albornoz, Nicolás, ed. 1985. *La modernización económica de España 1830–1930.* Madrid: Alianza Editorial.

Sandberg, Lars G. 1974. *Lancashire in Decline: A Study in Entrepreneurship, Technology, and Trade.* Columbus: Ohio State Univ. Press.

———. 1979. "The Case of the Impoverished Sophisticate: Human Capital and Swedish Economic Growth Before World War I," *J. Econ. Hist.,* 39, 1: 225–41.

———. 1982. "Ignorance, Poverty, and Economic Backwardness in the Early Stages of European Industrialization, *J. Europ. Econ. Hist.,* 11, 3: 675–97.

Sarfatti, Magali. 1966. *Spanish Bureaucratic-Patrimonialism in America.* Berkeley: Univ. of Calif. Press.

Sarton, George. 1956 [1951]. "Arabic Science and Learning in the Fifteenth Century: Their Decadence and Fall," in *Homenaje a [Jose Maria] Millas-Vallicrosa,* II, 304–22. Barcelona: Consejo Superior de Investigaciones Cientificas.

Sattaur, Omar. 1990. "WHO to Speed Up Work on Drugs for Tropical Diseases," *New Scientist,* 126, 1712 (14 April): 17.

Sauer, Carl O. 1966/1992. *The Early Spanish Main.* Berkeley: Univ. of Calif. Press.

Saul, S. Berrick. 1960. *Studies in British Overseas Trade 1870–1914.* Liverpool: Liverpool Univ. Press.

———. 1962. "The Motor Industry in Britain to 1914," *Business Hist. Rev.,* 5.

———, ed. 1970. *Technological Change: The United States and Britain in the Nineteenth Century.* London: Methuen.

———. 1970. "The Market and the Development of the Mechanical Engineering Industries in Britain, 1860–1914," in Saul, ed., *Technological Change,* pp. 141–70.

Sawers, Larry. 1992. "The Navigation Acts Revisited," *Econ. Hist. Rev.,* 45, 2 (May): 262–84.

Sawyer, John E. 1954. "The Social Basis of the American System of Manufacturing," *J. Econ. Hist.,* 14, 4: 361–79.

Saxonhouse, Gary R. 1974. "A Tale of Japanese Technological Diffusion in the Meiji Period," *J. Econ. Hist.,* 34, 1 (March): 149–65.

———. 1976. "Country Girls and Communication Among Competitors in the Japanese Cotton-Spinning Industry," in Patrick, ed., *Japanese Industrialization.*

Sayous, André-E. 1935. "Calvinisme et capitalisme: l'expérience genevoise," *Annales d'hist. écon. et soc.,* 7 (May): 225–44.

Scammell, G. V. 1981. *The World Encompassed: The First European Maritime Empires* c. *800–1650.* Berkeley: Univ. of California.

———. 1992. *The First Imperial Age: European Overseas Expansion c. 1400–1715.* London: Routledge.

Schama, Simon. 1992. "They All Laughed at Christopher Columbus," *The New Republic,* 5 and 13 January, pp. 30–41.

Schib, Karl, ed. 1954. *Johann Conrad Fischer, 1773–1854: Tagebücher.* Schaffhausen: Fischer.

Schneider, Bertrand. 1996. *Le scandale et la honte.* Paris: Club de Rome; Editions du Rocher.

Schran, Peter. 1994. "Japan's East Asia Market, 1870–1940," in Latham and Kawakatsu, eds., *Japanese Industrialization,* pp. 201–38.

Schreiner, Stefan, ed. 1985. *Die Osmanen in Europa: Erinnerungen und Berichte türkischer Geschichtsschreiber.* Graz: Styria. Selections from Richard F. Kreutel, ed., *Osmanische Geschichtsschreiber.* 10 vols. Graz: Styria, 1955–81.

Schultz, Theodore W. 1988. "On Investing in Specialized Human Capital to Attain Increasing Returns," in Ranis and Schultz, eds., *State of Development Economics,* pp. 339–52.

Schumacher, Martin. 1968. *Auslandsreisen deutscher Unternehmer 1750–1851 unter besonderer Berücksichtigung von Rheinland und Westfalen.* Cologne: Rheinisch-Westfälisches Wirtschaftsarchiv.

Schwartz, Stuart B. 1985. *Sugar Plantations in the Formation of Brazilian Society: Bahia, 1550–1835.* Cambridge: Univ. Press.

Scobie, James. 1964. *Revolution on the Pampas: A Social History of Argentine Wheat.* Austin: Univ. of Texas Press.

Scott, James C. 1985. *Weapons of the Weak: Everyday Forms of Peasant Resistance.* New Haven: Yale Univ. Press.

Scoville, Warren. 1960. *The Persecution of Huguenots and French Economic Development, 1680–1720.* Berkeley: Univ. of Calif. Press.

Seagrave, Sterling. 1995. *Lords of the Rim: The Invisible Empire of the Overseas Chinese.* New York: Putnam.

Searle, G. R. 1971. *The Quest for National Efficiency: A Study in British Politics and Political Thought, 1899–1914.* Oxford: Basil Blackwell.

Seed, Patricia. 1995. *Ceremonies of Possession in Europe's Conquest of the New World, 1492–1640.* New York and Cambridge: Cambridge Univ. Press.

Seers, Dudley, and Leonard Joy, eds. 1971. *Development in a Divided World.* Harmondsworth: Penguin.

Sejersted, Francis. 1992. "A Theory of Economic and Technological Development in Norway in the Nineteenth Century," *Scand. Econ. Hist. Rev.,* 40, 1: 40–75.

———. [1993]. "The Norwegian 'Sonderweg': Aspects of the Modernization Process in Norway." Typescript. English version of material in his *Demokratisk kapitalisme* (Oslo, 1993), esp. ch. 5.

———. 1995. "Science and Industry: Modernisation Strategies in Norway 1900–1940," in Caron, Erker, and Fischer, eds., *Innovations in the European Economy,* pp. 255–76.

Sella, Domenico. 1968. "The Rise and Fall of the Venetian Woollen Industry," in Pullan, ed., *Crisis and Change,* pp. 106–26.

Semo, Enrique. 1993. *The History of Capitalism in Mexico: Its Origins, 1521–1763.* Austin: Univ. of Texas Press.

Sen, Amartya. 1981. *Poverty and Famines: An Essay on Entitlement and Deprivation.* Oxford and New York: Oxford Univ. Press.

————. 1988. "The Concept of Development," in Chenery *et al.*, eds., *Handbook of Development Economics,* I, 9–26.

————. 1994a. "Freedoms and Needs," *The New Republic,* 10 and 17 January, pp. 31–38.

————. 1994b. "Population: Delusion and Reality," *New York Review of Books,* 41, 15, (22 September), pp. 62–71.

Shammas, Carole. 1990. *The Pre-industrial Consumer in England and America.* Oxford: Clarendon Press.

————. 1994. "The Decline of Textile Prices in England and British America Prior to Industrialization," *Econ. Hist. Rev.,* 47, 3 (August): 483–507.

Shcherbak, Yuri M. 1996. "Ten Years of the Chornobyl Era," *Scientific American,* 274, 4 (April): 44–49.

Sheridan, Richard B. 1965. "The Wealth of Jamaica in the Eighteenth Century," *Econ. Hist. Rev.,* 2d ser., 18, 2 (August): 292–311.

————. 1973. *Sugar and Slavery: An Economic History of the British West Indies 1623–1775.* Baltimore: Johns Hopkins Univ. Press.

————. 1985. *Doctors and Slaves: A Medical and Demographic History of Slavery in the British West Indies, 1680–1834.* Cambridge: Univ. Press.

————. 1987. "Eric Williams and *Capitalism and Slavery:* A Bibliographical and Historiographical Essay," in Solow and Engerman, eds., *British Capitalism,* pp. 317–45.

Shimada, Shingo. 1995. "Social Time and Modernity in Japan: An Exploration of Concepts and a Cultural Comparison," *Time & Society,* 4, 2 (June), 251–60.

Shumway, Nicolas. 1991. *The Invention of Argentina.* Berkeley: Univ. of Calif. Press.

Singer, Charles, E. J. Holmyard, A. R. Hall, and Trevor I. Williams, eds. 1957. *A History of Technology.* 5 vols. Oxford: Clarendon Press.

Singleton, John. 1991. "Showing the White Flag: The Lancashire Cotton Industry, 1945–65," in Rose, ed., *International Competition,* 129–49.

Sinoué, Gilbert. 1997. *Le dernier Pharaon: Méhémet-Ali (1770–1849).* Paris: Pygmalion.

Sirageldin, Ismail, and Alan Sorkin. 1988. *Research in Human Capital and Development: A Research Annual.* Vol. 5. *Public Health and Development.* Greenwich, CT: Jai Press.

Sivan, Emmanuel. 1988/1995. *Mythes politiques arabes.* Paris: Fayard.

Sivin, Nathan. 1978. "Imperial China: Has Its Present Past a Future?" *Harvard J. Asiatic Studies,* 38, 2: 449–80.

————. 1990. "Science and Medicine in Chinese History," in Ropp, ed., *Heritage of China,* pp. 164–96.

Smil, Vaclav. 1993. *China's Environmental Crisis: An Inquiry into the Limits of National Development.* Armonk, NY: M. E. Sharpe.

Smith, Alan G. R. 1972. *Science and Society in the Sixteenth and Seventeenth Centuries.* London: Thames & Hudson.

Smith, Anthony D. 1986. *The Ethnic Origins of Nations.* Oxford: Basil Blackwell.

Smith, David C. 1989. "Climate, Agriculture, History: An Introduction," *Agricultural History,* 63, 2 (Spring), 1–6.

Smith, Merritt Roe. 1977. *Harpers Ferry Armory and the New Technology: The Challenge of Change.* Ithaca: Cornell Univ. Press.

Smith, Neil. 1987. " 'Academic War over the Field of Geography': The Elimination of Geography at Harvard, 1947–1951," *Annals of the Assn. of Amer. Geographers,* 77, 2: 155–72.

Smith, Thomas C. 1961. "Japan's Aristocratic Revolution," *Yale Review,* 50 (Spring), 370–83.

———. 1970. "Okura Nakatsune and the Technologists," in Albert M. Craig and Donald H. Shively, eds., *Personality in Japanese History*. Berkeley: Univ. of Calif. Press, pp. 127–54.

———. 1988. *Native Sources of Japanese Industrialization, 1750–1920*. Berkeley: Univ. of Calif. Press.

Smith, Tony. 1981. *The Pattern of Imperialism: The United States, Great Britain, and the Late-Industrializing World Since 1815*. Cambridge: Univ. Press.

Smout, T. C., ed. 1979. *The Search for Wealth and Stability: Essays in Economic and Social History Presented to M. W. Flinn*. London: Macmillan.

Snooks, Graeme Donald, ed. 1994. *Was the Industrial Revolution Necessary?* London: Routledge.

Solow, Barbara, ed. 1991. *Slavery and the Rise of the Atlantic System*. Cambridge: Univ. Press.

———, and Stanley L. Engerman, eds. 1987. *British Capitalism and Caribbean Slavery: The Legacy of Eric Williams*. Cambridge: Univ. Press.

Soustelle, Jacques. 1961. *The Daily Life of the Aztecs on the Eve of the Spanish Conquest*. London: Weidenfeld & Nicolson.

Soutif, Michel. 1995. *L'Asie, source de sciences et techniques: Histoire comparée des idées scientifiques et techniques de l'Asie*. Grenoble: Presses universitaires.

Sowell, Thomas. 1994. *Race and Culture: A World View*. New York: Basic Books.

Spear, Percival. 1932/1963. *The Nabobs: A Study of the Social Life of the English in Eighteenth Century India*. Rev. ed., Oxford: Oxford Univ. Press.

Spence, Jonathan. 1974. *Emperor of China: Self-Portrait of K'ang-Hsi*. New York: Knopf.

———. 1990. *The Search for Modern China*. New York: W. W. Norton.

———. 1992. *Chinese Roundabout: Essays in History and Culture*. New York: W. W. Norton.

Stannard, David E. 1992. *American Holocaust: The Conquest of the New World*. New York: Oxford Univ. Press.

Starkey, Otis P. 1939. *The Economic Geography of Barbados: A Study of the Relationships Between Environmental Variations and Economic Development*. New York: Columbia Univ. Press; Westport, CT: Negro Universities Press.

Staunton, George Leonard. 1797. *An Historical Account of the Embassy to the Emperor of China, Undertaken by Order of the King of Great Britain*. London: Stockdale. American ed.: *An Authentic Account of an Embassy from the King of Great Britain to the Emperor of China*. 2 vols. Philadelphia, 1799. French ed: *Voyage dans l'intérieur de la Chine et de la Tartarie*. 4 vols. Paris, An VI (1798).

Stavrianos, Leften Stavros. 1981. *Global Rift: The Third World Comes of Age*. New York: William Morrow.

Steele, Brett D. 1994. "Muskets and Pendulums: Benjamin Robins, Leonhard Euler, and the Ballistics Revolution," *Technology and Culture*, 35, 2 (April), 348–82.

Steensgaard, Niels. 1990. "The Growth and Composition of the Long-distance Trade of England and the Dutch Republic before 1750," in Tracy, ed., *Rise of Merchant Empires*, pp. 102–52.

Stein, Burton. 1988. " 'Arrested Development': But When and Where?", in Dewey, ed., *Arrested Development*, pp. 49–65.

Stein, Stanley, and Barbara H. Stein. 1970. *The Colonial Heritage of Latin America: Essays on Economic Dependence in Perspective*. New York: Oxford Univ. Press.

Stern, Steve J. 1982/1993. *Peru's Indian Peoples and the Challenge of Spanish Conquest: Huamanga to 1640*. 2d ed., Madison: Univ. of Wisconsin Press.

———. 1993. "Africa, Latin America, and the Splintering of Historical Knowledge: From Fragmentation to Reverberation," in Frederick Cooper *et al.*, *Con-*

*fronting Historical Paradigms: Peasants, Labor, and the Capitalist World System in Africa and Latin America*. Madison: Univ. of Wisconsin Press, pp. 3–20.

Stevens, William K. 1993. "The High Risks of Denying Rivers Their Flood Plains," *New York Times*, 20 July, pp. C-1, 8.

———. 1993. "The Heavy Hand of European Settlement," *New York Times*, 10 August, p. C-1.

Stopford, John, and Susan Strange, with John S. Henley. 1991. *Rival States, Rival Firms: Competition for World Market Shares*. Cambridge: Univ. Press.

Strien-Chardonneau, M.M.G. van. 1993. *Le voyage de Hollande: Récits de voyageurs français dans les Provinces-Unies 1748–1795*. Leiden: E. J. Brill.

Strong, Frank. 1899. "The Causes of Cromwell's West Indian Expedition," *Amer. Hist. Rev.*, 4, 2 (January), 228–45.

Stoianovich, Traian. 1994. *Balkan Worlds: The First and Last Europe*. Armonk, NY: M. E. Sharpe.

Stuart, Gene S. 1981. *The Mighty Aztecs*. Washington, DC: National Geographic Society.

Studeny, Christophe. 1995. *L'invention de la vitesse: France, XVIII^e–XX^e siècle*. Paris: Gallimard.

Subrahmanyam, Sanjay. 1990a. *The Political Economy of Commerce: Southern India, 1500–1650*. Cambridge: Univ. Press.

———, ed. 1990b. *Merchants, Markets and the State in Early Modern India*. Delhi: Oxford Univ. Press.

———. 1993. *The Portuguese Empire in Asia 1500–1700: A Political and Economic History*. London: Longman.

———. 1997. *The Career and Legend of Vasco da Gama*. Cambridge: Univ. Press.

Suehiro, Akira. 1989. *Capital Accumulation in Thailand 1855–1985*. Tokyo: Centre for East Asian Cultural Studies.

Suleri, Sara. 1992. *The Rhetoric of English India*. Chicago: Univ. of Chicago Press.

Summers, Robert, and Alan Heston. 1988. "A New Set of International Comparisons of Real Product and Price Levels: Estimates for 130 Countries," *Rev. Income and Wealth*, 34: 1–25.

———. 1991. "The Penn World Table (Mark 5): An Extended Set of International Comparisons, 1950–1988," *QJE*, 106, 2 (May), 327–68.

Sun, Jingzhi, ed. 1988. *The Economic Geography of China*. Hong Kong: Oxford Univ. Press.

Sundararajan, V. 1970. "The Impact of the Tariff on Some Selected Products of the U.S. Iron and Steel Industry, 1870–1914," *QJE*, 84, 4 (November): 590–610.

Supple, Barry E., ed. 1963. *The Experience of Economic Growth: Case Studies in Economic History*. New York: Random House.

———. 1964. *Crisis and Change in England, 1600–1642*. Berkeley: Univ. of California Press.

———. 1990. "Official Economic Inquiry and Britain's Industrial Decline: The First Fifty Years," in Furner and Supple, eds., *The State and Economic Knowledge*, pp. 325–53.

———. 1994. "Fear of Failing: Economic History and the Decline of Britain," *Econ. Hist. Rev.*, 47, 3 (August): 441–58.

"A Survey of Multinationals." 1995. *The Economist*, 24 June.

Svedenstierna, Eric T. 1973. *Svedenstierna's Tour [of] Great Britain 1802–3: The Travel Diary of an Industrial Spy*, edited with introd. by M. W. Flinn. Newton Abbot: David & Charles.

Sylla, Richard, and Gianni Toniolo, eds. 1991. *Patterns of European Industrialization: The Nineteenth Century*. London: Routledge.

Szirmai, Adam, Bart Van Ark, and Dirk Pilat, eds. 1993. *Explaining Economic Growth: Essays in Honour of Angus Maddison.* Amsterdam: Elsevier; North Holland.

Szostak, Rick. 1991. *The Role of Transportation in the Industrial Revolution: A Comparison of England and France.* Montreal: McGill-Queen's Univ. Press.

Tabb, William K. 1995. *The Postwar Japanese System: Cultural Economy and Economic Transformation.* New York: Oxford Univ. Press.

Taira, Koji. 1978. "Factory Labour and the Industrial Revolution in Japan," in Mathias and Postan, eds., *Cambridge Economic History of Europe,* VII, 2, 166–214.

Takekoshi, Yosoburo. 1930; reprint 1967. *The Economic Aspects of the History of the Civilization of Japan.* 3 vols. London: Allen & Unwin; reprint: Dawsons of Pall Mall.

Taton, René, ed. 1964. *A General History of the Sciences.* Vol. II. *The Beginnings of Modern Science from 1450 to 1800.* London: Thames & Hudson. French ed.: *La science moderne.* Paris, 1958.

Tavakoli-Targhi, Mohamad. 1996. "Orientalism's Genesis Amnesia," *Compar. Studies of South Asia, Africa and the Middle East,* 16, 1: 1–14.

Tawney, R. H. 1926. *Religion and the Rise of Capitalism.* London: John Murray.

Taylor, Alan M. 1992a. "Three Phases of Argentine Economic Growth." Part of a Ph.D. thesis at Harvard Univ. Typescript.

———. 1992b. "External Dependence, Demographic Burdens, and Argentine Economic Decline after the *Belle Epoque,*" *J. Econ. Hist,* 52 (December), 907–36.

———. 1994. "Mass Migration to Distant Southern Shores: Argentina and Australia, 1870–1939," in Hatton and Williamson, eds., *Migration,* pp. 91–115.

Teich, Mikuláš, and Roy Porter, eds. 1996. *The Industrial Revolution in National Context: Europe and the USA.* Cambridge: Univ. Press.

Teich, Mikuláš, and Robert Young, eds. 1973. *Changing Perspectives in the History of Science: Essays in Honour of Joseph Needham.* London: Heinemann.

Teichova, Alice, Maurice Lévy-Leboyer, and Helga Nussbaum, eds. 1986. *Multinational Enterprise in Historical Perspective.* Cambridge: Univ. Press; Paris: Maison des Sciences de l'Homme.

Teitel, Simon, and Francisco E. Thoumi. 1986. "From Import Substitution to Exports: The Manufacturing Exports Experience of Argentina and Brazil," *Econ. Devel. and Cult. Change,* 34 (April), 455–90.

Temin, Peter. 1964. *Iron and Steel in 19th Century America.* Cambridge, Mass.: MIT Press.

———. 1997a. "Two Views of the British Industrial Revolution," *J. Econ. Hist.,* 57, 1 (March): 63–82.

———. 1997b. "Is It Kosher to Talk about Culture?" *J. Econ. Hist.,* 57, 2 (June): 267–87.

Temin, Peter. 1997c. "The Golden Age of European Growth: Review Essay," *European Rev. Econ. Hist.,* I, 1: 127–49.

Tenenti, Alberto. 1967. *Piracy and the Decline of Venice 1580–1615.* Berkeley: Univ. of Calif. Press. Italian ed.: *Venezia e i corsari, 1580–1615* (Bari: G. Laterza, 1961).

Tenner, Edward. 1996. *Why Things Bite Back: Technology and the Revenge of Unintended Consequences.* New York: Knopf.

Thomas, Hugh. 1993. *Conquest: Montezuma, Cortes, and the Fall of Old Mexico.* New York: Simon & Schuster.

Thomas, Keith. 1973. *Religion and the Decline of Magic: Studies in Popular Beliefs in Sixteenth- and Seventeenth-Century England.* London: Penguin University Books (originally London: Weidenfeld & Nicolson, 1971).

———. 1994. "Cleanliness and Godliness in Early Modern England," in Fletcher and Roberts, eds., *Religion, Culture, and Society.*

Thomas, Robert Paul. 1965. "A Quantitative Approach to the Study of the Effects of British Imperial Policy on Colonial Welfare," *J. Econ. Hist.*, 254: (December), 615–38.

———. 1968a. "The Sugar Colonies of the Old Empire: Profit or Loss for Great Britain?" *Econ. Hist. Rev.*, 2d ser., 21, 1 (April), 30–45.

———. 1968b. "British Imperial Policy and the Economic Interpretations of the American Revolution," *J. Econ. Hist.*, 3, 28 (September), 436–40.

Thomson, Guy P. C. 1985. "Protectionism and Industrialization in Mexico, 1821–1854: The Case of Puebla," in Abel and Lewis, eds., *Latin America*, pp. 125–46.

Thorens, Justin, *et al.*, eds. 1993. *1492: Le choc de deux mondes. Ethnocentrisme, impérialisme juridique et culturel, choc des cultures, droits de l'homme et droits des peuples*. Actes du Colloque international organisé par la Commission Nationale Suisse pour l'UNESCO. Geneva, 17–18 September 1992. N.p.: ELA La Différence ("Mobile matière").

Thuillier, André. 1974. *Economie et société nivernaises au début du XIXᵉ siècle*. Paris and The Hague: Mouton.

Thuillier, Guy. 1959. *Georges Dufaud et les débuts du grand capitalisme dans la métallurgie, en Nivernais, au XIXᵉ siècle*. Paris: SEVPEN.

———. [*c.* 1966]. *Aspects de l'économie nivernaise au XIXᵉ siècle*. Paris: Armand Colin.

Thuillier, Pierre. 1995. *La grande implosion: Rapport sur l'effondrement de l'Occident 1999–2002*. Paris: Fayard.

Thurow, Lester. 1993. *Head to Head: The Coming Economic Battle Among Japan, Europe, and America*. New York: William Murrow; Warner Books.

Tibawi, A. L. 1979. *Second Critique of English-Speaking Orientalists and Their Approach to Islam and the Arabs*.

Tibi, Bassam. 1990. *Islam and the Cultural Accommodation of Social Change*. Trans. Clare Krojzl. Boulder: Westview.

Tidrick, Kathryn. 1989. *Heart Beguiling Araby: The English Romance with Arabia*. Rev. ed., London: Tauris.

Tilly, Louise A. 1994. "Connections," *Amer. Hist. Rev.*, 99, 1 (February), 1–20.

Tilly, Richard H. 1986. "German Banking, 1850–1914: Development Assistance for the Strong," *J. Europ. Econ. Hist.*, 15, 1 (Spring): 113–52.

Tipton, Frank B. 1995. "Regional History: West Jutland in a Theoretical and Comparative Context," in "West Jutland and the World, II; Second Conference on Regional History." Sponsored by the Museum Councils of the Counties of Ringkobing and Ribe, Lemvig, 3–5 April.

Tisch, Sarah J., and Michael B. Wallace. 1994. *Dilemmas of Development Assistance: The What, Why, and Who of Foreign Aid*. Boulder: Westview.

Todorov, Tzvetan. 1982. *La conquête de l'Amérique: La question de l'autre*. Paris: Seuil.

Toland, John. 1970. *The Rising Sun: The Decline and Fall of the Japanese Empire, 1936–1945*. 2 vols. New York: Random House.

Tomlinson, B. R., ed. 1993. *The New Cambridge History of India*. Vol. III. *The Economy of Modern India, 1860–1970*. Cambridge: Univ. Press.

Toniolo, Gianni. 1990. *An Economic History of Liberal Italy 1850–1918*. London: Routledge.

Tortella, Gabriel. 1994. "Patterns of Economic Retardation and Recovery in Southwestern Europe in the Nineteenth and Twentieth Centuries," *Econ. Hist. Rev.*, 47, 1 (February), 1–21.

———. 1995. "La pénurie d'entrepreneurs: Explication du retard espagnol?" *Entreprises et histoire*, 8: 63–73.

Totman, Conrad. 1993. *Early Modern Japan*. Berkeley: Univ. of Calif. Press.

Toutain, Jean-Claude. 1996. "Comparaison entre les différentes évaluations du produit intérieur brut de la France de 1815 à 1938 *ou* L'histoire économique quantitative a-t-elle un sens?" *Rev. économique*, 47, 4: 893–920.

Tracy, James D., ed. 1990. *The Rise of Merchant Empires: Long-distance Trade in the Early Modern World 1350–1750*. Cambridge: Univ. Press.

Travis, Anthony S. 1993. *The Rainbow Makers: The Origins of the Synthetic Dyestuffs Industry in Western Europe*. Bethlehem, Pa.: Lehigh Univ. Press.

Trebilcock, Clive. 1981. *The Industrialization of the Continental Powers, 1780–1914*. London: Longmans.

Trevor-Roper, H. R. 1967. *Religion the Reformation and Social Change*. London: Macmillan.

Troitzsch, Ulrich, ed. 1981. *Technologischer Wandel im 18. Jahrhundert*. Wolfenbüttel: Herzog August Bibliothek.

Tsuru, Shigeto. 1993. *Japan's Capitalism: Creative Defeat and Beyond*. Cambridge: Univ. Press.

Tsurumi, E. Patricia. 1994. "Colonial Education in Korea and Taiwan," in Myers and Peattie, eds., *Japanese Colonial Empire*, pp. 275–311.

Tucker, Barbara M. 1984. *Samuel Slater and the Origins of the American Textile Industry, 1790–1860*. Ithaca: Cornell Univ. Press.

Tulard, Jean—see Humboldt, Alexander von.

Turnbull, S. R. 1977. *The Samurai: A Military History*. New York: Macmillan.

Turner, Anthony J. 1985. *The Time Museum*. Vol. I. *Time Measuring Instruments*. Part 1. *Astrolabes. Astrolabe Related Instruments*. Rockford, IL: The Time Museum.

Turner, Frederick. 1980. *Beyond Geography: The Western Spirit Against the Wilderness*. New York: Viking.

Turshen, Meredeth. 1984. *The Political Ecology of Disease in Tanzania*. New Brunswick: Rutgers Univ. Press.

Tweedale, Geoffrey. 1987. *Sheffield Steel and America: A Century of Commercial and Technological Interdependence, 1830–1930*. Cambridge: Univ. Press.

Uchitelle, Louis. 1997. "Like Oil and Water: A Tale of Two Economists," *New York Times*, 16 February, p. 3,1.

Ui, Jun, ed. 1992. *Industrial Pollution in Japan*. Tokyo: United Nations Univ. Press.

Uno, Kathleen S. 1991. "Women and Changes in the Household Division of Labor," in Bernstein, ed., *Recreating Japanese Women*, pp. 17–41.

Uselding, Paul J. 1972. "Technical Progress at the Springfield Armory, 1820–1850," *Explorations Econ. Hist.*, 9, 3 (Spring): 291–316.

Usher, Abbott Payson. 1920. *An Introduction to the Industrial History of England*. Boston: Houghton Mifflin.

———. 1954. *A History of Mechanical Inventions*. 2d rev. ed., Cambridge, MA: Harvard Univ. Press.

Valignano, Alexandre. 1990. *Les Jésuites au Japon: Relation missionnaire (1583)*. Paris: Desclée de Brouwer; Bellarmin.

Vandenbroeke, Christian. 1987. "The Regional Economy of Flanders and Industrial Modernization in the Eighteenth Century: A Discussion," *J. Eur. Econ. Hist.*, 16, 1 (Spring): 149–70.

Van Niel, Robert. 1988. "Dutch Views and Uses of British Policy in India around 1800," *Itinerario*, 12, 1: 17–31.

Van Strien, C. D. 1993. *British Travellers in Holland During the Stuart Period: Edward Browne and John Locke as Tourists in the United Provinces*. Leiden: E. J. Brill.

Vargas, Llosa Mario. 1990. "Questions of Conquest: What Columbus Wrought and What He Did Not," *Harper's* magazine, 281 (December), 45–53.

Vega, Garcilaso de la, El Inca. 1609/1616–17/1966. *Royal Commentaries of the Incas and General History of Peru.* Trans. Harold V. Livermore. Austin: Univ. of Texas Press.

Veliz, Claudio, ed. 1965. *Obstacles to Change in Latin America.* London: Oxford Univ. Press.

———, ed. 1967. *The Politics of Conformity in Latin America.* London: Oxford Univ. Press.

Verley, Patrick. 1997. *L'échelle du monde: essai sur l'industrialisation de l'Occident.* Paris: Gallimard.

———. 1997. *La Révolution industrielle.* Paris: Gallimard; "Folio/Histoire."

Verlinden, Charles. 1970. *The Beginnings of Modern Colonization.* Ithaca: Cornell Univ. Press.

Verma, Rupalee. 1995. "Western Medicine, Indigenous Doctors and Colonial Medical Education," *Itinerario,* 19, 3: 130–41.

Vernet, Juan. 1985. *Ce que la culture doit aux Arabes d'Espagne.* 2d ed., trans. from the Spanish, 1978, Paris: Sindbad.

Vernon, Raymond. 1971. *Sovereignty at Bay: The Multinational Spread of U.S. Enterprises.* New York: Basic Books.

———. 1989. *Technological Development: The Historical Experience.* Economic Development Institute Seminar Paper 39. Washington, DC: World Bank.

Veyrassat, Béatrice. 1995. "Mais où est donc la différence? Modèles comparés de développement technologique (XIXe siècle)," in Etémad, Batou, and David, eds., *Pour une histoire économique,* pp. 205–28.

Vicens Vives, Jaime. 1969. *An Economic History of Spain.* Princeton: Princeton Univ. Press.

Vickers, Daniel. 1994. *Farmers and Fishermen: Two Centuries of Work in Essex County, Massachusetts, 1630–1850.* Chapel Hill: Univ. of North Carolina Press.

Villiers, Patrick, and Jean-Pierre Duteil. 1997. *L'Europe, la mer et les colonies XVIIᵉ–XVIIIᵉ siècle.* Paris: Hachette.

Vincent, Bernard. 1991. *1492: "L'Année admirable."* Paris: Aubier.

———. 1993. "Rôle de l'Espagne aux XVᶜ–XVIᶜ siècles," in Thorens *et al., 1492,* pp. 93–100.

Vivero, Rodrigo de (1564–1636). 1972. *Du Japon et du bon gouvernement de l'Espagne et des Indes.* Trans. and ed. Juliette Monbeig. Paris: SEVPEN.

Vizenor, Gerald. 1991. *Heirs of Columbus.* Middletown, CT: Wesleyan Univ. Press.

Vlekke, Bernard H. M. 1960. *Nusantara: A History of Indonesia.* Rev. ed., Chicago: Quadrangle Books; The Hague and Bandung: W. van Hoeve.

Vogel, Barbara, ed. 1980. *Preussische Reformen 1807–1820.* Konigstein/Ts.: Anton Hain; Verlagsgr. Athenaum, Hain, *et al.*

Volti, Rudi. 1996. "A Century of Automobility," *Technology & Culture,* 37, 4 (October): 663–85.

Von Tunzelmann, G. Nicholas. 1978. *Steam Power and British Industrialization.* Oxford: Clarendon Press.

———. 1993. "Technological and Organizational Change in Industry During the Industrial Revolution," in O'Brien and Quinault, eds., *Industrial Revolution,* pp. 254–82.

———. 1995. "Time-saving Technical Change: The Cotton Industry in the English Industrial Revolution," *Explor. Econ. Hist.,* 32: 1–27.

Vries, Jan de. 1974. *The Dutch Rural Economy in the Golden Age, 1500–1700.* New Haven: Yale Univ. Press.

———. 1993. "Between Purchasing Power and the World of Goods: Understanding the Household Economy in Early Modern Europe," in Brewer and Porter, eds., *Consumption and the World of Goods,* pp. 85–132.

————. 1994. "The Industrial Revolution and the Industrious Revolution," *J. Econ. Hist.*, 54, 2 (June): 249–70.

Wade, Nicholas. 1974. "Sahelian Drought: No Victory for Western Aid," *Science.* 185 (19 July), 234–37.

Wadsworth, A. P., and Julia de L. Mann. 1931. *The Cotton Trade and Industrial Lancashire.* Manchester: Manchester Univ. Press.

Wakeman, Frederic, Jr. 1985. *The Great Enterprise: The Manchu Reconstruction of Imperial Order in Seventeenth-Century China.* 2 vols. Berkeley: Univ. of Calif. Press.

————. 1993. "Voyages," *Amer. Hist. Rev.*, 98, 1 (February): 1–17.

Waldron, Arthur. 1990. *The Great Wall of China: From History to Myth.* Cambridge: Univ. Press.

Waley-Cohen, Joanna. 1993. "China and Western Technology in the Late Eighteenth Century," *Amer. Hist. Rev.*, 98 (December), 1525–44.

Waller, Richard D. 1990. "Tsetse Fly in Western Narok, Kenya," *J. African Hist.*, 31: 81–101.

Wallerstein, Immanuel. 1974/1980/1989. *The Modern World-System.* 3 vols. New York: Academic Press.

————. 1982. "Dutch Hegemony in the Seventeenth-Century World-Economy," in Aymard, ed., *Dutch Capitalism,* 93–145.

————. 1995. *After Liberalism.* New York: New Press.

"War of the Worlds: A Survey of the Global Economy." 1994. *The Economist,* 1 October.

Ward, J. R. 1978. "The Profitability of Sugar Planting in the British West Indies, 1650–1834," *Econ. Hist. Rev.*, 2d ser., 31: 197–213.

————. 1994. "The Industrial Revolution and British Imperialism, 1750–1850," *Econ. Hist. Rev.*, 47, 1 (February), 44–65.

Washbrook, David. 1988. "Progress and Problems: South Asian Social and Economic History, *c.* 1720–1860," *Modern Asian Studies,* 22, 1.

Watkins, M. 1963. "A Staple Theory of Economic Growth," *Canad. J. Econ. and Polit. Sci.*, 29.

Watts, David. 1987. *The West Indies: Patterns of Development, Culture and Environmental Change Since 1492.* Cambridge: Univ. Press.

Waugh, Evelyn. 1960. *Tourist in Africa.* Boston: Little, Brown.

Weatherill, Lorna. 1988. *Consumer Behaviour and Material Culture, 1660–1760.* London: Routledge.

Weber, Max. 1904–05. "Die protestantische Ethik und der 'Geist' des Kapitalismus," *Archiv für Sozialwissenschaft u. Sozialpolitik,* 20: 1–54; 21: 1–110. Reprinted in his *Gesammelte Aufsätze zur Religionssoziologie* (Tubingen: Mohr, 1920).

Weber, W. 1975. "Industriespionage als technologischer Transfer in der Frühindustrialisierung Deutschlands," *Technikgeschichte,* 42: 287–306.

————. 1981. "Probleme des Technologietransfers in Europa im 18. Jahrhundert: Reisen und technologischer Transfer," in Troitzsch, ed., *Technologischer Wandel,* pp. 189–217.

Wei-ming, Tu, ed. 1996. *Confucian Traditions in East Asian Modernity: Moral Education and Economic Culture in Japan and the Four Mini-Dragons.* Cambridge, MA: Harvard Univ. Press.

Weiss, John. 1996. *Ideology of Death: Why the Holocaust Happened in Germany.* Chicago: Ivan R. Dee.

Welsh, Frank. 1993. *A Borrowed Place: The History of Hong Kong.* New York: Kodansha International.

Wengenroth, Ulrich. 1994. "Igel und Füchse: Zu neueren Verständigungproblemen über die Industrielle Revolution," in *Industrialisierung: Begriffe und Prozesse. Festschrift für Akos Paulinyi.* Darmstadt: Technische Hochschule Darmstadt;

Stuttgart: Verlag für Geschichte der Naturwissenschaften und der Technik, pp. 9–22.

Wesseling, H. L. 1992. "The Expansion of Europe, the Division of the World and the Civilisation of Modernity," in Keiji Yamada, ed., *The Transfer of Science and Technology Between Europe and Asia, 1780–1880.* Second Conference on the Transfer of Science and Technology Between Europe and Asia since Vasco da Gama, 3–7 November 1992. Kyoto and Osaka: International Research Center for Japanese Studies, pp. 241–52.

West, John. 1971. *The History of Tasmania.* Sydney: Angus & Robertson for the Royal Australian Historical Society.

Westebbe, Richard M. 1956. "State Entrepreneurship: King Willem I, John Cocker-ill, and the Seraing Engineering Works, 1815–1840," *Explor. Entrepr. Hist.,* 8, 4 (April), 205–32.

Westerfield, Ray B. 1915. *Middlemen in English Business Particularly Between 1660 and 1760.* New Haven: Yale Univ. Press.

Westwood, J. N. 1964. *A History of Russian Railways.* London: Allen & Unwin.

Whigham, Thomas L. 1978. "The Iron Works of Ybycui: Paraguayan Industrial De-velopment in the Mid-Nineteenth Century," *The Americas,* 35: 201–18.

White, Lynn, Jr. 1940. "Technology and Invention in the Middle Ages," *Speculum,* 15: 141–59. Reprinted in White, *Medieval Religion,* pp. 1–22.

———. 1971. "Cultural Climates and Technological Advance in the Middle Ages," *Viator,* 2, 74: 171–201.

———. 1978. *Medieval Religion and Technology: Collected Essays.* Berkeley: Univ. of Calif. Press.

Whitley, Richard. 1992. *Business Systems in East Asia: Firms, Markets and Societies.* London: Sage.

Wiarda, Howard J., ed. 1974. *Politics and Social Change in Latin America: The Distinct Tradition.* Amherst: Univ. of Massachusetts Press.

Wickham, Chris. 1985. "The Uniqueness of the East," *J. Peasant Studies,* 12: 166–96.

Wiener, Martin J. 1981. *English Culture and the Decline of the Industrial Spirit, 1850–1980.* Cambridge: Univ. Press.

Wilke, Jurgen. 1988. "Der Einfluss der Hugenotten auf die gewerbliche Entwick-lung," in S. Badstubner-Groger *et al., Hugenotten in Berlin,* pp. 227–280. Berlin: Union Verlag.

Wilkinson, Endymion. 1990. *Japan versus the West: Image and Reality.* London: Penguin. Earlier edition: *Japan versus Europe: A History of Misunderstanding.* London: Penguin, 1983.

Williams, Eric. 1944. *Capitalism and Slavery.* Chapel Hill: Univ. of North Carolina Press.

Williams, John Hoyt. 1972. "Paraguayan Isolation Under Dr. Francia: A Re-evaluation," *Hisp. Amer. Hist. Rev.,* 52, 1 (February), 102–22.

Williams, Karel. 1981. *From Pauperism to Poverty.* London: Routledge & Kegan Paul.

Williams, Karel, John Williams, and Dennis Thomas. 1983. *Why Are the British Bad at Manufacturing?* London: Routledge & Kegan Paul.

Williamson, Jeffrey G. 1990. "New Views on the Impact of the French Wars on Ac-cumulation in Britain." Harvard Inst. of Economic Research, Discussion Paper No. 1480.

———. 1994. "Economic Convergence: Placing Post-Famine Ireland in Comparative Perspective," *J. Econ. Soc. Hist.,* 21: 1–27.

———. 1995. "The Evolution of Global Labor Markets since 1830: Background Evidence and Hypotheses," *Explorations Econ. Hist.,* 32: 141–96.

Wills, Garry. 1990. "Goodbye, Columbus," *New York Review,* 22 November, pp. 6–10.

Wills, John E., Jr. 1993. "European Consumption and Asian Production in the Seventeenth and Eighteenth Centuries," in Brewer and Porter, eds., *Consumption and the World of Goods,* pp. 133–47.

Wilson, Charles. 1965. "Economy and Society in Late Victorian Britain," *Econ. Hist. Rev.,* 2d ser., 18, 1 (August), 183–98.

Wilson, Derek. 1994. *Rothschild: A Story of Wealth and Power.* Rev. ed., London: Mandarin.

Wilson, John F. 1995. *British Business History, 1720–1994.* Manchester: Manchester Univ. Press.

Windshuttle, Keith. 1996. *The Killing of History: How a Discipline Is Being Murdered by Literary Critics and Social Theorists.* Paddington, NSW (Austr.): Macleay Press.

Wink, André. 1988. " '*Al-Hind*': India and Indonesia in the Islamic World-Economy, c. 700–1800 A.D.," *Itinerario,* 12, 1: 33–72.

Winslow, Charles-Edward Amory. 1943. *The Conquest of Epidemic Disease: A Chapter in the History of Ideas.* Princeton: Princeton Univ. Press; paperback reprint, Madison: Univ. of Wisconsin Press, 1980.

Wittfogel, Karl A. 1957. *Oriental Despotism: A Comparative Study of Total Power.* New Haven: Yale Univ. Press.

Wolff, Edward N., and Maury Gittleman, "The Role of Education in Productivity Convergence: Does Higher Education Matter?" in Szirmai, Van Ark, and Pilat, eds., *Explaining Economic Growth,* pp. 147–67.

Wolman, William, and Anne Colamosca. 1997. *The Judas Economy: The Triumph of Capital and the Betrayal of Work.* New York: Addison-Wesley.

Womack, James P., Daniel T. Jones, and Daniel Roos. 1990. *The Machine That Changed the World.* New York: Rawson Associates.

Wood, Peter. 1979. *The Spanish Main.* "The Seafarers." Alexandria, VA: Time-Life Books.

Woolf, S. J. 1962. "Venice and the Terraferma: Problems of the Change from Commercial to Landed Activities," *Boll. dell'Istituto di Storia della Società et dello Stato Veneziano,* 4: 415–41.

World Bank. 1993. *The East Asian Miracle: Economic Growth and Public Policy.* New York: Oxford Univ. Press.

———. 1994. *Adjustment in Africa: Reforms, Results, and the Road Ahead.* New York: Oxford Univ. Press.

———. 1995. *Will Arab Workers Prosper or Be Left Out in the Twenty-first Century?,* Regional Perspectives on World Development Report 1995. Washington, DC.

Woronoff, Denis. 1984. *L'industrie sidérurgique en France pendant la Révolution et l'Empire.* Paris: EHESS.

———. 1994. *Histoire de l'industrie en France du XVIᵉ siècle à nos jours.* Paris: Seuil.

Woronoff, Jon. 1992. *Asia's "Miracle" Economies.* 2d ed., Armonk, NY: M. E. Sharpe.

Wray, William D. 1984. *Mitsubishi and the N.Y.K. 1870–1914: Business Strategy in the Japanese Shipping Industry.* Harvard East Asian Monographs No. 108. Cambridge, MA.: Harvard.

Wright, Gavin. 1986. *Old South, New South: Revolutions in the Southern Economy Since the Civil War.* New York: Basic Books.

Wright, J. F. 1979. *Britain in the Age of Economic Management: An Economic History Since 1939.* Oxford: Oxford Univ. Press.

Wright, Ronald. 1992. *Stolen Continents: The Americas through Indian Eyes Since 1492.* Boston: Houghton Mifflin.

———. 1993. "The Two Cultures: Cortés, Moctezuma and the Fall of the Greatest City of the Americas," *TLS,* 17 December, pp. 3–4.

Wrigley, E. A. 1961. *Industrial Growth and Population Change*. Cambridge: Univ. Press.
———. 1967. "A Simple Model of London's Importance in Changing English Society and Economy, 1650–1750," *Past & Present*, 37: 44–70. Reprinted in Wrigley, *People, Cities and Wealth*, pp. 133–56.
———. 1987. *People, Cities and Wealth: The Transformation of Traditional Society*. Oxford: Basil Blackwell.
———. 1988. *Continuity, Chance and Change: The Character of the Industrial Revolution in England*. Cambridge: Univ. Press.
———. 1994. "The Classical Economists, the Stationary State, and the Industrial Revolution," in Snooks, ed., *Was the Industrial Revolution Necessary?*, pp. 27–42.
Wrigley, E. A., and R. S. Schofield. 1981. *The Population History of England 1541–1871*. Cambridge, MA: Harvard Univ. Press.
Wythe, George. 1949. *Industry in Latin America*. New York: Columbia Univ. Press.
Yamada, K., ed. 1994. *The Transfer of Science and Technology Between Europe and Asia since Vasco da Gama (1498–1998)*. Kyoto: International Research Center for Japanese Studies.
Yamamoto, Shichihei. 1982. "A Protestant Ethic in a Non-Christian Context," *Entrepreneurship: The Japanese Experience*, 1: 1–9. Tokyo: PHP Institute.
———. 1983. "The Capitalist Logic of the Samurai," in *Entrepreneurship: The Japanese Experience*, 7: 1–11. Tokyo: PHP Institute.
Yamamura, Kozo. 1978. "Entrepreneurship, Ownership, and Management in Japan," in Mathias and Postan, eds., *Cambridge Economic History of Europe*, VII, 2, 215–64.
Yasuba, Yasukichi. 1975. "Anatomy of the Debate on Japanese Capitalism," *J. Japanese Studies*, 2, 1 (Autumn), 63–82.
Yasuba, Yasukichi, and Likhit Dhiravegin. 1985. "Initial Conditions, Institutional Changes, Policy, and Their Consequences: Siam and Japan, 1850–1914," in Ohkawa and Ranis, eds., *Japan and the Developing Countries*, pp. 19–34.
Yates, Frances A. 1964. *Giordano Bruno and the Hermetic Tradition*. Chicago: Univ. of Chicago Press.
———. 1967. "The Hermetic Tradition in Renaissance Science," in Charles S. Singleton, ed., *Art, Science, and History in the Renaissance*. Baltimore: Johns Hopkins Univ. Press, pp. 255–74.
Yergin, Daniel. 1991. *The Prize: The Epic Quest for Oil, Money, and Power*. New York: Simon & Schuster.
Young, Alwyn. 1991. "Learning by Doing and the Dynamic Effects of International Trade," *QJE*, 106, 2: 369–405.
———. 1992. "A Tale of Two Cities: Factor Accumulation and Technical Change in Hong Kong and Singapore," *NBER Macroeconomics Annual 1992*. Cambridge, MA: MIT Press.
———. 1994a. "Lessons from the East Asian NICs: A Contrarian View," *Amer. Econ. Rev., Papers and Proceedings* (May).
———. 1994b. "The Tyranny of Numbers: Confronting the Statistical Realities of the East Asian Growth Experience." *NBER Working Paper* Series 4680 (March).
———. 1995. "The Tyranny of Numbers: Confronting the Statistical Realities of the East Asian Growth Experience," *QJE*, 110, 3 (August): 641–80.
Young, Arthur. 1793. *Travels During the Years 1787, 1788 and 1789*. 2 vols. Dublin.
Young, Eric Van. 1983. "Mexican Rural History since Chevalier: The Historiography of the Colonial Hacienda," *Lat. Amer. Res. Rev.*, 18, 3: 5–61.
Youngson, A. J. 1959. *Possibilities of Economic Progress*. Cambridge: Univ. Press.
Zahedieh, Nuala. 1986. "Trade, Plunder, and Economic Development in Early English Jamaica, 1655–89," *Econ. Hist. Rev.*, 2d ser., 39, 2 (May), 205–222.

———. 1994. "London and the Colonial Consumer in the Late Seventeenth Century," *Econ. Hist. Rev.*, 47, 2 (May), 239–61.

Zanden, J. L. van. 1993. "The Dutch Economy in the Very Long Run—Growth in Production, Energy Consumption and Capital in Holland (1500–1805) and the Netherlands (1805–1910)," in Szirmai *et al.*, eds., *Explaining Economic Growth*, pp. 267–283.

———. [1994]. "Pre-Modern Economic Growth: Rate, Structure and Spread. The European Economy 1500–1800." Typescript, in Dutch and English.

———. 1995. "Tracing the Beginning of the Kuznets Curve: Western Europe During the Early Modern Period," *Econ. Hist. Rev.*, 48, 4 (November): 643–64.

Zerubavel, Eviatar. 1992. *Terra Cognita: The Mental Discovery of America.* New Brunswick: Rutgers Univ. Press.

Ziegler, Jean. 1988. *La victoire des vaincus: oppression et résistance culturelle.* Paris: Seuil.

Zonderman, David A. 1992. *Aspirations and Anxieties: New England Workers and the Mechanized Factory System 1815–1850.* New York: Oxford Univ. Press.

Zysman, John, and Laura Tyson, eds. 1983. *American Industry in International Competition: Government Policies and Corporate Strategies.* Ithaca: Cornell Univ. Press.

# Index